STASI

STASI

THE UNTOLD STORY OF THE EAST GERMAN SECRET POLICE

JOHN O. KOEHLER

Westview Press
A Member of the Perseus Books Group

Published in 1999 in the United States of America by Westview Press, 5500 Central Avenue, Boulder, Colorado 80301-2877, and in the United Kingdom by Westview Press, 12 Hid's Copse Road, Cumnor Hill, Oxford OX2 9JJ

Library of Congress Cataloging-in-Publication Data
Koehler, John O.
Stasi : the untold story of the East German secret police / John O. Koehler.
p. cm.
Includes bibliographical references and index.
ISBN 0-8133-3409-8 (hardcover)
1. Germany (East). Ministerium für Staatssicherheit—History.
2. Secret service—Germany (East)—History. I. Germany (East).
Ministerium für Staatssicherheit. II. Title.
HV8210.5.A2K64 1999
363.28'3'09431—DC21 98-26742
CIP

Design by Heather Hutchison

The paper used in this publication meets the requirements of the American National Standard for Permanence of Paper for Printed Library Materials Z39.48-1984.

10 9 8 7 6 5 4 3 2

To the victims of totalitarianism

CONTENTS

PHOTOS

Photos

ACRONYMS

ADN	Allgemeiner Deutscher Nachrichtendienst; the East German government's official news agency
ANC	African National Congress
AP	Associated Press
BfV	Bundesamt für Verfassungsschutz; the (West) German Office for the Protection of the Constitution
BKA	Bundeskriminalamt; the (West) German equivalent of the U.S. FBI
BND	Bundesnachrichtendienst; the (West) German Federal Intelligence Service
BRD	Bundesrepublik Deutschland; the Federal Republic of (West) Germany (FRG)
CDU	Christliche Demokratische Union; Christian Democratic Party (German conservative)
Cheka	Vserossiiskaia chrezvychainaia komissiia po bor'be s kontrrevoliutsiei i sabotazhem; the Soviet Extraordinary Commission for Combating Counterrevolution and Sabotage (the first Soviet secret police organization, 1917–1922)
CIA	U.S. Central Intelligence Agency
CIC	Counter Intelligence Corps (of the U.S. Army)
CPSA	South African Communist Party
DDR	Deutsche Demokratische Republik; the (East) German Democratic Republic (GDR)
DKP	Deutsche Kommunistische Partei; the name adopted by the West German Communist Party after the 1950s ban on communist parties was lifted; previously known as the KPD
DM	deutsche mark; the (West) German currency
ERP	People's Revolutionary Army (El Salvador)
FDP	Freie Demokratische Partei; Free Democratic Party (German liberal)
FMLN	Farabundo Marti Revolutionary Front (El Salvador)

FPL	Popular Liberation Forces (El Salvador)
FRG	Federal Republic of Germany
FSLN	Sandinista National Liberation Front (Nicaragua)
GPU	Glavnoe politicheskoe upravlenie; Soviet Main Political Administration (secret police, 1922–1923)
GRU	Glavnoe razvedyvatel'noe upravlenie; the Soviet Main Intelligence Directorate
gulag	Glavnoe upravlenie ispravitel'no-trudovykh lagerei; the Soviet Main Administration of (Corrective Labor) Camps
HVA	Hauptverwaltung Aufklärung; the Main Administration for Foreign Intelligence
IM	*inoffizieller Mitarbeiter*; secret police informer
KGB	Komitet gosudarstvennoi bezopasnosti; the Soviet State Security Committee (1954–1992)
KgU	Kampfgruppe gegen Unmenschlichkeit; Battle Group Against Inhumanity
KOKO	Kommerzielle Koordinierung; Commercial Coordination, a Stasi-controlled clandestine trading group
KPD	Kommunistische Partei Deutschlands; the name borne by the Communist Party of Germany before the post–World War II ban on communist parties in West Germany
LPB	Libyan People's Bureaus; Libya's foreign embassies
MAD	Militärischer Abschirmdienst; West German military counterespionage service
MfS	Ministerium für Staatssicherheit; Ministry for State Security (Stasi)
MGB	Ministerstvo gosudarstvennoi bezopasnosti; Soviet Ministry of State Security (1946–1953)
MK	Umkhonto we Sizwe; Burning Spear (South African terrorist group)
MVD	Ministerstvo vnutrennikh del; Soviet Ministry of Internal Affairs (1953–1954)
NATO	North Atlantic Treaty Organization
NKGB	Narodnyi komissariat gosudarstvennoi bezopasnosti; the Soviet People's Commissariat of State Security
NKVD	Narodnyi komissariat vnutrennikh del; (Soviet) People's Commissariat of Internal Affairs (1934–1946). During World War II, the counterespionage functions of the NKVD were delegated to the newly formed NKGB,

which after the war was put under the aegis of the MGB.

NSDAP Nationalsozialistische Deutsche Arbeiterpartei; National Socialist German Workers' Party (Nazi)

NVA Nationale Volksarmee; East German National People's Army

OGPU Obedinennoe gosudarstvennoe politicheskoe upravlenie; the Soviet State Political Administration (secret police)

OIBE Offizier im besonderen Einsatz; (Stasi) Officer on Special Deployment

PDS Partei des Demokratischen Sozialismus; Party of Democratic Socialism (new name of the East German Socialist Unity Party, the SED)

PMAC Ethiopian Provisional Military Administrative Council (also known as Derg)

SED Sozialistische Einheitspartei; East German Socialist Unity Party (communist)

SIM Servicio Investigacion Militar; Military Investigation Service (Spanish Civil War secret police)

SMA Soviet Military Administration (in post–World War II Germany)

SPD Sozialdemokratische Partei Deutschlands; Social Democratic Party of Germany (left wing)

UFJ Untersuchungsausschuss Freiheitlicher Juristen; Investigating Committee of Free Jurists

USAREUR the U.S. Army European Command

Vopo Volkspolizei; East German People's Police

ZAIG Zentrale Auswertung und Informationsgruppe; the Stasi's central analysis and information group

ACKNOWLEDGMENTS

When I began the research for this book, after the fall of the Berlin Wall, I knew that I would need to tap many sources. People's responsiveness to my requests for information and guidance was overwhelming, and I wish to express my deepest appreciation for their unselfish support. My thanks to Günther Buch, Berlin, former chief archivist of the Ministry for All-German Affairs; Andreas von Bülow, Bonn, former federal minister for research and technology and member of parliament; the late William Colby, Washington, D.C., former director of the U.S. Central Intelligence Agency; Ernst Cramer, Berlin, vice chairman of Springer Verlag; Ambassador and former state secretary Günter Diehl, Bonn, who supplied important data; Edward J. De Fontaine, Alexandria, Virginia, a superb journalist and my close friend for thirty-five years, whose skillful editing of the manuscript kept it from becoming twice as long as the Bible; Otto Doelling, New York, general executive of Associated Press World Services; Eduardo Gallardo, Santiago, Associated Press bureau chief for Chile; Presiding Judge Klaus Forsen, Düsseldorf; Judge Wolfgang Frank, spokesman for the High Provincial Court, Frankfurt am Main; Ambassador and former Undersecretary of Defense Karl-Günther von Hase, Bonn, a member of the Council of Elders of the Christian Democratic Party who opened important doors; Tony Helling, Bonn, former *Financial Times* correspondent and my tenacious research assistant; Dr. Rosemarie Hoffmann, Munich, whose medical knowledge was essential during my interviews of a Stasi disinformation agent; Ray Kendall, Lyon, France, director general of the International Criminal Police Organization (Interpol) and former Scotland Yard chief superintendent; State Criminal Police Director Manfred Kittlaus, Berlin, chief of the Central Government Criminality Investigation Office; Rainer Laabs, Berlin, chief archivist of Springer newspapers; Paul Limbach, Bonn, special correspondent for *Focus* magazine; A. F. "Fritz" von Marbod, retired Air Force lieutenant colonel, ace counterintelligence specialist, and good friend; John Mapother, Potomac, Md., a retired CIA officer who was stationed in Berlin during a critical Cold War period; Presiding Judge

Ina Obst-Öllers, Düsseldorf; Rosario Priore, investigating magistrate and specialist on terrorism, Rome; Johannes Legner and Cornelia Bull, in the Berlin press office of the federal commissioner for the Stasi archives; Eva Schübel and Rolf Hannich, in the press office of the federal prosecutor general, in Karlsruhe; the chief prosecutors for Berlin, Celle, Dresden, Magdeburg, Neuruppin, Schwerin, and Stuttgart; Herbert Romerstein, expert on Soviet intelligence for the U.S. government; the late Colonel Franz Ross, an ace U.S. Army intelligence officer and my former commander; Colonel (Ret.) Werner Schofeld, Bonn, Military Counterespionage Service (MAD); archivists Günther Schreiber and Rüdiger Stang, Berlin, who patiently helped me sift through thousands of documents from Stasi archives; William L. Stearman, Washington, D.C., former member of the U.S. National Security Council and adjunct professor for international affairs at Georgetown University; Dieter Steiner, New York bureau chief for *Stern* magazine; Harald Strunz, chairman of the Association of Victims of Stalinism for Berlin and Brandenburg; Christa Trapp, a Stasi kidnapping victim now living in the United States under a different name; John Willms, former liaison chief of the 513th and 66th Military Intelligence Groups in Germany, under whom I served as an intelligence officer on several occasions; and attorney Jürgen Wischnewski, joint plaintiff in the murder trial against Stasi chief Erich Mielke, Berlin. Finally, I wish to express my special thanks to the many present and former government officials in Germany and in the United States who generously shared their knowledge but wished to remain anonymous.

John O. Koehler

STASI

INTRODUCTION

THE FIRST TIME I MET Erich Mielke, the notorious chief of the communist East German secret police, was in February 1965, during a reception for Alexei N. Kosygin, successor to Nikita S. Khrushchev as premier of the Soviet Union. Kosygin had come to East Germany to help celebrate the 700th anniversary of the Leipzig industrial fair and to provide a visible display of Soviet support for the Deutsche Demokratische Republik (DDR), the German Democratic Republic. As I was then Berlin correspondent for the Associated Press, it was my job to cover this event. At the time, the fair was the only opportunity for a Western journalist, especially an American, to catch a glimpse of life inside the "workers' and peasants' state." The communist regime had cleared me for travel to the event, but I still lacked the official credentials guaranteeing access to the new Soviet leader. I eventually obtained the necessary documents through Oleg Panin, who served as chief of protocol at the Soviet embassy in East Berlin. I had first met Panin during the highly charged days in October 1962 when U.S. and Soviet tanks faced off, gun barrel to gun barrel, at Checkpoint Charlie on Berlin's east-west border. Panin had begun to court me assiduously—at the outset, probably because he enjoyed the lavish lunches in West Berlin for which I paid because he had no West marks. Later he suddenly had the West marks to spend, and it became obvious that he thought he could recruit me as a spy. Panin did not know that I was on to him. I knew he had been a captain in the Soviet secret police, the NKVD, when he first came to Berlin at the end of World War II. Years later he returned as a "diplomat" and a full colonel in the KGB. Panin oozed politeness when I told him what I needed, and he eagerly provided me Soviet passes and invitations to all events attended by Premier Kosygin.

On February 28, I headed for the Altes Rathaus, the Leipzig city hall built in 1556—still the most beautiful Renaissance-period city hall in Germany. East German Premier Willy Stoph was hosting a reception there for his Soviet counterpart. With my Soviet invitation, I was quickly waved through by the guards and passed into the narrow, dark ceremonial hall. Centuries of grime and communist neglect had made it a dingy place. Like all East German public buildings, the place reeked of lavatory disinfectant and cheap tobacco. Tables laden with crystal bowls of caviar, plates of sturgeon and other delicacies, and the inevitable liters of iced vodka had been strung together in a fifty-foot line through the center of the hall. At the end, the hall widened into a larger room, which was cut off by another long table bearing food and drink. There, looking down the dingy hall at a hundred or so East German apparatchiks stuffing themselves and guzzling vodka, stood Kosygin with a small entourage including Soviet Ambassador Piotr A. Abrassimov and Stoph. General Pavel Koshevoi, commander of Soviet forces in East Germany, was spooning caviar into his mouth from a crystal bowl and taking bites from a slab of dark bread, washing it down with vodka. Between the right end of the long table and the wall was a gap through which one could pass to the VIP area. It was guarded by East Germans and Soviets.

When Oleg Panin spotted me, he motioned to join him in front of the VIP enclave. "I want you to meet a friend of mine," he said, leading me toward a group of goons, one of whom I recognized from photographs. It was Erich Mielke, a three-star general (awarded four stars in 1980) and head of the Ministry for State Security (MfS), the secret police, popularly referred to as the "Stasi." Mielke was already the most feared man in East Germany. Wearing a dark blue suit, white shirt, and somber tie, Mielke, although broad-shouldered and stocky, looked about two inches shorter than my five feet nine and a half. His hairline was receding and his dark, graying hair was combed straight back. His flabby jowls sported a five-o'clock shadow, and the bags under his dark eyes were huge.

"Herr Mielke," Panin said, "this is Mr. Koehler of the Associated Press and a friend of mine. Jack, please meet Herr Mielke." As we shook hands, I said, "Oh, I know Herr Mielke very well." Mielke looked puzzled. "I don't think we have met before," he said. "How do you know me?" I smiled and replied, "A wanted poster with your picture has been hanging at Checkpoint Charlie for years." Panin's eyes widened. "Please don't say things like that to our guest," he admonished me. But Mielke smiled, and with a wave of his hand, said, "Ach, I am only a journalist like you." I could not suppress a grin. "Yes, I know, you were a reporter for the *Rote Fahne,*[1] but that was before you were involved in the murder of those two police captains."[2] Panin was squirming uncomfortably, but Mielke seemed to take my taunt in stride. "You are right; after that, I had to move to the Soviet Union." Then he picked up a bottle of vodka, filled two glasses, and handed one to me. "Prost! It is good to meet a friend of Oleg's."

After I finished the drink, Mielke apparently expected me to leave. But I still had a job to do for the Associated Press (AP). I asked Panin to

Celebrating the Stasi's twentieth anniversary, in 1969: Walter Ulbricht, secretary-general of the East German Communist Party; KGB General Vladimir Biroschkov; Major General Markus Wolf, chief of foreign espionage; and Colonel General Erich Mielke, minister of state security. (Courtesy MfS Archive)

tell Ambassador Abrassimov that I wanted an interview with the Soviet premier. Panin did so reluctantly. The white-haired envoy conferred with Kosygin, then turned and motioned me into the VIP area. Mielke watched and listened intently as I talked to Kosygin for about thirty minutes. It was the first interview the new Soviet leader had granted a Western journalist.

The following day Kosygin visited the fairgrounds. Panin had instructed me to meet the official party in the East German pavilion. When I reached the entrance, there stood Mielke, personally checking the credentials of those who were trying to enter. It was an astounding sight—after all, he held a cabinet post and a general's rank. When he saw me, he grinned and exclaimed loudly, "Aha, it's you! Because of the nasty things you said last night, you are not going to get in here!" I shrugged and held out my Soviet pass for his inspection. "Well, then, our friends will be disappointed if they don't see me," I said, placing special emphasis on *our*. "Oh, yes, I remember now, you are a friend of Oleg's, so please come in," Mielke said, waving me toward the door obsequiously. I felt more than a bit queasy later that day when I reflected on my encounter with the secret police chief.

The Stasi's function in East Germany was identical to that performed by secret police organizations in other communist-controlled nations: It was the primary instrument by which the ruling party—in this case, the Sozialistische Einheitspartei (SED), or Socialist Unity Party—retained power. Mass arrests of the leaders' political opponents, including many veteran communists who disagreed with current policies, had been reported. It was rumored that half a dozen prisons were filled with tens of thousands of such political prisoners. East Germany had become a police state; and when the Berlin Wall was built in 1961, the entire population became the state's prisoners.

Because of the communists' penchant for extreme secrecy, and people's fear of the secret police, evidence of the extent of the oppression was as hard to come by as were the details of intraparty struggles. However, the facts of East Germany's espionage operations began to surface more frequently in the West by the mid-1950s, when the numbers of spies arrested increased as a result of improved West German counterespionage methods. In addition, an occasional defector from the Ministry for State Security (MfS) revealed operational secrets.

Nonetheless, the true extent of the terror exercised by the Stasi over the German people, and the depth of its espionage apparatus, remained hidden until the fall of the Berlin Wall on November 9, 1989. The communist regime collapsed within weeks of that event, and the secret police organization quickly disintegrated. Although Stasi officers tried at the last minute to destroy incriminating documents, most of the organization's archives were saved. As the Stasi's secrets gradually were unveiled, German citizens became increasingly outraged.

Twice in the previous half century, a cabal of ruthless ideologues had claimed for itself the sole right to rule in the name of "social justice." After World War II, the western part of Germany had developed into a modern, economically powerful democracy governed strictly by the rule of law while the other Germany wallowed in a morass of government-sponsored crimes, its hapless citizens having passed from one dictatorship to another.

This book chronicles the distasteful and ruthless activities of the Stasi under the leadership of Erich Mielke—activities without which the dictatorship could not have maintained its grip on power. To be sure, the East German regime also could not have existed without the backing of the armed might of the Soviet Union. In the same token, there would have been no West Germany without the protective shield of the United States and its North Atlantic Treaty (NATO) allies.

KGB Chairman Viktor M. Chebrikov and Stasi minister Erich Mielke pose before a bronze relief of Karl Marx after signing an agreement on cooperation between the Soviet secret police and the Stasi in 1987. (Courtesy MfS Archive)

Anticipating difficulties in obtaining accurate information on the activities of the MfS during the previous four decades, I sought assistance from Ambassador Georg Wieck, who until September 1990 had been president of the Bundesnachrichtendienst (BND), the West German Federal Intelligence Agency—roughly equivalent to the U.S. CIA. Ambassador Wieck arranged a meeting for me with Rainer Wiegand, a former MfS colonel who had defected to the West in 1990 after two years of advance planning. The BND vouched for Wiegand's sincerity and the veracity of his information. I was told that the CIA and the French and British intelligence services, which also had interrogated Wiegand, expressed a similarly high regard for his straightforwardness and frankness.[3]

In the MfS, Wiegand had been assigned to the counterespionage directorate and had reported directly to Mielke. His specific job was chief of Arbeitsgruppe Ausländer, a task force responsible for all matters involving foreigners. This allowed him unique access to nearly all of the MfS directorates and departments. Wiegand's headquarters was in Berlin, but he had officers stationed in each of the fifteen Stasi district offices in East Germany. He was in almost constant communication with KGB officials. The former colonel often traveled to Moscow and other European cities and the Middle East. During weeks of debriefing, Wiegand revealed the most closely guarded secrets of the MfS. He detailed espionage and subversive operations against the United States and other nations; the training and harboring of international terrorists; murder; kidnapping; blackmail; coercion; election fraud; and many other crimes and flagrant abuses of human and civil rights. Wiegand's erstwhile chief, former Lieutenant General Günther Kratsch, confirmed much of this information in a separate interview.

Some of the most stunning testimony about East German espionage activities emerged during my interviews with Karl Grossmann, a former colonel who had retired in 1986. He had helped General Markus Wolf in the early buildup of the foreign intelligence department. He told of numerous Americans who had betrayed highly sensitive U.S. military secrets to the Stasi. Colonel Heinz Busch, who was Wolf's chief analyst, supplied rich detail about spies in the U.S. military forces and defense industry as well as in NATO. Another source produced samples of secret U.S. documents that these renegades had sold to the East Germans and that were subsequently found in the Stasi archives.

Although Wiegand provided rare insights into the personality and career of Erich Mielke, he was unable to fill in important gaps. "I always found it strange that he never said a word about what he did in the Soviet Union during his years before and during the war. The official biographies lacked significant details, which puzzled not just me, but my colleagues as well," Wiegand said.

Finally, in spring 1991, I obtained access to a dossier on Erich Mielke that had been found in his personal safe. This file contained materials assembled by a Berlin court in the 1930s, and included details of Mielke's activities as a young communist thug and agitator; police reports of his involvement in the 1931 murder of two police officers in Berlin; and records of his schooling in the Soviet Union. These documents bolstered information I had obtained from other sources, enabling me to assemble as accurate a profile of Mielke as is currently possible, given that the KGB has not yet opened its relevant files.

In August 1993, I was called to testify before a Berlin court that was trying Mielke for the 1931 murder of the two policemen. My earlier encounter with Mielke, during which he had not denied his involvement, was considered crucial evidence in this case. Mielke was found guilty and sentenced to six years in prison—a virtual life term for a man who was then eighty-six.

1

REVENGE VERSUS THE RULE OF LAW

"Worse than the Gestapo."
—Simon Wiesenthal, Nazi hunter

LESS THAN A MONTH after German demonstrators began to tear down the Berlin Wall on November 9, 1989, irate East German citizens stormed the Leipzig district office of the Ministry for State Security (MfS)—the Stasi, as it was more commonly called. Not a shot was fired, and there was no evidence of "street justice" as Stasi officers surrendered meekly and were peacefully led away. The following month, on January 15, hundreds of citizens sacked Stasi headquarters in Berlin. Again there was no bloodshed. The last bit of unfinished business was accomplished on May 31 when the Stasi radioed its agents in West Germany to fold their tents and come home.

The intelligence department of the Nationale Volksarmee (NVA), the People's Army, had done the same almost a week earlier, but with what its members thought was better style. Instead of sending the five-digit code groups that it had used for decades to message its spies in West Germany, the army group broadcast a male choir singing a children's ditty about a duck swimming on a lake. There was no doubt that the singing spymasters had been drowning their sorrow over losing the Cold War in schnapps. The giggling, word-slurring songsters repeated the refrain three times: "Dunk your little head in the water and lift your little tail." This was the signal to agents under deep cover that it was time to come home.

With extraordinary speed and political resolve, the divided nation was reunified a year later. The collapse of the despotic regime was total. It was a euphoric time for Germans, but reunification also produced a new national dilemma. Nazi war crimes were still being tried in West Germany, forty-six years after World War II. Suddenly the German government was faced with demands that the communist officials who had ordered, executed, and abetted crimes against their own people—crimes that were as brutal as those perpetrated by their Nazi predecessors—also be prosecuted.

The people of the former Deutsche Demokratische Republik (DDR), the German Democratic Republic, as the state had called itself for forty years, were clamoring for instant revenge. Their wrath was directed primarily against the country's communist rulers—the upper echelon of the Sozialistische Einheitspartei (SED), the Socialist Unity Party. The tens of thousands of second-echelon party functionaries who had enriched themselves at the expense of their cocitizens were also prime targets for retribution.

Particularly singled out were the former members of the Stasi, the East German secret police, who previously had considered themselves the "shield and sword" of the party. When the regime collapsed, the Stasi had 102,000 full-time officers and noncommissioned personnel on its rolls, including 11,000 members of the ministry's own special guards regiment.[1] Between 1950 and 1989, a total of 274,000 persons served in the Stasi.[2]

The people's ire was running equally strong against the regular Stasi informers, the *inoffizielle Mitarbeiter* (IMs). By 1995, 174,000 had been identified as IMs, or 2.5 percent of the total population between the ages of 18 and 60. Researchers were aghast when they found that about 10,000 IMs, or roughly 6 percent of the total, had not yet reached the age of 18. Since many records were destroyed, the exact number of IMs probably will never be determined; but 500,000 was cited as a realistic figure.[3] Former Colonel Rainer Wiegand, who served in the Stasi counterintelligence directorate, estimated that the figure could go as high as 2 million, if occasional stool pigeons were included.[4]

"The Stasi was much, much worse than the Gestapo, if you consider only the oppression of its own people," according to Simon Wiesenthal of Vienna, Austria, who has been hunting Nazi criminals for half a century. "The Gestapo had 40,000 officials watching a country of 80 million, while the Stasi employed 102,000 to control only 17 million."[5] One might add that the Nazi terror lasted only twelve years, whereas the Stasi had four decades in which to perfect its machinery of oppression, espionage, and international terrorism and subversion.

To ensure that the people would become and remain submissive, East German communist leaders saturated their realm with more spies than had any other totalitarian government in recent history. The Soviet Union's KGB employed about 480,000 full-time agents to oversee a nation of 280 million, which means there was one agent per 5,830 citizens. Using Wiesenthal's figures for the Nazi Gestapo, there was one officer for 2,000 people.[6] The ratio for the Stasi was one secret policeman per 166 East Germans. When the regular informers are added, these ratios become much higher: In the Stasi's case, there would have been at least one spy watching every 66 citizens! When one adds in the estimated numbers of part-time snoops, the result is nothing short of monstrous: one informer per 6.5 citizens. It would not have been unreasonable to assume that at least one Stasi informer was present in any party of ten or twelve dinner guests.

THE STASI OCTOPUS

Like a giant octopus, the Stasi's tentacles probed every aspect of life. Full-time officers were posted to all major industrial plants. Without exception, one tenant in every apartment building was designated as a watchdog reporting to an area representative of the Volkspolizei (Vopo), the People's Police. In turn, the police officer was the Stasi's man. If a relative or friend came to stay overnight, it was reported. Schools, universities, and hospitals were infiltrated from top to bottom. German academe was shocked to learn that Heinrich Fink, professor of theology and vice chancellor at East Berlin's Humboldt University, had been a Stasi informer since 1968. After Fink's Stasi connections came to light, he was summarily fired. Doctors, lawyers, journalists, writers, actors, and sports figures were co-opted by Stasi officers, as were waiters and hotel personnel. Tapping about 100,000 telephone lines in West Germany and West Berlin around the clock was the job of 2,000 officers.[7]

Stasi officers knew no limits and had no shame when it came to "protecting the party and the state." Churchmen, including high officials of both Protestant and Catholic denominations, were recruited en masse as secret informers. Their offices and confessionals were infested with eavesdropping devices. Even the director of Leipzig's famous Thomas Church choir, Hans-Joachim Rotch, was forced to resign when he was unmasked as a *Spitzel,* the people's pejorative for a Stasi informant.

Absolutely nothing was sacred to the secret police. Tiny holes were bored in apartment and hotel room walls through which Stasi agents filmed their "suspects" with special video cameras. Even bathrooms were penetrated by the communist voyeurs.[8] Like the Nazi Gestapo, the Stasi was the sinister side of *deutsche Gründlichkeit* (German thoroughness).

After the Berlin wall came down, the victims of the DDR regime demanded immediate retribution. Ironically, their demands were countered by their fellow Germans in the West who, living in freedom, had diligently built *einen demokratischen Rechtsstaat,* a democratic state governed by the rule of law. The challenge of protecting the rights of both the victims and the accused was immense, given the emotions surrounding the issue. Government leaders and democratic politicians recognized that there could be no "quick fix" of communist injustices without jeopardizing the entire system of democratic jurisprudence. Moving too rapidly merely to satisfy the popular thirst for revenge might well have resulted in acquittals or mistrials. Intricate jurisdictional questions needed to be resolved with both alacrity and meticulousness. No German government could afford to allow a perpetrator to go free because of a judicial error. The political fallout from any such occurrence, especially in the East, could prove fatal to whatever political party occupied the chancellor's office in Bonn at the time.

Politicians and legal scholars of the "old federal states," or West Germany, counseled patience, pointing out that even the prosecution of Nazi criminals had not yet been completed. Before unification, Germans would speak of *Vergangenheitsbewältigung* ("coming to grips with the past") when they discussed dealing with Nazi crimes. In the reunited Germany, this word came to imply the communist past as well. The two were considered comparable especially in the area of human rights violations. Dealing with major Nazi crimes, however, was far less complicated for the Germans: Adolf Hitler and his Gestapo and *Schutzstaffel* (SS) chief, Heinrich Himmler, killed themselves, as did Luftwaffe chief and Vice Chancellor Hermann Göring, who also had been the first chief of the Gestapo. The victorious Allies prosecuted the rest of the top leadership at the International War Crimes Tribunal in Nürnberg. Twelve were hanged, three received life terms, four were sentenced to lesser terms of imprisonment (up to twenty years), and three were acquitted.

The cases of communist judges and prosecutors accused of *Rechtsbeugung* (perversion of justice) are more problematic. According to Franco Werkenthin, a Berlin legal expert charged with analyzing communist crimes for the German parliament, those sitting in judgment of many of the accused face a difficult task because of the general failure of German justice after World War II. Not a single judge or prosecutor who served the Nazi regime was brought to account for having perverted justice—even those who had handed down death sentences for infringements that in a democracy would have been considered relatively minor offenses. Werkenthin called this phenomenon *die Jauche der Justiz,* the cesspool of justice.

Of course, the crimes committed by the communists were not nearly as heinous as the Nazis' extermination of the Jews, or the mass murders in Nazi-occupied territories. However, the communists' brutal oppression of the nation by means including murder alongside legal execution put the SED leadership on a par with Hitler's gang. In that sense, Walter Ulbricht or Erich Honecker (Ulbricht's successor as the party's secretary-general and head of state) and secret police chief Erich Mielke can justifiably be compared to Hitler and Himmler, respectively.

Arrest warrants were issued for Honecker and Mielke. The Soviet government engineered Honecker's escape to Moscow, where he became the ward of Soviet President Mikhail S. Gorbachev. When the Soviet Union crumbled, the new Russian President Boris Yeltsin expelled Honecker. He was arrested on his return to Germany, but a court decided against a trial when he was diagnosed with liver cancer. Honecker flew to Chile with his wife Margot to live with their daughter, a Chilean citizen by marriage. His exile was short, and he died in 1994. Mielke was not so fortunate: His KGB friends turned their backs on him. He was tried in Germany for the 1931 murder of two police officers, found guilty, and sentenced to six years in prison. Other charges, including manslaughter, were dismissed because of his advanced age and poor health.

Three other members of the twenty-one-member ruling Politburo also have been tried. Former Defense Minister Heinz Kessler was convicted of manslaughter in connection with the order to kill people who were trying to escape to the West. He received a seven-and-a-half-year term. Two others, members of the Central Committee and the National Defense Council, were tried with Kessler and sentenced to seven and a half years and five years, respectively. Politburo member Harry Tisch, who was also head of the communist trade union, was found guilty of embezzlement and served eighteen months. Six others, including Egon Krenz (Honecker's successor as party chief), were charged with manslaughter. Krenz was found guilty, and on August 25, 1997, was sentenced to six and a half years in prison.

However, eight years after reunification, many of the 165 members of the Central Committee have not yet been put under investigation. In 1945, Nazis holding comparable or lesser positions were subject to automatic arrest by the Allies. They spent months or even years in camps while their cases were adjudicated. Moreover, the Nürnberg Tribunal branded the Reich and its Corps of Political Leaders, SS, Security Service (SD), Secret State Police (Gestapo), SA (Storm Troopers), and Armed Forces High Command criminal organizations. Similarly sweeping actions against communist leaders and functionaries such as

Stasi officers were never contemplated, even though tens of thousands of political trials and human rights abuses have been documented. After the East German regime fell, German judicial authorities scrupulously avoided the appearance of waging witch-hunts or using the law as a weapon of vengeance. Prosecutors and judges made great efforts to be fair, often suspending legal action while requesting rulings from the supreme court on possible constitutional conflicts.

The victims of oppression clamored for revenge and demanded speedy prosecution of the erstwhile tyrants. They had little patience for a judicial system that was handicapped by a lack of unblemished and experienced criminal investigators, prosecutors, and judges. Despite these handicaps, the Berlin Central Police Investigations Group for Government Criminality, mindful that the statute of limitations for most communist crimes would expire at the end of 1999, made significant progress under its director Manfred Kittlaus, the able former director of the West Berlin state police. Kittlaus's major task in 1998 was to investigate wrongful deaths, including 73 murders, 30 attempted murders, 583 cases of manslaughter, 2,938 instances of attempted manslaughter, and 425 other suspicious deaths. Of the 73 murders, 22 were classified as contract murders.

One of those tried and convicted for attempted contract murder was former Stasi collaborator Peter Haak, who was sentenced to six and a half years in prison. The fifty-two-year-old Haak took part in the Stasi's 1981 Operation Scorpion, which was designed to pursue people who helped East Germans escape to the West. Proceedings against former General Gerhard Neiber, whose Stasi directorate was responsible for preventing escapes and for wreaking vengeance, were still pending in 1998.

Peter Haak's murder plot was hatched after he befriended Wolfgang Welsch and his family. Welsch was a thorn in the side of the Stasi because of his success in smuggling people out of the DDR. Haak joined Welsch and the latter's wife and seven-year-old daughter on a vacation in Israel, where he mixed a gram of thallium, a highly poisonous metallic chemical element used in rat poison, into the hamburgers he was preparing for a meal. Welsch's wife and daughter vomited immediately after ingesting the poison and recovered quickly. Welsch suffered severe aftereffects, but eventually recovered: He had consumed a large amount of beer with the meal, and an expert testified that the alcohol had probably flushed the poison from his system.

Berlin Prosecutor General Christoph Schäfgen revealed that after the DDR's demise 15,200 investigations had been launched, of which more than 9,000 were still active at the beginning of 1995. Indictments were handed down in 153 cases, and 73 perpetrators were convicted.[9] Among those convicted were the aforementioned Politburo members as well as a number of border guards who had killed people who were trying to escape to the West.

Despite widespread misgivings about the judicial failures in connection with some Nazi crimes, a number of judges and prosecutors were convicted and jailed for up to three years for perversion of justice. In collusion with the Stasi, they had requested or handed down more severe sentences in political cases so that the state could collect greater amounts when the "convicts" were ransomed by the West German government. (The amount of ransom paid was governed by the time a prisoner had been sentenced to serve.)

The enormity of the task facing judicial authorities in reunified Germany becomes starkly evident when one examines the actions they have taken in all five former East German provinces and in East Berlin. From the end of 1990 to July 1996, 52,050 probes were launched into charges of murder, attempted murder, manslaughter, kidnapping, election fraud, and perversion of justice. A total of 29,557 investigations were halted for various reasons including death, severe illness, old age, or insufficient evidence. In those five and a half years, there were only 132 convictions.[10]

The problem is even more staggering when cases of espionage are included. Between 1990 and 1996, the office of the federal prosecutor general launched 6,641 probes, of which 2,431 were terminated before trial—most due to the statute of limitations. Of 175 indictments on charges of espionage, 95 resulted in convictions. In addition to the cases handled at the federal level, the prosecutor general referred 3,926 investigations to state authorities, who terminated 3,344 without trial. State courts conducted 356 trials, resulting in 248 convictions.[11] Because the statute of limitations for espionage is five years, the prosecutor general's office told me in 1997 it was unlikely that more espionage trials would be conducted.

It is important to emphasize the difference between the statute's application to so-called government crimes committed in East Germany before the collapse and to crimes, such as espionage, committed in West Germany. The Unification Treaty specifically permits the belated prosecution of individuals who committed acts that were punishable under the East German criminal code and who due to official connivance were not prosecuted earlier. There is no statute of limitations for murder. For most other crimes the limit is five years; however, due to the obstacles created by previous government connivance, the German parliament in 1993 doubled this time limit for prosecution of the more serious crimes. At the same time, the parliament decreed that all cases must be adjudicated by the end of 2002. For less serious offenses, the statute would have run out on December 31, 1997, but the parliament extended it to 2000.

A number of politicians, jurists, and liberal journalists pleaded for a general amnesty for crimes committed by former DDR leaders and Communist Party functionaries. A former West German supreme court judge, Ernst Mahrenholz, said the "sharp sword of justice prevents reconciliation." Schäfgen, the Berlin prosecutor general, had this answer for the former high court judge and other amnesty advocates:

> I cannot agree. We are raising no special, sharp sword against East Germans. We must pursue state-sponsored injustice in exactly the same manner as we do when a thief steals or when one human being kills another. If one wants to change that, then we would have to do away with the entire criminal justice system, because punishment always hurts. We are not criminalizing an entire people but only an ever shrinking, small portion.[12]

German Foreign Minister Klaus Kinkel, who was West Germany's minister of justice when the nation was unified, said this at a session of parliament in September 1991: "We must punish the perpetrators. This is not a matter of a victor's justice. We owe it to the ideal of justice and to the victims. All of those who ordered injustices and those who executed the orders must be punished; the top men of the SED as well as the ones who shot [people] at the wall." Aware that the feelings against communists were running high among their victims, Kinkel pointed to past revolutions after which the representatives of the old system were collectively liquidated. In the same speech before parliament, he said:

> Such methods are alien to a state ruled by law. Violence and vengeance are incompatible with the law in any case. At the same time, we cannot tolerate that the problems are swept under the rug as a way of dealing with a horrible past, because the results will later be disastrous for society. We Germans know from our own experience where this leads. Jewish philosophy formulates it in this way: "The secret of redemption is called remembering."

Defense attorneys for communist officials have maintained that the difficulty lies in the fact that hundreds of thousands of political opponents were tried under laws of the DDR. Although these laws were designed to smother political dissent and grossly violated basic human rights and democratic norms, they were nonetheless laws promulgated by a sovereign state. How could one justly try individual Stasi officers, prosecutors, and judges who had simply been fulfilling their legal responsibility to pursue and punish violators of the law?

Opinions varied widely on whether and how the Stasi and other perpetrators of state-sponsored crimes should be tried. Did the laws of the DDR, as they existed before reunification, still apply in the east? Or was the criminal code of the western part of the country the proper instrument of justice in reunified Germany? However, these questions were moot: As Rupert Scholz, professor of law at the University of Munich and a Christian Democratic member of parliament, pointed out, the Unification Treaty specifies that the penal code of the DDR and not that of the Federal Republic of Germany (FRG) shall be applied to offenses committed in East Germany.[13] Scholz's view was upheld by the Bundesverfassungsgericht, the supreme court. Most offenses committed by party functionaries and Stasi officers—murder, kidnapping, torture, illegal wiretapping, mail robbery, and fraud—were subject to prosecution in reunified Germany under the DDR's penal code. But this would not satisfy the tens of thousands of citizens who had been sent to prison under East German laws covering purely political offenses for which there was no West German equivalent.

Nevertheless, said Scholz, judicial authorities were by no means hamstrung, because West Germany had never recognized the East German state according to international law. "We have always said that we are one nation; that the division of Germany led neither to full recognition under international law nor, concomitantly, to a recognition of the legal system of the DDR," Scholz said. Accordingly, West German courts have consistently maintained that West German law protects all Germans equally, including those living in the East. Therefore, no matter where the crimes were committed, whether in the East or the West, all Germans have always been subject to West German laws. Applying this logic, East German border guards who had either killed or wounded persons trying to escape to the West could be tried under the jurisdiction of West Germany.

The "one nation" principle was not upheld by the German supreme court. Prior to the court's decision, however, Colonel General Markus Wolf, chief of the Stasi's foreign espionage directorate, and some of his officers who personally controlled agents from East Berlin had been tried for treason and convicted. Wolf had been sentenced to six years in prison. The supreme court ruling overturned that verdict and those imposed on Wolf's cohorts, even though they had obtained the most closely held West German secrets and handed them over to the KGB. The maximum penalty for *Landesverrat,* or treason, is life imprisonment. In vacating Wolf's sentence, the court said he could not be convicted because he operated only from East German territory and under East German law.

However, Wolf was reindicted on charges of kidnapping and causing bodily harm, crimes also punishable under East German law. The former Stasi three-star general, on March 24, 1955, had approved in writing a plan to kidnap a woman who worked for the U.S. mission in West Berlin. The woman and her mother were tricked by a Stasi agent whom the woman had been teaching English, and voluntarily got into his car. He drove them into the Soviet sector of the divided city, where they were seized by Stasi officers. The woman was subjected to psychological torture and threatened with imprisonment unless she signed an agreement to spy for the Stasi. She agreed. On her return to the American sector, however, the woman reported the incident to security officials. Wolf had committed a felony punishable by up to fifteen years' imprisonment in West Germany. He was found guilty in March 1977 and sentenced to two years' probation.

Those who have challenged the application of the statute of limitations to communist crimes, especially to the executions of citizens fleeing to the West, have drawn parallels to the notorious executive orders of Adolf Hitler. Hitler issued orders mandating the summary execution of Soviet Army political commissars upon their capture and initiating the extermination of Jews. An early postwar judicial decision held that these orders were equivalent to law. When that law was declared illegal and retroactively repealed by the West German Bundestag, the statute of limitations was suspended—that is, it never took effect. Many of those convicted in subsequent trials of carrying out the Führer's orders were executed by the Allies. The German supreme court has ruled the same way as the Bundestag on the order to shoot people trying to escape to West Germany, making the statute of limitations inapplicable to such cases. The ruling made possible the trial of members of the National Defense Council who took part in formulating or promulgating the order. A number of border guards who had shot would-be escapees also have been tried and convicted.

Chief Prosecutor Heiner Sauer, former head of the West German Central Registration Office for Political Crimes, was particularly concerned with the border shootings.[14] His office, located in Salzgitter, West Germany, was established in 1961 as a direct consequence of the Berlin Wall, which was erected on August 13 of that year. Willy Brandt, at the time the city's mayor (later federal chancellor) had decided that crimes committed by East German border guards should be recorded. At his behest, a central registry of all shootings and other serious border incidents was instituted. Between August 13, 1961 and the opening of the borders on November 9, 1989, 186 border killings were registered. But when the Stasi archives were opened, investigators found that at least 825 people had paid with their lives for trying to escape to the West. This figure was reported to the court that was trying former members of the National Defense Council. In addition to these border incidents, the registry also had recorded a number of similar political offenses committed in the interior of the DDR: By fall 1991, Sauer's office had registered 4,444 cases of actual or attempted killings and about 40,000 sentences handed down by DDR courts for "political offenses."[15]

During the early years of Sauer's operation, the details of political prosecutions became known only when victims were ransomed by West Germany or were expelled. Between 1963 and 1989, West Germany paid DM5 billion (nearly US$3 billion) to the communist regime for the release of 34,000 political prisoners.[16] The price per head varied according to the importance of the person or the length of the sentence. In some cases the ransom amounted to more than US$56,000. The highest sum ever paid to the East Germans appears to have been DM450,000 (US$264,705 using an exchange rate of US$1.70 to the mark). The ransom "object" in this case was Count Benedikt von Hoensbroech. A student in his early twenties, von Hoensbroech was attending a West Berlin university when the wall went up. He was caught by the Stasi while trying to help people escape and was sentenced to ten years at hard labor. The case attracted international attention because his family was related to Queen Fabiola of Belgium, who interceded with the East Germans. Smelling money, the East German government first demanded the equivalent of more than US$1 million from the young man's father as ransom. In the end, the parties settled on the figure of DM450,000, of which the West German government paid DM40,000 (about $23,529).[17] Such ransom operations were fully controlled by the Stasi.

Political prisoners released in the DDR could not be registered by the West Germans because their cases remained secret. The victims were admonished to keep quiet or face another prison term. Nonetheless, in the first year after reunification, Sauer's office added another 20,000 documented cases, for a total of 60,000. Sauer said he believed the final figure of all political prosecutions would be somewhere around 300,000. In every case, the Stasi was involved either in the initial arrest or in pretrial interrogations during which "confessions" were usually extracted by physical or psychological torture, particularly between the mid-1940s and the mid-1960s.

Until 1987, the DDR imposed the death penalty for a number of capital crimes, including murder, espionage, and economic offenses. But after the mid-1950s, nearly all death sentences were kept quiet and executions were carried out in the strictest secrecy, initially by guillotine and in later years by a single pistol shot to the neck. In most instances, the relatives of those killed were not informed either of the sentence or of the execution. The corpses were cremated and the ashes buried secretly, sometimes at construction sites. In reporting about one executioner who shot more than twenty persons to death, the Berlin newspaper *Bildzeitung* said that a total of 170 civilians had been executed in East Germany. However, Franco Werkenthin, the Berlin official investigating DDR crimes, said he had documented at least three hundred executions. He declined to say how many were for political offenses, because he had not yet submitted his report to parliament. "But it was substantial," he told me. The true number of executions may never be known because no complete record of death sentences meted out by civil courts could be found. Other death sentences were handed down by military courts, and many records of those are also missing. In addition, German historian Günther Buch believes that about two hundred members of the Stasi itself were executed for various crimes, including attempts to escape to the West.[18]

SAFEGUARDING HUMAN DIGNITY?

The preamble to the East German criminal code stated that the purpose of the code was to "safeguard the dignity of humankind, its freedom and rights under the aegis of the criminal code of the socialist state," and that "a person can be prosecuted under the criminal code only in strictest concurrence with the law." However, many of the codified offenses for which East German citizens were prosecuted and imprisoned were unique to totalitarian regimes, both fascist and communist.

Moreover, certain sections of the code, such as those on "Treasonable Relaying of Information" and "Treasonable Agent Activity," were perversely applied, landing countless East Germans in maximum security penitentiaries. The victims of this perversion of justice usually were persons who had requested legal exit permits from the DDR authorities and had been turned down. In many cases, their "crime" was having contacted a Western consulate to inquire about immigration procedures. Sentences of up to two and a half years' hard labor were not unusual as punishment for such inquiries.

Engaging in "propaganda hostile to the state" was another punishable offense. In one such case, a young man was arrested and prosecuted for saying that it was not necessary to station tanks at the border and for referring to border fortifications as "nonsense." During his trial, he "admitted" to owning a television set on which he watched

West German programs and later told friends what he saw. One of those "friends" had denounced him to the Stasi. The judge considered the accused's actions especially egregious and sentenced him to a year and a half at hard labor.[19]

Ironically, another part of this section of the criminal code decreed that "glorifying militarism" also was a punishable offense, although the DDR itself "glorified" its People's Army beyond any Western norm. That army was clad in uniforms and insignia identical to those of the Nazi Wehrmacht, albeit without eagles and swastikas. The helmets, too, were differently shaped, but the Prussian goose step was regulation during parades.

A nineteen-year-old who had placed a sign in an apartment window reading "When justice is turned into injustice, resistance becomes an obligation!" was rewarded with twenty-two months in the penitentiary. Earlier, the youth had applied for an exit visa and had been turned down. A thirty-four-year-old father of two who also had been denied permission to leave the "workers' and peasants' state" with his family similarly advertised that fact with a poster reading "We want to leave, but they won't let us." The man went to prison for sixteen months. The "crimes" of both men were covered by a law on "Interference in Activities of the State or Society."[20]

Two letters—one to a friend in West Germany, seeking assistance to legally emigrate to the West, and another containing a similar appeal to Chief of State Honecker—brought a four-year sentence to their writer, who was convicted under two laws: those on "establishing illegal contacts" (writing to his friend) and on "public denigration" (writing to Honecker).[21] The Stasi had illegally intercepted both letters.

The East German party chiefs were not content to rely only on the Stasi's millions of informers to ferret out antistate sentiments. Leaving nothing to chance, they created a law that made the failure to denounce fellow citizens a crime punishable by up to five years' imprisonment. One man was sentenced to twenty-three months for failing to report that a friend of his was preparing to escape to the West. The mandatory denunciation law had its roots in the statutes of the Socialist Unity Party, which were published in the form of a little red booklet. I picked up a copy of this booklet that had been discarded by its previous owner, a Stasi chauffeur, who had written "Ha, Ha" next to the mandate to "report any misdeeds, regardless of the person responsible, to leading party organs, all the way up to the Central Committee."[22]

Rupert Scholz, member of parliament and professor of law at the University of Munich, said many East Germans feel there is little determination among their Western brethren to bring the Stasi criminals to trial. "In fact, we already have heard many of them say that the peaceful revolution should have been a bloody one instead so they could have done away with their tormentors by hanging them posthaste," Scholz told me.[23]

The Reverend Joachim Gauck, minister to a Lutheran parish in East Germany, shared the people's pessimism that justice would be done. Following reunification, Gauck was appointed by the Bonn government as its special representative for safeguarding and maintaining the Stasi archives. "We must at least establish a legal basis for finding the culprits in our files," Gauck told me. "But it will not be easy. If you stood the millions of files upright in one line, they would stretch for 202 kilometers [about 121 miles]. In those files you can find an unbelievable number of Stasi victims and their tormentors."[24]

Gauck was given the mandate he needed in November 1991, when the German parliament passed a law authorizing file searches to uncover Stasi perpetrators and their informants. He viewed this legislation as first step in the right direction. With the evidence from Stasi files, the perpetrators could be removed from their public service jobs without any formal legal proceedings. Said Gauck: "We needed this law badly. It is not reasonable that persons who served this apparatus of oppression remain in positions of trust. We need to win our people over to accepting that they are now free and governed by the rule of law. To achieve that, we must build up their confidence and trust in the public service."

Searching the roughly six million files will take years. A significant number of the dossiers are located in repositories of the Stasi regional offices, sprinkled throughout eastern Germany. To put the files at the Berlin central repository in archival order would take one person 128 years.[25] The job might have been made easier had the last DDR government not ordered the burning of thousands of Stasi computer tapes, ostensibly to forestall a witch-hunt. Thousands of files dealing with espionage were shredded and packed into 17,200 paper sacks. These were discovered when the Stasi headquarters was stormed on January 15, 1990. The contents of all of these bags now have been inspected. It took two workers between six and eight weeks to go through one bag. Then began the work of the puzzlers, putting the shredded pieces together. By the middle of 1997, fewer than 500 bags of shredded papers had been reconstructed—into about 200,000 pages. Further complicating matters was the lack of trained archivists and experts capable of organizing these files—to say nothing of the 37.5 million index cards bearing the names of informers as well as persons under Stasi surveillance—and interpreting their contents. Initially, funding for a staff of about 550 individuals was planned, at a total of about DM24.5 million annually (about US$15 million using an exchange rate of US$1.60). By 1997, the budget had grown to US$137 million and the staff to 3,100.[26]

Stasi victims and citizens who had been under surveillance were allowed to examine their Stasi files. Within four years of reunification, about 860,000 persons had asked to inspect their case files, with 17,626 of those requests being received in December 1994 alone. By 1997, 3.4 million people had asked to see their files. Countless civil suits were launched when victims found the names of those who had denounced and betrayed them, and many family relationships and friendships were destroyed.

The rehabilitation of Stasi victims and financial restitution to them was well under way; but Gauck believed that criminal prosecution of the perpetrators would continue to be extremely difficult. "We can already see that leading SED functionaries who bear responsibility for the inhumane policies, for which they should be tried, are instead accused of lesser offenses such as corruption. It is actually an insult to democracy that a man like Harry Tisch is tried for embezzlement and not for being a member of the Politburo, where the criminal policies originated."

The "Stasi files law," as it is popularly known, also made it possible to vet parliamentarians for Stasi connections. Hundreds were fired or resigned—and a few committed suicide—when it was discovered that they had been Stasi informants. Among those who resigned was Lothar de Maiziere, the last premier of the DDR, who signed the unification agreement with West German Chancellor Helmut Kohl. He was a member of the East German version of the Christian Democratic Union, which like all noncommunist parties in the Eastern bloc had been totally co-opted by the regime. After reunification, he moved into parliament and was awarded the vice chairmanship of Kohl's Christian Democratic Union. A lawyer, De Maiziere had functioned for years as an IM, an informer, under the cover name Cerny. De Maiziere at first denied he was Cerny, but the evidence was overwhelming. It was De Maiziere's government that had ordered the destruction of the Stasi computer tapes.

THE COMMUNISTS' POLITICAL SURVIVAL

De Maiziere, who had been a driving force behind prompt reunification, soon passed into oblivion; but twenty members of the old Communist Party, the SED, are still members of parliament. The SED changed its name in late 1989, when the DDR was collapsing, to the Party of Democratic Socialism (PDS). Its new leadership arrogantly dismissed their bloody past as irrelevant now that the word *democratic* had been adopted as part of their party's name. If the elections of summer 1990 had taken place just a few months later and thus had been conducted under the law of reunified Germany, these individuals would not have won parliamentary seats. The West German electoral rules governing the proportional representation system require that a party garner at least 5 percent of the vote before it may enter parliament. In addition to choosing a party, voters cast a second ballot for a specific person. This is called a direct mandate. If any party falls below 5 percent but gets at least three direct mandates, that party is seated in parliament. As a one-time compromise in consideration of East Germany's smaller population, the Bonn government accepted a 3-percent margin of party votes. Even so, the PDS barely made it into parliament.

In the 1994 general election, the first after reunification, the party polled 4.4 percent. Had it not been for the votes electing four persons by direct mandate, the PDS would have been excluded. The direct mandates all came from East Berlin districts heavily populated by unemployed, former Communist Party and government officials. One of the men elected directly was Gregor Gysi, a communist lawyer who had been accused of informing on his clients to the Stasi. Gysi denied the allegations and had obtained a temporary injunction barring a former East German dissident from making the assertion. However, a Hamburg court lifted the injunction in December 1994 on the basis of Stasi documents that indicated Gysi had no case.

Another candidate directly elected to parliament was Stefan Heym, a German-born writer who had emigrated to the United States after Hitler came to power, had changed his name from Helmut Flieg, and had become a U.S. citizen. He served in the U.S. Army as an officer during World War II, but switched sides in 1952 to live in East Germany, forfeiting his U.S. citizenship in order to become an East German citizen and a member of the Communist Party. A year later, on June 17, 1953, the East German people rose up in a revolt that was crushed by the Red Army. Had it not been for the intervention of the Soviets, Heym wrote afterward in the communist daily newspaper *Berliner Zeitung,* "the American bombing would have already begun. The shots against the rebels were fired to prevent war, rather than to begin one." And when Stalin died, just four months earlier, Heym used the same newspaper to mourn the butcher of an estimated twenty million people as the "most loved man of our times." Finally, in a speech on January 31, 1995, at a demonstration marking the 62nd anniversary of the Nazi takeover, the unrepentant Heym, now eighty-two years old, had the gall to say that the present climate in Germany was "very similar to that in 1933, and this frightens me." It was a grotesque spectacle when Heym was accorded the "honor" of delivering the opening address of the 1965 parliamentary session traditionally reserved for the body's oldest member. Despite vehement protests, parliamentary president Rita Süssmuth ruled to uphold the tradition.

One of the PDS members also retaining his seat was Hans Modrow. Modrow, a veteran communist, was SED district secretary in Dresden. It was a most powerful communal political position. Modrow was a vital cog in the apparatus of state repression. The local Stasi chief, Major General Horst Böhm, reported directly to him. Modrow was the one who ordered the Vopo, the People's Police, to resort to violence in putting down massive protests during the turbulent days in fall 1989, just before the Berlin Wall fell. Hundreds of protesters were severely beaten and jailed. Böhm, the Dresden Stasi boss, was found shot dead in his office in early 1990, just before he was to appear before a commission that had been convened to settle the future of the communist state. His death was listed as a suicide. However, an unsubstantiated rumor has it that he was murdered to prevent him from testifying about Modrow's despotic rule. Modrow was found guilty of election fraud in May 1993. The DDR hierarchy, according to the evidence, had ordered that the number of votes opposing the official slate in the 1989 election had to be fewer than in 1985. Modrow reported that only 2.5 percent of the ballots in his district were cast in opposition; but the true number was at least four times higher. The judge issued him a mere rebuke, refusing to imprison or fine him. The federal high court, which reviews sentences, ordered in November 1994 that Modrow stand trial again because the sentence "was too mild." After a new trial in 1996 on charges of perjury, Modrow was sentenced to six months' probation. A year later, parliament was still considering whether he should be deprived of his seat.

Unlike the Nazi Party's finances and property, which were confiscated by the victorious Allies and turned over to the first West German government in 1949, the SED's millions were inherited by the PDS, which spirited part of those funds out of the country when the East German government collapsed. The PDS also became custodian of the archives of the SED and refused anyone outside the party access to them. Shortly after reunification, in 1990, the courts ruled that the archives were state property. Judicial authorities as well as scholars were permitted to research them. Nevertheless, the SED archives were almost lost. In 1994, the German news magazine *Focus* discovered a letter dated March 1991, sent by Gregor Gysi in the capacity of PDS party chief to Vladimir A. Ivashko, assistant secretary-general of the Soviet Union's Communist Party. In this letter, Gysi pleaded with Soviet leaders either to put pressure on German Chancellor Helmut Kohl to return the archive to the PDS, or if Kohl felt this was politically impossible, to destroy it. The opening of the archive, Gysi wrote, was a "genuine catastrophe," because it contained many secret documents. Publication of the documents would have "extremely unpleasant results not only for the PDS but for the Communist Party of the Soviet Union as well," Gysi wrote. But his Soviet friends were no longer able to help him. The archive holds documents on Politburo decisions and directives that might prove crucial in prosecuting the former East German party hierarchy. In the end, the PDS offered to settle for 20 percent of the SED's ill-gotten funds, forfeiting the rest as a gesture of goodwill toward the new state.

Not all observers were impressed by this compromise. Peter Gauweiler, Bavaria's minister for development and ecological affairs at the time of reunification, and a member of the Christian Democratic Party, demanded that the PDS and the Deutsche Kommunistische Partei (DKP, the West German Communist Party), be outlawed: "Every month we learn of new crimes committed by the SED—terrible things, gruesome things," Gauweiler said. "We cannot tolerate a successor organization to such an extremely criminal gang."[27] It was not the party's politics that Gauweiler questioned:

> There will always be a party to the left of our Social Democratic Party. That is not the point. The transformation of the SED into the PDS was equivalent to the Nazi NSDAP's (National Socialist German Workers' Party's) changing its name in 1945 to the SAP, or Socialist Workers' Party. Then, after changing their spots, they said the Nazi ideology was okay but its application was abominable. "Now we begin anew, and because we want to be dear and loving toward one another, we demand only 20 percent of Nazi property." In other words, it would be like the converted Nazis saying they wanted only 20 percent of Hitler's Eagle's Nest. Anyone even considering such a move would have been locked up in an insane asylum for life.[28]

Gauweiler accused the DKP of acting as a "fifth column." Stasi documents proved that DKP members had been trained in East Germany on weapons, explosives, and guerrilla tactics so that they could perform terrorist acts in West Germany in the event of war. "This West German sister of the SED was a treasonable organization from its inception," Gauweiler told me.

At the same time as he demanded that both parties be outlawed, Gauweiler called for using PDS and DKP funds to cover the cost of financial restitution to the victims of communist oppression. Although

Gauweiler's proposals have been ignored by the German leadership, it is worthwhile to consider his arguments:

> Our people would be justified to declare us insane if this were paid out of public funds. Our people were not the ones who harmed those who were persecuted for their political beliefs. If we don't make the communists pay, it could lead to new schisms. Make them pay, and then forget about going after every little fellow traveler. We want to be one nation again, we want to advance. Our future is called Germany and Europe. In any case, there is enough guilt to go around. The entire West is guilty. Our inaction disheartened the people of East Germany.[29]

What Gauweiler meant by his last remark was that East Germans who were not communists or communist sympathizers had been driven into apathy and inaction by a series of traumatic events. The first was the 1953 uprising, when thousands of East Germans were imprisoned and many were shot. The Soviet Army smashed the insurrection, and the Western powers limited themselves to verbal protests. In 1956, the Germans witnessed the Soviet invasion of Hungary while the West stood idly by. The promise made by U.S. Secretary of State John Foster Dulles that the United States would "help those who help themselves" turned out to be empty as far as the "captive nations" were concerned.[30] The Hungarians' anguished cries for help, broadcast over Budapest radio, went unheeded. In 1961, tens of thousands of East Germans began to vote against communism with their feet; the Berlin Wall was built to stop their mass exodus. President John F. Kennedy, cowed by Soviet Premier Nikita S. Khrushchev at a summit in Vienna two months earlier, agonized for three days before telling the U.S. forces in Berlin to do nothing.[31] Seven years later, the "Prague Spring" was turned into another ice age by a massive invasion of the Soviet Army and the forces of its Warsaw Pact allies, including the People's Army of the DDR. Although military intervention by NATO might have led to World War III, the West could have pursued a number of other, nonmilitary measures to demonstrate its staunch opposition, instead of communicating virtual acquiescence.[32]

Another blow to opponents of the communist dictatorship was the retreat of U.S. military forces from Vietnam, which provided the communists with a great psychological victory. The final insult was the photograph of their tormentor, Erich Honecker, seated between U.S. President Gerald Ford and West German Chancellor Helmut Schmidt at the 1975 Helsinki Conference on Security and Cooperation in Europe. The Helsinki Conference dealt in part with the human rights and freedom of movement of the people of signatory nations. Both Ford and Schmidt knew about Honecker's order to shoot would-be escapees, and the East German people knew that the DDR regime was violating the Helsinki Agreement even as Honecker signed it. The photograph triumphantly adorned the front page of the Communist Party newspaper *Neues Deutschland,* as evidence of the DDR regime's acceptance as an equal by Western nations. The West German parties' fawning over Honecker during his 1987 state visit was not lost on the East German people: They were watching coverage of the events on television. They could see that the Social Democrats and many liberal Free Democrats were particularly anxious to please the DDR's leaders. The leading officials of those two parties had tried for years to have the Central Registration Office and its files on communist crimes destroyed.[33] It is understandable, therefore, that most East Germans, even those who did not join the party, chose to accommodate the regime.

As for prosecuting former Communist functionaries, Gauweiler echoed former Lithuanian President Vytautas Landsbergis, who had suggested that an International Tribunal should be formed. In 1990, Gauweiler told me: "Such a tribunal would be the 'court of the victims,' judging the communist chiefs of the entire communist imperium—Poland, the Baltics, the DDR, Bulgaria, Ukraine, and so on. They should not be prosecuted for personal enrichment but for crimes against humanity."

Even before the courts turned Honecker loose because of his terminal illness, Gauweiler said he had opposed calls for Honecker's trial by a West German court:

> West German justice has essentially granted Honecker an amnesty. Back in 1987 they changed laws so they could roll out the red carpet for his state visit, to which he was invited by the Bonn government. He was hailed as the great visitor. Now they want to try him, and that is being two-faced. After all, we already knew at that time that he had issued the order to shoot people at the border. His visit was problematic at the time, but we did it! The others who committed capital crimes, murder and manslaughter and torture, must also be tried. But for the rest who went along with the regime, the hundreds of thousands of SED members, there should be an amnesty. We don't know how we would have acted if we had been forced to live over there.[34]

Nazi hunter Simon Wiesenthal, whose views are opposed to those of Landsbergis and Gauweiler, has been supported by the German government. Wiesenthal maintained that the Nürnberg Tribunal never would have been convened had it not been for a world war and its millions of victims: "It is important that each of the former communist countries come to grips with its own history; and therefore they must put their own house in order, and not with some kind of international tribunal." Wiesenthal particularly emphasized that East German officials should be prosecuted quickly:

> They not only terrorized their own people worse than the Gestapo, but the government was the most anti-Semitic and anti-Israeli of the entire Eastern bloc. They did nothing to help the West in tracking down Nazi criminals; they ignored all requests from West German judicial authorities for assistance. We have just discovered shelves of files on Nazis stretching over four miles. Now we also know how the Stasi used those files. They blackmailed Nazi criminals who fled abroad after the war into spying for them. What's more, the Stasi trained terrorists from all over the world.[35]

All but one of the Stasi officers connected with training the international terrorists to whom Wiesenthal was referring were arrested and held briefly for investigation in summer 1991. One officer was tried, convicted, and sentenced to four years in prison for his role in the bombing of a French cultural center in West Berlin by Carlos "the Jackal" in 1983. However, a Berlin court ordered the release of the others and suspended further action while the supreme court deliberated on which laws—East or West German—were applicable. These Stasi officers, including the chief of the "counterterrorism" directorate, trained hundreds of German, Arab, and Latin American terrorists. In addition, they provided logistical support and safe haven to such figures as Carlos, Abu Nidal, and Abu Daoud, who have participated in and organized murders around the world.

The Stasi officers who did such things were not acting on their own initiative. They were following orders from Honecker and Mielke. Egon Krenz, who served briefly as SED secretary-general and the state's chief executive after Honecker was deposed, is facing prosecution only in connection with the government's order to shoot people who were trying to escape to the West. Yet he was also the Politburo member responsible for security affairs, and he worked closely with Stasi chief Mielke. Krenz, Honecker, and Mielke met frequently to discuss terrorist matters. At one meeting they decided to turn a blind eye to Libyan preparations for a bombing attack in West Berlin that resulted in the deaths of three American soldiers and wounded more than two hundred civilians.

Markus Wolf also was involved with international terrorism. His espionage service, the Hauptverwaltung Aufklärung (HVA), the Stasi's Main Administration for Foreign Intelligence, was closely linked to terrorists abroad. In fact, Wolf's agents made the first official East German contacts with such individuals. The former general has denied having had a hand in terrorist actions, but his knowledge of them is well documented, as is explained in a later chapter of this book.[36]

German authorities probing into Wolf's activities seemed mainly interested in the espionage operations of the HVA, which was composed of 4,286 officers. Virtually every West German government department was thoroughly infiltrated, including the intelligence agencies. Had the regime not collapsed, the West German counterespionage operation probably would have been rendered ineffective against Wolf's spies because of a major defection. One Stasi spy was even a close adviser to Chancellor Willy Brandt, who was forced to resign when the mole was unmasked.

Stasi espionage case officers did not limit themselves to ferreting out West German secrets. They covered the globe. Among their primary targets were NATO, U.S. diplomatic posts, and the U.S. armed forces intelligence operations. Money, and lots of it, was a key HVA tool; few American traitors were motivated by ideology. East German intelligence also maintained dossiers on top U.S. leaders, including a surprisingly accurate political profile of President Ronald Reagan.[37] A similar, more extensive dossier on President George Bush, complete with a psychological profile, was destroyed in the Stasi's waning days.[38]

Wolf has cynically defended himself and his men by insisting that they had been *Aufklärer für den Frieden,* reconnoiterers for peace. They had stopped "Western aggression" by knowing in advance of plans to attack the "peaceful" DDR. Yet as late as 1988, Stasi chief Mielke told a small circle of his officers that the next war in Europe would "commence with an attack of the Warsaw Pact forces on the Federal Republic (West Germany)."[39] Indeed, shortly after reunification, Bonn defense ministry officials discovered the Warsaw Pact's attack plan, which consisted of some 25,000 documents. Contrary to the contingency plans of the North Atlantic Treaty Organization (NATO), the communists' plans were strictly offensive. Nuclear strikes were to be employed within two days after the start of the invasion. A separate, detailed plan for the invasion of West Berlin, complete with the names of persons to be arrested, also surfaced in Stasi archives.

Wolf also insisted that his department was an entity separate from the Ministry for State Security and that he and his men were merely concerned with espionage, like all Western intelligence agencies. Of course, he said, he had absolutely nothing to do with the oppression of the population. Wolf probably believed that the HVA's most incriminating documents had been destroyed. He was mistaken. A document now held by federal prosecutors reports on a speech Wolf made to his staff in 1983 in which he emphasized that the HVA was not independent but was an integral part of the MfS.[40] He added that the Stasi's political operations against dissidents could not succeed without the information supplied by his spies.

In the immediate aftermath of the DDR's demise, only about a hundred former Stasi officers publicly repented and revealed their knowledge of the terror and espionage apparatus. Most members of the once 102,000-strong secret police organization remained silent, claiming they were still bound by an oath that they had been obliged to take by the last government of the DDR. The oath eventually was declared null and void, and a numbers of case officers were forced to testify against West Germans who spied for the East.

A PRESENT AND FUTURE THREAT

Meanwhile, the former secret policemen pose a serious internal security problem. Seething with anger over their rapid fall from power, loss of privileges, unemployment, and severe cuts in pensions, they are a potentially volatile group.[41] Several former Stasi officers who have cooperated with authorities have received death threats, as have former political prisoners who named their persecutors. Rüdiger Knechtel, a former border guard who had been imprisoned for writing to a U.S. Army radio station and requesting a song, was threatened with an acid attack and placed under police protection. Knechtel had appeared on a television talk show in a debate with a former Stasi officer, who was hidden by a curtain to shield his identity. The former secret police officer was totally unrepentant and railed against the "persecution" of honorable men who had done nothing more than protect the state. He called Jutta Limbach, then Berlin's senator for judicial affairs, who was pushing for action against Stasi criminals, a "crab louse that needs to be squashed underfoot."[42] Limbach was appointed to the German supreme court in 1993.

Despite obvious trends in the other direction, PDS diehards still believe that their brand of socialism will eventually triumph. They ignore the drop in membership of their party from a peak of 2.1 million in 1989, when the SED changed its name, to about 150,000 paying members in 1996. In conversations with the author, former Stasi officers kept insisting that "not all the SED did was bad" and cited free education, medical care, and all-expenses-paid vacations. One of them, former Colonel Manfred Kleinpeter, who was a controller of American spies, fell into an icy, enraged silence when I equated such statements to the Nazis' saying that not everything was bad under Hitler, because after all, he had built the autobahns.

In fall 1991, the incorrigibles began to emulate former members of the Nazi SS in other ways as well. After World War II, SS men formed a group code-named Odessa that spirited many murderers abroad to escape prosecution. The Stasi alumni call themselves the Organization of Officers of the Ministry (ODOM). Manfred Kittlaus, director of Berlin's government crimes investigation unit, said at a 1993 parliamentary commission hearing that the former communist functionaries were an example of a "classic form of organized crime." One of his criminologists, Uwe Schmidt, told the commission probing into the DDR's past that former Stasi officers were working hand in glove with the Russian mafia. "It is a domestic security problem of the first order," Schmidt declared.

EVERY DICTATOR NEEDS A SECRET POLICE

Like all communist regimes, the DDR dictators could not have existed without the secret police. The Stasi was a tool used by the SED to keep itself in power. The Ministry for State Security was founded on Lenin's theory and Stalin's practical application of "the defense of the revolution." One of the first acts of Lenin after the October 1917 Revolution was the establishment of a secret police, the Cheka. The secret police organizations were the natural offspring of the Marxist-Leninist parties. Soviet secret police structures and practices of social control through terror were in every respect the models for Mielke. Like the KGB and other communist security organizations, the Stasi was no aberration of history but the "shield and sword" of the party, the weapon enforcing its claim to absolute supremacy.

The party's claim was based on Lenin's general theory of class struggle, imperialism, legitimate socialism, and the dictatorship of the proletariat. The Stasi was not a state within a state. It was subject to strict control by the party hierarchy, ensuring that the dog could not bite its master. Discipline was drilled into all members of the Stasi. That is why the perpetrators of DDR-sponsored crimes, like the Nazi criminals before them, defended their actions with the statement that they had just been following orders.

Lenin, in his report of October 22, 1918, said that "the principal link in the chain of revolution is the German link, and the success of *world* revolution depends more on Germany than upon any other country." It was preordained, therefore, that the Stasi would also become the KGB's most important surrogate. Having defeated Germany in 1945 and having occupied a large portion of it, the Soviet Union would resort to any measures to maintain its foothold there. In 1947, Stalin told Edvard Kardelj, then prime minister of Yugoslavia, "We Russians will never get out of Germany."[43] To achieve the goal of world revolution, any sentiments against communism had to be totally suppressed, or better still, eliminated. During the five years after the destruction of the Third Reich, the NKVD (and later, the Soviet Ministry of Internal Affairs [MVD] and the Soviet Ministry of State Security [MGB]) maintained a number of concentration camps that had been established by the Nazis, including such infamous death camps as Buchenwald and Sachsenhausen. At first, the inmates were ex-Nazis—many of them token party members without any leadership responsibilities—and war criminals. This changed in 1946 after the merger of the Social Democratic Party (SPD) and the Communist Party of Germany (KPD) into the SED. Thousands of anti-Nazi social democrats and communists who opposed the merger wound up in the camps as well.

When the war ended, Erich Mielke had become the Soviet Union's man in Germany. He was a loyal vassal who systematically built the Stasi into a vast secret police and espionage organization. Like Joseph Fouché, the shadowy figure who helped destroy six French governments in the late eighteenth and early nineteenth centuries, during the Reign of Terror in France, Mielke was a master of intrigue and the art of survival. Although lacking the intellectual prowess of Fouché, he nevertheless displayed the same sagacity and skill as he maneuvered through purges and intraparty witch-hunts. Mielke was the longest serving state security chief in the Eastern bloc. His relationship with the Soviet secret police was symbiotic and dated back to 1931, when he had fled Germany for Moscow after murdering two Berlin policemen. He was an intimate of nearly every Soviet secret police chief. Like Fouché, Mielke relished directing clandestine activities personally. Feliks Dzerzhinski, the founder of the Soviet Cheka, was his idol, and Mielke often referred to himself as a Chekist.

In sum, the Stasi was a criminal organization founded and operated by a monopolistic party—a combination of Red Gestapo and mafia—in which Mielke played the dual role of Heinrich Himmler and Don Corleone. To understand the dynamics of this powerful secret police organization that trampled on basic human rights and on the dignity of the individual, it is essential to examine the life of its leader.

2

ERICH MIELKE

Moscow's Leader of the Red Gestapo

IT WAS MIDMORNING, August 9, 1931. Erich Mielke and a fellow communist, Erich Ziemer, were in a hurry as they walked rapidly past a dingy block of working-class tenements in Berlin. They had just volunteered to commit murder, and they barely noticed the fresh graffiti on the walls and fences, which screamed threats at policemen: "For One Worker Shot, Two Policemen Will Die!!! The Red Front Takes Revenge!" Mielke and Ziemer were on precisely such a mission of revenge.

As the pair headed across Bülowplatz, dozens of men were milling around the entrance to Karl Liebknecht Haus, the headquarters of the Kommunistische Partei Deutschlands (KPD), the German Communist Party. Two days earlier, on August 7, a jittery young riot squad member fresh from the police academy had shot a young communist who attacked him during a street battle. Violence had become a daily event around the tenements of Moabit, Wedding, Prenzlauerberg, Neukölln, and Gesundbrunnen, home to hundreds of thousands of laborers and their families. Mielke and his comrade finally reached their destination, the Lassant beer hall—a popular hangout for blue-collar workers and communists. A guard at the door took them to an empty room and told them to wait.

In another room, two communist deputies of the Reichstag, the parliament of the Weimar Republic, were plotting the murder for which Mielke and Ziemer had been picked as hit men. The conspirators were Hans Kippenberger and Heinz Neumann. Their victim: Paul Anlauf, the forty-two-year-old captain commanding the 7th Police Precinct,

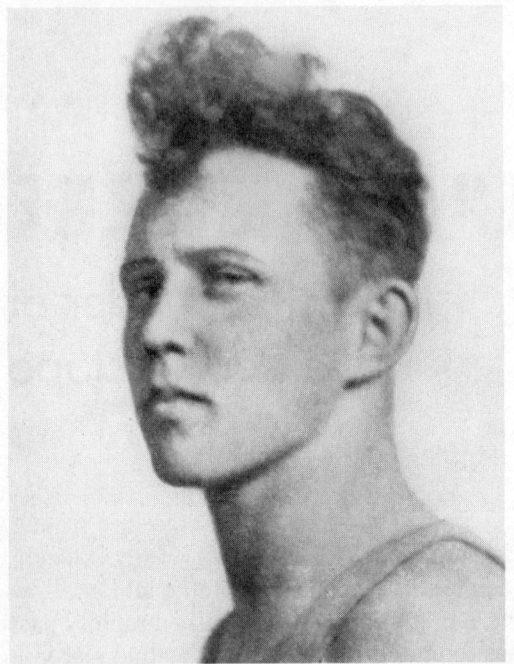

The young Erich Mielke as a member of the German Communist Party's military apparatus. Ullstein.

Erich Ziemer, Mielke's partner in the murder of Berlin police captains Paul Anlauf and Franz Lenck in 1931. Ziemer escaped to Moscow with Mielke and later participated in the Spanish Civil War, where he reportedly was killed in action. Ullstein.

Hans Kippenberger, who together with Heinz Neumann planned the murder of Berlin police officers Paul Anlauf and Franz Lenck. Private collection.

Heinz Neumann, communist firebrand and member of the Reichstag, who planned the murder of Berlin police officers Paul Anlauf and Franz Lenck in 1931. Neumann assigned Erich Mielke and Erich Ziemer to carry out the assassination. Ullstein.

Berlin police captain Paul Anlauf, murdered August 9, 1931 by Erich Mielke. Mielke, who would later become head of the Stasi, was sentenced to six years' imprisonment for the crime in 1993. Private collection.

whom the communists had nicknamed *Schweinebacke,* or Pig-Face. Of all the policemen in strife-torn Berlin, the reds hated Anlauf the most. His precinct included the area around KPD headquarters, which made it the most dangerous in the city. The captain almost always led the riot squads that broke up illegal rallies of the Communist Party.

Kippenberger and Neumann were furious. Their plan to have Anlauf murdered the previous evening had failed. They were still angry over their dressing-down by Walter Ulbricht, the Communist Party leader for the Berlin-Brandenburg region and the instigator of the plot. Ulbricht was a carpenter from the Saxonian city of Leipzig, the birthplace of the German socialist movement in the late nineteenth century. For weeks he had been itching to tangle with the police. "At home in Saxony we would have done something about the cops a long time ago," he had told Kippenberger and Neumann a week earlier. "Here in Berlin we will not fool around much longer. Soon we will hit the police in the head."[1]

Now Ulbricht's henchmen were determined to see Anlauf dead at any cost. Kippenberger, at the time a member of parliament, had been an infantry officer in World War I, decorated with the Iron Cross first class for heroism. A philosophy graduate from Hamburg University, he had led a group of leftist students and participated in the 1923

Communist rabble-rouser Walter Ulbricht addresses a 1931 mass rally in Berlin, at a time when the communists were still collaborating with the Nazis to bring down the social democratic Weimar Republic. On the left is Joseph Goebbels, the Nazis' chief propagandist. After the rally a pitched battle erupted that resulted in more than a hundred wounded. Ullstein.

abortive communist uprising in that North German port city. Wanted by police, he had fled to Moscow, where he was recruited personally by General Jan Karlovich Berzin, the first chief of the *Glavnoe razvedyvatel'noe upravlenie* (GRU), the Soviet military espionage service. Trained in the Soviet Union, Kippenberger later became the most important link between the Soviet secret service and Germany's Communist Party, functioning at various times under the code names Alex, Adam, and Wolf.[2] After the German government amnestied those who took part in the Hamburg revolt, Kippenberger returned to Germany and settled in Berlin. There he became Stalin's surrogate for controlling the many-faceted, secret KPD organizations—the M, N, Z, and T groups. M stood for military; N for *Nachrichten,* or intelligence; Z for *Zersetzung,* meaning subversion; and T denoted terrorism.

Neumann, too, was no run-of-the-mill communist. He was Soviet trained and was close to Stalin, whom he had visited many times in the 1920s and with whom he maintained a lively correspondence. Kippenberger and Neumann were joint chiefs of the *Parteiselbstschutz,* or Party Self-Defense Unit. This was the Communist Party's combined version of the brown-shirted Nazi storm troopers and the SS, whose members wore black uniforms adorned with a silver skull and crossbones. (The initials SS stood for *Schutzstaffel,* which translates into Security Squad.)

Like their Nazi counterparts, the Selbstschutz men were thugs who served as bouncers at party meetings and specialized in cracking heads during street battles with political enemies. Besides the Nazis, their arch foes included the Sozialdemokratische Partei Deutschlands (SPD)—the Social Democratic Party of Germany—and radical nationalist parties. They always carried a *Stahlrute,* two steel springs that telescoped into a tube seven inches long, which when extended became a deadly, fourteen-inch weapon. Not to be outdone by the Nazis, these goons often were armed with pistols as well.

While Mielke and Ziemer were cooling their heels, Kippenberger, who during strategy sessions liked to refer to himself as chief of the general staff, issued orders with military precision to two four-man groups of Selbstschutz men.[3] Michael Klause, a thirty-six-year-old unemployed laborer who had also emerged from the Great War as a highly decorated hero, was designated the field commander of the attack. Friedrich Bröde, the doorman at the Bülowplatz party headquarters, was a forty-seven-year-old veteran of many bloody street battles. In 1920 he had lost a leg when an explosive he was testing detonated prematurely. Kippenberger told the men that Mielke and Ziemer had been selected as the hit team because they had acquitted themselves well as members of the Selbstschutz.

The twenty-three-year-old Mielke had joined the Communist Youth Movement at the age of fourteen, and in 1927 he had been admitted to full KPD membership. Mielke was a special protégé of Kippenberger's, having taken to his paramilitary training with the enthusiasm of a Prussian Junker. World War I veterans taught the novices how to handle pistols, rifles, machine guns, and hand grenades. This clandestine training was conducted in the sparsely populated, pastoral countryside of Brandenburg province surrounding Berlin. Mielke also pleased Kippenberger by being an exceptional student in classes on the arts of conspiratorial behavior and espionage, taught by comrades who had studied at the secret M-School of the GRU in Moscow.

Kippenberger dismissed the group and joined Mielke and Ziemer. A third man, Max Thunert, also came into the room. He had just been handed a Luger pistol by another comrade, Max Matern, who told Thunert: "Now we're getting serious. . . . We're going to give

Schweinebacke something to remember us by." Turning to Mielke and Ziemer, Kippenberger asked, "Are you sure that you are ready to shoot Schweinebacke?" Ziemer nodded, but said he did not know what Anlauf looked like. "Thunert here will point him out to you," Kippenberger said. Mielke, a man who never had much to say but who was prone to violent outbursts when he was riled, stiffened. "Natürlich" ("of course"), he said in a loud voice, as if insulted by the question, adding that he knew Anlauf well from previous encounters during raids on party headquarters. Mielke exuded self-confidence. Although he was not tall—he stood about five feet five inches—he was well built, muscular, handsome, and very athletic. Tucked in his waistband and concealed under his jacket was a nine-millimeter Luger pistol—the artillery corps version, with an eight-inch barrel. The pistol had been given him by Klause, who also functioned as the armorer of the Selbstschutz. Ziemer was armed with a Dreyse automatic, a .32 caliber weapon carried by the police before they switched to the heavier caliber Luger.

"This evening you will go to the Bräustübl," Kippenberger ordered, referring to a Berlin beer hall that was situated next door to the police station. "From the first floor you can overlook the entire Bülowplatz. Don't forget that Schweinebacke is never alone. Hussar is always with him." Hussar was the communists' nickname for Senior Sergeant Max Willig. "When you spot Schweinebacke and Hussar, you take care of them." Then the parliamentarian explained that two groups of four men each would be their backup. "They will create a diversion after the attack so that you can get away. You know the route you have to take. Go to your homes and wait for further instructions." At that moment, Thunert was looking out the window. "There is Schweinebacke now," he said. Ziemer came to the window to see Anlauf walking slowly toward the square and in the direction of KPD headquarters. As usual, the heavyset captain with the Hitlerian mustache was trailed by Sergeant Willig. Both were wearing the distinctive police duty shako—a stiff, cylindrical military dress hat with a flat top and a silver police badge at the front. It was shortly after eleven o'clock in the morning. The weather had been hot and dry for weeks in Berlin, but that morning it had turned cool and it was raining lightly. Groups of Communist Party agitators were milling around a polling station. They were shouting slogans at burghers who were arriving to vote in a hotly contested plebiscite that had been called to determine whether or not the Prussian parliament should be dissolved.

As was often the case when it came to battling the dominant SPD, the KPD and the Nazis had combined forces during the pre-plebiscite campaign. At one point during this particular campaign, Nazi propaganda chief Joseph Goebbels even shared a speaker's platform with KPD agitator Walter Ulbricht.[4] Both parties wanted the parliament dissolved because they were hoping that new elections would oust the ruling SPD, the sworn enemy of all radicals. That fact explained why the atmosphere was particularly volatile this Sunday. "So, that's it," Kippenberger said. "Don't go near any trouble spots," he admonished his gunmen. "Lie low until six o'clock and then go to the second floor of the Bräustübl, and watch. Be alert! I don't want another failure."

It was still drizzling at eight o'clock Sunday evening.[5] Radio Berlin was featuring tenor Joseph Schmidt singing Italian operatic arias. George Bernard Shaw, who had arrived from Moscow that morning, was dining in serene elegance at the posh Adlon Hotel, Berlin's most exclusive hostelry, on Unter den Linden boulevard near the Brandenburg Gate. Berlin was a schizophrenic city in those days. At the luxury hotels, diners appeared in black tie, even in tails. Glittering movie houses and variety shows did a brisk business in the downtown area near Kurfürstendamm boulevard, as if the city was the most carefree in the world. The atmosphere could well have been the setting for a theatrical farce. Two miles from the scenes of lighthearted gaiety was the Bülowplatz. As dusk fell, the square was filling with a mob of several hundred people who were jeering and howling and waving red hammer-and-sickle flags at a small contingent of police. Like matadors taunting bulls, the agitators waved their red banners at the cops, daring them to swing their rubber truncheons at the crowd. The battlefield was communist turf, and this time no Nazi brownshirts challenged the Reds with the usual, venomous, shouted slogans: The two groups were fighting a common enemy. The mob roared when they heard the oscillating, high-low sound of police sirens signaling the arrival of riot units in their distinctive open assault trucks holding twelve men each. The riot cops wore blue-gray uniforms and showed that they meant business when they fastened the chin straps on their shakos. Holding their Mauser rifles across their chests, they charged against the mob. Shortly after eight o'clock Mielke spotted Captain Anlauf and his top sergeant approaching the square. They were accompanied by a third police captain, Franz Lenck, who normally was assigned to factory safety and health control duties. Because Berlin police had been placed on high alert, Lenck had been assigned to work with the 7th Precinct that evening.

Mielke and Ziemer sprinted downstairs but remained hidden in a doorway until the trio had passed. Then they hurried after the policemen, who were heading slowly in the direction of the Babylon movie theater at the corner of Bülowplatz and Kaiser Wilhelm Strasse. The Babylon was showing a double feature: Greta Garbo starring in *The Goddess* and Ramon Navarro playing in *The Youngest Lieutenant.*

Berlin police officer Franz Lenck, murdered August 9, 1931. Private collection.

When they reached the movie house, someone shouted: "Schweinebacke!" Anlauf turned. At that moment Mielke and Ziemer fired at point-blank range. Captain Anlauf was hit twice. Lenck caught a bullet in the chest. Sergeant Willig, wounded in the left arm and stomach, sank to his knees. Still he drew his Luger and fired a full clip at the assassins, who stormed past him into the theater: Willig's aim was wide of the mark. Lenck staggered to the theater entrance, where he died. The sergeant then dragged himself to where Anlauf lay on the cobblestones. Shot in the neck, Anlauf looked at Willig and gasped: "Wiedersehen . . . Gruss . . . " ("So long . . . Good-bye . . . "). Then he pulled his shako from his head and died.[6] Anlauf, whose wife had died three weeks earlier of a kidney ailment, left three daughters.[7] Captain Lenck was married but had no children.

THE ASSASSINS' ESCAPE

Mielke and Ziemer ran through the darkened theater and escaped through an emergency exit. They tossed their guns over a fence, where they were later found by detectives of the elite Berliner Mordkommis-

The Babylon movie theater in East Berlin, outside which Erich Mielke and Erich Ziemer murdered police captains Anlauf and Lenck. Private collection.

sion, the homicide squad. The pair headed northwest toward Gesundbrunnen, where they lived only a block apart—Mielke, at his parents' apartment at 25 Stettinerstrasse, and Ziemer, as a boarder at 25B Biesenthaler Strasse.

Back at Bülowplatz, the killings had triggered a major police action. At least a thousand officers poured into the square, and a bloody street battled ensued.[8] Rocks and bricks were hurled from the rooftops. Communist gunmen fired indiscriminately from windows and from the roofs of surrounding apartment houses. As darkness fell, police searchlights illuminated the buildings. Using megaphones, officers shouted: "Clear the streets! Move away from the windows, we are returning fire!" By now the rabble had fled the square, but shooting continued as riot squads combed the tenements, arresting hundreds of residents suspected of having fired weapons. The battle lasted until one o'clock the next morning. In addition to the two police officers, the casualties included one communist who died of a gunshot wound and seventeen others who were seriously wounded.

Kippenberger became alarmed when word reached him that Sergeant Willig had survived the shooting. Not knowing whether the sergeant could talk and identify his attackers, Kippenberger was tak-

A typical scene in front of Communist Party headquarters at Berlin's Bülowplatz on January 22, 1933, nine days before Hitler came to power. In the foreground Nazi storm troopers prepare to confront the assembled communists. Portraits of Vladimir Lenin, Karl Liebknecht, and Rosa Luxemburg adorn the front of the building. The slogan on the facade reads: "Move forward in their spirit in the battle against the dangers of war, fascism, and cold, for work, bread, and freedom." The slogans on the right urge the election of "Red workers' councils in the spirit of Leninism" and "strengthening the revolutionary labor union opposition." Ullstein.

ing no chances. He directed a runner to summon Mielke and Ziemer to his apartment at 74 Bellermannstrasse, only a few minutes' walk from where the two lived. When the assassins arrived, Kippenberger told them the news and ordered them to leave Berlin at once. The parliamentarian's wife Thea, an unemployed schoolteacher and as staunch a Communist Party member as her husband, shepherded the young murderers to the Belgian border. Agents of the Communist International (Comintern) in the port city of Antwerp supplied them with money and forged passports. Aboard a merchant ship they sailed for Leningrad.[9] When their ship docked, they were met by another Comintern representative, who escorted them to Moscow.

Virtually from the moment he arrived in Moscow, Mielke avoided contact with other German Communists living there in exile. He was following orders of the *Obedinennoe gosudarstvennoe politicheskoe upravlenie* (OGPU), Stalin's secret police organization—the successor to Feliks Dzerzhinski's Cheka. Young Mielke met with OGPU chairman Vyacheslav Menzhinsky, who had already been advised by Kippenberger through the Soviet embassy in Berlin of his arrival. Even though Mielke had proved his loyalty to the communist cause, he was ordered to provide a detailed handwritten biography.[10] This was the first of many biographies that Mielke would write for the Soviets. Handwritten biographies were primary tools of the Soviet secret police investigators, who watched for any deviations in data that might implicate the writers as "capitalist agents." Woe to the hapless writer if he later wrote something different than what he had supplied in previous versions.

"I, Erich Mielke, was born on December 28, 1907, in Berlin (Prussia)," he wrote.[11] "My father was a poor, uneducated woodworker, and my mother died in 1911. Both were members of the SPD and joined the KPD when it was formed in 1918. My stepmother was a seamstress and she also belonged to the KPD. My younger brother Kurt and my two sisters were communist sympathizers." Mielke was a master of obfuscation. He mentioned that his father had once quit the party, then rejoined, quit once more, and again returned to the fold. Apparently Mielke was not sure of his father's ideological convictions. In the end, anyone reading the paper would have had to give him the benefit of the doubt: Perhaps Papa Mielke was indeed a true comrade. The rest of the statement retained by the cadre division of the Comintern (Classified Secret No. 2458) read as follows.[12]

> Besides the distribution of leaflets to policemen, etc., I worked since the end of 1930 in the party cadre. We took care of all kinds of work; terror acts, protection of illegal demonstrations and meetings. The last work I accomplished with another comrade was the Bülowplatz affair. My parents had an inkling that I participated in it, but they are in all matters dependable and can be used as an address for me. I was arrested twice, released after five days of investigative detention, and then sentenced to four days [in jail] and fined 20 marks. The second case is pending.

For comparison, the OGPU had a personal history statement Mielke had written years earlier in Germany, when he had joined the KPD.

The OGPU's vetting of Mielke was completed within a few weeks. While he waited, he took intensive courses in Russian. He had an ear for languages and already spoke some French and English. The Comintern cadre division gave Mielke the temporary pseudonym of Scheuer and assigned him to the M-P school—the secret academy where the Soviet Union trained its most promising cadres in military science, political affairs, and espionage.

Mielke had not always been a good student. In fact, he left the Köllnisches Gymnasium in Berlin because, as school director F. Goss certified on February 19, 1929, he was "unable to meet the great demands of this school."[13] The Köllnisches Gymnasium was a high school that emphasized the humanities, and it was generally the preserve of the privileged; but a few children of the working class were admitted if they could pass stringent examinations. The future secret police chief, it seems, was smart enough to get into the school but not to graduate. Or perhaps he neglected his studies because he was too busy training as a communist thug. In any case, to make sure that no one could suspect him of having a bourgeois family background, he had carefully noted in his biography that he attended the school for two years "free of charge," on scholarship.

Mielke received better than average marks from his Soviet instructors. Even before he graduated from the spy school, a resolution of the Central Committee of the German Communist Party in exile recommended he attend the elite Lenin School, the ideological cadre factory. Study at the Lenin School was a must for prospective leaders, especially for those who had been selected for future secret operations. Again the OGPU and the International Committee of the Comintern approved the recommendation, and Mielke was given a new cover name, Paul Bach—a name he would use for the next few years.

Using mafia parlance, Mielke was "a made soldier" of the OGPU and the Comintern, a man who would fit into a secret army that would obey orders without hesitation and whose members had no moral scruples when it came to fighting for the cause. The need for such an army was more urgent than ever. Germany, the great obstacle to Lenin's world revolution, had been taken over by Adolf Hitler and his Nazis, and the Communist Party there was in shambles. Thousands of comrades had been arrested and thrown into prisons and concentration camps, and hundreds had gone into hiding. The KPD leadership had fled abroad, most of them to Moscow. Their dream of a "Sowjet Deutschland," a Soviet Germany, had been shattered, but they were convinced they would live to fight another day.

In mid-March 1933, while attending the Lenin School, Mielke received word from his OGPU sponsors that Berlin police had arrested Max Thunert, one of the conspirators in the Anlauf and Lenck murders. Within days, fifteen other members of the assassination team were in custody. Mielke had to wait six more months before the details of the police action against his Berlin comrades reached Moscow. On September 14, 1933, Berlin newspapers reported that all fifteen had confessed to their roles in the murders.[14] Arrest warrants were issued for ten others who had fled, including Mielke, Ziemer, Ulbricht, Kippenberger, and Neumann.

Ziemer also attended the M-P and Lenin Schools, under the name Georg Schlosser, but he was not in the same class as Mielke. In 1934, however, the two were reunited at a special Comintern school. Both spent a year lecturing on military and political subjects to other German communists, who were arriving in Moscow in droves since the Nazi takeover. Meanwhile, Kippenberger and Neumann were safe in Moscow. Ulbricht had escaped to Austria, where he continued his subversive activities for the Comintern. Eventually, he too would emigrate to Moscow.

Absorbed in his tasks at the Comintern school, Mielke had little time to ponder the trial in 1934 at which Klause, Matern, and Bröde were sentenced to death. Others received terms ranging from nine months to fifteen years at hard labor. Matern was guillotined and Bröde hanged himself in his prison cell. Klause's sentence was commuted to life imprisonment because according to a court report, he had "rendered valuable assistance in solving the case." In Mielke's eyes, Klause and four other men against whom charges were dropped or who were acquitted were obviously traitors to the cause.

All the while Mielke had maintained close links with the Soviet secret police, which by then had changed its name to *Narodnyi komissariat vnutrennikh del* (NKVD), the People's Commissariat for Internal Affairs. Its new chairman was Genrikh Grigorevich Yagoda, former assistant to OGPU chief Vyacheslav Rudolfovich Menzhinsky, who had died.

This was a time of new peril for the arrivals from Germany, whom Stalin soon began to view as a new threat to his power. The dictator had already eliminated some of his closest associates who had opposed the forced collectivization of Russian farmers. Tens of millions already had been murdered by the OGPU, had perished in labor camps, or simply had been left to die of starvation. Stalin's secret police agents, among them Mielke, reported "factionalism and deviationist trends" among the German exiles, whose elite was housed at the Comintern-operated Hotel Lux. It was true that many German communists abhorred his methods. Nevertheless, they were loyal to the cause as a whole and had deluded themselves into believing that ruthless methods were necessary for the eventual triumph of the international proletariat. The German communists had never been particularly cohesive. Various factions had opposed one another for years. There had always been tension between high-minded intellectuals and men like Ulbricht and Mielke, who came from the poor, uneducated, blue-collar class. It was a struggle that the intellectuals were destined to lose. They never seemed to comprehend that the millions born into abject poverty or who had become jobless during the horrendous inflation that followed World War I were the backbone of the KPD.

On May 13, 1935, Stalin finally decided he would deal with his real and imagined enemies once and for all. He ordered a final, great purge that lasted until September 1936 and that was designed to eliminate "counterrevolutionary elements" from the ranks of the Soviet Communist Party. Hundreds of foreign communists who had sought safe haven in Moscow, including Germans, were caught in Stalin's net as well. Ultimately, the purge served to terrorize Stalin's own party into absolute obedience.

Squads of NKVD troops armed with rifles and revolvers raided the Hotel Lux night after night. Hundreds of German communists—chiefly the intellectuals—disappeared. Some landed in labor camps, in the gulag. The more prominent were brought before military tribunals. Among them were Kippenberger and Neumann, the strategists of the 1931 Berlin murders. Both men were sentenced to death and shot. Kippenberger's wife, Thea, died in the gulag. Their daughter Margot, then nine years old, was packed off to an OGPU-controlled boarding school and later to a prison camp in Siberia. She was not told the fate of her parents until she was finally allowed to leave the Soviet Union for East Germany in 1958.[15] Neumann's wife Margarete also survived imprisonment but was turned over to the Nazi Gestapo after Stalin made his pact with Hitler in 1939. During all of these events, Mielke remained a shadowy figure working diligently for the NKVD. Was the proletarian Mielke the man who fingered his erstwhile intellectual comrades and mentors for Stalin's executioners? The question is legitimate, based on the existent (admittedly slight) circumstantial evidence; but it will remain unanswered until Mielke's dossier is released by the keepers of the KGB archives in Moscow.

MIELKE HEADS FOR SPAIN

Erich Mielke, alias Paul Bach, took yet another name in September 1936. As Fritz Leissner, he traveled with Ziemer to Spain and a new assignment in that country's civil war. It was a chance to advance his career as an NKVD man, or "Chekist," as he liked to call himself. It seemed as if Mielke felt that the "Chekist" label provided proof positive that he was loyally following in the footsteps of Stalin's secret policemen, who protected the state by murdering millions of their own people.

General Alexander Orlov headed NKVD operations in Spain. He urgently needed more agents to work with the Servicio Investigacion Militar (SIM), the Loyalists' military security service. Although Spanish communists were nominally in charge of the various SIM offices, the service was created by the Soviets to control "deviationists" and others who might disagree with Stalin's policies. Its ranks, however, lacked the expertise that men like Mielke and Ziemer could provide.

Adhering rigidly to the conspiratorial rules of the NKVD, Mielke managed to appear under various guises. For a while he was assigned as a captain and adjutant to the staff of "General Gomez," whose true name was Wilhelm Zaisser. A veteran German communist, Zaisser enjoyed the trust of Stalin and the NKVD. For years he was one of their top espionage and subversion agents in China. In Spain he commanded for a time the 13th International Battalion, composed mostly of East Europeans and Germans. Eventually, Zaisser was appointed chief of staff of the International Brigade, with headquarters at Albacete. There the SIM, with NKVD assistance, worked overtime checking into the background of all brigade members in leadership positions down to the level of company commanders. Mielke found himself in a familiar milieu.

Walter Janka, a German company commander stationed at Murcia, was summoned to the SIM in the winter of 1936 and confronted by Captain Leissner. A communist writer who had been living in exile in Czechoslovakia since 1933, Janka had made his own way to Spain rather than being assigned there by Moscow. Mielke, alias Leissner, interrogated the man harshly. He was especially interested in what he was doing in Spain and how he got there. Janka told Mielke to get lost. A few weeks later the feisty company commander was demoted to private and transferred to another unit. Mielke personally delivered Janka to the new unit's frontline position. Considering what had happened to others who came into conflict with SIM inquisitors, the new private was lucky. However, Janka later vented his anger to friends: "While I was fighting at the front, shooting at the fascists, Mielke served in the rear, shooting Trotskyites and anarchists."[16]

In Spain, Mielke and Ziemer would be a team again, albeit for only a short time. Mielke was stationed at the headquarters of the International Brigade at Albacete. He requested that the German cadre section write the following letter on August 26, 1937, to the commander of the Tank Regiment Archena stationed at Murcia.[17]

> Esteemed Comrade!
>
> You have a comrade Georg Schlosser in your unit. Since we intend to deploy the comrade in accordance with his qualifications, we cordially request you to release Georg Schlosser and send him to the Albacete Base. The deployment here of the comrade is very urgent and we therefore ask you to comply with our wish as quickly as possible.
>
> In friendship,
> Greetings,
> Cadre Division, German Section

Ziemer, alias Schlosser, was sent to Mielke's unit, and two months later he was dead. The circumstances under which Ziemer died remain mysterious. That it happened just after he was assigned to

Mielke's unit, however, certainly raises suspicions. Was Mielke systematically eliminating witnesses to the 1931 murder? The planners of the crime, Kippenberger and Neumann, were wiped out by Stalin. The others who abetted the crime had either been liquidated by the Nazis or were languishing in concentration camps or penitentiaries. By 1945, they too were dead.

Mielke was always careful to cover his tracks, but his membership in the SIM alone had stigmatized him. Military tribunals were kept busy adjudicating the cases of victims of the SIM, which used torture to extract "confessions" just as its agents had been taught by their Soviet advisers. Prison cells were so small that inmates could barely stand. Prisoners were subjected to deafening noises, icy baths, hot irons, and severe beatings. Executions ran into the hundreds, perhaps thousands, during the course of the three-year civil war.[18]

The carnage finally ended in 1939, and Mielke fled across the Pyrenees mountains to southern France, where he was interned with thousands of his comrades. He was still in a French camp when World War II began on September 1, 1939. Agile as always, he managed to flee to the Soviet Union a few months later. Secrecy once more shrouded Mielke, and his role during the war remains a carefully guarded secret.

RETURN TO GERMANY

In 1945, Germany was baking in an unusually hot and dry summer. A yellowish haze enveloped Berlin months after the last shot was fired and the last flames from incendiaries were put out. The smell of burned wood and musty, centuries-old masonry permeated the air. Here and there among the ruins the stench of decaying flesh lingered. What British and American bombers began, thousands of heavy Soviet artillery pieces had completed. The once vibrant city had become a giant pile of rubble, and survivors ambled listlessly past the facades of burned-out buildings.

While some Soviet soldiers distributed loaves of black bread to the starving, others raped and plundered. The first German words they learned were *Frau, komm* ("Woman, let's go"); and *Uhry* (an incorrectly pluralized, Russianized form of *Uhr,* the German word for watch), indicating that the owner was to hand over the desired object. It was not unusual to see a woman desperately clutching the handlebars of her battered bicycle and a grimy "Ivan"—the Germans' nickname for all Russians—pulling on the rear wheel, determined to claim it as his own. Passersby ignored such scenes, self-preservation being the order of the day. No one wanted to tangle with the NKVD—or the "GPU," as the Germans still called the Soviet secret police—whose agents were sweeping the city for Nazis. This was the Berlin to which Erich Mielke returned after a fourteen-year odyssey through intrigue, treachery, and war. At the age of thirty-six, the fanatic communist could once more set foot in his hometown without worrying about the outstanding warrant for his arrest on charges of murder. All judicial functions had been taken over by the Soviet Military Administration, and a loyal comrade was not about to be arrested on charges of killing two Prussian police officers back in 1931 when the communists were fighting for power.

There is little doubt that Mielke and Wilhelm Zaisser, his old commander in Spain who had also escaped to the Soviet Union, returned to Germany as special members of the Soviet secret police. They were joined by Ernst Wollweber, another loyal fighter against fascism. Wollweber moved to Denmark in 1933 and assumed leadership of the Seamen and Dockworkers International. Seven years after that, he fled ahead of invading German troops to Sweden. There he led a team of explosive experts in blowing up at least six freighters carrying goods destined for Germany, Italy, and Japan.[19] But his sabotage activities were short-lived: Wollweber was caught stealing explosives and jailed until he was extradited to the Soviet Union in 1943 after Moscow claimed that he was a fugitive who had embezzled government funds. It was a clever ruse to extricate one of their valuable secret agents, and the Swedes were only too happy to get rid of him.

The trio had one thing in common—all had attended Moscow's secret M-P school and the International Lenin School. Much of Zaisser's wartime service is known: He was in charge of the "antifascist school" at Krasnogorsk. There, in exchange for better food and treatment, thousands of German prisoners of war of all ranks, including several generals, allowed themselves to be brainwashed and turned into believers. The activities of Mielke and Wollweber, however, remained closely guarded secrets. Mielke's exploits must have been substantial. By war's end he had been decorated with the Order of the Red Banner, the Order of the Great Patriotic War First Class, and twice with the Order of Lenin. It is likely that he served as an NKVD agent, at least part of the time with guerrilla units behind the German lines, for he knew all the partisan songs by heart and sang them in faultless Russian.[20]

It is significant that Mielke, Zaisser, and Wollweber were not brought back to Germany in April 1945 aboard the special Soviet aircraft with the handful of men who were to assume leadership positions of a Soviet-controlled German civil administration. Among that group was the man who gave the order for the murders committed by Mielke in 1931, Walter Ulbricht. For the time being, the Soviets must have wanted to keep Mielke, Zaisser, and Wollweber out of the reach of public scrutiny as they began their work for the NKGB, the People's Committee for State Security, which had been created in 1943 to deal with guerrilla and subversive activities, counterespionage, and foreign espionage. The NKVD continued to exist separately until 1946, when it was elevated to the ministerial level as the Ministry for Government Security (MGB), which controlled the NKGB and the police and border guards.

Marshal Georgy K. Zhukov, supreme commander of Soviet Forces in Germany and head of the Soviet Military Administration (SMA), issued his SMA Order No. 2 on July 10, 1945, legalizing the establishment of "antifascist" political parties such as the KPD. Five days later, Mielke walked into KPD headquarters and offered his services, saying that he was already working with street cells of the KPD. In completing the obligatory party membership questionnaire, Mielke camouflaged his NKGB assignment, lying boldly about his wartime activities.[21] That he was successful in hiding the pertinent facts proves that he had the absolute backing of the Soviet Military Administration, the MGB, and the NKGB. Without this protection, lying on official documents would have been fatal. "The Soviets trusted Mielke implicitly," said Bernd Kaufmann, former director of the Stasi's espionage school. "He earned his spurs in Spain."[22]

When asked if he had ever been arrested or tried for a political offense, Mielke wrote: "I was sentenced to death in absentia (Bülowplatz)." That was the first lie. His name was mentioned in the 1934 trials but he was never tried. Next he said that he had moved to Belgium after being released from internment in France, following the Spanish Civil War, and that he had worked there for a Communist Party underground newspaper using the cover name Gaston. The third lie: Mielke attested that he had returned to France under the name Richard Hebel and had served there in the Organisation Todt (which he misspelled as *Tod*), an auxiliary paramilitary group for the construction of defensive positions, airfields, and roads, which was attached to the Wehrmacht. There was no way he could have joined the organization abroad. All German members were recruited or drafted in Germany, where their identities were easily checked by the Gestapo.

The questionnaire also provided this further evidence of Mielke's role in delivering German communists to Stalin's firing squads: "During my stay in the SU (Soviet Union), I participated in all Party discussions of the KPD and also in the problems concerning the establishment of socialism and in the trials against the traitors and enemies of the SU."

To impress his new Berlin comrades, Mielke bragged about the awards he had received, "including the sports medal of the Soviet Union." In closing, he wrote:

> I was a guest on the honor grandstand of Red Square during the May Day and October Revolution parades. I became acquainted with many comrades of the Federation of World Communist Parties and the War Council of the Special Commission of the Comintern.
>
> I will never forget my meeting with Comrade Dimitrov, the chairman of the Comintern whom I served as an aide together with another comrade. I saw Comrade Stalin during all demonstrations at Red Square, especially when I stood on the grandstand. I mention these meetings because all these comrades are our models and teachers for our work.

The KPD questionnaires were handed over to the MGB/NKGB headquarters that had been set up in the Berlin suburb of Karlshorst. The man in charge there was Colonel General Ivan Serov, who years later would become known as the "Butcher of Budapest" for his part in snuffing out the Hungarian Revolution. As might be expected, Mielke's account of his past was approved by the Soviets. Had Serov not been part of the conspiracy, Mielke would have been instantly arrested or at least subjected to an intense investigation because of his membership in the Nazi Organisation Todt, which used thousands of slave laborers. But he was cleared in record time, and by the end of June the Soviets had installed him as a station commander of the newly formed Volkspolizei (Vopo), the People's Police.

MIELKE'S NEW JOB

Mielke's future in the new Stalinist Germany was now assured. When the Soviet Military Administration on August 16, 1947 created the first German political police since the days of the Nazi Gestapo, Wilhelm Zaisser was put in charge and Mielke became his deputy. The Soviets gave the organization the cover name "Komissariat 5"(the Fifth Commissariat, or K-5), and attached it formally (although it operated independently) to the regular criminal investigation department of the Vopo. The subterfuge was necessary because the rules of the Allied Control Commission banned reestablishment of a German political police.

The K-5 was essentially an arm of the Soviet secret police. Its agents were carefully selected veteran German communists who had survived the Nazi era in Soviet exile or in concentration camps and prisons. Their task was to track down Nazis and anticommunists, including hundreds of members of the Social Democratic Party. Mielke and his fellow bloodhounds performed this task with ruthless precision. The number of arrests became so great that the regular prisons could not hold them. Thus, Serov ordered the establishment or reopening of eleven concentration camps, among them the former Nazi death camps of Buchenwald and Sachsenhausen.

Until spring 1946, inhabitants of the Soviet-occupied zone merely shrugged at the wave of arrests, believing that the victims were former Nazi officials and war criminals. Then the Soviets ordered the fusion of the KPD and the Social Democratic Party, which had been an arch foe of the Communists since the 1918 German revolution. The new party was named the Sozialistische Einheitspartei Deutschlands (SED), the Socialist Unity Party. Outwardly, the wedding appeared to proceed smoothly. In reality, however, thousands of rank-and-file socialists who opposed it were arrested and thrown into prisons and concentration camps. They were joined by people who had been denounced for making anticommunist or anti-Soviet remarks, among their number hundreds who were as young as fourteen years.[23] Although these arrests were made by Germans purporting to be officials of the criminal police, the existence of the K-5 political police eventually was exposed. Mielke, however, had risen to the post of vice president of the German Administration for Interior Affairs—the equivalent of the NKVD—and continued his manipulations from behind the scenes.

Mielke's days of anonymity were numbered, however. In January 1947, eight months before the establishment of K-5, two old-time Berlin policemen recognized him during his participation at an official function. They told their story to the head of the Kriminalpolizei (Kripo), the criminal investigation department, in West Berlin, and demanded that he be arrested for the 1931 murders. The Kripo chief reported the situation to Wilhelm Kühnast, prosecutor general for the Kammergericht, the highest court in Berlin, which was located in the Soviet Sector. Kühnast was a veteran jurist with an anti-Nazi background. A search of the archives was ordered, and to Kühnast's astonishment the files of the 1934 trial had survived the World War II bombings. Mielke's name figured prominently in testimony implicating him as one of the murderers of Police Captains Anlauf and Lenck. On February 7, 1947, the prosecutor general issued a new warrant for Mielke's immediate arrest.

At that time, the city administration, including the police, was under the control of the Allied Control Commission, which consisted of U.S., British, French, and Soviet military officers. All actions by city officials, including the judiciary, were to be reported to the commission. The Soviet representative alerted the MGB. Action was swift. Marshal Andrei Sokolovsky, who had replaced Zhukov, protested, and his representatives at the commission launched a vigorous campaign to discredit Kühnast. They unleashed a vicious barrage of accusations against the jurist. Kühnast, the Soviets said, was suspected of criminal offenses and of having belonged to the Nazi People's Court of Roland Freisler, the most bloodthirsty judge of the Third Reich, who sentenced hundreds of anti-Nazis to death. These blatant lies show the lengths to which the Soviets would go to protect their agent. The vehemence of the Soviet attacks was sufficient to cow the three western Allies into agreeing to remove the prosecutor general from his post and place him under house arrest. At the same time, the Soviets confiscated all documents on the case, including the 1934 court records.[24] For now, Mielke was saved again. The MGB valued his services and had still more important tasks in mind for him in the continuing Stalinization of East Germany.

Kühnast remained under house arrest for fourteen months at his home in the Soviet sector. Only the fact that the western Allies were involved in the case saved him from landing in prison or in a Soviet concentration camp. When the Soviets walked out of the Allied Control Commission and began their blockade of Berlin in July 1948, Kühnast was able to escape to the American sector, where he was granted political asylum.[25]

CLIMBING THE PROMOTION LADDER

At about the time of the prosecutor's escape, Mielke was given a new task. He became chief of the Deutsche Wirtschaftskommission, the German Economic Commission, which had been established by the Moscow-controlled provisional government. Concealed behind this innocuous name was a second secret police operation (in addition to Komissariat 5), which was charged with safeguarding confiscated property against "misuse and sabotage" as well as with investigating "economic crimes." Protection of the economy had become a major secret police function, and it included the pursuit of East Germans escaping to the Western zones. In the first year after the war, 1.6 million had left the Soviet zone, creating a serious shortage of skilled workers and specialists. Thousands were fleeing communist terror every month. Those caught at the border where rounded up and forced to work under wretched conditions in mines, digging uranium ore for the Soviet Union's atomic bomb project. Mielke's new group was intimately tied to this operation as well.

Though busy directing the roundup of state enemies, Mielke found the time to satisfy his libido. An affair with a seamstress, Gertrud Müller, produced a son in autumn 1948. They named him Frank, though papa Mielke always referred to him by the Russianized diminutive "Frankuschka." According to the communist code of behavior, it was evidently all right to commit murder for the good of the party or to imprison and torture human beings for opposing communism; but it simply would not do for a rising star in the party hierarchy to have an illegitimate child. He had to be a family man. Ten days before his forty-first birthday, on December 18, 1948, Erich married Gertrud. The Mielke family moved into a modest bungalow in the countryside north of Berlin.[26]

Mielke could not have spent much time being a devoted husband and father, for he continued to earn the plaudits of party chief Walter Ulbricht, and more importantly, of the Soviet secret police. The year after the adoption of the constitution of the Deutsche Demokratische Republic (DDR), the German Democratic Republic, by the German People's Council became crucial in Mielke's quest for absolute police power. At that time, the Soviet Military Administration (SMA) ceded judicial functions to its German communist minions. On January 14, 1950, the new chief of the SMA, Marshal Vasili Chuikov, informed the provisional government of the Soviet-occupied zone that all Soviet-controlled "internment" camps had been closed. In the five years since the end of World War II, the Soviets and their vassals had arrested between 170,000 and 180,000 Germans. Some 160,000 had passed through the concentration camps, and of these about 65,000 had died, 36,000 had been shipped to the Soviet gulag, and another 46,000 had been freed.[27] The remainder, according to Marshal Chuikov, had been turned over to German authorities to continue serving the sentences handed down to them by military tribunals. The Soviet actions coincided with the establishment of a Ministry for State Security (MfS), which the East German people immediately dubbed the "Stasi." The new ministry's staff was composed entirely of K-5 functionaries. The German Economic Commission also became part of the MfS. Wilhelm Zaisser, veteran GRU agent, was appointed minister. The Soviets approved the loyal Chekist Mielke as Zaisser's deputy with the rank of state secretary, and the party showed its appreciation of Mielke's diligence by electing him to its Central Committee.

Mielke tackled his new job with characteristic zeal, displaying the organizational talents that the Soviets had recognized in him long ago. He systematically structured the new ministry along the lines of the Soviet MGB, in three major departments: counterespionage, sabotage, and subversion.

NEW TARGETS FOR MIELKE

Western espionage, particularly the efforts of the CIA and of U.S. military intelligence, had become a major concern for the Soviets. Although neither American organization had the resources after World War II to keep tabs on the Soviet military in East Germany or on

Wilhelm Zaisser, longtime Soviet agent and head of the International Brigade during the Spanish Civil War. He was the first Stasi minister, from 1950 to 1953. Ullstein.

Moscow's political maneuverings there, they did have former Wehrmacht General Reinhard Gehlen: The former chief of military intelligence for the eastern front had made a deal with the Americans. When he surrendered in 1945 after initially hiding in the Bavarian Alps, he offered his own services and those of his staff. His files on the Soviets were transferred intact. Gehlen's quid pro quo was that he and his people would serve as an independent agency financed by the United States until Germany regained its sovereignty.

U.S. intelligence accepted the deal, especially since both American and British counterespionage agents were picking up hundreds of Russians disguised as refugees, who were sent to the Western-occupied zones a mere year after the last shot of the war was fired in Europe. In May 1946, a Soviet NKGB agent defected to the American zone and brought with him Secret Order No. 24, which listed seventeen agents and their locations in the West. The U.S. Army's Counter Intelligence Corps (CIC) responded immediately, and the seventeen agents were arrested. During interrogation these agents named hundreds of others, setting the stage for a spectacular CIC coup.

On June 21, 1946, the CIC launched Operation Bingo, the first and most concentrated postwar effort to neutralize Soviet spies. A top secret CIC directive ordered the arrest, interrogation, or surveillance of 385 persons who had been positively identified as agents or who were prime suspects.[28] Most were Soviet citizens residing in camps for displaced persons, including Red Army officers up to the rank of full colonel. These Soviets had been captured by the Germans. Threatened with repatriation—which would almost certain land them in the gulag, or worse—most accepted NKGB assignments. A few were trained intelligence officers who had allowed themselves to be taken prisoner in a classic infiltration ploy. They became double agents for the Abwehr, the Wehrmacht's counterintelligence service, or for the Gestapo.

Thus, the expertise of Gehlen and his men was needed not only to collect information on the Soviets and on East German political developments but also to assist in counterintelligence efforts. Conversely, Mielke became indispensable to the Soviets in combating Gehlen's organization.

THE COLD WAR

Soviet belligerence assumed new dimensions when the United States offered assistance through the Marshall Plan to war-torn Europe (including the Soviet Union and all of Eastern Europe). Stalin rejected this American gesture because it interfered with his own plans for Eastern Europe and Germany. He became alarmed in July 1947 when Czechoslovakia decided to participate in the recovery plan. Two months later, the Soviet Union responded with the formation of the Communist Information Office, known as Cominform, at a meeting in Warsaw. All East European communist party leaders, as well as those of France and Italy, attended. Stalin made it plain that Cominform had been created solely to defeat the Marshall Plan.[29] The first major objective of Cominform was to destabilize France and Italy with massive strikes by communist-controlled labor unions. When this effort failed, Stalin decided to consolidate Eastern Europe, where his army had remained since the war. Because of its borders with the West, Stalin felt that Czechoslovakia in particular needed to be firmly tied to the Soviet Union. A Moscow-led coup succeeded in toppling the democratic government there in February 1948.

West European governments as well as those of the United States and Britain, already alarmed by the militarization of East Germany, became even more concerned at the communist takeover of Czechoslovakia and the Soviet blockade of Berlin. Thus, in April 1949, the North Atlantic Treaty Organization (NATO) was formed by the United States, Britain, France, Belgium, the Netherlands, Luxembourg, and Portugal as a defensive alliance. The invasion of South Korea by communist North Korea paved the way for the membership of newly sovereign West Germany. In 1950, NATO was transformed into a military alliance.

As the Cold War intensified, living conditions in Soviet-occupied East Germany showed little improvement beyond the postwar level of bare subsistence. The new government of the DDR—a mere puppet of the Kremlin—relied more and more on the Stasi to quell discontent among factory workers and farmers. Ulbricht, claiming that the social unrest was fomented by capitalist agents, once ordered Mielke to personally visit one large plant and "arrest four or five such agents" as an example to the others.[30] The Stasi deputy chief "discovered" the agents in record time.

HATCHET MAN

Meanwhile, the East German leadership (i.e., the SED) had already passed through purges initiated by the MGB and later the MVD, the secret police having been renamed once again after Lavrenty Beria assumed command in March 1953. Dozens of high-ranking SED functionaries were expelled as "enemies of the working class." Most of those expelled were veteran communists who had sought exile in the West when Hitler came to power rather than escaping to the Soviet Union. They were accused of collaborating with Noel H. Field, the "American secret service agent." Field, an American communist working in Switzerland during World War II for the Quakers, was used by Allen Dulles of the U.S. Office of Strategic Services (OSS), the forerunner of the CIA, as a contact with the communist underground. Noel was particularly close to German exiles operating within the French Communist Party's underground movement.

Similar purges were conducted in Czechoslovakia, Hungary, and Bulgaria, where Field appeared as a witness in show trials that resulted in some death sentences. The Soviets simply distrusted all Communist Party members who had sought exile in the West. All the while, Erich Mielke remained untouched and continued to serve as the deputy secret police chief. His survival reinforced the belief that he had spent the war years in the Soviet Union instead of France and Belgium as he had claimed in the 1945 questionnaire.

Josef Stalin died on March 5, 1953. The following day the Central Committee of the SED met for a special session to mourn the dictator's passing, eulogizing him as "great friend of Germany who was always an adviser of and help to our people."

Two months later, on May 5, the SED celebrated the 135th anniversary of the birthday of Karl Marx by increasing work quotas for industrial plants. The city of Chemnitz was renamed Karl-Marx-Stadt and the Order of Karl Marx was created as the DDR's highest award. The party seemed to be enjoying a period of unity and political tranquility. It lasted but a fortnight. Mielke had been reporting secretly that a group of party officials were plotting against the leadership. This resulted in more expulsions from the Politburo and the Central Committee.

Discontent among the workers over increased work norms without corresponding wage hikes reached the breaking point June 16, 1953, at Stalinallee in Berlin. Probably encouraged by Stalin's death, nearly a hundred construction workers gathered for a protest meeting before starting work. Word spread rapidly to other nearby construction sites, and soon several hundred men and women marched to the House of Ministries, the government seat that once had housed Hermann Göring's Nazi aviation ministry. They chanted in protest for five hours until a minister decided to speak to them. His cajoling was met with jeers, and he retreated into the heavily guarded building. People's police riot units were called out of their barracks but made no move to break up the demonstrations. The protesters returned to Stalinallee, and a general strike was called. The following day, some 100,000 protesters marched through East Berlin; about 400,000 took to the streets in other towns.[31] Their demands were everywhere the same: free and secret elections.

The American radio station in West Berlin (RIAS) and several West German stations reported the protest marches and the plans for a general strike. These broadcasts were picked up throughout the Soviet zone, and 267,000 workers of major state-owned plants in 304 cities and towns spontaneously went on strike. In 24 towns, irate burghers stormed prisons and freed between 2,000 and 3,000 inmates.

Mielke was nowhere to be seen in public, but his secret police agents and the Vopo were out en masse, and bloody street battles erupted. Hundreds of policemen defected to the side of the workers, police stations were overrun, and government offices were sacked. The leadership had already retreated to its residences in the heavily guarded compound in the Pankow district of East Berlin. At 1 P.M. the Soviet commandant for Berlin, Major General P. K. Dibrova, a sixty-year-old Chekist who had never seen wartime combat, declared martial law. Stasi agents and people's policemen opened fire. Drumhead courts handed down death sentences that were carried out on the spot. The rioting continued, and by late afternoon Soviet tanks accompanied by infantry and MVD troops had rolled into East Berlin and other major cities in the Soviet zone. This made the people even angrier. At Berlin's Potsdamer Platz, which bordered the American sector, irate protesters ignored machine gun fire and the menacing barrels of tank guns. They ripped cobblestones from the streets and hurled them at the tanks.

The massive and brutal use of Soviet power—two armored divisions—against the unarmed protesters in 121 major cities and small towns broke the back of the revolt within twenty-four hours. By nightfall June 18, relative calm had been restored in the Soviet zone, and Stasi flying squads swept through the cities. Provisional prison camps were set up to hold the thousands of Stasi victims. Nearly 1,500 persons were sentenced in secret trials to long prison terms.

On June 24, Mielke issued a terse announcement that one Stasi officer, nineteen demonstrators, and two bystanders had been killed during the uprising. He did not say how many were victims of official lynching. The numbers of wounded were given as 191 policemen, 126 demonstrators, and 61 bystanders.

Alarmed by the events in East Germany, Beria, head of the Ministry for Internal Affairs (MVD), which had replaced the MGB, flew to Berlin. He wanted to know why the staff at his most important foreign outpost had failed to prevent an uprising by not recognizing the signs of extreme discontent and not taking early repressive measures.[32] He conferred with MfS Minister Zaisser and with Mielke, both of whom he had known since the early 1930s. True to form when treading dangerous waters, Mielke handled himself with circumspection. He was well aware that Zaisser's ties with Beria had been close for three decades. Beria decided to replace several hundred MVD officers, including Major General Ivan Fadeykin, the MVD chief for the DDR. The MfS generally remained untouched except for the arrests and dismissals, for dereliction of duty, of a handful of officers in the provinces. One high-ranking Stasi officer shot himself.

Calm returned to the streets of the Soviet zone, yet escapes to the West continued at a high rate. Of the 331,390 who fled in 1953, 8,000 were members of the Kasernierte Volkspolizei, the barracked people's police units, which were actually the secret cadre of the future East German Army. Also among the escapees were 2,718 members and candidates of the SED, the ruling party.[33]

Within the Communist Party and the government, however, turmoil persisted. Max Fechner, the minister of justice, declared that "illegal arrests" had been made as a result of the uprising. Belonging to a strike council or suspicion of being a ringleader, the justice minister observed, was not sufficient grounds for arrest and conviction. This was enough cause for Mielke to personally arrest Fechner. Hilde Benjamin, who became known as "Red Hilde" or "The Red Guillotine" after she appeared as a judge in a number of show trials, was appointed minister of justice. Fechner was convicted as an "enemy of the party and the state." He spent three years in the Stasi's notorious Bautzen prison. The prison was nicknamed the "Yellow Misery" because its yellow building housed political prisoners under the most inhuman conditions.

MVD chief Beria was arrested shortly after his return to Moscow from his Berlin inspection trip, and charged with plotting against the new Soviet leadership. Mielke, either encouraged by Beria's arrest or on direct orders from Moscow, used the Stasi's failure to keep the DDR quiescent as a pretext for a power play against his boss and fellow Cheka comrade, State Security Minister Wilhelm Zaisser. He told a party commission looking for scapegoats that Zaisser was advocating a change in the party hierarchy. Mielke also accused Zaisser of calling for rapprochement with West Germany because "he believed the Soviet Union would abandon the DDR."[34] What Zaisser had really said was that "it is the highest duty of a communist to remain always loyal to the Soviet Union, in good times and during bad days as well. . . . Even if the Soviet Union abandons the DDR tomorrow, you must remain loyal."[35]

The party chose to believe Mielke. Zaisser was stripped of his job, expelled from both the Politburo and the Central Committee, and deprived of his party membership.[36] Mielke must have expected to be awarded for his loyalty to the Soviet Union and to the party with a promotion to the post of minister of the MfS. Instead the party decided to downgrade the MfS and place it under the Ministry of the Interior. Ernst Wollweber, the old saboteur known in the West as the "miserable creature with the brain of an evil scientist," was named the new chief of the state security secretariat. Mielke remained on staff as his deputy.

Since his return from the Soviet Union in 1945, Wollweber had not held any known secret police posts, serving instead in various capacities in the Ministry of Transport. Immediately prior to being named state security chief, he was head of the State Secretariat for Sea Transport. In that capacity, he used his expertise in blowing up ships by establishing a special course at the DDR's merchant marine school. From each graduating class of two hundred, twenty men were selected for training with explosives and taught how to sabotage engines and navigational equipment and how to transmit secret messages. Although there were reports of numerous acts of sabotage aboard Western merchant and naval vessels in 1953, there was never any firm evidence that Wollweber's pupils were involved.[37]

As a direct consequence of the uprising and the attempts by Zaisser and associates to change the party and government leadership, the

Ernst Wollweber, a saboteur for Soviet intelligence who specialized in blowing up ships, succeeded Zaisser as Stasi minister from 1953 to 1957. Ullstein.

Ministry for State Security was put under rigid control of the Communist Party. Walter Ulbricht, who had risen to the all-powerful position of secretary-general of the SED and first secretary of the Central Committee, transformed the Stasi into an instrument for retaining power. Ulbricht prohibited the Stasi from keeping leading party functionaries under surveillance and from otherwise interfering in the party apparatus. Mielke had become Ulbricht's most loyal servant—at least outwardly, as he would later discover—and declared the MfS the "shield and sword of the state." It was not Mielke's brilliance that inspired this logo, however. He had simply copied it from the newly created Committee for State Security of the Soviet Union, the KGB.

Mielke and Wollweber, who had also advanced to the Central Committee, made an excellent team for four years. Their service had scored significant successes against espionage operations run by the CIA-sponsored organization of General Gehlen and by U.S. Army Military Intelligence. At the same time, the Stasi had expanded its network of secret informers, which would eventually penetrate every facet of life in the DDR. The Stasi's work was rewarded. The secret police was restored to the status of a full ministry in 1955, and Mielke obtained the rank of state secretary.

Mielke still nursed greater ambitions, but Wollweber stood in his way and had to be discredited. Mielke knew that Ulbricht had numerous disputes with the secret police chief. Ulbricht was particularly disturbed by Wollweber's stubborn emphasis on hunting "foreign spies" rather than on strengthening his corps of informers to watch over the population. Encouraged by Ulbricht, Mielke charged Wollweber with "ideological subversion" against the state and the Communist Party. As evidence Mielke cited his chief's contacts with high-ranking members of West Germany's Social Democratic Party, who had been exploring a modus vivendi with the DDR.[38] Ulbricht already knew that yet another group had formed within the Politburo and the Central Committee that opposed his policies. The new opposition was led by Politburo member Karl Schirdewan. Wollweber had taken Schirdewan's side.

On November 1, 1957, Wollweber resigned as minister for state security, citing ill health.[39] Mielke was appointed minister for state security the same day. He began at once to restructure the Stasi into a duplicate of the Soviet KGB, which was then headed by Mielke's old mentor Ivan Serov. The restructuring included the establishment of military ranks. Ulbricht gave Mielke the rank of major general, which he held until 1959 when he was promoted to the three-star rank of lieutenant general. Within a year he created the Hauptverwaltung Aufklärung (HVA), the Main Administration for Reconnaissance. Markus Wolf, appointed a major general, became Stasi deputy minister and chief of the HVA, which was put in charge of all foreign espionage operations.

Wolf was born in 1923, the son of a radical communist physician and writer who had emigrated with his family to the Soviet Union to escape Hitler. In Moscow, Markus attended the Karl-Liebknecht Schule, a middle school for the children of German communists in exile. While attending the school, he reportedly had connections to the GPU and was alleged to have served as a secret informer on the teaching faculty. Several male and female teachers were subsequently arrested during Stalin's 1936–1938 purges and disappeared in the labor camps.[40] Whether some of the arrests resulted from young Wolf's activities was never reliably established.[41] It is noteworthy, however, that Wolf and his family were among the very few German communist intellectuals who survived the purges.

Wolf became a Soviet citizen and member of the Soviet Communist Party in 1942 and adopted the alias of Kurt Förster. Together with other young German communist men and women he was sent to a Comintern school at Kushnarenkovo, a village about a thousand miles east of Moscow. The school was camouflaged as an agricultural college, while its curriculum actually consisted of espionage and sabotage training to prepare the students for clandestine assignments behind German lines. As the war turned in favor of the Red Army in 1943, the school was shut down, and Wolf returned to Moscow for assignment to Scientific Research Institute No. 205. His Stasi personnel card indicated that he was radio commentator and editor at the institute.[42] When I mentioned this fact to a former high-ranking Stasi officer, he guffawed and said, "The 205 was run by the NKVD."[43]

Two weeks after the end of the war, Wolf turned up in Berlin. Exactly how is unclear, but one report said he was then a captain assigned to the First Belorussian Front under Marshal Georgy Zhukov.[44] Be that as it may, Wolf became a commentator for Soviet-controlled Radio Berlin, and for a time was assigned to cover the Nürnberg war crimes trials. By that time he had taken back his real name. Fluent in Russian and with excellent contacts to influential Soviet officials, he was sent to Moscow in 1951 as a counselor to the DDR's first diplomatic mission, a post in which he served for one year.

East Germany's espionage service was the brainchild of Semyon D. Ignatyev, the chief of the KGB's forerunner, the MGB. He had persuaded the Soviet government to take advantage of the unique intelligence opportunity created by the defeat and division of Germany. In the immediate years following the end of the war, Soviet intelligence, assisted by the Polish and Czechoslovak services, had already been operating in the Western-occupied zones, as was shown by the U.S. counterintelligence operation code-named Bingo.

Until the creation of the sovereign Federal Republic of Germany, the Eastern communist bloc had considered the United States its main enemy. Now the new democratic West Germany became main enemy number two. Intentions of uniting Germany under Moscow's control had been nipped in the bud, and the Cold War assumed new dimensions. East German espionage became imperative in Ignatyev's view, because it could benefit immeasurably from the commonalities of German language and culture. In addition, the remnants of the prewar Communist Party of Germany, the KPD, and personal ties would be valuable assets. The Soviets knew they could trust their German vassals and profit from their zealous pursuit of perfection.[45] Markus Wolf was such a trusted minion.

Camouflaged as the Institute for Scientific Economic Research, the spy service was attached administratively to the MfS in 1953, with Wolf, then thirty years old, as its director. But its headquarters was in a Berlin suburb, and much to Mielke's distress, it operated more or less independently. At one point, the Stasi chief accused Wolf and his service of being "ideological subversives who underestimated the dangers of Western infiltration."[46] In his earlier days, Mielke had little use for waging espionage against the West, saying time and again that it was more important to catch Western spies and enemies of the party.

The oppressors meet for lunch (l-r): Walter Ulbricht, SED secretary-general (1946–1971) and head of state (1949–1971); Erich Honecker, successor to Ulbricht (1971–1989); Colonel General Erich Mielke, minister for state security; KGB General Vladimir Biroschkov; Lieutenant General Bruno Beater, deputy to Mielke; and Major General Markus Wolf, chief of foreign espionage (1969). Courtesy MfS Archive.

But Wolf's spies already had scored notable successes against Western targets, and the general was able to weather Mielke's attacks. Ulbricht's suspicious nature, however, helped Mielke obtain approval to move the espionage headquarters to his ministry's compound in central East Berlin.

The creation of the HVA, with the internal security and counterespionage services under one roof, completed Mielke's consolidation of power—a power he would wield for nearly four decades. Mielke managed to build the MfS into an instrument for the ruthless oppression of East Germany's population as well as into one of the world's most effective espionage services.

MIELKE TIGHTENS THE SCREWS

With foreign espionage operations firmly in the hands of Markus Wolf, Mielke concentrated on building up the internal security divisions of his ministry in order to dam the steady stream of East Germans seeking freedom in the West. The border with West Germany had been hermetically sealed for years, and the only escape hatch left was Berlin. The border between the two parts of the city was open because the city still was under four-power rule. It was a festering thorn in the communists' side, although the number of people leaving the "first German workers' and peasants' state" had dropped from a high of 331,390 in 1953, the year of the revolt, to 143,917 in 1959.[47]

When Ulbricht admitted the failure of his drive to persuade farmers to voluntarily join collectives, the East German party's Politburo agreed that force should be applied. The job fell to Mielke. In November and December 1959, Mielke ordered the arrest of all recalcitrant farmers on charges of "engaging in activities hostile to the state." Hundreds were deprived of their property and sent to prison. Thousands more left for the West.

Ruthless Stasi collectivizers were awarded medals and cash bonuses by Mielke. One of the highest awards, the Fatherland Medal of Merit in Silver, went to an especially merciless friend of Mielke, Major General Alfred Kraus. The general, a Communist Party member since 1930, when he was twenty years old, had led the collectivization drive in the Baltic coastal district of Rostock, where he was chief of the Stasi district command. In a report to Mielke, Kraus described his actions against farmers and other "state enemies" as having been "a lot of fun for us Chekists." In the citation accompanying the medal, Mielke wrote: "The Chekist is the political combatant. He is the loyal son of the class, the workers' class. He stands at the head of the battle to strengthen the power of our workers' and peasants' state."

Dissatisfaction with the confiscatory collectivization, however, was not limited to the farmers and the general population. Mielke's undercover agents and informers also reported grumbling among party officials. More than a hundred top functionaries of the country's fifteen SED districts were sacked, including seven first secretaries. New consternation arose among the population when the rubber-stamp parliament, the People's Chamber, promulgated a "Right to Work Law" guaranteeing equal pay for equal work but failing to mention the right to strike even though this right was anchored in the constitution. This was taken to mean that any disputes between workers and those who ran the state-owned industries could result in criminal charges.

On the economic front, new food shortages appeared. Deputy Premier Willy Stoph admitted in June 1961 that "at the moment there are difficulties in supplying meat, milk, and butter." Party leader Ulbricht was quick to reply in a meeting with party journalists that butter was withheld deliberately because it was an unhealthy substance—a remark that evoked bittersweet laughter among the populace.

Well aware of the economic advances made by their West German brethren and fed up with political oppression, East Germans began a new wave of defections. In 1960, 199,188 East Germans had voted with their feet. Most were highly skilled workers, technicians, engineers, educators, medical professionals, and youths avoiding service in the People's Army. Mielke's secret police were working feverishly to stem the westward flow with little success, though the number of political prisoners steadily filled Stasi prisons. At the same time, Mielke ordered his department charged with surveillance of the "political underground," the Twentieth Directorate, to find a way of stopping reception of West German television stations. Thousands of so-called IMs, unofficial Stasi collaborators, were sent through residential areas of East Germany to spot any television aerials pointed westward. With this information in hand, Mielke enlisted the leadership of Freie Deutsche Jugend (FDJ), the Free German Youth organization, which was the communist equivalent to the Hitler Youth, who sent out squads of blue-shirted youngsters to climb roofs and turn the aerials around or tear them off.

The fragile domestic situation raised Ulbricht's concern for the security of the party hierarchy to a new high. Since 1949 they had been living in a compound within the densely populated Pankow district of East Berlin. The compound was guarded by heavily armed members of Mielke's elite Guard Regiment Feliks Dzerzhinski, named in honor of the Soviet Union's first secret police chief. However, the guards would not have been able to withstand a massive assault during any general uprising. These fears were undoubtedly reinforced by the misfortunes of the Hungarian Communist Party elite during the 1956 uprising: They too had been living in a populated area of Budapest and were pummeled by irate demonstrators; a dozen or so officers were even killed. Thus, on May 5, 1960, Ulbricht issued a secret directive ordering all members of the Politburo and a select number of top functionaries to move to a new compound outside Berlin. It was located in an idyllic forest that bordered a pristine lake near the village of Wandlitz, twenty-three miles north of the city. It bore the innocuous name of Waldsiedlung Wandlitz—Wandlitz Forest Settlement. It consisted of two dozen villas, shops, and recreation facilities including an indoor swimming pool. A number of less pretentious buildings housed lesser officials, servants, and Stasi guards. The compound was more closely guarded by Stasi forces than an ammunition depot. Agents personally selected by Mielke, who lived in Villa No. 8, enforced a rigid code of silence. There was never a leak about the activities of the Waldsiedlung residents. Of course, the burghers had an inkling about their special privileges. However, the extent of the luxury in which these sons of the proletariat wallowed would not become known until East Germany collapsed.

The same developments that prompted the Communist Party bigwigs to move out of East Berlin were also watched from Moscow with increasing alarm. The Soviets could not afford to have their most important trading partner and comrade in arms end up in chaos, perhaps even anarchy. They decided to take action before it was too late.

THE WALL

Soviet Premier Nikita S. Khrushchev called for a meeting of the Warsaw Pact in March 1961 to discuss the situation. Ulbricht was accompanied by Erich Honecker, Politburo member and Central Committee secretary for security affairs, and Stasi chief Mielke. Ulbricht pleaded for sealing the border with West Berlin, the only escape hatch for refugees. But the other East European leaders supported Khrushchev, who had rejected such a move months earlier, and opposed Ulbricht's plan.[48] The Soviet leader wanted to keep Berlin neutral territory, needing both a geostrategic Achilles' heel in the Western security system and a European Hong Kong, a trade link between the communist East and capitalist West Germany.[49]

Ulbricht did not give up. Late in June, he invited Mikhail Pervukhin, the Soviet Ambassador to East Germany, to his villa in the Wandlitz forest for a talk. Mielke was present to provide facts on the security situation. The ambassador reported to the Kremlin that Ulbricht said the exodus from the DDR was so serious that if nothing was done, another revolt could not be excluded. And if that happened, he believed the West German Bundeswehr would become involved "and that would mean war."[50] Pervukhin closed his report by saying that if the border with West Berlin remained open, collapse would be "inevitable."

Pervukhin's report, as well as the Western allies' determination to hold on to West Berlin, finally persuaded Khrushchev to give in to the nagging Ulbricht. Instead of barbed wire barricades, he suggested a wall and told the ambassador to share his idea with Ulbricht and to ask Marshal Ivan I. Yakubovsky, commander of Soviet troops in the DDR, to work out a plan for dividing Berlin.[51] After his meeting with Ulbricht, Honecker, and Mielke, Ambassador Pervukhin reported to Moscow that "Ulbricht beamed with pleasure" and said: "This is the solution. This will help. I am for this."[52]

Shortly after this meeting, Ulbricht met with Western reporters to advance again his determination to transform Berlin into a "Free City" without the presence of the Western allies. "Does this mean," asked one of the journalists, "that according to your judgment the national border will be established at the Brandenburg Gate? And are you prepared to accept the consequences of such an action?" Ulbricht's answer was a blatant lie: "I understand your question in this way, that there are people in West Germany who wish us to mobilize the construction workers of the capital of the DDR in order to erect a wall. I am not aware of any such intention. The construction workers are fully occupied mainly with building houses. Nobody has any intention to erect a wall."

But throughout July, Central Committee Secretary for Security Honecker worked with Mielke and the top leadership of the People's Police and the National People's Army (NVA) on plans to do just that.

The morning of August 12, Mielke summoned his division chiefs and announced that all members of his Berlin headquarters as well as the Berlin MfS district office were to report to their offices immediately. Then he informed his deputies of the Politburo decision that all traffic between East and West Berlin would be cut off at midnight. The task of the MfS was to man strategic road crossings and guard against defectors from units of the National People's Army, the police, and the border guards, which were to choke off the sector border.[53] While Mielke was exhorting his underlings and threatening any who talked with a firing squad, the stream of refugees continued into the West. By nightfall, more than 2,400 persons had joined the 3,241 escapees who had come across in the previous two days.[54]

Mielke's threat and the total isolation of all troops the moment the orders for dividing Berlin were received achieved absolute secrecy. It was not until a few minutes after midnight of August 13 that West Berlin police patrols spotted the communist units stringing barbed wire along the border. There were no major incidents, although at one point People's Police units formed a human chain to hold back about 1,500 persons who were heading for West Berlin. Mielke had done his job well.

THE HATCHET FALLS ON ULBRICHT

The Stasi chief's devotion to his job had by 1970 reached workaholic proportions. Besides dealing with surveillance of the population, counterespionage, and foreign espionage and maintaining relations with international terrorists, Mielke closely watched developments within the party. In April of that year, he had learned that Moscow was becoming increasingly disturbed by Ulbricht's obstreperous behavior. The then seventy-seven-year-old Ulbricht was favoring the establishment of a confederation with West Germany, which he felt might save his economically feeble state. Ulbricht was encouraged by the newly elected West German Social Democratic Chancellor Willy Brandt and his new *Ostpolitik*, a policy aimed at rapprochement with Eastern Europe, particularly with the Soviet Union and East Germany.

Walter Ulbricht toasts Minister of State Security Erich Mielke on the Stasi's twentieth anniversary in 1970. A year later Mielke was instrumental in removing Ulbricht from the posts of party secretary-general and head of state. Courtesy MfS Archive.

Brandt's motto was cooperation, not confrontation. The Soviets were suspicious, however. Soviet Premier Kosygin warned Ulbricht that Brandt's policies, like those of NATO, were "aimed at the entire socialist camp."[55]

Ulbricht persisted, maintaining that trade relations needed to be strengthened with West Germany to bolster his own economy. Soviet Communist Party Secretary-General Leonid Brezhnev finally decided to be more blunt. On July 28, 1970, following a meeting of Warsaw Pact nations, the Soviet party leader summoned Erich Honecker, a member of the Politburo since 1958, to a meeting in Moscow at which only an interpreter was present. Brezhnev told Honecker to take the initiative in removing Ulbricht as head of the party and chief of state. "We will react to any moves on Walter's part regarding unity of leadership and the party," Brezhnev said. "I tell you very openly that it will not be possible to undertake any moves against you and other comrades of the Politburo. After all, we have our troops there with you."[56]

On his return to Berlin, Honecker met with Mielke to brief him on his encounter with Brezhnev. Honecker, who held the titles of secretary for security affairs and secretary of the National Defense Council, knew that Mielke would be essential for a successful overthrow of Ulbricht: No Soviet leader had ever been removed from office without the active support of the secret police.

During the rest of 1970 Honecker built up support within the Politburo and the Central Committee against Ulbricht. A meeting of the Central Committee was held from December 9 to December 11. The session was marked by a series of acrimonious debates between Ulbricht and Honecker, a spectacle that the 160 members and 60 candidates from throughout East Germany had not expected. Stasi officers handpicked by Mielke intensified their surveillance of the population and of party functionaries in particular. By mid-April they were able to report that the population was no more restive than usual; and more importantly, the Stasi had the names of die-hard Ulbricht supporters.[57]

The 16th Plenary Session of the Central Committee was scheduled for May 3, 1971. The night before, Mielke assigned his most trusted minions a variety of delicate tasks. A detail of Stasi men was posted at the entrances to the meeting hall, to check the credentials of participants. They compared the bearers' names to a list of Ulbricht supporters, and denied admission to anyone whose name was on the list.

The most sensitive part of this operation was the replacement of Ulbricht's regular Stasi bodyguards by two Mielke confidants. These men picked up an unsuspecting Ulbricht at his home and drove him to the State Council building in downtown East Berlin. Their assignment was to keep Ulbricht away from his office, where he had a direct telephone link to the commander of the National People's Army. Mielke feared that if Ulbricht realized that he was about to be booted out, he might become irrational enough to call out the army. Since he was the chairman of the National Defense Council, the military would have followed his orders.[58]

Instead of escorting Ulbricht to the meeting hall, the bodyguards took the protesting Ulbricht for a long walk along the river Spree, which ran behind the building. After an hour or so, the bodyguards were informed by radio that Ulbricht could be brought to the session. When he arrived, he was informed that Erich Honecker had been elected secretary-general of the party, first secretary of the Central Committee, and chairman of the National Defense Council. Ulbricht himself was "promoted" to chairmanship of the State Council, a ceremonial office devoid of any power.[59]

Honecker's election to the party's top leadership position brought Mielke's career to its zenith. Honecker rewarded Mielke with a candidacy to the Politburo and a new house in the party elite's compound outside Berlin. Five years later Mielke would be voted in as a full Politburo member. He was also promoted to the four-star rank of General of the Army.

Mielke was the longest serving secret police chief in the Eastern bloc. He was on the most intimate of terms with eleven Soviet secret police chiefs, and he survived them all. Subservient to a fault while they were in power, Mielke switched loyalties without missing a beat when they were fired. His allegiance was not to a person but to the joint KGB/Stasi venture in the quest of maintaining and expanding the power of communism.

3

KGB and STASI

Two Shields, Two Swords

THE SOVIET LEADERSHIP considered the part of eastern Germany that its forces had occupied in 1945 critical to its plans for communist expansion into Western Europe. With the advent of the Cold War, the Soviet zone—later the "sovereign" DDR—became a security and intelligence outpost for the Soviets as well as a communist beachhead in Western Europe. As the Soviet Union's westernmost satellite, East Germany was the front line in the ideological battle against capitalism. The protection of Soviet security and military forces stationed in East Germany against defection and Western espionage was as vital as the suppression of any anticommunist stirrings among the populace. In both efforts the Stasi was an essential tool, controlled completely by the Soviets until the mid-1950s.

The linchpin of Soviet control was General Ivan Aleksandrovich Serov. As a reward for having effectively applied his secret police expertise to the Sovietization of Eastern Europe, Serov was promoted to the chairmanship of the newly created KGB in March 1954. The Kremlin leadership judged Serov's accomplishments in the Soviet-occupied zone of Germany particularly meritorious, an uprising a year earlier notwithstanding. Blame for that failure was attributed to secret police chief Lavrenty Beria, providing yet another reason for Beria's execution. By the time Serov departed East Germany in the late 1940s, he had established a well-organized apparatus that he could confidently leave in the capable hands of the Soviets' well-trained and obedient servant, Erich Mielke.

In 1957, as the East German internal situation had stabilized and communist control had become absolute, the KGB relinquished overt command, and Mielke became head of the East German Ministry for

State Security (MfS). This outwardly trusting gesture was deceiving, however. Until the Soviet Union's end in 1990, the KGB maintained liaison officers in all eight main directorates of the Stasi. Each liaison officer—in most cases, a full colonel—had his own office inside the Stasi's Berlin compound. The KGB placed special importance on Markus Wolf's foreign espionage directorate, which occupied three offices in that compound. In addition, the KGB was ensconced in every one of the fifteen Stasi district headquarters around East Germany, occupying thirty separate offices. KGB officers had access to all information collected by the Stasi. In its structure, East Germany's state security ministry had become a clone of the Soviet KGB.

Slowly the KGB-Stasi association evolved from a dictatorial, military occupation–type regimen to more "fraternal" relations. This process gained momentum once the Stasi had proved its mettle in espionage, subversion, and foreign and domestic counterintelligence. Collaboration between the two became so close that the KGB invited its East German ally to establish operational bases in Moscow and Leningrad for the surveillance of visiting East German officials and tourists. Stasi officers considered themselves equals to their Soviet counterparts. Stasi Minister Mielke, in staff meetings and official directives, continually stressed that MfS officers were to consider themselves "Chekists of the Soviet Union."[1] He never tired of swearing absolute loyalty to the "close relations and alliance" between members of his Stasi and the KGB. There was hardly a public speech between 1946 and 1989 in which Mielke did not pay homage to the Soviet "Chekists" and extol the virtues of the KGB-Stasi brotherhood, even when he spoke at collective farms and before factory workers.

For twenty years MfS-KGB relations were based on informal understandings between Mielke and whoever was in charge of Soviet security and espionage. Then on March 29, 1978, the first protocol on collaboration between the KGB was signed by Mielke and Yuri Andropov, who later replaced Brezhnev as head of state. The Stasi chief saw to it that KGB officers in East Germany were accorded the same rights and powers they enjoyed in the Soviet Union, with the exception of the right to arrest DDR citizens. The KGB contingent in the DDR had become the largest outside Moscow and covered all espionage operations in Western Europe.

Four years later, on September 10, 1982, KGB Chairman Vitaly V. Fedorchuk signed a formal agreement with Mielke, who pledged total logistical support for the entire KGB operation in East Germany and its staff of roughly 2,500.[2] The Stasi provided office buildings, recreational facilities, and kindergartens, as well as automobiles and their maintenance. Living quarters in villas and apartments were completely furnished. The exact cost to East German taxpayers could never be ascertained, but it must have run into tens of millions of marks. The normal cost of furnishing just one such apartment was nearly US$19,000 at the time.

General Serov established KGB headquarters in the Karlshorst district of Berlin, with a staff ranging at various times from 800 to 1,200, including families. Until the mid-1950s, the entire district was a heavily guarded military compound that also housed the Soviet Military Administration. Later the barbed wire was removed, but the main KGB buildings remained hidden behind a six-foot wall.[3]

Five of the KGB's six major departments were installed at Karlshorst, including espionage against Western governments and political targets; counterintelligence and infiltration of Western intelligence organizations; logistical support for agents in Western Europe; economic and technological espionage in Western Europe and beyond; and espionage against the West German military establishment.

A sixth department, subordinate to the Second Main Directorate (counterespionage), resided at the Cecilienhof in Potsdam, the former summer residence of Prussian kings and kaisers, where the World War II Allies met in 1945 to hammer out an agreement that established a common policy for dealing with defeated Germany. There, about 1,000 intelligence officers controlled the activities of Soviet military intelligence (the GRU) in Germany and oversaw the recruitment of non-Germans residing in West Berlin. The latter activity became an important part of KGB operations in Turkey and the Middle East. Turkish and Arab citizens were recruited in West Berlin, trained in East Germany, and sent back to their native countries. Mielke's Stasi provided training facilities, safe houses for clandestine meetings, and travel documents.

Periodically, Mielke and the KGB chiefs would renew their pledges of collaboration in what were called *Perspektivpläne*—plans for future joint operations. The last such document, covering plans for the years from 1987 to 1991, was signed by Viktor M. Chebrikov and Mielke. It reflected the same hard line that had prevailed before Mikhail Gorbachev came to power in 1985. Despite his reform agenda, Gorbachev obviously had decided to retain that hard line in state security policy. The document declared:

> The strengthening of joint efforts in the battle against hostile secret services is necessitated by conditions developing out of drastically worsening international military-political situations created by the adventurous policy of American imperialism. The USA, its NATO allies, and other states have developed hostile actions of espionage and subversion by their secret services and propaganda organs against the national and uni-

> fied armed services of the USSR, the DDR, and other states of the socialist community.[4]

The KGB's reliance on the Stasi permeated all areas of secret police operations. Its central focus, however, remained on foreign espionage and counterespionage. "Legends," or personal backgrounds, were falsified by the Stasi for Soviet espionage agents operating worldwide, and particularly for those in West Germany. Those operating under an East German identity, including agents who had infiltrated other countries as "refugees," were provided genuine East German documents. Others were outfitted with forgeries produced in Stasi laboratories. Many KGB agents inserted with Stasi help as deep cover agents—or "illegals," as they are known in the intelligence trade—can be assumed to be still in place. The chances of their discovery by Western counterspies are slim, since the Stasi retained no records of these agents. It will take a few talkative high-ranking Soviet defectors to expose even a few. East Germany also acquiesced to take the heat in the event that a Soviet deep cover agent operating under KGB-manufactured identity was caught in flagrante delicto while Moscow was attempting to appear conciliatory vis-à-vis the West. The agents were instructed to insist that they were operatives of General Wolf's foreign espionage directorate. Not only would this lie enable the Soviet government to save face but it also would make it easier for the Soviets to repatriate such spies by exchanging them for captured Western spies or for Eastern-bloc political prisoners.

The Soviets benefited in yet another way from the close cooperation between the KGB and the Stasi: All information obtained by Wolf's spies was immediately turned over to them, sometimes even before Stasi analysts had a chance to review the material. This was particularly true in the penetration of Western intelligence services, top military commands, NATO headquarters, and science and technology sectors. Without a doubt, the East Germans' activities saved the Soviet Union hundreds of millions of dollars in high-tech research and development costs.

THE POLISH PROBLEM

Internal security concerns in the Soviet satellite nations of Eastern Europe were the top priority of the KGB's Second Main Directorate. For years, however, KGB operatives had difficulty in conducting operations in those countries. This was particularly true of Poland, where anti-Russian and anti-Soviet sentiments were as pervasive in the security organs as they were among the broader population. "You Germans and the Bulgarians are okay, but we can forget the others, and the Poles we can forget altogether," high-ranking Stasi officers were told repeatedly when visiting their colleagues in Moscow.[5] When visiting with their Polish counterparts, the Germans were told "the KGB gets nothing from us."

Thus, Lieutenant General Günther Kratsch, head of the Stasi's Second Main Directorate (domestic counterintelligence), was not surprised when Mielke ordered him in December 1981 to establish an operational group in Warsaw. Mielke had been asked for help by KGB Chairman Yuri V. Andropov. He briefed party chief Erich Honecker, who ordered him to comply without even bothering first to inform the Politburo. Honecker had been watching the growth of the independent labor movement Solidarność (Solidarity) under Lech Walesa for some time. However, neither he nor Mielke could have imagined that the restiveness of the Polish workers signaled the downfall of communism. Analyses of the Solidarity movement rated it a "typically Polish" development. "We are going to show those Poles" was the attitude expressed during Stasi meetings at which operations in Poland were being planned. Party functionaries, obsessed with the idea of their ideology's infallibility, blamed the events in Poland on *polnische Schlamperei*—Polish sloppiness.

Nevertheless, Honecker told Mielke that one could not completely dismiss the possibility "that the Polish germ could spread to East Germany." The KGB request, therefore, could not have been made at a more propitious moment. The struggle over the security of the East German communist regime was shifted to Poland. Besides using the resources of the Stasi's domestic counterintelligence department, Mielke also ordered General Wolf's foreign espionage directorate to provide additional manpower. The Fourth Counterintelligence Task Force was created at MfS headquarters, and a ruthless communist stalwart, Colonel Willi Buchner, was placed in overall command. Mielke traveled to Warsaw to supervise the establishment of the Stasi's war room headquarters at the East German embassy under Colonel Karl-Heinz Herbrig. The veteran counterintelligence specialist maintained personal contact with the leadership of the Polish secret police. Stasi agents were assigned to East German consulates throughout Poland. Networks were established to shadow church and labor leaders, whose meetings and street contacts were photographed and videotaped. Offices and telephones were bugged.

In the early stages of the operation, collaboration between the KGB and the Stasi was extremely close, particularly in the recruiting of informants among military officers and officials of the Polish secret police. Stasi officers took advantage of the general shortage of food and luxury goods. They bribed their "colleagues" and other Polish officials and many ordinary workers into becoming Stasi informers with Western cigarettes, food, and other scarce items, such as soap. Later, the East German regime awarded their minions with medals and money.

An East German freelance journalist, identified only by the code name Josef, was recruited to keep tabs on labor leader Lech Walesa. The journalist had met Walesa in the winter of 1980 and had written a series of articles about their meetings, all of which had been rejected by East German publications. Then he wrote a letter to a West German publishing company, hoping to peddle his story there. That letter was intercepted by the Stasi. Officers of the Fourth Task Force visited the man, who readily agreed to spy on his Polish friends. He skillfully inveigled his way into the inner circle of the Solidarity movement. From then on, nothing happened within Solidarity that was not relayed to the Stasi and the KGB. Of priority interest to the Soviet–East German secret police alliance was the foreign financial support: Where the antigovernment leaflets were being printed inside and outside Poland, and who were Solidarity's Western contacts. Josef took hundreds of photographs of Solidarity members. All of this material was turned over to the KGB. As a result, the Soviet leadership knew the Polish situation intimately. The Soviet Union's western security cordon was in danger of collapsing. The supply line to the 380,000 troops of the Western Group of Soviet Forces stationed in East Germany was threatened. Leonid Brezhnev and the Soviet military decided on an invasion of Poland unless General Wojciech Jaruzelski declared martial law and smashed the opposition. The Polish leader, knowing that his army would rebel if Poland was invaded, crumbled under Moscow's ultimatum. The KGB-Stasi data, particularly that gathered by Josef, was handed over to the Polish secret police. This information facilitated the arrests of hundreds of Solidarity members within a few hours after martial law was declared.

Sensing that the turmoil in Poland could well be the first pebble of a rock slide that would bury the communist system, U.S. President Ronald Reagan decided to act. He ordered CIA Director William Casey to provide secret support to Solidarity and to supply the anticommunist labor movement with printing and communications equipment. President Reagan also sought the collaboration of the Vatican. The Polish-born Pope John Paul II enthusiastically accepted the proposition and directed his church officials in contact with Poland to act as conduits for money and equipment.

East German and Soviet counterintelligence spotted the intensified underground activities, and by mid-1982, they had responded by deploying about 300 Stasi officers in Poland. All telephone and telegraph traffic as well as the mail into and out of Poland was under Stasi control. Hundreds of other agents kept track of about 34,000 Poles who worked in East German industry. The operation had become so huge that Stasi chief Mielke ordered that the temporary Fourth Task Force be transformed into a permanent Tenth Department of the Second Main Directorate (counterintelligence).

Antigovernment opposition was increasingly evident also in other East European countries, including the DDR. In Moscow, where Mikhail Gorbachev was just settling in as the new head of state, leaders knew that a collapse of the regime in Poland, Czechoslovakia, or Hungary would threaten the Soviet Union's hold on East Germany. After a meeting with KGB officials and Honecker in summer 1985, Mielke ordered further expansion of the Tenth Department and dispatched operational groups to Prague and Budapest.

The Stasi's frenetic activities in the "fraternal socialist countries" during the next four years were but fingers in dikes, which leaked under the pressures of militant populations. The first significant breach came in Hungary, when the government ordered the dismantling of fortifications and barbed wire barriers along its border with Austria, in August 1989. Word spread rapidly to East Germany, and thousands of freedom seekers poured into Hungary. The remaining East German border guards made feeble attempts to stem the exodus. Hungarian Foreign Minister Gyula Horn ignored pressures by the DDR, including Stasi threats, to close the border. The battle was lost, and a few months later, Germans began to dismantle the Berlin Wall.

MOSCOW APPROPRIATES STASI TECHNOLOGY

Over the years, a valuable KGB asset for the Stasi was the Soviet computer operation known as the System of Joint Acquisition of Enemy Data (SOUD). The system was actually created by Stasi engineers using stolen or illegally obtained Western technology, but the Soviets had insisted that it be based in Moscow. All information acquired worldwide by the intelligence and security services of the Eastern bloc was stored in the SOUD computer. The Stasi was by far the largest contributor; but at Stasi headquarters, only a handful of top-ranking officers, mostly of the counterintelligence directorate, were cleared for access. Those who belonged to this privileged class were not always happy with Moscow. They complained that the KGB received far more than it was willing to provide. Far from being a quid pro quo, the relationship was often a one-way street.[6]

KGB-Stasi collaboration was not limited to Europe. In the western hemisphere, Stasi engineers under Major General Horst Männchen built and operated jointly with the KGB the computerized electronic espionage facility in Cuba—a listening post capable of monitoring all U.S. microwave telephone traffic. Männchen also developed a system for tracking U.S. warships. Operating out of Cuba, Soviet and East German electronic specialists manned fishing cutters outfitted with technology that could locate and track all U.S. strategic submarines.[7]

RELATIONS WITH MOSCOW

During the early years, Mielke guarded his contacts with the KGB like a jealous husband. However, Markus Wolf, the foreign espionage chief, was allowed access to Mielke's Soviet counterparts without the Stasi chief's prior permission. Mielke knew that Wolf had nearly as much clout with the KGB as he had. All others had to go through the Tenth Directorate under Major General Willi Damm, who answered only to Mielke. Eventually, however, this system became so unwieldy that Mielke had no choice but to loosen the reins. Personal relationships—exactly what Mielke always tried to prevent—developed that in some cases, have endured the disintegration of the Soviet empire. KGB department heads frequently invited ranking Stasi officers, particularly those of the counterintelligence directorate, to Moscow, where they were entertained in a manner befitting heads of state. To appease those who could not travel to the Holy Grail at Dzerzhinski Square, the KGB leadership in Karlshorst periodically hosted lavish parties. This amicable generosity was designed to tie Stasi officers ever more closely to the KGB. From time to time, the Soviets also awarded medals to their Stasi clones, including the Order of Lenin and the Order of the Red Banner. Both medals were highly coveted by East Germany's secret policemen.

OPERATION MOSES

KGB-Stasi operations involved all main directorates, to varying degrees. While the Polish operation was in full bloom, another significant joint venture began in May 1982, When Mielke was informed by the head of the KGB's Second Main Directorate, General Ivan Alekseevich Markelov, that he would be sending his most trusted aide to Berlin for a conference.[8] Markelov provided no further details except that the visitor would be Colonel Vladimir Anatolevich Kremakovski, head of the Fourteenth Department of Markelov's directorate. Mielke knew that the Second Directorate was responsible for internal security and counterintelligence and that Markelov himself was a deputy KGB chairman. Further, the Fourteenth Department was the KGB general's personal command and central control center, through which all counterintelligence matters concerning the Soviet Union were routed. Thus, Mielke knew that whatever Kremakovski wanted to discuss was of supreme importance, and he treated General Markelov's message as an order to prepare for a state visit.

The Stasi chief ordered his counterintelligence director, Lieutenant General Kratsch, to take Kremakovski under his wing. Not knowing why Kremakovski was coming to Berlin, Kratsch pulled out all the stops: He directed a top aide, Colonel Kurt Schenk, and Colonel Rainer Wiegand to be prepared to deal with any and all counterintelligence matters of joint Soviet and DDR interest. Wiegand was the director of Arbeitsgruppe Ausländer (AGA), a task force responsible for surveillance and control of all visitors to the DDR and foreigners living in East Germany, including diplomats assigned to foreign embassies in East Berlin. Using double agents, the AGA also handled penetrations of various organizations based in West Berlin. Wiegand, hoping to learn more about the purpose of Kremakovski's visit, contacted Colonel Boris Smirnov, the KGB liaison officer assigned to Stasi counterintelligence. Smirnov said he knew nothing, but he advised Wiegand that Kremakovski was one of the most powerful officers in the Second Main Directorate.

On May 5, 1982, a delegation composed of Wiegand, Schenk, and a protocol officer as well as the KGB liaison officer assembled at the VIP section of East Berlin's Schönefeld airport to meet the illustrious visitor. After the "ordinary" passengers had left the Aeroflot Ilyushin jet by the rear door, stairs were rolled up to the front. Only then did Comrade Kremakovski appear. A bear of a man in his early sixties, he descended majestically in slow, measured steps, like a potentate about to be received by his underlings. His dour expression reminded Wiegand of Andrei Gromyko, the late Soviet foreign minister who always looked as though he was suffering from severe heartburn. The colonel was followed by a younger man, who was introduced as a lieutenant colonel and a specialist in Israeli affairs.

The KGB liaison officer, Colonel Smirnov, greeted the distinguished visitor with exaggerated reverence and led him to the Stasi officers, who had formed a receiving line. When Smirnov started to introduce the group, Kremakovski merely barked, "Poshli!" ("let's go!"). No handshake, no greeting. Without a word, the KGB visitor stepped into the Mercedes limousine that the East Germans brought out for special occasions.

Kremakovski was silent during the entire thirty minutes it took to reach "Projekt Ufer," a posh villa overlooking a scenic lake in the suburb of Grünau. The place was used by the Stasi as a guest house for visiting dignitaries. General Kratsch was on hand to greet the Soviet visitor and lead him into the "hunt room"—an oak-paneled salon decorated with trophies from Stasi deer, elk, and boar hunts. When Kremakovski was seated, Kratsch said, "And now, Comrade Colonel, allow me to have Colonel Schenk give you an overview of the security situation in the DDR." Kremakovski merely nodded. As he listened, his facial expression became one of icy tension. Schenk had talked for some ten minutes when Kremakovski abruptly slammed his fist on the conference table, toppling bottles of mineral water and crystal glasses. He turned to the liaison officer and bellowed something rapidly in Russian. Colonel Smirnov's face turned crimson with embarrassment. Hesitatingly, he translated, "Comrade Kremakovski asks how long this is going to last. He is not here to listen to political discourse." Later he told Wiegand what Kremakovski had really said. "How long is this idiot going to blather about this stuff that doesn't interest me."

"I am only interested in your operations against the Israeli intelligence service. Furthermore, I want to hear what you know about the misuse of former Soviet citizens living in West Berlin. Please report!" Kremakovski's behavior was unlike any Stasi officers had experienced since the 1960s. Kremakovski, Wiegand would recall, lived in the world of yesteryear: He was a Stalinist of the old school for whom the Germans were the vanquished.

General Kratsch, seething with anger, struggled out of his armchair—not an easy task for this man who was as obese as Hermann Göring, the Nazi *Reichsmarschall.* He reportedly said: "Comrade Colonel, you can continue this meeting with my staff. If I have time, I will receive you at the end of your mission. First I have to consult with the chief of your headquarters here." Without waiting for a response, Kratsch stormed out of the room. That evening Kremakovski was summoned to KGB headquarters in Karlshorst for a meeting with General Oleg Shumilov, the head of the KGB for East Germany and Western Europe. After that, the visitor's demeanor was somewhat more subdued, although his attitude was fundamentally unchanged.

Finally explaining his mission, Kremakovski said he had studied the reports Wiegand had been submitting to the KGB. These dealt with the activities of Soviet citizens living in the DDR and in West Berlin who were engaging in serious criminal activities such as smuggling and currency speculation, which made them highly desirable subjects for coercive recruitment as informers. Colonel Wiegand also had provided surveillance reports indicating that Western intelligence agencies were focusing considerable attention on Soviet Jews who had been allowed to emigrate and who had eventually settled in West

Berlin. These reports had prompted Kremakovski to travel to Berlin for a personal assessment. He wanted to determine whether the situation could be used to enhance his directorate's efforts toward infiltrating Jewish organizations, particularly the Mossad, Israel's espionage organization.

The conference lasted more than a week, during which time Stasi officers noted that the Soviet visitor went to the KGB Karlshorst headquarters every morning to consult with General Shumilov, and by telephone, with General Markelov in Moscow. Each day he demanded more information and precise answers to his questions. In an effort to change Kremakovski's attitude toward the Germans, Wiegand scheduled sightseeing trips and excursions in a Stasi motor yacht on the rivers, canals, and lakes of East Berlin. The vodka flowed. To play on his ego, Kremakovski was given the ship captain's hat. Standing at the helm, Wiegand photographed him in various poses and continued to snap away even when he ran out of film.

In the end, the day before his departure, Kremakovski demanded that Wiegand's task force enter into a "joint venture" with the KGB for "combating operations of Western intelligence services against the Soviet Union." Kremakovski suspected that Jewish immigrants from the Soviet Union were being used as agents by the Israeli and U.S. intelligence services. The KGB-Stasi team's primary focus would be on the Mossad. The KGB also needed eyes and ears inside Jewish communities, keeping tabs on Soviet Jews who still had relatives in the USSR and who might be useful in ferreting out dissidents and potential espionage agents. The East German had no choice but to agree. Wiegand was ordered to appear in Moscow within three months with a concrete program and plans.

Before Kremakovski departed, Wiegand decided to stroke him a bit more. He and his aide were taken on a shopping spree through East Berlin department stores and special hard currency shops on the Stasi's tab. Then, laden like two Santa Clauses (as Wiegand put it), the two officers were driven to the airport. By the time Kremakovski boarded the Aeroflot jet, the colonel's attitude had indeed been transformed, and he bade his Stasi "friends" a gracious farewell. As he shook Wiegand's hand, Kremakovski smiled. "We will name our joint venture 'Moses,'" the colonel said with a guffaw. "I never thought he was capable of a smile, much less of hilarity," Wiegand recalled.

When Mielke had been briefed on the conference, he ordered that Operation Moses be conducted entirely by Wiegand's task force.

In August 1982, Wiegand flew to Moscow, where he was met by Kremakovski and taken by Chaika limousine to the new KGB headquarters at Dzerzhinski Square. Wiegand had visited the Soviet capital as a tourist and was familiar only with the old Lubyanka building, where the Soviet secret police was previously housed. He recalled: "From the outside, the new building looked like any other big government complex. But when I entered, it took my breath away. There was a huge hall paneled in noble woods, with marble columns, crystal chandeliers, thick red carpets—the best of the finest the Soviet Union could produce. I thought I was visiting the palace of Tsar Nicholas. Everywhere stood the obligatory busts of Lenin, Dzerzhinski, and so on." Wiegand could not refrain from asking what the building had cost. Kremakovski replied icily, "An organization like ours, which amounts to something in our country, has to make a prestigious impression."

The office of Kremakovski, who held a Soviet rank equivalent to Wiegand's in East Germany, was as posh as the quarters of the party's secretary-general that Wiegand had seen depicted in Soviet movies. But the East German could not suppress a smile when he also noted the weaknesses of the Soviet system. Next to the colonel's desk was a table holding sixteen telephones. When one phone rang, Kremakovski had to put his ear to each receiver in order to determine which one it was. They all sounded alike. According to Wiegand: "Sometimes he grabbed the wrong one, and near chaos ensued. It was pure slapstick. Obviously, since the secretary had to handle the connections, she also had sixteen telephones. And the higher-ups probably had twenty." When Wiegand asked why the KGB didn't use a modern switchboard, Kremakovski didn't understand the question. The East German had to explain that it would save manpower, and above all, material such as copper. "We don't find that necessary—we are a rich land," the Soviet colonel replied.

Instead of getting down to business, Kremakovski summoned a number of subordinates to his office for a get-acquainted party. The colonel's hospitality was profuse. He may not have changed his attitude toward the Germans, but he was not going to be outdone by them. Rounds of vodka were interspersed with cups of strong tea accompanied by chocolate pralines and fresh fruit. They toasted each other's success. No business was discussed. After a couple of hours, Wiegand was taken to a KGB apartment, where he managed to sleep off the alcohol. In the evening, a KGB officer took him to one of Moscow's finest restaurants, the Azerbaijan on Gorki Street, for the real welcome. "It was a *prazdnik,* a Russian orgy that I will never forget," Wiegand recalled. "I lost count of the toasts, which began with drinking to Brezhnev's health, the memory of Lenin, and when they ran out of communist leaders, they switched to labor unions and finally to our mothers and fathers. In between we munched on *zakuski,* the Russian hors d'oeuvres of fatty herring and smoked bacon, tomatoes and cucumbers. By the time we got to the main course, I was so drunk that I never remembered what I ate."

The next morning, Wiegand sat in Kremakovski's office with a throbbing headache. The Soviet colonel pointed to a stack of files on a coffee table, saying, "Operation Moses; take a look." The KGB had already translated their original material into German. Wiegand was astounded. Soviet counterintelligence had organized an extensive espionage network in Israel many years earlier. Four double agents already were operating successfully within the Mossad. KGB case officers disguised as tourists met clandestinely with their agents in Bulgaria and other Eastern bloc countries. In addition to the four double agents, the KGB had recruited sixteen more who had been dispatched to Israel as immigrants.

Wiegand was puzzled. Why, he asked Kremakovski, did the KGB need the assistance of Stasi counterintelligence when the operation was already proceeding so smoothly? "It is not working as well as you think," Kremakovski replied gravely. "The first four are doing good work, but none of the others has made contact with us, and there is no way we can send our case officers there to find them." Kremakovski then told Wiegand the KGB wanted Stasi officers to travel to Israel, locate the wayward agents, and build a fire under them.

The East German became agitated: "Vladimir Anatolevich, you must be joking! It is hard enough for any German to try anything like that in Israel, but for an East German it is even worse. The Mossad is good, and they would catch us in no time. They know what an anti-Semitic government we have. They are already angry that the DDR has refused to pay even a single mark in reparations. They are just waiting for us to do something stupid so they can step on us."

Although Wiegand knew that the KGB—especially a man of Kremakovski's character—did not take kindly to expressions of dissent, he refused the request, being convinced that in this case Mielke would back him. He was relieved when Kremakovski merely shrugged and answered, "So, then, let's go to the plans you brought with you."

The Stasi had developed a comprehensive program for surveillance and recruitment of Soviet citizens in the DDR. Emphasis was placed on the Soviet wives of numerous East German government and political officials as well as on officers of the National People's Army and the Stasi who had married while studying at various institutions in the Soviet Union. Their wives were maintaining contacts in West Berlin with the "Russian mafia." It was relatively easy for them to engage in smuggling and currency speculation, because as privileged residents of the DDR, they were not subject to customs controls. Some even worked as prostitutes in West Berlin to earn hard currency. Wiegand told Kremakovski that even if the husbands suspected or actually knew of their wives' criminal activities, they were unable to do anything about it. "All husbands, even a major general I know, are totally henpecked," he told Kremakovski gleefully. "Some of the women even beat their husbands. They are spineless cowards." The Soviet colonel smiled and approved the plan.

Kremakovski then reached for another file. "Go ahead and work on the wives, but make this one, *Schlange* [Snake], your priority." Wiegand learned that *Schlange* was the code name for Maria Brauner, a woman born in Lwów, Poland (formerly Lemberg) and raised in Latvia. Wiegand recognized the name at once. She was the wife of Artur Brauner, a wealthy and well-known West Berlin motion picture producer. The Soviets had given her the nickname Larissa.

The KGB counterintelligence files alleged that Frau Brauner was a "devout enemy of the Soviet Union who caused great harm to the Soviet economy by smuggling diamonds, icons, and paintings out of the Soviet Union to the West." The KGB, Wiegand read, had information that the woman had organized an extensive smuggling network in West Berlin with the help of the Russian mafia. Furthermore, the KGB suspected that Brauner also worked for the Mossad, the Israeli intelligence service.

The East German colonel asked his Soviet counterpart why Mrs. Brauner had not been arrested in the Soviet Union, in view of the evidence the KGB claimed it had already amassed. Kremakovski replied that he wanted to identify her network, including her contacts in the Soviet Union, and using threats of arrest, to turn her associates into agents who could infiltrate the Mossad as well as keep an eye on the Jewish community.

After Wiegand had studied the Schlange case file, he was told that Operation Moses had two other prongs. The first was "Scout," the code name for a Palestinian who had studied in Kiev and had married a Soviet woman. He had been recruited by the KGB. Wiegand was to take the Palestinian under his wing and bring him to the attention of Mossad case officers attached to the Israeli embassy in Bonn, in the hope that he would be recruited.

The third prong of Operation Moses was *Fuchs* (Fox), a.k.a. Nina Albrot, a plump, forty-two-year-old woman who also had come to Berlin from Latvia. The Soviets knew only that she was somehow connected with Maria Brauner and traveled often to the Soviet Union. "Find out how Nina fits in," Kremakovski said, and ended the consultation.

Immediately on his return to East Berlin, Wiegand assigned a half dozen counterintelligence officers to start recruiting informants and double agents. They located yet another Latvian-born woman who lived in East Berlin and who was tailor-made for recruitment because she, too, was involved in smuggling and currency speculation. This was Irina Rehse, a tall, good-looking blonde in her early thirties. Confronted by Stasi officers, Rehse agreed to become an agent rather than go to prison, and she was assigned the code name Anna. Three other agents also were successfully recruited from among the "Russian mafia" in West Berlin.

By mid-1983, Wiegand told me, his task force had not only confirmed the KGB's allegations and suspicions but controlled the group with which Brauner was involved. Everything that Mrs. Brauner and the "Russian mafia" undertook was reported to Wiegand, who in turn informed Kremakovski in Moscow. The East German colonel claimed he verified that "the smuggling of valuables out of the Soviet Union amounted to millions of rubles."[9] Surveillance of the woman was so tight that she could not make a move without the Stasi knowing about it. Her home was bugged and her telephone tapped. Conversations outside the home were picked up by directional microphones. Wiegand said he soon recognized that Mrs. Brauner was an "extremely imaginative businesswoman who had her money everywhere—in porno shops, peep shows, and diamond and icon smuggling." In several cases, according to Wiegand, East German counterintelligence officers "were able to connect her with crimes committed by the Russian mafia operating in West Berlin." Nina Albrot was also identified. Wiegand said she was a partner in Brauner's alleged smuggling activities, and at the same time, a competitor in illegal enterprises, such as peep shows and small private shops. The network reaching into the Soviet Union and her connections to smugglers was uncovered and reported to Kremakovski in Moscow. From time to time Kremakovski reported the arrests in Moscow of agents of Mossad and other Western powers, but he never revealed the details, keeping his East German allies largely in the dark.

Suboperation Scout also had been successfully launched: The Palestinian had traveled to West Germany, shepherded by Stasi agents. He was told to visit bars and nightclubs that the Stasi knew were being frequented by Mossad agents, and to drop disparaging remarks about the Soviets and communism. He was soon recruited by the Mossad, and Wiegand's team began their control measures. Surveillance of his meetings with Israeli case officers was total. Through extensive telephone taps the KGB was able to identify the Mossad station chief as well as other agents and their informants. But it soon became apparent that "Scout" was not kosher. "We learned that he was playing a first rate confidence game, deceiving both the Soviets and the Mossad while actually working for the security branch of the Palestine Liberation Organization, the PLO," Wiegand told me. Nevertheless, the KGB decided to retain him: "Scout" furnished genuine information from time to time, and because of Stasi surveillance, his PLO contacts were also exposed to the point where they could be brought under communist control.

As a result of the visual and electronic surveillance of the Mossad residency at the Israeli embassy in Bonn as well as of Mossad officers operating in West Berlin, Wiegand claimed he learned something else. "Mrs. Brauner's involvement in criminal activities apparently was too much even for the hard-bitten Mossad, and they dropped her." Before he had a chance to report this turn of events to Kremakovski, Wiegand's watchers presented him with one of the most sensitive dilemmas of his career: Surveillance agents had reported that Mrs. Brauner frequently met in East and West Berlin with individuals who were identified as officers of the KGB's First Main Directorate based in Karlshorst. Photographs showing Mrs. Brauner passing items to the Soviets and vice versa, Wiegand said, convinced him that the woman was working for the KGB's foreign espionage directorate. Wiegand went to Karlshorst to confront Colonel Feliks Vinogradov,[10] chief of the directorate's Second Department, which was responsible for counterintelligence in Germany.

"On the one hand we are assigned by the KGB to work this woman over, and on the other she is working for you," Wiegand said to Vinogradov. "What's going on, Feliks?" Vinogradov became highly agitated and implored Wiegand not to report this to Kremakovski and to cease all operations against Mrs. Brauner. It now became clear to the East German that what he had long suspected was true: The rift within the vaunted KGB was so deep that officers of the one department lied to their colleagues in the other. "They deceived one another left and right." Wiegand said Vinogradov would not reveal details of Mrs. Brauner's work for the foreign espionage department. Wiegand knew that corruption was rampant within the KGB and thought it was possible that KGB officers might be part of the smuggling operations. Had Kremakovski been told by someone in the highest echelon of the KGB to keep his hands off Mrs. Brauner? Or had Vinogradov made a deal with Kremakovski? Whatever the case, Wiegand said that Mrs. Brauner changed her usual travel route to Moscow after he talked to Vinogradov. Instead of traveling eastward through Poland—the most direct route—she made her way via Sweden and Finland. KGB counterintelligence never caused her any trouble.[11]

Meanwhile, Irina Rehse, agent Anna, had become an enthusiastic Stasi collaborator. After all, why not take advantage of the Stasi connection, which would provide her the protection she needed for her smuggling operations? Kremakovski had assured Wiegand that Anna could pursue her "business" in the Soviet Union as well, so long as she delivered the required information from within the Jewish community in West Berlin.

OPERATION NEEDLE

While Operation Moses was running smoothly for the KGB Second Main Directorate in Moscow, Colonel Vinogradov of the First Directorate stationed in East Berlin approached Wiegand for help. The KGB leadership in the DDR had become concerned over the increasing concentration of former Soviet citizens, especially Jews of German extraction, in West Germany. Analysis of telephone intercepts and reports from moles buried inside the West German security services were alarming. The BND, the Bundesnachrichtendienst (Federal Intelligence Service) and the BfV, the federal counterespionage service, had stepped up recruitment of agents from among the emigrants. These agents, the Soviets had learned, were to be employed against military targets in the DDR and against Soviet citizens residing there.

Besides the pipeline into Israel established by Kremakovski's department, Vinogradov revealed that the foreign espionage directorate had recruited a number of Soviet Jews, who were "allowed" to emigrate. Wiegand's task force was to assist in controlling these agents once they had infiltrated Jewish organizations in Western Europe, especially those located in West Berlin. In addition, some of those agents were to penetrate specific offices of the West German intelligence services, the U.S. Central Intelligence Agency, and the U.S. Army's Intelligence and Security Command.

These offices were located at refugee and emigrant reception centers at Traiskirchen near Vienna, Ostia near Rome, and Marienfelde in West Berlin. East German *Instrukteure,* agents providing moles in place with funds and communications, were to be deployed. Vinogradov told Wiegand that this operation was important to him personally. He explained that he was preparing to return to Moscow and take over the Second Department at Moscow Central. This department was headed by Colonel Mikhail ("Misha") Skorik, who had been designated to assume command of the KGB contingent in the DDR. Skorik was a highly acclaimed officer who had recruited and controlled BND officer Heinz Felfe.[12] But Skorik fell victim to internecine intrigue.[13] Wiegand reported Vinogradov's proposition to his boss, General Kratsch, who authorized the colonel to cooperate. The new operation was code-named *Nadel* (Needle), and another successful KGB-Stasi joint venture ensued. Within six months, Wiegand reported to Vinogradov that the agents were in place, mainly as interpreters. Thus, the KGB was able to keep track of emigrants recruited as agents by the West as well as to obtain information revealed by emigrants during interrogation.

Operation Moses also continued to develop. Agent Rehse proved how good and "loyal" an informant she was. At one point she came to Wiegand with information so explosive that he suggested to the counterintelligence chief, General Kratsch, that it be relayed quickly and directly to Mielke, without a paper trail. "Anna" had reported that the Soviet mother-in-law of a Stasi officer was smuggling gold and other contraband from the USSR to West Berlin. The Stasi officer himself was peripherally involved, a fact which by itself needed not necessarily be disastrous for the Stasi. But the officer, First Lieutenant Thomas Kleiber, turned out to be a member of Wiegand's own task force, which was a calamity. Moreover, he was also the son of a powerful member of the Politburo, Minister for Science and Technology Günther Kleiber. His father had used his connections to get Thomas the Stasi job. He was appointed a lieutenant, and before he served even a day on the job, he was detailed to study journalism at Leipzig University. There he met and married a Soviet girl who was also a student. When Wiegand was told to accept him in his unit, he refused. An extraordinarily gutsy and dedicated professor said in a written final evaluation that young Kleiber had been the worst student he had ever instructed. "He was stupid, lazy, and arrogant, and he tried to bribe me with Western goods he had obtained in Wandlitz."[14] Although Mielke was fully aware of Thomas Kleiber's background, he had overruled Wiegand's objection.

Now Mielke was forced to make a distasteful decision. Dismissal and punishment? Recognizing the Stasi chief's dilemma, General Kratsch seized the moment to further ingratiate himself with the boss. The general decided to retain Kleiber in his counterintelligence directorate but transfer him to the Thirteenth Department, which was responsible for the surveillance of journalists. Mielke accepted this solution, and the matter was closed. Mielke ordered Wiegand to maintain silence and not to inform the KGB. Kleiber was not told that he and his family had been tagged as criminals. Kleiber's mother-in-law, known only as "Elena," retained her job at Radio Volga, the Soviet armed forces' station in East Germany. She and young Kleiber continued business as usual.

Irina Rehse, alias Anna, had proved her loyalty and ability as an agent and was elevated from a mere informant to *inoffizieller Mitarbeiter mit Feindberührung* (IMB). This designation, unofficial collaborator with enemy contact, was the highest Stasi "rank" given to an operative who was not a commissioned officer. It was reserved for tested agents who operated both inside and outside the DDR. In agreement with the KGB, the Stasi then sent Rehse on a mission to Israel, using a genuine West German passport. She was thoroughly briefed on how to make herself conspicuous to Israeli security officials at Lod Airport in Tel Aviv. Stasi officials hoped this would result in her recruitment by Israeli intelligence. The ploy worked. The Stasi alliance obtained a valuable insight into the operation of Mossad in West Berlin and in the DDR.

A year before Kremakovski retired in 1988, he told Wiegand that he had a first-class agent whom he wanted "Anna" to introduce to the Mossad for recruitment. "Kremakovski characterized this agent as extremely dependable, and unfortunately we believed him." In late fall 1989, shortly before the Berlin Wall came down, "Anna" made another trip to Israel, after which Wiegand received disturbing information from another double agent. It appeared that the Mossad suspected "Anna" of being a double and that she was no longer trusted. Mossad officials told "Anna" that her services were being terminated because the risk had become too high. The Israelis, Wiegand believed, decided against arresting her because they feared that this might prompt the Soviets to interfere with Jewish emigration.

Colonel Wiegand was convinced that there was a serious leak in Moscow. He flew to the Soviet capital to confront Kremakovski's successor, a younger and less experienced lieutenant colonel. In an effort to stonewall, the colonel told a tale rife with clumsy contradictions that Wiegand knew was pure fiction. The confrontation became heated, and the East German threatened to return home unless he was provided with truthful answers. The threat worked, probably because the political situation in the DDR was already shaky and the KGB did not want to alienate its allies.

Wiegand was astounded to learn that Kremakovski's agent was not of proven loyalty or ability but merely a woman who had applied for an exit visa. The KGB had approached her and told her that she would be contacted shortly by an Israeli agent, and when that happened, she should contact the KGB at once. "Anna" made contact, and the new recruit not only informed the KGB but also used relatives in the West to inform the Mossad. It became clear that Kremakovski's successor, and perhaps Kremakovski himself, had been playing a cynical game of betrayal in order to prove their worth as spy catchers.

By the time Wiegand returned to East Berlin, shortly before the Berlin Wall came down, the MfS was in turmoil and many of its agents had already broken off their Stasi contacts. There was no chance to warn Anna. Months later, Wiegand learned that Rehse, accompanied by Kleiber's mother-in-law Elena, had made another "business" trip to Moscow, where she was promptly arrested. "Interestingly, Elena, the real culprit, was released and returned to East Germany, while Rehse was kept in prison." Despite efforts by the Stasi and the East German government to obtain the latter's release, she was still in KGB custody when Germany was reunited. Wiegand said he felt "used and betrayed."

Operation Moses functioned until November 1989, when the Berlin Wall fell and the Stasi disintegrated. None of the smugglers and speculators operating in the DDR had ever been arrested. However, a West Berlin police detective who insisted on anonymity said an investigation of Mrs. Brauner was under way in the 1980s but was stopped by the police president. The detective maintained that the case file, to which he had contributed, had disappeared.

THE KGB-STASI ALLIANCE DISSOLVES

During their participation in Operation Moses, Stasi officers discovered that information that originated with the MfS and was relayed to the KGB's headquarters in East Germany was subsequently presented by the latter to the Moscow leadership as KGB morsels. By 1986, the Stasi had become so disgusted with the KGB's duplicity that staff morale had sunk, compelling Mielke to complain to KGB Chairman Chebrikov. Several KGB officers stationed in East Germany were demoted and recalled to Moscow. Chebrikov also wrote a letter to all KGB units in the DDR in which he emphatically warned officers "not to deceive their MfS colleagues in the future." The letter continued, "The MfS officers also are good experts, and the KGB officers better use their own eyes a bit better."[15] This improved the atmosphere, at least so long as Chebrikov remained head of the KGB. Even then, however, relations were not always harmonious.

It also nettled the East Germans that KGB operatives routinely recruited DDR citizens under "false flag"—the East Germans were misled to think they were working for their own country's Ministry for State Security. The Stasi was generally informed of such instances, if for no other reason than to ensure that these individuals were not arrested in the course of Stasi investigations. Germans who were aware of their KGB employment also were carefully protected by the Soviets. However, foreigners who happened to be targeted for KGB recruitment while traveling in East Germany were not always so fortunate.

A particularly unfortunate case was that of Anton Ivankovic, a businessman who was kidnapped in Leipzig on April 27, 1988.[16] The fifty-three-year-old owner of Ost-West Montage (OWM), a Swiss firm supplying manpower to Western construction firms, was frantically sought by his employees, who knew only that he had disappeared and that work in progress at five major projects was in danger of shutting down. Negotiations over OWM's participation in the construction of a luxury hotel already had collapsed when Ivankovic failed to show up at a scheduled meeting. Ten days later, Ivankovic finally telephoned his East Berlin office manager, Achim Fassman, from Budapest. The normally gregarious Yugoslav sounded deeply distraught, and Fassman immediately booked a flight to the Hungarian capital. On his arrival, he found a spiritually broken man who had been physically tortured and who was suffering from extreme paranoia. Ivankovic, who always dressed elegantly, was disheveled and penniless. With great effort, Fassman extracted from him an incredible story, one so monstrous that Fassman had difficulty believing it.

Ivankovic was in Budapest on business when he had received a telephone call, on April 26, from an East German business partner. This partner asked Ivankovic to travel to East Germany to complete negotiations that had been under way for several months with another Swiss company, Schulzer-Eschowitz. A representative of that firm, Michael Schneider, would meet him in the East German city of Leipzig to sign the contract. Ivankovic was eager to comply. For months he had been in contact with Horst Virgens, owner of a consulting firm at Singen, near Lake Constance on the Swiss border. Virgens had offered Ivankovic a part in the construction of a power plant at Tomsk in the Soviet Union. Over the telephone, Ivankovic's East German business partner told him that he would be awarded a contract worth 20 million Swiss francs (about US$13.6 million). Ivankovic flew to Leipzig the next day.

Virgens met the Yugoslav businessman at the Hotel Merkur, where he introduced him to Schneider, saying that the latter would handle the deal. Virgens then excused himself and left Ivankovic alone with Schneider. After a twenty-minute conversation about the contract, Schneider invited Ivankovic to his apartment on the outskirts of the city for a talk *unter vier Augen*, a confidential chat. When they arrived, Ivankovic was attacked by Schneider and a second man who was already at the apartment and whom he had never met. Neither was a match for Ivankovic, a well-built six-footer: Schneider was several inches shorter. The stranger was about the same height and build as Schneider, wore glasses, and as Ivankovic recalled, "looked mean." Ivankovic fought back, and his jacket was torn off. The melee ended when Schneider pulled a pistol he had carried concealed beneath his jacket and threatened to shoot. Ivankovic was shoved into what appeared to be a child's bedroom and pushed onto a bed. His wrists were tied and his arms were stretched above his head and lashed to a wrought iron headboard. His legs were tied as well. Around his neck the attackers placed a noose designed to strangle him if he moved. Schneider then held Ivankovic's nose shut while the second man poured a sleep-inducing solution into his mouth.

When Ivankovic awakened, he again faced his attackers, who now introduced themselves. Schneider said he was a member of the Ministry for State Security of the DDR. The other man gave no name and merely said he was an officer of the Soviet KGB. The reason for his detention, Schneider told Ivankovic, was that during the years he had worked in East Germany, he had "caused damage to the DDR and other East European socialist countries" and that he was charged with "economic sabotage and political subversion." The accusation was that he did not "honor the trust" put in him by the foreign trade ministry and DDR firms that had contracted to supply manpower to "major construction projects of socialism." Specifically, his captors said, Ivankovic had "merely raked in money and cheated socialism by not paying proper taxes and commissions." These accusations were interspersed with threats and beatings. Several times Schneider released the clip from his pistol and showed Ivankovic that it was loaded with live shells. He was deprived of food and drink. Not allowed to go to the toilet, Ivankovic soon lay in urine and excrement.

"We are going to finish you off," the nameless tormentors said after Schneider accused Ivankovic of "collaborating with Western intelligence against the DDR and other socialist states." The punishment for espionage was death, he told the Yugoslav. From time to time, telephone calls were made or received in an adjoining room during which Schneider said he was relaying preliminary reports to headquarters. And all the while Ivankovic tried to figure out just what these men wanted. He knew he had broken no laws. By midnight the first day, his wrists and ankles were bleeding. Then he was given another drug that put him to sleep.

The torture and threats continued the second day. Ivankovic maintained his innocence and repeatedly asked that he be brought before a normal court. The situation became more tense, and suddenly Schneider went out of the room and returned with a rifle. The weapon was loaded, the ropes with which Ivankovic was lashed to the bed were cut, and he was told stand up. A death sentenced was pronounced and a shot was fired. Ivankovic fainted. The "execution" had been a perverse sham. When he regained consciousness, Schneider said, "So now you either do what we demand, or you will be shot for real." There were only two demands: financial restitution to the DDR and socialism, and signing an agreement to work for the Stasi and the KGB against the West. In physical and mental agony, Ivankovic agreed to cooperate. He was given another sedative and fell asleep.

On the third day, Ivankovic was released from the bed and blindfolded. His wrists were still tied. Schneider led him to a telephone in another room and forced him to call a bank in Vienna, where he maintained a special account used only to cover business expenses incurred in East Germany, to determine the amount of the current balance. All the while Ivankovic could feel the muzzle of the pistol pressed to the back of his head. Schneider was surprised that the balance in the account was no longer DM1 million (US$625,000)—the amount specified by a bank reference earlier, when Schneider was "negotiating" with Ivankovic—but only 300,000 marks (US$187,500). In the interim, Ivankovic had withdrawn the bulk of the money to pay salaries. Schneider pressed the pistol to Ivankovic's temple and forced him to call the bank again and to request a credit of DM700,000. When the bank refused, Ivankovic was told to order the transfer of the remaining DM300,000 to his account at the Handelsbank in East Berlin. In a third telephone call, Ivankovic was forced to inform the East Berlin bank of the upcoming transfer and to authorize withdrawal of the money by one of his representatives. That completed, he was made to write on his firm's stationery a one-page agreement volunteering his services to the Ministry for State Security of the DDR and to the KGB for espionage assignments against the West. Even then, however, Ivankovic remained shackled.

The fourth day, a Saturday, began with new beatings. Later that day Ivankovic was given official forms from his East Berlin bank to complete, designating Schneider as his representative for the withdrawal of funds. Then came a new twist: Ivankovic was informed that after much deliberation it had been decided not to "ruin your business in the DDR and Switzerland," even though his guilt had been established. Instead, his firm could continue and could even receive assistance. This "magnanimous" offer of redemption was predicated not only upon his spying for the Stasi and the KGB but also on his financing Stasi and KGB operations in the West, "in the spirit of further restitution." For the time being, DM2 million (US$1.250 million) were to be paid in installments every two weeks in the following two months. Payment would be made during clandestine meetings in Vienna and Zurich with Schneider, who would function as his "case officer." The role of the "KGB officer," who had not uttered a single word during Ivankovic's ordeal but who excelled in brutality, was characterized by Schneider as that of the executioner: "If you break the agreement or fail to pay, he will hunt you down and will execute you no matter where in the world you hide."

Psychologically broken and physically tortured, Ivankovic was ready to agree to anything to stay alive. On the fifth day, he was allowed to visit the toilet and clean himself up. Then he was given some food and drink. But after he had eaten, Ivankovic was tied again to the iron bedstead, and the torture continued. The scene changed from being left alone to beatings and threats with the pistol, again and again the threat of being shot. The Yugoslav's situation once more became critical on the sixth day—Monday, May 2. His tormentors were suspecting that Ivankovic had played a trick on them because the money had not been deposited in East Berlin. Numerous telephone calls ensued. Later that day the bank finally confirmed receipt of the money. Ivankovic was told to clean up again and get ready to leave for the Leipzig airport. Before Schneider and the "KGB officer" led him out of the apartment, they took all of his cash in various hard currencies as well as his travelers' checks and other valuables.

At the airport, Ivankovic was given a ticket to Budapest, 300 West marks (about US$187), and his passport. Before boarding the plane, he was instructed to check into Hotel Thermal. He was warned not to leave the hotel and to wait for "control telephone calls." Ivankovic obeyed. Indeed, the next day he did receive two calls. It was Schneider making more threats and setting a date for the first clandestine meeting, which was to take place in two weeks. Ivankovic was told to bring with him to the meeting the first installment of 250,000 West marks (US$156,250).

It took Ivankovic another day to regain sufficient strength over body and mind to call his office manager in East Berlin. The Yugoslav spoke haltingly and with great difficulty. Achim Fassman listened incredulously. Things like that just didn't happen in the DDR. Finally convinced that Ivankovic was telling the truth, Fassman now had to persuade him to return to East Berlin and report the crime to the police. It took some effort, but his boss finally agreed.

Arriving at Schönefeld airport the morning of May 6, the two men went directly to People's Police headquarters at Alexander Platz in downtown East Berlin. A criminal investigator listened patiently while Ivankovic told him the entire story. Then the detective dismissed him, saying that he didn't believe a word of it. Nevertheless, a report was forwarded to the Ministry for State Security. Because it involved a foreigner, the report eventually landed on the desk of Colonel Wiegand. The colonel remembered meeting Ivankovic several times at the Ministry for Foreign Trade. Although highly skeptical, he decided to look into the case because Ivankovic did not seem the type to make up such a story. His decision meant, however, that he had to "deconspire" himself—Stasi jargon for revealing his true identity. The Yugoslav had known him only as "Herr Falk," a government official dealing with investment projects of foreign firms in the DDR.

Wiegand ordered Major Klaus Schilling, a section chief in his department, to pick up Ivankovic at the Metropol Hotel and question him at a Stasi safe house. He, too, had trouble believing the man. When Wiegand read the statement Ivankovic made to the major, he still had doubts.[17] But there was a ring of truth to the story, and Wiegand handled the second interrogation of Ivankovic himself. "Ivankovic was stunned when he saw me and I identified myself as a ranking member of the MfS." The colonel offered the man a brandy to put him at ease and then produced several pistols of different make. "Is there a weapon here of the type that you were threatened with?" Ivankovic picked out a nine-millimeter Makarov, the standard issue sidearm carried by both the Stasi and the KGB. There was also something familiar about the formulation of the espionage agreement the Yugoslav was made to sign. The wording was very close to the form used by both the Stasi and its KGB allies. Were the kidnappers intelligence officers turned common criminals? It wouldn't have been the first time. Years earlier, Wiegand had caught a Stasi major who had killed his two informants so he could put the money he was to pay them in his own pocket.[18] Wiegand decided to give Ivankovic the benefit of the doubt. As a next step, he had Ivankovic examined by a team of doctors assigned to the Stasi. "The result was a shocker. Even days after his release, the man's ankles, legs, and wrists clearly showed the marks of shackles and rope burns," Wiegand recalled. "His entire body showed subcutaneous hemorrhages, ugly bruises that the doctors said could only have been caused by severe beatings. A blood test removed all doubt. It showed traces of chemicals identical to those used in sleep-inducing pharmaceuticals. The doctors diagnosed physical exhaustion, sleeping disorder, traumatic fear, and an irregular heartbeat."

A search of the Stasi computer, in which personal data and photos of all persons entering the DDR were stored, showed that a representative of the Swiss firm Schulzer-Eschowitz named Schneider had traveled to the DDR on several occasions. However, the travel dates did not correspond to the period during which the Ivankovic kidnapping had taken place. Ivankovic's description of Schneider was different, too. Next, the MfS checked out Horst Virgens, who had originally introduced Schneider to the Yugoslav businessman. Computer data showed the man had been in East Germany during the dates in question and had entered the DDR from West Germany in the company of another man, whose photograph was shown to Ivankovic. Without hesitation, he identified Uwe Königsmark, a twenty-four-year-old, self-employed car dealer from the West German town of Tuttlingen, as

"Schneider, the MfS officer." The computer data on Virgens also showed that in addition to Königsmark, he was often accompanied by two other West Germans, Norbert Fuchs and Helmut Masannek. The latter was an engineer employed by the West German firm Mannesmann, a giant conglomerate producing heavy industrial equipment as well as electronics. Ivankovic identified the thirty-one-year-old Fuchs as the nameless KGB officer but said he had never seen or heard of Masannek. To Wiegand's regret, the computer check also revealed that all four men had left East Germany the day Ivankovic was put on the plane to Budapest.

Until then, the investigation had been conducted in the strictest secrecy and knowledge of the results had been limited to Wiegand, his deputy Major Klaus Schilling, and the medical team. At this point they would have to inform the boss, General Kratsch, and provide Mielke with an interim report. Mielke approved the collaboration with the special criminology department of the Ninth Main Directorate, which was responsible for internal investigations and liaison with prosecutors and the courts. Wiegand briefed Major General Pycka, an experienced criminologist, with whom he had worked previously on other criminal cases. "But he didn't display much interest and made a few remarks which showed that he was not taking the matter seriously." Next he sought the help of Colonel Armin Waals, chief of the investigations directorate's First Department, which passed final judgment on all espionage cases prior to turning them over to prosecutors. "He was an old pro. All the spy cases that had ever been uncovered in the DDR had passed through his hands. I needed him, because after all, the crime had been passed off as a joint MfS-KGB action. He promised to help, but nothing happened." At this point, Wiegand officially opened the investigation into the Ivankovic affair and assigned it the code name Alligator.

Exasperated by the inaction of the other Stasi departments, Wiegand formed a small Alligator task force staffed by his own officers. Since the Saxonian city of Leipzig had been the scene of the crime, Wiegand also summoned Lieutenant Colonel Günther Reum, deputy chief of the local counterespionage department, to Berlin. Reum didn't believe Ivankovic's story, but he agreed to work with Wiegand because he had known him for many years and respected him as a solid professional. Returning to Leipzig, Reum reported to his district chief, Lieutenant General Günther Humitsch, and requested additional manpower. Humitsch refused, saying his officers were too valuable to be wasted on a wild goose chase.

With Reum getting organized in Leipzig, Wiegand requested access to the computer in the Twelfth Department, which only Mielke could authorize. Next to ZAIG, the central analysis and information group with access to the Moscow KGB computer, the Twelfth Department was the most highly restricted section of the Stasi. "I was actually a little surprised when Mielke allowed me to dig there," Wiegand said. The digging paid off. Virgens and Masannek were listed as "registered by order of the chief of the Twelfth Department." This terminology indicated that the men were top agents employed by the KGB group stationed in East Germany. The special wording generally protected such KGB agents from arrest by the Stasi.

Next, Major Schilling took Ivankovic to Leipzig in an attempt to jog his memory and locate the apartment were he had been held. On the last day of his imprisonment in Leipzig he was allowed to go to the toilet, where he had looked out of the window. He had noticed a small park and a large chestnut tree next to which was parked a dark red Moskvich sedan. Schilling was joined by Reum, and together they drove Ivankovic through the outskirts of the city for two days. Then Ivankovic excitedly pointed to an apartment building. "That's where they held me." The building stood opposite the park and the tree he had described earlier. A dark red Moskvich sedan was parked next to the tree.

The apartment was rented to Dana Grimmling, a teacher who neighbors said was on vacation in Sochi, on the Black Sea.

Schilling reported his findings to Wiegand, who drove to Leipzig with a forensic unit of the Stasi's Special Commission for Criminalistics to make a surreptitious search of the apartment for evidence. Forensic scientists established beyond any doubt that this was the place where Ivankovic had been held and tortured. Bloodstains found on bed sheets and on a piece of rope matched the Yugoslav's blood type. A bullet hole was found above the iron bedstead on which Ivankovic had been tortured, attesting to the truth of his statement about the mock execution. Wiegand was elated. "The forensic experts were the best we had in the DDR, and they found everything I needed—even the fingerprints of Ivankovic and the perpetrators."

All foreigners visiting the DDR, including West Germans, were under almost constant surveillance by the Stasi. Even when they stayed in private homes, their presence had to be registered in a *Hausbuch,* a ledger kept by a trusted tenant. The ledger was inspected daily by a representative of the People's Police. It was easy, therefore, for Stasi officers to discover that in addition to being acquainted with Dana Grimmling, Virgens had a lover whose name was Kerstin Albrecht and who was a teacher. Ivankovic was shown photographs of Albrecht and Grimmling. He did not know Grimmling, but he said that Albrecht had posed as Virgens's secretary at a negotiating session in Vienna. A file check revealed that she had never been issued an East German passport and there was no record of her ever having been authorized to visit a noncommunist country. Wiegand was now convinced that the KGB was directly involved in the case. He knew that the Ministry for State Security had been supplying the KGB with genuine blank DDR passports, official seals, and exit permits.

Meanwhile, investigators had confirmed that money had been transferred from the Viennese Bank to Handelsbank in East Berlin on the date provided by Ivankovic. Furthermore, bank officials revealed that Horst Virgens had established an account at the Handelsbank a few days before the kidnapping and that he had been the recipient of the blackmail money. Additional incriminating facts began to pile up. A car rented by Virgens was discovered and found to have been the vehicle in which Ivankovic had been driven to the Leipzig airport.

According to Ivankovic, Virgens never appeared after their "negotiation," just before the kidnapping. Yet Wiegand was sure he had been the man directing the operation, especially since the car was rented by him. The colonel figured that Virgens probably was on the other end of the line when the telephone calls were made to the Leipzig apartment. As an experienced espionage agent, Virgens would have known that all telephone calls from hotels were being monitored. Thus, he might have used a public telephone somewhere along the autobahn between East Berlin and Leipzig. All telephone calls made from public facilities as well as from service stations along the major highways through East Germany were also recorded by the Stasi. Within a few hours the surveillance station in Potsdam had located the tapes of three calls placed at a service station near Berlin by a West German to a number in Leipzig. That number belonged to Grimmling. The tapes were damning. Virgens had, indeed, masterminded the events. Wiegand heard him say, "Beat him to a pulp, and when that doesn't work do the execution like we discussed."

At this juncture, Wiegand was summoned to report to State Security Minister Mielke. "I am going to have Colonel Malkov report to you for a meeting," Mielke told the colonel. "Tell him everything you have uncovered, and let's see what he says. In the meantime, the investigation is to be handled in such a way that no one else finds out about the KGB connection." The Stasi chief emphasized that Ivankovic was not to be told either. Lastly, Mielke ordered Wiegand to provide him with an update by eight o'clock every morning.

Colonel Alexander A. Malkov, from 1970 to 1978 the KGB station chief at the Soviet Embassy in Bonn and then assigned to the foreign intelligence Second Directorate at Karlshorst, listened attentively as Wiegand detailed the case. The Soviet colonel said he would take the information to his superiors. However, the Karlshorst KGB headquarters remained silent. Wiegand prodded Malkov at a second meeting but got nowhere. Wiegand complained directly to Major General Gennady F. Titov, chief of the KGB in Germany.[19] "Titov told me to piss off. It was typical Titov." But Wiegand pressed on. "Finally, probably out of fear that the crime and the KGB connection would become public, they were ready to tell the truth about their connection with Virgens and Masannek." The two men had attended the Leipzig Industrial Fair in spring 1985, where they visited the Soviet pavilion and volunteered their services to the ever present KGB representatives. For a short time they collaborated with officials of the Soviet Industrial Representation, unaware that they were dealing with the KGB. Then the two West Germans were provided cover stories and taken over as regular agents by the Fourth Department, which was responsible for scientific and technical espionage. Demanding increasingly higher pay, Virgens and Masannek provided a wealth of information and technical goods embargoed by NATO nations for sale to communist countries. They also spied against military targets. Masannek copied documents to which he, in his position as a well-placed engineer at Mannesmann, had access. Later, the pair began introducing scientists and secretaries to KGB case officers. Now it was clear to Wiegand why the Soviets had been so determined to stonewall and protect their agents. Virgens and Masannek obviously were first-class assets. But the East German colonel knew only part of the Virgens/Masannek saga—the part that Titov, the KGB chief in East Germany, wanted him to know.

As Wiegand was wrestling with the problem of how to turn over the kidnappers to judicial authorities without revealing the KGB connection—as Stasi chief Mielke had ordered—he received volatile information through a back channel. For several years, Wiegand had worked closely with Colonel Anatoly Mananikov, who was assigned as a KGB liaison officer to the Stasi's counterespionage directorate. Wiegand recalled: "Mananikov was the type of 'honest' Russian who began his career in 1946. As a young officer he participated in the ruthless extermination of the resistance in the Baltic states. After many talks with him, I realized that his conscience had begun to bother him—he was suffering because of his past. His trust in me was boundless, and I, of course, helped him whenever I could." Mananikov now volunteered information to help Wiegand put the Stasi-KGB dilemma in perspective.

Apparently, Virgens and Masannek were not making enough money from their "genuine" activities. They had begun to manufacture false information and forged documents. In mid-1987, Moscow Central became suspicious. Analysts were puzzled by the extensive and massive supply of information and documents. Concurrently, counterespionage specialists began to question the agents' abnormal lack of fear in situations of high risk—behavior that might indicate that they had made "hostile contact." Their case officer had praised the agents highly and reported the large sums they were being paid. The reports also described the gifts that the pair had been offering their case officer. All these circumstances led Moscow Central to suspect Virgens and Masannek of being double agents, working for a Western service to disseminate false or doctored material.

Moscow had told Titov to consider terminating the services of Virgens and Masannek, but the ambitious general was reluctant to do so. Without the significant successes this duo had brought him, he knew he would not inherit the top job. Titov therefore devised a counterstrategy. He discredited the case officer, who was known to the East German investigators only by his cover name, Alexei. Then he upgraded the status of the two "ace agents" and presented them to Moscow as indispensable to foreign intelligence collection. Wiegand's friend, Colonel Mananikov, confided that the case officer had been charged with suspected treason and had been brought back to Moscow under guard. After his first interrogation by a special KGB investigating panel at the Dzerzhinski Square headquarters, "Alexei" had committed suicide. "He was my friend," Mananikov told Wiegand, but he declined to reveal the agent's true name. "He was a dedicated officer, and he shot himself out of shame and desperation."

Titov told Moscow that the suicide was evidence that there had been at least an attempt by a Western intelligence service to recruit Alexei. Moscow agreed and at the same time ordered that the Virgens-Masannek operation be discontinued forthwith. But according to the KGB liaison officer, Titov ignored the directive and secretly planned to continue using Virgens and Masannek as agents. To cover his tracks, Titov first had to rid himself of those intimately acquainted with the case. Charging that they were responsible for the death of Alexei, he relieved Lieutenant Colonel Sergei Maskolniv, chief of the Fourth Department, and all other officers of that department above the rank of captain, and sent them back to Moscow. At the same time, he cunningly transferred the operation to the counterintelligence department of the foreign espionage directorate and assigned Colonel Malkov as the new case supervisor. In turn, Malkov assigned a lieutenant colonel, known only as "Eugen," as the new case officer and the direct contact to Virgens and Masannek. It would be Titov's alibi in case the operation went sour and Moscow got wind of his disobedience. He could always say that he had assigned Malkov in order to follow up on the suspicion that Alexei had been approached by the "enemy." On the other hand, if Virgens and Masannek continued to deliver, the general was in a position to show off his successes as the master spy handler. No wonder Titov's colleagues had dubbed him "the Crocodile."[20] Wiegand described him as "the most unscrupulous Russian" he had ever met. Karl Grossmann, former colonel and deputy head of counterintelligence in the Stasi's foreign espionage directorate, described Titov simply as a pig.[21]

Wiegand now was sure that Malkov, the very KGB officer to whom Mielke had complained, and the new case officer Eugen were somehow involved in the crime. In his next report to Mielke, Wiegand said he did not think that the crime had been a full-blown KGB operation but that the two officers had known something of Virgens's plans. Faced with the evidence, Mielke agreed that Wiegand should confront Malkov again.

Meeting in a luxuriously appointed visitors' room at Stasi headquarters, Wiegand told the Soviet colonel all that he knew about the crime. "I must admit that I felt good when I saw Malkov squirm as I revealed all the KGB internal dirt that I had heard from my friend Mananikov." Playing from a position of strength, with Mielke's support, Wiegand demanded that the KGB summon the four men to a meeting in East Berlin. "We want Virgens to be questioned by you, and we want a recording of that meeting," Wiegand told the Soviet colonel.

Within a few days Virgens, accompanied by Königsmark the bogus Stasi officer and by Masannek, arrived in East Berlin. Fuchs, who had played the KGB role, did not make it. While awaiting the arrival of the kidnappers/extortionists, Wiegand had spent his time well. He had his Stasi technicians break into the KGB office at the Soviet Industrial Representation to install their own bugs. The rendezvous took place as the Soviet colonel had said it would. Wiegand sat in an office above, wearing earphones. He listened as Malkov, accompanied by Eugen, demanded to know what had happened. There was no question that the KGB man had known what Virgens had planned. "But I told you that Ivankovic would make a top source, with his connections in the West," Wiegand heard. "And I also told Eugen that we may have to use force, . . . that without force it wouldn't work, and he said 'well, you must do what you think will work.'" Neither Malkov nor Eugen responded. Virgens did not mention the money he had extorted from Ivankovic, which convinced Wiegand that Malkov was not an accomplice to that act. "What shall I do now?" Malkov told him to sit tight at his hotel until he heard from him. "We will straighten it out, don't worry." Before leaving, Virgens handed Malkov the passport that the KGB had supplied for Albrecht. "She has to go to London on an important business matter; please give her the exit visa." Colonel Wiegand heard it all. To his astonishment, Malkov summoned an assistant, who stamped the passport then and there. Until then, the Stasi had not known that the covert KGB office in downtown Berlin was equipped to issue phony visas and thought that a special documentation section at Karlshorst headquarters handled such matters.

Before General Titov had a chance to contact Mielke, a team of Stasi officers arrested the trio. Virgens's lover Kerstin Albrecht also was taken into custody with the KGB-issued passport in her possession. Dana Grimmling, the owner of the apartment where Ivankovic had been tortured, was apprehended at Schönefeld airport when she returned from her Black Sea vacation. Admonished once more by the state security minister that the KGB's involvement must remain secret, Wiegand circumvented the civil courts. Instead, he turned the case over to the High Military Tribunal and the military prosecutor. Interrogated by both the Stasi and the prosecutor, Virgens maintained that he merely wanted to coerce Ivankovic into spying for the KGB. Königsmark, the phony MfS officer, admitted to nothing except that he "acted on orders of the highest authorities." Masannek said he was merely spying for the KGB. He was released and allowed to return to West Germany, where he was later tried for espionage and sentenced to four years at hard labor. Both Albrecht and Grimmling turned state's evidence and were released.

Again Wiegand tried to contact Titov, who by then had been promoted to the top KGB post in East Germany. True to form, Titov had sensed—as Wiegand put it—"dass er tief in der Scheisse steckt" (that he was stuck in deep shit), and had refused to see the East German. Instead, he met again with Malkov and another colonel whom he had never seen and who introduced himself only as "Vasily." "Now, comrades, I want to know everything about those men you had registered as your agents, and I want to know why," Wiegand told the Russians. Malkov was fidgety. "Eh, we must first ask Comrade Colonel General Titov. You know, in such big things the general decides everything." Wiegand lost his patience. He gave a brief summary of what the Stasi knew: "So, and now I must tell you that we, even I, my dear friends, suspect that you have something to do with this case and you must now disprove it. We have collaborated for a long time, but that you commit crimes on our territory is, of course, a new twist." Malkov tried to protest, but the East German colonel cut him off. "I want you to tell General Titov that we have informed the permanent representative of the BRD [West Germany] that we have arrested three of their citizens. As you know, we have to do this in accordance with our agreement with them. I also know that a journalist is already on the trail of this story, and in a few days something is to appear in the press. I can't believe that it would enhance the present policy of the Soviet Union when headlines appear that say 'KGB kidnaps and tortures West European in the DDR.'" It pleased Wiegand when he sensed panic in Malkov and Vasily as they hastily departed. He knew that the Soviets had finally understood the seriousness with which the Stasi viewed the incident.

Within hours, Malkov called and said he had the files; but he tried one last time to stonewall, saying that there was nothing the Stasi could do with them, as the documents were all written in Russian. "Don't tell me that," Wiegand replied. "You know very well that I have an excellent translator. Let's have them quickly." The documents were on his desk by late evening. The translator worked all night. By morning Wiegand had the full story. Virgens and Masannek had, indeed, been top agents.

The military judicial authorities ruled that the kidnapping, extortion, and robbery of Ivankovic was a "common crime" and that the case would be tried in a civilian court at Leipzig. Prior to the trial, Virgens and Königsmark were threatened with more severe punishment if they ever told any "outsider" of their KGB connection. The ban included their court-appointed lawyers.

Simultaneously with the military tribunal's decision, Stasi chief Mielke sent a special courier to Moscow with a copy of the final investigation report, to be hand delivered to KGB Chairman Vladimir A. Kryuchkov. In turn, the KGB chief notified Foreign Minister Eduard A. Shevardnadze. Less than a week later, the Soviet Ambassador to the DDR, Vyacheslav Ivanovich Kochemasov, sent a note to Mielke. The Soviet envoy declared that Virgens and Masannek had had "business contacts" with representatives of the Soviet foreign trade mission in the DDR, but "at no time did they have a connection with the KGB." General Titov, too, wrote a letter in which he stated that "the claims by Virgens and Masannek that they had contacts with the KGB are false." Both letters were handed to the military tribunal and prosecutor, who informed the civil court judges but swore them to secrecy.

Virgens and Königsmark were charged with unlawful detention, causing bodily harm, and robbery. They were sentenced to eight and four years in the penitentiary, respectively. A warrant was issued for Fuchs and sent to West Germany. Just days before German reunification in October 1990, Virgens was granted a furlough from prison and failed to return. When he was recaptured, he told police that he felt the sentence given him by the East German court no longer had legal validity.

Meanwhile, Norbert Fuchs, the "KGB officer," had been apprehended in southwestern Germany. His trial on charges of kidnapping took place on May 21 and 22, 1992, before the provincial court in Rottweil. Virgens and Königsmark were brought from Berlin to testify. The star witnesses, however, were Ivankovic and the former MfS colonel Wiegand. The court commented favorably on the Stasi's investigation and its "meticulous development of the chain of evidence in accordance with the rule of law."

Both Virgens and Königsmark told the court that they had told their KGB case officer Eugen of their intention to recruit Ivankovic by force but that they had not revealed the ransom scheme.

Virgens attempted to play down his role as the mastermind of the crime, but Königsmark and Fuchs testified that Virgens had threatened them with the KGB when they tried to quit on the third day of the kidnapping because Ivankovic was not cooperating. "Virgens also gave me and Fuchs only part of the money, 25,000 West marks (about US$16,600), because he said the KGB had confiscated the rest," Königsmark claimed. Wiegand learned something new. Virgens had taken away their passports so that they could not quit before Ivankovic was sent to Budapest.

In view of Fuchs's full confession that he had played the role of the KGB officer in the scam, the court sentenced him to only three years' imprisonment.

Earlier, a court in eastern Germany had ordered Virgens to make restitution, but Ivankovic was able to recover only about half of the money that was extorted from him.

General Titov was recalled to Moscow in 1989 to take over the KGB's Second Main Directorate, responsible for counterintelligence. KGB chief Kryuchkov once more took his protégé under his wing. In August 1991, Kryuchkov and Titov were involved in the putsch against President Gorbachev and were arrested when the coup failed. Titov was stripped of his rank and kicked out of the KGB. Along with other conspirators, Kryuchkov and Titov later were released from prison, after the Russian parliament ordered their pardon.

Occasional irritations and Soviet heavy-handedness notwithstanding, the KGB-Stasi collaboration had been a successful enterprise for nearly half a century. In suppressing political opposition and oppressing a restive people, the secret police alliance had provided both the Soviet Union and the East German Communist Party "two shields and two swords."

4

THE SWORD OF REPRESSION

The dignity, liberty, and rights of the human being are protected by the criminal laws of the socialist state. The socialist society is guided by the respect for human dignity, even vis-à-vis the violator of the law, that is the steadfast mandate for the activity of the state and of justice.

—***Constitution of the DDR, Article 4***

STASI MINISTER ERICH MIELKE once said at a memorial rally for victims of fascism, "The DDR is a state that guarantees its citizens freedom, democracy, and basic human rights." Had he been honest, he would have added that these noble ideals were valid only so long as citizens did not question or oppose the will of the party. However, hundreds of thousands of citizens did test the state's guarantees, and they paid dearly for it—many with their lives.

HORST ERDMANN: FROM FIGHT TO FLIGHT . . .

One of those who yearned passionately for freedom was Horst Erdmann. When he tried to obtain it, he promptly became a target of the Stasi.[1] Erdmann was twenty-six years old and a second-year medical student at the University of Greifswald on the Baltic Sea. After months of debating their lot under the tyranny of communist dictatorship, he and six friends had distributed a stack of leaflets calling for free elections. During the night of May 29, 1953, Erdmann scattered more such leaflets around town. At seven o'clock the next morning, he was awakened by a pounding on the door of his furnished room. "When I opened up, I saw five men pointing pistols at me," Erdmann recalled. "One showed me an ID card and said they were from state security and that I should come along to 'clear up a certain matter. They had no arrest warrant, and I didn't ask to see one; one never questioned the Stasi about such legal niceties."[2]

At Stasi headquarters he was ordered to strip naked, after which his anus and penis were probed by a warder. The "penis search" puzzled Erdmann. Perhaps the warder was a sexual deviate, he had thought. Later he discovered that male inmates often slid ballpoint pen fillers into their urinary tracts to be used later for writing messages and diaries. The young medical student was held overnight in a small cell at the local Stasi headquarters without being questioned. At dawn he was given two slices of black bread with jam and a cup of *Muckefuck,* slang for ersatz coffee made of roasted barley. After this meager breakfast Erdmann was led into a courtyard surrounded by a twelve-foot wall topped with shards of broken glass and barbed wire. A large van with *H. O. Backwaren* stenciled on it was parked near a gate. The van was a Black Maria—the Germans called it a "Green Minna"—disguised as a bread delivery vehicle of the state-owned trading organization. Erdmann, now handcuffed, was placed inside the van, in a cell with a bare wooden bench, just large enough to accommodate one seated prisoner. The van held five such cells and a larger space for the guard. Erdmann sensed that the other cells were being filled as well. The guard had prohibited all talking, an order that he emphasized by slapping a rubber truncheon against the palm of his hand. The message was clear.

> Nobody told me where I would be taken. After driving for several hours, the van stopped. When the door opened, I was taken out of this cage and led into the cellar of a large building. There I was put into another cell. When the door banged shut, I looked around me. I was appalled. The place was filthy, the mattress on the iron cot was filthier, the toilet bowl was a stinking, cracked receptacle.[3]

The cell had no window, and the only incoming air flowed through a small ventilation duct.

For weeks the Stasi tried to break Erdmann by depriving him of sleep. Then there were seven weeks when he was not questioned at all and his only human contact was the warder who silently slipped food into the cell. Erdmann did not know where he was until months later, when another prisoner was put in his cell and told him he was in what prisoners called the *Hundekeller,* the "dogs' cellar" of the Stasi's district headquarters in Berlin. "At first I refused to sign any statements, and they repeatedly kicked me in the kidney, even threatened to put my mother in the cell next to mine," Erdmann continued. "'Well, eventually you'll sign anything!'—and I did."

It was almost a year after his arrest when Erdmann was told that he would be tried for crimes under Order No. 160 of Soviet Military Administration Directive No. 38. He didn't find out until his secret trial on March 1, 1954 that his crime was engaging in "sabotage and fascist propaganda that endangered the peace." His six friends were tried with him. His fellow medical student Horst Strobel had already been tried earlier and sentenced to six years at hard labor and now was facing another charge. All six had court-appointed attorneys, but none had much to say during the three-hour proceeding before a trial judge and two "jurors"—a female social worker and a stonemason.

Erdmann received eleven years at hard labor and Strobel got another five years, bringing his sentence to a total of eleven years. The other five defendants received sentences of between three and a half and nine years each. Erdmann described the attorneys as useless panderers and the prosecutor as a figurehead. The Stasi set the terms, and the judge gave them the rubber stamp. After pronouncing sentence, Chief Judge Götz Berger launched into such a tirade that it seemed he must have studied under Chief Judge Roland Freisler of the Nazi People's Court.[4] Freisler's rantings, as when he handed down death sentences to those involved in the 1944 attempt to kill Adolf Hitler, are among the darkest moments of German judicial history.

Erdmann was separated from his friends after the trial and taken to the Stasi's bedbug-infested special treatment plant, Rummelsburg prison in Berlin. He worried about his fifty-seven-year-old mother, and found out after his release that she had been kept in the dark about her son's arrest and trial until November 1954. Her letters to East German President Wilhelm Pieck only evoked replies denying any knowledge of him.

In September 1954, Erdmann and other political prisoners were loaded aboard a train nicknamed the "Grotewohl Express," after Otto Grotewohl, then the DDR's prime minister. Like the prison truck, it had tiny cells and stopped at numerous places to pick up more prisoners during its journey of almost two days. When they arrived, they realized that they had been sent to the "Yellow Misery" penitentiary, notorious for its yellow-painted exterior and its dismal treatment of prisoners inside. The prison is located in Bautzen, a small town about two hundred miles southeast of Berlin.

After reunification, West German authorities estimated that about 16,000 prisoners had died in Bautzen, especially in the early years, when the Soviets still had some control.[5] "The dead were taken out of their cells and piled on trucks," said Erdmann. "Then a warder would stab into the pile with a long pole that had a steel point, to make sure no living prisoner had been smuggled among the dead. The bodies were taken to an area on the periphery of Bautzen that was known popularly as *Karnickel Berg* [Rabbit Hill], thrown into pits, and covered with lime. Today the area is a housing project."

Erdmann spent six years in Bautzen under conditions that equaled those in the worst of Nazi prisons. After a year in solitary confinement, he was put into a cell designed for only one person that held three or four. The former medical student had to empty latrine buckets for his cell block. The wooden buckets dated back to the era of the kaisers, when the prison was built. The buckets leaked, and often there was no chlorine to cover the stench. Although it was a filthy job, Erdmann considered it a godsend: "At least it got me out of that horrible cell."

Because he was fluent in English and French, Erdmann was eventually assigned to what was called the "Construction Bureau," where he translated specialized Western magazines—including *Aviation Week* and other American aviation publications—for the Ministry of Defense. Erdmann lasted nearly two years at the prison's most pleasant job. Then he was denounced by a fellow prisoner, who had been recruited by the Stasi, for making an anticommunist remark. After that, Erdmann was put to work in a weaving plant, a move he described as leaving heaven and descending into hell: "We worked eight hours a day, seven days a week on ancient looms that seemed to date back to when the Frenchman Jacquard invented the machine, in the eighteenth century. The daily fare, standard for all DDR prisons, was meager—for example, twenty-one ounces of dark bread and an ounce of marmalade and lard."[6] Lunch was two pints of soup. Potatoes were served only on Sundays. Those who performed especially heavy work received extra lard and a slice of sausage. Black ersatz coffee was served twice a day.

Prisoners who worked and whose behavior was certified as good were allowed to receive food packages from relatives twice a year, on their birthdays and at Christmas. No package could exceed 6.6 pounds, and the contents were strictly regulated. Medicine, toilet articles, candy, and tobacco were taboo. In the eleven years of his imprisonment, Erdmann received four parcels from his mother. Another sixteen were denied him because of various infractions of the rules—some real, most imagined. When the packages were handed out, the nastiness of the Stasi warders came to the fore, as they would maliciously pour the sugar over the butter or dump the jam over the sausage.

Despite the severe conditions of prison life, Erdmann and his fellow politicals at least enjoyed a camaraderie based on a common bond: their loathing of communism. But this dynamic changed as soon as the authorities realized that they were failing to make the political prisoners more compliant and to reeducate them as good communists.

In 1956, the Stasi, which controlled all prisons, changed the housing rules: Mimicking common practice in the Soviet gulag, it began to lock up criminal convicts—murderers, robbers, burglars, sexual deviates, and petty thieves—together with political prisoners. "This became a terrible psychological burden," Erdmann told me. "Until then we were soul brothers. Now our things were stolen, such as a bit of food we had saved. Soon we didn't know who was a political anymore. The criminals had no conscience and worked as informers for the Stasi, to get better treatment or early discharges. They told the Stasi things that weren't even true." New charges were brought against Erdmann for breaking prison rules, based on denunciations by criminal prisoners.

After six years at "Yellow Misery," Erdmann was moved to Brandenburg prison, a more modern, maximum security institution. The treatment still was harsh. For a while he worked in the kitchen peeling potatoes. Then he was assigned to a factory that produced steel treads for tanks and tractors—a dangerous place, given the total absence of safety equipment. Many prisoners working there were killed or badly injured in accidents. "I had a few more years to serve, and I was not about to lose an arm or a leg, so I refused to work there," Erdmann said. His rebellion earned him twenty-one days in solitary confinement. However, in the end, he had his way: After he was released from the "hole," Erdmann was assigned to a tailor shop that produced uniforms for the People's Army. There he was reunited with his old friend Horst Strobel, the medical student who had been tried with him seven years earlier. Strobel was to be released in summer 1961 and was planning to move to West Berlin. To stay in touch, the two friends worked out a code: Strobel was to visit Erdmann's mother and tell her to copy the letters she received from her son, word for word, and send the copy to Strobel. She was also to copy the letters she would receive from Strobel and send the copies on to Erdmann. "We had to do this, because I could only write to my mother and no one else," Erdmann told me. "That was how I found out that he had settled in West Berlin just before the wall was built on August 13, 1961."

In April 1964, Erdmann received a letter from his mother. He decoded the message from Strobel, which said that Erdmann would be smuggled into West Berlin as soon as possible after his release, which was scheduled for June 1. "I replied that I was ready to do anything except remain in the DDR. Early in May I was informed by the prison director that my release had been set for June 26. Through another letter to my mother, I told Strobel of the release date," Erdmann said.

By now Strobel had resumed his medical studies at West Berlin's Free University, but his primary extracurricular activity was getting people out of East Berlin: He had joined one of several dozen groups that were smuggling human beings to freedom. In the eyes of the communists, the smugglers were arch-criminals. Strobel sent another message to Erdmann, instructing him to meet a contact in East Berlin on June 27.

> I was astonished that it was a young lady who was also a medical student in West Berlin. She held a West German passport, and for that reason she could enter East Berlin. I was told that I would be taken to West Berlin on August 13. I was to hide in the bushes of a small park in an area near the wall that was usually fairly quiet. An American car driven by an army officer would come to the area and turn around. While turning, the car would back up against the bushes. The trunk would not be locked but loosely tied down with string, and I was to rip it open, jump in, and pull it shut. The Americans were not searched at the Checkpoint Charlie crossing, and so the officer would drive me to freedom.[7]

The day of Erdmann's planned trip to freedom arrived, but his friends in West Berlin had made a serious miscalculation. "When I tried to get to the park, I saw that all hell had broken loose. August 13 was the third anniversary of the [building of the] wall. I could hear an angry crowd shouting and chanting on the Western side. On my side, the place was crawling with border guards and Stasi officers. I guess they expected trouble. The streets were blocked by armored cars and water cannons. There was no way I could get even close to the pickup point." Erdmann never knew the name of the American officer who was to bring him to West Berlin, except that it was a woman who held the rank of major; nor did Strobel. Both thought she might have been a U.S. Army nurse, since Strobel's co-conspirators were all medical students, many of whom had American friends.

Just a few hours after the fiasco, Erdmann was contacted and told he would be brought out the next day. Two Jordanian students, who were permitted to use the Checkpoint Charlie crossing reserved for non-Germans, would pick him up in a car. "By now my nerves were stretched to the limit, and when I saw the car I nearly gave up," Erdmann recalled. The rescue vehicle was a tiny, two-seater French Renault powered by a rear engine. Between the engine and the backrests of the seats, the rescuers had ingeniously built a compartment of thin steel plates. Erdmann was jammed into this compartment, which was just over a foot wide, four feet long, and three feet deep. The journey began.

> I was cramped in there like a contortionist, not able to move even a finger. If I had not lost so much weight in prison, I would never have fit in that box. Pretty soon the steel on the engine side got boiling hot. At that

> point the car stopped. The engine was turned off, and I could hear the voices of the border guards. I was worried that I might cough, and just then I heard them say, "Drive on!" I heard the engine turn over and over, but that thing wouldn't start. Then one of the border guards said in an angry tone, "Get that thing out of here." I thought my heart would stop when the border guard said to the Jordanians, "What's the matter, do you have somebody stashed in that thing?" One Jordanian laughed and said, "Of course, we have two in here, but come on, help us push." The car started moving, and the sound of the hobnailed boots told me the border guard was pushing. Suddenly the engine coughed and started. A few seconds later we were across the line and in West Berlin.[8]

Erdmann was immediately offered a place in the Free University's medical school. "But I couldn't take it. I was now thirty-seven, and knew that I could not compete with the twenty-year-olds. I had not seen a medical textbook in eleven years." He decided he needed to earn some money immediately, and friends helped him find a job as an intern at Radio Free Berlin. "I wanted to do all the things we had dreamed about in prison: . . . See West Germany, Italy, France, and perhaps the United States. I wanted a normal life and to get married." A friend invited him on a trip to the Spanish island of Majorca. "It was like a trip to fairyland, because within a couple of days there I met Margarete, a beautiful woman. We had much in common. Her brother, too, had been a Stasi prisoner for eleven years, on trumped up charges of espionage. He was merely a member of a group of students opposed to communism." A year later they were married.

Horst Erdmann's ordeal was shared by thousands of East German university students and academics. In 1962, the German Association of University Students published the names of 1,118 professors and students who had been caught in the Stasi web for various political offenses. Of those, 8 were sentenced to death, 27 died in prisons, and 87 disappeared without a trace. Later statistics could not be compiled, because the construction of the Berlin Wall made reporting impossible. When the regime fell, many records were destroyed.

. . . TO FIGHT AGAIN

In 1981, after surviving three heart attacks and bypass surgery, Erdmann had to retire from his job at Radio Free Berlin, where he had risen to production manager in the political news department. When the Berlin Wall fell, he began to wage a new battle to bring his judge, Götz Berger, to justice. "Berger was a most foul and despicable minion of the party," his victim charged. "He helped create East Germany's terror of justice. He trained so-called 'people's judges' who had no formal legal training and had merely to be solid communists. Berger served as an instructor of other judges at political trials in 1952 during which 32 persons were sentenced to death, of whom 26 were executed." According to court records, Berger handed down sentences totaling about 4,000 years at hard labor for political offenses.

Erdmann discovered in 1991 that Berger had retired with a monthly pension of about US$2,200. In addition, he was collecting a special pension of US$1,100 for "fighters against fascism." The latter was instituted by the communist regime in 1949, and in the reunification treaty of 1990 the West German government agreed that it would be continued. And in 1992 Berger was still lecturing at a college in the eastern part of Berlin.

Before reunification became official but after the new noncommunist government had been installed, Erdmann wrote to the chief prosecutor in East Berlin and demanded action against Berger for perversion of justice. On July 11, 1990, he was officially informed that no action could be taken, since any offenses Berger might have committed fell under the statute of limitations. However, the judiciary of reunited Germany later decided otherwise, and a pretrial investigation was launched. Action was still pending in 1996, when Berger died at the age of ninety-one.

RÜDIGER KNECHTEL: UNWILLING BORDER GUARD

After Germany's reunification, hundreds of the politically persecuted, like Erdmann, began to bombard the mass media and publishers with their stories of horror in an effort to prod the government into action. Former East German border guard Rüdiger Knechtel put together a booklet exposing forty of the most appalling cases of human rights abuses.[9] Knechtel himself had spent two and a half years in a military prison after being confined for ten months in the Stasi's notorious Hohenschönhausen political prison in Berlin.

Born in 1941, Knechtel was drafted to serve as a border guard when he turned twenty. He was already married and had an infant son when he was assigned to the orderly room of a unit guarding the Berlin Wall, near the U.S. Army's Checkpoint Charlie. On his first day on the job, he found a photo in his desk of a young man who had been shot in the head. When he asked his commander, a captain, what the photo meant, the officer answered laconically, "A cadaver of one who tried to flee." Knechtel had to pull himself together lest he reveal his abhorrence. "I soon discovered that this inhuman callousness characterized almost all officers and noncoms," he told me. "This reinforced my vow to make it my task to convince fellow soldiers not to shoot at in-

Rüdiger Knechtel stands guard at the Berlin Wall. Knechtel was sentenced to two and a half years in a military prison in 1963. His crime: tossing a bottle over the wall, containing a letter to a radio station in which he described his disgust with the regime and requested a song. Private photo.

nocent people. It was strictly prohibited to have any contact with people on the western side of the wall. We couldn't even return friendly greetings, but there was hardly anyone in my platoon who obeyed. We could trust each other—except one, Bernd Jakobs, who was an SED minion."[10]

Knechtel and his friends were right not to trust Jakobs: In August 1963, his entire platoon and three-quarters of the company—about a hundred men in all—were arrested by the Stasi on charges of espionage. The SED comrade was not among them. A month earlier, Knechtel had tossed a bottle over the wall, which contained a letter to the American Forces Network (AFN) radio station in Berlin, explaining his plight and requesting a song. The word *Schandmauer* (Wall of Shame) also appeared in the letter. AFN was just celebrating an anniversary, and in a special program dedicated to the occasion, the announcer described Knechtel's letter as "congratulations from the other side." The letter was posted on the station's bulletin board, alongside congratulations from President John F. Kennedy and West German Chancellor Konrad Adenauer. A Stasi spy saw it, and together with the reports of Stasi

Spitzel Jakobs, this was "evidence" sufficient to convict the young border guard of espionage. In total, the men arrested with him received between twenty-five and thirty years' imprisonment at hard labor. Jakobs was promoted to sergeant, received a cash bonus, and was awarded the post of regimental secretary of the Free German Youth (FDJ), the Communist Party's equivalent to the Hitler Youth.

After his release from prison, Knechtel was put under constant Stasi surveillance. His church attendance was duly noted. Instead of resuming his profession as a geological engineer, he chose to work as a nurse's aide in a home for psychiatric patients. In July 1982, he was arrested again, this time for "illegal possession" of five valuable antique paintings he had intended to sell. He was released, but the paintings were confiscated and sold in West Germany to earn foreign currency for the state.

In May 1988, Knechtel's son Ralf was arrested by the Stasi. Ralf had been born in 1966, five years after the Berlin Wall was built. He was baptized at the age of twelve, and when he turned fourteen, he was the only student in his class who had refused to submit to *Jugendweihe,* the atheist ritual that had replaced confirmation. Ralf was nabbed by police when he threatened at Vopo headquarters to demonstrate at a monument of Karl Marx unless he received an exit permit. His sentence was one year at hard labor, but he was ransomed by the West German government after serving six months.

JOSEF KNEIFEL, REBEL

Another object of prosecutorial wrath was Josef Kneifel, at the time undoubtedly a man much hated by the Stasi. Chief Prosecutor Sauer, the former head of the registration center of DDR crimes, has described Kneifel as the most rabid opponent of the regime on record. Kneifel's story is one of horror, disgust, and incredible courage.[11]

A longtime factory laborer with a home of his own in Saxony, Kneifel began in the early 1960s to protest against the regime's politicization of the workplace. He was aware of the risks, and had no desire to go to prison. "But to live in this state called the DDR as a human being was not possible, and just to plod along like a dazed animal was against my nature," he told me during a conversation in 1993. Because Kneifel's skills as a welder and lathe operator were needed and he was a top performer, the party functionaries at first did nothing but issue warnings. However, as Kneifel remained active in the Lutheran church and continued to speak out against instances of communist oppression, the regime gradually became fed up with his attitude. In 1975, Kneifel was arrested by the Stasi, having been denounced for

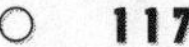

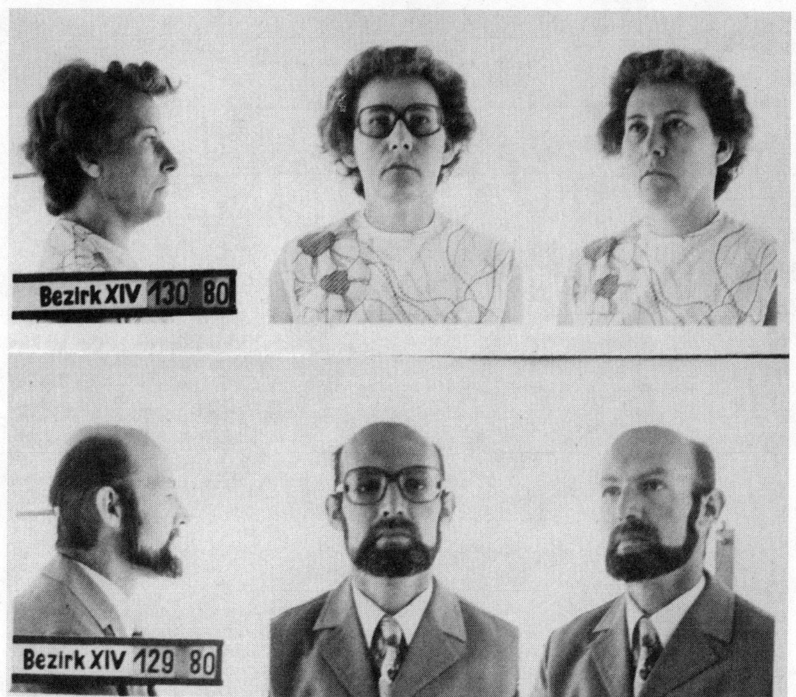

Irmgard and Josef Kneifel after their arrest by the Stasi. Kneifel was sentenced to life imprisonment and his wife was given a two-year prison term although she had no knowledge of her husband's activities. Courtesy MfS Archive.

telling his coworkers that Stalin had committed gruesome crimes against humanity. Kneifel also had described the SED and its affiliated parties as having "prostituted themselves to become vassals of Moscow." Sentenced to ten months at hard labor, Kneifel suffered the usual beatings and dehumanizing chicaneries at the hands of Stasi warders. He was then thirty-three years old. When he was released, his regular identity card was replaced with the Stasi's PM-12, a temporary document that had to be renewed every twelve months. Such identification papers were issued only to convicted criminals, known political opponents, or to persons with mental problems. The Stasi might as well have branded him: Whenever he applied for a job, the card had to be shown. Even employers sympathetic to his cause would not have dared hire him.

During the next four years Kneifel worked at odd jobs that provided him and his family of three the barest subsistence. When Soviet troops

Soviet tank memorial damaged by Josef Kneifel's homemade bomb. Courtesy MfS Archive.

invaded Afghanistan to prop up the embattled communists, Kneifel became enraged. Every time he bicycled past a Soviet monument featuring a tank, to him a symbol of bloody communist aggression, Kneifel inwardly cringed. One day, his growing sense of outrage got the better of him. Kneifel approached two like-minded friends, one of whom was a sergeant and tank commander in the People's Army, for help in planning a meaningful act of protest. "We thought long and hard over what we could do before we decided we would make the biggest impact by blowing up the monument tank. We agreed to make sure that innocent people would not be hurt, or not to do it at all. We are not murderers."[12]

Having determined the right explosive composition, they poured the material into a hundred-pound steel hydrogen tank. Kneifel fashioned an electric detonator and a crude timing device. When the day came to set off the bomb, Kneifel prevailed on his friends to stay at home because "they were younger than me and had small children."

On the evening of March 9, 1980, the third Sunday of Lent, Kneifel loaded the bomb into his old, rickety gray Trabant car. In his pockets he carried a revolver and five hand grenades, all homemade: "I was sure I would be caught, and I was determined not to be taken alive," he explained. Kneifel parked his car on a side street about a hundred yards from the memorial. Although it was dark and sleeting, he could clearly see the monument on its massive red granite pedestal, awash in the glare of floodlights from the People's Police barracks, which stood directly opposite. The surrounding area looked deserted. Kneifel, wet and exhausted from lugging the bomb, climbed the pedestal and shoved his load as far as he could beneath the tank. He set the timer for ten minutes, jumped off, and walked to his car. A moment after he was inside and had slammed the door, there was a deafening boom accompanied by a tremendous flash. The explosion was immense. A chunk of the tank's steel tread was catapulted against the high wall surrounding the police barracks. As the police stormed out of the building, Kneifel made his escape.

The regime imposed a blackout on reportage of the event, but news of the bombing spread throughout East Germany by word of mouth. Horst Knechtel, the border guard turned anticommunist activist, remembered the incident well: "While special Stasi units and all the Vopos were looking for the perpetrator, the people were gleefully rubbing their hands."[13]

For a while Kneifel escaped detection. Eventually, however, he made a grievous mistake, confiding in his pastor and other church friends. Kneifel later came to believe that there was an informer in the group or that the pastor's apartment was bugged. On August 18, five months after the blast, Kneifel was arrested as he entered the plant where he had a temporary job. Three Stasi men who had concealed themselves behind a pile of rocks rushed at him with pistols drawn. At about the same time, another Stasi squad arrested his wife, Irmgard. A few days later they grabbed the couple's eighteen-year-old son Friedeman (which translates roughly into "Man of Peace"). Kneifel's two accomplices also landed in prison.

The secret trial of Kneifel began March 9, 1981, at the heavily guarded courthouse in Karl-Marx-Stadt. Of course, the prosecutors, judge, and jurors were all members of the Communist Party. "I was determined to boycott the farcical proceedings," Kneifel later told me. "When the judge began to read the sentence, beginning with the phrase 'in the name of the people,' I shouted: 'Enough of this misuse of the people's name, you lackeys! I will not accept a sentence from you.'" Two Stasi men immediately dragged Kneifel from the courtroom. He did not hear the life sentence pronounced.[14]

A prison van delivered him to the Brandenburg penitentiary on March 16. He was shoved into a tiny cubicle in the van, his left hand manacled to steel bars, and his right, to a steel ring bolted to the floor. He had no choice but to remain in this contorted position for the entire three-hour ride. He was clad only in a thin shirt and pants, and it was bitterly cold. Shaking from the cold and from pain, he screamed,

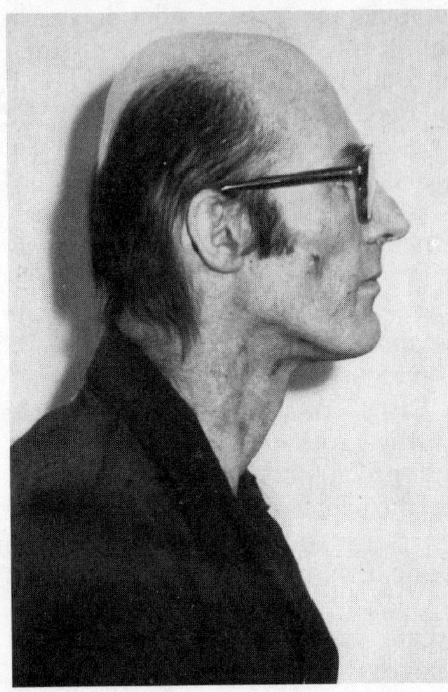

Josef Kneifel, described by West German officials as the most courageous political prisoner held by the East German communists, shown here prior to his release from prison in 1987, on the eve of Erich Honecker's state visit to West Germany. Courtesy MfS Archive.

"You dogs, stop torturing a political prisoner!" A fat warder stuck his rubber truncheon through the bars and smashed it over his head. "My teeth smashed together, and I spit blood. When they dragged me out of the van, I was only able to moan."[15]

At Brandenburg, Kneifel was assigned a tiny cell measuring no more than six feet square. It was unheated. Later he was locked up with two felons. One had been a married party official who had seduced a female comrade. She later began to blackmail him, and he killed her. This murderer, the warders told Kneifel, was supposed to "modernize" him. In protest against such attempts to "criminalize" political prisoners, Kneifel began the first of many hunger strikes. This strike lasted several months. From time to time he was brought to a prison hospital, where he was force-fed. "Despite the malicious directives of Stasi Major Arndt, who wanted me to die, a Dr. Hoffmann, a man of unshakable medical ethics, eventually hauled me out of my hole and saved my life," Kneifel told me.

Irmgard Kneifel, meanwhile, had been sentenced to two years at hard labor for "failing to report a crime" to the Stasi, even though her husband had never told her of his plans. "When the Stasi questioned me, they kept urging me to divorce my husband and said I would be immediately released. But I refused."[16] Her treatment was nearly as brutal as her husband's. Kneifel's son was sentenced to ten months in the penitentiary but was released after four and a half months and placed on probation for two years. The People's Army sergeant was sentenced to fourteen years, and Kneifel's other friend received six and a half.

A year passed before Kneifel was told about his family's plight. Six months after her release, Irmgard Kneifel was allowed to visit her husband at the prison hospital for one hour. They were forbidden to embrace or hold hands. She was not allowed to talk about her time in prison, so Kneifel did not know how terribly she had been treated. "But I could tell by looking at her. She was forty years old and looked like fifty."

In 1984, the Stasi decided that the obstreperous Kneifel should be moved to a more austere punitive environment. Bautzen I, the "Yellow Misery," was just the place for him. There the Stasi had established a special isolation ward dubbed the *gesonderte Kommando.* For the next year Kneifel vegetated in a dark, dank, one-man cell.

Kneifel refused to be identified with common criminals, and throughout his imprisonment, he used to shout, "Kneifel, political prisoner of the communists, reporting!" It earned him so many brutal beatings that he lost count. The beatings were almost invariably administered by privileged felons. One of the worst of these torturers was a former Communist Party member and People's Police officer named Thierfeld. A giant of a man, he was serving a second term for abusing children. His first conviction had been on charges of sexually assaulting his daughter. His specialty in prison was twisting arms out of their sockets. But there was also a warder, Master Sergeant Wolfgang Schmidt, who liked to handle matters himself. In the dead of winter he enjoyed pouring buckets of cold water over Kneifel.

From time to time Kneifel would be moved to a larger cell containing three or four other prisoners, all convicted felons, including murderers. Because of his stubborn resistance to "reeducation," it never lasted long. A year of close arrest followed each such episode. All the while, he thought up new ways to mock the regime and prison officials. Using the jagged end of a broken plastic spoon, he cut veins in his legs and collected the blood in a plastic cup. Before it could coagulate, he painted caricatures on the whitewashed cell wall, ridiculing Stasi warders and communism. Another time, he used his blood to daub the label "Political Prisoner" on the yellow stripes of his prison trousers. At this point, Kneifel's health rapidly declined. His feet had swollen to mere lumps.

In August 1985, Kneifel was moved to a prison hospital near Leipzig. In an adjacent room was patient Johannes Zuber, a twenty-two-year-old student from Erlangen, West Germany who was serving time for "banditry," having helped East Germans escape to the West. The prisoners never saw each other. There were moments, however, when guards were distracted and the two could exchange a few fleeting whispers through their adjacent windows, which were barred but could be opened. When Zuber revealed that he would be released and returned to West Germany, Kneifel hurriedly prepared a *Kassiber,* a secret message. It got through, and within days Kneifel's message was published in a small West German newspaper aptly titled *Der Patriot.* The headline over Kneifel's incredible story of Stasi torture and courageous resistance was "A Call for Help from the Other Side." At the same time, the young student informed the West German government and Lutheran church officials of Kneifel's dire situation.

The "call for help" had little immediate effect. As time passed, Kneifel began to change his style of reporting when warders entered his cell, often saying, "Cell occupied by two felons and a political prisoner of the Honecker gang." By 1987, Kneifel's head was covered with scars left by beatings. Some of the wounds had been sutured; others had healed without medical attention: "There were times when I was left with untreated sores and cuts," Kneifel recalled. "I licked them or poured my own urine over them to ward off infection. Once when I was brought to the dispensary with another head wound, I complained to the doctor, who said only, 'You shouldn't bump your head so much.'"

But there was another doctor whom Kneifel considered an angel of mercy: "This was Dr. S. C. Rogge. Though a lieutenant colonel, he was a humanitarian of the first order who saved many lives, including my own. Not all the East German officials were scoundrels. We prisoners were very much afraid that the Stasi would catch up with him some day." Years later Kneifel would discover that the Stasi did, indeed, get wise to the humanitarian traits of Dr. Rogge. However, a lack of concrete evidence saved him from imprisonment.

One of the Stasi-led warders' favorite torture instruments was a special handcuff called *die Acht,* or the Figure Eight—so named because of its configuration. Lacking the swivels that connect normal handcuffs, it was rigid to prevent any movement of the hands. On January 2, 1987, a special order arrived at Bautzen from General Wilfred Lustik, the man in charge of all prisons in East Germany, whose office was in Berlin. Incensed by the reports of Kneifel's resistance that landed on his desk nearly every day, he had ordered "special treatment for the recalcitrant prisoner."[17] Kneifel was thrown onto a bare metal cot in an isolation cell, clad only in a thin shirt and trousers. There was no mattress. In the scuffle with the felons who were assisting the warders, his shirt had slipped above the waist, and the steel springs cut into his back. His arms were stretched out, and his hands and feet were cuffed together with an *Acht.* There was no heat. He was not released from this position even to urinate into a bucket, and his trousers quickly became soggy, the urine dripping onto the concrete floor. "After a day Captain Braune entered the cell, pinching his nose. He asked only, 'Are you finally willing to be reasonable?' I declined. He slammed the cell door shut. Two days later, the same dialogue." General Lustik also denied Kneifel medical treatment.[18] After reunification, Lustik said: "My prisoners had it good. After all, they didn't have to do anything for themselves. Food and lodging were free, and they received 80 marks in pocket money. And don't forget, they were criminals. I was only the executive organ."[19]

After spending five days on the steel springs, during which he had refused all food, Kneifel felt near death. Then two mattresses and a wooden stool were brought into the cell. The shackles were taken off, and he was visited by Lieutenant Colonel Heinz Gerhard, the chief medical officer at Bautzen I. Kneifel described what followed: "I looked on as he tore off the rounded tip of a rubber catheter. He used this sharp end to probe into my nasal passages and throat. Blood gushed over the apron they had hung over me. During this procedure, or rather torture, the colonel's assistant, a young sublieutenant, left the room in obvious disgust." After the examination, Kneifel was fed. "When the first drops of soup reached the stomach, my body slackened and I suddenly could hardly see anything. The muscle system seemed to have become paralyzed. The second stomach filling made me feel better." The mattresses and the stool were removed when the doctor left. In the evening one mattress was returned. The next day he was given another bowl of a hot liquid consisting of eggs, milk, and sugar. As he began to swallow, he felt something solid between his teeth and bit down on it. "I knew the taste. It was the kind of pharmaceutical chalk used in binding tablets, and since I was able to move around a little better, I figured it must have been a muscle relaxant." After two weeks of this new regime, Kneifel's vision improved.

Although he was now feeling better physically, Kneifel's hatred of Dr. Gerhard and his "treatment" got the better of him. He used the sharp end of a bedspring to cut his finger and began a new protest in blood, covering the whitewashed walls of his tiny cell once more with his defiant scrawl. Kneifel was taken out of his cell while the walls were scrubbed by other prisoners. For the next two months he vegetated in a dark chamber, and then pent-up anger exploded once more.

Throughout the month of April he repeatedly drew blood, which he poured against the lock of his cell door. When a warder opened the cell, Kneifel sprayed him with blood he had collected in a metal bowl. The warder called for assistance, then beat him with a baton made of steel springs.

So it went until July 13, 1987, when Kneifel was visited by Johannes Hempel, the Lutheran bishop of Saxony. "I was astounded when he embraced me and said, 'Brother Kneifel, I bring you an offer from the chairman of the State Council. You are free and are allowed to leave for West Germany with your wife.'" Three days later, Stasi officers drove Kneifel to the city of Eisenach, near the border. There he was released into the bishop's custody. His wife was already there, and they were driven together to West Germany. "When we arrived in Bavaria, I experienced the last infamy of the Stasi. When I unwrapped my sparse belongings, I found they had stolen my personal documents—all court papers, my driver's license, wristwatch, and the mail from my wife."

The reason for Erich Honecker's "act of mercy" became clear less than two months later when he made his state visit to West Germany. He had wanted to appear humane and generous. As part of the deal for his freedom, Kneifel was not allowed to reveal his experiences to the news media. It was a time when conservatives, social democrats, liberals, and the church—especially the Lutherans—were hell-bent on "normalizing" relations with a state that everyone knew was ruled by a criminal clique.

The Social Democratic Party and the Liberal Free Democrats were particularly anxious to please Honecker and his gang. The leading officials of both parties tried for several years to have the Central Registration Office of SED crimes closed and its files destroyed. Only the fierce resistance of the conservative Christian Democratic Party kept the office intact.

Kneifel and his wife settled in a small town in Bavaria. In fall 1991, Kneifel's doctors prescribed a regimen of kidney dialysis. The forty-eight-year-old man looked sixty-eight. His wife, who was fifty-four, also appeared twenty years older. Kneifel had entered prison a healthy man, five feet nine inches tall and weighing nearly 180 pounds. He weighed less than 140 pounds when he was freed and had not gained much since. His health was ruined, although like most former political prisoners, his spirits remained intact. He filed charges against various Bautzen prison officials, some of whom were still at their posts. Only criminal convicts remained. The torture-happy Dr. Gerhard was still the chief medical officer. The "Kremlin Bedbug"—First Lieutenant Scherch—and several other warders also still held the same jobs.[20]

In spring 1992, Kneifel was invited by the custodians of Stasi files to view his own dossier—8,000 pages of it—which had been found in Chemnitz. His faith in humanity was once again severely jolted. In the dossier he discovered the reports of spies who had informed on him and his wife. To his astonishment, these included Jürgen Meier, the lawyer in whom his wife had confided. Then he spotted the names of several pastors and family friends. "I realized then that the DDR was even a greater cesspool than anyone could have imagined," Kneifel commented.

Kneifel and his wife Irmgard enjoyed their life in freedom, often traveling with their camper through the scenic Black Forest and the Bavarian Alps. But Kneifel's tranquillity was to last only five years: Irmgard died in July 1993 of cancer.

MIELKE PURSUES THE DEVIATES

The experiences of Erdmann, Knechtel, and Kneifel were typical of men and women who became prisoners of the Stasi. Until about 1955, many of the people arrested as enemies of the state were turned over to the Soviets, who shipped them to the gulag. This was particularly true of communists who had dared to disagree with the SED leadership. Leo Bauer, a party member since 1932, was arrested in 1950. After being deprived of sleep for two days, he was interrogated by Mielke personally. Mielke, who was then the Stasi deputy chief, forced Bauer to confess that he was an "imperialist agent." Bauer later told his wife that Mielke had beat him "worse than a dog" and that once he screamed "I will have your head hacked off."[21] Bauer was thirty-eight years old at the time.

Bauer had spent the Nazi years in Soviet exile. After World War II he was elected to the parliament of the state of Hesse in the U.S.-occupied zone. While serving as the leader of the West German Communist Party (KPD) delegation, Bauer belonged to a group that openly criticized the policies of then East German Communist Party leader Walter Ulbricht. The SED lured him to Berlin with an offer of a job as chief editor of the state radio, hoping that he would reform. Bauer did not, and continued to speak out against the division of Germany favored by Ulbricht.

Bauer was tortured into signing his 180-page "confession," then was handed over to the Soviets. A military tribunal tried Bauer for "counterrevolutionary activities" and sentenced him to death. However, Stalin died before the sentence was carried out, and Bauer was sent to Siberia. Pardoned in 1955 and sent to West Germany, he joined the Social Democratic Party and eventually became an adviser to Chancellor Willy Brandt.

Also lured to East Germany in March 1950 was the head of the KPD for Lower Saxony and member of the West German parliament, Kurt Müller. Müller was summoned to East Berlin ostensibly to participate in an important meeting. Accused of being a Trotskyite and an enemy agent, Müller too was brutally interrogated by Stasi chief Mielke. He spent six years in total isolation in the Stasi's special Hohenschönhausen prison. He returned to West Germany after his release and joined the Social Democratic Party. Müller's chief accuser was Max Reimann, head of the KPD in East Germany. Ironically, even Reimann's son Josef did not escape the wrath of the Stasi. When young Reimann returned from a Soviet prisoner of war camp shortly after the war, his father persuaded him to join the People's Police in the Soviet-occupied zone. In 1949 he defected and returned to West Germany, where he sought the protection of British authorities. After several weeks, however, he disappeared under mysterious circumstances and was presumed kidnapped. He spent the next three years in the Stasi's special prison, then was sentenced to fifteen years at hard labor and transported to the Soviet Union. There is no evidence that his father ever lifted a finger to seek his release.

The Stasi and the Soviet secret police employed every imaginable form of brutality—physical and mental—to eradicate enemies of the state. The kidnapping of anticommunists operating in West Berlin was almost a weekly occurrence between 1945 and the early 1960s. Günther Buch, a top official of the Institute for All-German Affairs, which kept track of communist human rights violations, said that more than five hundred cases were being investigated by Berlin police in spring 1995. Many of the victims disappeared without a trace.

THE RESISTANCE

It was inevitable that the political oppression in East Germany would spawn a number of anticommunist groups in West Berlin and in the U.S.-occupied zone. The first was the so-called Ostbüro (East Bureau) of the Social Democratic Party (SPD) of the Western-occupied zones of Germany and West Berlin.

SPD membership in the Soviet zone had soared between December 1945 and March 1946, from 376,000 to nearly 700,000. East German Communist Party membership at the same time was about 600,000. Fearing that they would lose the election scheduled for late fall 1946 in the Soviet zone, Communist Party leaders had received Stalin's permission to seek an amalgamation with the Social Democrats. The SPD agreed to put the question to a membership vote, but the vote was banned by the Soviet Military Administration (SMA). The Soviets, aided by the fledgling Stasi, then resorted to mass arrests of SPD members who opposed the merger. In addition, Soviet officials corrupted some top SPD officials with expensive gifts and other favors.[22] On April 22, 1946, the leadership of the Soviet zone's SPD, without the consent of the rank and file, signed the merger document. The new party, under firm control of the communists, named itself the Sozialistische Einheitspartei Deutschlands (SED). All of the SPD functionaries who betrayed social democratic ideals by signing the agreement were awarded high posts.

The SPD East Bureau was established immediately after the forced amalgamation, initially to provide moral support to Social Democrats who had been sold out. Later, the bureau engaged in widespread propaganda campaigns. Working with the East Bureau, or merely espousing SPD ideals, was dangerous. By 1950, some 400 Social Democrats had lost their lives by execution or by maltreatment during their imprisonment in the Soviet gulag, or had simply disappeared. More than 5,000 were imprisoned. Two hundred of these were sentenced to a total of 10,000 years.[23] Until 1950 all sentences were pronounced by Soviet military tribunals—in every sense of the word, kangaroo courts in which thousands of "trials" lasted no more than ten minutes. These tribunals also had mail-order proceedings, meaning that they met in the Soviet Union and sent the convicts' sentences by post to wherever they were incarcerated.

As the terror escalated, Berlin humanitarians and anticommunists not directly affiliated with any political party decided to create a new organization that would operate less clandestinely—and more aggressively—than the SPD East Bureau. It would become known as the Kampfgruppe gegen Unmenschlichkeit (KgU), the Battle Group Against Inhumanity. Its founder was Rainer Hildebrandt. An examination of Hildebrandt's background is necessary to grasp the motivation that led him to become one of the most passionate defenders of human rights in postwar Germany.

Rainer Hildebrandt was born in 1914. His father was an art historian and an anti-Nazi who was stripped of his university teaching job in 1937, after his name appeared on the Nazis' blacklist due to his publications and his wife's "degenerate" paintings. (Mrs. Hildebrandt was an artist and a Jew.) With his father on the Gestapo's surveillance list, Rainer and his mother were in grave danger. Sworn statements sent to the "racial authorities" in Germany by Rainer and by family friends living abroad persuaded the Nazis to classify Rainer's mother as "half Aryan."

Rainer Hildebrandt wanted to become a physicist and began his studies at Berlin's Technical University. In his spare time he read the writings of philosopher Oswald Spengler, the author of *Decline of the West,* who viewed the Nazis' theory of Aryan blood as reprehensible.[24] Spengler's philosophy, as well as the writings of the Weimar Republic Foreign Minister Walther Rathenau, prompted young Hildebrandt to change course and pursue a doctorate in the social sciences. In 1940 he attended the lectures of Albrecht Haushofer, professor of geopolitics. Deeply impressed by the professor's idealism, Hildebrandt befriended him and was drawn peripherally into a circle of anti-Hitler patriots. In fall 1940, the professor told him that he believed he was being watched by the Gestapo and asked him to deliver a letter to Johannes Popitz, the former Prussian minister of finance. Thus young Hildebrandt became part of the 1944 conspiracy to assassinate Hitler, albeit playing a minor, unwitting role.

Rainer Hildebrandt was drafted into the Wehrmacht in 1943 and served as an interpreter for a year until he was arrested by the Gestapo and imprisoned without charge. Released in June 1944, he was assigned as a guard to an internment camp that primarily held Polish prisoners of war. He was questioned again after the attempt on Hitler's life. His friend and mentor Haushofer was executed in April 1945. Former Minister Popitz, to whom Hildebrandt had delivered that letter in 1940, was hanged from a meat hook at Berlin's Plötzensee prison in October 1944. When it became clear that the war was drawing to a close, Hildebrandt, fearing a massacre by SS troops, supplied a group of Polish officers with a pistol.

After the war, Hildebrandt returned to Berlin to write a number of treatises on the anti-Nazi resistance and a book chronicling Haushofer's life. Even as he was engaged in combating fascism, Hildebrandt sensed that a new and equally dangerous dictatorship was tightening its grip on the East German population. In June 1948, when the Soviets started their Berlin blockade to drive out the Allies, the Cold War was on, and Hildebrandt shifted gears. Coining the slogan "silence is suicide," he began to exhort citizens to speak out against communist violations of human rights. He organized rallies of West Berliners and invited prisoners who had been released in summer 1948 to appear there as guest speakers. When he was not holding public rallies, Hildebrandt and a small group of Berlin university students questioned returning prisoners about the conditions in camps and penitentiaries. The names of those still in communist custody and the circumstances of their arrest were registered. Hildebrandt's organizational and oratorical talents began to bring results. He soon convinced U.S. occupation authorities to broadcast a statement over the American-controlled German-language radio station RIAS-Berlin—the most popular station in the Soviet zone, initially because of its jazz programming. Hildebrandt's first message was: "Fellow Germans in the

Soviet zone! We want to help you. From now on, we will broadcast every week the truth about the conditions under communist dictatorship. We urge you to join us in shedding light on Soviet slavery. Silence is suicide." The effect was immediate. Thousands of anguished letters poured into the RIAS studios. The management had to add staff to cope with the flood.

Hildebrandt's campaign and the initial RIAS broadcasts alarmed Soviet occupation authorities. A representative of the SMA remonstrated with Brigadier General Frank L. Howley, the U.S. commander, demanding that he punish the RIAS announcer. Howley, a crusty old U.S. Army cavalryman, rejected the Soviet demand. "There was no way I was going to accommodate the sons-of-bitches," he commented later. "The bastards had it coming to them."[25]

Hildebrandt's zeal and idealism were infectious. Soon the Student Association of West Berlin's Free University, the Christian Democratic Party's youth organization, and the Social Democratic Party called a mass meeting. Hildebrandt responded promptly. Under the new slogan *Nichtstun ist Mord* (inaction is murder), the meeting was convened on October 17, 1948, at the Titania Palast, the city's largest movie theater, with five hundred seats. There was standing room only.

The audience listened in embarrassed silence as former inmates of Soviet concentration camps and a teenager who had fled from forced labor in a uranium mine related their experiences. They heard that conditions inside the camps, which once held prisoners of the Nazis, were worse than they had been before 1945. At the Sachsenhausen camp, illnesses including tuberculosis were reaching epidemic proportions; in addition, between sixty and eighty prisoners were dying each day of starvation and malnutrition. In 1948 the camp housed about 6,400 prisoners, about 1,000 of whom were later deported to corrective labor camps in the Soviet Union.[26]

Hildebrandt told those assembled that on the basis of the eyewitness accounts, one could surmise that the entire Eastern zone resembled "a concentration camp in which only the warders and those who hand out the food can still live well." He described Stalinism as the "third and last ultimatum given the Western world to be unified in all basic matters confronting humanity." Hildebrandt announced his intention to create the "Battle Group Against Inhumanity." Six months later, the Allied command headquarters—minus the Soviets, who had walked out a year earlier—approved the KgU as a political organization.

THE COMMUNIST COUNTEROFFENSIVE

Until that point, the Soviets and the East German communists had limited their countermeasures chiefly to propaganda campaigns. Now they moved quickly to create a special Stasi task force to directly combat the KgU and its emissaries in East Germany. Chosen to head the Stasi detail was Otto Knye, a Communist Party veteran who had been trained by the NKVD in the Soviet Union, where he had found asylum after the Nazi takeover. Knye, who had fought with Soviet partisans behind the German lines during World War II, was described as an absolute ideologue who behaved at times "like someone not quite right in the head."[27] Nevertheless, he was unquestionably a secret police professional par excellence. Knye's first order of business was to recruit agents to infiltrate the KgU—an effort that proved highly successful.

Hildebrandt's KgU soon numbered about eighty full-time staff members, including Ernst Tillich, a thirty-eight-year-old anti-Nazi theologian who had spent three years in concentration camps and prisons. After the war Tillich had joined the Social Democratic Party and had become active in charitable organizations. Tillich was a prolific writer on church and social issues. His outspoken anticommunism drew him into Hildebrandt's circle of like-minded idealists and to membership in the KgU.[28]

The first KgU offices were set up in a rented single-family house practically next door to the home of the British commandant in Berlin, which was guarded around the clock by a detail of British military police. This provided protection as well for the KgU office. Almost from the beginning, the office was visited each day by between 100 and 150 former prisoners and relatives of persons reported as missing and believed arrested in the Soviet zone. By June 1949, the KgU had received 12,000 missing persons requests and had registered more than 8,500 arrests.[29]

While the KgU staff was busy with paperwork, Hildebrandt devoted most of his time to organizing clandestine groups throughout East Germany. Besides reporting secret police arrests, members distributed anticommunist leaflets detailing the extent of the oppression and encouraging the populace to resist. Tens of thousands of helium-filled toy balloons carried thousands of leaflets beyond the Iron Curtain. Small firecrackers with long-burning fuses were attached to the balloons, causing them to burst and spread the KgU messages.

The success of the KgU was not lost on U.S. Army Counter Intelligence Corps (CIC) officials, who viewed the group as an ideal vehicle for augmenting their operations in the East. Overtures made by Colonel Severin F. Wallach, head of the CIC in Berlin, were rejected by Hildebrandt because he did not want to have the KgU branded as an espionage organization.[30] However, in the long term, expenses that initially had been covered by private contributions were outpacing receipts, which prompted Hildebrandt to accept the colonel's proposition of cooperation.

"We needed money, and the Americans had it," Hildebrandt remarked later. "I rationalized that we and the Americans were fighting essentially the same battle. But I made it very clear to Colonel Wallach that I subscribed to the philosophy of Mahatma Gandhi and would not tolerate any violent acts to further our struggle for freedom. He assured me that he would abide by my wishes."[31]

As the several hundred KgU volunteers in the Soviet-occupied zone became more proficient in their propaganda activities, the Stasi team under Colonel Knye worked overtime to smash the resistance. By summer 1949, secret police agents were making arrests of KgU sympathizers who had been distributing literature. Sentences of twenty-five years on charges of espionage or "anti-Soviet activities" were the norm.

The Soviet authorities and the East German communist regime prodded their secret police services into high gear. Hildebrandt was put on the Stasi's most wanted list, with a reward of 15,000 East marks promised to anyone delivering Hildebrandt into Stasi hands. Nonconvertible East marks were useless in the West, but in East Berlin this was a tidy sum. In June 1949, West Berlin police who were guarding the KgU chief spotted a car with Soviet zone license plates that had been parked for hours near Hildebrandt's residence. Officers questioned the four male passengers but had to release them: Although the police suspected that these men planned to kidnap Hildebrandt, there was no evidence on the basis of which to detain them.[32]

A month later, on July 23, a number of Hildebrandt's neighbors became leery of a car that had been parked nearby for nearly four hours, though periodically it was moved from spot to spot. The car held four passengers in addition to the driver. Police were alerted. A search of the car turned up a Mauser automatic pistol stowed beneath a seat. The five men, all Germans residing in the Soviet sector of Berlin, were arrested and tried for attempted kidnapping. Four of them were sentenced to two years in the penitentiary. The driver was acquitted when he proved he had been unwitting tool in the operation. Over the next year, the Stasi received at least three more orders from the Soviets to kidnap the KgU leader. All failed because Colonel Wallach's CIC agents had succeeded in recruiting a member of the planning group as a double agent.[33]

Having botched all plots to kidnap Hildebrandt, the communist secret police tried a new tack. Its agents within the KgU had reported that the Americans had complained about Hildebrandt's sloppy bookkeeping practices and at one time suspected that he was slipping funds into his own pocket for personal use. An audit had disproved these suspicions, reassuring them that Hildebrandt was not an embezzler but merely a careless bookkeeper.[34]

Mid-1950 saw Hildebrandt's tenure drawing to a close. Under the influence of his deputy Tillich, who had become increasingly more radical, the nonviolent character of the Kampfgruppe began to change. The previously rather harmless antics of throwing stink bombs into Communist Party offices and meeting places were abandoned for more serious efforts. Tillich began to order acts of sabotage. Railroad tracks were blasted with homemade explosives, KgU operators burned Communist Party propaganda banners, and a bridge across a canal in East Germany was damaged by a bomb. Rather than compromise his ideals, Hildebrandt decided to quit as head of the Battle Group Against Inhumanity. By then, the financing and direction of the KgU had been assumed by the newly created U.S. Office of Policy Coordination (OPC), which was charged with running clandestine operations.[35] Although staffed with CIA officers, the OPC was not initially under the control of the CIA director. Instead, the first OPC chief, Frank Wisner, received his marching orders from, and reported to, a committee composed of officials from the departments of state and of defense.

In the meantime, Otto Knye's Stasi agents had thoroughly infiltrated the KgU, and hundreds of arrests were followed by a number of show trials in the Soviet zone. On October 3, 1951, eighteen persons—high school students, their parents, and several teachers—were sentenced to a combined total of 124 years at hard labor. The students had been charged with producing anticommunist leaflets; the teachers and parents with failing to curb the activities of the youngsters, the youngest of whom was sixteen years old.

Although they knew KgU plans were being leaked to the Stasi and the Soviet MVD, Tillich and his U.S. sponsors continued to send their agents on sabotage and propaganda operations in the Soviet zone. One show trial followed after another. By 1951, two KgU men had had their heads severed at the district prison in Dresden by the same guillotine that had been used by the Nazis. Dozens more had received life sentences. Hildebrandt was appalled that these setbacks did not induce the KgU to stop its operations. He put the blame squarely on the CIA. During my 1992 interview with him, he suddenly exploded in rage, shouting: "I wish I had a chance to look the former CIA director in the eyes and tell him what a criminal one of his men was! Men were killed, hundreds went to horrible prisons for a long time. That man knew it and still he kept sending them out. He was a swine!"

The man who had aroused Hildebrandt's ire was Henry Heckscher, the executive officer of the CIA's Berlin station, who was charged with running the KgU as part of the Office of Policy Coordination's covert activities. Heckscher, then about forty years old, was born in Hamburg and had studied law at Berlin University until 1934, after which he emigrated to the United States. He served in Berlin from 1950 until 1954. His later assignments included Laos and Chile. After retiring from the CIA, he briefly served as an adviser to George Bush during the latter's campaign for the presidency.[36]

There is no doubt that Heckscher knew KgU operatives were being arrested en masse; and even a simpleton would have suspected betrayal.[37] Was he criminally negligent, as Hildebrandt charged? Was he a psychopath, or a man devoted to furthering his career at any cost—or both? George Bailey, former Berlin correspondent for *Reporter Magazine* and an executive for Radio Free Europe, answered the question this way:

> Heckscher was a cross between a joke and a loose cannon and a monumental jerk. He was a braggart with a direct line to Washington, a dangerous nut with clout in some high places, a damned fool who liked to throw his weight around. Heckscher was really an asshole and an arrogant son-of-a-bitch! When he was operating in Turkey, Iran, and Iraq, the Kurds he was in contact with gave Heckscher the nickname "Thousand and One Nights."[38]

Peter Sichel, Berlin CIA station chief and Heckscher's boss, said he could not fathom how Heckscher, a refugee from the Nazis, could wind up "acting like a Nazi—he was a nut."[39]

West German politicians who were anxious to achieve rapprochement with the East became increasingly concerned about the operations of the Kampfgruppe and the resulting drumbeat of propaganda in the Communist Party newspaper *Neues Deutschland.* In a newspaper interview, West Berlin Mayor Willy Brandt, who later became chancellor of West Germany, called the KgU a *Mistverein,* a dung heap.[40] Minister for All-German Affairs Ernst Lemmer likened the KgU to a "pigsty."[41] This pressure, including a highly critical study conducted by the West Berlin Senate, finally led to the KgU's dissolution on March 11, 1959. Even feeling the way he did, there was nothing the CIA Berlin station chief could do to rein in Heckscher's activities, since the OPC was independent. Besides, as Bailey pointed out, Heckscher had friends in high places.

Free Jurists: A Soviet Creation

No study of the battle against communist oppression would be complete without examining the Untersuchungsausschuss Freiheitlicher Juristen (UFJ), the Investigating Committee of Free Jurists, founded officially in West Berlin in 1950. It is a saga of Soviet counterintelligence tradecraft and Western security agency failures. The UFJ was the brainchild of Major General Nikolai I. Melnikov of the Soviet MGB.[42] Melnikov also was instrumental in shaping the Polish secret police, the Urzad Bezpieczeństwa (UB), between 1944 and 1948, when he was assigned to the Soviet-occupied zone of Germany.

Working under General Ivan A. Serov, who headed Soviet secret police operations in Germany, Melnikov organized networks of informants to observe political parties, labor organizations, and religious groups. He set up headquarters in Belzig, a small town southwest of Berlin, where he commanded about a hundred MGB officers. A short, stocky man of about forty-five years, Melnikov could exude charm or the chill of an icicle, whichever suited the circumstances of the moment. He was known to slap subordinates for minor infractions or mercilessly beat soldiers caught fraternizing with German women. The general liked his vodka and enjoyed hunting rabbits at night in the glare of spotlights.[43]

Also in Belzig was Horst Johannes Karl Erdmann, who arrived there during the turbulent summer of 1945.[44] It was a time when community officials faced the difficult task of coping with thousands of refugees and former prisoners of war who had no identity papers. Erdmann was one of these dispossessed. He told local authorities that he had been in a concentration camp in Silesia for having made anti-Hitler remarks and had been liberated by the Red Army. He claimed to have been born in Lübeck in 1919 and to have moved with his family to Breslau, where he later studied law. In the biography that the authorities required before issuing him identification documents, Erdmann wrote that he had served as a court assistant but had been fired when it was discovered that his mother was a Jew. The German communist authorities believed Erdmann's story and issued him a license to practice as an attorney. However, the monitoring of attorneys also fell within the purview of Melnikov's office. In scrutinizing Erdmann's activities, investigators found out that the attorney also was maintaining an office in West Berlin. Further exploration into his background, particularly as compared with the handwritten biography, raised enough questions to warrant interrogation. The MGB decided that Erdmann was not a spy but a common confidence man and a fairly good forger. A check of the university archives at Breslau, which was then in Polish hands, revealed that Erdmann had studied law briefly but never graduated. Moreover, the Soviets found that he was born in Breslau, not in Lübeck. They also located an old Breslau telephone book in which he was listed as a *Stammführer*—a leader of the Hitler Youth.

General Melnikov decided that Erdmann could be used to form a phony anticommunist organization directly controlled by the MGB. In his plans, Melnikov drew on the experience of NKGB operatives in the Baltics who had formed their own "partisan" group in 1946, ostensibly fighting the Soviet occupiers who were being battered by Latvian underground units.[45] In this way they gained the confidence of the real guerrillas so as to identify and exterminate them.

Given a choice between jail and collaboration, Erdmann chose to become a Soviet agent.[46] The new agent was instructed to stick to the background that the MGB had exposed as false. To buttress his legend, the MGB forgery shop provided Erdmann with documents attesting that he was half Jewish and had been imprisoned in a concentration camp. They also provided him a fake university diploma indicating that he was a doctor of jurisprudence. On Melnikov's instructions, Erdmann traveled to Berlin and contacted Rainer Hildebrandt of the KgU, to whom he proposed merging "his" jurists' group with the fighters against inhumanity. Erdmann claimed he had already begun to recruit lawyers and friendly officials in the province of Brandenburg. Hildebrandt, sensing a potential rival whose background he did not know, turned him down. Erdmann's approach to Hildebrandt was obviously a ploy to attract the attention of the CIC. It worked. CIC officials provided Erdmann with cash and instructions to operate out of Belzig. In those days, residents had unrestricted access to the western sectors of Berlin. For several months Erdmann provided his CIC handlers with information carefully prepared by Melnikov's staff. The Americans were pleased to have gained another asset in the Soviet zone, if only for a few months.

In April 1950, Erdmann showed up again in the American sector of Berlin, this time as a refugee. The Americans readily accepted his claim that operating out of Belzig had gotten too hot and that he intended to establish himself in the West. He hung out his shingle as Horst Erdmann, Attorney-at-Law, but the CIC made him take it down. He was also given a new name: Theo Friedenau, born 1919 in Berlin. After all, it was the rule of the intelligence game that the true identity of a valuable agent needed to be protected with a cover name. With the blessing of U.S. intelligence, he then set out to carry out General Melnikov's order to organize an "anticommunist" association of lawyers for investigating human rights abuses in the Soviet zone. Melnikov's purpose was to establish a system by which the MGB could monitor the judicial system in the Soviet zone to assure that the will of the communist regime was diligently carried out. Next to the Stasi, the judiciary was the party's most important instrument for political oppression.

Theo Friedenau garbed himself in tailor-made suits, using the money CIC officials had paid him from their "confidential funds." Sporting a neatly trimmed mustache, the slightly built Friedenau made an effort to appear elegant. For Günther Buch of the Institute for All-German Affairs, however, it was a thin veneer. "He always gave me the impression of a pimp."[47] Nevertheless, Erdmann's gift of persuasion made him acceptable to the West Berlin lawyers and city officials whom he contacted to advance "his idea." The con man par excellence told them that his group would refrain from propaganda and sabotage operations, concentrating instead on digging up human and civil rights abuses and exposing the culprits. He was enthusiastically accepted, and the UFJ was born.

The CIC provided Erdmann with a posh villa that it had rented from a German importer. Money began to flow in Erdmann's direction from various sources, including the West Berlin city government and the Ministry for All-German Affairs. No sooner had the Investigating Committee of Free Jurists begun to take shape than the U.S. Army Counter Intelligence Corps was once more obliged to relinquish its asset to the more powerful Central Intelligence Agency. The change of overseers was a godsend for Friedenau. Not that the CIC was miserly with its funds; but the CIA had far more ready cash. As a cover for providing the UFJ with money, CIA officials established the Gesellschaft für ein Vereinigtes Deutschland, the Society for a United Germany. The patrons of the society were ostensibly beer brewers of German descent living in Milwaukee, Wisconsin.[48]

As Friedenau was busily establishing his investigating committee, General Melnikov's MGB scouts searched for another lawyer who could be funneled into the UFJ. Melnikov probably wanted someone who could keep an eye on the shifty Erdmann, alias Friedenau. In January 1950, they found the ideal candidate in Walther Rosenthal, born in 1917 in a small town near Berlin, and a graduate of Berlin University's faculty of law.

Rosenthal had served as a lieutenant in the German Wehrmacht from 1939 until the war's end, mostly on the eastern front, and according to Stasi files, as a Soviet agent.[49] He had been decorated with the German Cross in Gold, a medal ranking just below the coveted Knight's Cross. Exactly when and how he became a Soviet agent during World War II is not known. But after the war, it was clear that Rosenthal had become a good comrade. In 1948 he passed a state examination for jurists in the Soviet zone and was appointed a prosecutor at the Potsdam provincial court. A bit later he was promoted to the post of judge. On January 7, 1950, Rosenthal signed the following statement: "I hereby pledge to perform for Soviet authorities required intelligence tasks. I will keep this matter secret. For the purpose of maintaining secrecy I will sign my report with the cover name Schmidt. I have been instructed regarding the consequences in the event that I violate the secrecy pledge."[50] Five months later, Rosenthal was promoted to chief judge at the high court of Brandenburg province, apparently to boost his professional stature before his planned "flight" to West Berlin two months later.

The Americans swiftly approved Rosenthal's application to work with the jurists' investigation committee, which had grown rapidly to include eighty full-time case workers. The case workers' initial task was to recruit agents among the East German population who would watch for human rights abuses committed by prosecutors or judges. Within a year, the UFJ could rely on some 12,000 watchers, including a number of Communist Party members. After the UFJ had pinpointed individuals who committed human rights violations, culprits received warning letters containing statements such as: "Someday you will be held to account not because you are a communist but because you are committing wrongful acts. It is up to you to decide whether or not you want to carry this guilt on your shoulders." The letters had the desired effect. Hundreds of their recipients were traveling to West Berlin to seek rehabilitation. Many were arrested on their return home and landed before Soviet military tribunals and in prisons.

What Melnikov apparently had not counted on was that Friedenau could not prohibit other operations proposed by his staff without arousing suspicion. One was the issuance of a flyer that told Soviet zone residents to "pay your taxes, but not more than absolutely necessary" and suggested ways in which this might be achieved. Another was a campaign to explain why the East Germans should no longer sign up for life insurance: "In the so-called DDR, life insurance premiums are no longer invested in traditionally secure stocks and bonds or real estate. Instead, they wind up in the emaciated government treasury and the insured loses the security."

The result of this campaign became starkly evident when the number of policies written in just one town near Berlin dropped by 40 to 50 percent in a single year. The only individuals who suffered were the insurance agents, who at the time could still pursue their jobs in relative freedom. Aware of their plight, UFJ specialists instructed them in how they could fill their quotas by writing accident and fire policies.

The Stasi Fights Back

Still working under strict Soviet control, the East German state security service began offensive operations against the UFJ in 1952, although agents Friedenau and Rosenthal, who had risen to deputy UFJ chief, were still controlled by the MGB. The East German government apparently convinced Moscow that UFJ activities were getting out of hand and the organization had to be eliminated.

At 7:22 P.M. on July 8, 1952, Walther Linse, a lawyer and head of the economics section of the UFJ, left his home in the American sector of Berlin. A taxi with a driver and one passenger was parked nearby, its engine running. A Volkswagen delivery van drove up and parked a few yards behind the taxi. A man leading a dachshund ambled by. As Linse walked down the street, two men approached him from the opposite direction. When they reached Linse, near where the taxi was parked, one of the men asked the lawyer for a light. Linse reached into his pocket, and at that moment the man grabbed him by the wrist and twisted, causing both to fall to the ground. The second man pounded his fist against Linse's temple. The taxi's passenger opened the rear door, and the men shoved Linse inside and jumped in after him. The most brazen of the many Stasi kidnappings that made headlines in Berlin in the late 1940s and early 1950s was under way.[51]

When he saw the attack, the man who was walking his dog pulled a police whistle from his pocket and blew it furiously. He was an unarmed Linse bodyguard. A woman nearby screamed for help. While the taxi holding Linse and his attackers was turning around, the Volkswagen van, which also belonged to the bodyguard detail, started up and swung around to block the taxi. One of the attackers pointed a pistol out of the taxi window and fired two shots at the Volkswagen's driver. The bullets missed, but the driver failed to stop the cab. Upon hearing the police whistle and the gunfire, passersby ran into the street at an intersection toward which the taxi was heading, to block the way. Another shot was fired, and the crowd dispersed. The gunman threw about twenty tetrahedron spikes onto the road, which were designed to puncture the tires of any vehicles in pursuit. The kidnappers sped off.

Inside the cab, Linse lay face down on the floor, struggling violently. He kicked out at the driver. The gunman fired twice, and a bullet smashed into Linse's calf. The lawyer lost consciousness as the cab drove at high speed to a border crossing near the suburb of Teltow, less than three miles from Linse's home. There the kidnappers left the cab and joined Stasi Major E. Sabbath and Captain Heinz Marozoeck, who were waiting for them at the border. The cab took Linse to a special Stasi prison.

The kidnapping, code-named Operation Lehmann, had been meticulously planned for two months after Stasi Minister Wilhelm Zaisser gave the order that Linse be "arrested." The planning group of nine Stasi officers included Colonel Bruno Beater, who later became a Stasi general and deputy minister, and Colonel Otto Knye, who was leading the assault on the Battle Group Against Inhumanity. The Stasi had recruited four petty criminals to carry out the actual abduction. They were led by Harry Bennewitz, a thirty-one-year-old seaman given the Stasi code name Barth and described as a "typical leader of bandits." He was the shooter. Six other petty criminals were recruited to reconnoiter and act as lookouts.

Berlin newspapers headlined the kidnapping the following day and accused the communist secret police of the crime. Editorials condemned the communist regime, and politicians of all stripes protested. Two days after Linse's abduction, a mass rally was held in West Berlin. It was attended by Lord Mayor Ernst Reuter, a Social Democrat; the U.S., British, and French commandants; and representatives of all democratic political parties and labor unions. Stasi secret agent "Procontra" observed a crowd of about 10,000. The agent reported that a speaker opened the demonstration with a description of the abduction and the crowd went wild, demanding that Max Reimann, the West German Communist Party leader, be seized and held as a hostage. "They screamed: 'We demand vigilante rule! . . . Give us weapons! . . . Throw them (West Berlin Communist Party members) into penitentiaries!' . . . The place became a witches' cauldron." The agent's report, which filled three pages, closed with the observation that not much was needed to incite the masses to wage a "pogrom" against West Berlin communists: "After all, it was officially proclaimed by Reuter today that they [the communists] are agents of the Soviets and accomplices to kidnapping." Apparently, the loyal agent firmly believed his employers would never stoop to such a crime and that somebody else must have done it. To help the authorities catch the perpetrators, he had included a description of Linse in his report.

The U.S. High Commissioner for Germany Walther J. Donnelly sent a note to General Vasili Chuikov, head of the Soviet Military Administration, protesting the kidnapping and demanding Linse's immediate return. Chuikov replied that the Soviet authorities had no information about Linse's whereabouts. Linse's wife Helga sent a telegram to Prime Minister Otto Grotewohl in which she demanded the immediate release of her husband, "if you yourself do not want to be seen as a criminal." There was no reply. Either the Stasi intercepted the telegram, or Grotewohl sent it to them, as it was later found in Linse's Stasi file.

In the meantime, Linse had been assigned the number 505 and was being interrogated by Stasi officers, at times in the presence of MGB representatives. He shared his cell with another man who was either a Stasi officer or a prisoner co-opted by the secret police, as he wrote daily reports of his conversations with Linse. On July 11, three days after the kidnapping, the informer wrote that Linse said his leg wound had been satisfactorily treated. But he complained that despite the wound, he had been questioned for eighteen straight hours by a "Russian." "But he commented favorably about his general treatment." Eventually Linse's cell mate was exchanged for another and his cell was bugged. The inmates' conversations and the long prayers that the devout Linse recited every day were recorded and meticulously transcribed.[52] Between his abduction on July 8 and December 12, 1952, Linse was interrogated thirty-four times. Confronted with evidence that he had been under surveillance since late fall 1951 and that his mail had been systematically intercepted, Linse admitted that he had collected economic information while visiting East Germany. He also named thirty-five persons living in East Germany who had cooperated with the Free Jurists.[53]

When the Stasi had finished with Linse, they turned him over to the MGB. On September 23, 1953, Soviet Military Tribunal No. 482 in Berlin found Linse guilty of espionage, counterrevolutionary activities, and propaganda, and sentenced him to death. He was shipped to Moscow, where on December 15, 1953, the Superior Court of the USSR confirmed the sentence. One hour after this final verdict, Linse was shot at Butyrka prison. His body was cremated at the Donskoy monastery.[54] He was fifty years old.

Linse was dead, but the Stasi had no end of problems with the criminals they had recruited for the kidnapping. Each was provided with a completely furnished house or apartment. According to Stasi records, the gang was held in reserve for other jobs. But they became useless when a defector told Western authorities the story. The kidnappers and their helpers refused to pursue legitimate jobs and became involved in various petty crimes. At one point, Erich Mielke, who was then Stasi deputy minister, wanted to pack them off to Poland; but this plan apparently was not carried out. Finally, when the various gang members began to brag about their escapades during drunken orgies, the Stasi decided it had had enough of them. All were arrested and jailed. It is not known whether Stalin silenced them forever, but all were dead by the time Germany was reunified.

The Stasi offensive against the UFJ continued unabated. On July 27, 1952, East Germany's High Court convicted seven UFJ members of espionage for the "American espionage organization Committee of Free Jurists." The seven were accused of undermining the DDR and "furnishing Western imperialists with information used in preparing for war." Two men were sentenced to life, and the others received penitentiary terms ranging from ten to fifteen years.

In October 1955, Walther Rosenthal was apprehended by West Berlin police on suspicion of espionage. Someone had sent police a copy of his pledge to work as a communist agent signed five years earlier. However, police investigators were unable to substantiate the suspicion, and Rosenthal was released. Who sent police the document remains a mystery.

Linse's successor as head of the UFJ economics department, Erwin Neumann, was kidnapped by Stasi agents who boarded his sailboat on the Wannsee in Berlin on August 20, 1958. Neumann's sailing companion, his assistant Wolfgang Weidhaas, had prepared the way by putting a sleep-inducing drug into his boss's beer. Neumann, an economist, was sentenced to a life term and died at the age of forty-eight, after nine years in an isolation cell. He left a wife and a daughter, who eventually emigrated to the United States. To camouflage Weidhaas's role in the abduction, a court sentenced him to three years and six months in the penitentiary. In reality, the twenty-nine-year-old was secretly promoted to first lieutenant and sent as a Stasi representative to Bulgaria.

The year of Neumann's abduction, the CIA abandoned its support and direction of the UFJ. The organization was disbanded in 1968 and some of its personnel were integrated into the West German government's Institute for All-German Affairs as civil servants. One of them was Götz Schlicht, a jurist who was the director of East Germany's School for People's Judges when he was arrested in 1952 for distributing UFJ leaflets. Sentenced to twelve years in prison, he was released after serving five, and returned to work for the Free Jurists. When East Germany collapsed and the Stasi files became available, it was found that he had been recruited in prison to spy for the Stasi. Schlicht, whose code name was Dr. Lutter, betrayed at least twelve individuals who wound up in Stasi prisons. In return for his good work for the Stasi, he received five decorations, including the Combat Medal for the People and Fatherland in Gold. Ironically, the West German government also awarded him the Federal Cross of Merit First Class, which was taken away when his spy activities were discovered. Because of his age—he was born in 1909—and his failing health, he escaped prosecution.

THE STASI GATHERS FORCE . . .

In 1953, Stasi personnel numbered about 4,000. The people's revolt that June had prompted the regime to order a massive buildup and reorganization of the secret police. By 1973 the Ministry for State Security had been restructured along military lines and its ranks had swelled to 52,707. Stasi chief Mielke also built up his own fighting force of 16,000 officers and men, equipped with armored cars, heavy infantry weapons, and antiaircraft guns. He called it the F. E. Dzerzhinski Guard Regiment in honor of his idol, the first Bolshevik secret police chief.

To raise the educational standards of his officers and perfect their ideological obedience, Mielke established a training academy called Juristische Hochschule, College of Justice. Attendance was mandatory for all officers aspiring to promotion above lieutenant colonel. One colonel received his diploma as a "jurist" after he wrote a thesis on how best to combat political dissidents. The thesis, written in 1988, was promptly classified as a state secret.[55]

Antistate political activities and Stasi oppression eased considerably after the Berlin Wall was built in 1961. Exact statistics on the numbers of arrests and political trials cannot be located, because the East German judiciary did not keep separate records on political cases, all of which were criminalized; in addition, countless files were destroyed when the DDR collapsed. However, other evidence indicates the numbers decreased significantly around this time.

The relative calm lasted until 1975, when the party leadership pushed the panic button as a result of the Helsinki Conference on Security and Cooperation in Europe (CSCE). Erich Honecker, the SED leader and the head of state, viewed the CSCE agreement as a grave threat to his regime. His fears proved justified: When people became aware of the contents of the agreement that Honecker had signed, which indicated that the DDR would respect "human and basic rights, including freedom of thought, conscience, religion, and conviction," resistance groups began to form. This spurred an even more rapid buildup of the Stasi. Within two years of the Helsinki Conference, Stasi strength had risen by more than 10,000. Mielke, a Politburo member, was accorded new, wide-ranging powers. The Stasi became the leadership's personal instrument of power to an extent not known since the demise of Stalin except perhaps in Romania under Nicolae Ceausescu. The oppression became even greater than it had been in the half decade after World War II when the Soviet secret police wielded total power.[56]

In 1979, Mielke ordered his district commanders to draw up plans for a system of internment camps. By 1984, twenty-four locations had been designated as sites for "isolation and internment." Each location was assigned a code name (for example, the medieval Ranis castle in the province of Thuringia was *Rosenstock*, rosebush). Stasi Major General Josef Schwarz, who held a doctorate of law, issued an order in which he specified six categories of persons to be arrested and detained.[57] These included anyone who had ever been under surveillance for antistate activities, including the members of peace movements not sponsored by the state. Those to be detained if Mielke issued his emergency order code-named Schild (shield) ran into the tens of thousands. About 2,600 were on detention lists in a small area of Thuringia alone. The Stasi's plans for isolation and internment camps were a carbon copy of how the Nazi concentration camps got their start after Hitler came to power in 1933.

. . . AND REFINES ITS METHODS

The Stasi's recruitment and deployment of secret informants became a science when Mielke issued his *Richtlinie 1/76,* a manual of standard operating procedures.[58] This top secret document outlined the surveillance of the population down to the last detail. Stasi officers, especially those assigned to the Twentieth Main Directorate, were assigned quotas for recruiting informers. The directorate, commanded by Lieutenant General Paul Kienberg, was responsible for the surveillance of state entities, political parties, churches, hospitals, doctors, youth, and sports groups. It was in overall charge of combating underground political movements. Assigned to its headquarters in Berlin alone were 391 officers, assisted by more than 1,300 informants. The majority of Twentieth Directorate personnel, about 1,800 officers, was stationed around the provinces in the 15 Stasi district offices and 214 substations. Each officer supervised at least 30 regular informers, for a total of more than 54,500. About 55 clandestine monthly meetings per officer with stool pigeons was the norm. Some Stasi snoops were as young as twelve years, and the oldest in one district was eighty-nine.

The Twentieth Directorate's closest collaborators were the Second Main Directorate (domestic counterintelligence) headed by Lieutenant General Günther Kratsch and the Third Main Directorate under Major General Horst Männchen. The Second Directorate, composed of about 4,400 officers, included Department M, which was charged with postal surveillance. The 6,000 officers of the Third Directorate handled electronic surveillance. About 3,000 officers were assigned to tap telephones. Telephone confidentiality was guaranteed by law, which provided stiff penalties for violations; however, as in other spheres, the Stasi operated above the law. One former high-ranking Stasi officer with whom I spoke said he could not remember a judge's ever having issued a warrant for a wiretap.[59]

The inviolability of postal communications also was guaranteed by law. Nevertheless, Division M had deployed its officers at every post office. All letters and parcels sent to or received from a noncommunist country were opened surreptitiously. The operation was established to catch spies and enemies of the regime; but over the years, it evolved into organized mail robbery. Money sent by West Germans to their relatives in the East for the purchase of goods available only in hard currency shops was systematically removed. According to DDR law, the money should have been returned to the senders. Instead, about 6.5 million West marks (more than US$4 million) wound up in Stasi accounts during the last three years of the DDR's existence.[60] As the Stasi began to disintegrate in late 1989, West Berlin suddenly became flooded with five-mark notes, which had not been printed for years and were being replaced by coins. Authorities surmised that these bills came out of the Stasi coffers. When the notes appeared, some Berliners sarcastically called them "Pankow dollars," after the East Berlin suburb of Pankow, which housed top communist officials. Of some 20 million parcels sent to East Germans each year, about 200,000 never reached their destinations.[61] Beginning in 1984, a parcel sent from West Germany to East Germany in error was no longer returned to its senders. Instead, it wound up in the Stasi's Objekt Freienbrink, a huge warehouse outside Berlin surrounded by barbed wire and guard towers, where the contents were plundered.

The Stasi's oppression machine, in its never-ending search for state enemies, dissidents, spies, and would-be escapees to the West, employed every possible means of surveillance. When irate citizens stormed Stasi offices after German reunification, they discovered rooms with shelves holding thousands of canning jars. The jars, labeled with only a number, contained pieces of cloth. Mystified, the people searched for files that would shed light on this peculiar discovery. They found lists of names that corresponded to the numbers. Further Stasi reports revealed that the pieces of cloth were impregnated with the body odors of suspected dissidents who could thus be tracked by bloodhounds. The Stasi got the idea from a method employed by the KGB in the 1970s to track personnel of the U.S. embassy in Moscow. KGB agents had sprayed a special chemical on the sidewalk in front of the embassy. The chemical adhered to shoe soles, and dogs could be used to trail anyone departing the building. The Stasi perfected the method, as former Stasi Colonel Wiegand put it, *mit deutscher Gründlichkeit,* with characteristic German thoroughness: Suspected dissidents were summoned to regular police stations for "conversations" during which men were told to place a specially treated cloth in their armpits, women in their crotches. These body odor depositories were found in Stasi offices throughout East Germany. Several thousand samples were located in East Berlin alone.

Stasi officers with degrees in criminology from East Berlin's Humboldt University were important cogs in the oppression apparatus.

One of the professors was Heinz Felfe, who learned his trade as an SS officer under the Nazis.[62] Extensive use of criminological techniques by the Stasi included graphological examination of handwritten leaflets, anonymous letters, and dissident slogans daubed on walls. Writing samples were obtained surreptitiously during postal examinations or at the time when dissidents were obliged to provide their body odors to the Stasi. The Eighth Department of the Twentieth Directorate maintained a library of videotapes of church meetings, rallies, and other public events in which the participation of dissidents was suspected. Persons showing up repeatedly at certain events were placed under special observation.

Watchmen at the Wall

Stasi officers assigned to Checkpoint Charlie acted as if they expected an invasion whenever a prominent Western personage, especially an American, showed up near the wall or entered East Berlin. What were these foreigners up to? Were they spies? Provocateurs, planning an action to embarrass the regime? To Mielke's legions, every foreigner was a potential enemy and harbored dastardly intent. The Stasi's paranoia was acute.

On the morning of December 1, 1978, East German border guards noticed a group of photographers and a television camera crew on the western side of the checkpoint, apparently awaiting someone important. What follows can only be described as grotesque and was minutely recorded in an eight-page dossier complete with six photographs.[63] At 10:30, the photographers and camera team filmed "two persons, a male and a female, in front of the checkpoint shack" the report noted. "The filming stopped at 10:40. There was no hindrance of traffic." At 2:22 P.M., a black Plymouth sedan bearing a license assigned to the U.S. mission in Berlin drove to the eastern side of the checkpoint to enter East Berlin. "The car was driven by a (U.S. Army) specialist 4 in uniform. The others in the car showed their U.S. passports issued in the names of Reagan, Ronald, born February 6, 1911; Reagan, Nancy, born July 6, 1921 . . . ."

Obviously, the Stasi's watcher had no idea who the Reagans were, for he closed his report saying that "the two persons using the name Reagan were identical with the persons filmed in the morning." An unmarked car followed the visitors on their sightseeing trip through East Berlin, and the report closed by noting that the "persons departed at 15:18, again without incident."

When it became known that Ronald Reagan would visit Berlin as U.S. president on June 9, 1987, Mielke put his secret police on general alert with a three-page order.[64] Because the plans called for a spectacular visit, especially the rally at the Brandenburg Gate, "we must count on provocative and slanderous abuse of the DDR," the Stasi chief wrote, and ordered "the highest amount of vigilance." The secret police were particularly edgy about the Reagan visit because of intensified dissident activities in East Berlin.

Watchdogs at the Press

In the late 1970s, Western news organizations were permitted to open offices in East Berlin. The DDR was the last Eastern-bloc regime to open its doors to Western journalists and did so primarily in order to gain greater stature and recognition in the West. But the communist rulers thereby created a new problem for themselves: Western news correspondents had to be kept from close contact with ordinary citizens who might divulge information that could embarrass or discredit the regime. Thus, the Western journalists were under rigid surveillance by officers assigned to the newly created Thirteenth Department of the counterespionage directorate. In addition, every Western news office in East Berlin was obliged to hire all support staff, from secretaries to office assistants, from a special local labor pool selected and overseen by a department of the foreign ministry. Nearly all of the local hires were Stasi IMs, unofficial collaborators. All telephone lines were monitored around the clock, as were the lines of all news organizations based in West Berlin. Besides being subjected to visual observation, journalists were videotaped while going about their work.[65]

Under the most intense, around-the-clock observation was the East Berlin chief correspondent of the Associated Press, Ingomar Schwelz, as well as all AP journalists assigned temporarily to cover events in the communist capital. The author has obtained copies of the Stasi's AP dossiers, which together weigh just under fourteen pounds. The dossier starts with a copy of Schwelz's original job application and a series of letters sent to him while he lived in Stuttgart, West Germany, by the AP chief editor based at the news agency's Germany headquarters in Frankfurt, West Germany. These documents could only have been supplied by a mole in the Frankfurt office. The secret police dossier also makes it clear that at least one Stasi IM, codenamed Anett Müller, was a close associate. Remarks made by Schwelz in his office and plans for news coverage were reported before he even had a chance to carry them out. These reports all were labeled "Top Secret—Special Source Protection"—the Stasi's way of indicating that they originated with a human source. Reports based on telephone intercepts were marked as such.

The Stasi's immense expenditures of time and money to spy on journalists were mind boggling, considering that East Germany was on the brink of insolvency. Witness a "special operation" to cover an

East Berlin reception in 1995 to introduce Schwelz, an Austrian citizen, as AP's new East Berlin chief. The party was attended by about a hundred people, including communist functionaries, diplomats, and journalists from both East and West. To watch over them, the Stasi used three informers and one OIBE (a regular officer working under deep cover). The affair was recorded on 134 pages, all classified as top secret. Each informer wrote detailed reports on their conversations with the participants.

As the activities of East German dissidents intensified in 1987, so did the surveillance of journalists. At least eight informers were assigned to the AP man. Hundreds of pages cover Schwelz's contacts with dissidents and his attendance at antiregime church rallies. Some of his contacts were arrested and expelled to West Berlin. The reports ended abruptly shortly before the wall came down in November 1989.

Internal Discipline: Carrot and Stick

The Germans coined a word to describe the regime's incredibly vast network for surveillance and intimidation of the populace: *flächendeckend,* meaning that nothing was left uncovered. The stick was not always visible, but the people always knew it was there. Even Stasi officers were not immune. With his own, however, Stasi chief Mielke employed the carrot as well.

By East German standards, Stasi officers were well paid.[66] A lieutenant earned 1,900 marks a month, double the national average and more than a managing director of a medium-sized factory employing several hundred workers. Majors and above were able to acquire weekend cottages located in the most scenic areas of East Germany at a fraction of their actual cost. Much of the land used had been confiscated from those who were imprisoned as state enemies or who had fled to the West. In addition, all personnel were entitled to free vacations at any of twenty-four Stasi spas. The higher ranks were entitled to shop in special stores for Western goods. From time to time, the generals and colonels were summoned to the warehouse of the postal surveillance department to collect sealed metal boxes containing goods pilfered from parcels sent to East Germans by their Western relatives.[67]

Mielke's stick—which was as often used as the carrot—was political and personal discipline reminiscent of the early French Foreign Legion. For starters, newly recruited Stasi personnel were made to swear an oath pledging to "fight alongside the state security organs of all socialist countries against all enemies of socialism." Violators of this solemn oath were threatened with "the severest punishment under the republic's laws, and the contempt of the workers." In addition, personnel were made to sign a secrecy pledge that was valid for life. They could never visit capitalist countries and had to report any receipt of mail or visitors from the West. Their immediate family members also were included in these restrictions. Violations of the oath or the security pledge meant expulsion from the security service and prohibition of work in any meaningful job. Serious infractions were tried before secret military tribunals and could end in execution by beheading or a shot in the neck, as happened to about two hundred Stasi officers.[68] "There was only one way to leave the MfS without being haunted for the rest of your life," one former colonel commented. "You either retired, or you died. After you signed up, if you did not agree with policies and said so openly, you were finished. If you didn't land in prison, or worse, you became an unperson. It happened to several thousand. In a way, they too were victims of the oppressive regime."

5

THE INVISIBLE INVASION

Espionage Assault on West Germany

"The principal link in the chain of revolution is the German link, and the success of the world revolution depends more on Germany than upon any other country."

—*V. I. Lenin, Report of October 22, 1918*

THE STASI'S ESPIONAGE WAR against capitalist enemies abroad was hugely successful and ended only when the diehard communists realized that their dream of clinging to power at home had been shattered. On May 31, 1990, Stasi spies in West Germany sat by their radios, poised to copy the five-digit code groups that for years had been used to relay instructions from their controllers behind the Berlin Wall. On that day, however, the familiar, monotonous female voice said only "Wittenberg" three times. Then there was silence. *Wittenberg,* the name of the town where Martin Luther broke with Catholicism and started the Protestant Reformation, was also the code word ordering the recall of about three hundred Stasi operatives on special deployment—OIBEs, in Stasi jargon—who served as espionage case officers in West Germany. The agents scurried back to East Germany, abandoning their Western collaborators.

Six days earlier, the intelligence division of the People's Army had told its spies by radio that the game was over. In contrast to the Stasi announcer, the army men apparently had to boost their courage with schnapps: Giggling and slurring their words, they sang a children's ditty about a duck swimming in a lake, dunking its little head in the water and lifting its little tail. Staging this broadcast may have been hilarious to the alcohol-stimulated singers in East Berlin; not so to the spies who listened.

These two broadcasts ended espionage operations that had functioned successfully for nearly four decades. The Hauptverwaltung Aufklärung (HVA, the Stasi foreign intelligence service) and the military intelligence service of the DDR were dead. Eighty percent of all East German espionage operations in West Germany had been run by the HVA. The military played a smaller but no less successful role, with 20 percent.[1]

Within months, some Stasi spy handlers had talked, and dozens of officials—some highly placed—in all of the government ministries found themselves under investigation or in prison. In the first three years after October 3, 1990, when Germany was reunified, hardly a week passed without sensational arrests. Although dozens of East German spies as well as Soviet and Polish operatives had been arrested annually over four decades, the infiltration was far worse than had been suspected. It became clear that the entire government was infested, as was every political party, West Germany's industry, banks, the church, and the news media. The Bundesnachrichtendienst (BND, the Federal Intelligence Service) and the nation's counterespionage service Bundesamt für Verfassungsschutz (BfV, the Office for the Protection of the Constitution) also had been covertly invaded. The Ministry of Defense's Counterintelligence Service, the Militärischer Abschirmdienst (MAD), had as well. One female Stasi mole in the BND, an East German agent for seventeen years, had been entrusted with the job of preparing the daily, top secret intelligence summary for Chancellor Helmut Kohl. The West German security services had failed miserably.

Joachim Gauck, federal commissioner charged with maintaining and evaluating the Stasi archive, estimated that at least 20,000 West Germans had spied for the Stasi.[2] He based his estimate on the reconstruction of dossiers that had been shredded. "This estimate is a conservative one. When the reconstruction process is completed, we may find that the figure is closer to 30,000."[3] But even if all spies were exposed, none could be prosecuted because the statute of limitations for espionage is five years.

Nevertheless, a staggering number of espionage cases have been solved. According to the Federal Prosecutor General, about 6,600 investigations were conducted between 1990 and 1996.[4] Forty percent involved West Germans; 25 percent, East Germans who had spied in the West; and 35 percent, regular Stasi officers. West German spies for the Stasi came from all walks of life. In addition to government employees and politicians, they included high-ranking provincial police officers, journalists, university professors, and employees of defense plants. Some 4,000 cases that the federal prosecutor considered less serious were handed over to provincial prosecutors. There are no central statistics to show the outcome of these cases. Hundreds were dismissed because of the defendants' old age or illness. Many others brought mild sentences of probation or fines, particularly when the accused had been coerced into committing espionage. About 130 cases were still awaiting adjudication in 1998. Finding those who had spied for East German military intelligence was made extremely difficult because the DDR's last defense minister, Rainer Eppelmann, had ordered several tons of files burned. Eppelmann, a prominent dissident and Protestant minister, was appointed by a government that thought it could still salvage the DDR as a reformed socialist country governed by democratic ideals.

A MONUMENTAL SECURITY LAPSE

West Germany's most spectacular security failure began on November 14, 1955, when Werner Sikorski, press spokesman for the Investigative Committee of Free Jurists, interviewed an informant identified only as "M.A." In his report on their meeting, Sikorski wrote that M.A. drew attention to a photographer named Günter Guillaume, a member of the Communist Party employed by a state-owned publishing house.[5] "It is conspicuous that this man often failed to show up for work without explanation," the report stated. "When his department head began to make inquiries, he was told by the party leadership not to bother about things that were not his business. Finally, G. was sent to a lengthy training course. Normally the school to which a man has been delegated becomes public knowledge very quickly. But this case was treated with great secretiveness." The informant revealed that Guillaume had often been sent to West Germany: "Four weeks ago he left the publishing house for good, obviously so he could devote himself to work in the West." Since he expected that Guillaume would cross into the West more often, the informant recommended that "it would certainly be useful to take a closer look at this man."

The informant's hunch was correct. Guillaume and his wife Christel had been recruited as long-range agents by Colonel Paul Laufer of the Stasi's Hauptverwaltung Aufklärung, the foreign espionage directorate. Laufer was a secret Communist Party member in the late 1920s and at the same time openly held membership in the Social Democratic Party in Berlin. This master in conspiratorial operations, whose cover name was *Stabil* (Sturdy), spied on the socialists for the

N Apparat, the communists' intelligence service before Hitler came to power.[6] It was fitting, therefore, that Laufer would assign Guillaume to infiltrate the West German Social Democratic Party.

Sikorski's report was sent to the political section of West Berlin's criminal investigation department, where it remained untouched for nearly a year.[7] A detective eventually scrutinized the report and recommended that the Bundeskriminalamt (BKA), West Germany's equivalent to the FBI, be notified. But to do this, he needed a more detailed description of Guillaume, which the Free Jurists were unable to supply. The report therefore landed in the central registry and was forgotten. By then, Guillaume and Christel—twenty-eight and twenty-seven years old, respectively—had settled in the West German city of Frankfurt. To avoid intensive questioning by West German security officials, the couple did not register at a refugee camp, a procedure usually followed by escapees from the East. Instead, the Guillaumes registered with the local police, a requirement of all persons living in Germany. They gave the address of an apartment rented days earlier by Christel Guillaume's mother, Erna Boom, who also came from East Germany. Because she was a Dutch citizen, Boom herself was exempt from registering with the refugee authorities, but the Guillaumes still had to comply with this formality. Thus, Erna Bloom wrote a letter to the authorities requesting refugee status for her daughter and son-in-law. Her request was granted without much delay.

Guillaume worked for various firms as a clerk and for a while helped his mother-in-law manage a variety store. Every Wednesday evening, he listened to the Stasi's shortwave spy messages. After the birth of their son Pierre in 1957, a message from their control officer directed the Guillaumes to join the Social Democratic Party (SPD). Christel became secretary to a party official dealing with refugee affairs. Later she was promoted to work for federal parliament member Wilhelm Birkelbach, a Social Democrat.

Meanwhile, the electronic surveillance division of the federal border police had intercepted and decoded several messages the Stasi had sent to its agents over the frequency 6.5 megahertz. One spy was code-named Georg. Messages to him were preceded by the number 37. Georg received requests such as "Observe problems within faction, most importantly the trip of the club president."[8] The monitors concluded that "faction" referred to a political party's parliamentary faction and the club president must have been the party chief. But intelligence analysts could neither pinpoint the party nor the agent for whom the messages were intended. From time to time there were messages of a personal nature or expressing delight with the agent's work (congratulations on the birth of a child and on finding a job). There also were three separate birthday greetings.

Günter Guillaume was devoting himself to SPD affairs—at first, to taking photographs at party meetings, and later, in 1962, as an employee of the party newspaper *Der Sozialdemokrat.* Guillaume did his job so well that he was made a salaried district SPD secretary and became a member of the Frankfurt city council. A relatively short and paunchy but not unattractive man, Guillaume exuded energy at work and play. He often finished the day at bars and restaurants, trading party gossip with his socialist colleagues, among whom he was well liked. What Christel Guillaume lacked in physical appearance, she made up for in efficiency at the job, and her career blossomed. Her boss Wilhelm Birkelbach was appointed a state secretary and aide to Georg Zinn, minister president (the equivalent of state governor in the United States) for the state of Hesse. It was natural that Birkelbach would take along his trusted secretary. Now Christel could supply her husband with sensitive information that flowed into the Hesse government office.

Applying the tradecraft he had learned at the Stasi's foreign espionage school at Belzig, Guillaume photographed documents his wife acquired at her new job, including reports on NATO maneuvers, using an Exacta camera he had brought with him from East Germany. Reports were sometimes reduced to microdots by using a special small camera. A sheet of typing paper could be reduced to a negative the size of a pinhead. The dots were hidden beneath stamps on letters going to cover addresses in East Berlin. Guillaume's handlers were particularly interested in reports dealing with the strengths and weaknesses of socialist functionaries who might make good candidates for recruitment as spies. The Guillaumes were a perfect espionage team, the wife also having been trained at the East German espionage school.

As Guillaume rose through the party ranks, the HVA decided to improve his communication methods and ordered the infiltration of two highly experienced couriers. The team, a married couple using different identities, arrived separately as refugees in West Germany and established legal residences in different cities.[9] Then the two met each other "by chance" at a ski resort in Bavaria. Soon they were married a second time and settled in Munich. Their code names were Arno and Nora. Periodically one or the other, or sometimes both, would rendezvous with Christel or Günter Guillaume in hotels and restaurants of various cities to receive material the two had gathered.

Günter Guillaume: Rising Star

During the 1969 general election campaign, Günter Guillaume functioned as campaign manager for Georg Leber, a prominent Social Democrat and labor union leader. Guillaume tackled the task with his usual fervor. In the fall, Leber was elected to parliament by a wide margin. The Social Democrats won enough votes to form a coalition with the liberal Free Democratic Party. Willy Brandt, former West Berlin mayor and foreign minister in the CDU-SPD coalition government, was elected chancellor. Leber became postal and telecommunications minister in the Brandt cabinet and moved quickly to reward his loyal campaign chief. He recommended that Guillaume be named an assistant aide in the chancellery's department responsible for maintaining liaison with labor unions and employers' associations. On November 13, 1969, Leber introduced Guillaume to Brandt's chief of staff, Chancellery Minister Horst Ehmke, to whom he also wrote a letter extolling Guillaume's virtues: "He proved himself by carrying out his assignments with diligence, devotion, dexterity, experience, and intelligence," Minister Leber gushed. "What I especially valued was his dependability and his sense of responsibility in standing up for a life in freedom and for democracy. In many difficult situations in which I found myself, he proved his absolute trustworthiness."

Guillaume received the appointment, pending completion of the usual personal history statement required for security purposes. He received the form within a few days. Concurrently, the chancellor's security office sent queries to the criminal investigation agency (BKA), the federal foreign intelligence service, the counterespionage agency, and the refugee affairs authority.[10] The latter two agencies replied that they had no derogatory information on Günter Guillaume or his wife Christel. The criminal investigation agency also had no records of the couple but sent an inquiry to the Berlin police, which replied with a teletyped summary of the report the Free Jurists had provided in 1955. The BND also found an index card that said that in 1954 a Günter G. was said to have been employed by a publishing company and traveled to West Germany on espionage assignments. The BND added, however, that the accuracy of this information could no longer be established. Nevertheless, the BND liaison office in Bonn asked headquarters whether the source of the information was reliable. The answer was affirmative, and the chancellery's security officer was so informed. Chancellery Minister Ehmke then ordered BND Chief General Gerhard Wessel to brief him on the situation personally at a meeting in Bonn on December 23. However, the general was ill, and instead he sent a teletype to the chancellery.[11] It reiterated that the source was indeed reliable and recommended that "Guillaume be confronted and specifically asked if the assertions are true." From his reaction one might draw relevant conclusions, the general wrote, adding that Guillaume could, for example, say he accepted a spy job only as a pretense. In any case, the general recommended that the former photographer from Berlin not be hired for the chancellery position but given a job in some other government agency. Finally, the intelligence chief wrote that "the 1964 report alone was no reason to disadvantage Guillaume but that it necessitated a comprehensive background check by the counterespionage agency." Ehmke showed the teletype to Egon Bahr, a state secretary and confidant of Chancellor Brandt. Bahr agreed that Ehmke should question Guillaume but warned that "even if he makes a positive impression, a certain security risk will remain."

Guillaume was questioned on January 7, 1970, by Minister Ehmke, a party functionary and dilettante in intelligence matters. Witnessing the amateurish interrogation were Guillaume's new department head Herbert Ehrenberg and Franz Schlichter, the chancellery's security representative. Obviously, they were no match for the highly trained spy. After the meeting, Ehmke discussed the meeting with Ehrenberg and both agreed that Guillaume had made "a self-confident and relaxed impression and that there was nothing to the suspicions."[12] At the end of January, the Federal Office for the Protection of the Constitution informed Ehmke that there was no reason not to grant Guillaume access to classified material up to and including that designated as secret.

The Star at Its Zenith

Guillaume signed his employment contract on January 28 and began his new job that same day. The Stasi now had a master spy inside Palais Schaumburg, the seat of the West German Chancellor in Bonn. He performed so well that by July he was being considered for promotion to a position requiring a top secret security clearance, which was promptly granted. Two months later he was appointed a full-fledged *Referent,* or official adviser, handling liaison duties with labor and employers' groups. Guillaume's monthly salary was boosted from DM2,650 to DM3,308—about US$828 and US$1,034, respectively—a respectable sum at the time. He relinquished his Frankfurt city council seat, and the family, including Guillaume's mother-in-law, moved to Bonn. Grateful for Christel Guillaume's services, the Social Democratic Party's Hessian branch awarded her the job of running its guest house in Bonn.

Following the parliamentary election in fall 1972 Guillaume moved up another notch in the chancellery ranks. The head of the liaison department won a Bundestag seat, and Günter Guillaume replaced him in November, receiving another pay increase to DM4,399 marks, or about US$1,375. The stellar performer received the ultimate award six months later when he was appointed one of three personal assistants to Chancellor Brandt, a rank equivalent to that of deputy assistant to the president of the United States. Guillaume's job was to represent

West German Chancellor Willy Brandt (left) and his top aide Günter Guillaume, a long-range Stasi agent who wormed his way into the Social Democratic Party leader's confidence. Guillaume spied eighteen years before he was arrested in 1974 and sentenced to thirteen years in prison. He was later exchanged for Western spies caught by the Stasi. Ullstein/Agentur Simon.

the head of government in dealing with the Social Democratic Party and its parliamentary faction and with other parties and associations. It was a position of extraordinary power and access.

Guillaume ingratiated himself with Chancellor Brandt as he had with his previous superiors. The spy worked long hours, and except for brief vacations, he never missed a chance to be at the German leader's side, often accompanying him on official and private trips. It was a time when Brandt was immersed in pursuing his *Ostpolitik,* a policy designed to achieve rapprochement with the Eastern bloc, particularly with East Germany. Guillaume was able to pilfer documents on negotiating positions being developed not only by the West German government but also by its allies, including the United States. Like all information obtained by East German spies, Guillaume's booty was automatically shared with the Soviets. This placed the three Western allies controlling West Berlin in an extremely disadvantageous position during the 1972 negotiations with the Soviets over access to the divided city. "The Russians knew our position from the start," remarked Kenneth Rush, former U.S. envoy to West Germany and one of the negotiators, who later became deputy secretary of state.[13]

Guillaume also could supply the Stasi with situation reports sent to Brandt by the BND, and with interrogation protocols from refugee camps where escapees from East Germany were questioned before they were resettled. The minutes of all discussions between Brandt and top politicians, as well as with West Germany's allies, and correspondence to and from world leaders on emergency contingency plans, found their way eastward. Guillaume also participated in top secret domestic and foreign policy discussions.[14] By now his couriers had been recalled to East Berlin, and the HVA had supplied Guillaume with the latest in what the counterespionage experts called "A-1" radio equipment.[15] These small transmitters were fed with strips of celluloid bearing messages in the form of tiny holes punched out by miniature coding devices with keys resembling those of a typewriter. A sharp twist of a crank, and the radio would transmit the message in a fraction of a second, making it impossible to detect the sender's location. Guillaume transmitted from his car at various locations near the West German capital. He used this method of communication only to inform his control officer on the location of *tote Briefkästen* (TBKs), dead letter drops. The TBKs would be located at such places as a hollow tree on the banks of the Rhine river or behind a loose brick of a cemetery wall and would be used to transmit rolls of filmed documents.

Under Suspicion

Heinrich Schoregge, a senior investigator of the federal counterespionage agency, sat in his Cologne office in early March 1973, studying the case of a Frankfurt journalist suspected of working for the East Germans.[16] It was the beginning of the end of the spy careers of Guillaume and his wife. When Schoregge noticed that the suspected spy had been a friend of Guillaume, he remembered that the name also had appeared in two other cases. In 1965, Guillaume was questioned about a woman who worked for the press department of the Frankfurt SPD and who was arrested for espionage. The other case, in 1972, concerned a labor union official who was arrested as he met his East German courier. When the man's apartment was searched, investigators found a number of notes, one of which bore the name Guillaume. Schoregge, a former police detective, smelled a rat. His intensive research turned up the report that the Free Jurists Committee had provided Berlin police seventeen years earlier.

Deciphered spy messages were rechecked, especially those containing personal greetings.[17] Dates were compared with those in the Guillaume dossier—and the tenacious Schoregge hit pay dirt. Birthday wishes to "Georg" sent on February 1 corresponded with the date Günter Guillaume was born. Another congratulatory message was broadcast on his wife's birthday, October 6, and a third when his son was born on April 8, 1957. The counterspy's fifty-four-page report, listing thirty such suspicious coincidences, was turned over on May 24, 1973 to Günther Nollau, president of the Office for the Protection of the Constitution. Five days later Nollau informed his immediate superior, Interior Minister Dietrich Genscher, a liberal party member, who at once relayed the suspicion to Brandt. The chancellor was told to act as usual toward Guillaume because the spy catchers wanted to collect solid evidence before making an arrest. Brandt told only State Secretary Horst Grabert, responsible for chancellery administration, and his office manager about the suspicion.

In the meantime, counterspies placed the Guillaumes under tight, although not around-the-clock, surveillance. Despite more than 150 observation operations stretching over nearly eleven months, watchers were unable to catch Guillaume red-handed.[18] However, they noted that Guillaume periodically exhibited the behavior of a trained agent. He would enter department stores, railroad stations, or hotels through one door and slip out through another.

In early April 1973, Guillaume informed Brandt that he would travel by car to Lyon, France on a brief vacation. Interior Minister Genscher passed this information on to the counterespionage agency. From past cases the spy catchers knew that Stasi agents operating in West Germany often met with their case officers in France. Therefore, they requested surveillance assistance from the Service de Documentation Extérieure et de Contre-Espionage (SDECE), the French counterespionage service. German and French agents shadowed Guillaume during the entire trip without noting anything suspicious.

Toward the end of June, Chancellor Brandt was planning a vacation with his wife Rut and his youngest son Matthias near scenic Lake Mjosa, at Hamar, Norway, where they owned a rustic log cabin.[19] Brandt's wife was a Norwegian whom he had met while in exile in Norway. Since Guillaume had been a frequent travel companion, Brandt was told to take him along lest he become suspicious. The fact that the pudgy, mild-mannered spy was not under surveillance during that time later created an enormous controversy. In any case, Guillaume and his family left Bonn by car for Norway on July 2, 1973. The Brandts and the security detail flew to Norway a few days later. Halfway through the 662-mile journey that took them through Denmark and Sweden, the spies stopped at the small town of Halmstad, on Sweden's west coast, and checked into Hotel Hallandia. Guillaume's luggage included two identical attaché cases. After deciding that the place would be suitable for a *Treff* on the way back, Guillaume wrote a postcard. "Gudrun and Peter await you with ardent anticipation at Hallandia hotel July 31," Guillaume wrote. He had picked the spot knowing that Sweden was a Cold War neutral and was not as security conscious as states belonging to NATO, the North Atlantic Treaty Organization.

A Parting Flourish

At the Brandts' vacation spot in Hamar, seventy-three miles north of Oslo, the Guillaumes were billeted at a local youth hostel, which also housed the security staff and served as a command center. As the only personal aide present, the spy had unlimited access to the chancellor's mail and teletype messages. Departing again ahead of the Brandt party, Guillaume handed the chief of the security detail a locked attaché case, saying he did not want to carry classified material in his car and asking that he lock it in his safe upon returning to the chancellery. What it actually contained, however, were knickknacks Guillaume had purchased in souvenir shops. The other case, crammed with highly sensitive material classified as high as "cosmic," the highest NATO classification reserved mostly for wartime nuclear contingency plans, had already been stowed in the trunk of Guillaume's car. The correspondence file contained a top secret letter from President Richard M. Nixon detailing serious differences in Franco-U.S. relations.

On arrival at the hotel in Halmstad, Guillaume went to the hotel bar, where he met the East Berlin case officer and slipped him the key to his room. The officer went to Guillaume's room, photographed the documents, and within an hour was on his way home. The next day the Guillaumes continued their return trip to the West German capital. No one took any notice when Guillaume arrived at the chancellery with the attaché case, since he had carried it often in the past. He took it to his office and then asked his secretary to bring him the case the security officer had given her to lock in the safe. After a while he took the documents to Chancellor Brandt's office, one floor below his own. The switch had been the epitome of simplicity. It was the master spy's grand finale.

Caught!

Surveillance of Guillaume continued whenever he left the chancellery building throughout 1973, with no concrete results. Although Guillaume's behavior had become increasingly suspicious, he was not yet being watched inside the workplace. One month into the new year, the interior minister summoned Nollau, the head of the Office for the Protection of the Constitution, and demanded a decision on the Guillaume case.[20] Nollau, whose agency did not have arrest powers, submitted on March 1 a final report with facts so tenuous that Federal Prosecutor General Siegfried Buback declined to seek an arrest warrant.[21] But Buback ordered that the case and all information concerning it be turned over to the BKA. As the government's law-enforcement arm, the BKA was subject to stringent supervision and direction by both the interior minister and the prosecutor general. The criminal investigators and the counterspies collaborated in watching Guillaume, particularly when the spy took another brief vacation in southern France in April. Again, tight observation revealed nothing. When the Guillaumes returned home, criminal police officials became worried that the spy might have detected the surveillance and might try to escape to East Germany. They persuaded Prosecutor General Buback to ask the federal court to issue arrest warrants for both Günter Guillaume and his wife Christel.

At 6:32 A.M. on April 24, 1974, four BKA detectives went to the spy's apartment. His eighteen-year-old son Pierre answered the knock on the door, thinking it was the bakery delivering fresh breakfast rolls. Instead he faced four criminal police officials with the arrest warrants. His father had just finished shaving and was still in the bathroom. When Guillaume was told he was under arrest on espionage charges, he blurted out: "I am an officer of the National People's Army of the DDR and a member of the Ministry for State Security. I beseech you to respect my honor as an officer."[22] The arresting officers were relieved by the contemporaneous confession, for until then, they had been acting on circumstantial evidence. A search of the apartment turned up the microdot camera and a camera disguised as a wristwatch. Guillaume and his wife were led away in handcuffs, leaving behind a son who had known nothing about his parents' espionage activities nor that his father held the rank of a Stasi captain.

Falling Stars

Later that morning Chancellor Brandt returned to Bonn from a meeting in Cairo with Egypt's President Anwar Sadat. Waiting at the airport was Interior Minister Genscher with news of the arrest, which was already sweeping the capital like a firestorm. Chancellery officials attempted to downplay Guillaume's importance until journalists confronted them with a directory showing that Guillaume was one of the sixty-one most important aides out of a staff of 279. Former Chancellery Minister Ehmke, who had bungled the questioning of Guillaume four years earlier and was now postal and telecommunications minister, refused to meet with reporters. The Guillaume spy case was the most damaging political scandal in West Germany's postwar history.

The scandal occupied the front pages of newspapers for weeks. Each day produced headlines with new revelations, including lurid stories about Guillaume acting as a pimp for the chancellor. It had been rumored for years that Brandt frequently stepped out on his wife. He was also said to have been more than a social drinker, which earned him the nickname "Weinbrand Willy" (Brandy Willy) during his tenure as mayor of West Berlin. The scandal could not have come at a worse time for Brandt. The winner of the Nobel Peace Prize had been under fire for some time for leadership failures in domestic affairs. In March, his party was soundly defeated in local elections in Hamburg, traditionally a socialist stronghold. Coincidentally, another Western government leader was under siege as well. Across the Atlantic, Richard M. Nixon was battling to hang onto the U.S. presidency as the Watergate affair assumed ever greater dimensions.

On May 6, 1974, Willy Brandt resigned as chancellor of West Germany. In a statement that was televised nationwide, he said he was resigning "out of respect for the unwritten rules of democracy and also to prevent my political and personal integrity from being destroyed." This was clearly a reference to the rumors that Guillaume had threatened to reveal spicy details of Brandt's private life if he were not released and allowed to return to East Germany. Referring to reports alleging that he was being blackmailed all along by his former aide, the chancellor said: "Whatever may yet be written about it, it is and remains grotesque to think a German federal chancellor would be subject to blackmail. In any event, I am not." Brandt was replaced on May 16 by Helmut Schmidt, also a member of the Social Democratic Party.

Nineteen months after Brandt's resignation, on December 15, 1975, Günter Guillaume was found guilty of high treason and sentenced to thirteen years in prison. His wife Christel was given an eight-year term for treason and complicity in espionage. Before pronouncing the sentences, Presiding Judge Hermann Josef Müller of the provincial high court in Düsseldorf said the mild-mannered espionage agent had "endangered the entire Western defense alliance." The judge confirmed that Guillaume had passed to his East Berlin control top secret letters to Brandt from President Nixon, one of which described a meeting with French Foreign Minister Michel Jobert. After the sentencing, government spokesman Klaus Bölling said the Guillaumes would not be exchanged for Western spies held in East German prisons. However, in October 1981, Guillaume was freed in exchange for eight West German spies who had been sentenced to long prison terms. His wife had been exchanged seven months earlier for six persons and was reunited with her son and mother, who had resettled in East Berlin shortly after the trial.

Heroes' Welcome

Lieutenant General Markus Wolf, head of the Stasi's foreign espionage directorate, embraced his returning spy warmly when Guillaume reported to him at East Berlin's Stasi headquarters. "Welcome home, Günter," Wolf said, smiling broadly. Stasi chief Mielke presented Christel Guillaume with a bouquet of red roses. This scene was filmed for posterity, but the public did not see it until the communist regime collapsed in 1990: The film had been locked away in the Stasi's secret archives.

The Guillaumes were accorded the highest honors. Günter was promoted to Lieutenant Colonel by Stasi Minister Mielke. Erich Honecker, party secretary-general and head of state, awarded the spy and his wife East Germany's highest decoration, the Order of Karl Marx. They were assigned a state-owned villa on a quarter acre abutting a scenic lake northeast of Berlin. The communist regime made sure that their show-and-tell "reconnoiterers for peace," as Markus Wolf called his spies, were well provided for. Guillaume's bank account, into which the Stasi had been paying his captain's pay of 1,425 East marks plus hardship bonus of 250 marks every month since June 1956, had burgeoned to well over 500,000 marks, not counting dividends.[23] For a man who had never attended high school, Guillaume had done well.

Christel Guillaume would not enjoy the new riches for long. Shortly after arriving back in East Berlin, her husband, then fifty-four years old, divorced her and married a nurse twenty years his junior. Until his retirement in 1989, Guillaume lectured three times a week at the Stasi espionage school. His son, who had spent his developing years in West Germany, never could come to terms with life under communism. In February 1988, Pierre, then thirty-one and married with two small boys, officially requested an exit visa.[24] His father called him a traitor, and the Stasi placed him under surveillance as they would have any other "enemy of the people." Stasi officers also pressured him to remain—first with threats and later with promises of material rewards, good schools for his children, and the possibility of travel abroad. Pierre remained adamant, and in March the family was allowed to leave for West Germany, where they live under a new identity.

In 1993 Günter Guillaume was summoned again to the very courtroom where he had stood trial eighteen years earlier. This time he was called as a witness in the trial of his old boss, Markus Wolf, who stood accused of treason. This time Guillaume answered questions about his spy career with relish. He described in detail the caper with the two attaché cases in Norway, about which he had been silent at his own trial. Two years later, this communist spy who had brought down a German chancellor died of heart disease and a stroke.

THE SPYING COUNTERSPY

Klaus Kuron was popular with his subordinates and superiors at the Office for the Protection of the Constitution (BfV).[25] He had joined its headquarters in Cologne in 1962, after a stint in West Germany's federal border police. His devotion to the job and his intelligence—though he had never attended high school—earned him numerous promotions until he became a section chief in the Fourth Department, the counterespionage arm of the BfV. His section specifically dealt with "countermen" (CMs). These were agents who started out as spies for the Stasi but were "turned" to work for the BfV. It was one of the most sensitive positions in the counterspy agency, with access to its innermost secrets.

Over the years Kuron earned the accolades of his BfV superiors, but his salary was stagnating. He had reached a civil service rung that paid him a net of DM4,000 (about US$1,770) a month. It was enough to make payments on a modest house and to take occasional vacation trips to the Alps or Spain with his wife Agnes and four sons. Kuron's lack of formal education barred him from promotion to the senior civil service ranks without attending a special government academy. He was doing his job so well, however, that his superiors felt they could not spare him for an academy course. He became increasingly frustrated, especially because he felt that less intelligent and less industrious colleagues kept getting the promotions he coveted.

Kuron's frustration and greed prompted him in fall 1981 to place a letter in the mailbox of the permanent representative of the DDR, as the East German quasi-diplomatic representative in Bonn was called.[26] The letter was an application for a new job, the counterespionage expert's first step toward committing treason. Kuron wrote that he was prepared to work for the Stasi, and if there was interest in his services, he should be so informed over the spy radio during its morning transmissions. He would be listening at 8 A.M. In the letter he included a banknote, the first five numbers of which were to be read at the start of the message. The remaining numbers would signify the date and place for a noon meeting. He named three possible *Treffpunkts*: Number one was the house where Mozart was born, in

Salzburg, Austria; two, the so-called theater jetty on the northern end of Lake Zurich in Switzerland; and three, the Mannekin Pis statue in downtown Brussels, Belgium.

Several days after depositing this "job application," Kuron heard the identifying number, followed by numbers setting a meeting for October 24 in front of the statue of a urinating little boy in Brussels. Kuron was on time, but his contact failed to show up. He was later told that a Stasi team, suspecting a trap, had watched the area and photographed him. What followed was, like so many happenings in espionage lore, bizarre. Kuron angrily telephoned Stasi headquarters, asking what had happened to his contact. The Stasi operator noted his call and hung up on him.

Contact was finally made in late June, in Austria, where Kuron betrayed the first of many Stasi agents whom his agency had turned into a double. He was rewarded with DM5,000 (about US$2,110) in cash and was assigned, appropriately, the code name *Stern* (Star). In October, Kuron and his wife traveled to Austria, where they met Colonel Gunther Nehls of the Stasi's foreign espionage department, in charge of counterintelligence. Nehls handed Kuron a diplomatic passport and drove the couple to Bratislava in Czechoslovakia. From there they were flown aboard a government plane to Dresden, East Germany. At a luxurious Stasi guest house they were met by spy chief Markus Wolf and several other high-ranking officers, and the bargaining began. Kuron demanded a onetime payment of DM150,000 (nearly US$62,000) and a salary of DM4,000 a month. Wolf agreed. In addition, Kuron was appointed a Stasi colonel and told that after fifteen years he would be able to retire at 60 percent of this "salary." Kuron made an additional demand: Agents he betrayed were not to be arrested at once, lest his superiors in Cologne began to suspect a mole in their midst. Wolf agreed that the agents would be quietly and carefully placed into positions in which they could no longer effectively spy.

The Ultimate Betrayal

Although the counterespionage agency did have a need-to-know rule, Kuron's popularity enabled him to obtain details on sensitive cases over coffee with colleagues in the cafeteria while exchanging professional experiences. He picked up internal gossip about counterspies who were alcoholics, had extramarital affairs, or were in debt. All these tidbits went to East Berlin for possible use in recruiting new agents. Sometimes Kuron would hand the information to couriers. Mostly, however, he used the telephone. Using an early laptop computer, he would encode the information and record it on a miniature tape recorder equipped with rubber cups that fit over a telephone

72558	18849	01262	49122	85787
12502	99790	12481	74253	88625
43122	22563	76052	31814	48322
67021	62236	85287	93075	74820
10006	29134	93444	49798	05118
43475	75456	71272	98984	15583
09486	51783	81350	58922	84646
51611	40026	77103	89422	32346
85229	18333	96750	74057	30742
61811	89735	53759	54185	42376
19025	92703	39524	49969	89905
37313	02650	50752	46441	54139
88771	90373	81352	08207	16589
41752	52312	15207	13525	98854
22291	70623	54190	03727	66644
94634	99880	97931	31939	05533
70070	41523	05848	49806	90813
38425	14888	31031	61024	60431
17699	38390	15411	90060	12015
40891	56664	78639	30709	22200
58098	70533	68411	96676	15779
84525	40076	60473	39295	73367
73988	50981	51352	74198	65790
40360	52568	54642	13968	55064

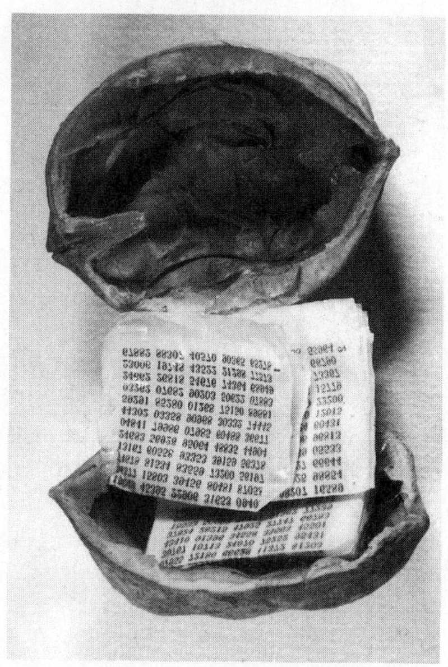

Stasi cipher pads hidden inside a walnut. Private photos.

mouthpiece. Then he would look for a public telephone booth,[27] sometimes roaming Cologne for hours until he found a suitable booth in an area where he could easily spot possible surveillance. Having found the most ideal place, Kuron would simply dial a special number in East Berlin and activate the recorder. The message was sent in seconds. The Berlin number was changed often, and knowing the electronic interception capabilities of the federal border police, Kuron rarely used the same telephone booth twice.

The Burned Doubles

Horst and Gerlinde Garau were double agents directed by Kuron. The couple were known in their East German town of Kalau as staunch members of the SED. Horst Garau was an education councillor, in charge of the local school district. His wife, also an educator, had close contacts to Minister of Education Margot Honecker, wife of the party secretary-general and head of state. The Garaus were also Stasi informants. Their membership in the highest elite of the regional party organization afforded them extraordinary privileges, such as frequent trips to West Germany. From time to time during such trips they functioned as espionage couriers. On one jaunt to West Germany in 1976, Horst Garau was contacted by a counterspy of Kuron's section. Offered a goodly sum of West marks, which compared to the unconvertible East marks was equal to payment in gold, Garau agreed to become a double agent. Operating under the code name *Schneiderwerkstatt* (Tailor Shop), the Garaus became valued agents, although exactly what they were able to convey to the West Germans was never revealed. When Kuron betrayed them to the Stasi, Markus Wolf kept his word. Instead of being arrested, they were simply deprived of their travel privileges.

Early in August 1985, Heribert Hellenbroich put the BfV on alert footing after Klaus Tiedge, a group leader in the counterespionage department, defected to East Berlin and the Stasi. Never before had a member of the BfV gone over to the communists. Tiedge was an obese alcoholic and gambler and deeply in debt even before his wife died in 1982. He decided defection was the only way out of the abyss. Hellenbroich knew that any amount of damage control would be useless. Tiedge knew too much.[28] "We knew that *Schneiderwerkstatt* would be over," Hellenbroich said later. Of course, the head of West German counterespionage did not know that the Garaus had already been betrayed by Kuron.

With Tiedge in East Berlin, the Stasi no longer feared that an arrest of the Garaus might endanger Kuron. On the morning of August 15, 1985, the couple was picked up and taken to a Stasi villa in Berlin for

Hans Joachim Tiedge, a high-ranking West German counterespionage official who defected to East Germany in August 1985 and betrayed his agency's innermost secrets. After reunification he fled to Russia, where he was granted asylum. Courtesy AP/Wide World.

interrogation. Gerlinde Garau would later describe the days of questioning as "psychological terror," as she was threatened with never seeing her husband again.[29] "I was scared to death. . . . I thought they would shoot us."

Four months later Frau Garau was released. Her husband was sentenced to life imprisonment at Bautzen II, the prison dubbed the "Yellow Misery." "I was allowed to see my husband every other month," Gerlinde Garau recalled in a 1992 interview with *Quick* magazine. "He deteriorated more and more, spoke as if in a trance, and was hardly able to concentrate. When he shook my hand, he seemed totally without strength."

In a letter dated July 6, 1988, Garau had written to his wife: "Don't be sad, be confident. Someday we will be together again. I will see it through."[30] Apparently he had been hoping that he would be exchanged for East German spies jailed in the West. Six days later Gerlinde Garau was summoned to the military prosecutor, who reported tersely and without emotion that her husband had committed suicide. The official version was that he had hanged himself with a blanket on a bedpost in his cell. The absence of a death certificate or medical examiner's report made Gerlinde Garau suspicious. She refused to believe the suicide story, and demanded to see the body, which had been taken to a judicial medical facility in Dresden. Her husband's body was covered with a white sheet, which she pulled aside, despite attempts by a Stasi officer to stop her. "I saw head wounds and bloody hair, but no signs of strangulation on the neck," she told *Quick*'s reporter.

The Doctoral Thesis

While Kuron continued betraying his agents, Tiedge was put on a stringent diet by the Stasi and spent some time in a hospital, drying out.[31] Then the Stasi persuaded him to write a dissertation, which would "earn" him a doctorate of law from East Berlin's Humboldt University. The "dissertation," entitled "The Counterintelligence Task of the Office for the Protection of the Constitution of the Federal Republic of Germany," was in reality nothing more than a compilation of what Tiedge had told his Stasi interrogators.[32] Classified as "secret," Tiedge's 245 pages exposed all of the counterespionage methods employed by the BfV, including the organization's electronic surveillance operations.[33]

The communist regime began to crumble in November 1989. Three months later, new elections wiped out the old guard. The Stasi told both Kuron and Tiedge that they could seek refuge in the Soviet Union. Tiedge, who had since married a Stasi secretary, accepted. The East German espionage service always took good care of their spies, and despite the deplorable financial condition of the country, continued its generosity. Tiedge received "severance" pay of DM150,000 (US$93,167.70) and was flown to Moscow aboard a Soviet military plane.

A clandestine meeting with a KGB officer was arranged for Kuron beneath a railroad bridge in Berlin. The contact took Kuron and his wife to the KGB compound in the East Berlin suburb of Karlshorst. Greedy to the last, Kuron accepted DM10,000 (US$6,211), then said he would need time to decide, and returned to West Germany by train, leaving his wife behind in Cologne. During the trip, Kuron hatched a plan to salvage his career. He checked into a hotel in Hannover and called BfV headquarters, saying that he had made a KGB contact and that he needed to meet with BfV President Gerhard Boeden immediately upon his return to Cologne that next day. What he had in mind was to come clean and request to be sent to Moscow and work for the Soviets as a double agent.[34] But Boeden, a former high-ranking police detective, heeded his intuition and immediately informed the BKA, requesting that a team be sent to the Hannover hotel at once to detain Kuron. Realizing there was only way he would be spared a possible life sentence, Kuron confessed.

Klaus Kuron, section chief of West Germany's counterespionage agency, who was convicted in 1992 of spying for East Germany and sentenced to twelve years in prison. Kuron volunteered to spy for the Stasi in 1982 and gave himself up when the East German regime fell in 1990. The information he divulged to the Stasi resulted in dozens of arrests of West German agents and in at least one death. Courtesy AP/Wide World.

The Trial

Facing a possible life sentence on a charge of aggravated treason, Kuron went to trial before the high provincial court in Düsseldorf on January 8, 1992. The presiding judge was Klaus Wagner, a highly experienced jurist who had tried more than a hundred espionage cases. During questioning by Judge Wagner and Senior Federal Prosecutor Ekkehard Schulz, Kuron readily described in detail how he had betrayed the double agents who were his charges. The court heard how Kuron and one of his double agents had traveled to Argentina. There they searched cemeteries for the personal data of deceased German immigrants, for use in creating new identities. What Kuron did not reveal was that he also took a trip to Mexico with the deputy chief of the HVA's counterintelligence division at the time—Karl Grossmann—on an identical mission.[35]

The traitor's case officers, former Colonel Gunther Nehls and Major Stefan Engelmann, also were called to testify, and both talked freely. At the time, both men were facing indictment for espionage, perhaps even treason, and may have felt that their cooperation would stand them in good stead in a future trial.[36] When Nehls entered the courtroom, he approached his former agent, shook his hand, and said, "I cannot change anything about your situation."

Kuron's testimony left no doubt that his motive for committing treason was unmitigated greed. The court learned that he had collected a total of DM680,000 (US$422,360, at the 1990 exchange rate) in cash. In addition, the Stasi bought him a vacation bungalow in Spain. On February 7, 1992, Kuron was sentenced to twelve years in prison. In pronouncing sentence, the judge said that Kuron had largely destroyed the counterespionage operations of his department. Whatever money he had left and all his properties were to be confiscated. Kuron told the court he had spent all of the money, partly on the education of his sons. It was suspected, however, that the bulk of the cash was stashed in a secret Swiss bank account.

No Remorse

Georg Mascolo and Georg Bönisch, top reporters for the German news magazine *Der Spiegel,* interviewed Tiedge in Moscow in December 1993. Tiedge said he was living well as a pensioner and that he worked occasionally as a legal consultant to Russian firms doing business in Germany. Blaming his treachery on his superiors for not having rescued him when he was down and out, Tiedge said defection was the only solution: "I lacked the courage to commit suicide." He also blamed security officials for their sloppiness in conducting the obligatory background checks every five years. He had worked sixteen years without his security dossier being updated as was required to retain clearance. Asked by *Spiegel*'s reporter whether he viewed himself as a traitor, Tiedge arrogantly replied, "Of course I am a traitor." The statute of limitations for treason will run out in 2005, after which Tiedge still hopes to receive his German government pension of DM800 or 900 a month. He will be disappointed. Convicted federal officials and those who have evaded prosecution are not entitled to their civil service pensions. Instead, they are paid just enough from a welfare insurance fund to eke out a living and not fall through the social safety net.[37]

German law specifies that a convict may ask for probation after serving 50 percent of his sentence, including pretrial detention. Kuron applied but was rejected by the court. However, he was moved to a halfway house. On weekends he visited his wife. Kuron felt aggrieved that he had to associate with murderers and robbers. "Real riffraff, the scum of the earth.[38] For people like us, there should be special jails." He felt absolutely no remorse; but his wife, Agnes, whom Kuron told early on of his treachery, showed a trace of it. "I did not know the extent of his activities. I thought, What that man does is right. Today I think, If only I had offered more resistance."[39]

MOLES IN THE MAD

After the Berlin Wall was torn down, a number of Stasi officers held their fingers to the wind. What they felt was that the communist regime was not long for this world. They struck Faustian bargains with the very West German intelligence service they had once viewed as a creation of the devil. In rapid succession, dozens of Stasi moles serving in high places were dragged out of their holes.

Alas, one of the first and most dangerous spies to be exposed had already been dead for three years. In 1990 Colonel Joachim Krase, assigned to MAD, the German equivalent to the U.S. Army's Counterintelligence Corps, had been a spy for eighteen years.[40] His treachery was not restricted to delivering MAD agents into the hands of the Stasi's counterespionage operatives: Krase also provided the details of Poseidon missile sites, the top secret locations of U.S. tactical nuclear weapons in West Germany. Map coordinates of the sites enabled the Soviet to retarget their weapons, ensuring accuracy within 100 meters.[41]

A Wehrmacht lieutenant in World War II, Krase joined the new West German Bundeswehr as an armored officer in 1956 after eking out a living in menial jobs. He was thirty years old and married at that time. Two years later Krase, now a captain, was detailed to the MAD intelligence school at Bad Ems, and then to the Baltic seaport of Kiel as an investigations officer. Those who served with Krase remembered him as a friendly but reserved officer and a happy boozer during parties with fellow officers. Ideologically he seemed sympathetic to the social democrats and might have been an SPD member. His wife was a friendly type but not particularly attractive, and lacking in social graces. Fellow officers felt that Krase suffered because of his wife's shortcomings. His superiors valued his professional ability, and over time he gained a certain popularity because of his operational successes. Yet Krase apparently became frustrated when younger officers were promoted above him and he was declared ineligible to attend the general staff academy.

Operating out of Kiel, Krase took part in numerous operations along the border with East Germany during which he acquired detailed knowledge of patrol activities of both East and West German border police. In February 1968, the colonel appeared at the border, waving a letter at a communist patrol. It was at a spot where no antipersonnel mines had been planted because it was used to funnel Stasi agents to

West German Navy Captain Hans Cohancz, commander of a military counterespionage group, presents a door prize to Major Joachim Krase at a military ball in 1968—the year Krase began his espionage career for communist East Germany. After eighteen years of spying, Krase retired from Stasi service in 1987 as a colonel. He died a year later. Private photo.

the West. An East German border guard came to the fence and accepted the letter, which offered his services to the Stasi and suggested dates and places for a face-to-face meeting. Suspicious of an MAD colonel who offered to become a traitor, the Stasi did not respond at first. Eventually Krase was summoned to East Berlin for a meeting with Colonel Klaus Bothe of the First Chief Directorate, responsible for military and border security. Bothe reported the encounter to Stasi chief Mielke, who ordered that Major General Günther Kratsch, deputy head of the Second Chief Directorate take over personally. Kratsch invited Krase to a luxurious Stasi safe house on the Baltic island of Ummanz, where the MAD colonel's future secret work for the communists was programmed.

After that first meeting, Kratsch and Krase would meet three or four times a year at Wirchensee castle, where the Stasi trained Chilean and Palestinian guerrillas, and in various European cities such as Helsinki, Prague, Vienna, and Budapest. Besides travel expenses, Krase was paid DM5,000 (about US$2,700) after each meeting—a paltry sum, compared to what other spies were paid. Krase also sent encoded messages to East Berlin, directly to General Kratsch, over a special telephone that Kratsch had secured in a vault. The numbers were changed frequently. In brief, Krase employed the same technology used by Kuron and many others.

Kratsch was promoted to lieutenant general and chief of the Second Directorate in the early 1970s, after which his deputy, Major General Wolfgang Lohse, became an additional control officer. By then, Krase's wife had died of cancer. It is perhaps indicative of Krase's character that he completely neglected her grave and remarried almost immediately.

On his promotion to the rank of lieutenant colonel, Krase was named chief of the MAD office in Hamburg, thus becoming the primary liaison officer to all West German intelligence substations in that city and to the local CIA representative. He had easy access to the most sensitive information. He also was in a position to spy on the General Staff Academy as well as on the Military University, which were based in Hamburg.

With Krase's promotion to full colonel and chief of staff of the MAD, Lohse was assigned as his primary controller. In the meantime, the MAD had become a hotbed of internecine intrigues and internal scandals. This trend intensified with the appointment of Brigadier General Paul Albert Scherer, a member of the Social Democratic Party, as head of the military counterespionage service—a position to which West German Navy Captain Konrad Koch had aspired. But as they say in Bonn, Koch owned the wrong party book. He was a conservative Christian Democrat, and the Socialists were in power. Compared to Koch, an ace intelligence officer with years of experience, General Scherer was an utter dilettante. To get rid of his rival, Scherer transferred Koch to Kiel. Scherer's six-year tenure was characterized by numerous scandals. He illegally ordered the surveillance of Luftwaffe pilots. Without a court order, he had a listening device placed in the bedroom of a secretary to Defense Minister Georg Leber. For the amusement of colleagues in his Bonn office, Scherer played the taped exchange of passionate declarations of love between the woman and a married ministerial director of the Defense Ministry.

Navy Captain Koch found solace by plunging into a torrid affair with his secretary, described as a "full-blooded, buxom redhead with eyes that seemed to pierce through a man's suit and strip him naked." She accompanied the captain on weekend trips in his official Mercedes, and he charged their expenses to the government. When Koch's Bonn chief found out, he requested an independent investigation conducted by a defense ministry colonel. Koch vehemently termed the charges malicious slander and turned incriminating facts into misunderstandings. No action was taken against the captain. In fact, he was eventually transferred back to Bonn and became deputy chief of the MAD.

These incidents were fodder for the traitor Krase, whose Stasi employers were constantly searching for dirt with which to compromise officials and recruit them as spies. Former West German intelligence officials still cannot fathom why the defense ministry took no action to clean out the MAD. There were numerous indications of a possible mole within its ranks as counterintelligence operations against the East Germans became increasingly ineffective.

In fall 1978, with the Munich Oktoberfest in full swing, the 66th U.S. Army Military Intelligence Group sponsored a three-day joint conference with the German military counterespionage service and the Landesamt für Verfassungsschutz (LfV) of the province of North Rhine–Westphalia. U.S. intelligence officers revealed their top secret wartime contingency plans in minute detail. The proceedings were recorded, and a transcript was made available to all attendees. Because the Americans knew that Krase spoke no English, the presentation was translated and enhanced by graphics and photographs projected on a screen.

Count Hardenberg, head of the LfV in Düsseldorf, lectured on his methods and techniques of counterintelligence operations. The lecture was followed by a discussion period, during which there was a free exchange of ideas. Every detail of Count Hardenberg's operations was examined and tape recorded. A few months later, three of the count's agents were arrested in East Berlin and sentenced to several years in prison. Hardenberg suspected the MAD of sloppy security work. Since he was unable to produce any proof, the case was filed away.[42] When the agents were bought out of East German prisons in 1984 and returned to the West, they were intensely interrogated but were unable to provide clues as to what had led to their arrest.

Krase retired for health reasons in April 1985, but he kept on spying. While visiting MAD offices around the country, he took advantage of his comrades' loose tongues as they discussed ongoing operations and sought his advice. Meetings with his East German handlers continued until 1987, when he met for the last time with Major General Lohse in Salzburg, Austria. A year later Krase died of cancer at the age of 60. His burial was attended by high officials of the intelligence community, including the Bonn station chief of the CIA.

Krase's son Wolfgang was mystified when in July 1988, two months after the funeral, he received a package containing DM5,000 (US$2,793) and a cassette tape. He played the tape and was astonished to hear the voice of his father, saying that the money, along with an apartment he had bought for Wolfgang in Tübingen, were his legacy. His father also urged him to work for the East German secret service. The son had been unaware of his father's treachery. He gave the contents of the package to a family friend, Gerhard Boeden, former deputy chief of the Federal Criminal Police Agency, who had been promoted to lead the counterespionage office (BfV). Reaction was one of shock and consternation when the news reached officials at the chancellery, the defense and interior ministries, and the prosecutor general's office.[43] "It was quickly agreed to keep the scandal quiet, because luckily, the man had died in time," an intelligence official later told me. "From now on officialdom was ruled by the maxim: 'Don't touch anything: danger of explosion!'"[44] Although rumors about a top mole circulated throughout the West German capital, it was not until the collapse of the East German regime and the discovery of Stasi files that Krase's treachery became public. A close examination of the tape eventually showed that it had been spliced together from other tapes made of Krase's voice: Krase's Stasi handlers were thumbing their noses at the West Germans, deliberately exposing the treachery in order to create suspicion among the military's spy catchers.

In another case of MAD infiltration, Gisela Gieren, at age sixty-eight, was convicted of treason and sentenced to eight years' imprisonment in March 1995.[45] Her younger sister, forty-eight-year-old Dagmar Sdrenka, got off with four years and six months. Gieren and her husband Günther, who died in 1989, had been running a spy ring in Hannover for General Kratsch's domestic counterespionage directorate since 1964. Using phony CIA credentials produced by Stasi forgers, and with the persuasion of his wife, Günther Gieren recruited his sister-in-law Dagmar and told her to apply for a government job. On July 1, 1968, Dagmar began work as an administrative assistant for the Hannover office of the MAD. Like the MAD's Colonel Krase, she became a valuable operative for the communists—thinking all the while, however, that she was serving the Americans. From the position of typist she gradually advanced to the job of registrar of all classified material. In the latter post she succeeded in photographing countless top secret and "cosmic top secret" documents, the latter dealing with nuclear weapons and planning. She also betrayed the Poseidon Objekte in North Germany—air force units with nuclear capability, as well as Lance and Nike missile sites. Dagmar's sister Gisela delivered the material to case officer, Lieutenant Colonel Kurt Ulbrich. Because of the importance of the spy ring, it was closely controlled by General Kratsch and his deputy, General Lohse. Federal prosecutors termed the betrayal "espionage of the highest significance." Also belonging to the Gieren conspiracy was Ute Barth, a twenty-two-year-old secretary at the counterespionage office for Lower Saxony. She was put on probation for two years and fined DM30,000 (about US$18,700). At the age of twenty, while she was working as a typist for a military court, Sabine Gieren was likewise recruited by her spying mother Gisela. Sabine was given fifteen months' probation and was fined DM20,000 (about US$12,500).

The Gieren spy ring was paid DM360,000 altogether (about US$225,000). In addition, the Stasi put money into an East Berlin bank account as a retirement nest egg. There was about DM140,000 in that account when the regime collapsed. Gieren's case officer said he took out the money and handed it to a courier who was to deliver it to Gieren. No trace of the money was ever found.[46]

STASI AGENTS IN THE BND

West Germany's Bundesnachrichtendienst (BND), the federal intelligence service, severely tightened its personnel security procedures in the 1950s following the exposure of a number of moles working for the KGB. But security checks were not sufficiently thorough to withstand the relentless efforts by the Stasi's Hauptverwaltung Aufklärung (HVA) to place its spies inside the BND compound in Pullach, near Munich. The polygraph (lie detector), a useful though not infallible tool for detecting spies, was disdainfully rejected as an "unreliable American gadget." But few other tools were available to ascertain trustworthiness. Thus, apart from revelations made by the occasional defector, the most dangerous moles would not be unearthed until East Germany collapsed.

In late summer 1990, a Stasi defector volunteered that a woman employee of the BND had been an agent since 1971 for the Fifth Section of HVA's Ninth Division for counterintelligence.[47] The defector described the mole as about forty years old, holding a doctoral degree, single, and the ward of a disabled child. A lengthy and thorough investigation revealed that the spy was Gabriele Gast. Gast had joined the intelligence service in 1973, two years after she graduated from Aachen University with a Ph.D. in political science. At the moment she was on vacation, mountain climbing in the Swiss Alps.

Gast's private telephone was tapped, and when she returned home she was placed under constant surveillance.[48] On September 29 she received a telephone call from a man who did not identify himself but asked that she meet him, without mentioning where. The next morning she drove onto the autobahn and headed for Austria. Authorities had to act quickly, because once in Austria, Gast would be unreachable: The Austrian government did not permit the extradition of persons accused of offenses with political overtones. Normally travelers were not required to show identification at customs posts. However, when Gast stopped at the West German customs post on the Austrian border, she was asked to present her identification. When she did, she was promptly arrested.

Gast's career as an East German spy had its genesis in a 1968 visit to Karl-Marx-Stadt, East Germany (renamed Chemnitz after German reunification). She was working on her dissertation on "The Political Role of Women in the DDR," and her professor suggested she travel to East Germany for research. At Chemnitz she immersed herself in discussions with women unionists and female members of the Volkskammer, the communist version of parliament. After one such meeting she was approached by a man who expressed interest in her work. He introduced himself as Karl-Heinz Schmidt ("call me 'Karliszek,'") and invited her to accompany him on excursions to other cities. He was tactful, charming, a good dancer, and jovial. Gabriele, an attractive, slender brunette, was smitten by Karliszek, and before long they landed in bed together. She was twenty-five years old, he eight years older. What he did not reveal was that he was an OIBE, an officer on special deep cover assignment for the Stasi, and that his real name was Karl-Heinz Schneider.

The Romeo Ploy

Gabriele Gast had fallen for a typical "Romeo," as the Stasi called its agents whose assignment was to seduce lonely and vulnerable women and when they had them hooked, persuade them to work as spies. The Romeos were particularly active in the 1960s and 1970s. With millions of men killed in the war, there was a great shortage of eligible men for the lonely secretaries working in the Bonn ministries. It was a ruthless game that landed dozens of women in prison after they were unmasked as spies. Naturally, the Romeos escaped punishment.

Karliszek played his role well, waiting until Gabriele's third visit to Chemnitz before introducing her to his "friend" Gotthard Schiefer, one of the aliases used by Major Egon Lorenz. Another alias he used was Gotthard Schramm. Lorenz was chief of the Stasi's foreign espionage subdetachment in Chemnitz. He revealed Karliszek's real name to Gabriele and told her that he worked for the Stasi. The recruitment began. Gabriele's lover played on her emotions, saying that they could never see one another again if she didn't help him. They didn't want her to spy but only to talk a bit about her university and its people. She was given a forged West German passport to be used for future trips to the East and the code name Gisela. "It took me a while before realizing that at this point I had crossed the Rubicon," she would later

A camera so small that it fits inside a matchbox. Cameras like this one were used by Stasi espionage agents to photograph documents. Private photo.

tell the court. But love for a man won over love for country. She also claimed that she had undergone an ideological transformation. The more she traveled to the DDR, the more she said she believed the communist regime was not the warmongering cabal it was portrayed as in the West. Besides, her new friends in the East were not evil but nice, charming men. Gast had apparently become afflicted with what Judge Klaus Wagner called *Betriebsblindheit,* selective blindness: "It allowed her and so many others to shut their eyes to realities of socialism such as the uprising against the regime in 1953, the Berlin Wall, Hungary, and the brutal suppression of the Prague Spring."[49]

In 1970 Gabriele Gast made another trip to Chemnitz, this time to celebrate her "engagement" to Karliszek. In the meantime she had undergone a crash course in espionage communications, clandestine photography, and handling specially prepared pocketbooks and cosmetic items for use in secreting coded messages. From then on, every Tuesday evening she received Karliszek's encoded love notes over shortwave radio. After graduating in 1972, Gast was hired by the Institute for Security and International Affairs, a think tank financed by the conservative Christian Socialist Union, the Bavarian wing of the Christian Democratic Party. A year later she applied for a position with the Ministry of Foreign Affairs, after which she was approached with a job offer from the Bundesnachrichtendienst (BND). She accepted the offer, and using the invisible ink process she had been taught in Chemnitz, notified her Stasi lover by letter. Gast started her

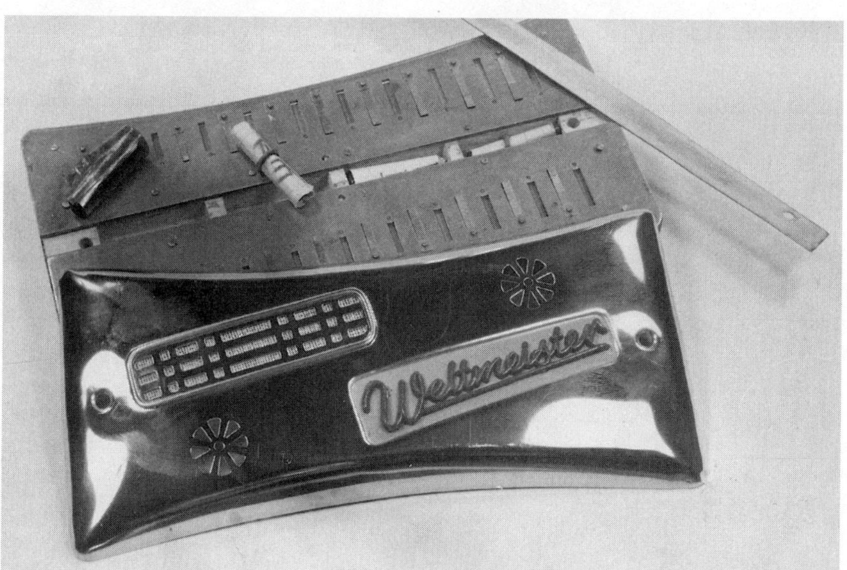

Cipher pads hidden inside a harmonica. Private photo.

new job on November 1, 1973. Like all BND employees, she was issued identification papers and a passport bearing a new name—she was now Gabriele Leinfelder. Her first assignment was to the BND's Soviet affairs department.

As Gast's offerings became more valuable, her spymasters decided to provide her with special couriers. An East German couple was infiltrated into West Germany via London and settled in Hagen, about forty-five miles northeast of Bonn. They brought with them two cans of a deodorant spray that had false bottoms for hiding film. If the bottoms were not unscrewed properly, a chemical would be released to destroy the film. Gast periodically met with the woman, who called herself Cordula Naumann, at hotel or restaurant rest rooms to exchange the cans. In the mid-1970s the courier couple was suddenly withdrawn to East Germany. The Stasi had learned that the Federal Criminal Police Agency had perfected a system of identifying enemy agents, referred to as *Rasterfahndung.* On a June morning in 1976, BKA detectives arrested more than thirty people in cities throughout West Germany for espionage. All had entered the country under assumed identities from East Germany or from a third country, posing as refugees. *Rasterfahndung* was merely a method of identifying spies or terrorists by establishing whether they fit certain typical profiles.

A Stasi agent's Minox camera, concealed in a beer can. Private photo.

False bottom in an instant coffee container, used by Stasi espionage couriers to transport exposed film and to hide cipher pads. Private photo.

Before the development of supercomputers, it was painstaking work requiring the efforts of hundreds of detectives and counterespionage officials to sift through and assemble the pieces of the puzzle. Coinciding with the withdrawal of Gast's couriers, Gast was instructed by radio to cease her activities for security reasons. Several months later she was reactivated.

Gast moved steadily up the career ladder. Her value to East German intelligence correspondingly increased to the point where spy chief Markus Wolf requested in 1975 that she meet him in a small resort town on Yugoslavia's Adriatic coast. She felt flattered that the top man wanted to see her. Gast told her BND colleagues she would be vacationing in Ireland; and in fact, she did fly to Dublin, where she spent a few days before going on to Rome. There she was met by Karliszek, and together they drove to Yugoslavia. Wolf was his charming self. Gast was impressed by his intellect. Wolf soon had her eating out of his hand as so many had done before. (Others who have had direct dealings with Wolf have described him variously as possessing the mingled qualities of a snake and a pious priest; as a *Halunke* [a scoundrel]; and as a *Charakterschwein* [a person with the character of a pig]—the latter being an insult to the pig.) Gast met Wolf again on two other occasions in East Germany, traveling on her West German passport to Sweden, then crossing the Baltic by ferry on an East German diplomatic passport. Wolf always lavishly entertained Gast and her lover, who had been promoted to the rank of major.

By the mid-1980s Gast had reached the grade of *Regierungsdirektorin,* which is roughly equivalent to the military rank of lieutenant colonel—a rank commanding a monthly salary of DM7,000 (about US$4,300). Using the alias Leinfelder, she traveled the world on official business. In Langley, Virginia, she conferred and exchanged information with CIA officials. In London she met with officers of the British Secret Intelligence Service (SIS), and in the Middle and Far East she visited other friendly services. Her experience made her a top expert of the BND. Finally she was handed an assignment that made her Wolf's treasure: Gast was given access to every piece of top secret information the BND was gathering worldwide. Her new job was preparing the daily intelligence digest for Chancellor Helmut Kohl. Markus Wolf, Stasi chief Erich Mielke, and the communist leadership were reading the chancellor's daily intelligence mail until the end of the German Democratic Republic.

In December 1961, Gast sat before Presiding Judge Ermin Briessman of the Bavarian High Court in Munich, answering questions freely though at times with a faint sob. She testified that she never accepted money, even paid her own expenses when traveling to meet her handlers. No evidence to the contrary was presented. This may have been a mitigating factor in sentencing, as Gast served only six years and nine months in prison.

Many other communist moles, like Gabriele Gast, operated for years inside the BND without being caught. Another case that subsequently came to light is that of Alfred Spuhler. Two years after entering the BND's service in 1968, the twenty-seven-year-old Spuhler decided that the portrayal of the Eastern bloc as militarily superior to the West was a myth and that therefore the intense rearming, especially of West Germany, was endangering peace.[50] He therefore sought contact with the West German Communist Party, whose ideological espousal of a fair and just socialist society was closer to his personal beliefs. During a visit to Berlin in 1972 he volunteered to spy for the Stasi in order to contribute toward establishing a military balance. Then he recruited his brother Ludwig, a technician at Munich's Max Planck Institute, Germany's eminent research center encompassing all scientific disciplines. Alfred stole the secrets, including reports from BND agents operating in the East, and brother Ludwig acted as courier. Ludwig would leave the material in dead drops, secret hiding places in southern Germany and Austria. Periodically he would meet with case officer Lieutenant Colonel Günther Böttcher at various sites in Greece, Yugoslavia, and Austria.

In 1989, the BND was tipped off, and placed the Spuhler brothers under surveillance. Counterspies observed a secret rendezvous in Greece, which led to Ludwig's arrest on circumstantial evidence. The same defector who led to the downfall of Gabriele Gast furnished the details that made both men confess. In November 1991, the same judge that sentenced Gast, Ermin Briessman, gave Alfred Spuhler ten years in prison and brother Ludwig five and a half. During the trial it was revealed that Alfred had been paid nearly DM280,000 (about US$175,000), and his brother about DM260,000 (about US$162,500). Alfred had been assigned the rank of a Stasi major and was awarded the East German Fatherland Order of Merit in silver and gold. Ludwig was given the same decoration in silver.

ROMEOS AND SECRETARIES

Markus Wolf's espionage directorate HVA began recruiting good-looking single men throughout East Germany in the mid-1960s. Following intensive training at the HVA's intelligence school, they became Wolf's stable of Romeos. Some were sent under phony identities to the West German capital of Bonn. Others roamed southern European vacation spots that the Stasi knew were favorites of single West German women seeking sunshine and fun. The Romeos' assignment was to ferret out and woo love-starved secretaries employed by the federal government and political parties. Once these women had fallen head over heels in love and having been promised marriage, the men revealed themselves as East German agents and pleaded for help in their espionage assignments, claiming they would otherwise have to return home. How many of the hapless women fell for it may never be known; but in the ten years prior to 1980, fifteen were uncovered by counterspies, five of them in 1979 alone. Günther Buch of the Institute for All-German Affairs believes that at least 50 women spied for East Germany. Some were able to escape to East Germany, others were sent to prison for as many as five years.[51]

Dagmar Kahlig-Scheffler was thirty-one years old in 1977 when she was sentenced to four years and three months in prison on charges of espionage. The attractive brunette had worked as a secretary in the chancellery of Helmut Schmidt since 1975. She was roped into spying for East Germany in 1973, when she vacationed at Varna on Bulgaria's Black Sea coast, where she was approached by a handsome young man who showered her with compliments. He introduced himself as Herbert Schröter, an engineer from Berlin. Recently divorced, Dagmar was delighted to meet such an attractive fellow German. She fell for him hard, and by the time she learned that her lover lived in East Berlin, she no longer cared that it was the communist part of the city. "With Herbert I had my first orgasm," she would later tell the court. Her recruitment was routine for the HVA. At the time, Kahlig-Scheffler worked for Bonn University.

Over the following year, she visited Schröter and took courses in espionage. She was instructed to take English lessons and apply for a chancellery job. A ten-month background check turned up nothing derogatory, no debts and no relatives behind the Iron Curtain. Dagmar got the job in the chancellery's European department, where she spied industriously, photographing and copying the chancellor's secret papers. The latter included correspondence between Helmut Schmidt and U.S. President Jimmy Carter.[52] A year later she went to East Berlin and was married to Herbert Schröter. She would not know until her arrest that Schröter was already married and that her marriage ceremony was a diabolical fake engineered by Markus Wolf and his Stasi cohorts. Another thing she did not know was that Schröter was also the lover of Gerda Ostenrieder, a secretary in the Ministry of Foreign Affairs who betrayed foreign policy secrets. Schröter had turned Ostenrieder's head in Paris, where she was studying French.

The Nun and the Daily Communicant

Certainly one of the most egregious and humanly devastating operations that was ever conducted by a Stasi Romeo involved a former nun of the Order of the Sacred Heart who had served as a missionary in Brazil from 1957 to 1965. Edith Drexler returned to West Germany and quit the Order to study at Munich University and later went to Rostock in East Germany, where she was recruited for the Stasi by a Romeo. The thirty-five-year-old, wooed with bouquets of red roses, fell in love, and succumbing to the old line "You have to help me in my work or I will have to pay dearly," she agreed to become a spy. Back in West Germany, Drexler joined a scientific institute that had a consulting contract with the Ministry for Research and Technology, advising on policy toward the DDR and Eastern Europe. She was apparently a highly regarded source, since the Stasi assigned a pair of deep cover couriers living in West Germany specifically to handle her. From time to time Drexler would see her lover on clandestine trips to East Germany because he told her he was not allowed to visit the West. Naively, she believed him until her arrest in 1991. She never saw him again. Although charges had already been filed against Edith Drexler, Chief Prosecutor Manfred Kieling of Koblenz displayed a magnificent sense of compassion. The German code of criminal procedures provides that a prosecutor may petition the court that he be allowed to withdraw charges filed. Pleading that the case was a "bagatelle," Kieling asked to be allowed to withdraw the charge on condition that Drexler contribute DM10,000 (about US$6,250) to charity. Presiding Judge Joachim Vonnahme agreed.

The Danish Lover

An equally dastardly operation lured Margarethe Lubig and her sister Marianne Lenzkow into the Stasi's net. It began in 1960 when Anita Brünger, a nightclub barmaid in Bonn, invited Lenzkow to celebrate her engagement in Berlin, where she might also meet a man. The trip would be paid for by Brünger's fiancé Eric Michaelson, a singer at the nightclub. The Danish-born Michaelson was an East German spy aptly code-named Singer, and the barmaid worked with him as a recruiter and courier. Lenzkow, a divorced thirty-one-year-old teletype operator for the Interior Ministry, which supervised the counterespionage agency, was ready for a fling, and she readily accepted. In Berlin, Michaelson introduced Lenzkow to "Kalle" Schramm and Kai Petersen, both attractive men claiming to be members of the Danish Military Mission. In reality, the men were officers of the HVA. In fact, Schramm was the same man who played a decisive role in the recruitment of Gabriele Gast of the Federal Intelligence Service (BND). Petersen had been an East German actor named Roland Gandt when he was recruited by Schramm as a Romeo. His code name was Venske.

Following a few more flings in Berlin with Schramm, Lenzkow was invited to spend a weekend at the "guest house of the Danish Mission" in Plauen, near Chemnitz. Her girlfriend, Anita Brünger, was now out of the picture. At the Stasi's rustic Plauen safe house, where BND spy Gast had also spent time with her lover, Schramm and Gandt asked the woman to gather information for them. They explained that Denmark was obliged to gather information secretly because their country was a relatively small one and was not being taken seriously by its NATO partners.[53] Naive beyond belief, Marianne Lenzkow signed a pledge to work for the "Danish Intelligence Service" and began delivering secret teletype messages, including those listing wanted espionage agents.[54] Her couriers were the barmaid and the singer.

In 1961, Marianne's sister Margarethe Lubig, twenty-five years old and unsuccessful in finding a man, spoke of her loneliness and of how she wished she would meet a man. Marianne sent a message to Schramm proposing that Gandt meet her and her sister in Vienna. Knowing that Lubig worked as a foreign-language secretary for the Department of Defense, the Stasi spymaster quickly agreed, for Lubig had been on his list of targets all along. In the Austrian capital, the suave Gandt was a generous host, and Lubig, having found the love of her life, was exultant. Before the sisters left Vienna a week later, Magarethe had agreed to spy for Denmark. Her Stasi code name was Rose. Lubig met Gandt in Vienna three more times. During the last rendezvous, Margarethe lost her virginity and the couple celebrated their engagement.[55] Gandt gave her an expensive diamond ring bought with Stasi funds.[56] She reciprocated with copies of secret military documents. Later she occasionally received an expensive piece of jewelry, and once, DM5,000; but authorities never determined her total compensation for espionage.[57]

Between 1963 and her early retirement in 1989, Lubig served at the office of the West German military representative at NATO headquarters, in Fontainebleau, outside Paris, and later for the military attaché in Rome. In those positions she was able to copy or photograph sensitive documents relating to defense policy and armament production planning. During a winter vacation at Arosa, Switzerland, Lubig—a deeply religious, daily communicant—told her fiancé she wanted to clear her conscience. She said she wished to confess her sins to a priest, and if necessary, to her superiors.[58] Alarmed to the danger this represented, Gandt suggested they travel to Copenhagen, where she could make the confession and meet his "chief" for a discussion. Lubig agreed. Gandt alerted his control officer Schramm, who concocted an elaborate and diabolical plan.

The following summer Lubig went on leave for several weeks and traveled to Denmark to learn some Danish and prepare herself for the confession. Meantime, the Stasi had rented two houses outside the

Danish capital. One was the ostensible residence of Gandt's phony superior. The other was represented to Lubig as the home of Gandt's "mother," where they would stay. The bogus mother was an East German communist and Stasi informant living in Sweden. On Lubig's arrival, Gandt introduced her to his superior, a "general." Playing that role was a Danish Communist Party member of German descent. Afterward Gandt took Lubig to a nearby Catholic church to meet the German-speaking "priest," who was actually Stasi informant Karl-Heinz Hüppe, working for spymaster Egon Lorenz. The woman confessed her espionage involvement, but Hüppe was successful in soothing her. He told her, "On the one hand the actions cannot be condoned, but on the other hand they are not reprehensible."[59] The next day Lubig returned to NATO headquarters and continued to spy.

The game continued until early 1990, when Heinz Busch, a colonel in charge of military analysis for the East German foreign intelligence directorate, defected after Stasi Major General Ralf-Peter Devaux threatened him with bodily harm.[60] Busch, a sensitive intellectual never really at ease in his job, was appointed by the new espionage chief Werner Grossmann to represent him at the so-called roundtable talks. These talks between government officials and dissidents (who had the upper hand after the fall of the Berlin Wall) were aimed at dissolving the Ministry for State Security. The assignment delegated to the good-natured and friendly Busch was to plead that those who had spied for East Germany were doing so in the interest of peace and that it was now imperative to protect them from arrest. Busch soon realized, however, that he was a pawn of Grossmann and Wolf. The latter had retired in 1987 but still wielded influence behind the scenes. Both wanted to keep the foreign espionage service intact as an instrument for a new "socialist government with a democratic face." When Busch realized that the DDR was doomed, he switched sides and became one of the most valuable assets of the BND. He talked about working with highly secret documents pilfered by spies. Though he knew only the code names of the agents, Busch deduced from the kind of information they supplied where they might be located. Investigators were able to assemble the puzzle, and numerous arrests followed, including that of Magarethe Lubig, who immediately confessed. Because of her willingness to tell all and the compassion of Judge Ina Obst-Öllers of the Düsseldorf court, Lubig got off lightly. Because she was sixty years old, she was given an eighteen-month suspended sentence. Her sister Marianne Lenzkow died before the trial was held. Spymaster Lorenz died in 1989.

Romeos and Romiettes

East German espionage services also used homosexual Romeos to entice gay officials into compromising situations for which they were later blackmailed into committing espionage. For this reason authorities have always been extremely reluctant to grant security clearances to known homosexuals. Egon Streffer, a civil servant in the Ministry of Defense, was recruited by his friend Dieter Poppe, who was a deep cover agent for East German military intelligence. Streffer spied from 1969 until shortly before he died in 1989, at the age of forty-three. He gave Poppe top secret minutes of ministerial meetings and defense plans. Before his death he was deputy chief of the ministry's secret archives. Streffer was a well-liked official—so much so, that Defense Minister Gerhard Stoltenberg eulogized him in a newspaper obituary as a "loyal and popular colleague."[61] Recruiter Poppe, who had volunteered his services to communist military intelligence in 1966, was arrested in 1990 after a defector gave him up. He had collected at least DM110,000 (about US$68,750) from his spymasters.[62] Convicted of aggravated espionage in December 1991, Poppe was sentenced to six years in prison.

Other variations on the Romeo ploy were used with equal effect: Many East Berlin prostitutes were recruited by the Stasi to lure officials and businessmen into situations for which they could be blackmailed. These women were regulars at the bars of East Berlin's luxury hotels. Interestingly, however, I found only one instance in which a man, a diplomat, had succumbed to a latter-day Mata Hari.

Heinrich Lummer, a popular Christian Democratic Party politician formerly responsible for interior affairs in West Berlin's senate, was personally targeted by spy chief Markus Wolf. Using a sexy Stasi "swallow" named Susanne Rau to entice Lummer into an East Berlin hotel bed, Wolf's officer took a series of photographs showing Lummer naked on top of the woman. When Stasi officers showed the pictures to Lummer and tried to blackmail him, the politician told them to get lost, and informed counterespionage authorities. An American journalist found himself in a similar situation. When he returned to his hotel room one evening, he found two strangers in his room. Asked what they were doing there, one of the men pointed to the bed, on which a dozen eight-by-ten-inch photos were spread out, showing the journalist having intercourse with a woman who was obviously a "swallow." Sensing immediately what was in the offing, the journalist kept his wits about him. Smiling, he pointed a finger at each photograph and said: "Wunderbar! . . . I'll take two of this one, one of this one . . . ". The Stasi men left in a hurry, leaving the pictures behind.[63]

SPYING POLITICIANS

The Stasi was able to place a number of spies in the federal chancellery. Few, however, were as devastatingly effective as Günter Guillaume. For the most part, they were secretaries with limited access to the West German leader's secrets. At least two were able to flee to East Germany before they could be arrested. There was also no shortage of diplomats and politicians of all parties who were willing to betray their country. Most of the latter group, however, belonged to the Social Democrats—a party that espoused an ideology close to that of the communists.

Federal criminal investigators searched three years to find a spy code-named Töpfer, whom they suspected was a highly placed official at the chancellery. In 1993, researchers for the federal prosecutor general's office found a "clear" name (a real name as opposed to a pseudonym) in Stasi documents that pointed to material delivered to the Stasi by Töpfer. During an unrelated investigation of a diplomat, Federal Prosecutor Joachim Lampe, who had tried hundreds of espionage cases, casually dropped the name "Töpfer."[64] The diplomat was an espionage suspect because his name had shown up in a computer search for individuals who had traveled to Vienna when spy chief Markus Wolf also was known to have been there. After the interrogation session, the diplomat was asked to come to the Foreign Office. There a former Stasi officer who had been Töpfer's case officer (he did not know the spy's true name) and who was willing to come clean was asked whether the diplomat was his former charge. He said he had never met the man. The former Stasi officer then casually asked the diplomat where he would spend the next few days. He answered, "At my friend Knut Gröndahl's house." Gröndahl had been under suspicion, but detectives had found no concrete evidence against him. Now he was detained for questioning, during which the Stasi officer made a positive identification.

Gröndahl's arrest sent another shock wave through Bonn's bureaucracy and the Social Democratic Party. The spy was a close collaborator of SPD Vice Chairman Wolfgang Thierse. Gröndahl, a socialist ideologue, was recruited by the Stasi while studying law in the mid-1960s, picked specifically as a long-range agent to infiltrate the government. He complied, and embarked on a fast career track, first joining the Ministry for All-German Affairs, which dealt with the situation in communist East Germany. There he was able to betray ministry informants who furnished political and economic information as well as to provide top secret policy documents. For two years, from 1986 to 1988, Gröndahl served as political adviser in the office of West Germany's permanent representative to the DDR in East Berlin, a quasi-diplomatic post. This position made him privy to all political correspondence with and policies toward East Germany emanating from Chancellor Helmut Kohl's office. That was why counterspies thought the mole had to be located there. Gröndahl's moral corruptness and unbelievable hubris is exemplified by the love affair he had with the wife of a colleague. The colleague found out and told the head of the East Berlin office, who confronted Gröndahl, telling him he would be returned to Bonn for fear that he could be blackmailed by East German spy recruiters. Gröndahl admitted the affair and agreed that he had become a candidate for blackmail.[65]

During his trial Gröndahl admitted that he had used the name of his diplomat friend when he traveled to meet HVA General Wolf. He had other covert meetings in Copenhagen, Paris, Venice, and Florence. During his last meeting with Wolf's successor, General Werner Grossmann, in East Berlin in spring 1990, he was assured that all documents showing his activities had been destroyed; but Grossmann had not counted on a defector from his ranks. Gröndahl never was paid for his espionage services except for reimbursement of travel expenses, and from time to time, expensive gifts. Gröndahl received a prison sentence of three and a half years, which a higher court reduced to three years.

Karl Wienand, the former manager of the Social Democratic Party (SPD) parliamentary faction, was sentenced in June 1996 to two and a half years in prison and fined DM1 million (about US$750,000). The sixty-nine-year-old politician and confidant of SPD leaders including Chancellors Willy Brandt and Helmut Schmidt had spied for the East Germans for thirteen years. Wienand vehemently denied the charges, but the evidence was overwhelming. Former Stasi Colonel Alfred Voolkol, confronted with a file found in the Stasi archive, acknowledged that he was the contact for Wienand, whose code name was *Streit.* The indictment said Wienand received DM10,000 per month (about US$5,000) from the Stasi.

Bodo Thomas, a member of West Berlin's city parliament and of the mayor's cabinet, hanged himself in May 1995, before he could be tried as a spy for the communists. A social democrat who was fond of elegant suits, fine cigars, and his collection of tin soldiers, Thomas had been accused of working for the Stasi for twenty-six years.

William Borm, former liberal Free Democratic Party (FDP) parliamentarian and the party's chairman emeritus, who died in 1987 at the age of ninety-two, had spied for the East Germans since at least 1973. Borm had served nine years in an East German prison on charges of warmongering and spreading hatred against the regime, a typical charge against dissidents. He had been arrested in 1950 while driving through East Germany and was apparently brainwashed in prison. Borm was deputy chairman of the FDP at the time. After his imprisonment, he settled in Bonn, became a member of parliament, and served on committees for intra-German and foreign affairs. An outspoken advocate of reconciliation with the East German communist regime, Borm attracted the attention of counterespionage authorities as early as 1973, but no evidence that he was a spy could be found. Stasi files discovered in 1991 proved that he had delivered the minutes of secret policy discussions to the East and that he was an agent of influence. Many of his speeches and newspaper articles had been written for him by Wolf's disinformation experts.[66] Borm was personally decorated by spy chief Wolf in 1983—which attests to the value of the service he had performed.

When asked to comment on the report that Borm had been an agent, FDP Chairman Count Otto von Lambsdorff answered laconically: "The news did not surprise us. We knew it."[67] One of Borm's secretaries was Johanna Olbrich, who was sixty-seven years old when she was sentenced in 1961 to two and a half years in prison. Formerly a teacher in East Berlin, Olbrich had volunteered for idealistic reasons to spy for the Stasi in 1966. She was given the identity of Sonja Lüneburg, a West Berlin hairdresser who had moved to East Germany. Olbrich was sent to West Germany via France with the assignment to apply for a job with Borm. Whether he knew that she was also a spy was never established. In any case, Borm later recommended her for other jobs within the government. Warned that she was about to be arrested after counterespionage computers fingered her as a spy, Olbrich escaped to East Germany. She was apprehended after the DDR faded into oblivion.

Unsuccessful in getting a job with the all-German affairs ministry—his assignment when he agreed to become a long-range agent for the HVA in 1972—Rainer Ott recruited his twin brother Reinhard. Reinhard held a doctorate in economics and was a member of the conservative Christian Democratic Party (CDU). As an economic adviser to the CDU provincial parliamentary faction of North Rhine–Westphalia, he was privy to many party secrets. In addition, he managed to elicit other highly sensitive information from top officials. The Ott brothers were arrested in 1992 and found guilty of espionage in August 1994. Rainer the recruiter received a mild sentence of one year's probation, and Reinhardt was sentenced to a four-year prison term, a fine of DM250,000 (about US$156,000), and loss of civil rights for three years.

THE CIVILIAN POLICE: RIDDLED WITH SPIES

There was hardly a major West German police department that had not been corrupted by the Stasi. Valuable information such as wanted lists and emergency plans were routinely betrayed by police officers who had sworn to uphold the law. The same was true for the Landesämter für Verfassungsschutz (LfV), the various provincial-level offices for the protection of the constitution, which were responsible for investigating left- and right-wing radicalism and espionage.

Personal financial problems led Rolf Grunert, a Hamburg detective captain and chairman of the Association of German Police Detectives, to seek employment with the Stasi. In the early 1970s Grunert traveled to East Berlin and asked a border guard to put him in touch with a representative of the Ministry for State Security. Anyone showing up at the border with such a request was automatically turned over to General Kratsch's domestic counterintelligence directorate. Kratsch was delighted to have a volunteer who was not only a top detective but also a member of the personnel council of his department, and Grunert's offer was eagerly accepted. However, his career as a spy, during which he turned over to the Stasi all of the internal secrets he could get his hands on, did not last long. In 1978 counterespionage agents traced a telephone call made to East Berlin and uncovered Grunert. He was put under surveillance and caught when he met with a courier. A telephone number found on him was identified as belonging to a Stasi cover.[68] He was sentenced to two and a half years in prison.

West Berlin Detective Captain Harald Weichert also lived beyond his means and sought to augment his police pay with the Stasi's marks. His father, a Communist Party veteran, had provided Harald's first Stasi contact in 1968, when he was twenty-seven years old. Harald, in turn, recruited his elder brother Hans, a truck driver, as his courier. According to court testimony, Harald Weichert provided reports on personnel structure and strength, readiness orders, and wanted lists, and even tapped into the police computer. The spying brothers were equipped with an infrared device with which they could signal across the Berlin Wall to arrange for meetings with case officers. The Stasi files gave them away after reunification. Considering the seriousness of their betrayal, in return for which the brothers netted at least DM70,000 (about US$43,750), their sentences were extremely mild. Harald was put on probation for two years and fined DM6,000 (about US$3,750), and his brother Hans was sentenced to half that punishment.

Former Detective Sergeant Maria Trautman was let off with eighteen months' probation and a fine of DM1,500 (about US$940) when she was caught as a spy. Trautman had quit her job with the police department in the Bavarian city of Regensburg in 1986, angry at not getting an assignment for which she felt better qualified than many of her male colleagues.[69] "Also, I resented being pawed by my colleagues." She wrote a letter to the Stasi asking if there was a job for her. They took her up on the offer, on condition that she withdraw her resignation or apply for a job with the counterespionage agency in Munich. She was promised an enlistment bonus of DM20,000 (about US$12,500) and a monthly salary of DM2,000 (about US$1,250). Before she could become an effective spy, however, the DDR collapsed; Trautman never received a single pfennig from the Stasi.

THE INFILTRATION OF COUNTERESPIONAGE AGENCIES

When the provincial counterespionage and antisubversion offices (LfV) were established in 1952 in addition to the federal BfV, their staffs consisted mainly of experienced detectives recruited from various police departments. This led to lapses in the thoroughness of background investigations, as detectives who had served previously with an unblemished record were assumed uncorrupted. As a result, every LfV in the eleven German provinces was infiltrated by communist spies. The communist espionage onslaught severely overtaxed the resources of the federal and state protectors of the constitution, who also had to keep their eyes on left- and right-wing radicals.

Next to the betrayals by Kuron and Tiedge of the federal counterespionage office, the case of Hans-Joachim Adam was among the more serious on the regional level. Frustration in their professional lives drove numerous officials into becoming volunteers for Stasi service, and so it was with Adam. The fifty-year-old senior police inspector dialed a telephone number of the HVA to which he had access in his job as a counterspy and asked to be connected to the counterintelligence division. He told them he had information as to the whereabouts of Werner Stiller, a first lieutenant assigned to Markus Wolf's division for technical and scientific espionage. Stiller, then thirty-one years old, had defected to the West in 1979 and revealed the identities of dozens of agents working for his division. The damage to Stasi espionage was so great that Stasi chief Erich Mielke had offered a reward of one million East marks (about US$578,000) for Stiller's capture dead or alive. Adam, who worked for the LfV for Lower Saxony state in Hannover, never did deliver Stiller; but the Stasi employed him anyway. Until November 1989, he met his case officers twenty-three times to deliver films of top secret counterespionage documents showing the methods employed to track down agents. The Stasi, according to the federal general prosecutor, paid him at least DM300,000 (roughly US$188,000). Based on a Stasi defector's tip, Adam was arrested in October 1990, and six years later he was sentenced to seven years' imprisonment.

Another spy catcher in Lower Saxony, Wilhelm Balke, was punished with a nine-year prison term in 1994 for thirteen years of spying. He also had to repay the DM250,000 (about US$156,000) that he was given by the Stasi, and his civil rights were suspended for five years. The court said Balke's treachery resulted in his office's counterespionage effort having come "to a total standstill."

The federal border police, which among other tasks is charged with guarding all federal buildings in Bonn, also did not escape Stasi infiltration. The most egregious case was that of Police Director Alexander Dahms, whose ideology was to the far left. In 1963, as a twenty-one-year-old, Dahms had volunteered to spy for the Stasi. He was recruited as a long-range agent and directed to study law with the aim of becoming a diplomat. While working toward his law degree, he reported on the activities of an anticommunist organization and on a Christian Democratic Party parliamentary member for whom he worked part-time. After graduation, Dahms applied for the diplomatic service but failed the entrance examination. He then applied to the border police and was accepted. He rose steadily through the ranks while delivering anything that was of interest to his communist spymaster. At his trial in 1991, the prosecution revealed that Dahl had furnished East Berlin with details on a new forgery-proof West German identity card, wanted circulars, and requests for assistance from the BND and the BfV. He had had meetings with case officers throughout Germany and Europe, including Greece, Switzerland, Italy, Britain, Austria, and Finland. On his twentieth anniversary as a spy, Dahl was awarded the rank of a Stasi lieutenant colonel. He also collected DM20,000 (about US$32,500) in pay during those years. A defector betrayed Dahms after German reunification, and in February 1991, he was sentenced to six years and six months behind bars.

SPYING DIPLOMATS

The West German diplomatic corps had at least a dozen spies in its midst. Most had been recruited while they were studying at universities during the turbulent 1960s and early 1970s, when student protests against the Vietnam war were popular on West German campuses. Many students were sympathetic to the communists, believing that they were the true guardians of world peace.

While studying law at West Berlin's Free University in 1959, Klaus von Raussendorf was drawn into a circle of leftists. He attended ideological discussions in the communist part of the city and was recruited as a long-range agent in 1960, when he was twenty-four years old. Everything went as the Stasi had planned. In 1961 Raussendorf was hired as an attaché in the higher diplomatic service by Bonn's Ministry of Foreign Affairs. He served at a number of embassies, rising steadily until he reached the rank of embassy counselor.

According to testimony at his trial in 1991, Raussendorf met his couriers clandestinely twice a year between 1963 and 1972, each time turning over two to five tiny films with images of secret foreign service documents he had photographed. At those meetings he also made oral reports. In addition the diplomat used so-called "traveling dead letter drops," hiding material in a preselected toilet of an express train destined to travel through East Germany. The last covert meeting during which he passed documents to the courier took place in October 1989, a month before the Berlin Wall crumbled.

Raussendorf's services were terminated at a final meeting with his case officer in the Ruhr Valley city of Essen on November 22, 1989. He was the acting ambassador to the United Nations Educational, Scientific, and Cultural Organization (UNESCO) in Paris when he was arrested on April 9, 1990, at the age of fifty-five. Investigators were unable to establish exactly what secrets the diplomat had betrayed. However, a Stasi defector said analysts judged his contributions "satisfactory to good," and in a few instances, "very good."[70] At his trial in June 1991, the court noted that the value of Raussendorf's espionage was "illuminated" by the fact that he was received twice by HVA chief Markus Wolf and that he had held the rank of a Stasi lieutenant colonel. Raussendorf was paid at least DM100,000 (about US$62,500) for his treachery. Found guilty on charges of espionage and venality, he drew a prison term of six years.

Hagen Blau, an embassy counselor convicted of espionage and venality in November 1990, was also sentenced to a prison term of six years. His recruitment path and diplomatic career were nearly identical to Raussendorf's. Blau, too, joined the diplomatic corps in 1961 and had served at the West German embassies in Tokyo, Vienna, and London, and lastly, as deputy ambassador at Colombo, Sri Lanka. Blau was equipped with a miniature camera built into a cigarette case, produced in East Germany for espionage work. During his assignment in London, he was in constant consultation with West Germany's allies, working out common positions for negotiating multilateral balanced force reduction (MBFR) with the Soviets. In addition, Blau participated in negotiations for Great Britain's entry into the European Economic Community. Everything to which Blau was privy he reported to Wolf's spy shop, where it was analyzed and shared with the KGB, giving Soviet officials a distinct advantage at the MBFR negotiating table. According to the German federal prosecutor general, Blau also provided the communists with the position of West Germany and other western nations toward China. His value as a spy was spotlighted by a meeting with Wolf. Blau, according to his own testimony, never wanted money from the Stasi but twice accepted $6,000 at the urging of his case officer during their secret meetings in Sri Lanka. Blau has been described by some as a brilliant analyst. In contrast, retired Ambassador Günter Diehl told me: "I gave him an unsatisfactory appraisal while he worked for me in Tokyo for a year. He was a rather intelligent man, but his muddle-headed and convoluted way of thinking produced nothing tangible." Asked why he thought Blau spied for the communists, Ambassador Diehl said: "The man had a complex of self-importance. He was convinced that he was morally right, and things like the Berlin Wall and the oppression of the East German people didn't matter to him."

Ludwig Pauli, a senior counselor in the foreign ministry, had an affair with a "swallow" and then was blackmailed into becoming a spy. So far as I have been able to determine, Pauli was the only man who fell into a honey trap and was later exposed. He paid for his transgression with a conviction for espionage and venality, for which he went to prison for four years in 1992. Had he reported his misstep and the Stasi contact to his superiors, he probably would have received no more than a slap on the wrist or a one-grade demotion.[71] Pauli's downfall was a German "journalist" whom he met while he was assigned to the West German embassy in Belgrade. The journalist enticed the diplomat into a sexual escapade with a Yugoslav beauty. That accomplished, the "journalist" identified himself as a Stasi officer and threatened that if Pauli refused to spy for the Stasi, he would expose the affair.

Operating under the code name Adler, Pauli received intensive training in cryptography, document photography, clandestine radio communications, and the use of secret dead letter drops.[72] In more than two decades of spying, he copied nearly every document of interest that came across his desk at various consulates around Europe and at the Ministry of Foreign Affairs, where he was assigned when detectives put him in handcuffs. After the fall of the Berlin Wall and the collapse of the communist government, Pauli had met with his case officer in East Berlin and agreed to continue spying for the new DDR government. Pauli had been instructed to watch for certain chalk marks on a preselected wall in Bonn, a sign that his case officer wanted a meeting. The chalk marks never appeared, he told the court.

INFILTRATION OF GOVERNMENT AND INDUSTRY

Whether it was West Germany's economic condition, defense readiness, or nuclear research, Stasi spies kept the leadership of the communist regime east of the Elbe river constantly up to date. Werner

Stiller told West German intelligence officers after his defection that for every 5 million marks it spent on industrial and scientific espionage, the DDR saved 300 million in development and research costs. Stiller was a first lieutenant and case officer for agents spying for the foreign espionage directorate's scientific and technology division. Details of new Western armament systems landed in East Berlin even before the systems were put into service.

Wolf-Heinrich Prellwitz was one of the most dangerous moles in the defense ministry. He was recruited by a "businessman" who said he was connected to wealthy French lobbyists. Would Prellwitz be interested in a lucrative sideline? Although he told the court later that he suspected the offer came from East German intelligence, he accepted it anyway. In his more than twenty-one years as a spy, Prellwitz photographed more than 100,000 pages of top secret documents with a miniature camera hidden in a cigarette package, and delivered them to Stasi couriers.[73] Among the secrets he sold for a total of DM820,000 (about US$512,000) were diagrams of weapons systems, including the newly developed multipurpose Tornado fighter jet and West Germany's Leopard II tank. Prellwitz's case officer wanted to prevent him from being tempted to live beyond his means in his hometown of Bonn, so his treasonous earnings were paid into a numbered Swiss bank account. Prellwitz used the money to pay for expensive vacations outside Germany.[74] He was arrested in April 1991, on a tip from a Stasi analyst who said the material Prellwitz provided was rated "extremely valuable" and "valuable." The Stasi shared the booty with the Soviet KGB. In May 1992, Prellwitz was found guilty of treason and prostituting himself and was sentenced to ten years in prison by Presiding Judge Klaus Wagner of the Düsseldorf High Provincial Court.

Heinz Werner, serving in the West German navy as a noncommissioned officer, wrote a letter to the East German propaganda radio station "Soldatensender 904" offering to sell information.[75] He was hired by the military intelligence service of the People's Army. Werner, then twenty-six years old, was a highly desired trophy because he was assigned as a teletype and cryptographic noncom. In 1974 he was promoted to chief petty officer and assigned to the defense command in Nürnberg as custodian of super secret cryptographic material. Werner was equipped with a miniature camera and an attaché case with a secret compartment in which he transported documents he had copied. The fact that he escaped detection when he stole a complete Electrotel coding machine, an extremely secret device, is mind-boggling. A defector told investigators that the Soviet military intelligence service GRU rated Werner's material "extremely valuable."[76] For his betrayal he received DM250,000 (about US$156,000) and several decorations, including the Battle Medal of the People's Army in Gold. Arrested in January 1991, Werner was tried nine months later and found guilty of treason, venality, and violating official secrecy rules. His crimes brought him a nine-year prison term.

Walter Liewer was recruited by the Stasi's foreign intelligence directorate in 1976 as a long-range agent. He studied at West Berlin's Technical University and graduated with a doctorate in physics. He had been trained in clandestine radio communications, document photography, and in the use of invisible ink. During his three-year employment, starting in 1983, at the government's Nuclear Research Center at Karlsruhe, Liewer regularly delivered films showing a variety of secret documents. Liewer was later transferred to the government-financed Association for Applied Natural Sciences in Bonn. Until 1989 he deposited his films in preselected secret hiding places aboard express trains heading for East Germany. His conviction in February 1994 brought him a three-year prison term.

Spies in industry could fill another book. The most damaging of these included Peter and Heidrun Kraut, both mathematicians. Peter was employed by the arms production firm Messerschmitt-Bölkow-Blohm (MBB), and Heidrun, by the Industrie Anlagen corporation. This husband-and-wife team was recruited in 1970 under false flag: The Stasi officer who made the pitch pretended to be an agent of U.S. military intelligence. Although the couple knew by 1971 that they were working for the communists, they did not break off their activities.[77] The loss of their extra income of several hundred thousand marks would have been too much to contemplate. The couple worked as a team for twenty years, betraying, among other secrets, the technical details of tanks and aircraft. Their code names were Siegfried and Kriemhild, two heroes of ancient Germanic saga. Stasi files gave them away in 1991, and a year later they were found guilty of treason. Peter Kraut went to prison for nine years, and his wife for seven.

Peter Koehler was the highest paid East German spy, according to the federal prosecutor, who said that in just four years he had received DM1.1 million (about US$685,700). Koehler was employed as an engineer by a West German subsidiary of Texas Instruments. He delivered information on the production of computer chips and circuit configurations that were embargoed for export to a communist country. Koehler was fifty years old when he was sentenced in 1993 to four years' imprisonment and fined DM460,000 (about US$287,500).

Karl-Paul Gebauer, an employee of IBM Special Systems at the North Sea port of Wilhelmshaven, volunteered to work for the Stasi in 1975, when he was about fifty years old. His company was working closely with the West German navy's supersecret Research and Testing Facility No. 71 at Eckernförde, near Kiel, on the Baltic Sea.[78] That Gebauer was cleared by the military counterintelligence service for access to classified material remains a scandal of epic proportions: The man had a criminal record that included a prison term in connection with the death of an American GI shortly after World War II.[79] His appointment as the company's security representative responsible for all classified material bordered on criminal negligence.

Early in his espionage career, Gebauer provided the Stasi with details of Projekt Tenne, a communications command system developed by IBM for NATO naval units. Because of Gebauer's betrayal, a potential enemy was in a position to jam the system and prevent the fleet commander's orders from reaching his naval units—effectively destroying his ability to command.[80] This would have forced individual commanders to make decisions without having the information that only the fleet commander possessed. Projekt Tenne documents also revealed that the coding device "Ecrovox," classified as "crypto top secret" (next to "eyes only," the highest classification), was to be used. In 1976 Gebauer delivered 13,000 documents recorded on six rolls of film into the communists' hands.

Before IBM Special Systems was disbanded in early 1980 and Gebauer lost his job, he had stolen forty secret file folders, each two inches thick, which he was supposed to destroy. Although he could no longer deliver any secret data, Gebauer met again with Stasi officers on later occasions until in 1986 he was deactivated. For his services the Stasi paid Gebauer the relatively paltry sum of DM70,000 (about US$43,700). A defector divulged the information that led to Gebauer's arrest in 1990, and a Berlin court tried and sentenced him to twelve years behind bars.

SPYING JOURNALISTS

Dozens of West German journalists were arrested as Stasi spies in the first years after reunification. Some worked for the country's major news organizations. A few went to prison for their treachery; most merely lost their jobs after getting away with suspended sentences and fines.

Karl-Heinz Maier, one of the most prominent post–World War II newsmen, died in January 1996. At a memorial service, Berlin Mayor Eberhard Diepgen called his death a "heavy loss" for Berlin's journalistic establishment. Someday, he said, one will recall the time when "Karl-Heinz Maier, with his usual circumspection and human warmth, coaxed those who governed into revealing their secrets."[81] A month later Diepgen would find out why Maier did so much coaxing, when the federal prosecutor general revealed that since 1994, authorities had been investigating Maier for espionage. The newsman was the West Berlin correspondent for the large Rhineland daily newspaper *Westphälische Rundschau* in the 1950s, and in 1968 switched to the government radio station Deutsche Welle, serving as its Berlin chief until his retirement. For many years he served as chairman of the Berliner Presse Konferenz, a prestigious and influential position to which he was elected by his admiring peers. He was honored by the West German, British, and Austrian governments with high decorations. Maier would issue the highly coveted invitations for the press association's annual dinner. His guests over the years included the U.S. Secretaries of State George Shultz and James Baker, French President François Mitterrand, Israeli President Chaim Herzog, and Austrian Chancellor Bruno Kreisky. His work for the Stasi continued over three decades. According to documents uncovered after reunification, he did exactly what Mayor Diepgen said: He wheedled secrets out of officials. How he became a spy and what rewards he received from the communists is not known. For the East German espionage service, according to its own files, he was a "interesting partner who delivered important information." The tip that Maier had been an agent reportedly came from the CIA, to whom a former Stasi general had sold microfilms showing the code and clear names of about 2,000 German spies in high places.

Consternation and disbelief was the reaction of managers and editors of the left-leaning weekly news magazine *Der Spiegel* on December 11, 1990, when the federal prosecutor general announced that the magazine's Berlin bureau chief, Diethelm Schröder, had been an East German spy for thirty years. Born in 1930 in the East German city of Greifswald, Schröder had been a member of a Hitler Youth antitank squad during the last days of the war. He was captured by Soviet troops and interned for three months. It is probable that Schröder expressed his enthusiasm for communism while in captivity, since other youths were held for years, even sent to the Siberian gulag. After his release he went back to high school. Following his graduation, Schröder worked for a newspaper in the Soviet zone, taking correspondence courses in journalism and Marxism offered by the University of Leipzig. In 1956 he was recruited as a long-range agent by the HVA and sent to West Germany as a "refugee."

Schröder worked for various news organization, including the Associated Press in its Bonn bureau. Eventually he was hired by *Der Spiegel* to cover military affairs, a job that brought him into contact with the top military echelon and defense department officials. In 1964, counterespionage officials questioned him after intercepting

Stasi radio messages to an agent code-named Schrammel. There was no hard evidence for an arrest, but suspicions remained. Subsequently Schröder became a close friend of Defense Minister Manfred Wörner, with whom he discussed military affairs. The Defense Minister would like to have appointed him his press spokesman, but he belonged to the wrong political party, the Social Democrats.[82] Schröder also covered Allied maneuvers, during which he was briefed by NATO Commander General Alexander Haig and later by Haig's successor Bernard Rogers. His case officers were impressed by the wealth of information he supplied. In mid-1980 Schröder, for reasons known only to himself, quit spying. Ten years later he was betrayed by his former case officer. Schröder was sentenced to twenty-one months' probation in November 1992 and was fired by *Der Spiegel,* where he had been earning an annual salary of DM280,000 (about US$175,000).

HOW WOLF ACHIEVED SUCCESS

These great successes of the East German intelligence apparatus were no accident, but the predictable results of foresight and long-range planning. Not content merely to milk contacts that they had established before 1945, Markus Wolf and his Soviet mentors perceived unprecedented opportunities as well as challenges in the division of Germany and the evolving Cold War. West Germany, its eastern borders abutting two communist countries, the DDR and Czechoslovakia, had become NATO's first line of defense. Upward of 600,000 U.S., British, French, Canadian, and Belgian troops were stationed in the Federal Republic of Germany. The country's economic power was steadily increasing, and its democratic government was stable and gaining in influence on world affairs. In contrast, East Germany was languishing in isolation from the West. Thus, West Germany was a prime target for military, political, and industrial espionage as well as for attempts at destabilization through disinformation campaigns and agents of influence from the East. The Soviet intelligence services and their Polish, Czechoslovakian, and Hungarian allies also were active in West Germany. But most clandestine activities were left in the hands of the Stasi: The East Germans enjoyed the distinct advantages of a common cultural heritage and a shared language with the West Germans, facilitating infiltration, communication, and control. In addition, hundreds of thousands of West Germans had relatives in the DDR, making it relatively easy for the Stasi to coerce many of the former group into becoming agents by threatening the well-being of their loved ones in the East. Thus, in the late 1950s, the farsighted Wolf—then a major general and deputy minister of the Stasi—ordered the recruitment of a wave of new, young cadres, many of whom had just graduated from high school or university. These young men and women were trained in espionage techniques and sent to West Germany as *perspektiv Agenten,* long-range agents. Some, like the chancellery spy Guillaume, spent years worming their way into the upper ranks of the government and industry before being activated.

This period witnessed the coming of age of the Stasi, signaled by the espionage service's move into the ministerial compound and by its formal designation as the Hauptverwaltung Aufklärung (HVA). Wolf was allocated ever increasing amounts of personnel and funding. Within two or three years, the HVA's structure consisted of thirteen departments directing espionage or counterintelligence operations. Administrative, logistical, and analytic/evaluative services and special scientific units were organized in another fourteen departments and working groups, including one for forging documents. The Stasi had become a formidable communist weapon.

6

THE STASI AGAINST THE UNITED STATES AND NATO

WHITMONDAY IN 1956 FELL on May 20. As had been their tradition for centuries, Germans celebrated the three-day Pentecost weekend with family gatherings and outings to enjoy the new foliage and blooming fruit trees. The more faithful Christians visited their churches to celebrate the descent of the Holy Spirit upon the Apostles. Horst Hesse, however, had no inclination either to tour the countryside or to attend church services. He was taking advantage of a monumental security blunder to do major damage to his employer—the military intelligence service of the U.S. Army.[1]

At 12:30 A.M. on May 20, Hesse entered the two-story villa at 4 Eisenmannstrasse, a quiet and affluent neighborhood in Würzburg, in northwestern Bavaria. The villa housed a detachment of the 522nd Military Intelligence Battalion of the U.S. Army, which was responsible for conducting espionage in Eastern Europe. The German had no trouble entering the villa: He had the keys to the front door, and he had every right to be there. Hesse was a recruiter and principal agent for U.S. Army intelligence.

Inside the building, Hesse punched the code numbers into the security lock that opened the steel gate barring unauthorized entry to the second floor. Then he made his way to the office of Captain James G.

Campbell, the station commander. Behind a desk stood two olive-colored Mosler field safes. Each weighed 110 pounds and measured 12 3/8 inches in height, 15 7/16 inches in width, and 17 inches in depth. They were the most secure containers the captain had for storing highly secret documents. When these safes were first built, during World War II, military specifications did not require them to be protected against forced entry but merely against unauthorized or surreptitious entry. The safes were similar to the padlocked strongboxes carried by stagecoaches in bygone days. However, instead of a simple lock-and-key mechanism that might be quickly demolished by a six-shooter, they were secured by dial locks that opened only to a particular combination of code numbers. Because the safes could be carted away easily, army regulations had decreed that they be fastened to the wall by a massive chain. In many army offices they were chained to radiators. The captain had neglected such security measures.

Hesse knew that a sergeant was always on guard duty on the second floor, but he was unconcerned. He knew from past experience that the man on duty that night always sacked out on a field cot. True to form, the sergeant was sleeping soundly in an adjacent room. Nevertheless, Hesse moved quietly. He had no difficulty hefting the first safe and lugging it downstairs after stowing it in a heavy canvas U.S. Army mailbag he had found in the captain's office. Hesse was lean and strong, five feet ten inches tall and weighing 170 pounds. He placed the safe on the rear seat of his bone-white Mercedes Benz 190 SL convertible and returned to the house to get the second safe. The sergeant was still asleep.

Within fifteen minutes Hesse was on a country road, driving northeast toward the autobahn some seventy miles away. The car's gasoline tank was full, the weather was good—with only a few, scattered clouds—and the temperature was mild. Although the road was narrow with tricky curves and on hilly, wooded terrain, Hesse made good time, slowing only as he drove through a half dozen sleepy villages. Shortly before 3 A.M. he drove onto the four-lane superhighway, and fifteen miles farther north he turned onto a secondary road. The border of the DDR now was only twenty miles ahead. Hesse would reach the communist part of Germany—and safety—well before daylight, just as he had planned. Hesse was only a mile or two from the border when suddenly he saw a red light being waved and his headlights picked up two uniformed figures. He slowed down and stopped when he realized it was a patrol of the Bundesgrenzschutz, the West German border police.

When asked for his papers, Hesse nonchalantly produced credentials issued by the refugee affairs section of the U.S. Army's European Command Department for Public Opinion Research. Actually, there was no such unit in the U.S. Army. This was, in fact, the cover name for the clandestine branch of U.S. Army military intelligence. If his heartbeat and pulse rate increased, Hesse never showed it. He was confident that the document would pass any inspection; after all, it was of genuine U.S. Army issue. He coolly eyed the patrol officer who was carefully scrutinizing the identification card, which called on "all Allied Forces to assist the bearer." It stated further that "all documents and other items carried by the bearer are the property of the United States Government and cannot be inspected or confiscated without permission of the issuing authority." Recognizing the document as legitimate, the officer knew at once that he was dealing with a U.S. intelligence agent and immediately relaxed his stance. He passed the card to his companion, who merely shrugged and grinned. Before he was waved on, Hesse offered each of the border patrolmen a cigarette, then gave them a mock salute as he drove off.

Fifteen minutes later Hesse was stopped again, this time by the East German border police. He had made it, his mission complete at only a few minutes past five o'clock in the morning—or so he thought. Rather than being welcomed as a hero returning from enemy territory, Hesse was greeted with skepticism by the border guards, and not without reason. The only papers he was carrying were a West German identity card and a U.S. Army pass. The guards refused to notify Stasi headquarters in Berlin as Hesse demanded. Instead, the officer in charge placed him under guard and called his own headquarters for instructions.

At dawn Hesse was driven to the border police headquarters at Rudolstadt, about thirty miles away. More questioning followed, and finally a call was made to Berlin. Incredibly, no one answered the number Hesse had memorized. Finally it dawned on him that the comrades, too, were celebrating Pentecost and had taken the day off. Although it was a Christian holiday, the atheistic communist regime had never abolished it. Evidently the leadership feared that doing away with a centuries-old tradition would further aggravate a populace that to a large extent was already hostile.

Hesse's carefully constructed plan, the most important element of which was taking advantage of the quiet holiday weekend, was turning into a nightmare. Border police officers refused to help him break open the safes despite Hesse's pleas that time was of the essence. Not until Tuesday morning when Berlin resumed normal office hours were orders given to release him. Hesse was instructed to bring his booty to Berlin, where the safes finally were opened—more than twenty-four hours after Hesse had hauled them out of the Würzburg intelligence station.

U.S. INTELLIGENCE ALERT

Captain Campbell—known to his German agents as John C. Walker, Johnny, or Dr. Jansen—was furious when he reached his office. The sergeant, who had alerted his commander when he discovered the safes missing shortly after dawn, knew he was in deep trouble. Campbell realized that his predicament was even worse than the sergeant's. The safes had contained the names and locations of twenty-five principal agents his station controlled in East Germany, as well as other highly sensitive material. There was no time for damage control, no time to summon a mason to install the obligatory wall anchors and chains. Campbell notified his headquarters at the IG Farben Building in Frankfurt, even though he had not yet identified the thief.

Upon hearing the report, the commanding officer of the 522nd Military Intelligence Battalion, Lieutenant Colonel Edward W. ("Big Ed") Crawford realized that he was dealing with the most serious penetration to date of U.S. Army intelligence in Europe. The colonel took charge personally. He issued orders to recall all agents whose identities and locations in East Germany had been kept on file cards in one of the safes. Then he drove to Würzburg to relieve Captain Campbell of his command, a measure the colonel did not relish. The captain, a twenty-seven-year-old regular army officer, had been touted as the unit's "hot ticket." He was the fair-haired boy not only of his commander but also of the intelligence staff of the USAREUR, the army's European Command at Heidelberg. Campbell had built his reputation as a first-rate intelligence officer by setting up a highly efficient and reliable espionage network in East Germany. No one then suspected that he was also a skilled flimflam artist.[2]

The Würzburg station was a vital link in the defense of Europe against a Soviet attack. Its primary mission was the surveillance of rail facilities from the Polish border to the Fulda Gap, a broad, flat valley cutting through the hills west of the Thuringian Forest. U.S. military strategists viewed the Fulda Gap, as well as the Cheb Gap farther south and east, on the Czechoslovakian border, as the likeliest routes for Soviet armor units striking at the center of U.S. defenses.

In 1956, electronic devices for listening in on Warsaw Pact communications had not yet been perfected. Thus, the Würzburg station's network of agents was essentially an early warning system. The agents were chiefly East German railroad personnel equipped with the latest miniaturized radios. They would watch for concentrations and movements of flatcars (on which tanks can be moved rapidly through hilly and mountainous terrain). They also kept their eyes on any changes in the strategic stockpiles of coal needed for the aging steam engines that were still in use in Eastern Europe.

The compromise of any agent at that time was an intelligence disaster. Top U.S. commanders had become apprehensive when the Soviets moved large infantry units of Central Asian troops to the border area.[3] Traditionally, the Soviets had used such units as first-line assault groups—in other words, as cannon fodder. A large number of military men also had sent their families home, even though no orders had been issued to evacuate dependents.

The Würzburg station's carefully established and smoothly operating spy network was falling apart. Less than a day after the safe caper, nine of the twenty-five active agents had heeded the emergency radio warning and arrived at predetermined locations in West Germany, some with their families. They were met by their American "handlers" and taken to Würzburg station. The fate of the other sixteen would not be known for some time. Had the Stasi in Berlin been on the job instead of taking advantage of a Christian holiday, none would have returned.

While the commander of the 522nd MI Battalion was making his on-the-spot damage assessment, counterespionage specialists began to question personnel at the Würzburg station. No one had a clue to the thief's identity. Of the dozen German agents employed there, eight had arrived at the station when summoned. The other four, including Hesse, were on preplanned assignments and could not be contacted. No one figured at the time that the theft had been perpetrated by one of the station's own agents; instead, everyone thought it was an outside job, although that seemed a bizarre scenario. Some intelligence experts viewed the safe thefts as a prelude to more trouble, perhaps even a Soviet attack.

Major William G. Leyden, commander of the battalion's station in the North German port city of Bremen, received a coded teletype message, which he said alarmed him as much as if a war were about to start. In the message he was told that hit teams of the East German State Security Service were planning to assault all stations of the 522nd in search for classified material. Major Leyden ordered his men to arm themselves at once. The only weapons available, however, were .38 caliber snub-nosed Colt revolvers. "Hell, there were no U.S. troops of any consequence in Bremen at that time," Leyden later recalled: "So I requested a shipment of heavier weapons. I knew the army was jittery, so we fortified the little house we occupied and got ready for a firefight." The fight never came.[4]

After a few days, all units were ordered to stand down. Questioning residents living near the Eisenmannstrasse office, special agents of the

Army's Counter Intelligence Corps (CIC) hit pay dirt. A man coming home late that night said he had noticed that lights were on in a second-floor room of "the mystery house," as the locals called it. He remembered that he saw a man loading a heavy sack into a car. He thought it was odd because it was in the middle of the night, and on a holiday at that, when hardly anybody was working. The car, he said, was a white Mercedes Benz 190SL convertible. That clinched it for the investigators. Only recruiter/principal agent 0065–09, known as Horst Berger (the Army's cover name for Horst Hesse), drove such a car. A bulletin with his description was sent to U.S. military and German police, saying he was wanted for theft of U.S. government property. Within hours came the bad news; a border police post reported that two officers had checked the identification of Berger and that he was last seen driving toward the East German border.

Commanders in High Dudgeon

At Fort Holabird, in Baltimore, Maryland, Major General Boniface Campbell was fuming over news of the Würzburg fiasco. The veteran combat commander had only recently been chosen to head the U.S. Army's Intelligence Center, which included the counterespionage school. At the same time, the Army Chief of Staff had ordered General Campbell to reorganize the army's worldwide intelligence activities. "This screwup proves that army intelligence deserves every bad name it's got," he told Colonel Franz H. Ross, his newly appointed chief of staff, whom he had called to his office. Noting Ross's perplexed expression, General Campbell handed him a long teletype marked "top secret." The colonel quickly scanned the message, then muttered, "Oh, sh—I mean, that's a heck of a note." Colonel Ross never swore in the presence of a general officer. General Campbell nodded. "Exactly!" he exclaimed. "Thank God that this Captain Campbell isn't a relative of mine."[5]

Like the general, Ross was new to Fort Holabird and to military intelligence. The general had picked Ross as his chief aide when the colonel was discharged from Walter Reed Army Medical Center after having stomach surgery. The crusty artillery officer from Savannah, Georgia, who had enlisted in 1940 and worked his way up from buck private, was ideal for the job ahead. He was well known to dozens of general officers for his professionalism, integrity, and no-nonsense approach to any job he had ever held. He was also known as a straight shooter, never hesitating to tell the truth to his superiors when he encountered mismanagement or lack of leadership. Standing just under six feet tall, Ross exuded confidence and experience. Had he lived a century earlier, he probably would have been a sheriff or a U.S. marshal, six-shooters strapped to his hip, chasing outlaws. His men called him a "tough bird"; his four bronze stars for valor and three air medals had earned him respect. "Don't bother getting settled just now, Franz," General Campbell said. "I want you to hightail it over there and find out what the hell is going on. Get back here in two weeks and tell me how we can clean up that mess."

In addition to investigating the safe caper at the 522nd Battalion, Colonel Ross was ordered to take an especially close look at the 513th Military Intelligence Group, which had just been formed at Camp King in Oberursel, a small town in the Taunus Mountains near Frankfurt. Before the U.S. Army took over the camp in May 1945, it had been a Transit Camp/Air where Luftwaffe intelligence officers interrogated U.S. Army Air Corps members who had parachuted down over German or occupied territory before shipping them to regular prison camps. Oddly, the camp was a fairly pleasant place. Prisoners were housed in bungalows resembling small farmhouses, in a park-like setting. No rubber hoses were used to extract information here: Instead, prisoners were taken to the Frankfurt opera and to the local swimming pool for recreation. This milk-and-honey treatment was the rule, and some prisoners succumbed, including a colonel who later faced charges of high treason. When the war ended, the U.S. Army used the camp to hold interned high-ranking German civilians, and it was known as the European Intelligence Center. The first espionage operations against the Soviet Army east of the Elbe river were planned there, after Stalin's bellicosity began to be viewed as a serious threat to the West.

East Berlin Reveals the Safe Caper

On May 29, ten days after Hesse had disappeared with the safes, the Prime Minister of East Germany, Otto Grotewohl, spoke before the Volkskammer, the communist rubber-stamp parliament. He revealed that a long-time German employee of the U.S. intelligence service had defected to the DDR: "As a gesture of goodwill, he brought with him a safe containing the entire files of an American espionage headquarters. On the basis of those files, 137 agents have been arrested." He did not name the defector, nor did he elaborate.[6] However, rumors had already circulated through Würzburg that documents had been stolen from the Eisenmannstrasse villa and transported to East Germany. In response, a U.S. Army spokesman issued a statement claiming that Grotewohl's assertion was false.

When Grotewohl made his announcement, Colonel Ross had already spent a few days with the 513th MI Group, going through every section of the command. He was appalled at what he had found. If the surgeons had not already removed most of his stomach, they certainly would have had to do so after this inspection tour. Rather than directing and closely supervising all of the army's covert intelligence activities in Europe, the group was functioning as nothing more than an administrative support unit. Its commander did not have the slightest idea of what was happening in the field, nor did he have the authority to direct and supervise the operations of intelligence units supposedly under his command. Ross also probed the Würzburg incident in depth, questioning members of the 522nd MI Battalion for many hours.

Disgusted, Colonel Ross traveled to the USAREUR headquarters in Heidelberg. Living up to his reputation for straight talk, he did not mince words when he explained the deplorable state of affairs to Major General John M. Willems, the USAREUR assistant chief of staff for intelligence. "The clandestine people are all doing their own thing without properly accounting to anyone," he told the general.[7] One by one, General Willems confronted his staff officers in the presence of the irascible colonel. All admitted that what Ross reported was true. Clandestine units responsible for intelligence collection reported results to Heidelberg staff officers but were not subject to any kind of supervision. There was no centralized control over funds used for espionage operations. "The commander of the 513th is out in left field and is treated like an errand boy until something goes wrong, then all hell breaks loose and he is blamed," Ross said, making no effort to tone down his anger. "It stinks!"

Ross also had discovered that some of the USAREUR brass had made "field trips" to Würzburg station, where the resourceful Captain Campbell treated them to spine-tingling demonstrations of how agents were being inserted into East Germany through its closely guarded border. Sitting in the basement of 4 Eisenmannstrasse, the captain would place a pointer at a spot on a map showing the border. "Our agent has just reported that he is approaching the spot we have previously reconnoitered," he would tell the assembled staff officers from Heidelberg. "We know the schedules of the communist patrols, and in a minute the area will be clear for infiltration." Then the radio would crackle and a voice would say in heavily accented English, "I am at the barbed wire . . . no guards in sight." With suspense equaling that of a James Bond movie, the agent would describe his crawling through the barbed wire fence. Then they would hear a volley of shots, and finally a voice reporting, "I am through." A day later, the same brass would hear the exfiltration as the agent returned with the desired information. When some officers asked to actually go to the border to see the drama, Captain Campbell would tell them that it was too dangerous and talked them out of it.

"Now, gentlemen, I would like you to listen closely," Ross said in his Georgia drawl, pursing his lips—a signal to those who knew him well that he was about to "lay one on": "I know about those infiltration demonstrations, and I can tell you that you have been flim-flammed. That Captain Campbell is a resourceful officer all right, but he pulled the wool over your eyes. What you witnessed was nothing but an elaborate charade. What you heard was one of his trained seals sitting in a meadow a few miles from the station. It was a sham. Oh, he had some good agents and obtained valid information. But as far as I am concerned, Würzburg station was nothing more than a big cathouse." Then he added with a chuckle: "When I made this observation to Campbell, he claimed the women going in and out where only *Putzfrauen,* cleaning ladies. Cleaning ladies, he tried to tell me, by God!" The officers were stunned, and Ross recalled later that there were "a lot of red faces."

Back at Fort Holabird, General Campbell was still absorbing his chief of staff's report when he received a call from the army's assistant chief of staff for intelligence at the Pentagon. He was told that the European commander in Heidelberg wanted Ross as the new chief of the 513th MI Group. Would the general release him? "Only if Franz gets a star," Campbell replied.[8] But Ross would not become a brigadier general. Because of his stomach problem, he had been stricken from the general officers' promotion list. No one had paid any attention to the fact that he had an ulcer thirteen years earlier when there was a need for junior combat officers and regulations were relaxed so he could attend Officer Candidate School. He had seen combat in Korea and in Europe, bad stomach and all. Ironically, he had been promoted unusually quickly. Apparently his stomach was judged good enough to withstand the extreme hazards of operating ahead of the infantry as a forward artillery observer but not the stresses of a general's command.

Ross did go to Germany as the 513th MI Group commander, but he was awarded no star—just the responsibility of commanding some 3,000 officers, enlisted men, and U.S. civilian intelligence specialists. In keeping with his character, Ross took these circumstances in stride. He was determined to mold the 513th MI Group into an efficient and highly successful unit. But before assuming command, he again reported to USAREUR headquarters, where the deputy assistant chief of intelligence, Colonel Charles Johnson, listened to his demands. Johnson directed Ross to write the reorganizational and operational orders. Although Ross thought this was unheard of, if not irregular, the colonel complied, and the European Commander did not change a comma. According to the orders, all espionage operations in Europe and all operational funds were put under his command.

The Propaganda Tool

On July 10, 1956—fifty-two days after the Würzburg caper—the Ministry for State Security presented Horst Hesse to a news conference in East Berlin.[9] In contrast to the sloppily clad Communist Party functionaries who were also present, the dark-haired spy was dressed in a natty gray double-breasted suit and white shirt. His conservative tie was carefully knotted in Windsor fashion, as he had been taught by his American "friends." He appeared calm and self-assured. This was his big show. In addition to the representatives of the communist-controlled press, reporters from West Berlin and foreign correspondents with the Associated Press, United Press, Reuters, and Agence France Presse were present.

Flanked by a Stasi colonel, Hesse read a statement saying that he had been recruited by the U.S. military intelligence service in 1954, while working in the East German city of Magdeburg. Because of his good work, he said, he was transferred to Berlin and later to Würzburg, where he became the chief recruiter of agents. "By virtue of this position I had a relatively large insight into the Würzburg branch's efforts to recruit agents in the DDR," he said. Then he detailed U.S. operations against various targets, including transportation facilities and the Soviet and East German military. He admitted stealing the two safes. Despite his poise, he sounded like an automaton carefully programmed by his Stasi handlers: "After many doubts arose in my mind concerning the correctness of my work and activities, I decided to break with this secret service and go to the DDR. As evidence of my good will and sincerity in making this break, and hoping to compensate somewhat for my wrongful acts, I made the decision to take the already mentioned safes, along with their important contents, to the DDR with me."

Hesse maintained that one safe contained names of agents, but he did not repeat the number provided earlier by Prime Minister Grotewohl. The other safe, he said, held 2,000 West German identity cards, 100 West German press cards, about 100 identification cards of the Heidelberg Detective Agency, and nearly 250 ID cards of the German Detective Association. There were also U.S. Army ID cards for the Office of Public Opinion Research and the Graphic Surveying Commission, both cover names for intelligence units.

Hesse then revealed the names of fellow recruiters in Würzburg and in West Berlin and the name of his chief, Captain John Walker (Campbell's cover name). He described the captain as an unscrupulous lout who enjoyed "humiliating, oppressing, and intimidating" his staff. "He looked upon all Germans as 'fair game' so to speak, who, without a mind of their own, should unconditionally and blindly carry out his directives," Hesse read from the statement. Then Hesse paused dramatically before he delivered what he and his Stasi bosses may have thought would be the knockout punch: "This means, for example, that an agent who refuses to carry out his mission will be shot. Proof of this is contained in the safe that I brought to the DDR with me. Associates and confederates are also threatened with being shot or otherwise murdered if they dare to act against the orders and directives of the MID."

Neither Hesse nor the Stasi ever displayed the "proof" of this assertion, and whether Captain Campbell actually made such threats may never be known. However, the captain was described by Colonel Ross as a "rough son-of-a-bitch." In closing, Hesse revealed the names of East Germans who had been targeted for recruitment but who had refused to "play the dirty game."

Reporters began pressing for details. How did he manage the escape? What kind of car did he use? Did anyone help him? Was he paid by the Stasi? What kind of work was he doing now? Before Hesse could reply, he was silenced by his watchdog Stasi colonel, who indicated that his charge had "many West German helpers."

The Stasi carefully concealed the fact that Hesse was not just an ordinary citizen disillusioned with the warmongering policies of the West; that in fact he had been commissioned a lieutenant in the Stasi after he was recruited by the Americans. Western correspondents began leaving the conference when it became more and more obvious that they would be kept in the dark about much of the affair. "In any case," the newspaper *Main-Post* of Würzburg editorialized, "the East was bent on making political capital out of the entire affair."[10]

The Investigation Continues

At Camp King intelligence headquarters, analysts dissected Hesse's statement and found nothing that added to what was already known. They were hoping to learn more about the number of arrested agents—137—revealed by Prime Minister Grotewohl, but the figure was not repeated at the Hesse news conference. Was there something investigators had missed? Initial questioning of Captain Campbell had established that the files of only twenty-five principal agents were kept in one of the safes, and nine of them were able to escape. But the analysts also thought that the figure could be true. Principal agents operate networks that could consist of up to a dozen or more subagents. Only the principal agent is known to, and maintains contact with, his control officer, who might not know the size of the network.

In an attempt to explain the discrepancy, Ross ordered new and more intense interrogations of all U.S. Army personnel assigned to

Würzburg station. Finally the truth emerged. Captain Campbell had withheld the fact that he was employing about thirty principal agents whom he had not registered with headquarters. It was permissible to make a one-time payment to a source without assigning a code and reporting the act to higher authorities. But using an "uncoded source" more than once was a direct violation of regulations established by the intelligence chief at USAREUR headquarters. It was then assumed that all of Captain Campbell's uncoded sources had been arrested by Stasi counterespionage as well.

Meeting with his counterintelligence staff, Colonel Ross ordered that inspection teams visit all field stations to scrutinize all records and assure that all "uncoded agents" were either discontinued or properly registered. "Maybe the East Germans just lied about the number of arrests they made," he said. "But by God, I want security as tight as we can make it, and I want everyone to know that there'll be hell to pay for the slightest violation." Then he revealed that Captain Campbell had been ordered to return to the United States. However, he was not transferred home immediately. On August 6, 1956, General H. I. Hodes, commander in chief of the U.S. Army in Europe, let the captain off lightly with an administrative reprimand. It was better than a court-martial, but he would have to work hard for further promotion. The sleeping sergeant, Glenn D. Wood, also was reprimanded by General Hodes.

On October 15, 1956, Chief Warrant Officer Cecil C. Lacy Jr. reported to the commander of the 522nd MI Battalion that five of Würzburg station's agents had been tried by the East Germans in Magdeburg. Lacy was the assistant source (or agent) control officer at the intelligence division of the European headquarters of the army in Heidelberg. He had based his information on a Berlin newspaper report, which said the judge had handed down sentences ranging from thirteen months to seven years at hard labor. No other trials of agents betrayed by Hesse were made public.

Troubles Mount

In the meantime, the nine agents who had been extricated from East Germany spent four months at the Würzburg station awaiting West German government recognition as refugees. They were fed and provided with pocket money. When their status was approved, the former agents were paid cash settlements ranging from DM500 to 1,500 (US$125 to $375), for which they were made to sign quitclaims. This was shabby compensation at best. After all, while performing a dangerous service for the United States, they had lost their homes and personal property and had nearly lost their freedom, thanks to a U.S. Army officer's negligence.

The cavalier treatment of the compromised agents backfired in January 1957. Five former agents filed a claim for additional compensation with the European Command Headquarters, which bucked the hot potato to Lieutenant Colonel Crawford, the chief of the 522nd MI Battalion. In a letter classified as secret, Crawford replied that in view of the original denial that the safe caper had occurred, the only appropriate answer was a reiteration of the denial: "It is considered that any admission of the validity of such claims would create a precedent which could possibly result in hundreds of such claims by dropped sources of this unit."[11] Undoubtedly, Crawford felt he was acting in the best interest of the government. These agents were not just "dropped sources"; they were victims of betrayal. Nevertheless, acting on the colonel's recommendation, the Judge Advocate General in Heidelberg, the U.S. Army's highest legal authority in Europe, denied the claims.

For almost two years the intelligence brass at European headquarters sat on their hands, probably hoping the claims would evaporate with the passage of time. By now, all nine of the compromised agents had filed claims. Then, in December 1987, Chief Warrant Officer Quinton B. Shafer, an agent control officer, was forced to reopen the matter. Despite the original rebuff, the former agents had continued to press their claims and as a result were being watched constantly by CIC agents. The surveillance established that the "Würzburg Nine" had hired an American attorney, George C. Dix of New York. "Continuing CIS [counterintelligence surveillance] indicates Dix is taking an active interest in the case and that the claimants are passing extensive data to Dix to substantiate the claims," the CIC reported to Shafer.

While Shafer was trying the decide how to cope with the new information, he received another unsettling report. A former Würzburg agent had written to the U.S. Commander in Berlin demanding payment of "DM7,850 [US$1,962]—DM6,000 as indemnification, and the remainder for unpaid operational expenses and salary while employed."

This new claim prompted Shafer to send a memorandum to the chief of the section that handled transportation intelligence at Heidelberg headquarters.[12] "This development puts an entirely different light on our problems with this group, as it will undoubtedly lead (the new claimant) into contact with other former Würzburg sources residing in West Berlin and West Germany," Shafer wrote. Horst Hesse's safe caper was still having repercussions—repercussions that had assumed dimensions over which Stasi officers must have been gloating: When communist agents were caught in the West or managed to escape before being nabbed, the Stasi generously awarded them monetary bonuses, new apartments, and jobs.

Shafer must have taken a deep breath before recommending that an "equitable settlement" be reached with the group. Even then, he was still pinching pennies. "It is believed that such settlements should range from a minimum of DM5,000 [US$1,250] to a maximum of DM10,000 [US$2,500]," he wrote. To justify his figures, Shafer wrote that some of the group "lost considerably more than others; some are comparatively young and have adjusted, while others have difficulty in obtaining satisfactory employment due to their age." Finally, Shafer suggested that settlements be paid by "intelligence personnel directly to the claimants and not through negotiations with Dix." He figured that this method was necessary because the judge advocate had officially discredited the claims. "In addition, through use of intelligence personnel we can officially disclaim the attempt in the event of misfire." In closing, Shafer warned that even if his recommendations were implemented, the files on the incident could not be completely closed: "Numerous sources were arrested and imprisoned in the East Zone and may appear at a later date requesting assistance."

Shafer's memorandum went unanswered for two months. At that point, he wrote another plea for a "thorough review" of the matter, rehashing his earlier memorandum, and because he sensed that any recommendation for an appropriate settlement would again go unheeded, adding a new twist: He proposed that the Bundesnachrichtendienst (BND), the West German Federal Intelligence Service, be asked for "assistance in putting pressure on the group to have the claims withdrawn."

Shafer's superiors stewed another two months over the new memorandum. Eventually they decided to wash their hands of the matter and let Colonel Ross of the 513th MI Group settle it. By then, Ross had completely reorganized the unit. Operations in East Germany were running more smoothly, although the Eastern-bloc intelligence services were formidable opponents. In an article attacking "American secret service gangsters," the Czechoslovakian Communist Party newspaper *Rude Pravo* called Colonel Ross "the gray ghost." The moniker had been coined by a KGB general stationed in Prague, who was quoted as saying Ross would appear at trouble spots and disappear as suddenly as he had arrived. Ross was proud of the label, and it became a badge of honor. Meanwhile, he was plagued by an occasional defector from the American ranks and an occasional penetration from the East. However, no one else had damaged the U.S. Army's intelligence effort in Germany as much as had Hesse. Ross had heard about the claims and was not surprised when he was requested to put an end to the matter. He knew just how to do it: His ace in the hole was John H. Willms, who had become Ross's most dependable troubleshooter. Bilingual in French and German, Willms had arrived in Germany during the war as a captain in counterintelligence. He had been involved in Operation Paperclip, locating German rocket scientists to work for the United States—among them Wernher von Braun, who developed the rocket used in the first manned flight to the moon. When the war ended, Willms chose to remain in Germany as a civilian employee of the Department of the Army. His rank as chief of the 513th MI Group's special liaison section was equivalent to that of colonel. Many German officials he had helped during the lean postwar years with food and such luxuries as American soap, chocolate, and cigarettes now held top government positions. His friends were mayors, police chiefs, lawyers, and above all, ranking members of the Bundesamt für Verfassungsschutz (BfV), the West German counterespionage agency. No other U.S. intelligence official in Germany, the CIA included, was as well connected as Willms.[13]

"John, Heidelberg wants us to clean up the Würzburg claims mess," Ross told Willms at a meeting in the colonel's austere office, furnished by nothing more than a desk and a few straight back chairs. Its only adornments were a photograph of President Eisenhower and a U.S. flag. "It burns my ass, the way they have treated those agents," Ross said heatedly, and rose out of his chair. "First they just about threw them out; told them they ought to be lucky to be alive. Then they denied the claims, and now those people in Heidelberg are running scared."

Willms knew that if anyone would act resolutely to resolve the claims issue quickly and equitably, it would be Ross. He once was called to a conference with a CIA official who had asked Ross's help in getting a prominent chemist out of East Germany. The CIA man had hemmed and hawed about the money it would cost. The colonel cut him short, saying, "Stop moaning, I'll spend 10,000 dollars." It was vintage Ross. A week later the chemist was safely in the West.[14]

"I can't imagine what got into Heidelberg, suggesting that I beg the BND to put pressure on those people to drop the claims," Ross said as he handed Willms the memorandum written by Chief Warrant Officer Shafer. The memorandum had been sent to Ross for action, without comment from headquarters. "Damn it, John, those agents risked their necks for us, and I'm going to do right by them." Then Ross gave Willms another sheaf of papers. It was a scathing three-page reply to the assistant chief of staff for intelligence, Major General Willems, rejecting all his recommendations. The liaison officer read the letter and grinned. "I know what you're going to say, John, but I'm not sending it," the colonel said, pursing his lips. "We'll settle this mess and then tell 'em, right?" Problem solving was Willms's forte. He looked at Ross and said, "Can do."

On April 30, 1959, Willms drove to the headquarters of the BfV in Cologne. He knew the counterespionage agency had a special department handling resettlement cases. BfV President Manfred Schrübbers and Willms met for thirty minutes, and the claims problem was solved. The former Würzburg agents were offered well-paying jobs and new apartments, and for the next five years they were exempted from paying income tax. All accepted happily and swore to keep their espionage activities for the Americans, and the settlement, secret.

The Real Horst Hesse

For ten years the Stasi sent Hesse around East Germany lecturing on his exploits at party meetings, schools, and to members of the paramilitary Society for Sports and Technology. By 1966 he had reached the rank of lieutenant colonel, but his health had deteriorated, and he was allowed to retire. In 1975, when U.S. intelligence officials had forgotten the safe caper and Colonel Ross had been retired for twelve years, Hesse was trotted out once more. He was glorified in a movie as the hero who served the "workers' and peasants' state" in a dangerous assignment. Trying their best to make it into a James Bond–type thriller, the communist propagandists even gave the film the title "For Eyes Only."

The film extolled the virtues of Horst Hesse as a "heroic comrade," a "reconnoiterer for peace" who had insinuated himself into a U.S. intelligence service. The official Communist Party newspaper *Neues Deutschland,* in describing the movie, provided details suggesting that the safe caper was the result of a carefully planned operation. U.S. Army counterintelligence analysts were unable to verify the veracity of the new information. Their skepticism was not without foundation, since experts readily identified several lies. For example, the communists claimed that an American military court had sentenced Hesse to death, "in absentia, of course." German civilians were never tried by U.S. courts-martial. U.S. military government courts, which did adjudicate crimes committed by Germans against the occupation forces, were dissolved when West Germany regained its sovereignty more than half a decade before Hesse stole the safes.

When the communist government collapsed in 1989, the Hesse case came to life once more as former East German intelligence officers were being debriefed. Former Colonel Rainer Wiegand revealed that propagandists' lies and half-truths notwithstanding, the operation had indeed been meticulously planned.[15]

Hesse, born in 1922, had been seriously wounded during his service as an infantry corporal in World War II. He was taken prisoner by the

British Army but quickly released because of his war wounds. In 1945 he returned to his hometown of Magdeburg on the Elbe river, which was part of the Soviet zone of occupation. He joined the Communist Party there and worked for a short time as a mechanic. Then he volunteered for the People's Police, the Vopo, and was assigned to a border guard unit. In 1954 the state security ministry ordered the discharge of anyone—including Communist Party members—who had been a prisoner of the Western allies. Since the Soviets had recruited agents from among prisoners of war, the Stasi naturally figured, wrongly, that the Western forces had done likewise.

After his stint as a Vopo sergeant, Hesse was working again as a mechanic at a machine factory when he received a letter from a Siegfried Voigt inviting him to visit Berlin. Hesse recalled Voigt as a former neighbor who had moved to Berlin. Hesse did not know Voigt well but knew he was an idler who had gotten mixed up in a theft before "fleeing the republic." Now this sudden contact. What was Voigt up to? Hesse recalled the lectures on espionage that he had attended during his People's Police service. The instructor had described unexpected letters from former acquaintances as one of the methods employed by spy recruiters. Hesse seized the chance to prove his loyalty to the party, and informed the Stasi's Magdeburg district office, which in turn alerted Berlin.

Stasi counterespionage officers established that Voigt was indeed employed by U.S. Army intelligence as a recruiter and a principal agent. Even though the state security service had been elevated to a ministry only three years earlier, it had a cadre highly experienced in the conspiratorial modus operandi of counterintelligence. Among them was Colonel Josef Kiefel, a German Communist Party veteran who had fled to the Soviet Union when the Nazis came to power in 1933. During World War II he was trained as a combat intelligence agent and earned Soviet decorations for fighting behind the German lines with partisan units. Just before the end of the war he parachuted into Czechoslovakia and established an espionage cell. Now working as chief of counterintelligence for the MfS in Berlin, Kiefel had designed a plan to infiltrate Hesse into U.S. Army intelligence.

Hesse was told to visit his old neighbor in Berlin and allow himself to be recruited. The ruse worked perfectly. Hesse's initial assignment for U.S. Army intelligence was to apply for a job with the Soviet Army as a mechanic—a job that would allow him access to Soviet military installations. Colonel Kiefel alerted the KGB, which arranged for Hesse to be employed at the Soviet Army garrison in Magdeburg.

Once settled in his new job, Hesse reported back to Voigt in Berlin, and U.S. Army intelligence issued its first order. He was to photograph the interior of the installation, concentrating on the buildings that housed administrative offices, on tanks and armored vehicles showing unit numbers, and on anything else he thought might be important. The information was sorely needed by U.S. intelligence specialists assigned to assemble the order of battle, the organization of the Soviet forces in Germany. Within a matter of months, Hesse had a considerable reputation as a spy for the U.S. Army. His photographs and reports on Soviet troop movements were highly prized. Hesse would bring his material personally to West Berlin, as the border was still wide open at that time.

Colonel Kiefel was puzzled by the Americans' ready acceptance of this material and their failure to question the agent about how it was obtained. "You know," Hesse later told students at the MfS counterintelligence school in Potsdam, "I would have fallen on my ass very quickly if the Americans had asked the right questions."[16] He explained that all the photographs were taken by KGB officers: "I never saw the pictures. I just delivered the exposed film. If I had been asked what time of day they were taken, from what angle, at what exposure, and so forth, I wouldn't have been able to answer correctly." This fact had bothered his superiors, who refused to believe that the Americans were accepting Hesse's work at face value. They were convinced that eventually he would be exposed. Therefore, Colonel Kiefel decided to speed up the process of forcing the Americans' hand. Hesse was only of marginal value so long as he operated inside East Germany. He was needed inside the U.S. Army's intelligence establishment, where he would have access to information pointing to agents whom the Stasi had not been able to detect.

Hesse had been reporting to his Stasi controllers that Voigt was a careless man who kept records of his espionage activities in a desk at his apartment. Colonel Kiefel came up with a perfect plan. After completing the next delivery to West Berlin, Hesse told Voigt that he needed some rest and recreation from his nerve-racking job and suggested that they go to a nightclub. Voigt was only too happy to oblige his ace agent, and said he would bring his girlfriend along. While the trio was sipping champagne at the expense of U.S. Army intelligence, a Stasi burglar entered Voigt's apartment and made off with lists of agents and their assignments and locations. One of the lists included Hesse.

Hesse, the loyal Stasi man and would-be U.S. spy, was also a good actor. "You idiot!" he screamed at Voigt after he was told about the burglary. "You have not only endangered me but other agents. There's no way I can go home again without getting arrested. I have to stay here now and leave my family behind." The Americans agreed, never suspecting that the burglary was a carefully directed Stasi ploy to discredit Voigt and boost Hesse's credibility. Anyone willing to forsake his family had to be true blue. To underpin Hesse's bona fides, a Stasi officer arrested Hesse's wife—and in broad daylight, to make sure that the neighbors would see it. Interrogators questioned Hesse's wife for several hours and then released her. She and Hesse's teenage son were left believing that their husband and father had turned traitor.

Before Hesse was transferred to the Würzburg station he was subjected to polygraph examination. He later claimed that he had been strapped to lie detectors four times and had passed with flying colors. What probably happened was that the Berlin test proved "inconclusive." U.S. Army polygraph operators at the time were few and far between and lacked experience and expertise. As a result, if examinations showed that a person could be lying but the operator was not absolutely sure, the tests were labeled "inconclusive" and passed to a more experienced operator for a second reading. If that resulted in still another "inconclusive," a second test would be scheduled for six months to a year later.[17] Hesse apparently made his move to escape with the safes before he was retested.

The safe caper was the first major compromise of agents operating in communist East Germany for the U.S. Army as a result of hostile infiltration. Conversely, for the Ministry for State Security, it was the first successful penetration of a U.S. intelligence service. The coup could not have come at a more propitious moment—a time when the Stasi still had to prove itself as the praetorian guard of the Communist Party hierarchy and as a reliable partner of its Soviet masters. The contents of the safes provided grist for the anti-American propaganda mills. There now was "proof" of what the party had been telling the East German people all along, that the evil imperialists were out to destroy the peace-loving DDR and socialism.

Aside from having proved its value to the party and to the Soviet comrades, the Hesse operation had another significant effect on the MfS hierarchy. Until then, East German espionage operations had been almost exclusively directed at West German targets. The U.S. Army in Europe as well as NATO as a whole had been the concern of the Soviet services, the KGB and the GRU. The Hesse operation had exposed the weaknesses of the U.S. military and pointed to future possibilities. The MfS leadership, especially Mielke and his espionage chief Markus Wolf, had tasted blood. The United States had become a major espionage target of East Germany.

THE HOSTAGE WHO HELD OUT

Stasi spymaster Markus Wolf was desperate in 1955 to recruit someone with access to sensitive information gathered by the West Berlin mission of the U.S. High Commission for Germany (HICOG). They had one agent, Heinz Bielke, but he was a low-level employee in HICOG's labor section. He did, however, furnish the Stasi with personality profiles of persons in higher positions who might be persuaded to become agents. One of those he fingered was Christa Trapp, a twenty-six-year-old secretary and administrative assistant to the chief of the Eastern Affairs division. Christa Trapp lived with her mother, who was then fifty-two years old. Her father was a prisoner of war in the Soviet Union and had died shortly after his release. To supplement her salary, Trapp gave private English lessons.

Early in 1955, Trapp's neighbor Hildegard Diskowski invited her to a theater performance, saying she had an extra ticket and that her husband could not attend. Trapp accepted. During the intermission, the neighbor met a "friend." They greeted each other warmly, and Diskowski introduced him to Trapp as Henry Gerlach, an ostensibly well-to-do businessman. A few days later Diskowski contacted Trapp again to tell her that Gerlach wanted to learn English and to ask whether she would accept him as a pupil. Trapp agreed. A week later, Gerlach invited his teacher to join him for dinner. The vivacious and pretty Christa Trapp declined, but Gerlach persisted, showering her with flowers and boxes of bonbons. "He was not unattractive, but not my cup of tea," she would say later. "He was not up to my cultural standards."[18] On June 16, 1955, Gerlach begged her again to join him for dinner, and this time she accepted on condition that her mother accompany them. Gerlach agreed, and came to pick up the women in a chauffeured car. The two women got into the car, and after a few minutes' drive, Trapp asked Gerlach where he was taking them, because he was heading toward the lower middle-class Neukölln district. Gerlach replied that he had some business to take care of and that it would take only a few minutes. The car drove into a street that led straight to the Soviet sector. At the border, the car was stopped by a People's Police (Vopo) border guard.

Trapp realized at this point that she was being kidnapped. Had she known that one of her colleagues, Elizabeth Erdmann, had been seized by the Stasi on April 24—just two months earlier—she would have refused the dinner invitation. Erdmann, a secretary for the mission's political affairs division, was abducted while returning from West Germany to Berlin by bus.[19] At the communist checkpoint, Erdmann was pulled off a bus by Vopo officers and taken to a Stasi office in nearby Potsdam. She was interrogated throughout the night and pressured to sign an agreement to spy. She refused, and eventually she was released. Erdmann promptly reported the incident to her superior. For some unexplained reason, the U.S. government kept quiet about it until 62 days after the Trapp kidnapping, when both incidents were revealed at a news conference.[20]

Undaunted, the quick-witted Trapp opened the car door and pulled her mother out, and the two tried to run back to the American sector. They stopped when the Vopo drew his gun, bellowing that he would shoot. The car with her "pupil" still inside drove off. The two women were separated and driven off in cars that had been idling nearby. Christa Trapp and her mother had become victims of a carefully constructed plan designed to force the young woman into spying on her American employers when the Romeo approach failed.

The plot was hatched by Stasi Major Horst Jänicke, a former Luftwaffe soldier who was persuaded to become a communist while a prisoner of war in the Soviet Union. The other signatory to the eight-page kidnapping plan was Captain Werner Prosetzky, a former clerk with a grade-school education, and a long-time Communist Party member.[21] The two men submitted the plan to their chief Markus Wolf on March 23, 1955, recommending that the abduction take place on April 4. "Except for changes in connection with crossing of the sector border and the cover of 'Stein,' approved," Wolf wrote on the top margin, and signed it on March 30. Stein was the cover name of Henry Gerlach (or whatever his real name was), who was described as a "GM," or *geheimer Mitarbeiter* (secret collaborator). His chauffeur was a Stasi officer. Since Trapp had resisted Gerlach's dinner invitations for so long, Stasi agent Gerlach had apparently been under pressure to produce results, and in desperation he agreed to her mother coming along. That's when the Stasi plan went awry.

According to the detailed scenario, Gerlach's car was to be stopped by a Vopo, who after pretending to check a wanted list, was to inform Trapp that she must accompany the two detectives to their station. Gerlach was to be placed under arrest, and Trapp was to be told that he was wanted for engaging in illegal East-West trade. The two "detectives" were Prosetzky and another Stasi man. "In the event that 'T' causes trouble, such as screaming at the border, Stein is to prevent this by force, and the story will be changed accordingly, that he is our collaborator." They had not counted on Trapp's jumping out of the car and pulling her mother after her. Thus Gerlach's cover was preserved.

Prosetzky took Trapp to a Stasi safe house where Jänicke awaited them. There the two men subjected her to a recruiting pitch. "They told me that they knew I worked for HICOG and wanted me to talk about my job in detail and about my superiors and colleagues," she told me. "Then they described the Eastern bloc as a 'peace camp' and threatened that when they took over West Berlin I would be held to account for having worked for the Americans against the German people." Her account jibed exactly with the recruitment scenario of the kidnapping plan. They offered her a salary of DM500 (US$125) a month and promised her a bonus of DM10,000 (US$2,500) after three years, as well as help in securing emigration to the United States. "If you don't sign a pledge to work for us," Jänicke told the frightened Trapp, "you will never see your mother again."[22] In an icy tone of voice, he added: "You will not get out!" This latter threat, too, was made according to plan, though with a slightly different variation, since the Stasi men had not expected Trapp's mother to be present: "In the event that 'T' does not accept our offer, she is to be pressured (arrested on charges of working against the DDR)."

Trapp's intelligence, decisiveness, and fortitude had been abysmally misjudged by General Wolf, Jänicke, and Prosetzky. They were misled in this by Trapp's neighbor Hildegard Diskowski, who turned out to be a Stasi agent code-named Gisela. She had described Trapp as apolitical but as often expressing fear that West Berlin might someday be occupied by the Soviets: "She does not have much willpower, displays a certain insecurity and fickleness, and is relatively easily influenced."[23]

Trapp once had had ambitions of becoming an actress, and the kidnapping and the Stasi pressure gave her a chance to play the role of a frightened damsel to the hilt. "Let me go home and think over your proposal," she told the Stasi officers. "You must understand that it is not easy for me to go behind the backs of my employers."[24] Prosetzky said soothingly that he understood fully, and congratulated her for having misgivings. But Jänicke, who played the "bad cop," yelled that she had to decide immediately, and threatened her again with prosecution. At last she agreed, but she refused to put the agreement in writing: "Why do I have to do that? You have my word." They applied more pressure, and she complied. She was given DM300 (US$75), for which she had to sign a receipt that according to the scenario, "is to be detailed and worded in compromising language." Before she was released, she was given her assignment: to make carbon copies of all the reports she wrote; to hand in all of her shorthand pads; to report the opinions of the Americans and the German employees; and to report all personnel changes.

At dawn Trapp was driven to the border of the American sector, where her mother was waiting under Vopo guard. The two crossed into West Berlin and took a taxi home. When she arrived for work, Trapp immediately notified her superior and handed over the money Jänicke had given her. Trapp later received a number of telephone calls from the Stasi ordering her to meet with couriers and turn over the material she had been told to gather, but she ignored them. U.S. State Department security officers and U.S. Army CIC agents kept an eye on her until she emigrated with her mother to the United States in 1956.

THE DOUBLE DIPPER

Sergeant James W. Hall III borrowed a dog from his neighbor and went for a morning walk in November 1982, in the upper-class Grunewald district of West Berlin. When he reached the villa occupied by the Soviet consulate, Hall pulled a letter from his pocket and dropped it into the consulate's mailbox. Written in English, the letter expressed interest in "working for you." If there was interest, someone should meet him at the rest stop on the Avus speedway at 7 P.M. that evening. He would be wearing a checkered shirt. The meeting came off, and that same evening Hall was taken by two Soviets to East Berlin. They rode the elevated railway to the Friedrichstrasse station, the border checkpoint. There the Soviets took him through a secret passage used by East German and Soviet intelligence officers to and from West Berlin on clandestine missions. They showed special passes to the border guards, and Hall was allowed through without having to produce identification. A waiting car took them to a villa near the KGB compound in suburban Karlshorst. During a two-hour meeting with KGB officers, Hall told them of his assignment as a U.S. Army signal intelligence and electronic surveillance expert assigned to Field Station Berlin. This was the most sensitive installation in the divided city, operating atop the Teufelsberg, Devil's Mountain. The 300-foot-high hill was built from the rubble of buildings destroyed during World War II by Allied bombers and Soviet artillery. Because of its elevation, it was an ideal electronic espionage location from which the army and the U.S. National Security Agency monitored all military and civilian communications originating in the flat expanse of East Germany and beyond. It was a vital early warning post, and in wartime, could wreak havoc with the command communications of the communist Warsaw Pact armies. Hall had been granted the highest security clearance for access to top secret/sensitive compartmented information.

The Soviets were obviously delighted by the valuable volunteer and agreed to "hire" him. The twenty-three-year-old sergeant from Sharon Springs, New York, had become a traitor. Apparently the KGB, as is usual in dealing with walk-ins, watched him carefully for a while to make sure that he was not a double agent for U.S. intelligence. Before he was taken back to West Berlin, Hall was told that the first working meeting would be in early 1982.

Hall, who enlisted in 1976 and was assigned to the Army Security Agency, first was stationed at Schneeberg, another listening station, at a 2,224-foot elevation near the Czechoslovakian border. It was there that he met a local girl, Heidi. His marriage to her coincided with his transfer to Berlin in 1981, and with Hall's volunteering to spy for the Soviets. Because he had married a foreign national, he needed a waiver to retain his special clearances. Hall had established a fine record on the job; his wife's background was checked, and the waiver was granted.

For the next two years Hall would smuggle the most secret documents out of the Teufelsberg station, hiding them inside his battle fatigue jacket or in a gym bag the Soviets had given him that had a false bottom. He would drive his car to an isolated spot and photograph the loot with a so-called rollover camera also supplied him by the Soviets. This special spy camera with a built-in light source was electrically operated and held enough film to photograph about forty documents. Wide enough to cover half a sheet of 11- by 8-inch paper, the user would place it on top of a document and pull it across the paper in a sweeping motion. Hall's Soviet handlers, whom he met secretly once a month, had struck a mother lode. They received top secret manuals on electronic surveillance, documents detailing the radio frequencies used by American intelligence, and actual intercept of Warsaw Pact military communications.

The sergeant's treasonous activities entered a new phase in 1983. Working as a civilian employee at the Berlin Field Station's auto hobby shop was Huseyin Yildirim, an ace Turkish mechanic who was well-liked by enlisted soldiers and officers. The GIs had nicknamed him "Der Meister," the Master, for his expertise. Hall frequented the shop to work on his car and struck up a friendship with the Meister. One day they were discussing money, and the Turk said he was thinking of quitting to set up his business with a bank loan.[25] "It's easy to make money," said Hall. "Just sell secrets." Der Meister thought it was a good idea and told Hall he had some Turkish friends who would pay well for secrets. And so Hall began to "double-dip."

Hall quickly realized that there were no Turks interested in U.S. secrets, that in fact Der Meister was dealing with the East German foreign intelligence service. Before long Yildirim acknowledged this and told Hall the East Germans wanted to meet him. How? Because of his sensitive position, Hall was prohibited from entering communist territory. The Turk explained that rather than crossing to the East through a checkpoint at the Wall, the East Germans would meet him at the outskirts of the city, at a place surrounded by a series of high fences. The East Germans would slip him through a hole in the fence at a spot used for infiltrating agents. This was located in an isolated area amid stands of trees and clumps of brush at the southeastern suburb of Zehlendorf, bordering on the East German village of Klein Machnow. Hall agreed to the meeting.

The sergeant, wearing civilian clothes, showed up at the border where two Stasi officers were waiting. They introduced themselves as Wolfgang and Horst, took him through the fence, and drove him to a Stasi safe house. The Stasi officers were Colonel Wolfgang Koch and Lieutenant Colonel Horst Schmidt of the Hauptverwaltung Aufklärung's Division Nine, the Stasi's foreign counterintelligence arm.[26] Hall brought no documents—these were delivered by Yildirim, who acted as their courier. Hall's discussions with Koch and Schmidt, during which he did not reveal that he was already working for the KGB, concentrated on future operations, and most importantly, money. Koch agreed to pay $10,000 at each meeting, maybe more later on, and assigned him the code name Paul, which was later changed to Ronnie. Hall, who coveted the finer things of life that his army pay could not support, was pleased. He returned to West Berlin by the same route. At a subsequent meeting the East Germans gave him a British passport issued in the name of R. S. Hillyer and a vaccination certificate in the same name.

During the four years he was assigned to the Teufelsberg, Hall betrayed hundreds of supersecrets. Among the most sensitive was Project Trojan, a worldwide electronic surveillance network that in wartime would have been able to pinpoint armored vehicles, missiles, and aircraft by recording their signal emissions. Worse, Hall's betrayal immobilized a computer program that had been designed to spot gaps in the Soviet military communications network. The resulting damage was estimated in the hundreds of millions of dollars.[27] The East Germans expressed their pleasure with Hall by summoning him to an East Berlin meeting with Stasi minister Erich Mielke and his espionage chief Markus Wolf for the presentation of a decoration. He was handed the Battle Medal of the Ministry for State Security and a $5,000 bonus. Hall was allowed to finger the medal and read the citation, but he had to hand them back.

Meanwhile, the KGB was becoming leery of documents they were receiving from their German colleagues because they had obtained a great deal of the same material from their own agent. At a meeting at the Karlshorst KGB headquarters the two services realized they were working with the same agent. Since the Soviets were getting everything the East Germans collected anyway, why should they spend their own good money? After this meeting, Hall became the exclusive agent of the Stasi until late April 1985. At that time, Hall sent a message to Colonel Koch in East Berlin informing him that he was being transferred to the 513th Military Intelligence Group stationed at Fort Monmouth, New Jersey. The East German espionage service lacked an

Top Stasi counterintelligence officers celebrate the recruitment of U.S. Army Warrant Officer James Hall III. Colonel Karl Grossmann, deputy chief of the foreign espionage directorate's counterintelligence department; Colonel Wolfgang Koch, Hall's case officer; and Major General Harry Schütt, chief of the counterintelligence department. Private photo.

infrastructure for servicing spies in the United States because years before, the KGB had assumed primacy over espionage in the United States with the exception of political and economic spying.[28] Therefore, Hall again became an agent for the Soviets. They worked out an elaborate system of dead letter drops in New Jersey, New York City, and Long Island, where Hall could stash his films. He used the Long Island drop once but never again because it was too time consuming due to heavy traffic in the New York metropolitan area.[29] While Hall was in New Jersey, Field Station Berlin was awarded the coveted "NSA Oscar" for superior performance in 1985, a time when the entire Teufelsberg operation had been compromised.

Hall served only a year at Fort Monmouth, but during that time he flew to Vienna to contact the KGB, using a telephone number he had been given before leaving Germany.[30] There Hall met with a Russian who was an expert in signal intelligence. He had no documents with him but gave him an oral report. Toward the end of meeting, the KGB agent told Hall the KGB knew that he had been providing information to the East Germans and had ordered him to stop. The sergeant explained the difficulty with the dead letter drops. The KGB case officer understood and provided him with specially treated paper to use for invisible letter writing as well as a cover address. Hall never used either the paper or the address. In fact, he lost them while packing to return to Germany with a promotion to staff sergeant after only a year at Fort Monmouth.[31]

With his new assignment to the 302nd Military Intelligence Battalion of the Fifth U.S. Army Corps in Frankfurt, Hall's spying activity became frenetic. Security was so lax that he was able to "borrow" hundreds of secret and top secret documents. Yildirim the Meister had to come down from West Berlin to help. Hall was back in business with the Stasi. He acquired a panel truck solely for photographing documents. Later this became too cumbersome, so Hall rented an apartment near his headquarters. The East Germans paid the rent and other expenses, including the purchase price of a portable photocopier that Hall could take along on military maneuvers so as to continue his spying without missing a beat. There was hardly a sensitive document crossing Hall's desk that was not copied or photographed for the communists. While in Frankfurt, Hall learned that his unit's personnel would be subjected to polygraph examination. Alarmed about having to take a lie detector test, he sent an urgent message to his East Berlin control, asking for instructions on how to beat the "box." He promptly received the information, but it was so technical (terms such as *cardiovascular* were used) that he had trouble comprehending it.[32] As it turned out, he need not have worried. The army did not have enough trained polygraph operators, and the examinations were scrapped.

Despite his lucrative treasonous sideline, Hall remained a top performer in his unit, with excellent efficiency reports, which got him selected to attend a warrant officer training school in the United States. He graduated in February 1988 and was assigned to G-2 (intelligence) of the 24th Infantry Division at Fort Stewart, Georgia, just west of Savannah. Yildirim had also moved to the United States and was living in Belleair Beach, Florida with Peggy Bie, whom he had met in Berlin and who sponsored his immigration. In addition to his espionage courier job, the Turk smuggled diamonds into Europe and the United States from Sierra Leone, West Africa, though that sideline may not have been as lucrative as the spy business.[33]

THE SHOPLIFTER

Colonel Wolfgang Koch's ace agent had dried up and he was diligently exploring ways to reactivate Hall. Furthermore, he had lost contact with five other members of the Berlin Field Station's listening post staff, albeit in positions not as advantageous to the communists as Hall's.[34] All had been recruited by the Turkish auto mechanic. At the same time, the Stasi colonel had developed misgivings about the further use of Yildirim as a courier, for reasons that have never been clearly established.[35] It might have been that Koch felt the Turk's diamond smuggling made him too vulnerable to arrest. To prepare for Hall's eventual return to Germany, Koch decided to find a new courier. Koch needed someone who could speak English to deal with Hall in the West because the warrant officer had let it be known that he no longer wanted to crawl through the hole in the border fence. The lot fell to Joachim Reiff,[36] a professor of languages at East Berlin's Humboldt University, who had been used as a courier years earlier but had been dropped as unreliable.[37] Without obtaining the required permission from Lieutenant General Günter Möller, head of the Main Directorate's Cadre and Training, Koch hired the professor.

Briefed on his assignment to scout locations for possible dead letter drops and clandestine meetings, the professor was sent to West Berlin carrying false identification papers in early August 1988. The linguist had not been in the West for some years and was dazzled by the well-stocked shops. The Stasi had given him just enough West marks to cover expenses and no more. After completing his scouting assignment, the professor went to a department store to browse. As he looked over the goods unavailable in East Germany, temptation got the better of him. Oblivious to the surveillance cameras, he slipped various items into his briefcase and was promptly challenged by a security officer and turned over to police.

"I want to see somebody from the Staatsschutz," the professor blurted out before police had a chance to question him.[38] Staatsschutz is a section of the city's criminal investigation department responsible for political offenses including espionage. Staatsschutz listened to the professor's tale and contacted the Berlin CIA Station, since it involved an American and a civilian whose names he did not know. But whoever was on duty that late afternoon was not interested in the matter.[39] Instead of dropping the matter then, a detective called U.S. Army intelligence. The duty officer also did not seem to show much interest, remarking that there were too many cases of persons who had been arrested for minor crimes claiming to have knowledge of espionage. Nevertheless, Colonel Stuart Herrington, a brilliant intelligence officer with two decades of counterespionage experience, took charge and opened an investigation on August 24, 1988. A team of agents was dispatched to West Berlin. They interrogated the professor and told him he had to return to East Berlin to gather more information and establish his bona fides. They also promised that if he cooperated, his family would be resettled in the West under new identities. Professor Reiff agreed. By fall, Colonel Herrington had zeroed in on James Hall III and Huseyin Yildirim. The involvement of Der Meister must have come as a shock to Herrington. While stationed in Berlin as commander of counterespionage, the colonel also had frequented the auto shop and was on friendly terms with the Turk. However, his emotions in no way deterred him from pursuing the pair of spies with the determination for which he had become known during his two tours of duty in Vietnam.[40] Herrington was the last man to board the final helicopter leaving the U.S. embassy in Saigon on April 18, 1975.

Court-approved wiretaps were installed on both suspects' telephones and legal mail intercepts were put into place. The telephone surveillance uncovered that Yildirim was also using the alias Mike Jones, particularly when he called Hall. Dozens of officers and enlisted men who had served with Hall were questioned. Both Hall and the Turk were watched around the clock by U.S. Army counterintelligence agents. Sophisticated surveillance equipment was installed in areas frequented by Hall. By the end of November, the FBI was brought in on the case.

In early December, Hall was contacted by a man using only the first name Phil. He had met Phil a few months earlier and had accepted him as a fellow conspirator. This time Phil said he wanted to arrange a meeting with an official of the Soviet embassy, who would travel from Washington to Savannah. Hall, eager to get his spy business going again, agreed to a rendezvous the evening of December 20, 1988, at a Days Inn in Savannah.

At the Days Inn, Phil introduced Hall to Vladimir Kossov, who spoke English with an unmistakable Russian accent, and left the room. After a few minutes of chit-chat, Kossov got down to business, saying that the KGB wanted to take over the operation again, in cooperation with its "East German friends." The Soviet told Hall that this was necessary to make sure that he was "safe and secure," and secondly, because "we can help you much more." Hall was noncommittal. Kossov said he was new on the case and wanted to know a bit more about Hall's operations. They chatted for about two hours, Hall relating how he worked with Yildirim, methods they used and how he hated to crawl beneath the border fence in Berlin. "My superiors have been looking at some of the things we have been receiving through our East German friends," Kossov remarked. "They think that you're a very valuable person and the material you have been giving them is very valuable, very valuable. Now, to speak frankly with you, my superiors in Moscow, they thought that the way our friends handled the whole thing could have been done much better for two important reasons. One is your personal safety and security, which is number one for everybody involved. And the second one, we think that, uh, because the material that you provided was so good and so valuable, we think that they should've taken—how you say in America?—better care of you."

As the conversation progressed, Hall became increasingly profuse in describing the material he had supplied the East Germans. He told of a plan to release a special kind of dust over enemy communications centers: "When it goes into electronic equipment, it implodes it. Like if you blow dust into a TV and turn the TV on, it just puff, it shuts it down." One of the most sensitive systems Hall betrayed was capable of intercepting and cutting into Warsaw Pact communications, enabling U.S. military linguists to issue confusing commands to combat commanders. This system was in communist hands even before it was installed at the Teufelsberg electronic warfare facility. "So before you even turned it on, our side knew already?" asked Kossov. "I hope so," Hall replied. "Don't know, personally. . . . As long as I get my money, you can do what you like with whatever it is I give you." This prompted Kossov to ask, "So you did it just for money?" Hall: "Oh yeah. It's not because I am anti-American. I wave the flag as much as anybody else."

Kossov then opened his attaché case and took out bundles of money. He took out six packets, saying Moscow had decided to make up the difference in underpayment to him by the East Germans. "Five thousand, ten thousand, twenty, twenty-five, that's thirty." Hall, slouching in his chair, took the money and nonchalantly tossed it into a shopping bag. Kossov produced a receipt stating that the money was payment for past services and asked Hall to sign it. "Boy, you guys are tightening the reins, aren't you? I used to just scribble my name across it. Now I have to sign my full name." Kossov smiled. "Well, you know, bureaucracies are the same on both sides." He took out another $30,000 and handed the bundles to Hall. "This is for services you will provide in the future. Please write out another receipt." Hall copied the wording from the first receipt and signed.

In closing, the two discussed plans for the delivery of future secrets, including the rental of a post office box. Before leaving the room, Kossov made a little speech: "Well, I know you told me before that you do it for, uh, for money; but still, I want to thank you on behalf of my country and on behalf of socialism. I'm sure you probably don't believe in socialism. But, uh . . . ." Hall: "Well, I do have my personal problems with it." Kossov shrugged. "But, uh, well, I do honor socialism. And I thank you in the name of socialism. And, uh, I do think we can work together." The warrant officer replied that Kossov should call him the next day and he would give him his post office box number.

When Hall walked out of the Days Inn, Colonel Herrington watched with deep satisfaction as his men arrested him and put him in handcuffs. Vladimir Kossov's performance was worthy of an Oscar. Kossov turned out to be FBI Special Agent Dimitry Dourjinsky, and Phil was a U.S. Army counterintelligence agent. The entire meeting had been videotaped.[41] FBI and Army agents immediately searched Hall's home in Richmond Hill, Georgia. They found a briefcase holding four passports, his own and those of his family; family medical records; and $5,000, plus some foreign currency. A search of Hall's pickup truck turned up a manila envelope containing $4,150 in fifty-dollar bills. Hidden in a duffle bag was the British passport in the name of R. S. Hillyer but bearing Hall's photograph and a British vaccination certificate issued to Robert Hillyer. Most damning was another duffle bag that held top secret intelligence documents including a letter addressed to "Dear Friend" and detailing the kind of intelligence information Hall needed to procure. While the search of Hall's home was under way, a team of agents combed through Yildirim's house in Florida, discovering false identification papers.

Confronted with unassailable evidence, Hall confessed fully and agreed to cooperate with investigators. He was facing a possible death sentence. However, prosecutors told him if he pleaded guilty and agreed never to reveal the details of what he had betrayed, they would asked for a forty-five-year prison term. Hall complied. At his general court-martial at Fort McNair in Washington, D.C., on March 10, 1989, a tearfully contrite Hall said he felt his betrayal "to the bone." His father, James W. Hall Jr., told the court his son loved the U.S. Army and that he was shocked when he learned of the espionage charge. When he met his son after the arrest, the father said, "I felt like punching his lights out . . . but then I threw my arms around him." Colonel Howard C. Eggers, a military judge, sentenced Hall to forty years at Leavenworth military penitentiary, a fine of $50,000, and a dishonorable discharge. The Soviets and the East Germans had paid the traitor a total of about $300,000. His pay as a warrant officer was $25,894 a year plus allowances.

Huseyin Yildirim, then sixty-two years old, was tried in Savannah, vehemently denying that he had been a spy. He told such convoluted lies that one intelligence officer remarked that the Turk was a "cultural phenomenon whose manhood is enhanced by the size of his lies that are believed." Yildirim claimed that Hall had instigated the operation, and that Yildirim merely took the documents to guard them from falling into the wrong hands. To buttress his claim, Yildirim con-

U.S. Army Warrant Officer James Hall III caught on videotape accepting $60,000 from an agent of the FBI who Hall believed was a Soviet KGB agent. Courtesy U.S. Army.

fided to his court-appointed defense attorney Lamar Walter, a former U.S. Attorney, that he had hidden many documents in the wine cellar of an apartment building in West Berlin and in two water jugs buried in a cemetery. Walter, accompanied by FBI agents, flew to Berlin, where they found about 10,000 pages of highly sensitive National Security Agency and Army signal intelligence documents.[42] No one believed the Turk's tale. It seemed more likely that he had stashed the material away for a rainy day, as a sort of private retirement plan under which he would give the East Germans a few pages whenever he was short of cash.

At one point during the two-day trial before U.S. District Judge B. Avent Edenfield, an FBI expert testified that he lifted Yildirim's fingerprints from a $50 bill found in Hall's truck as well as from the "Dear Friend" letter. There was also testimony that a copy of the "Dear Friend" letter was found in one of the water jugs dug up in the cemetery. An FBI counterespionage expert testified that the letters were typical of those sent by Soviet intelligence requesting information from agents. The evidence against Yildirim, including the Hall videotape, was overwhelming. The prosecution called about thirty witnesses. The defense called none and rested. Walter had defended Yildirim to the best of his ability under extremely trying circumstances that included a

Huseyin Yildirim, a Turkish auto mechanic who helped Hall copy top secret documents and who delivered the copies to the Stasi. Yildirim is shown leaving the court after he was sentenced in 1989 to life imprisonment. Unlike Hall, who made a full confession and cooperated with investigators, Yildirim pleaded innocent and claimed that he was actually working for U.S. intelligence. Courtesy U.S. Army.

threat on his life by the Turk's girlfriend Peggy Bie.[43] She was dissatisfied by the way he handled Yildirim's defense, maintaining that he should have tried the case in the press, which is what she had attempted to do. Peggy Bie had contacted ABC television, which aired her story that her live-in lover had been framed by U.S. intelligence, in particular by Colonel Herrington. Attorney Walter would later describe Peggy Bie as a "space cadet."[44] After six and a half hours of deliberation, the jury returned a verdict of guilty. Yildirim was sentenced to life imprisonment, and banishment from the United States forever if he was later paroled. Interviewed by counterespionage officials from time to time in the Lompoc, California federal prison, Yildirim has steadfastly denied having been part of the Hall espionage conspiracy. Although spy chief Markus Wolf has said that Yildirim recruited "several" Americans, the Turk has refused to discuss this claim. His request for a reduction of his sentence was denied in 1996.

The Hall/Yildirim espionage conspiracy was one of the U.S. Army's worst security failures. "It was the Army's Walker case," commented a Washington source intimately familiar with the affair. (Navy War-

Hall is escorted by military police to his 1989 court-martial. He was sentenced to forty years in prison for spying for the East Germans and the Soviets. Courtesy U.S. Army.

rant Officer Arthur J. Walker sold codes and other information to the Soviets, rendering the Navy's worldwide communications useless. Walker was arrested in 1985 and subsequently sentenced to life imprisonment.)

HALL'S TWIN

Paul Limbach and Heiner Emde, tenacious and well-connected reporters for the now defunct German magazine *Quick*, made a contact in East Berlin in January 1990 who sold them several thousand documents from General Wolf's espionage archive. Among the documents were original U.S. intelligence manuals and reports classified as top secrets. The reporters' contact, a former Stasi officer, said he procured the documents from two Americans. He named Hall as one but knew only the alias of the other—Jens Karney—and his address in East Berlin. Limbach contacted his friend Gerhard Boeden, the head of the Office for the Protection of the Constitution. After examining the papers, Boeden decided to hand over copies to the CIA station chief in Bonn, Ed Pechus.[45] In summer 1990, I obtained copies of these documents along with Karney's name and address. Karney reportedly lived in an apartment building in the Friedrichshain district of East Berlin, but residents there denied knowing anyone by that name. Karl Grossmann, former deputy chief of the Stasi's foreign counterintelligence department, later confirmed that Karney was an American who had spied for his department under the code name Kid, starting in 1982. Grossmann said he could not remember the agent's clear name—only that he was an air force sergeant who defected to East Germany in 1985: "He was a homosexual with real problems, but we gave him a job translating radio intercepts. We gave him the Jens Karney name and made him a Danish citizen because of his Scandinavian-like accent. Then when the MfS stopped functioning in January 1990, he got a job as a building superintendent at the Liebknecht Haus."[46] Officials at the Liebknecht Haus, traditional headquarters of Germany's Communist Party, denied in interviews that they employed Karney.

By summer 1990, Karney had been identified by American authorities as U.S. Air Force Sergeant Jeffrey Carney, of Cincinnati, Ohio. He had been assigned to the 6912th Electronic Security Group in Berlin from 1982 until 1984, when he was transferred to Goodfellow Air Force Base in Texas. He deserted his post there in the fall of the following year, heading straight back to Berlin, where he asked his Stasi contacts for asylum.[47] It remains a mystery why U.S. authorities did not arrest him in 1990, when Berlin was still governed by occupation law and the Allies had legal jurisdiction over their own. Was it a bureaucratic foul-up or had the CIA not informed the Air Force in time? Carney was finally seized by agents of the Air Force Office of Special Investigation in April 1991, at a time when full sovereignty had been restored to the city of Berlin. German judicial authorities had not been privy to the U.S. action. Thus, the Federal Attorney General's office confirmed in June 1997 that it had launched an investigation into the matter—particularly, whether CIA officials had flouted German law. The investigation was eventually terminated when the arrest was determined to have been legal under the Status of Forces Agreement governing the stationing and rights of U.S. military forces in Germany.

Jeffrey Carney was controlled by Colonel Heinz Schockenbäumer, who led a division of the Eleventh Department in foreign espionage against U.S. forces in West Berlin. Carney did not always go to the trouble of copying documents. He delivered *numbered* originals.[48] The documents he provided enabled the KGB, which had the greater expertise in this field, to spot and correct deficiencies in the communications security of the Soviet military and the Warsaw Pact. Carney provided much of the same information Hall had sold, which was ironclad confirmation for the East Germans and the Soviets that Hall's material had not been doctored. Particularly critical was a supersecret study code-named Canopy Wing, requested by the Joint Chiefs of Staff. Carney's unit was to work out methods that would prevent the Soviet general staff from effectively employing high frequency communications in controlling and leading combat forces. Warsaw Pact planners must have danced a jig when they received a forty-seven-page study of the weaknesses of Soviet general staff communications. The cost of the recommended U.S. countermeasures, according to the study, was estimated at $14.5 billion. The foregoing are but a fraction of the U.S. secrets Carney transmitted to East Berlin.

Jeffrey Carney apparently did not turn traitor for money. He was a homosexual with severe emotional problems, frequently suffering from deep depression.[49] Whether he was recruited by one of the Stasi's homosexual Romeos is not clear. He was, however, recruited, and did not volunteer after walking through a checkpoint at the Berlin Wall, as some reports have suggested. It is highly probable that Carney frequented the auto shop and came into contact there with "Der Meister" Yildirim, who spotted him for the Stasi. Money did not appear to be the reason for Carney's turning traitor, though after his defection he was provided with a car and a salary of 3,000 East marks a month—roughly the salary of a Stasi lieutenant colonel.

Carney might never have been caught if reporters Paul Limbach and Heiner Emde had not found the documents the sergeant betrayed. He was tried in secret before a general court-martial on November 4, 1991, at Andrews Air Force Base, near Washington, D.C. Carney pleaded guilty to charges of espionage, conspiracy, and desertion, and was sentenced to thirty-eight years' imprisonment and a dishonorable discharge.

OTHER MILITARY SPIES

Airman First Class Robert Glenn Thompson betrayed agents that the U.S. Air Force Office of Special Investigation (OSI) in West Berlin had operating behind the Iron Curtain. Thompson, who enlisted in the Air Force in 1952 at age seventeen, served as a mechanic at various bases until he was assigned as a clerk to the Berlin OSI office after he injured his back. Though he was court-martialed, demoted one rank, and fined $67 for dereliction of duty while drunk, he continued to have access to top secret information. This was a grave security failure in a unit responsible for counterespionage. After a night of drinking, Thompson crossed over to East Berlin and volunteered to work for the Stasi. In 1958 he returned to the United States for discharge—but not before the Stasi had handed him over to the KGB. He took leave to train in the Soviet Union in espionage techniques. Thompson was caught in 1965 because of the incompetence of his Soviet case officer. He pleaded guilty in federal court in New York and was sentenced to thirty years' imprisonment.

In 1978 Thompson was freed in a swap for Israeli flier Miron Marcus, held in communist-controlled Mozambique, and for Alan Van Norman, a twenty-three-year-old student from Winden, Minnesota who had been sentenced to two and a half years for attempting to smuggle people out of East Germany. On May 3, 1978, State Security Minister Erich Mielke sent a secret letter to all Stasi departments, in which he announced Thompson's arrival in East Germany in typical Stasi jargon: "As a result of determined political operations, we have succeeded in the battle to free a former IM for the MfS and the KGB, Robert Glenn Thompson, a citizen of the USA who had been sentenced to 30 years in prison," Mielke wrote. "On the basis of material supplied by him in the years 1957–1958, the MfS was in a position to unmask and arrest a great number of spies and agents of the U.S. secret services." He went on to explain the swap, and added: "The liberation of Thompson proves anew that all of our patriotic and inofficial workers, even those in difficult situations including arrest and sentencing by the enemy, can rely at all times on the active support and welfare of the MfS and the solidarity of our brother organs." He added that Thompson's swap was to be displayed as an example to Stasi spies in order to gain their confidence and trust.[50] My attempts to locate Thompson after the demise of the communist regime failed. Like others in his position, he might have been given sanctuary in Russia.

Frustrated in his job as an intelligence analyst and electronic signal interceptor, Sergeant Michael A. Peri stole a laptop computer, disks containing top secret information, and a Humvee all-terrain vehicle on February 21, 1989. He headed for a section of the East German border, near the Fulda Gap, that was patrolled by his unit, the 11th Armored Cavalry Regiment. This was an area that U.S. defense planners saw as the kind of terrain that communist armored units probably would use in a surprise attack on Western Europe. Peri left the vehicle near the border fence, which he scaled. He was picked up by East German border guards, relieved of the computer and accessories, and taken to East Berlin. After Peri was questioned by Stasi intelligence officers for thirteen days, during which time he told them he did not want to remain in the East, his computer and disks were returned. Peri was given $300, taken to Schönefeld airport outside East Berlin, and flown to Vienna. Having second thoughts about his desertion, he returned to his unit voluntarily. The Stasi's action in this case was unusual in that they did not pressure him to work for them. This odd behavior might be explained by the fact that the incident occurred nine months before the Berlin Wall fell, with the country in turmoil and many East German intelligence officers sensing that the end was near. When the laptop that Peri had carried was examined, it had been wiped clean. The absence of fingerprints told investigators that the disks had been copied. At his court-martial, the twenty-two-year-old sergeant from Laguna Niguel, California was tearfully repentant as he pleaded guilty to espionage. He was sentenced to thirty years in prison.

THE BUGGED HEADQUARTERS

Analysts of the HVA's task force on Indications and Warning were excited when they learned that a listening device, a bug, had been placed in the briefing room of the chief of staff of the 7th U.S. Army, at headquarters in Heidelberg.[51] The task force had been established at the prodding of Major General Lev N. Shapkin, a member of the Soviet Defense Council. It was integrated into the Warsaw Pact's early warning system. The Soviets felt that the East German espionage service was in the best position to obtain data on Western intentions because of its ability to recruit agents, particularly from among the U.S. military and German civilian employees. Lieutenant Colonel Siegfried Weber of the HVA's Eleventh Department, charged with conducting espionage against U.S. targets, was the Stasi hero who proved the Soviets right. Weber recruited a German civilian maintenance man working at the Heidelberg headquarters. Incredibly, the man had unsupervised access to an area that Major General Otis C. Lynn described as one of the two most sensitive areas in the command.[52] The other was the office of the commanding general. Lynn, now retired, was 7th Army chief of staff from 1980 to 1982, when the bug was operating. The German spy had affixed the bug, including a mini recorder, beneath the table of the briefing room. Over a period of several months, they regularly changed tapes and batteries. While the analysts thought the information was somewhat useful for early warning purposes, others found the bug of little value because of technical problems, and the operation was discontinued. An investigation of the maintenance man failed to produce any evidence against him, and no charges were filed.

Former Colonel Grossmann said the HVA had decided in the 1970s to go for quality rather than quantity. They would rather pay a million dollars to one spy than ten times a hundred thousand. Colonel Wolfgang Koch, who succeeded Grossmann and who was Warrant Officer Hall's case officer, confirmed this.[53] There is no question that damage resulting from penetration of the U.S. military establishment increased dramatically during the last two decades of East Germany's existence. The Ministry for State Security, of which General Wolf's Main Administration for Foreign Intelligence was a part, was a highly compartmentalized operation, and the protection of sources was paramount. By fall 1991, only a handful of former Stasi agent handlers had revealed the true identities of their agents. Most officers who were among those with access to clear names of agents, like Koch, steadfastly refused to give them up. They would divulge details of cases and mention code names, but nothing more: "Our honor as professionals is at stake," they would say. Thus, U.S. authorities have yet to expose dozens of Americans who have spied for the Stasi at one time or another. General Lynn's assessment of why U.S. counterespionage failed so miserably coincides with the views of former East German intelligence officers. They put the blame squarely on U.S. laws, such as the Privacy Act, which resulted from the hearings on intelligence in the 1970s chaired by Senator Frank Church. "The counterespionage people were deprived of the tools needed to uncover spies by being forced to be overly protective of a person's privacy," former Stasi counterspy Colonel Rainer Wiegand told me in a 1991 interview. "Counterespionage is at a disadvantage in an open, democratic society," he added.

Besides the Stasi spies who were stationed at the Teufelsberg electronic warfare and surveillance station, whose identities have not been made public, at least three other highly placed U.S. civilians remain hidden under code names. For example, "Optik" was an American engineer who walked into Stasi headquarters in 1982 and offered to sell highly classified documents pertaining to space research. All walk-ins were referred to the internal counterintelligence directorate. Thus, Colonel Rainer Wiegand met with the man, who wanted DM10,000 (about US$6,250) for papers that the colonel could not decipher because of their scientific nature.[54] Wiegand gave the man DM5,000 and told him there would be more if the information proved useful. He wrote down the fellow's name and address, and said he would be contacted. Wiegand's chief, Lieutenant General Günther Kratsch, locked the materials in his vault and forgot about them. Three years later Kratsch's directorate came under pressure from Stasi Minister Mielke for not having fulfilled its quota of catching spies. Kratsch remembered the walk-in, took the papers from the vault, and handed them over to the foreign espionage directorate HVA as his "big catch." The HVA's scientific department assigned Lieutenant Colonel Edgar Ziegner as the case officer. Wiegand remembered that the Stasi made contact with Optik in 1985 but said he knew nothing about what later transpired, other than that the spy had become "very valuable."

A U.S. Air Force master sergeant stationed in West Berlin in the early 1960s was recruited by the Stasi under blackmail.[55] A married man, the sergeant was working at a management post at Tempelhof Air Base when his German girlfriend had an abortion in East Berlin arranged by the Stasi. I was unable to uncover any information about what secrets the sergeant, code-named Tom, had betrayed while he was in Berlin. However, when he was later stationed in Thailand, during the Vietnam War, he reportedly relayed to his Stasi contacts the dates and times of U.S. Air Force combat missions, which resulted in the downing of three fighter jets.[56] After Tom's return to the United States, the Stasi lost contact with him. They believed he had been arrested for smuggling narcotics.[57] His control was Colonel Manfred Kleinpeter of the HVA's U.S. department, who was stationed in the 1970s as a "legal resident" in East Germany's U.N. mission in New York. In a conversation with me, Kleinpeter acknowledged "knowing about Tom" but refused to reveal any details. However, Kleinpeter spoke with glee about an unsuccessful attempt by the FBI to recruit Kleinpeter as a double agent.

A number of other Americans spied for the Stasi: Mice was a member of the U.S. Army, and Junior a civilian scientist who was reportedly paid $1 million by an OIBE, Stasi First Lieutenant Wolfgang August.[58] The scientist had access to long-range electronic planning and attended conferences at NATO that were so secret that he was required to send his conference notes to the United States by special courier. According to former Stasi Colonel Karl Grossmann, August operated under deep cover in Frankfurt, where he worked for a rubber products company for five years, until 1970, when he was recalled to East Germany.

A knowledgeable U.S. intelligence officer told me that he believes all these spies have been located but that the Department of Justice refuses to prosecute them. "If they are not 100 percent certain of a conviction, they will not prosecute, as a matter of preserving prestige."

WHAT OTHER SPIES HAVE BETRAYED

Files originating with General Wolf's foreign espionage directorate show that East German intelligence was successful in infiltrating most U.S. military and many government offices around the world.[59] These are but a few samples of what Americans sold to the East Germans:

U.S. Air Force order of battle listing all available aircraft and their locations (top secret); order of battle of 1st Armored Division during exercise "Cartel Card," February 25–March 3, 1972 (secret); training report of the 108th Military Intelligence (MI) Battalion, July 1987 (top secret); counterintelligence inspection report sent by the 504th MI Battalion to the assistant chief of staff for intelligence of the 1st Armored Division (top secret); U.S. Army Battle Concept against Armor, 1978 (top secret); report of counterintelligence inspection of building 5350, Hindenburg Kaserne (barracks), Ansbach, West Germany, signed by Pennington P. Smith, officer in charge of a counterintelligence field office (secret); military police security plans and transport schedules of the U.S. Army's European Command (secret); and organizational charts dated between 1975 and 1982, including officers' names and telephone numbers at forty-one army installations in Europe, the United States, Panama, and Asia. Some of the charts had pieces cut out in the upper margins, to hide a classification or a name that might have revealed the source.

Interestingly, the chart of the 8th Infantry Division stationed at Bad Kreuznach, West Germany, showed the name of Staff Sergeant Clyde L. Conrad, operations and security NCO in the office of the assistant chief of staff for operations with the 8th Infantry Division, who had retired and settled in Germany in 1985. Conrad was arrested in August 1988 on charges of treason. The investigation was led by Colonel Stuart Herrington, who also nabbed the electronic spy Hall. Conrad had betrayed U.S. defense plans classified as cosmic top secrets, including the use of tactical nuclear weapons in the event of a communist surprise attack. Incredibly, the U.S. Department of Justice was not interested in prosecuting the traitor, and the case was turned over to the West German prosecutor general.[60] Colonel Herrington testified that Conrad had spied for Hungarian intelligence since 1975. The chart found in Stasi files might well have been provided by the Hungarians. The prosecution said he had received about DM2 million (about US$1.250 million). After an almost six-month trial, Conrad was sentenced to life imprisonment, the most severe sentence handed down by a German court for treason since World War II. A German judicial official later described the investigation by Colonel Herrington and the agents of U.S. Army Foreign Counterintelligence as thorough and well organized.[61] Conrad died in prison in 1997.

TOPAZ

The headquarters of the North Atlantic Treaty Organization (NATO) in Brussels was a high-priority target for the Stasi's foreign espionage directorate. Although the Soviets had been able to penetrate NATO from time to time, the East Germans were profoundly more effective in recruiting moles with access to the secrets of the Western defense pact. Their recruitment efforts began in the late 1960s, when NATO had a shortage of well-trained and multilingual secretaries while West German ministries had a surplus. The transfer of West German secretaries to the Belgian capital prompted the Stasi to dispatch its Romeo recruiters.

Ingrid Garbe, a secretary at West Germany's diplomatic mission to NATO headquarters in Brussels, was arrested as an East German spy recruited by a Romeo in March 1979. The arrest triggered panic in another, more important spy: Ursel Lorenzen, secretary to the British director for operations in NATO's general secretariat, fled Brussels the night of March 5, 1979, leaving most of her personal effects behind. At the same time, an executive of the Brussels Hilton Hotel, Dieter Will, also disappeared. Suspecting that the Garbe arrest and the disappearances were no coincidence, NATO security officials investigated and found that Lorenzen had had access to the alliance's innermost secrets. Several weeks after her disappearance, Lorenzen appeared on East German television for a Stasi-managed propaganda interview. She said "pangs of conscience" caused to her to seek East German asylum. "I have experienced the inhuman planning which in fact is only directed toward a new war." The Hilton executive was the Romeo who had recruited her.

The flow of secrets did not end with Lorenzen's escape. In fact, it continued almost without interruption. Colonel Heinz Busch, military analyst for the Stasi's foreign espionage directorate, who knew Lorenzen and Will by the code names Mosel and Bordeaux, was provided with first-class NATO secrets also by an agent code-named *Topas* (Topaz).[62] Like Lorenzen and Will, Topaz was controlled by Colonel Klaus Roesler, whose HVA division dealt with NATO and the European Community, and his deputy Colonel Karl Rehbaum. Busch noticed that Topaz had been assigned the same internal registration number (MfS/XV/333/69) under which Lorenzen had been carried. "That was curious, because I have never seen this done before." When East Germany collapsed and Busch became the primary source for uncovering Topaz, NATO security officials speculated that it was not merely one person but an entire spy ring. They based this guess on the incredible volume of highly secret NATO documents—sometimes up to 3,000 pages per delivery—that flowed across Busch's desk. This need not be so, Busch told security chief Bartelli, because Lorenzen also produced an immense amount of material, albeit with the help of her Romeo, who assisted in photographing papers during her lunch hour. But there was no question that Topaz was the most extensive case of espionage inside NATO since the founding of the alliance in 1949.[63] Among the sensitive documents Busch analyzed was MC-161, classified "cosmic top secret"—a comprehensive study of the capabilities of Warsaw Pact armies and their order of battle.[64] It was the bible of western defense planners. No wonder the Stasi gave its agent the name of a gem. Busch did not know that *Topas* collaborated with *Türkis* (Turquoise), because that code name never showed up on transmittal slips attached to the NATO documents.

Detectives of the Bundeskriminalamt, the German FBI equivalent, and NATO security agents toiled for nearly three years, painstakingly piecing together the information supplied by former Stasi colonel Busch. They probed NATO personnel who had access to numbered documents discovered at the Stasi archive, comparing security records showing who had checked them out. The final lead came from a computer diskette on which a list of agents was recorded. Former Stasi Major General Rolf-Peter Devaux is said to have sold it to the CIA for $1.5 million.[65] Rainer Rupp and his wife Ann-Christine were on that list. Rupp worked in NATO's economic directorate, and his wife was a secretary in various departments, the last of which was the alliance's highly sensitive security service. On July 31, 1993, the couple was arrested while vacationing at Rainer's parents' home in Saarburg, in southwestern Germany, near the border with Luxembourg. Rupp was charged with treason, and his wife was prosecuted as an accessory.

Rupp was twenty-two years old and a student of economics in Düsseldorf when he participated in several left-wing demonstrations in the Rhineland. As one of thousands of young left-leaning idealists radicalized in the 1960s, Rupp railed against the "evils of capitalism" and America's role in the Vietnam war. After one rally in Mainz, he and fellow students went to a saloon for beer and goulash. When it was time to pay, they lacked 50 pfennigs (about 16 cents).[66] A man at a neighboring table who introduced himself as "Kurt" bailed them out and even sprang for another round of beer. The students and Kurt got into a discussion of politics and found they had much in common, though Rupp was not in favor of the type of communism practiced by the East German regime. Rainer Rupp met Kurt again and they gradually developed a friendship. Kurt eventually revealed himself as a Stasi recruiter and suggested to Rupp that he meet with "friends" in East Berlin—in other words, with members of Wolf's Hauptverwaltung Aufklärung. "At my first meeting I met Jürgen, who later became a leading man in the HVA," Rupp recalled after his trial.[67] Jürgen told him: "We do many stupid things here, and not everything works as it should. But if one day the DDR should disappear, the people will not allow capitalism to be reintroduced." This seeming openness on the agent's part, and Rupp's resultant perception that East Germany was not only improving economically but also becoming more liberal, in-

Rainer Rupp, code-named Topas, *was a top spy for the Stasi in the Brussels headquarters of the North Atlantic Treaty Organization for twelve years. Rupp is shown talking with his wife Ann-Christine after he was sentenced to twelve years in prison for treason. His wife was sentenced to twenty-two months' probation as an accessory to the crime. Courtesy AP/Wide World.*

fluenced the young leftist to turn traitor. Rupp was signed up as a *perspektiv Agent* and instructed to perfect his French by continuing his studies in Brussels.

Rupp's description of Jürgen fits Colonel Jürgen Rogalla, who earned his espionage spurs in the mid-1960s, when, disguised as a student, he was the HVA station chief in Ghana. At that time, Kwame Nkrumah was attempting to establish a communist-style dictatorship with massive assistance from the Soviet Union and other Eastern-bloc countries.[68] A military coup deposed Nkrumah in February 1966, and Major Rogalla was thrown in jail. He was later released in exchange for Ghanaian prisoners being held in East Germany. At the time of East Germany's collapse, Rogalla was a colonel in charge of espionage against the United States, Canada, and Mexico.

Rupp completed his studies, then joined the Brussels branch of a British commercial bank. One evening at a Brussels bar, friends introduced him to Ann-Christine Bowen. The sophisticated and highly attractive daughter of a retired British Army major from Dorchester, England, Ann-Christine had a secretarial job with the British military mission. It was love at first sight for Ann-Christine. She was two years younger than Rupp and impressed by his knowledge and intelligence.

In 1971 she took a job at NATO. Shortly after their wedding a year later, Rupp told his wife he was an agent for the Stasi and asked her to join him in his "work for peace."[69] She agreed.

Almost every working day for five years, Ann-Christine crammed NATO documents into her handbag and carried them to her husband, who photographed them with a miniature camera supplied by the Stasi. All of the documents were classified, some as highly as "cosmic top secret"—particularly those dealing with communications and defense plans. Periodically the Rupps would travel on weekends to cities outside Belgium, such as Amsterdam and The Hague. There they would meet with Colonels Roesler or Rehbaum, their Stasi case officers, to receive instruction. Rupp delivered the exposed film rolls, hidden in the false bottoms of beer cans, to couriers. The meeting dates and places were signaled to Rupp over shortwave spy broadcasts. In time, Rupp himself applied for a NATO job, and after a background investigation cleared him for access to the most sensitive classified information, he was hired in 1977.

According to the German federal prosecutor general, Rupp's betrayal of top secret material provided the Warsaw Pact leadership with reliable and up-to-date insight into NATO planning: "This insight made it possible to reliably judge the military potential of the NATO states and to exploit this knowledge in event of a crisis situation. This continual betrayal of state secrets to the MfS and the relaying of the information to the KGB resulted in serious disadvantages for the defense capability of the German Federal Republic and her allies."[70]

During the Rupps' trial in October and November 1994, Presiding Judge Klaus Wagner tried to establish whether Rupp regretted his betrayal. He said that he had also "served the interests of the German Federal Republic by trying to make it clear to the Stasi that I had recognized that NATO was not an instrument for an offensive war."[71] The judge then asked: "How could you be sure that some crazy Soviet defense minister would not use this knowledge to order an attack on Western Europe?" Rupp answered that in thinking it over, he could not be sure.

In his testimony, Rupp accepted all the blame for the couple's treachery and tried to protect his wife. He described how after the birth of their first son, in 1984, Ann-Christine had told him they should quit but he had talked her out of it. Judge Wagner thought Rupp's portrayal of his leading role plausible: "Rupp was intellectually and mentally superior to his wife."[72] Following the birth of the couple's second son two years later, Ann-Christine threatened to take the children to England unless Rainer stopped spying. This time Rainer said he had agreed but secretly had continued his covert activities. Even the birth of a daughter did not deter him. He would sneak into the wine cellar of the plush villa they had acquired with Stasi money and photograph the documents he continued to haul out of his office. "We felt sorry for Mrs. Rupp, who had been roped into his activities," Judge Wagner commented.

Federal prosecutor Ekkehard Schulz presented his summation on November 5, 1994, and demanded a fifteen-year prison term for Rupp and two years for his wife. The prosecution maintained that the Stasi paid Rupp about 800,000 marks (about US$500,000) in his twenty-one years of spying. After two weeks of deliberation, Judge Wagner sentenced Rainer Rupp to twelve years in prison and Ann-Christine to two years' probation.

SPIES IN THE U.S. EMBASSY

Like all U.S. and NATO installations vulnerable to Stasi infiltration, the U.S. embassies in Bonn and East Berlin were no exception. State Department security officials were acutely aware that infiltration occurred, though none was spectacularly damaging and no U.S. officials were involved. In Bonn, they caught some German embassy drivers and caterers, but they were mostly purveyors of gossip about officials' weaknesses and peccadilloes. However, one case in Bonn was somewhat more serious. Gabriele Albin, a German woman employed in the U.S. embassy teletype room, was recruited by a Romeo in 1977 after her marriage to a U.S. Army officer had failed. Her cover name was Gerhard. Her case officer was Lieutenant Colonel Heinz Keller of the department that ran operations against the United States. Albin had a limited access clearance that allowed her to work with classified material up to secret but only under the supervision of an American official. But the "supervision" edict was often violated. For about four years Albin delivered material of so little interest that military analyst Colonel Heinz Busch asked her case officer to instruct her in selecting documents more judiciously. For a while Albin provided more desirable information, such as reports on the reaction of politicians regarding the stationing of intermediate range nuclear weapons in Germany. Then, in 1980, the case officer told Busch that his connections to Gerhard had been broken off for reasons he refused to explain. Albin had been suffering from severe psychiatric problems and was in and out of hospitals.[73] Suddenly, in 1982, Busch received new material from agent Gerhard. Albin was active again, in a new job at the embassy's Office of Defense Cooperation. In contrast to her earlier spy work, Albin now delivered valuable military documents, including the stationing of Pershing II missiles and extracts of secret operating procedures covering the Pershing and Tomahawk systems. She also provided coded and encoded messages—valuable items for code breakers. She should never have been allowed even to see those documents because she still had only limited access clearance. However, she was a popular veteran embassy employee, and those responsible for security ignored the rules.

Albin had been reactivated by the man who recruited her earlier, an East German chemist who had tried to flee the country but was caught and became a Stasi Romeo and courier rather than go to prison. Seven years older than Albin, Rudolf Reck stowed films in secret hiding places aboard trains traveling to East Berlin, so-called rolling dead letter drops. Albin and Reck, whom the woman knew by the alias Frank Dietze, were arrested on March 13, 1991, and released on bail. A Stasi defector had betrayed them. Before he could be tried, the Romeo courier was killed when his car was hit by a train at a crossing. There was speculation that he was murdered to stop him from testifying, but a thorough investigation determined that his death was an accident.[74] At Albin's trial in August 1996, Presiding Judge Ina Obst-Öllers said Albin's "blind adoration" of her courier had led her to spy: "Although she never knew his address or telephone number, this extremely sensitive woman believed his promise to marry her," the judge remarked. "She was used in a perfidious manner."[75] However, Albin was a culprit as well as a victim. She was placed on probation for two years—a mild sentence, considering that the Stasi had paid her a total of about DM170,000 (US$106,250).

Erich Honecker, East German's Communist Party chief and head of state, was provided a daily top secret Stasi intelligence digest similar to that prepared by the CIA for the U.S. president. It dealt with current worldwide political and military developments as well as disputes between political leaders as reported by Stasi spies. The digest of March 16, 1987 reported the relief from command of the chief of the U.S. mission in West Berlin, John Kornblum, and his transfer to Brussels as deputy U.S. ambassador to NATO: "The transfer was prompted by his ongoing internal differences with the USA Ambassador to Bonn (Richard) Burt. He (Burt) accuses Kornblum of lacking the ability to secure American interests and giving too much consideration to BRD (West German) positions." Furthermore, the report said, Kornblum had been unable to restrict the scope of action of West Berlin's Mayor Eberhard Diepgen. "Conversely, Kornblum reproached Burt for constantly interfering in his areas of responsibility."[76] The report undoubtedly was produced by a mole who was never uncovered.

A TEST OF AMERICAN WATERS

Attorney General Robert Kennedy ordered the expulsion from the United States of a beautiful, exotic German woman on August 21, 1963, in total secrecy. Ellen Rometsch, twenty-seven years old and married to a Luftwaffe sergeant attached to the West German embassy in Washington, D.C., had less than a week to leave the country. Had it not been for Pulitzer Prize–winning reporter Clark Mollenhoff of the *Des Moines Register,* the incident might never have surfaced in the public eye. Two months after Rometsch and her husband left the United States, Mollenhoff reported that Senator John Williams, a Republican from Delaware, had obtained a nearly complete rundown of the woman's life in Washington since she had arrived there in 1961. "If the investigation brings out all the information reported to Williams and federal investigative agencies, the testimony could rock Washington in much the same way the Profumo scandal rocked London last summer," Mollenhoff stated. British War Minister John Profumo had been forced to resign after admitting he lied to Parliament about his relationship with Christine Keeler, a prostitute who also was being bedded by Soviet assistant naval attaché Eugene Ivanov.

Senator Williams told Mollenhoff he would not comment on the matter except that it was "an extremely sensitive and dangerous" one. Ellen Rometsch belonged to a stable of call girls working for Robert (Bobby) Baker, secretary of the Senate's Democratic majority and Lyndon B. Johnson's protégé. Baker made the girls available to senators and other powerful Washingtonians. At the time, Baker was being probed for financial irregularities. On September 30, 1963, Representative H. R. Gross, an Iowa Republican, said in a House speech that missile secrets might have been stolen by Rometsch, and called for an investigation. Gross said the woman once took a nude champagne bath at a party hosted by a defense contractor and attended by an official of the federal space agency. He did not reveal the names except to say that the contractor was president of a firm manufacturing missile components. The FBI was certain that the stunning German woman's clients included President John F. Kennedy.[77] FBI Director J. Edgar Hoover assumed that Rometsch, an East German from Pirna (near Dresden), who had fled to West Germany in 1956, was a spy.[78] The expulsion was in itself unusual in that the attorney general was personally involved. "That John F. Kennedy was involved with the woman would not surprise me," said University of Wisconsin history professor Evan C. Reeves, who wrote the Kennedy biography *A Question of Character: The Life of John F. Kennedy.* As to Robert Kennedy's unusual involvement in the Rometsch case, Reeves commented: "Why not, he did all the dirty work." After Rometsch left the United States with her sergeant husband, the case died, shrouded in secrecy.

In summer 1997 I was told by a German government official in Berlin who wished to remain anonymous that there were strong indications that Ellen Rometsch had been a long-range agent for the Stasi's foreign espionage directorate. Upon her return to Bonn, the cause of her expulsion was investigated by military counterintelligence department (MAD), which determined that it was an issue of moral turpitude. MAD had never received anything from the FBI.[79] A former German intelligence officer said Rometsch was most likely recruited in East Germany, specifically to be used against military targets: "She came over at a time when Wolf was sending out his *perspektiv Agenten.*" Rometsch had been married previously to a Luftwaffe officer, from whom she was divorced. She did not marry the sergeant until he had received orders posting him to Washington, D.C. The intelligence officer, who also wished to remain anonymous, said it was highly likely that the East Germans turned her over to the KGB when she left Germany because the United States was the domain of the Soviets. He continued: "Besides, the HVA had no courier infrastructure in America at that time. In any case, I am absolutely convinced that Mr. Hoover was correct, but I wish he had shared with us whatever information he had."

In November 1997, I spoke about the case with Oleg Kalugin, former chief of KGB counterintelligence, who once served as an intelligence officer at the Soviet embassy in Washington. Asked whether Rometsch had in fact been a Soviet agent, Kalugin replied, "Yes, I know of such a woman," but added that he was unable to remember any details.

Today Ellen Rometsch lives with her husband in an attractive bungalow on the Rhine River, near Bonn. Contacted by a friend of mine, a former intelligence officer, she refused to respond to questions, even though she no longer needed to fear prosecution because she is protected by the statute of limitations. "She still is a most attractive woman, and judging by the Rometsches' house and the new BMW sedan they own, they have money," the former intelligence officer said. Had she continued her lucrative sideline, pleasing lonely politicians in Bonn? Or are the rumors true that the Kennedys paid her hush money?

THE USEFUL IDIOTS

Lenin has often been quoted as saying that the Bolsheviks must employ Western liberals as "useful idiots" and have the "capitalists furnish the ropes with which to hang them." The Stasi's foreign espionage dossiers are replete with cases of Americans who unwittingly played the role Lenin envisioned for them. These include businessmen who attended the Leipzig industrial fair, where they met "friendly" East Germans who engaged them in seemingly innocent conversations. And by and by, these friendly men and women wheedled economic information and other data of intelligence interest out of the naive visitors. The Stasi referred to this activity as *abschöpfen,* skimming off the cream.

But businessmen were not the only target on which the Stasi had drawn a bead. Legions of recruiters scoured professional conferences and seminars held in Eastern Europe and attended by Westerners, searching for "useful idiots" some of whom might sign on as spies. Horst Scholz, a professor at the Leipzig commercial college, was signed up in 1976 as an informal Stasi collaborator (IM), with a specific assignment as such a recruiter. His code name was *Forschung* (Research).[80] He was controlled by Division Fifteen for foreign espionage, attached to the Stasi district headquarters at Leipzig.

In August 1985, Scholz attended a conference in Budapest, Hungary, where he identified Jacob Naor, professor of marketing at the University of Maine, as a potential source of useful information.[81] Scholz engaged his target in a conversation on marketing and related subjects. When he returned to East Germany, Scholz wrote a five-page report for his case officer Captain Horst Findeisen, which read:

> The political-ideological position of the KP [*Kontaktperson,* i.e., Naor] can be judged quite positive (insofar as this was possible on the basis of the brief conversations—in total, about six hours). He has quite a definite opinion of Reagan and his policies (domestic and foreign), on the different treatment of the races and skin colors in the USA on all levels of society, and toward the position and development of Israel, and he appeared to sympathize with the development of socialism in various countries. (In the latter area he is quite well informed, publishes in this area in the USA, and because of it has reaped the enmity of his college and some of his colleagues.) His stand on this: Those colleagues, also his dean (college director) are totally misinformed or not informed at all about socialist developments and are as a rule the most primitive kind of anticommunists (the latter is typical for the USA). He describes Reagan as a primitive politician, but typical for the Americans, who act according to the principle that anyone who in any way sympathizes or negotiates with socialism is against the USA and her strength. All those in opposition are therefore defamed and—according to the KP—systematically eliminated from public life. In a sense, he views this also as a personal danger and shapes his tactics accordingly. At the college he is considered a high-profile expert in the marketing area, and his director "needs him."

Judging by this report, the American professor seemingly went out of his way to ingratiate himself with the East German spy recruiter. He even went so far as to inveigh against Israel. When Scholz asked Naor why he had settled in the United States, Naor said that it was because of "widespread nationalism and the increasing 'fascism' within the Israeli army."

Naor, according to the recruiter's report, spoke at length about his private affairs: He said that his family owned a home bought for $40,000, paid a mortgage of $450 a month, owned three cars, spent about $100 a week on food, and paid between $900 and $1,000 a month on his daughter's education (she was studying engineering). "Mrs. N. is director of statistical services in the Maine state department of health. The statistical services maintains data on all residents of the State of Maine (about one million) and Mrs. N. *has full access* to all data." The underlined words are noteworthy, as in later reports she is listed as a possible intelligence target.

During this very first meeting, the spy recruiter reported, Naor offered to provide computer program information used by his college as well as by the American Marketing Association. The report stated further:

> In addition, the KP unveiled a second concrete offer: It concerns an export marketing program with supposedly the largest comprehensive database of 600 large USA firms, the USA in general, Canada, South Korea, and Sweden. It includes the so-called "Excellent Stores," the best exports of the USA. In this connection, the KP has created his own program at the University of Maine for analysis and comparison and has at his disposal the entire database.

The American professor, wrote the East German, said he would send some material to a Dr. Szabo at the Budapest Institute for Market Research, where "I could pick it up, because according to the KP, mail to Hungary was not subject to such rigid controls. He would deliver the large database in person when he visits Leipzig next year." What did Naor fear? In any case, the Stasi dossier contains a report that he did, indeed, send documents to the Hungarian cutout.

The Stasi case officer recommended that the Scholz-Naor relationship be maintained and expanded. His chief, Colonel Claus Brüning, approved, and Naor was given the code name *Flamme* (in English, Flame). A background check on Naor was ordered, which included a request to the Hungarian secret police to furnish data on the professor's travel to and within that country.

Preliminary Stasi vetting revealed that Naor was born in Vienna, Austria, in 1931, to a Christian mother and a Jewish father. His family name at the time was Neubauer. To escape Nazi persecution, the family emigrated to Israel in 1939. In 1952 Naor moved to the United States and later studied economics at the University of California, after which he worked as a financial analyst for the American President

Lines shipping company for five years, until 1971. Then he moved to Israel, where he worked as a teacher until 1974, when he returned to the United States. Naor lectured at the Universities of Wisconsin and Oklahoma before being hired as a professor at the University of Maine's College of Business Administration. He was granted tenure in 1983. Naor was listed as being married to a native-born American and as having two children, a daughter and a younger son. As citizenship, the Stasi listed: "USA and Jew."

Naor maintained an exchange of letters with Stasi recruiter Scholz in which he told him that he would try to have his 1986 trip to East Germany funded by the International Research and Exchanges Program (IREX), which is financed by the U.S. government. On May 28, 1986, he wrote his East German contact that his plans for IREX financing did not work out because "they don't have any money now (Reagan's fault)." Naor did travel to East Germany in July 1986, where he met with his Stasi contact. The Stasi dossier does not reveal whether Naor brought with him the comprehensive database he had promised or how his trip was financed.[82]

During a meeting in Leipzig, the Stasi recruiter asked Naor whether he expected "unpleasantness" because of his frequent trips to communist countries. "N. told me the following: He makes his reports at the university only to his dean because he furnishes the money for the trips. So far he has not spotted any interest on the part of the FBI or CIA. However, this could change, but he had a "clear conscience."

From East Germany Naor traveled to Hungary, flew from Budapest to Israel on Romanian Airlines to visit his father and brother, and returned to Budapest on Yugoslav Airlines. He reportedly told Scholz, whom he met in Budapest for three long sessions between August 22 and 26, that he used those airlines because they "posed a lesser risk with regard to terrorist attacks." During the clandestine meetings, Naor handed over "material from the University of Maine (microcomputer training)," Scholz's September 11 report to the Stasi said.

Over the next two years, Naor continued to travel to Eastern Europe, including East Germany, to study "socialist marketing." On each occasion he met with the East German professor cum spy recruiter who then wrote the usual elaborate reports for his Stasi handlers. The Forschung and the Flamme dossiers clearly indicate that the groundwork was being laid for recruiting the American as a spy. More importantly, Naor had told his East German "colleague" that he had asked University of Maine officials to invite him to Maine as a guest professor in 1988. For Stasi foreign espionage, getting one of their agents officially invited to the United States with freedom to roam would be a coup of the first order.

That Naor, described by a colleague in Maine as extremely intelligent, would inveigle an invitation for the East German was bizarre. Why would Naor choose to ignore the political unrest that was sweeping through East Germany at the time, which was widely reported in the American media? Was he a naive, muddleheaded, liberal academic who was bent on advancing his image as an expert on communist economics and commercial policy?

On May 5, 1987, the chief of foreign espionage at the Stasi's Leipzig headquarters, Colonel Brüning, shifted into high gear. He forwarded Naor's dossier to Colonel Armin Grohs, deputy chief of the HVA's Eleventh Department. This department was responsible for espionage against the United States, Canada, and Mexico. In an accompanying, explanatory letter, Brüning wrote:

> The political realism and the relatively progressive position which comes to the fore in the material seems an honest one, though perhaps not entirely free from bending with the wind. Flamme has a genuine scientific interest in building up his image as an expert on socialist countries and to assist socialism in becoming a strong adversary to the USA.

However, Colonel Brüning added, "The results of the background checks so far show that it may not be possible to successfully recruit him in 1987." Instead, Brüning recommended that operational emphasis be placed on preparing for the visit of Forschung to the United States—a visit that the appropriate Stasi authorities had already approved.

In the next eleven months, Scholz obtained permission to work in the United States, and the U.S. embassy in East Berlin issued him the appropriate visa. Early in May 1988, the Stasi recruiter was extensively briefed on his mission.[83] His official reason, or "legend," for the U.S. visit was to broaden his academic contacts, study the academic environment, and polish his English language skills. Scholz's real mission, however, was that of a classic espionage recruiter. It included the thorough study of all university activities, faculty and their living conditions, and the political climate on campus and in the environs, as well as the collection of material on microtechnology and development trends. Scholz was ordered to thoroughly investigate the Maine professor's personal life and to concentrate on Naor's son, then twenty years old and pursuing studies in chemical engineering. He was to try to establish a rapport with the son and "look for favorable indications on which to base future recruiting." In addition, Scholz was to scout out academicians who might be vulnerable for recruitment as Stasi spies, and students who could figure in a Maine-Leipzig student exchange.

The communist East German spy recruiter, with $2,500 in his pocket, arrived in New York via Helsinki. Then he flew to Portland, Maine, where he was met by his American host, Naor, who drove him to Orono to begin his three-and-a-half-month guest professorship. His academic performance was a flop. According to a faculty member of the college of business administration who asked to remain anonymous, Scholz's English was so bad that students rebelled because they could not understand him. Scholz nonetheless applied himself with zest to his recruitment and espionage efforts. He selected a few students for studies in East Germany and named at least one unwitting professor as a possibility for future recruitment. But he did not think Naor's wife would be a candidate: "Though she shares her husband's political position regarding Israel, regarding the political and social conditions in the USA itself she is more patriotic than her husband (she is a native-born American)." Scholz had a problem with Naor's son, saying that the young man spoke such terrible slang that he could hardly understand him and he did not care much for his dressing "like a rocker." "Nevertheless I was able to interest him in the DDR and I invited him to visit Leipzig in connection with the spring fair." Scholz wrote that he met the couple's twenty-five-year-old daughter a few times and found her totally disinterested in politics, adding that "Flamme is angry about that."

The Stasi recruiter left the United States on July 28. When he returned home, he wrote a nine-page report of his visit. His dossier also listed a number of items that he turned over to his case officer. These included a sketch, aerial photographs, and photos of "important objects" at the university; university projects planned for 1988; various university publications; and a map of the state of Maine.

The Stasi dossiers give no indication that any of the American students Scholz had invited ever traveled to East Germany. It appears that interest in the project was fading rapidly as the East German regime was heading toward oblivion. Naor made one more trip to study at the Leipzig Commercial College from January to June 1989, after which the dossier on Flamme was closed. The Berlin Wall was torn down five months later.

Professor Naor continued to teach at the University of Maine. His expertise on the socialist economies became history. According to former colleagues, he applied himself to studying emerging economies—that is, the former communist planned economies in transition to a free market, i.e., capitalism. His dream, as related by the Stasi dossier, of helping the communists forge "socialism into a strong adversary to the USA" remained just that—a dream. There is no evidence in the dossiers that Naor ever provided the spy recruiter any classified U.S.

government information or that he accepted any direct payments for his largesse. He betrayed no information endangering U.S. security. Whether or not he was engaging in economic espionage is a question that only judicial authorities could determine. Whatever Naor's motives, he fit Lenin's definition of a "useful idiot," and the material he turned over to the communists could easily be construed as a strand in the rope with which to hang capitalists, albeit a thin one. Professor Naor retired from the University of Maine in 1996 and moved to the Pacific northwest.

THE STASI'S FAILURES

General Wolf decided in 1973 to test the waters in the continental United States in competition with the KGB and Soviet military intelligence, the GRU. Major Eberhard Lüttich arrived in New York that year and established an "illegal residency," under deep cover and without diplomatic protection. Under the cover name Hanns-Dietrich Steinmüller he established a phony background in the West German port city of Hamburg. He had joined the East German espionage service in 1969 and after intensive training had been designated as *Offizier im besonderen Einsatz* (OIBE), or officer on special deployment. In New York he found a job as a salesman at the branch office of Schenker and Company, a huge West German transportation firm of international standing. Its business included the shipping of household goods for diplomats and the military between the United States and Europe. This position enabled Lüttich to gather information on personnel movements of intelligence interest. His assignment also included establishing contacts at universities with the aim of recruiting long-range agents among young academics. Over the years, Lüttich became a first-class agent. He sent his material in the form of microdots to letter drops in West Germany. He received his assignments via shortwave radio, directly from the DDR and from a clandestine station in Cuba. In July 1974, the United States and East Germany established diplomatic relations. Within the MfS it was debated whether Lüttich should be recalled and the "legal residency"—i.e., the DDR embassy in Washington, D.C.—relied on for information in future. However, because he worked so well, it was decided to leave the major in place. On November 22, 1979, he was arrested by FBI agents, but not because U.S. counterintelligence had sniffed him out. Instead, he was betrayed by an MfS defector, First Lieutenant Werner Stiller, who had crossed to West Germany the previous January. In the interval between the betrayal and the arrest, FBI agents had Lüttich under intensive surveillance to collect sufficient evidence. They were lucky to nab him: There obviously had been a lapse in MfS operations, in that not all agents known to the defector had been recalled. Lüttich confessed at once and furnished such valuable data that he was deported to West Germany and rewarded with a special amnesty.

According to a top former Stasi officer, Lüttich was the only long-term illegal agent who operated in the United States.[84] In any case, the Soviets had reserved the fields of military, scientific, and industrial espionage in America for themselves. However, the "legals" at East Germany's embassy in Washington delivered mountains of material that analysts deemed of relatively high reliability and of "great prognostic value." The most valuable source was Heinz-Joachim Switalla (under the cover name Siegel), counselor of the DDR embassy, who came from a prominent communist family. His father had been in exile in the Soviet Union, and together with Mielke, had founded the Stasi.

Another failure was the planned recruitment of a female CIA employee whom the internal counterintelligence directorate code-named *Fee* (meaning "Fairy").[85] The woman was transferred in 1983 from the U.S. embassy in Vienna to the embassy in East Berlin as an attaché. The U.S. State Department applied for her diplomatic accreditation, and the Stasi counterspies ran her name through a KGB computer in Moscow into which all Eastern-bloc intelligence services entered information. She was listed in the database as having been the target of Hungarian intelligence. Colonel Rainer Wiegand was dispatched to Budapest to confer with Colonel Laszlo Csordas, a forty-two-year veteran spy who had a file on Fee a foot thick. Csordas, working under cover as an attaché for the Hungarian embassy in Vienna, had conducted a close surveillance of the woman. A source inside the American embassy had drawn his attention to her. The Hungarians had bugged her apartment, where she frequently met after work for a drink with a secretary from her office. The two women would complain about the condescending attitude of their male colleagues, who they felt were intellectually and professionally inferior. They would also discuss the upcoming travel to Eastern Europe of CIA operatives, enabling communist counterintelligence officers to be a step ahead of the visitors. "These women would bitch and moan over their drinks and let out their frustration by gossiping about the human frailties of their fellow workers," Wiegand recalled. "It was a gold mine not only for the Hungarians but also for the KGB who got copies of everything Csordas collected. Through Fee we were able to unmask a colonel of the Yugoslavian defense ministry who was a longtime CIA source."

Wiegand returned to East Berlin, where General Kratsch decided that Fee should be recruited by the Stasi. Since all diplomatic apartments were assigned by the foreign ministry, the Stasi made sure that

Fee's would be properly equipped with listening devices and hidden video cameras. When Wiegand's people were nearly ready to make their move, the KGB intervened, claiming a primary right to recruit Americans. Wiegand resisted, and the Soviets complained to Stasi minister Mielke, who capitulated. Wiegand was visited by Colonel Felix Vinogradov, chief of KGB foreign counterintelligence in East Germany, who told him that a "specialist" fluent in English, who had lived for some years in the United States, would come from Moscow to handle the recruitment of Fee. Meanwhile, all documents on Fee were sent to KGB headquarters; but the Stasi withheld the fact that her apartment was under electronic and video surveillance. "We wanted to see how this big man from Moscow was going to handle her," Wiegand said.

The Moscow "specialist" arrived in summer 1984 and visited Fee's apartment one evening. The Stasi tapes and cameras were running to record the KGB officer introducing himself as an American who needed help. When she let him in, the "specialist" acted the proverbial bull in the china shop. He confronted her with the Vienna transcripts and "suggested" that she should work for the KGB if she wanted to save herself. "You should have heard her," Wiegand recalled gleefully. "I mean she was violent, called him an asshole and told him to piss off." The KGB officer apparently had expected a different reaction and retreated, saying he would contact her again. While Stasi officers exulted in the KGB man's tribulations, the "specialist" lingered menacingly outside Fee's apartment building. After a few days, he resigned himself to failure and left.

I interviewed Colonel Laszlo Csordas, who had retired in 1986, in Budapest in 1993. He confirmed the details of the operation, proudly describing how he and an assistant had rented an apartment above Fee's and installed listening devices and video cameras. "We knew everything about her and the Vienna CIA operation." If the woman had compromised herself by her indiscretions, why did he never try to recruit her? "We could have done that at any time, but I always felt she would rather risk exposure than work for us. Besides, she was more valuable to us in place. Had we recruited her, we never could have been sure that she was not playing a double game. As it turned out, I was right," Csordas said with a chuckle.

Was Felix S. Bloch the embassy insider who drew his attention to Fee? Bloch was the deputy ambassador accused of having spied for the KGB but was never tried, for lack of evidence, though he was fired by the State Department without a pension. "No, it was not Bloch . . . someone else. But we knew all about Bloch because the Germans had sent us a file on him and his sexual escapades when he was stationed in East Berlin. But I knew our Soviet friends had an eye on him. Whether they recruited him I don't know." Csordas took great delight in telling me that he was often invited to parties at the U.S. embassy and regularly lunched with the deputy U.S. military attaché. He named the attaché as Joseph Szilagyi; but that name was not on the list of foreign diplomats accredited to Austria. If that statement was a lie, how much of what Csordas revealed was true? With intelligence officers one can never be sure; but Csordas's account did jibe with the East German story.

ACTIVE MEASURES

In late 1986 the New Delhi newspaper *The Patriot* published an article in which the U.S. Army was accused of having created the AIDS virus in its bacteriological laboratory at Fort Detrick, Maryland. The newspaper quoted a Dr. Jakob Segal as having said that American scientists used genetic technology to combine the leukemia virus Visna, found in sheep, with the human leukemia virus HTLV-1, discovered by Dr. Robert Gallo, the eminent American virologist. The HIV virus, according to *The Patriot,* had been tested on felons, some of whom had been released and had spread the dread disease. The same story also was picked up by the Soviet news agency TASS and by Western news media.

The idea that AIDS was created by genetic technology was quickly pronounced rubbish by experts, including Meinrad Koch, head of the virology department of the Robert Koch Institute in West Berlin. Nevertheless, left-leaning newspapers and those with an anti-American bias had a field day. At the time, I was working as a consultant to Charles Z. Wick, director of the U.S. Information Agency, creating a task force to combat Soviet disinformation and propaganda. We quickly established that the Indian newspaper was being financed by the KGB and that its editor was the recipient of the Stalin Peace Prize. Thus it was determined that the AIDS story was a dastardly canard cooked up in Moscow by the active measures department of the Soviet secret police.

In research for this book in Berlin, I spotted Segal's name in Stasi documents. Born in pre-Soviet St. Petersburg, Segal had been a professor and head of the Institute for Applied Bacteriology at East Berlin's Humboldt University and was then retired. In a 1991 interview with me in Berlin, Segal presented himself as a die-hard Marxist, totally incapable of accepting the demise of communist East Germany. Segal, then eighty years old, insisted that his information on the origin of the HIV virus was solid, and he denied having had any contact with the

Stasi. He was lying. In 1992, two former officers of the Stasi's disinformation department published a book in which they described how they collaborated with the KGB to spin the AIDS yarn, using Segal and his scientific credentials to lend the story credence.[86]

As in the case of the AIDS lie, the Stasi active measures specialists often worked separately from the KGB, but always in tandem with Soviet policy. In the late 1970s the Soviet Union wanted to convince the world that the United States was preparing a first nuclear strike against the communist bloc. The Stasi created a number of pamphlets on the subject, using forged and real NATO documents supplied by spies and distributed to pacifist groups and the media under the names of fictitious publishers.[87] In June 1979, West European newspapers published a letter ostensibly written by outgoing NATO Commander Alexander Haig to Secretary-General Joseph Luns. The letter contained a discussion of U.S. war plans and the explosive statement, "We may be forced to make first use of nuclear weapons." The letter actually was written by Stasi forgers.

THE REAGAN FILE

East German Communist Party Chief and Head of State Erich Honecker aspired to visit the United States and meet with President Ronald Reagan to gain prestige for himself and polish the image of his police state. However, the visit never occurred, chiefly because of the DDR's support of international terrorism. However, to prepare for an eventual visit, the Stasi foreign espionage directorate compiled an extensive dossier on the U.S. president.[88] Most of the dossier consisted of top secret KGB and Cuban intelligence reports and analyses. President Reagan was described by the KGB as a "died-in-the-wool anticommunist who engaged in a campaign to drive progressive people out of the film industry and the unions." As a presidential candidate, it added, he promised to regain the "international leadership position the United States forfeited under President Carter." The KGB analysts expressed their low opinion of President Jimmy Carter by noting that he had "mismanaged the economy, reduced the morale of American business, and weakened the United States' position worldwide." A number of reports expressed the belief that Mr. Reagan would reverse this trend and quoted him as saying during the 1980 campaign: "No one wants to use atomic weapons, but the enemy should go to sleep every night in fear that we could use them."

The tone of many reports was one of reluctant respect: "Reagan is a firm and unbending politician for whom words and deeds are one and the same." In remarkably frank language, one KGB profile emphasized the president's "incessant attacks on the lack of political freedom, prohibition of free speech, restrictions on religious worship and travel, and economic failures of the socialist countries." In closing, the writer complained that Reagan ignored the positive attributes such as "efforts to achieve world peace and disarmament and the fulfillment of the Helsinki Accords by reuniting families." A twenty-nine-page Cuban intelligence analysis written in February 1986 expressed admiration for President Reagan: "Despite advanced age, despite health problems and the fact that he is in his second term, Reagan enjoys high personal popularity. He presents himself as a capable president and is able, if necessary, to participate in all important political events."

Much information appears to have been obtained from the perusal of newspapers, and perhaps to a larger extent, from agents' eavesdropping in Washington bars and restaurants on conversations of officials trying to impress others with their importance. It takes little imagination to assume that KGB and Cuban agents zeroed in on those who appeared in public with their White House or State Department passes dangling from their necks. However, information in one secret KGB report that reached the Stasi in May 1987 could only have come from a State Department or White House insider or from highly secret documents.[89] It revealed that Reagan hoped to unify the reaction of Western nations to the announced Soviet plan to withdraw intermediate range missiles from Europe. The report anticipated that the White House would announce its response at the seven-nation summit meeting in Venice, sometime between June 8 and 10. A handwritten marginal note said that U.S. intentions were not actually revealed until June 22, 1987.

Analysis of the Reagan Administration

The judgment of Stasi intelligence analysts about the eight-year Reagan administration proved remarkably accurate. Occasional lapses in insight are attributable to the analysts' blind faith in the eventual triumph of communism.[90] Seven months after President Reagan's first inauguration, Colonel Werner Bierbaum, chief analyst, wrote that the Reagan administration harbored the "illusion that it will be possible for the USA and her allies to force the Soviet Union and the other socialist states into arming themselves to death." This, of course, is exactly what President Reagan achieved. In an interview, Bierbaum told me that although he had accurate information from "both internal and external" sources, meaning Stasi and KGB spies, he was obliged to consider the "political ramifications."[91] In other words, to keep his job he had to play ball with the ideologues, even though Stasi insiders knew since 1983 that the communist economic system was headed for bankruptcy.[92] In the same interview, Bierbaum said: "I have to confess that President Reagan is the man who destroyed communism in Eastern Europe. No other Western statesman can take credit for that."

Officers like Bierbaum were hoping that the regime's leadership could "read between the lines." After all, hidden among ideological language in Bierbaum's analyses they could find first-class data on the U.S. economy and military preparedness, much of it taken from highly classified documents. For example President Carter's Directive No. 57, according to former National Security Council Soviet Affairs expert William L. Stearman, was top secret. It dealt with waging a global nuclear war. In discussing the military strategic concept of the United States, the analyst referred to "internal documents, drafts, substantive correspondence with allies, NATO position papers, and internal presentations to parliamentary committees." All of these documents at the very least would have been classified as secret.

NOT AN HONORABLE SERVICE

Markus Wolf's HVA unquestionably achieved remarkable results in its foreign espionage operations. Recruiting West Germans as spies was relatively easy: The common language, ties to family members living in the East, and personal frustrations, vulnerabilities, and character flaws were exploited. Ideology played a lesser role except among agents recruited in East Germany. Only three Americans—James Clark, Theresa Squillacote, and Kurt Stand, all indicted in 1997—said they had volunteered to spy for East Germany for reasons of ideology.

The claim that the HVA was no different in its modus operandi from the U.S. CIA, as Wolf and his officers asserted, is false. After the early 1950s, the HVA was not an independent organization. It was firmly integrated in the apparatus of the Ministry for State Security, designed for the purpose of political oppression. At a leadership seminar on March 3, 1971, Wolf lectured on the *Gesamtsystem,* the total system, of the Stasi: "The total system of our ministry can function only when all partial systems are correctly connected to and coordinated with one another." The foreign espionage directorate was never purely an information-gathering organ but was fitted into the political aims and strategies of the "class struggle" between communism and western democracies. The HVA was a participant in the surveillance and oppression of the domestic population.[93] For example, the Second Main Directorate, responsible for domestic counterintelligence, worked hand in glove with Wolf's foreign espionage directorate. When domestic counterintelligence officers sniffed out persons who exhibited anticommunist behavior or who were making plans to escape to the West, the officers would attempt to coerce them into accepting espionage assignments and then would turn them over to Wolf's HVA.[94] To assure proper coordination among all the Stasi's directorates, HVA officers were regularly posted to domestic security units. No one has been able to establish how much of East Germany's money was spent on such oppression and espionage efforts; but it surely amounted to many hundreds of millions and certainly contributed to the DDR's disintegration.

7

THE STASI'S SPY CATCHERS

SPY CATCHERS WORKING for the Stasi had an incredible advantage over their counterparts in the West. The eyes and ears of the secret police permeated every stratum of East German society. The responsibility for domestic counterespionage lay with the Second Main Directorate, under the command of Lieutenant General Günther Kratsch when the regime collapsed in 1990. Kratsch, an obese man just under six feet tall, was slavishly devoted to Stasi minister Mielke and the party. He commanded his subordinates with iron discipline and brutality.[1] Woe to anyone who voiced an opinion that could be interpreted as criticism of the party or the state! Kratsch reported directly to Mielke—a chain of command that conferred on him a power and an autonomy not enjoyed by most other directorate heads.

The counterespionage directorate had a full-time staff of 2,350, of which 1,962 served at the Stasi's East Berlin headquarters. The rest were stationed in the Stasi's provincial offices. "Considering that we had only about two hundred agents in all of Europe, it was not a fair fight," commented a senior U.S. counterespionage officer. Indeed, it was not. Years earlier, Mielke had issued a special directive on counterespionage, ordering the entire MfS staff of 108,000 to put all their resources at the disposal of the Second Directorate whenever their help was requested by any of the latter's officers.[2] The backbone of Stasi counterespionage, as of all other Stasi operations, were the IMs, the unofficial informers. The Second Directorate had a stable of between 2,500 and 3,000.

Major support for the counterespionage effort was provided by the 6,000 regular officers assigned to the Third Main Directorate, for elec-

Party chief and head of state Erich Honecker, shown here with Stasi Lieutenant General Günther Kratsch, Minister Erich Mielke, and Major General Werner Grossmann, successor to Markus Wolf as chief of the foreign espionage directorate. Courtesy MfS Photo.

tronic intelligence. This directorate was the brainchild of Major General Horst Männchen and included the installation and operation of telephone taps. For many years, Männchen's officers had tapped 2,200 telephones used by U.S. installations in West Berlin. The magnitude of this operation becomes clear when one considers the manpower required to operate just half of these taps manually, twenty-four hours a day. The rest of the taps were handled by computers that controlled the taping and storage of conversations for later analysis.

Lastly, there were the "mailmen"—Stasi officers assigned to every post office in East Germany—whose job it was to surreptitiously open and read thousands of letters destined for or arriving from the West. Every incoming parcel was x-rayed. Suspicious letters were chemically treated to expose messages written in invisible ink, or searched for microdots hidden beneath stamps or envelope flaps. The postal surveillance department was under the direct control of the counterespionage directorate.

No search or seizure laws bound the Stasi's counterspies. Search and arrest warrants were obtained more often than not after the fact, from co-opted judges and prosecutors. For many years, until the party decided that its regime ought to have some semblance of justice, Stasi minister Mielke personally signed all arrest warrants.[3] Thus, the rate of success in nabbing Western agents was high, particularly in the years between 1950 and 1965. Remarkably, the typically draconian sentences did not appear to deter East Germans who were disgusted with communism and Soviet occupation from enlisting in the silent war. Between 1952 and 1981, at least 126 such citizens, among them three women, were executed.[4] The exact number might never be known, because the Stasi turned hundreds of people over to the Soviets for trial. The bodies of the executed were secretly cremated and their ashes buried in mass graves. All records were ordered destroyed in 1989.

However, Dietmar Hildebrand, who headed a crematory in Dresden, disobeyed orders and hid his records, and turned them over to authorities after reunification. This is how many of the victims' relatives learned for the first time the fate of their parents, children, and spouses who had disappeared decades earlier, as communist authorities steadfastly had disavowed any knowledge of them. The death certificates all cited as the cause of death *akutes Herz- und Kreislaufversagen*—acute cardiac and circulatory failure. Hildebrand also revealed the location of a mass grave, in which sixty-one urns were found. In addition to the executions, at least twenty-eight life sentences were handed down between 1955 and 1960. Prison terms of less than ten years were rare. In contrast to this judicial rampage, there was not a single execution for espionage in post–World War II West Germany, And only one person was sentenced to life imprisonment. Despite the absolute control of state security organs over the East German population and the threats of severe punishment, Western intelligence scored successes, many of which led the Stasi to commit farcical errors. As the Western espionage services tightened their security procedures and improved the training of their agents in the early 1980s, arrests of the latter dropped to between thirty and fifty a year.[5]

THE DELICATESSEN SPY

In spring 1985, the Stasi's mail snoops found a secret message written in invisible ink in a letter posted to an address in West Germany. The message was of such great military importance that the initial analysis pointed to an American spy within the headquarters of the Group Soviet Forces Germany at Wünsdorf, south of Berlin. It dealt with top secret internal matters. A second letter was discovered that reported an upcoming secret visit of the commander of the Soviet Army. Stasi investigators checked with the chief of staff of the East German People's Army, the KGB, and the Soviet embassy. No one knew anything about such a visit. Nevertheless, the Soviet marshal arrived as the letter had predicted, and spent a week with troop units in the vicinity of Dresden. East German authorities were never informed. Stasi analysts deduced that the spy was either a member of the Red Army headquarters in the DDR or was serving on the general staff of the Soviet Army in the USSR itself and somehow managed to use East Germany as a mail drop. On the other hand, the letter, written in German superimposed over the invisible ink message, showed that the writer was conversant with the idiom of the German language, which pointed to a native German. The KGB was called in, and its agents were also stymied.

A special MfS/KGB commission of ninety counterespionage experts was created and labored for a full year on Operation Siren. The usual informants and telephone taps produced nothing. Dogged detective work finally produced a baffling result: The spy turned out to be Hella Zickmann, a rather nondescript woman in her early fifties. She lived in an apartment in Dresden that was nowhere near a Soviet headquarters, nor had she ever set foot in one. Frau Zickmann had not been sleeping with a talkative Soviet officer, either. She worked as an order clerk and dispatcher in Dresden's Markthalle, a wholesale food supply depot and a kind of super delicatessen. How could she possibly have gotten hold of secret military information? "Actually only because of our faulty socialist economy plagued by constant shortages," said former Stasi Colonel Rainer Wiegand cynically. What Wiegand, who worked on the case, meant was that these central depots were able to obtain food items unavailable to the average citizen unless one had "connections" or something valuable to offer as a bribe. Hella Zickmann's job included ordering food supplies for the Soviet Army. Soviet headquarters supply officers with ranks up to colonel were dependent on her goodwill when it came to the ordering and distribution of food. To curry favor with her, they often presented her with gifts. Sometimes the officers had to emphasize the importance of an order, particularly when they wanted such rarities as caviar, salmon, citrus, and tropical fruit and Frau Zickmann was not inclined to fill the request. "So-and-so is coming next week," they would say, and from the places to which the goods were to be delivered she could easily determine the VIP's itinerary.[6]

Having pinpointed Zickmann, investigators found out that her son had fled East Germany before the Berlin Wall was built and had settled in Hamburg. Until the wall was built, she had visited him several times a year, traveling via Berlin, where she caught a plane for West Germany. Her son had died in the early 1980s. The delicatessen spy was placed under surveillance, and her apartment was bugged with the goal of discovering whether she was a solo agent or belonged to a spy ring. Stasi monitors noted that three times a week she would get out of bed shortly after midnight, sometimes being awakened by an alarm clock, and turn on the radio. But monitors picked up no sound coming from the radio. Counterspies then decided to use what they called *Massnahme Dora,* boring tiny holes in the apartment walls for video observation. They saw Zickmann turn on the radio but listen to it through headphones while she was writing groups of numbers on a pad. A decision to arrest her was made when it was determined that the times she activated the radio coincided with those used by U.S. military intelligence broadcasting from West Germany. Her husband also was arrested.

Frau Zickmann talked freely about her recruitment by U.S. Army intelligence when she visited her son, who had also been a U.S. agent but was dropped when he began to have problems with alcohol and drugs. Until the Berlin Wall was built, she would report to her handlers in person, but after August 13, 1961, the connection was broken. In the mid-1970s Frau Zickmann was allowed to travel to West Germany to pick up the ashes of her son, who had died in Hamburg. There she again met with agents of U.S. Army Field Operations Intelligence, who gave her a crash course in using invisible ink and ciphers. When she returned to East Germany, she had no problem smuggling in such espionage paraphernalia as codes and special chemicals for mixing invisible ink. The incriminating items were hidden in the urn beneath her son's ashes.

For Stasi chief Mielke, the case was manna. He ordered propaganda specialists to construct a scenario with which to blast the lack of reverence of the American imperialists who would stoop to using an urn containing the ashes of a son for espionage purposes. Lo and behold, party chief and head of state Erich Honecker ordered Mielke to remain silent, explaining that this was not the time to burden the DDR's relations with the United States.[7]

Frau Zickmann's husband was released when she convinced her Stasi interrogators that he had not the slightest knowledge of her sideline. "I must admit that I respected how she pulled that off," commented former Colonel Rainer Wiegand. "She had been able to shut him out of this business completely during the ten years she worked for the American service, in other words, for MI." Hella Zickmann was convicted of espionage in 1987 and sentenced to twelve years in a penitentiary. She was automatically released when the country was reunited in 1990.

THE SECRETARY AND THE LAWYER

Elli Barczatis let out a piercing, heart-wrenching scream when prosecutor Wolfgang Lindner demanded that she and her boyfriend, Karl

Laurenz, be executed for espionage.[8] That was on the afternoon of September 23, 1955. Thirty-one days later both were dead, having been beheaded in a Dresden prison by the same guillotine used earlier by the Nazis. Barczatis was forty-three years old, and her friend was seven years her senior. Their bodies were immediately cremated. The couple's trial before the high court in East Berlin as well as the sentence and execution were classified as top secret. No one knows what happened to their ashes.

Elli Barczatis and Karl Laurenz had become friends in 1949 when both worked for the Ministry of Industry. She was single, not especially attractive, but intelligent and outgoing. Laurenz, a doctor of law and also single, was short and sported a brush mustache. His polite, kind, and cultured manners offset his physical appearance. Both were members of the SED (the East German communist party). In April 1950, Barczatis was promoted to a dream job—the post of secretary and administrative assistant to East German Prime Minister Otto Grotewohl. Laurenz, however, fell on hard times: He was expelled from the SED for political unreliability, having been a member of the Social Democratic Party when the latter was merged with the SED under Soviet duress. The expulsion cost Laurenz his government job. Blackballed in the legal profession, he decided to make a living as a freelance journalist for various newspapers in East and West Berlin.

On New Year's Eve 1950, a Stasi female informer code-named Grünspan spotted her two former acquaintances, Barczatis and Laurenz, at a cafe. The informer noticed Barczatis surreptitiously slipping Laurenz a "bundle of files." Although observant, Grünspan did not report the incident to her Stasi control until ten days later. Her report launched an investigation that would last four years. Because of Barczatis's position with Grotewohl, who valued her efficiency and devotion and had promoted her to chief secretary, the Stasi was obliged to tread carefully. For an entire year the case was handled quietly and unofficially. Had Barczatis worked elsewhere in the government, Mielke would have ordered the immediate arrest of Barczatis and her boyfriend and have had his interrogators sweat them in the Stasi's special Hohenschönhausen dungeons.

Toward the end of 1951, Mielke officially authorized Operation Sylvester. Barczatis and Laurenz were watched constantly and their mail was intercepted. Stasi officers probed deeply into their personal affairs and those of their friends. At least five informers were insinuated into Barczatis's surroundings, one of whom (code-named Lina) worked in her office. The Stasi even enlisted the help of the KGB. All efforts to prove that the couple was engaged in espionage were fruitless until a Stasi officer finally had a bright idea: Informer Lina was instructed in November 1954 to prepare an envelope with minute markings, place outdated and no longer sensitive documents inside it, and seal it. Ostensibly departing on a business trip, Lina handed the envelope to Barczatis "for safekeeping," saying that she would pick it up on her return. When she retrieved the envelope a few days later, Lina noticed that it had been changed and readdressed. On the sly she obtained samples from the typewriter used by Barczatis and gave them to her Stasi control officer. Analysts found that the type matched that on the new envelope. But the Stasi wanted to catch Barczatis redhanded. Another Stasi informer secretly took an impression of the key to the safe in Grotewohl's outer office, where Barczatis and Lina worked. The plan was for Lina to leave early one day, giving Barczatis an opportunity to get to the contents of the safe without being seen by anyone. The Stasi expected her to remove secret documents and take them home for copying. After Barczatis left for home, Stasi officers would go to the office and check the safe's contents against the document register. Lina was given the duplicate key the evening of December 6, 1954, to make sure it worked. The key did not fit, she informed her control. Two Stasi officers went to the office to verify this, and reported that the key was improperly copied. The officers decided to take the building security officer, who kept the safe key in his office, into their confidence and to swear him to secrecy. The safe was opened, and to their chagrin, all of its contents were accounted for. The Stasi had been so confident of catching Barczatis in the act that her arrest had been scheduled for that evening. Finally, nearly three months later, on March 3, 1955, Lina saw Barczatis slip a report on preparations for the Leipzig Industrial Fair between the pages of a business magazine that she was taking home.

Forty Stasi officers surrounded Barczatis's apartment building in the Berlin suburb of Köpenick early on the morning of March 4. Barczatis was arrested and taken to Hohenschönhausen prison. Laurenz was arrested a few hours later, after he returned to East Berlin from a visit to the Western sector. Stasi agents had observed his West Berlin meeting with two men they identified as agents of the Gehlen Organization, the West German espionage service, which at that time was still controlled by the CIA.[9]

Barczatis and Laurenz were brutally interrogated until June by three Stasi officers working in tandem, Lieutenants Gerhard Niebling, Carli Coburger, and Willi Damm—all of whom subsequently were awarded the rank of general. Immediately after her arrest, Barczatis was questioned for eighteen hours straight, and Laurenz, about the same period. Interrogations always took place at night and normally lasted about six hours. After two sessions with Laurenz on March 27 and 29,

Stasi Lieutenant Niebling wrote: "The accused became provocative, comparing the State Secretariat for State Security of the German Democratic Republic with the fascist Gestapo and the notorious Nazi Sicherheitsdienst (SD) [the SS's Security Service]. He remarked that the treatment of prisoners by the State Secretariat for State Security is worse than the treatment by the SD and the Gestapo." No wonder Laurenz confessed almost at once to having worked as a spy. Still, he held out nearly two months before divulging the details and giving away the names of his West German intelligence contacts. Until the end, however, Laurenz protected his girlfriend, saying that she never knew about his role as a spy but believed instead that he used the information she supplied as background for his newspaper articles.

What was the extent of Elli Barczatis's espionage? What did she betray that justified her execution? Incredibly, the interrogation record reveals not a single instance in which she furnished Laurenz with material so sensitive that it could be interpreted as having endangered the security of the communist state. She betrayed no military or defense secrets. She merely told her friend about letters her office received from the populace complaining about food shortages; mismanagement that created problems in industry; government personnel changes; and Westerners who visited Prime Minister Grotewohl. The absurdity of all communist regimes was that such tidbits of information were considered state secrets.

It is noteworthy that Barczatis and Laurenz refused legal counsel: A lawyer would have been of no help to them, since all East German lawyers were communist party members and the verdict was preordained. The judiciary did as the party and the Stasi commanded. The trial lasted a total of fourteen hours. Presiding Judge Walter Ziegler, a communist since the 1930s and a longtime member of the SED, alternately screamed and sneered at the defendants. Barczatis, after temporarily losing control when the prosecutor demanded the death penalty, pulled herself together and delivered a seven-minute plea for clemency, admitting her guilt and begging to be allowed to redeem herself.

Laurenz spoke eloquently for twenty minutes, telling the court that he had worked hard all his life until he was expelled from the party and barred from holding any job. "I held the Socialist Unity Party responsible for destroying my livelihood, and I joined the opposition. Had I not been unemployed against my will, I would not be here today." Laurenz, his voice firm, said he realized that he must be severely punished. "But I ask this high tribunal to apply the depth of humaneness, the magnificent principle on which the law of the German Democratic Republic rests." He said he would work hard behind prison walls as restitution for his crime. "I can still contribute toward building this land. No one derives any benefit from a dead Laurenz, and I ask you to temper justice with mercy." Presiding Judge Ziegler sarcastically bellowed, "Is that all?" Laurenz said "yes," and the court adjourned. Five minutes later, Ziegler and his two associate judges, Gerda Kleine and H. Löwenthal, returned to the court room. "In the name of the people," Lindner intoned, and pronounced the death sentence.

After Germany was reunited, in April 1994, Judge Gerda Kleine was charged with perversion of justice—but not in connection with this trial. She stood accused of having meted out excessive sentences to persons whose only crime was having expressed the wish to emigrate. "Her mission was to dispose of political opponents," Judge Inken Schwarzmann declared but then added that Kleine's record as "a superloyal party member" was a mitigating factor. Kleine was sentenced to two years' probation, a fine of DM4,000 (US$2,500), and 160 hours of community service. Judges Ziegler and Löwenthal had died before reunification and thus could not have been called to account. Prosecutor Lindner also was not held accountable for the death sentences meted out to Barczatis and Laurenz; but in 1994, a Dresden court sentenced Lindner to six months in prison for election fraud.

THE RAILROADER

Günther Müller, a corporal in the Luftwaffe's Ninth Parachute Regiment, had just celebrated his eighteenth birthday on the front line in Normandy when, in August 1944, he was taken prisoner by U.S. infantrymen. He and several other Luftwaffe paratroopers were shipped to an internment camp at Fort Sill, Oklahoma. In 1948 he was released and returned to his home, 140 miles northwest of Berlin—now part of the Soviet-occupied zone. Müller resumed his job with the railroad and married his childhood sweetheart, but life was hardly bearable. "I began to detest the Russians and their German stooges with a passion. I had enough of the communists, who were no different than the Nazis," Müller later recalled.[10] The Cold War was getting colder, and he decided to fight in his way. "I loved the Americans ever since I was their prisoner. I was astonished how well they treated me when I was captured and later in Oklahoma. It was like living in paradise, and now I wanted to do something for them." In spring 1953, shortly after the birth of his daughter, he traveled to Berlin's American sector. He visited former schoolmate Paul Perner, whom he told about his hatred of the communists and his desire to fight them. Perner confided that he was working for U.S. military intelligence. Did he want to join up?

Müller agreed at once. The Americans enthusiastically welcomed the volunteer, who was a strategically placed railroad dispatcher. He would become an important link in the then primitive early warning system of U.S. military intelligence. Müller, code-named Münzberger by the Americans, was handed a cheap box camera and told to go to work. Because he was a volunteer and spied for ideological reasons, he was reimbursed only for expenses.

Müller tackled his espionage assignment with zeal, photographing Soviet troop, tank, artillery, and vehicle transports moving through his station. He reported train numbers, departure points and destinations, and type of rail cars and their contents if noticeable. In the case of troop trains, Müller counted the passengers and the number of officers and their rank and uniform insignia. This information provided important clues for analysts in determining Soviet military strength in East Germany—whether it was being reinforced or merely moved to other locations. Periodically, Müller would be summoned to West Berlin's Kempinski Hotel for meetings with his handlers, who flew in from their headquarters in West Germany. At those meetings he would turn over his films and notes. In the event of especially heavy military movement, Müller or Perner (the two worked as a team) would head immediately for Berlin.

Toward the end of 1954, Müller and Perner were introduced to a new intermediary who called himself as Moosbach but said they should call him by his code name, Moritz. At this stage the operation became a bit more sophisticated. The cheap box camera had given out under heavy use, and the spying pair was given an 8mm motion picture camera and a tiny Minox camera to share. In addition they received several fountain pens containing an invisible ink solution and instructions on their use. They also were taught how to set up and use dead letter drops. Müller's code designation was changed to 2M, and Perner became 1M.

At 1:30 A.M. on November 20, 1955, the Müllers were awakened by a man's voice shouting Günther's name from the street below their second-floor apartment. Müller put on pants over his pajamas and went below to unlock the front door. A stranger pushed him aside, and with two other men, stormed upstairs into the apartment. One man rushed to the kitchen stove and stirred the ashes, another went to the bedroom, and the third demanded to see Müller's identity card. After inspecting the card, he pulled Müller's arms behind his back, handcuffed him, and dragged him out of the apartment. He had no chance to put on shoes or dress properly, though his wife managed to throw a jacket over his shoulders as she asked when he would return. Müller merely shook his head without saying a word. His two-year-old daughter was crying and clinging to her mother. The remaining men searched the apartment until the late afternoon. The only incriminating item they found was a tiny cassette of unexposed Minox film. All the while they never identified themselves or showed a search warrant. Irene Müller, of course, knew they were members of the feared Stasi.

The following morning the Stasi officers returned and searched again. After several hours they told Irene to get dressed, and one man pulled the wailing little girl from her mother. "She goes to your mother's, and you are coming with us," Irene was told. In reply to her question of whether she could take her daughter along with her, a Stasi man said: "You may never see your child again." When they reached the street, Irene was shoved into a car while her mother, who lived nearby, led the little girl away.

Wedged between two Stasi men, Irene Müller asked where they were taking her but received no answer. When she turned her head to look out the window, one of the Stasi men hit her head with his fist. It was already getting dark as the car drove through a gate into the backyard of a red brick building. They had arrived at the Stasi's prison and interrogation center on Lindenstrasse, in Potsdam. The building had served the Nazi Gestapo and the Soviet NKVD for the same purpose. Irene Müller was taken to a room and told to sit on a wooden stool that had been bolted to the concrete floor. Before her was a small table. The interrogation began. A man sat on the table, and another paced back and forth, asking why her husband always traveled to Berlin. "To buy medicine for our daughter and oranges or bananas." For hours they asked the same questions, over and over. Frau Müller's answer was always the same. By now she was sobbing bitterly.

Eventually a women relieved the interrogators and continued the questioning. Frau Müller described what followed:

> Since I could not give her any answers other than those I had given the men, she screamed at me and called me such names as 'dirty slut,' 'whore,' and 'boozing bitch.' When I held my handkerchief to my eyes, she grabbed my hands roughly, slammed them on the table, and hit them with her fist. Once, when my arms dropped to my side because I was exhausted after so many hours on the stool, she grabbed them so violently that my dress was torn. I told her that I had never met a woman like her in my life, which made her so mad that she punched me in the face.[11]

At that point Frau Müller soiled herself, her earlier request to use the toilet having been ignored.

In the morning the Stasi men returned and she was finally allowed to use the toilet under guard; but the door had to remain open. When she was returned to the room, a Stasi interrogator placed several typewritten sheets of paper before her and covered the writing with a blank sheet except for her name at the bottom. She was told to sign. "What does it say?" she asked. "Exactly what you have told us." When she lifted the cover sheet, her hand was slapped roughly. Frau Müller refused to sign. "Either you sign, or you will never see your kid or your mother again. We will send them to Siberia, and you will be behind penitentiary walls where you will have time to think over everything."

At midmorning, another Stasi man relieved the others. He took a thermos of coffee and a package of sandwiches from his briefcase. Grinning, he said: "Well, do you want to drink something too? First I will have my breakfast." He ate leisurely and gave Frau Müller nothing, although she had asked hours before for something to drink. The ordeal continued. Frau Müller was close to collapse when a man in uniform entered the room. One of the Stasi men spoke to him in Russian, and she could not understand what they were saying. "I was shaking and could no longer think straight. I don't know if I signed the paper or what they had written down." There was more talk that she could not understand. Then the man in uniform said "davai." There was not a German of her age who did not know that this Russian word meant "let's get started." Frau Müller was taken out of the room. At the top of a staircase, one of the Stasi men said to her, "Your husband is behind you." As she tried to turn her head, she was shoved down the stairs, taken to a car, and told to sit in the back seat. This time there was only a driver and another man seated next to him. Again they would not tell her where they were going. Shortly before noon the car stopped at her mother's house. "Now get out!" the driver yelled. The thirty hours of brutality without sleep, food, or drink had ended for Irene Müller.

Günther Müller was subjected to the same brutal questioning as his wife except that he was punched in the face more often and for the first few days his hands were cuffed behind his back while he sat on the stool. "By far the worst torturer was a woman who would scream and threaten. When I said to her, 'If you think you can squeeze me like a lemon, you are wrong,' she grabbed a large key ring and smashed it over my temple." Müller spent four months at the Lindenstrasse torture house, in cells without heat and with just enough food to keep him alive. "One of the Stasi men once said to me, 'Müller, if you are going to lie, you must do it logically,' and that's what I did."

From the questions being asked, Müller surmised that the Stasi knew about some of his activities but not everything, and certainly not those he considered the most damaging. For example, they did not know that he had spied since 1953. They also wanted to know what Perner looked like, which indicated that they had not arrested him. Thus, Müller told them that it was Perner who used the Minox camera and that he merely delivered the film. He admitted to starting in July 1955, a mere four months before his arrest. "Since they really did not know much about what I did, I was able to lie my way off the gallows; because if the whole truth had come out, I would not have gotten away with less than life in prison. I think I handled myself the right way." Following a one-hour trial on March 2, 1956, Günther Müller was sentenced to eight years' imprisonment and taken to Brandenburg penitentiary. "I estimated that of the 5,000 prisoners there, about 500 had been sentenced to long terms for espionage."

Müller heard nothing from his family for four years. Then his mother wrote that his wife had fled to West Berlin in 1956 and his daughter had died of leukemia in a refugee camp. "For me the world caved in, and I began to doubt God and justness. When I signed up with the Americans, I was told not to reveal my activities to anyone, not even to my wife, and I obeyed. In hindsight, I should have left a letter with instructions for my wife with someone I could trust in Berlin. Then she could have been helped by the Americans."

Müller's sentence was reduced to six years in September 1960 by a state clemency board, and fourteen months later he was released. But he was not yet free. Three months earlier the Berlin Wall had been built, shutting off the last escape hatch. Barred from returning to his railroad job, Müller worked on his parents' small farm, which had become part of a collective, and hatched plans to escape and join his wife in West Germany. He contacted two former colleagues whom he knew to be staunch anticommunists and who still worked for the railroad. They were willing to help.

Müller remembered having seen some prewar lead railcar seals while working at the railroad before he was arrested. He told his friends to remove all the seals from the freight car in which he would ride and replace them with the old ones, because if one seal were missing, the car would be opened and inspected. The right moment presented itself on the night of March 10, 1962. A freight car containing 400 sacks of cement, already sealed, was to be added to a train destined for West Germany. Müller and his friends removed all the seals, including one over a ventilation hatch. Müller removed his clothes and managed to squeeze his skinny body inside. The two railroad workers threw his clothes in after him, shut the hatch, and sealed it. With a pocket knife, Müller bored a tiny hole through the wooden wall of the car. It would enable him to see where the train was when daylight came. Twelve hours later the train stopped, and border guards inspected the seals. Shortly thereafter it stopped again for another inspection. Not knowing that all trains leaving East Germany were inspected twice before crossing the border, Müller almost knocked on the door to have it opened. But through his tiny peephole he saw the uniform of a border guard.

"God was on my side that day," Müller told me. "If they had had their dogs with them, I would have been finished; but it was a Sunday, and I guess they were too lazy to be thorough." At the third stop, Müller noted that it was a switching yard and that the track beds were higher and looked newer than those in East Germany. He took a chance, unhinged the sliding door, pushed until the seal broke, and burst out. A few yards down the tracks he spotted a railroad man checking a manifest. He walked up to him and asked the name of the station. "Büchen," the man answered. Müller was free at last. Railroad police questioned Müller and gave him a ticket to Mönchen-Gladbach, near the Dutch border, where he was reunited with his wife.

Müller was hired by the West German federal railroad, but none of the tests he had taken in East Germany were recognized, and he had to start over. He was, however, credited with past service years. By the time he retired in 1985, he was a senior administrator. The West German government paid him DM8,260—about US$2,750 at the exchange rate then prevailing—as compensation for his time in prison. He claimed nothing from the U.S. Army. With the restitution money and his salary, Müller was able to establish a new and full life.

As the years passed, the Müllers thought less and less about their ordeal, until the East German regime collapsed. When the German government announced that Stasi victims could peruse their files, Müller applied for permission to do so. On October 26, 1993, he sat in a small room in the former Stasi headquarters, seething with anger. He discovered why he had been arrested: The file contained a statement by a George Anschütz, a.k.a. Anderson, an agent of British intelligence who had sold out to the Stasi. For some unexplained reason, Müller's intermediary handler Moosbach had given Anschütz Müller's clear name and address. At best, this was a flagrant violation of procedures. Müller's partner, Paul Perner, apparently got wind of events while in Berlin but did not return to the East and thus was unable to warn his friend.

Müller received yet another shock. He found a letter by Stasi foreign espionage chief Markus Wolf to a Stasi colonel in charge of the area covering Müller's former hometown. Wolf wrote that according to a statement made by Müller to West German police after his escape, he was aided by railroad workers Werner Preuss and Heinz Lüdecke. Both men spent two years in prison for helping their friend. Wolf also had enclosed copies of teletypes originating in Düsseldorf with the West German counterespionage agency and the Criminal Investigation Bureau (Landeskriminalamt, or LKA) of the province of North Rhine–Westphalia, obviously provided by Stasi moles. Because West German security was rife with spies for the East, the identity of the mole who provided Wolf with the Müller teletypes might never be known. However, the most likely suspect was Ruth Wiegand, a teletype operator who worked for the Düsseldorf LKA office, which covered the city where Müller lived. She had been a Stasi spy since 1957 and had collected DM846,000 (about US$528,000) for furnishing more than 3,000 secret teletypes. She went to prison for three years. What really irked Müller was that the teletype from the counterspy agency said he was suspected of having been turned into a double agent while in prison and had his sentence reduced because of it. Müller wrote scathing letters to the German counterespionage agency and the U.S. embassy in Germany, accusing his handler, Moosbach, of treason.

THE MACHINIST

Werner Juretzko was sixteen years old in 1948 when he fled the Soviet-occupied zone, fearing arrest because of his anticommunist activities.[12] He wound up in the town of Kassel in the American zone, where he found a job as an apprentice in a heavy machinery plant. The German Communist Party's agitation and propaganda apparatus was in high gear at the time, trying to organize the plant's workers with little success. Juretzko's outspoken opposition soon drew the attention of the local criminal investigation section charged with combating political extremism of both right and left. He became an undercover operative and was instructed to change his view on communism, at least in public. The local communists accepted the new convert. He joined a peace group supported by East Germany and the communist Free German Youth, both of which were virulently anti-American. He kept police informed on upcoming demonstrations and the methods used by the East Germans to ship propaganda material to the West. U.S. military intelligence, which maintained a close liaison with the German police, liked Juretzko's diligence and recruited him as an agent in 1953. At the same time, Juretzko kept his job as a master machinist.

Juretzko was trained in various espionage techniques and was used mainly as a courier and on urgent assignments. Using false identity papers in the name of Werner Markus, he traveled throughout East Germany emptying dead letter drops. Having been born in Upper Silesia, where he learned to speak fluent Polish, he also was used on occasional assignments during which he used phony papers in the name of Stanislaw Swoboda. His frequent absences from his job, which he excused with ill health, became intolerable to his employer. He was given the option to resign or be dismissed. He quit. His espionage activities became a full-time job.

Between courier assignments, Juretzko spied on Soviet air bases and troop areas. For a time he worked as a crane operator at a base near Falkenburg, east of Leipzig, where the Soviet Air Force was extending and widening the runways. His orders were to stay until he could observe the type of aircraft being brought in. What he eventually reported to his handlers in Kassel was the arrival of the First Bomber Fleet, which hitherto had been stationed in Asia.

On August 13, 1955, Juretzko was sent to check a rumor that MiG-19 fighters had arrived at a Soviet base north of Berlin. Four days later he checked into a hotel in Schwerin. Before dawn he was awakened by someone rapping at his door. Juretzko sensed that it was the police, and he rushed to look out the window with escape in mind. His perception had been correct. The hotel was surrounded by what seemed an entire company of People's Police. Juretzko opened the door and faced two men in civilian clothes, one of whom demanded to see his identification and then checked it against what Juretzko noticed was a Stasi wanted list. After a perfunctory body search that yielded a few sketches, he was handcuffed and driven straight to the Hohenschönhausen prison in East Berlin. The building had been built by the Nazis as a giant kitchen where thousands of meals were prepared for workers in armaments plants. The Soviet secret police (NKVD) had it rebuilt in 1945 with an underground cell block for especially recalcitrant prisoners. All the cells were totally dark, and sixty-eight of them were so small that a person could only stand. To encourage confessions, the tiny cells could be filled with icy water up to a person's chest. Others were equipped with a sound system that would give off brain-scrambling noise. The Stasi inherited the place in the early 1950s. Prisoners called the underground dungeon the "U-boat."

During his interrogations Juretzko pretended to be politically disinterested. "I figured that if they thought I was a staunch opponent of communism and the DDR regime, they might hack my head off, so I played the mercenary." It did not take long for Juretzko to determine that he had been betrayed by someone who knew only his alias. "One of the Stasi guys said to me over and over, 'Markus, Markus, what a stupid pig you are. We know all about you, Werner Markus.'" What the Stasi wanted to know was whether he was part of a spy ring. Since he always worked solo or emptied dead letter drops, Juretzko had nothing much to give them. Assuming that agents who were loading the drops had been warned of his arrest, he would occasionally "remember" a drop location.

During part of his time in the U-boat, Juretzko shared a cell with Heinz Friedemann, an engineer and architect who had been part of a large espionage group working for British intelligence. Apparently he was an especially hard case for Stasi interrogators. In charge of the case was First Lieutenant Gerhard Niebling, who sent many to their death, including the hapless secretary Elli Barczatis. Niebling had been promoted since the Barczatis and Laurenz case. It seemed that the way to move up in the Stasi and the judicial system was to ignore humaneness, even truth, and go for the severest sentences. Juretzko told me: "One time Friedemann came back to the cell and he was sweating profusely and he stank terribly. Before they turned the light out I thought I saw that the sweat was pink. I thought he was really sweating blood." When Friedemann had calmed down, he told Juretzko that Niebling had said that the final protocol was almost complete and that his "noggin will roll." Just before Friedemann was taken away a few days later, he said: "Werner, please hug my family for me when you get out."

Juretzko spent more than a hundred days in the U-boat, until he made a full confession on December 27. He was taken out of the U-boat and transported to the prison in Halle known as the *Rote Ochse* (Red Ox). There he was sentenced to thirteen years for espionage. Inexplicably, Juretzko was tried a second time, resulting in a reduction of the original sentence to eight years. He would serve seven years before he was released on August 18, 1961 and expelled to West Germany.

Immediately after his release at age twenty-nine, Juretzko decided to begin a new life in the United States, where his three sisters had settled years earlier. His parents had died shortly after World War II. At the end of 1961 he arrived in Chicago, enrolled in school, and became an industrial engineer. He married in 1963. After retiring from a steel corporation, Juretzko set up his own business specializing in prototype engineering for industry and in aerospace components, in Wheeling, Illinois.

In summer 1992, Juretzko traveled to Berlin, where he found out that his cell mate Heinz Friedemann, then forty years old, had been executed on December 22, 1956—five days before his confession, which he now believed might well have saved his own life. Juretzko located Friedemann's seventy-three-year-old widow Irmgard and his two daughters and fulfilled his friend's last wish, giving them all a hug. Irmgard Friedemann told Juretzko that she had been informed in November 1955 that her husband was sentenced to death and that she had written immediately to DDR President Wilhelm Pieck, pleading for mercy. Her letter was never answered. On December 12 she wrote another letter, pleading for an answer. The second letter was found in the archive of the East German Prosecutor General. On it, someone whose signature is unreadable had written: "I feel it appropriate that Frau Friedemann not be told before the holidays that the sentence has been carried out."[13] That note was dated December 24, 1955.

The presiding judge in the Friedemann case was a woman named Lucie von Ehrenwall, director of the district court in Cottbus. The two lay judges assisting her were Hildegard Schrögelmann, a factory worker, and Friedrich Gubatz, a butcher. In 1992, prosecutors were preparing an indictment against von Ehrenwall, who was known as the "bloody judge of Cottbus" for having sent at least twelve persons to the guillotine. In one case she sentenced a man to fifteen years in prison for singing a song that was considered antistate. Von Ehrenwall, who was then seventy-nine years old, died before she could be tried for perversion of justice. Hildegard Schrögelmann also was dead. The butcher Friedrich Gubatz was alive, and Juretzko paid him a visit. They sat in the old butcher's well-tended garden.

Juretzko told me that Gubatz said he still could not figure out why he was chosen: "I was not even a party member." He said he had voted against the death penalty but that "Frau von Ehrenwall was so horrible, a five hundred fifty percenter, that nobody could convince her, and the other woman was also a convinced communist." Juretzko asked: "Were you able to sleep well that night? Can you imagine that Heinz Friedemann would also have liked to sit in a little garden?" The man did not reply. Juretzko handed him a copy of the certificate of execution. "Here is a present for you; sleep well." Gubatz looked at him and said quietly, "I am sure I won't."

Juretzko was not finished in his quest for revenge. In August 1992, he wrote the Berlin prosecutor general and demanded that former Stasi Major General Gerhard Niebling be charged with actively participating in the murder of Friedemann. At first he was notified that an investigation was pending, then that the case was closed. "I guess the Germans have lost their balls," he said resignedly. Juretzko said he plans to return to Berlin someday to read his Stasi file. When he does, he will find out who betrayed him.

THE CIA'S DOUBLE AGENT

Pursued by West German revenue agents for tax fraud, Hamburg businessman Dieter Vogel fled to Switzerland early in 1978. Vogel, who was recruited in 1974 by the U.S. Central Intelligence Agency, had some expert help in covering his trail.[14] His espionage activities had been minimal, furnishing mostly economic information he picked up on occasional business trips to East Germany. Now, with the tax man on his tail, Vogel was reactivated in a big way. His assignment was to travel to East Germany and volunteer his services to the foreign espionage directorate (HVA). The CIA wanted him to become a double agent in order to obtain information on HVA operations and anything else he could pick up about the Stasi.

On September 3, 1978, Vogel arrived in East Berlin and contacted Stasi headquarters. He was interviewed by Major Werner Poppe of the HVA's Fourth Department, which dealt with espionage against the West German military establishment. Consulting the West German police's wanted lists, Poppe could easily confirm Vogel's story that he was a fugitive. But his department determined that Vogel did not have the talent they required and offered him to Colonel Rolf Wagenbreth, head of the disinformation and active measures department (the HVA's Tenth Department). Wagenbreth and his deputy, Colonel Rolf Rabe, met with Vogel numerous times to get personal impressions of Vogel and how he could be used. Eventually he was assigned the code name Horn and designated an informal collaborator of Major Udo Jänert, whose section handled agents of influence. Provided with false passports and money, Vogel lived for a time in Canada, El Salvador, and Argentina, gathering data on persons of possible intelligence interest to the HVA. He duly reported all of his assignments to his CIA handlers.

One of the tasks of the Tenth Department was to mislead and discredit Western intelligence services. To accomplish this, the department was obliged to develop its own sources within these services. In this effort, Vogel was ordered to attempt to recruit an officer by the name of Keil, the chief of the emigration surveillance section of the West German Federal Intelligence Service (BND). The plan, devised in cooperation with the counterintelligence department, called for Vogel to approach Keil, posing as a CIA operative. The operation began in January 1980. About five or six months later, a Stasi agent inside the BND reported that Vogel had informed both the CIA and the BND of the operation and that Horn had been a CIA mole all along.

Vogel returned to East Berlin to make contact with his control officers on August 4, 1980, and was placed under surveillance. A week later he was arrested by officers of the counterespionage directorate and taken to the Hohenschönhausen dungeon. His interrogation and preparation for trial lasted nearly a year. On June 4, 1981, he was tried before the High Military Tribunal for aggravated espionage, sentenced to life imprisonment, and incarcerated in the notorious "Yellow Misery" prison at Bautzen. Prison officials reported that Vogel hanged himself in his cell on March 9, 1982.

When the Stasi archive became available after Germany's reunification, authorities discovered a microfilm of the official investigation of Vogel's death. Among other items, the microfilm contained a note indicating that the sworn affidavit from the Criminalistic Institute of the People's Police stating that Vogel had taken his own life was a forgery by members of the Stasi's operational and technical services directorate, which was then headed by Lieutenant Colonel Klaus Standtke.[15] Furthermore, the note said, the investigation in Vogel's cell was not conducted by a lieutenant of the People's Police but by a member of the Ninth Main Directorate, the Stasi's investigative arm. The official record of the investigation on file at the prosecutor's office in Dresden does not contain this note.

The personal file that the Stasi kept on Vogel during his imprisonment contains other material that also caused prosecutors to suspect that he was murdered. While in investigative detention before his trial, Vogel had complained in a letter to West Germany's permanent representative in East Berlin that he was being given injections even though he had no medical problem. That letter, intercepted by a censor, was never mailed. Another notation in the file said Vogel had asked to be included in prisoner swaps or to be ransomed by the West German government. However, the Stasi vetoed these requests because they wanted to obtain information about the CIA that interrogators felt Vogel was withholding. Vogel's death was still being probed in 1998.

A CIA COUP

The "mailmen" of the Stasi's counterespionage directorate randomly opened letters destined for West Germany, and West Berlin in particular, to test them for invisible writing. This method of spy catching was extraordinarily successful in tracking down a number of well-placed CIA agents. Wolfgang Reif, who held the subcabinet rank of state secretary in the East German foreign ministry, was arrested in 1984 after a letter written in invisible ink was traced to him.[16] Reif confessed to espionage and revealed that he had been recruited by the CIA in 1965, while serving as a vice consul at East Germany's embassy in Jakarta, Indonesia. He returned to East Berlin in early 1970, and seven years later he was posted again to Jakarta, this time as deputy ambassador. His access to the most secret foreign policy decisions with regard to East Germany's relations with the Soviet Union and other Eastern-bloc nations made him an extremely valuable CIA asset. The fifty-four-year-old Reif, whose CIA code name was Greif, had been sentenced to life imprisonment but was automatically released after reunification in 1990.

Gertrude Liebing, a communications technician for the Central Committee of the Communist Party, had written a letter in invisible ink to a CIA cover address in February 1966.[17] It was intercepted, and she was placed under investigation for seven months before she was arrested. During that time she wrote a number of other letters, all of which wound up in the hands of the Stasi mailmen. Because she was suffering from terminal cancer, it took relatively little effort for the Stasi to wring a confession out of Frau Liebing, who said she had been recruited by the CIA in West Berlin eleven years earlier. It was a major coup for the CIA when the woman joined because she had extensive and detailed knowledge of and access to all major government ministries. At the CIA's behest, Frau Liebing researched the technical possibilities for installing listening devices at Central Committee offices and supplied top secret telephone numbers and telephone books. The woman, whose CIA code name was Markus, was also an unofficial Stasi collaborator and reported to the CIA on the personalities of members of the Ministry for State Security with whom she came into contact.

A Stasi interrogation protocol said that prior to the erection of the "antifascist protective barrier," as the communists called the Berlin Wall, the CIA had supplied Liebing with ciphers that would enable her to decode radio messages. This was how she received her assignment after the Wall was built on August 13, 1961. CIA messages were preceded by the letters "Kta," followed by a number—for example, Kta/11—indicating the agent for whom the messages were intended. Frau Liebing apparently had no contact with other CIA agents in East Berlin, but she gave Stasi probers a list bearing forty-two names that she had relayed to the CIA as recruitment prospects.

Presumably working from that list, Stasi counterespionage officers were successful in identifying and arresting at least five other agents. All were employed in the Central Committee's telecommunications department and were obviously extremely useful to the CIA. Five other message recipients were only partially identified, and their fate is not known. One of the arrested was Harry Wierschke, a party member who had served one year in a Nazi concentration camp for refusing to serve in the military. He is believed to have supplied the CIA the tape recordings of secret party meetings, which he had been entrusted to destroy. Wierschke was sentenced to life imprisonment—a sentence that was later reduced to fifteen years. The sentences of the others ranged from five to twelve years. Gertrud Liebing received a twelve-year term and died of cancer in prison a year later. All the others had also died by the time their Stasi files were found in 1997. In the case of one Arno Heine, it could be ascertained that he had died in Bautzen II penitentiary, allegedly of cardiac arrest.

THE INNOCENT

The number of individuals imprisoned on false charges of espionage may never be known, but it might well range in the thousands.[18] Among the innocent was Günther Jahn, who was an apprentice aircraft mechanic when, at age sixteen, he was drafted into the Nazi Wehrmacht and assigned to a tank destroyer unit. He was wounded just five days before the war ended, taken prisoner by a U.S. Army unit, and sent to a British POW camp in northern Germany. He was released in July and assigned to work as a farm hand. After a bout with typhus, pneumonia, and pleurisy, Jahn headed for the Soviet zone to find his mother. His father had died in the concentration camp at Dachau, where the Nazis had confined him for resistance activities.

Jahn found his mother living near Berlin. The labor office there assigned him to clearing rubble and cutting down trees and later to a job on a bridge construction project. When the job was completed in 1948 Jahn and hundreds of other men were ordered to report for work in a mine in the Ore Mountains, to dig uranium for the Soviet atomic bomb project. Having heard of the miserable and dangerous conditions that existed in the mines, Jahn decided to flee to the American zone. However, as he was about cross the border, he was nabbed by a patrol of the People's Police. After interrogation by the K-5 criminal police, the forerunner of the Stasi, he was turned over to the Soviet secret police. He was confined to a room with seventeen other prisoners. They slept on a pile of straw, and an old water bucket was their toilet. "The food was so bad that I want to throw up just thinking about it," Jahn wrote to me later. For weeks, sometimes for months, the prisoners did not shave or bathe: "We looked like cave men and stank like pigs. If the lice with which we were infested had been dollars, we'd have been millionaires," Jahn wrote.

For weeks Jahn was questioned by a Soviet secret police captain, who was aided by a uniformed woman interpreter. He was accused of trying to reach the Americans and give them "secret" information about the bridge he had helped build. At one point he lost his temper, told the Soviet officer what he thought of him, and spat in his face. In return, he was beaten severely, and for good measure, the woman interpreter rammed a letter opener into his shoulder. The metal tip broke off, and no one made an attempt to extract it. From then on he was handcuffed to a heating pipe and his interrogations began with beatings. "I realized after a while that I would not leave the place alive if I didn't sign the statement of lies they had concocted," Jahn said. "So I signed all that shit." Three days later he stood before a Soviet military tribunal, and within five minutes he had been sentenced to twenty-five years in a labor camp.

Jahn was confined in Bautzen II penitentiary, where the treatment was as bad as could be. For talking to another prisoner a People's Police warder smashed his baton into Jahn's right kidney. For weeks Jahn's urine was pink. There was no medical treatment. For minor infractions prisoners were squeezed into a cell measuring about twelve by fourteen inches, the length of such confinement depending on the mood of the warder. "I had several experiences with that cell. If you were lucky you got out in two hours, if not you might be in for eight. When they opened the door you would just fall out," Jahn recalled. The food, already sparse and barely edible when he arrived, got even worse in 1950. On March 31, 1950, the prisoners rioted when they assembled in the mess hall. Warders fled, and armed People's Police units stormed into the prison yard. Guards used fire hoses to spray the mess hall windows and drive away the prisoners, who were chanting: "We call upon the Geneva Red Cross! . . . We are starving, starving, starving! . . . We want our freedom! . . . We are innocent!"[19] The prisoners could see people standing in nearby streets, waving at them. The onlookers ran off when Soviet troops and tanks surrounded the penitentiary. Suddenly the mess hall door swung open and police stormed in. The first wave was badly beaten; but in the end, the prisoners were reduced to a sad, moaning, and bleeding heap of humanity.

In December 1950, Jahn was called to the administrator's office, where he was received by Chief Commissioner Gustav Schulz (whom he called "Hunde Schulz"—"Schulz the Dog"). He was given paper and pencil and told to write down the poems he had written and distributed among the prisoners, one of whom obviously had informed on him. What poems? Jahn asked. Schulz beat him with a riding crop. Jahn wrote out the poems, all of which spoke of freedom triumphing over misery. The last stanza of one poem read: "Walls will collapse, bars will break, our precious possession shall always be the golden freedom, and then you laugh with teary eyes over pain long forgotten." His poetry earned him fourteen days in solitary. For eight days Jahn was in handcuffs and fed a bowl of soup every other day. Then the cuffs were removed and he received food every day. After his solitary confinement Jahn was assigned to a tailor shop where he said he learned a lot that he knew would stand him in good stead after his release.

Release came suddenly, on January 16, 1954. He and other prisoners were given new clothing, shoes, two packages of cigarettes, and a packet of sandwiches. Jahn and the others were told to sign a pledge that they would remain in East Germany, would never discuss prison conditions, and would work for the Stasi. "The main thing was to get out of there," Jahn explained. "Everything else could wait till later; I signed." He received ten marks, his discharge paper, and a railroad ticket to Strausberg, where his mother lived, near Berlin. When he arrived there, he registered with the police as required.

Instead of reporting back to the police three days later as he had been ordered, Jahn slipped into West Berlin, where he checked into a refugee camp. He was flown to another camp in West Germany, where he worked as a fitter in a metal shop. At government expense he was sent to a spa for four weeks of recuperation and removal of the tip of the letter opener that the Soviet woman translator had rammed into his shoulder six years earlier. At the spa in Bad Nauheim he met Helga Ramm, who was recuperating from five years of unspeakable torture and humiliation during Soviet interrogation in a number of prisons. She had been arrested by Stasi agents while visiting East Berlin. Ramm, then 19, had worked as a housekeeper for Rainer Hildebrandt, who led the anticommunist Battle Group Against Inhumanity (KgU). From time to time Hildebrandt gave her letters to deliver to a U.S. Army officer. The KgU was infiltrated by Stasi informers, who must have reported her name, and she was put on a wanted list. The young woman was turned over to the Soviets, who tortured her into signing a confession. Like Jahn, she was sentenced to twenty-five years in a labor camp. She was pardoned and released a day after Jahn regained his freedom.

Günther Jahn and Helga Ramm met on March 9, 1954, were engaged three days later, and married in April. Their daughter Birgit was born a year later, while the Jahns were still living in the refugee camp. Finally they were given a tiny apartment in a small town near Frankfurt. "The treatment we received from local officials was catastrophic," Jahn told me. "[They were] narrow-minded provincial bureaucrats in whose eyes we were interlopers and antisocial riffraff. They told us straight out, 'If you were in prison over there, you must have committed a crime.'" The young couple decided to turn their backs on Germany and emigrate to Australia to seek a new life. The beginning was tough, having to learn a new language and adapt themselves to the climate and culture. In time, Jahn got a job in a factory near Melbourne that manufactured blades for aircraft turbines. He worked his way up to head the toolmaking department. A second daughter was born in Australia in 1959. Both children are married and the Jahns have three grandchildren. The West German government paid them restitution, and Jahn was granted a pension, although it was 30 percent less than he would have received in Germany, because he and his wife are now Australian citizens.

THE AMERICAN NONSPY

Research for a doctorate in art history landed Ron Wiedenhoeft in a Stasi prison for nine months.[20] Wiedenhoeft was in East Berlin on September 5, 1967, photographing buildings constructed during the Bauhaus period and other architectural sites, including housing complexes built in the 1920s. He was taking pictures of a series of buildings at Normannenstrasse in the Lichtenberg district when he was arrested by a plainclothes Stasi officer. The thirty-year-old historian did not know that the building he was about to photograph was the Stasi's headquarters. He had made about thirty previous research excursions through East Berlin without incident.[21]

The Stasi arrest report, classified as top secret, asserted that Wiedenhoeft was arrested on "strong suspicion of espionage when caught red-handed as he photographed the building complex of the Ministry for State Security. This was confirmed when the confiscated film was developed." Other "damning evidence" was a Berlin city map carried by the suspected American spy. On this map, which showed both parts of the divided city, Wiedenhoeft had highlighted various areas. The Stasi checked out those areas that were in East Berlin, and the report described them as incriminating locations: "These areas included, besides the building of the MfS and adjacent apartment buildings, the MfS motor pool and a Soviet Army depot (underground ammunition bunker)." When Wiedenhoeft was searched, a notebook was found in his possession, in which he had made notes about the location of buildings he had already photographed, including the MfS headquarters.

Wiedenhoeft was taken to a prison that, based on the description he gave me, was most likely the Stasi's Hohenschönhausen interrogation center. Judging by the arrest and initial interrogation reports and by his own account, he was treated unusually well. He appears to have been the only American citizen arrested on suspicion of espionage during those years. The Stasi officer handling Wiedenhoeft's case made only two copies of his initial report, one of which was sent to the party secretary-general and head of state, Erich Honecker, and the other to Foreign Minister Otto Winzer. Honecker was anxious at the time to improve relations with the United States and to bolster the image and prestige of the German Democratic Republic and his own diplomatic recognition by Washington.[22] It is probably for this reason that Wiedenhoeft did not experience the brutal treatment that German suspects encountered and was spared a stay in the U-boat.

The Stasi was particularly intent on determining whether during his many visits to East Berlin Wiedenhoeft had smuggled in espionage equipment, because "the American intelligence service repeatedly established dead letter drops in historical buildings." Wiedenhoeft denied this charge as well as that he had had any contact whatsoever with the CIA. While in Stasi custody, Wiedenhoeft shared his cell for a time with a man who said he had been employed by the world-famous Zeiss optical firm and had been arrested after spying for the CIA for ten years. Wiedenhoeft was questioned periodically, but he told me that he was threatened only once: "The interrogator said if I didn't wise up and confess, I would still be sitting here when my daughters were getting married." His daughters were one and six years old at the time.

Meanwhile, President Lyndon B. Johnson became involved in trying to free the hapless American, enlisting the services of a New York attorney, Maxwell M. Rabb, President Dwight D. Eisenhower's Chief of Cabinet, who had previously tackled a number of delicate missions for the U.S. government.[23] Secretary of State Dean Rusk wanted Rabb to go to Berlin as a consultant for the CIA because that was only way they could pay the attorney. Rabb declined and paid his own way. Rabb was told that the U.S. government would not trade any communist spies imprisoned in the United States but would pay to get Wiedenhoeft out.

Rabb began his mission in April 1967. His first meeting was with Gerhard Beil, deputy minister for foreign trade, and several other top-ranking East Germans. "They were friendly . . . all smiles . . . when I told them my mission," Ambassador Rabb recalled in an interview with me. "They asked me what they would get if Wiedenhoeft were released, and I said 'goodwill.' Their attitude changed immediately. . . . They blew up, screaming 'You are debasing and maligning us,' and they yelled about the terrible things we were doing in Vietnam." Rabb left Berlin but later returned twice, bringing his wife and teenage son.

After the second meeting, which was more amicable, the Rabbs went sightseeing in East Berlin, followed by Stasi men, one of whom later introduced himself as Hans Fruck. Rabb did not know that Fruck was the deputy chief of the foreign espionage directorate and one of the most ruthless men that the Stasi had at the time. Fruck never showed his bad side to the American emissary. He was friendly and even invited the Rabbs to a sightseeing journey in Dresden. Fruck's demeanor as well as the attitude of other officials is further indication that they had been instructed by Honecker to be nice to the Americans.

At their third meeting, at the end of May 1968, Rabb was told that Wiedenhoeft would be delivered into his custody in a room of East Berlin's Metropol Hotel on June 3. Not only did the East Germans keep their word, they also provided a bottle of Rotkäppchen (Little Red Riding Hood) champagne to toast the release and paid for the hotel room. Considering the brutality with which the East German government treated others, these were extraordinary events. From then on, Ambassador Rabb was used as a private go-between and managed also to obtain the release of ten young Americans imprisoned for aiding East Germans attempting to flee. In all cases Rabb paid his own expenses.[24]

Wiedenhoeft returned to New York and finished his doctoral work at Columbia University in 1971. The title of his thesis was *Berlin Housing: Revolutionary German Reform in the 1920s.* He became a professor of liberal arts and international studies at the Colorado School of Mines. Reminiscing in an interview with the author about his imprisonment as a nonspy, Wiedenhoeft said: "Those guys in the MfS really were paranoid and they certainly were barking up the wrong tree. Although I would obviously have been a logical candidate to use the cover of being an American art historian to deliver information or help in efforts to get people out of the DDR, amazingly no one ever contacted me with such a request. I wonder if our guys were so incompetent that they weren't aware of my existence or whether they were so good that they didn't need me."

U.S. EMBASSY UNDER CONTROL

The U.S. embassy in East Berlin, like all noncommunist diplomatic missions, was obliged to employ only local help assigned by the Service Agency for Foreign Diplomatic Missions of the Ministry of Foreign Affairs. This agency was headed by an official named Neumann, who was actually an OIBE, a Stasi officer working under cover.[25] Neumann held the rank of colonel. Only those who signed a pledge to work for the Stasi as informers made the list. Thus, information flowed freely from the U.S. embassy to the Stasi for a while. However, within a short time, it slowed to a trickle. "What happened was that the Americans treated them well, gave them such things as oranges and bananas they couldn't buy in our shops," said former Stasi Colonel Rainer Wiegand. "As a result, the employees learned that the Americans were not the monopolistic, capitalistic, warmongering bloodsuckers our propaganda portrayed them as, and they just stopped informing on them."

The embassy employed only third-country nationals, such as Britons or Germans married to a U.S. citizen, for certain positions.

Following the spy scandal of the 1980s involving the U.S. embassy in Moscow, the State Department ordered its embassies in communist countries to dismiss their local help. For janitorial work, the embassy in East Berlin hired a number of citizens of various African countries, who were living in West Berlin. All were compromised the first day they crossed through the wall. Customs officials found them in possession of East German marks that they had bought in the West at the exchange rate of one West mark for ten nonconvertible East marks. Importing East marks was illegal, and rather than go to jail, they all signed up to work for the Stasi.[26]

Every U.S. diplomat was viewed as a spy by the Stasi hierarchy. Their apartments were bugged, and in some cases video cameras were installed. Around-the-clock surveillance was routine. Every East German who had any contact with U.S. diplomats was vetted, and in many cases placed under surveillance. This total control of U.S. diplomats was not only horrendously expensive but unnecessary. Counterespionage officers claimed they had no difficulty in identifying intelligence personal posing as diplomats.[27] Over the years they had learned that the Americans had reserved certain embassy personnel slots, such as counselor for economic affairs or second secretary in the political section, for intelligence officers. There was no deviation from this practice. Furthermore, Stasi counterespionage was able to check new arrivals through the KGB's SOUD computer, in which persons previously identified as intelligence operatives in other countries were registered. This computer stored precise descriptions that in most cases rendered the use of pseudonyms useless. If there were doubts, the diplomat's private residence was entered surreptitiously in search of confirmation.

In one case, the East Berlin apartment of a diplomat who had arrived as a second secretary in September 1987 was entered, and the black bag men struck pay dirt. They found a citation awarding a medal for the "diplomat's" superior performance at a Reserve Officers' Training Corps at the University of Massachusetts between 1981 and 1985. Besides the man's name and rank, the document listed his Army branch as military intelligence. In his wardrobe hung a uniform with military intelligence insignia on its lapels.[28] The Stasi put him down as an officer of the Defense Intelligence Agency.

Assuming correctly that all of their official and personal telephones were tapped, U.S. diplomats in East Berlin were among the most security conscious and adhered to rigid telephone security. What they did not know was that all public telephones within a 500-meter radius of the embassy were also monitored. This led to tragic consequences in early summer 1988.[29] Around noon, the embassy telephone operator received a call from a man who asked in broken German to be connected to someone who could speak Russian because he wanted to defect. The operator said it was the lunch hour and that he should come to the embassy in an hour. Monitors immediately alerted Stasi counterespionage that the call had been placed from a booth near the embassy. The Stasi also alerted the KGB, and a wide area around the embassy was cordoned off. Watchers spotted a man walking toward the embassy carrying a briefcase and wearing a raincoat that did not cover his uniform trousers. He was surrounded by KGB and Stasi men, tackled, and pulled into a car when he tried to run. The catch turned out to be a Soviet colonel commanding an intermediate range missile brigade. His briefcase held a collection of documents concerning the Soviet rocket system in East Germany. He was flown aboard a Stasi aircraft to Moscow, where he was executed. Major General Wolfgang Lohse, who led the Stasi arrest team, and Lieutenant Colonel Bernd Häseler, responsible for surveillance of the U.S. embassy, were decorated with the Soviet Order of the Red Banner.[30]

Increasing evidence of political dissent in 1987 put all Stasi units on high alert. General Kratsch's counterespionage directorate was almost entirely devoted to crushing the percolating rebellion. As a result, only one or two spies were uncovered in the years following 1985.[31] Kratsch maintained that socialism and its humaneness toward the people could not possibly generate any reasons for resistance: Ergo, resistance toward the regime was inspired and organized by outsiders and imported into the DDR. Therefore, Kratsch, whom his former subordinate Colonel Rainer Wiegand described as a man with "a head filled with concrete," suspected that the U.S. diplomats in particular had inspired and organized the political opposition. Kratsch ordered an even tighter watch over them. Lieutenant Colonel Häseler reported that Ralph Hirsch, one of the dissident leaders, had met with a CIA operative from the embassy at a cemetery in the dead of night and had handed over documents for which he received money. When I interviewed him, Hirsch denied ever meeting anyone at a cemetery and receiving money from any American:

> I am not an idiot. I knew they were watching all of us night and day. I met with anybody who was interested in our movement—foreign journalists, American and British diplomats. I didn't ask whether they were CIA, and I didn't care. There were many meetings in my apartment, but I assumed the place was bugged, and if we had something to discuss we met in parks. You can be sure they would have arrested me for espionage if the Stasi had seen me taking money. And the so-called documents I gave anyone who wanted them were copies of our underground newsletter.

Four of the most influential dissidents, including Hirsch, were indeed arrested on January 25, 1988 and charged with engaging in illegal political activities bordering on treason. They were held in the Hohenschönhausen prison, where according to Hirsch, they were harshly interrogated and injected with unknown drugs. On February 15 all four were presented with applications for exit visas and told to sign. They did, and within hours they were in West Berlin. The coerced deportation merely speeded up the resistance movement, with others, including church leaders and even former communists, taking their places.

A HOLE IN THE STASI'S NET

Despite the total surveillance of the population and Western visitors, Stasi counterespionage was not infallible. Numerous U.S. operations were highly successful and went undetected. In 1987, the KGB told General Kratsch that the main telephone cables to the East were tapped and that they suspected the Americans. The KGB said they had discovered taps in Moscow, and the taps were always at cable distribution points that could be accessed through manholes. Kratsch, agreeing with the Soviets that "the Americans were tops in electronic espionage," went to work and started Operation Dichter.[32] Some two hundred Stasi officers spent a week climbing down every telephone cable manhole in East Berlin and found nothing.

The KGB fed the Stasi new information, claiming that an American electronic spy gadget was buried next to the cable in the area of Hönoh, east of Berlin. Clandestine observation posts were set up throughout the area and manned day and night by counterspies. After a month the manned posts were replaced by hidden video cameras. The yield was zero, prompting the installation of an elaborate detection system by technicians responsible for electronic surveillance and countermeasures. When even these devices failed to locate the tap, General Kratsch figured that the cable must be tapped in the countryside, and requested a regiment of army engineers to dig up miles of cable reaching nearly to the Polish border. Again they toiled in vain. Until that time, Kratsch had acted solely on KGB information. Though the Soviets had convinced him that a tap existed, he tried another tack.

Telecommunications experts were ordered to examine the routing of the cable in East Berlin. To Kratsch's astonishment, they reported that the cable carrying traffic of the Central Committee and the National Defense Council ran alongside the building housing the U.S. embassy. Assuming that the cable was tapped from inside the embassy and that all sensitive electronic equipment can be detected by its emissions, sensors were installed in neighboring buildings. Helicopters with detection equipment circled above the embassy for weeks. The operation was costing millions. In the end, just before the wall came down in November 1989, Kratsch threw in the towel.[33] When this story was told to a high official with intimate knowledge of the U.S. electronic espionage, he responded with a broad grin. "So they didn't find it," he said, and clammed up.

THE STASI'S WILD-GOOSE CHASE

In the early 1980s, the counterespionage services of various Eastern-bloc countries, including those of Bulgaria, discovered a number of mysterious technical gadgets placed near strategic sites such as air bases and ammunition depots.[34] These gadgets were camouflaged as rocks, tree limbs, and other natural debris. The finders could not divine the purpose of the objects—seemingly mere pieces of metal. No one was able to determine how these gadgets worked or why they were deployed. They knew only that the gadgets had something to do with espionage. Then a Stasi counterespionage double agent who had been recruited by a U.S. intelligence service received three of the gadgets from his American handlers in 1983, to be placed near an ammunition depot outside Berlin. In addition, children playing near railroad tracks found one and handed it in to police. Stasi counterspies consulted their KGB counterparts and learned that the same gadgets had been found in the Soviet Union but no one had been able to figure out their purpose.

In the end, East German technicians believed they had solved the puzzle: The gadgets were sensors capable of recording traffic in and around air bases, munitions depots, and rocket bases, and according to former Stasi Colonel Wiegand, to register emissions from nuclear munitions. The data were transmitted at predetermined intervals to a U.S. satellite that crossed over East Germany. The problem was to find out how the sensors were serviced, since they either needed to be fed with new batteries or replaced. The double agent who originally had brought a sensor to the Stasi was unable to help. Whatever system the Americans used had yet to be discovered, and more intensive checks of persons crossing through the wall from West Berlin were ordered.

Attention focused in 1988 on a man and a woman crossing once or twice a month into East Berlin en route to Cottbus, a city southeast of Berlin. The man was identified as Jürgen Kockro, and the woman, as his live-in partner, Helga Rodrich. Stasi files were checked, and Kockro was found to have been a suspected espionage courier in the late 1950s and early 1960s, when he was a student at West Berlin Technical University. The Stasi suspected him of loading and emptying dead letter drops. Before he could be arrested, the Berlin Wall was built and he stopped coming to the East. A graduate communications engineer, he was employed by the U.S. command in West Berlin. Kockro worked at a compound that also housed a large contingent of U.S. Army intelligence as well as CIA personnel. The East Germans thought Kockro had to be the man who serviced the sensors. In summer 1989 General Kratsch launched Operation Phoenix, which involved tight surveillance every time Kockro and his companion traveled to East Germany. They were watched as they drove to a small village adjacent to an air base. Helga Rodrich would go to an old-age home, while Kockro would sit for hours in his car or go for walks near the base.

Weeks of observation were fruitless. The man never did anything that seemed suspicious. Stasi technicians then theorized that Kockro's car contained electronic equipment that was used to service the sensors they suspected were in place near the air base. The decision was made to detain Kockro and offer him DM1 million (about US$532,000) in cash in return for his knowledge of the sensor and satellite operations. But that decision came too late: The wall was being dismantled, and East Germany soon passed into history, and Operation Phoenix with it.

I contacted Kockro in 1991 and showed him the report a Stasi colonel had written about him. Kockro, then fifty-nine years old, began to read it, nodded, and said: "Yes, everything that's written here is correct. It's true that I was a courier while I was a student—not for the Americans, but for the Ukrainian underground movement NTS [Narodnyi trudovoi soyuz]. They were right that I worked for the Americans, but only as a telephone engineer, and in all my years with them I only visited the intelligence building once when they had a serious problem with their communication system." When he came to the part about his suspicious behavior while his companion was visiting the old-age home, he began to laugh convulsively. "My God, this is funny!" he said after he caught his breath. "Helga was visiting her mother, and I hated to go in there and spend my time with all those old people. . . . I just couldn't stand that, so I sat in the car or went for a walk." Then he mused: "Too bad they didn't act earlier. For a million marks I could have told them a whale of a tale!"

8

STASI OPERATIONS IN THE THIRD WORLD

AS MUCH TREASURE AS THE STASI spent on spying against the West, if not more, went to support the so-called liberation forces in the Third World. Erich Mielke's Ministry for State Security was the closest ally of the Soviet KGB in the communists' attempt to establish a foothold in the Third World. The two services' areas of responsibility were clearly delineated: The Soviets supplied military hardware, money, military advisers, and other support of an ideological and propagandistic nature. The Stasi organized and trained secret police forces and intelligence departments.

The Stasi's first major task abroad was in Cuba, after Fidel Castro and Vice Premier Anastas Mikoyan signed the Soviet-Cuban pact on February 13, 1960, officially placing Cuba in the Soviet bloc. As Soviet arms shipments began, Mielke sent a number of Stasi officers of General Wolf's HVA to Havana. Led by Colonel Siegfried Fiedler, they assisted in setting up what became a first-rate intelligence service and an oppressive secret police. As a result Cuba's relations with East Germany developed as closely as those with the Soviet Union. Intelligence gathered in the United States by the Cubans was routinely shared with the Stasi. Much of the information contained in the dossier the Stasi maintained on President Ronald Reagan, for example, originated with the Cubans.

THE STASI IN NICARAGUA

State Security Minister Mielke pondered ways the Stasi might aid the Sandinistas almost immediately after they had taken Managua and ousted the Somoza regime, spawning debates within the MfS against involvement in Nicaragua.[1] Mielke dismissed all objections out of hand. This was a great opportunity for his men to confront the "arch-enemy America" in its own backyard. Besides, he had to fulfill his pledge to Moscow. The Soviets had added Latin America to the DDR's list of responsibilities in the international class struggle and in support of so-called liberation movements. The East German leadership accepted this obligation in the mid-1960s.[2] In September 1979, East German Foreign Minister Oskar Fischer traveled to Managua to establish diplomatic relations with the Sandinista regime.

Sandinista training in Cuba in the mid-1970s for the takeover of Nicaragua had provided the Stasi officers stationed in Havana with the opportunity to become intimately acquainted with the leadership, especially with Tomas Borge. Shortly after the Sandinistas defeated the Somoza regime and seized power in July 1979, Colonel Fiedler set up a Stasi outpost in Managua. Over the years the size of the Stasi contingent fluctuated between 60 and 80 officers.[3] The primary task of this group was to systematically construct a Nicaraguan General Directorate of State Security (DGSE) that was identical in structure and operational doctrine to the Stasi.

In mid-March 1980, Nicaraguan Interior Minister Tomas Borge visited Moscow for meetings with KGB Major General Yakov P. Medyanik, deputy chief of the First Main Directorate, the KGB's foreign intelligence arm. Later that month Borge flew to Czechoslovakia, then to Sofia, where he consulted with secret police officials of the Bulgarian Ministry of the Interior. Before Borge left for East Berlin, Mielke received a report on a telephone call to Stasi headquarters from Bulgarian state security outlining discussions with Tomas Borge.[4] The Bulgarians said they had agreed to train forty Nicaraguans in general police work and twenty others in counterespionage and intelligence gathering. In addition, they planned to send a Bulgarian secret police officer to Nicaragua. Borge also presented his wish list for weapons, uniforms, and communications equipment. On these matters the Bulgarians were noncommittal. "The Bulgarian comrades coordinated all questions with the KGB in advance," the report said.

On April 1, 1980, Borge met with Mielke. Borge was accompanied by his deputy Hugo Torres, responsible for state security, and Marcos Somarriba, political commissar of Borge's ministry. With Mielke were Major Generals Horst Jänicke, deputy chief of foreign espionage, and Willi Damm, chief of the Tenth Department, which was directly under Mielke and handled international relations. Also present was Lieutenant Colonel Horst Scheel, whom Mielke had named to coordinate collaboration between the Stasi and the Nicaraguan Interior Ministry, which controlled all law-enforcement functions, including the secret police and customs.

A top secret protocol of the meeting quoted Borge as telling those assembled that Nicaragua's precarious economic situation precluded commercial purchases of needed equipment for military and paramilitary purposes.[5] Therefore, Borge pleaded for "solidarity assistance" by the furnishing of motor transport to provide greater mobility for state security forces. "For example," Borge said, "if the DDR could supply motorcycles, it would already be of great help." However, Borge did not stop at motorcycles. He requested pistols, uniforms, and communications and surveillance equipment. "This is especially necessary for the establishment of an effective personnel security force," he argued, "because plans of the enemy, particularly the CIA, to assassinate leading personalities of the revolution including myself have already been discovered." Stasi minister Mielke then asked Borge to provide an overview of the political situation in the country.

The Sandinista Liberation Front (FSLN), Borge replied, was experiencing opposition from the Social Christian Party, which had already succeeded in placing a mole inside the state security apparatus. "The chairman of that party and president of the Nicaraguan Human Rights Commission, Gonzalez, is discrediting and slandering the Sandinista Revolution abroad." As soon as he returned to Nicaragua, Borge vowed, he would "clear up this question and take appropriate measures." He also told Mielke that "repressive measures have already been taken against the so-called Communist Party, which in no way can be seen as communist-Marxist but is a politically unimportant group of Trotskyites and Maoists." Borge alleged that this group "has a relationship with the CIA, and we are endeavoring to create evidence in this regard." In closing, Borge declared that

- the Nicaraguan revolution was an irreversible process;
- the FSLN would become a Marxist-Leninist Party loyal to the principles of its founder Carlos Fonseca;
- the Soviet Union and the socialist camp were held in high regard;
- any open intervention would plunge the country into a civil war, i.e., create a new Vietnam. The FSLN was ready and armed for that.

Mielke responded by emphasizing the "strengthening and solidifying the organs of power, particularly the security organs" and that loyal citizens must be won over to the political aims of the Sandinistas. In other words, Mielke urged the establishment of a secret police system like that in East Germany. "If that does not succeed, other politically operational measures must be taken." What he meant was clear: If the Sandinistas were unable to come to grips with the opposition by lacing it with informers, stern repressive measures would be required. In that regard, Mielke said his ministry was prepared to train a specially selected secret police cadre in East Germany. He said he would order an immediate study regarding the supply of weapons and other equipment. This meeting set in motion one of the most massive Stasi efforts in support of the establishment of a communist police state in the Third World.

Following Borge's visit, Mielke became increasingly dissatisfied with the slow pace of other Eastern-bloc countries in providing assistance.[6] He decided to seize the initiative and told KGB Chief Yuri Andropov he wanted to convene a meeting in Berlin to rectify the situation. Andropov agreed. The two-day meeting, chaired by Stasi General Jänicke, convened on May 12, 1980. Besides Jänicke, the East Germans were represented by Stasi General Damm and People's Police General Reinhard Uhlig.

Taking part for the KGB were General Medyanik and Colonel S. Kolomyakov, chief of the Latin American section of the foreign espionage directorate. Others included Colonel Vlcek, head of the international department in the Czechoslovakian interior ministry; Colonels Platschkov and Mitev, Bulgaria's foreign espionage deputy chief and international department head, respectively; and Colonel Hamel Ruiz, deputy chief of Cuban counterespionage. Mielke had arranged an elaborate program of work and entertainment. The Bulgarians and the Cubans were flown to East Berlin aboard Stasi aircraft. They were greeted by Markus Wolf, who hosted a luncheon for them. He told his guests that the MfS and the Interior Ministry would diligently adhere to the decision of East Germany's Politburo to actively support the Nicaraguan revolution.

The first day was devoted to analysis and discussion of Nicaragua's political situation, which Ruiz of Cuba said was still in a state of flux.[7] He described the close ties of the FSLN to the Cuban Communist Party and said splits within the Sandinistas had largely been assuaged: "Measures are under way to restructure the Sandinista Front into a Marxist-Leninist Party." Remnants of the division "are being dealt with," Ruiz said. "Nevertheless, one must assume that in this area problems still may arise." He also detailed the activities of non-Sandinista political groups, saying that the socialist parties under Alvaro Ramirez and Luis Sanchez were coming to terms with the FSLN. Ruiz described the People's Action Movement (MAP) as a Maoist group whose leaders "display hostile (criminal) tendencies, and some of the leaders are now in prison and its newspaper has been banned."

In the judgment of the Cuban intelligence officer, the MAP had been destroyed, "although one cannot predict if the MAP or similar Maoist-oriented groups can reactivate themselves."

Discussing the Communist Party under Ali Altamirano, Ruiz said it has a small membership but a "certain influence upon the Labor Union CAUS, which had displayed a hostile attitude" toward the Sandinistas. "The Sandinista Front was forced to flex its power and defend itself by arresting a number of activists." Altamirano was not arrested, so as to avoid exacerbating the situation, Ruiz added. The Cuban's assessment in general was one of guarded optimism on the one hand and veiled pessimism on the other. This undoubtedly influenced Mielke's perception that for the Sandinistas' survival, Nicaragua needed to be shielded from outside influences as rigidly as his own police state.

While the East Germans pledged assistance, they said equipment of a technical nature would be forthcoming only after the Nicaraguans had received proper training. The Czechoslovakians and the Bulgarians told the meeting that they had already sent aid to Managua, including a total of 1,500 submachine guns, 50 light machine guns, 12,000 pistols, 8,000 rubber truncheons, and 18,000 lightweight uniforms and shoes. Ammunition shipments totaled two million rounds. In addition, the Bulgarians pledged an immediate shipment of two field hospitals and 500 field telephones with ten switchboards and sixty miles of cable.

KGB General Medyanik acknowledged that Cuba carried the main burden of support. "But since we know that Lenin's words about the difficulties of defending a revolution have been confirmed many times, we all have the obligation to do our share for strengthening and securing the revolution in Nicaragua. The United States will not acquiesce to the revolutionary changes in her own sphere of influence. She will attempt to destabilize the revolution and mobilize all opposing forces. Therefore, our consultations are of the highest significance." The Soviet general emphasized the importance of coordinating the selection of Nicaraguan cadres for training in the Eastern bloc, paying particular attention to security and background checks. "We have experienced that the enemy infiltrated the ranks of cadres selected for training so that we in the Soviet Union have trained some American and English agents."

Medyanik said Borge requested a great amount of technical material, which would involve "considerable" expense. Contrary to the other countries, the Soviet Union did not agree to or sign an official protocol covering the discussions with the Nicaraguan Interior Minister. Despite the absence of such a document, the KGB general said significant aid was already being shipped, though he did not elaborate and none of his subservient discussion partners asked for details. It seemed that Moscow was not yet convinced that the Sandinistas would be able to mold Nicaragua into a solid Marxist-Leninist state. In an aside, Medyanik said Borge had asked for 50 Lada sedans and 50 all-terrain vehicles, which he said was the most complicated problem. "These are not in the 1980 plan, and it is unlikely that we can fulfill this wish in the foreseeable future. Apparently it will become necessary to negotiate with the Nicaraguan comrades on a commercial basis." In other words, if the Sandinistas wanted the vehicles, they would have to pay for them.

Statements by Medyanik and Colonel Kolomyakov made it clear that the KGB was pursuing aims that differed from those of their "brother" services. Both were concentrating on how the Sandinistas could contribute to establishing a base for directing espionage operations throughout Central America. Kolomyakov dismissed the shipment of arms, uniforms, motor transport, and communications equipment as "elementary." For example, he said, facilities for creating false documents, electronic surveillance equipment, and a one-way radio transmitter for sending messages to agents were more urgently needed. To that list General Medyanik added invisible writing implements, special containers for transporting secret material, and training of Nicaraguans in the use of ciphers.

Toward the end of the two-day meeting, General Medyanik asked Ruiz what results had been achieved "in discovering and liquidating enemy agencies"—that is, clandestine espionage and sabotage groups. Ruiz replied that so far there were only indications, particularly based on "the behavior of U.S. citizens in collecting information, but there is no proof." Security officials were not concentrating on "legal residenturas," foreign intelligence operatives working under diplomatic cover. "There is a lack of surveillance personnel, and telephone monitoring is just beginning. The Americans are very active, presumably working with networks established during the Somoza era, but at this time we have no real information. The diplomatic representation of the USA is numerically very strong. The Americans are roaming through Managua totally unhindered." In connection with liquidating "enemies," Ruiz said construction of a new prison was urgent. "There is only one prison, and that holds more than 7,000 inmates. The large number of prisoners is due mostly to the fact that all members of the national guard and Somoza supporters who were suspected of being informers were arrested." He added that most of the prisoners had not had a trial and many had not even been interrogated because of the lack of investigators. "Can the army pose a danger to the revolution?" the KGB general asked. Ruiz maintained that all command functions were in the hands of loyal, battle-tested Sandinista commanders and that all Somoza officers had been removed. "The main problems with this army are disciplinary difficulties caused by such things as the hot-bloodedness of many commanders." He added, without elaborating, that there had been "many incidents."

Stasi minister Mielke ended the meeting with a speech in which he summarized the actions that must be taken in support of transforming Nicaragua into a "socialist" state. He said he called the conference because he felt progress in that regard was not proceeding as rapidly as he felt was necessary. In a rare criticism of the Soviet Union, the usually subservient Mielke said: "The Soviet comrades are the most competent in judging such situations, and we would have welcomed it if they had seized the initiative." In an obvious dig at the frequent heavy-handedness of Soviets operating in Third World countries, Mielke said all those dispatched to Nicaragua must conduct themselves in an unassuming manner, work effectively, and adhere to strict secrecy. "Of course, the enemy will find out that we are operating there. The appearance of our representatives working as a unit is of prime importance. Mutual agreement on all matters will be the requirement for transforming chekist principles, created by Dzerzhinski, into reality in Nicaragua. The Nicaraguan comrades must feel that the communists are on their side."

Within a few weeks after the East Berlin conference, Mielke dispatched four officers to train twenty-five bodyguards and supervise security preparations for the celebration of the first anniversary of the Sandinista takeover on July 19. Speedy establishment of a reliable security contingent was paramount because of Fidel Castro's participation in the ceremonies. Acting on Stasi liaison officer Colonel Münzel's report on alarmingly lax control procedures at Managua's airport and seaport and at border crossing points due to untrained and underequipped officials, a high-powered Stasi delegation flew to Nicaragua for a firsthand study. The group was led by Major General Heinz Fiedler, head of the Sixth Main Directorate, responsible for general border security including passport control, screening for persons wanted by the police, and surveillance of customs personnel. The Stasi group was accompanied by Michel Najlis, chief of immigration at the Nicaraguan interior ministry, her deputy Lila Aguilar, and Magdalena Calderon, chief of border crossing points. Fiedler also met with officials of Nicaragua's General Directorate for State Security (DGSE), including its chief, Lenin Cerna. In his report to Mielke, General Fiedler confirmed earlier reports and stressed the urgency of training and the need for modern equipment. Tightening up the border crossing points was most important to the DGSE in their quest to discover "spies and subversives." Before returning to East Berlin, Interior Minister Borge made Fiedler a gift of an Israeli Uzi submachine gun that he said was taken from "one of Somoza's most cruel policemen."[8]

The first group of Nicaraguan border control officials flew to East Berlin in January 1981, after the winter clothing they had requested arrived in Managua aboard a special flight of the government airline Interflug. Led by the chief of border control, Magdalena Calderon, the group included Javier Amador, deputy passport control chief at Managua airport, and other border control officials. They were intensively briefed on East Germany's extremely tough border control procedures. Stasi General Fiedler gave a special lecture on the construction of the "antifascist protective barrier," the Berlin Wall. Particular attention was paid to recognizing "forms and methods of enemy activities in traffic across the borders," which included political and ideological subversion. In Stasi lingo, this meant the smuggling of Western newspapers and books.[9] A two-week guided tour for the Nicaraguans included airports, ports on the Baltic coast, and border checkpoints. Fiedler reported to Mielke that the Nicaraguans also were also taken to a number of cultural institutions to acquaint them with the "results of the building of socialism and the spiritual and cultural life of our republic and the path of development from the destruction of fascism by the Red Army until the present. In this connection particular attention was paid to measures designed to solidify and protect the dictatorship of the proletariat, the power." At the end of their stay, the Nicaraguans were given instructional materials on recognizing forged passports, the significance of passport control, and security techniques. The East Germans had prepared well. All documentation had been translated into Spanish. In addition, the Nicaraguans received passport stamps with interchangeable plates, ink pads, and colors, and one million statistical entry and exit forms. It was the first step in the direction of making Nicaragua's border control as tight as East Germany's.

The first two intensive training classes of twenty-five men each lasted two months and were held in the spring of 1981.[10] All trainees were either secret police investigators or officials assigned to border control. In addition, Mielke approved the dispatch of $751,378 worth of equipment, including motorcycles, hand-held radios, cameras, binoculars, and fingerprinting equipment. Early in 1981, four Stasi specialists were sent to Nicaragua, two to supervise the establishment of a central secret police archive and two communications specialists to prepare facilities for wiretapping.

Over the next two years, hundreds of Sandinistas were brought to East Germany for on-the-job training at border crossing points. Special equipment, such as ultraviolet lamps for detecting forgeries, inks to place secret markings on passports of suspect travelers, surveillance video cameras, and one-way mirrors were provided by the Stasi. In September 1982, a reporter of the West Berlin newspaper *Berliner Morgenpost* wrote that procedures at Managua's Augusto C. Sandino airport were identical—as "one egg to another"—to those on the East German border. The article became part of the Stasi file on Nicaragua. What better proof that the Stasi's efforts were not in vain!

In line with Mielke's edict that the Sandinista secret police recruit informers, in-country schools taught the Nicaraguans how to cope with dissidents and "counterrevolutionaries." Toward this end, the instructors applied Stasi directives I/79 and II/79 to the letter. These secret directives set forth the methods employed in recruiting informers in such masses that the hydra of the DGSE would reach into all strata of society. That effort was a failure. Mielke's men had not counted on the cultural, societal, and behavioral makeup of a Latin people, and they underestimated the influence of the church.

Sandinistas selected for top leadership positions were brought to East Germany for six- and twelve-month courses at the top secret foreign training branch of the Stasi's so-called College of Justice. The curriculum was dominated by Marxist-Leninist ideological indoctrination. Prospective second echelon leaders were trained in terrorism, counterterrorism, and antiguerrilla warfare at various clandestine camps near Berlin by members of the Stasi directorates for personnel security and counterterrorism.

After their first meeting in March 1980, Mielke and Borge carried on a steady correspondence, Borge asking for more and more assistance, and Mielke agreeing to provide it.[11] In the early years Borge, who addressed the Stasi minister as "Compañero," would sign off with "revolutionary greetings" and the slogan "Free Fatherland or Death." By 1988, Borge had dropped the death pledge, signing off with "brotherly greetings." In his last letter to Mielke on October 21, 1989, seventeen days before the fall of the Berlin Wall, Borge merely wrote "fraternally" above his name.

In summer 1983 the Stasi liaison officer in Managua sent an urgent top secret cable to East Berlin, requesting additional equipment to achieve maximum control over U.S. citizens entering Nicaragua.[12] Following the closure of Nicaraguan consulates in the United States, Americans were issued 90-day visas when they entered the country. "This has created a new operational situation, inasmuch as 2,000 U.S. citizens enter Nicaragua monthly and a decrease is not expected," the cable said. In order to achieve greater control over the travelers, cameras were needed to photograph all travel documents "for operational analysis and to place them into archives." In addition, ten electric door locks were needed to "achieve control over entry and exit facilities" at Managua airport. The requested equipment was in Nicaragua a month later.

U.S. support of the Nicaraguan anti-Sandinista guerrilla fighters, the Contras, preoccupied Stasi analysts during the entire period of East Germany's presence in the Central American country. Although reports to the leadership repeatedly said there were no indications of intervention by U.S. forces, Cuba was preparing for a war that Cuban Deputy Defense Minister Ibarra Colome opined could mushroom into World War III. Colome made his comments during a November 1984 visit to East Berlin.[13] At that time, Colome told an officer with the Stasi's counterespionage directorate, Cuba had 8,000 advisers in Nicaragua, and he himself spent most of the year in that country. The Cubans were particularly active in preparing for modern jungle warfare. As far as Cuba proper was concerned, preparations were under way to outfit caves as emergency shelters for the population. "But first they have to rid them of bats, which carry the tuberculosis bacillus, and have asked the Soviet comrades for help in this regard," a Stasi report said. While the Cuban was talking all-out war, the Stasi was more concerned about the threats that Nicaragua's economic situation and internal political opposition posed to the Sandinista regime. However, in fall 1984, Stasi agents reported "preparations for a possible invasion of Nicaragua." A memorandum dated September 24, 1984 said:

> Indications are intensifying regarding a possible U.S. military engagement in Nicaragua. It has been learned from leading circles close to J. [Jesse] Jackson that the Reagan Administration is preparing for a direct armed intervention in Nicaragua. The time for military action has not yet been determined, but one must consider that in the event of worsening chances for Reagan's reelection, intervention by the USA even before the election cannot be ruled out. If the election campaign develops the way Reagan imagines, one can expect armed action by the USA with Honduras taking part. No serious steps on the part of the Soviet Union and Cuba are anticipated.[14]

Quoting sources close to President Reagan, the memorandum went on to say that the U.S. administration "holds the view that the USSR is not in a position to intervene militarily and that Cuba will not risk a military confrontation with the USA." By June 1986, the U.S. intervention talk had disappeared from Stasi reports, which were once more concentrating solely on economic problems that "increasingly become fertile ground for counterrevolutionary propaganda."

While massive deliveries of equipment designed for state security purposes continued at a fast pace, a well-nigh ridiculous shipment of food was sent to Managua. It was probably intended only for the upper crust. The shipment consisted of 2,000 jars of gooseberries; 8,000 jars of mixed vegetables; 3,000 jars of red cabbage; 1,000 jars of pickled mixed vegetables; 500 jars of celery; and 1,200 pounds of powdered milk. A seventh item, 1,900 jars of sauerkraut, had been crossed off the shipping list. Apparently a wise Stasi man realized that sauerkraut is not as popular in Latin countries as it is in Germany.

Stasi documents make it clear that Mielke did not rely only on his official representatives in Nicaragua for information. He made sure that every East German non-Stasi government delegation visiting that country included at least one IM, an unofficial collaborator. Upon their return to East Berlin, these informers filed elaborate reports. One such report, dated August 26, 1985, was written by a member of a group of economic and industry ministry officials as well as managers of various industrial plants whose task was to investigate Nicaragua's economic problems. His report dealt mainly with the Nicaraguan political and economic policy situation, which he described as "confusing": "The leadership of the FSLN is marked by various political ideologies ranging from Maoist tendencies to conservative views. The economic development of the country is based on private capitalism with strong participation of the state." The confiscation of land and industrial property, he lamented, affected only the Somoza clan. Other industrialists retained their plants and their power. "The official opinion is that pluralism in the economy and politics is and must remain the leitmotif of the government. Therefore, their philosophy is such that the classicists like Marx and Lenin are hardly mentioned and that Jose Marti is considered the pioneer of the revolution, which means it is possible that they will adopt the reforms of our European socialist development."

As had previous Stasi visitors to Nicaragua, the informer also decried the lack of censorship of the country's private newspapers and the fact that the leadership, in speeches to the population and government-controlled news media, avoided using the word *socialism*. "Sometimes we were even told that they are not striving for socialism but for a sort of South/Central American combination of socialism cum pluralism in which private capitalism must be retained. This neutral path, which they believe they can follow, is tenable at the most through 1985. After that they must decide whether they want to return to a capitalistic republic, which would enable a few families to regain power and dictatorship, or whether they consequently seek a path toward a Cuban-style revolution to decisively effect a change in property rights. It will become evident in the next months which direction the revolution will take and what the leaders of the revolution really want."

The report revealed a little known nugget of information that had been kept a state secret, at least from the East German population. At a time when the country was facing financial bankruptcy and a rapidly declining economy, the DDR regime had granted Nicaragua a credit of $50 million in addition to the tens of millions the Stasi spent on what Mielke called "solidarity shipments"—outright gifts. "There was little readiness to accept our argument that repayment is essential," said one report. "Instead, they view it as a debt of honor, that the socialist countries are simply duty bound to grant such credits, and someday, when Nicaragua is in a better position, they want to repay." The East Germans then suggested an alternative: Accept 50 percent in dollars for payment of coffee exported to the DDR, and put the other 50 percent toward repayment. "It was rejected out of hand," the report said. Needless to say, the loan of $50 million was never repaid. In addition to this loan, Erich Honecker used his personal slush fund for the purchase of more than $39 million worth of wheat, corn, and other foodstuffs for Nicaragua between 1981 and 1987.[15]

Mielke's traveling informer ended his report with a scathing attack on the East German embassy in Managua for failing to render his delegation the proper support and respect. "We needed a week to figure out how to tackle our assignment because the preparations by the embassy and the ambassador, Dr. Merz, were unsatisfactory." Documents on Nicaragua's economy and industry were supplied only in Spanish, and a thousand pages had to be translated, causing a further loss of time. "Furthermore, the embassy's information on the condition of the economy and the political situation was false. Our delegates rarely had contact with the embassy, and we were not even invited there." The informer recommended that "appropriate measures" be taken to assure that the DDR's interests "are effectively represented." "The self-portrayal of the embassy as an efficient organ is exaggerated. The work that is being done there was unsatisfactory. We constantly had to drive to the embassy to get clerical work done, and sometimes we could not even get into the building because the security people were not at work." The embassy's inability to supply the delegation with two typewriters forced them to have one flown in from Mexico and another from Cuba.

What the informer apparently did not realize was that the embassy staff was overburdened because it also maintained liaison with communist organizations in neighboring countries. Much of this work was handled personally by Ambassador Merz. For example, on September 13, 1985, he sent a top secret cable marked "Flash" to East Berlin, in which he dealt with the kidnapping of El Salvador President Duarte's daughter Ines the previous day.[16] The cable to Hermann Axen, chairman of the Central Committee's Department of Foreign Relations, said the abduction had been planned and executed by the Communist Party of El Salvador. This, the ambassador wrote, he had been told by "Comrade (Julio) Santiago," a member of the political commission of the Salvadoran Party's Central Committee. The kidnappers demanded the release of twenty-two imprisoned communists, including the party's deputy secretary-general, and medical care abroad for ninety-six wounded FMLN guerrillas. "Publicly, of course, the CP denies any responsibility, but the government is not convinced and had started a major campaign against Nicaragua." Merz's remark was written in a tone that suggested that Axen use his influence to stop such actions, as they would only exacerbate the volatile situation in Nicaragua. Eventually, President Duarte ordered the release of the prisoners and approved the departure of the guerrillas for Cuba in exchange for his daughter and thirty-three small-town mayors who also were being held captive. William L. Stearman, a Soviet-bloc specialist for Central America in President Reagan's National Security Council, told me that the cable was of significant historical importance:

> As far as I know, this is the first time such a documented admission has been discovered. It proves that the Communist Party continued to operate as such underground after it announced a split in 1972 into the Popular Liberation Force (FPL) and the People's Revolutionary Army (ERP). Of course, we always knew that the Communist Party was controlling the FMLN, but its leadership consistently denied this and claimed it was a homegrown, independent, and noncommunist liberation movement.

Throughout the nearly eleven years of Sandinista rule, all Stasi reports on the political progress toward absolute communist domination were couched in careful language: On the one hand the top leadership was striving for a Marxist-Leninist type of rule, but on the other some Sandinista commandantes and much of the public and the churches were against it. Nevertheless, dozens of Stasi delegations, often led by a general, visited Managua over the years and kept urging the continuation, even intensification, of material support. These communist officials did not merely wear ideological blinders but walked through this world permanently and totally blind, or worse yet, lacked the courage to tell the leadership the truth, though many said later they saw it coming as far back as 1983.

From 1980 through May 1989, when political turmoil was reaching its height in East Germany, Mielke showered the Sandinistas with gifts that according to records I obtained, totaled roughly $15.7 million. Most of the items supplied were intended for use in political control, such as electronics for wiretapping of practically every telephone in Nicaragua. Other shipments included surveillance cameras, optical instruments, uniforms, and to a lesser extent, medical supplies and food. In 1983 the Stasi chief approved $25,000 for installing a security system at the home of Interior Minister Tomas Borge. No records could be found covering the expenses incurred in flying Sandinistas to East Germany for training or by the various delegations from both sides visiting each other's countries. It would certainly add another few million. And then there were the personal gifts the Stasi presented to high officials—although in one such case the quality and value of the gift might have been less than one would expect. Stasi deputy minister Lieutenant General Gerhard Neiber once gave a watch to Javier Amador, deputy director of Managua airport. The watch stopped working after a few months, and Amador had it sent via a Stasi courier to East Berlin for repair. It took several cables to find out whether the repairs had been made. Finally, nearly two months later, comrade Amador received his repaired watch, courtesy of a Cuban official who had been in Berlin and who agreed to act as a courier.

The most bizarre aspect of the Stasi's involvement with the Sandinistas was that East Berlin officials made detailed plans in November 1989, the month the wall came down, for "solidarity" shipments through 1995 valued at roughly $240 million. Again, nearly all of the items listed were designated to maintain the technical inventory of Nicaragua's secret police and intelligence department. However, the shipment being readied in November 1989 included household items such as 400 frying pans; 9,000 pieces of china; 18,000 pieces of silverware, bed linens, and towels; and 36,000 bars of soap. The Stasi had not forgotten the needs of women, and planned to send personal items ranging from shoes, nightshirts, and panty hose to sweaters and sanitary napkins.

The first indication that the Sandinista regime was heading toward defeat came in a report of May 15, 1989, by Stasi Lieutenant Colonel Artur Herman, although one must read between the lines. Herman, assigned to the Twentieth Main Directorate, responsible for control of the churches, spent two months in Nicaragua. "A decisive influence on the attitude of the population is the Catholic religion, which is solidly embedded in the people, who are deeply devout," Herman wrote. "Of the 3.5 million Nicaraguans, 80 percent are Catholics. The church dignitaries have been supported for years by the United States and other reactionary powers, who elevated the church to a symbolic figure in an exposed position. Cardinal Miguel Obando has great influence, which he uses openly to confront the Sandinista movement." He went on to say that there was not a single area of Nicaragua's society that was not affected by the influence of the church, and that "the critical ideological debate is increasing." The colonel wrote that the deputy director of state security, Commandante Castillo, said technical methods need to be employed against the church and asked for Stasi assistance. What he surely meant was that he wanted to bug the churches, rectories, and confessionals, as the Stasi had done in East Germany for many years.

Included in an earlier Stasi "solidarity" shipment were ten document shredders. It must be assumed that these were working at capacity when the Sandinistas lost the election on February 29, 1990.

STASI SUPPORT FOR CHILE'S COMMUNISTS

Salvador Allende Gossens kept a busy international travel schedule in the 1960s that took him to North Korea, North Vietnam, and East Germany. Allende believed that the latter regime would provide him its ardent support. In East Berlin, Allende met with the party secretary-general and head of the government, Walter Ulbricht, and with Hermann Axen, the Central Committee secretary for international relations.[17] Axen's assignment was to function as liaison with communist parties throughout the world. Whether Allende met with Stasi Minister Erich Mielke is not known. However, cementing ties with Axen was more important at the time, because the level of support given fraternal parties by East Berlin's regime depended on Axen's recommendations. His contacts with leading communists around the world did not go unnoticed by Western intelligence organizations, particularly the CIA. U.S. President Richard Nixon was rightly alarmed by the developments. President Nixon and his national security adviser Henry Kissinger recognized that the former medical doctor was not the starry-eyed, benevolent agrarian reformer he was portrayed as by American liberals. Allende's Marxist fervor and the fact that Chile's Communist Party was the largest and best organized in South America made Chile a perfect target for expansion of the Soviet bloc in that part of the world. From a geopolitical view, the possible establishment of a Moscow-financed communist dictatorship presented a threat to the national security of the United States. Those who were reviled for their support of such Chilean political parties as the Christian Democrats were proved correct by subsequent events.

Allende was elected president of Chile, and the East German regime was ready to lend him Stasi support. Within weeks, a dozen specialists in covert operations and guerrilla warfare were dispatched to Santiago under diplomatic cover.[18] They were joined by other Eastern-bloc trainers, including officers from Czechoslovakia, as they set up camp near Valparaiso. The Soviets furnished the weapons and prefabricated huts. The "pupils" were young Marxist radicals of the Manuel Rodriguez Revolutionary Front.

When the September 1973 military coup resulted in the death of Allende and his regime, most Stasi men were able to extricate themselves using their diplomatic passports, and returned home. However, a few MfS officers remained in Santiago under diplomatic cover, helping dozens of leading communists, radical socialists, and prominent members of the Allende government and their families to escape to East Germany and asylum. Among them were Clodomiro Almeyda, an extreme left-wing socialist who held, at various times, the posts of vice president, foreign minister, and defense minister in the socialist-communist coalition of Allende, the former foreign minister and doctrinaire socialist firebrand Ricardo Nuñez, and the secretary-general of Chile's radical Socialist Party, Carlos Altamirano. Several hundred lesser-known hard-core left-wing radicals were also granted asylum. All were generously supported by the East German Government, chiefly because Erich Honecker's daughter had married a Chilean activist. Stasi minister Mielke ordered General Kratsch's domestic counterespionage directorate to assume responsibility for the protection of the exiles.[19] Its Foreigners' Task Force under Colonel Rainer Wiegand was ordered to recruit informers among the exiled Chileans to watch over political activities.

Demonstrating his continued attention to Chilean affairs, Mielke wrote to all Stasi departments on December 18, 1976: "The Chekists of the DDR welcome with enthusiasm and happiness the great victory of the international solidarity movement for (obtaining) the freedom of the secretary-general of the Communist Party, our friend and comrade Luis Corvalan."[20] Corvalan had been imprisoned in Chile. "Because of the powerful battle waged by all progressive powers in the world, especially those of the socialist camp and the international communist and workers' movement, the magnificent son of the Chilean people and distinguished revolutionary, Comrade Corvalan, was torn from the claws of the fascist military junta," Mielke wrote in one breathless sentence. He said the Soviet KGB used "certain special measures" that forced the junta to give Corvalan his freedom. What Mielke did not say was that the Chilean communist leader was freed in exchange for the release of Vladimir Bukovsky, the Russian writer who helped put the spotlight on Soviet practices of locking up dissidents in psychiatric wards. Nathaniel Davis, U.S. ambassador to Chile at the time of the coup, was ambassador to Switzerland and handled the final negotiations for the swap. "It may have been the first occasion in history," the ambassador wrote later, "where the Soviets exchanged 'political prisoners' with a regime like Pinochet's and acknowledged by their actions that Bukovsky was such a prisoner and not a simple criminal or psychiatrically disturbed person."[21]

Once the Stasi men remaining in Chile had completed their job of spiriting the enemies of the Pinochet regime out of the country, they assumed a liaison function with the Communist Party and particularly with the Manuel Rodriguez Revolutionary Front. When the Chilean Communist Party publicly declared it would no longer offer passive resistance but would switch to "armed struggle," the East German regime was ready. Officers of the Stasi's foreign espionage directorate established an underground railroad via Mexico by which Chilean communists were supplied with forged passports and socialist radicals were smuggled, first to Czechoslovakia and from there to East Germany.[22]

A top secret and heavily protected special training camp code-named Objekt Baikal was established east of Berlin, close to the Polish border. It was an idyllic spot situated between two lakes, surrounded by tall pines. The Chileans lived in six attractive bungalows and dined in a pine-paneled banquet hall.[23] Besides a security detail, there were two cooks and a housekeeping couple attending to the daily needs of the trainees. The installation originally served as a vacation hideout for members of the domestic counterespionage directorate. Mielke had assigned that particular directorate the task of training the Chileans. Mielke received his orders from party Secretary-General Erich Honecker, who was acting on the recommendations of Hermann Axen. At Objekt Baikal, the lesson plan included methods of sabotage, the manufacture of explosive devices, assassination, and Marxist-Leninist indoctrination. For weapons training the students were bused to a closely guarded firing range maintained by the Stasi personnel security directorate at Motzen, southeast of Berlin. As camouflage, the Chileans were dressed in traditional forest-green hunter garb whenever they were taken out of the Baikal compound. The courses lasted five months, usually beginning in March. The East German Party leadership, to assure that the Stasi adhered to its directives, closely supervised the curriculum. Functionaries of the Central Committee frequently visited Baikal to exercise control, issue new orders, and—as former Stasi Colonel Rainer Wiegand put it—"demonstrate to the Chileans the leadership role of the Party."[24] Although some guerrillas were schooled in Cuba, the most important training was handled by the Stasi.

Leftist urban guerrilla groups began a reign of terror in Chile in 1983 with bombings and assassinations, exactly the kind of actions for which the Stasi had provided training. Bombs were exploding in Santiago, Viña del Mar, Quilpué, Concepción, and Talca, damaging supermarkets, buses, government offices and four stores in Santiago's largest shopping center. Between 1983 and 1986 there were more than a thousand bombings attributed to the clandestine Communist Front and the Revolutionary Movement, which also was blamed for killing twenty-one military officers and policemen.[25] Between 1984 and 1988 the East Germans contributed $6,795,015 to the Chilean Communist Party for the financing of terrorism.[26]

In early August 1986, Chilean security forces discovered six arms and ammunition caches in the northern part of the country. According to security officials, the clandestine arsenals held 3,223 automatic rifles, 281 rocket launchers, three tons of explosives, 1,959 grenades, and two million rounds of ammunition. Twenty-one members of the Manuel Rodriguez Revolutionary Front were arrested and accused of unloading the arms from a Cuban fishing boat. Among the weapons were U.S.-made M-16 rifles captured by the North Vietnamese.

The most serious incident occurred the evening of September 7, 1986, when guerrillas attempted to assassinate President Augusto Pinochet in an ambush of his motorcade near Santiago. Pinochet survived unharmed, but five members of his escort were killed and ten others wounded. Twelve members of the Manuel Rodriguez Revolutionary Front attacked the president's convoy with gunfire and grenades. The government did not comment on their fate. Since no arrests were announced, it must be presumed that they were all killed. The attack prompted Clodomiro Almeyda to break with the communists, saying such violence would only push the Pinochet government into pursuing repressive measures at the expense of innocent people. Almeyda's action put his East German hosts in a precarious position. They could not simply drop him, as that might give rise to an embarrassing debate within the international communist movement. It was a tricky situation for the East Germans, since Carlos Altamirano, secretary-general of the radical Socialist Party, had left East Berlin for Paris after he became disenchanted with the oppressive regime. The socialist firebrand Ricardo Nuñez had also publicly voiced his disgust with the lack of freedom of the East German people. Thus, Honecker continued to finance Almeyda's stay in East Berlin until he returned to Chile in 1987. He was jailed because his return had not been sanctioned by the government but he apparently convinced authorities that his disgust with communism was genuine, and he was quickly released. Almeyda cooperated with the incoming government of Christian Democrat Patricio Alwyn. Almeyda's ideological conversion was awarded with a posting to Moscow as ambassador. He resigned when he became the center of furor for having granted sanctuary in the embassy to his old patron Erich Honecker, who was then a fugitive from German justice.[27] Almeyda died in August 1997, at age 74. Communist Party Leader Corvalan returned from his Moscow exile and ran for political office. He got only a handful of votes. By 1997, Altamirano and Nuñez had disappeared from the political scene.

Terrorist attacks did not cease after a democratically elected government took over from General Augusto Pinochet. In fact, 1990 was the most violent year, with police registering 2,422 attacks against individuals, mostly police officers, including the murder of Colonel Luis Fontaine. Leftists and human rights activists had accused him of serious human rights violations during the reign of Pinochet. In March and April 1991, gunmen killed Senator Jaime Guzman, a professor at Catholic University's law school and an adviser to Pinochet. The Manuel Rodriguez Revolutionary Front and the Popular Forces of Lautaro claimed responsibility. At a point when the Chilean economy had been rebuilt into the most successful in Latin America, terrorist attacks had reached such proportions that President Alwyn's government began to fear serious political and economic destabilization. "Chile's economy is prosperous, but the vulnerable point is terrorism and the problem of personal security," Treasury Minister Alejandro Foxley told journalists on April 5. Recognizing the seriousness of the situation, the Senate acted with extraordinary speed to authorize creation of a permanent commission on terrorism as well as a 550-percent increase in spending for the national police force and the department of investigations. The last action by the Manuel Rodriguez Revolutionary Front was the breakout on December 30, 1986 of four convicted terrorists from Santiago's maximum security prison, including two men who took part in the killing of Senator Guzman. A helicopter hovered over the prison yard and dropped a large basket fastened to a thirty-yard-long rope. The men jumped into the basket and were lifted away. Police were unable to trace the helicopter or the escapees. Investigative Judge Lamberto Cisternas said in 1997 that two Irish sisters took part in the breakout but that he had no "clear line" on their whereabouts. The judge said he was convinced that they fled Chile and spent some time in Brazil.

Until the fall of the East German communist regime, few suspected that more than two hundred of the most dangerous terrorists had been trained by specialists of the Stasi in East Germany. The last class graduated in August 1989, when the DDR was already heading toward disintegration. It appears that not all graduates of the last East German terrorism course for Chilean radicals returned to their homeland. A West European antiterrorist investigator told me, on condition of anonymity, that there were strong indications that some of them had joined the Basque separatist movement ETA, which had been terrorizing Spain for years. My request for information from the Spanish State Security Secretariat went unanswered.

MIELKE'S MINIONS ON THE AFRICAN CONTINENT

Stasi activities in Africa were designed to assist the Soviet Union in assuring that countries emerging from or seeking to throw off colonial rule developed into noncapitalist states. Altruism, however, and "solidarity with the oppressed" were not the regime's sole motives. Ostracized by most Western democracies, the East German regime pined for recognition as a "sovereign" state and it thirsted for trading partners outside Eastern Europe's communist bloc. In 1964, Zanzibar became the first African state to establish diplomatic relations with East Germany. Its leaders immediately asked for assistance in establishing a state security service.[28] At almost the same time in West Africa,

Kwame Nkrumah of Ghana was pursuing his pan-Africa policy, which included active support of liberation movements. Teams of Stasi espionage and counterespionage officers were sent to both nations. Those operating in Zanzibar stayed on when the island became part of Tanganyika. However, the overthrow of Nkrumah in 1966 ended the Stasi's presence in Ghana and resulted in the imprisonment of Stasi Major Jürgen Rogalla. Rogalla later was traded for Ghanaians who were being held by the East Germans. The Politburo formally decided in early 1967 to support African liberation movements with shipments of equipment for military and security use.[29] Erich Honecker was then secretary for security affairs in the Politburo, which made him the de facto supervisor of these activities. Stasi Minister Mielke did not become a Politburo member until 1976. Thus, the regime's top leadership issued its orders on the support of liberation movements to the Stasi through Honecker.

Southern Africa

The first group of Africans completed their five-month course at the Stasi's Department for International Relations in early 1971. These included members of the terrorist wing of the African National Congress, Umkhonto we Sizwe (literally, "Spear of the Nation"). This group was headed by a white South African communist, Ronnie Kasrils, who turned his charges into ferocious guerrilla fighters.[30] Subsequently, the East Germans trained members of liberation movements from Rhodesia, Mozambique, Namibia, and Zimbabwe in two distinctively separate groups. Military commanders received tactical schooling, including training in terrorism, at the huge Teupitz troop training area southeast of Berlin. Those slated for leadership positions in espionage, counterespionage, and general security attended the Department for International Relations. For practical exercises, the latter were bused to the Motz firing range of the personnel security directorate or to nearby Kallinchen, where training in handling explosives was conducted. I was unable to locate Stasi files showing the exact number of Africans who received training in East Germany. However, former Colonel Rainer Wiegand, responsible for surveillance of all foreigners, estimated they numbered at least 1,500. Most of those, he told me, came from the communist-controlled African National Congress (ANC) of South Africa. Soviet President Nikolai Podgorny and Cuba's Fidel Castro in a joint 1977 statement pledged "quick" establishment of additional training camps for Spear of the Nation terrorists in Angola, with East Germany and Cuba providing the instructors and the Soviet Union the weapons.

I also could not locate documents from which to calculate the total amount spent by the East German communists on propping up liberation movements and Marxist governments in Africa between the late 1960s and 1989. However, for 1988 alone, the Politburo authorized spending more than 1.134 billion marks, including 30.8 million "hard" (West German) marks.[31] According to a secret memorandum of the meeting, "this represents .43 percent of the annual national income of the DDR." Interestingly, the memorandum revealed that the regime used an exchange rate of 3.399 West marks to 1 East mark, although the communists always insisted their mark was just as solid as the hard deutsche mark. Upon entering East Berlin, visitors were forced to change at least five West marks, and the rate was always 1 for 1. Although the West German bank rate was more advantageous (it held at 10 to 1 for years), it was illegal in East Germany to import East marks from the West. Even when using the phony East German exchange rate, the value of the 1988 deliveries in U.S. dollars would come to roughly $444.7 million. This figure does not include the hundreds of millions sent abroad by the so-called Solidarity Committee of the DDR, to which all workers were obliged to contribute. In a September 28, 1988 letter to Kurt Seibt, Solidarity Committee president and Central Committee member, Mielke wrote that Stasi members alone had contributed 10 million marks between 1987 and 1988. Seibt thanked Mielke in a fawning letter that ended: "For Peace and Liberty! This is an obligation, which also is an expression of the class consciousness of members of your ministry to be the protective umbrella of our free socialist fatherland and the peaceful life of its citizens."

Most of the substantial Stasi financial assistance to the ANC was provided in the form of top quality counterfeit Rands, the South African currency.[32] Indeed, the Stasi's Technical Operations Sector (OTS) included a sophisticated currency counterfeiting unit under Colonel Kurt Lewinsky, a veteran Berlin forger whom the Nazis had imprisoned at Sachsenhausen concentration camp.[33] He managed to escape in 1945 as prisoners were being evacuated to keep them from falling into the hands of the Red Army. After World War II, Scotland Yard launched an extensive investigation into SS counterfeiting operations that produced such high-quality British pound notes that even Swiss banks failed to recognize them as bogus. In a secret 1947 Scotland Yard report, Kurt Lewinsky was named as one of the counterfeiters.[34]

Despite the tight secrecy imposed by all communist countries on their support for liberation movements, Western intelligence services became aware of it early on. Nevertheless, the Denton Subcommittee on Security and Terrorism of the U.S. Senate Judiciary Committee issued a report in November 1982 on Soviet, East German, and Cuban involvement in fomenting terrorism in southern Africa. While the Stasi had operatives in Mozambique, Rhodesia, Namibia, Angola, and Zimbabwe, I could find no evidence of their presence with the ANC on

South African territory. The Stasi apparently had decided to concentrate only on training ANC members in East Germany, since ANC activities were under the direct control of the South African Communist Party (SACP). The party was led by Joe Slovo, a white man born in Lithuania and believed by Western intelligence officials to have held the rank of colonel in the Soviet KGB.[35] Heading the ANC was Oliver Tambo, who during a visit to Moscow in the late 1980s, was awarded the Order of Lenin. Activities in South Africa were directed capably by longtime communists who had proven themselves ideologically and militarily trustworthy. In testimony before the U.S. Senate's Denton Committee, Bartholomew Hlapane, a former member of the ANC National Executive Committee and the SACP Central Committee, described terrorist activities in detail. "No major decision could be taken by the ANC without the concurrence and approval of the SACP Central Committee," he said. "Most major developments were, in fact, initiated by the SACP Central Committee." Less than a month after his testimony, Hlapane and his wife were murdered in their home in Soweto by an ANC assassin armed with a Soviet-made AK-47 automatic rifle.[36]

On February 11, 1990, Nelson Mandela, in his first major public address after his release from prison, lavishly praised the SACP, saying, "I salute the South African Communist Party for its sterling contribution to democracy." This, a *Washington Post* editorial two days later described as "passing uncomfortable." The author of the editorial asked whether the ANC "is about to create another of the cruel, undemocratic, and inefficient state-centered regimes that are collapsing in other parts of the world." In 1997, all vital cabinet posts of the Mandela government were in the hands of long-standing SACP members. Joe Modise was secretary of defense. His deputy was Ronnie Kasrils, the former head of the Spear of the Nation terrorist organization. The minister of foreign affairs was Alfred Nzo, and Pallo Jordan was minister for telecommunications and broadcasting. Takeover of the South African Army by the old ANC guard was completed in June 1998 when Lieutenant General Siphiwe Nyanda became army commander after George Melring went into early retirement. The forty-seven-year-old Nyanda received his military training in communist East Germany. "It is a textbook example of the ministries communist parties always covet as an essential first step to total control," said William Stearman, former U.S. National Security Council expert on Soviet Affairs and liberation movements. "Moreover, First Deputy President Thabo Mbeki, designated successor to seventy-eight-year-old Mandela, is also an SACP member," added Stearman.[37]

Besides training and supplying liberation movements in southern Africa, the East Germans also provided development aid, composed chiefly of civilian technicians who were party members. Those selected or who volunteered for such assignments underwent extensive vetting that sometimes lasted as long as a year. During this time, the candidates were constantly observed by Stasi informants. To assure that they remained loyal and would not defect to the West, once abroad they were under constant scrutiny by informers reporting to Stasi controllers based in all East German embassies. As an added security, only married personnel were chosen, and their families remained home as hostages. Over the years, there were only about a dozen defections out of some 2,000 workers serving in Africa at any one time.[38] Concern over defections at times resulted in bizarre machinations to protect the "workers' and peasants' state." Hermann-Hugo Kästner, a master mechanic from a small Thuringian town, often spoke of his opposition to the regime when he was among friends.[39] Privately, the twenty-five-year-old was consumed by thoughts of escape. In 1977 he applied for a foreign assignment and was rejected because he was not a party member. In 1984 he joined the party, married, and reapplied. A childhood friend who was a Stasi informer denounced him, saying he thought Kästner wanted the foreign job only so that he could defect. He was the kind of citizen the Stasi wanted behind bars. The Stasi arranged Kästner's acceptance and at the same time sent the informer along to collect evidence. In 1985 Kästner and the informer, appropriately codenamed Condor, were sent to Angola. In Luanda, Kästner immediately made his plans. Knowing that visiting the West German embassy was too dangerous, he eventually applied for a special harbor pass that would allow him to accompany trucks picking up supplies. He planned to reach a West German or noncommunist vessel and ask for asylum. The request for a pass was enough evidence for the Stasi. Kästner was ordered to return to East Berlin, ostensibly for treatment of an ankle he had sprained during a soccer game. He at first declined, but the East German ambassador insisted, so he returned aboard the government plane of party chief Honecker, who was visiting Angola. He was arrested by the Stasi as he left the plane, and later was tried, convicted, and sentenced to eighteen months in prison for attempting to defect. In the end, however, he was lucky, having served only eight months before he was ransomed by the West German government and allowed to leave East Germany.

Northeast Africa

The Stasi bloodied its hands by proxy wherever it was instrumental in setting up secret police organizations for Marxist governments. Nowhere was the bloodshed worse than in Ethiopia. Three years after overthrowing Emperor Haile Selassie in 1974, the Provisional Military

Administrative Council (PMAC), or Derg, of Marxist Lt. Colonel Mengistu Haile Mariam requested East German assistance in establishing a state security apparatus. Stasi Major General Gerhard Neiber was dispatched to Addis Ababa and arrived there at the start of Mengistu's reign of terror. Neiber's mandate was to contribute to the stabilization of Mengistu's powers by establishing an effective secret police. He was aided by about 100 other Stasi officers.[40] In addition, roughly 300 other East Germans from the People's Army and police assisted some 1,000 Soviet military advisers in training the Ethiopian army and police. Neiber systematically patterned the military dictator's state security service on the MfS. By the time Neiber returned to East Germany and promotion to lieutenant general in late 1978, the Mengistu reign of terror had reached its height. Between 40,000 and 100,000, mostly young people, were murdered.[41] Thousands more were imprisoned under extremely harsh conditions and tortured.

In the late 1970s the Ethiopian intelligence service established what former Stasi Colonel Rainer Wiegand called a "strong presence" in East Berlin. A number of their operatives had been trained at the Stasi's Center for International Relations. They collaborated with the HVA's Third Department and Wiegand's task force responsible for the surveillance of foreigners residing in East Germany. At the same time, roughly one hundred Ethiopians were being schooled at various East German educational institutions. "Here we had considerable problems from an internal security point of view," recalled Wiegand, whose group was subordinate to the counterespionage directorate. "For one thing, many of the Ethiopians lacked even an elementary education." They became targets of the anti-Mengistu Tigrean People's Liberation Front, which had established an office in West Berlin run by Colonel A. Teferre. "Teferre's people not only subversively influenced the students but also developed an entire movement of students who would defect to the West once their schooling was completed," Wiegand said. "This went so far that Mengistu, in a letter to Honecker, asked that this situation be stopped." During one of Teferre's trips to East Berlin, after Stasi agents observed him visiting the U.S. Army's McNair barracks, where they suspected a CIA detail was housed, the Stasi detained Teferre and questioned him for two days. "We knew that Ethiopian students fleeing to West Berlin were held there for four to six weeks, and we suspected that Teferre was working with the CIA," said Wiegand. "Of course, he did not admit it, but he also did not accept a lucrative recruiting offer, and he never returned to East Berlin." Under pressure from the party leadership, the Stasi began to detain Ethiopians after they completed their studies, placing them under guard on a direct Interflug flight to Addis Ababa. "This went on until it got too hot for me and I refused to continue, pointing out that our methods were bound to turn them into antisocialist zealots," Wiegand told me. "The party bought my argument, but frankly, I just felt sorry for those poor wretches. From colleagues who returned from Addis Ababa I heard all about how the Mengistu state security dealt with anyone suspected of being an enemy."

In June 1984, Stasi Minister Mielke and the Ethiopian Minister for State and Public Security Tessaye Wolde Selassie signed a five-point mutual cooperation agreement classified as top secret.[42] The preamble of the agreement said the two sides were "guided by the principle of proletarian internationalism and our mutual interests in the anti-imperialist struggle aimed at making an effective contribution in the battle against the imperialist secret services and other reactionary forces." They pledged to exchange information regarding plans and activities affecting the security of both states, particularly as it concerned Ethiopians residing in East Germany and East German citizens visiting socialist Ethiopia. In other words, you keep an eye on our people, and we'll watch yours. Mielke and Tessaye agreed they would exchange representatives based at each other's capital under diplomatic cover. The text of the agreement also stated that both sides would "conduct joint operations against subversive activities of imperialist and reactionary forces which are aimed against either of the two states." Mielke said his ministry would continue to provide free schooling at universities or other institutions for "a certain number of cadres." Furthermore, the Stasi would provide unspecified "materials and equipment" on a "solidarity basis"—i.e., gratis—and would assist in the acquisition and supply of other materials and equipment, apparently arms and munitions, against "cash payment."

I was unable to locate official figures on East German support for Ethiopia between 1977 and 1987. The German foreign policy journal *Aussenpolitik,* however, said it totaled nearly 100 million East marks. Using the East German exchange rate of 3.99 West marks to 1 East Mark and then converting it into dollars by applying the average rate over the years, the assistance would have amounted to $11,289,484. *Aussenpolitik,* in its 1996 issue, asserted that East Germany had stopped its support in 1987. On the contrary, on March 29, 1988, Honecker ordered "immediate" arms shipments to Ethiopia. Prime Minister Willi Stoph executed the order by directing the Commercial Coordination (KOKO) section, a trading organization controlled by the Stasi, to deliver weapons, ammunition, military equipment, and 100 trucks, valued at a total of US$14,134,078.[43] Stoph ordered finance of the shipment with a 2.5-percent annual interest government credit repayable in fourteen years. In addition, he decreed that used and overhauled weapons valued at US$1,396,648 be given to the Mengistu regime as a "solidarity gesture" free of charge, the money coming out of the East German budget. These shipments were made at a time when Soviet President Mikhail Gorbachev sought to disentangle the Soviet Union from the Ethiopian adventure but reluctantly went along with Moscow's hard-liners. Paul Henze, the foremost U.S. expert on Ethiopia, who served at the U.S. embassy in Addis Ababa and in the National Security Council, said that although the Soviets and Ethiopia had an agreement on delivery of arms, Moscow made it clear in 1988 and 1989 that not much more was coming. "In fact, we knew that the Soviets told them to 'go to the East Germans, they have lots.'" Edward M. Korry, who was assigned to Ethiopia as ambassador after his tenure in Chile, told me he was aware that the Soviets and East Germans were spending huge sums of money to prop up the Mengistu terror machine, and said: "I recommended to the State Department that we broadcast to the Soviet and East German people how much money their governments were pouring into Africa while their own economies were in dire straits. They turned me down on grounds that this would be merely seen as propaganda."

In addition to military equipment, the Stasi shipped building materials to Addis Ababa. In East Berlin and other cities and villages, apartment buildings were decaying at an incredible rate, and some had to be abandoned. Whole balconies were dropping into the streets for lack of construction materials. Yet, in January 1989, Stasi Major General Willi Damm, head of the international relations directorate, signed a protocol with the Ethiopian interior ministry pledging to deliver at Stasi expense items sorely needed in his own country. A list of 105 items delivered to Ethiopia between 1988 and June 1989 was attached to the protocol, including: 1,000 tons of portland cement, 331 tons of reinforced steel, window frames, 5,197 feet of various pipes, 8,563 feet of electric cable, and hundreds of electric switches. The 62 toilet bowls and 25 urinals, furniture, refrigerators, freezers, and steel safes scheduled for delivery in December 1989 never made it to the port. The Berlin Wall had been dismantled a month earlier, and the government was in disarray. But Ethiopian table tennis players were lucky: They received two Ping-Pong tables with nets and paddles in June.

The murderous Marxist regime ended in May 1991, with the resignation of Mengistu and his escape to Zimbabwe as Tigrean rebel units advanced on Addis Ababa. Most of the East German contingent had returned home a year earlier, but the Stasi men left something behind—their records. After retiring, Ambassador Korry returned to Ethiopia in late 1994, just as the trials of former Mengistu accomplices were getting under way. More than a thousand people, including former State Security Minister Tessaye Wolde Selassie, who signed the assistance agreement with Stasi Minister Mielke, were in prison. "An official of the new government told me that the East Germans had left behind files minutely detailing the crimes committed by the Mengistu people," Ambassador Korry told me. "These records are being used in the trials." Ironically, while many of the accused were sentenced to long prison terms or worse, their accomplices in the Stasi remained free.

STASI BASES IN THE MIDDLE EAST

Egypt and several other Arab countries broke diplomatic relations with West Germany in the mid-1960s and recognized East Germany as a result of Bonn's secret delivery of arms to Israel. Until then, Middle Eastern nations had refrained from dealing with East Germany because of West Germany's Hallstein Doctrine, which held that recognition of East Germany by any nation would be considered an unfriendly act. Egyptian relations with West Germany were reestablished in 1970 and 1971, when Chancellor Willy Brandt, a Social Democrat, was pursuing rapprochement with the communist bloc. It was during this hiatus of some five years that the Stasi's foreign espionage directorate gained a foothold in the Middle East, developing a close cooperation with the intelligence services of Egypt, Libya, and Syria.

Stasi activities in the Middle East increased in 1974 after State Security Minister Erich Mielke returned from consultations with the KGB in Moscow. Moscow's dream of establishing a solid political and military base on the Red Sea evaporated two years earlier when President Anwar Sadat ordered thousands of Soviet advisers to leave Egypt within a week. In an effort to maintain a Soviet presence in the strategic Gulf of Aden, Moscow continued to cultivate its alliance with South Yemen and asked Mielke to step up his efforts there.[44] One of the most pressing problems facing the Marxists were internecine battles among political parties and real or perceived intrigues by middle-echelon government officials against the leadership. The mandate to the Stasi's operational group of about a hundred agents led by Colonel Siegfried Fiedler, who had earned his spurs in Cuba, was to bring the disorganized state security apparatus under control—a task in which Soviet advisers had failed.[45] With a Stasi officer assigned to every department of the Yemeni intelligence and secret police agencies, the Stasi gained control and access to all operational matters. But they could do little to stop the high-level intrigues: President Ali Nasser Muhammad even sent his bodyguard to the cabinet room in 1985 to mow down the Politburo with a machine gun.[46]

The Stasi contingent in Aden also provided transportation and security for officials traveling to East Berlin to negotiate arms deals. It appears that all military hardware was supplied to South Yemen by commercial transactions, initially with the private London-based firm Dynawest, and later, directly with the Yemeni defense ministry. The 1982 contract with the London firm was for US$126,250 worth of ammunition. Between September 1987 and September 1988, the East Germans shipped 10,095 automatic rifles and Soviet Dragunov sniper rifles, and 33,760,800 rounds of ammunition, for which South Yemen paid US$2,937,232.[47] The East Germans did not seem to have been as generous with cash gifts to the South Yemen Communist Party as they were with other parties on the African continent and Latin America. Only US$526,638 was donated in 1985 by Honecker for construction of a Communist Party headquarters in Aden.[48]

South Yemen's port of Aden was also important to the East German communists for supplying Yasser Arafat's Palestine Liberation Organization (PLO) with arms. In 1983, the PLO purchased US$1,877,600 worth of AK-47 ammunition. Four years later, Lieutenant Colonel Ali Kaid of the South Yemen Ministry of Defense traveled to East Berlin on behalf of the PLO to negotiate a contract for 20 million rounds of ammunition, valued at US$1,541,899. At the same time South Yemen ordered 200 submachine guns with silencers, 200 telescopic sights, 200 mortars, and 10,000 mortar rounds.

Stasi officers in Aden, according to former Colonel Rainer Wiegand, who occasionally visited, "lived like kings." The government had assigned them villas once occupied by British officials, complete with servants. "When Fiedler was there he reigned like a Prussian governor, residing in a huge villa with a beautiful view of the gulf," Wiegand recalled. He said he had become disgusted with the behavior of his colleagues.

> Aden was the first time that I experienced German arrogance even among our own men. They had adopted a German colonialist attitude. For example, accompanied by a young MfS lieutenant, I was visiting the deputy minister of state security, who had the habit of picking his nose. The lieutenant would wave a finger at him, saying, "Ali, Ali, Ali." The man took his finger out of his nose but soon started again. The lieutenant got up from his chair, stepped in front of the deputy minister, and slapped him on the nose like you would a child. When they were recalled in 1989, they had a tough time readjusting to our "socialist" ways.[49]

9

THE STASI AND TERRORISM

The La Belle Bombing

SOLDIERS FROM THE U.S. ARMY garrison in West Berlin were enjoying their weekend passes at La Belle discotheque early Saturday morning, April 5, 1986. The less than elegant establishment in the American sector district of Friedenau was a favorite hangout of black GIs and their girlfriends. Unexpectedly, the revelry ended in a bloodbath. At 1:40 A.M. a powerful bomb exploded, ripping the dilapidated building apart. Sergeant Kenneth T. Ford and Nermin Hannay, a twenty-nine-year-old Turkish woman, were killed outright. Ford, a twenty-one-year-old black infantryman from Detroit, Michigan, had just finished a week of patrol duty along the communist wall that divided the city. Hannay, a pretty brunette, had emigrated to Berlin to escape the poverty of her homeland. After years of study and hard work, she was finally making good money as a secretary. Of the 234 persons injured, 41 were Americans. A second GI, twenty-five-year-old Sergeant James E. Goins, of Ellerbe, North Carolina, lost both legs and suffered multiple internal injuries. He died on June 7, only a few days after receiving the Purple Heart along with the other wounded soldiers.

The devastation was immense. Walls buckled, the ceiling collapsed, and a hole of more than four feet in diameter was blasted through the two-and-a-half-inch-thick concrete floor to the basement. Fortunately, there was only a small fire, which was extinguished by West Berlin firefighters who reacted with extraordinary speed. First Chief Commissioner Gerald Dörp, the top expert on terrorism for the state security division of the West Berlin police, led the investigation at the scene. The last time he had seen such mayhem was as a boy, after an air raid at the close of World War II. The discotheque held 284 people when the bomb went off. A police veteran of thirty years, the detective termed it a miracle that more of them were not killed. Dörp and his men sifted through the rubble for days, and kept finding bits of human flesh—from time to time, a finger or a foot. The blast was so intense that not enough fragments could be found to identify the construction of the bomb. But investigators discovered small jagged pieces of steel that had been mixed with the explosive. Many of these steel bits later were extracted from the bodies of the dead and wounded. There was hardly any chemical residue, which led the experts to deduce that a military explosive had been used—probably Semtex, produced in Czechoslovakia. That communist nation sold 2,000 tons of the explosive to Libya, and since then it had been a favorite of terrorists.[1] The bomb's weight was estimated at 1.7 kilograms (3.74 pounds).

Major General Thomas N. Griffin, the U.S. commandant in Berlin, had been at a dinner earlier that night where he was informed that the CIA had reliable information pointing to an imminent attack on a GI hangout. The general had ordered military police to make the rounds of dance halls and discotheques frequented by U.S. soldiers and "clear them out." The MP patrol destined for La Belle was just a few hundred yards away when the bomb went off.

Within days of the massacre, President Ronald Reagan told the world that he had incontrovertible evidence that the attack was carried out by terrorists under Libyan direction. He ordered retaliation, and ten days after the La Belle massacre, U.S. Air Force and Navy planes attacked military targets in Libya. At the same time, the U.S. charged that the terrorists were based in communist East Berlin and that the governments of East Germany and the Soviet Union could have prevented the murders.

Stasi Minister Erich Mielke had been party to many dastardly acts in his secret police career, but the bombing was the first that would enmesh him in a major international incident.[2] Mielke knew that the U.S. president was telling the truth. And so did Erich Honecker, the Communist Party leader and head of the East German government. The two men moved quickly to contain the damage to their already disreputable regime, and vehemently denied the accusation. The Soviet government, anxious to improve relations with the Reagan administration, also resorted to the "big lie." Neither the German communists nor the Soviets suspected that a high-ranking officer of East Germany's Ministry for State Security (MfS) had secretly been trying to prevent the Libyans from bombing the discotheque.

The Bar at La Belle discotheque in Berlin, devastated by a Libyan terrorist bomb on April 5, 1986 that also killed three people, including two American GIs, and wounded more than two hundred. The hole in the floor marks the spot where the bomb exploded. Courtesy Berlin Police.

The "renegade" was Colonel Rainer Wiegand, chief of Arbeitsgruppe Ausländer of the MfS's Second Main Directorate, charged with all counterespionage operations in East Germany. The directorate reported directly to Mielke. Wiegand himself had sole responsibility for investigating and combating attacks on his country's security by foreigners. The colonel had known for months that the Libyans were planning acts of violence in West Berlin, but his efforts to move against them were thwarted by East Germany's leadership. He was dismayed that his own clandestine efforts to prevent the bombing had failed.

Wiegand became aware in mid-1985 that the Libyan People's Bureau (LPB), the diplomatic mission accredited to the East German government, was rapidly enlarging its staff. He knew Libyans were being expelled from West European countries, especially after the killing in April 1985 of a policewoman in London. The killing occurred during a demonstration at the Libyan People's Bureau, as Colonel Muammar Qaddafi had renamed his embassies. The British government ordered the bureau closed and expelled its diplomats. In Bonn, the West German capital, two Libyan diplomats were declared personae non gratae

Colonel Rainer Wiegand of the Stasi's counterespionage directorate, who defected to West Germany in December 1989 and subsequently revealed details of the East German government's collaboration with Arab terrorists. Wiegand was killed in June 1996, in a crash in Portugal, shortly after he was slated to appear as a star witness in the La Belle discotheque bombing. Though there was no conclusive evidence, German judicial and intelligence authorities suspect that he was murdered. Private photo.

and expelled. Those who were allowed to remain were put under the closest surveillance. European governments also were being pressured by the United States to act against Libya after the Rome and Vienna airport shootings on December 27, 1985. Those massacres left eleven people dead and more than a hundred wounded, including five Americans and four terrorists. Wiegand had deduced that the Libyans were establishing a base for their attacks on Western Europe in his part of divided Berlin.

WIEGAND DEFIES MIELKE'S ORDERS

Ignoring repeated orders from Mielke to stay away from the Libyans, Wiegand had recruited a Libyan official as an unofficial collaborator. The man came to the colonel's attention for his whoring, frequent drunkenness, and foreign currency deals on the black market—a felony offense for which nondiplomats could be jailed. Rather than risk exposure, the Libyan had signed an agreement to serve as an agent. The new agent, code-named Mustafa, would become a key to unraveling the Libyan terrorist scene in East Berlin.

On November 29, 1985, Wiegand met with Mustafa in a *konspirative Wohnung,* a secret Stasi apartment maintained for clandestine meetings. The agent first disclosed the names of the Libyan secret service agents who were operating under diplomatic cover out of the LPB villa in the Karlshorst district of East Berlin, less than a mile from the German headquarters of the Soviet KGB. Then he described how he had witnessed the arrival at the LPB of a suitcase that contained pistols equipped with silencers and of rectangular packages that Mustafa thought were explosives. The agent went on to explain that he had overheard conversations about planned attacks against the West and the liquidation of anti-Qaddafi Libyan exiles. The colonel's tape recorder caught it all.

Wiegand could hardly conceal his excitement. What he suspected had been confirmed. He drove back to his office in the dingy gray building on Ruschestrasse, part of the huge Stasi complex that stood like a fortress amid shabby apartment houses. He took a circuitous route to make sure he was not being followed. In addition to Western intelligence services operating out of their embassies, the espionage services of "friends" like Libya, South Yemen, Iraq, and Syria also spied on the East Germans. Wiegand, a counterintelligence veteran of twenty-seven years' experience, vitally needed to protect his source. After arriving at his fourth-floor office in Building 2, he transcribed the recording himself. He would not trust his secretary to do the job—Mielke had informers everywhere. Then Wiegand called Lieutenant Colonel Wolfgang Stuchly to a meeting in his office. Stuchly, Wiegand's colleague of two decades and in the latter's words, "a very decent man," was head of Section 15 of the Stasi's Berlin district office, which handled security and protection of Third World embassies.

Stuchly read the transcript, which Wiegand already had stamped *Streng Geheim—Besonderer Quellenschutz* (Top Secret—Special Source Protection). It listed the names and titles of a number of Libyan People's Bureau diplomats: Juna M. Ahmed, administrative officer; Omar Faruk M. O. Alfaghi, liaison officer; Ali I. O. Keshlaf, consular officer; El Amin El Shames, financial officer; Omar Ali Shalbak, consular officer; Ibrahim Ramadan Hamuda, diplomat, and Abdusalam E. Alregee, acting secretary.

Stuchly told his associate that he knew them all. His agents Alba and Mario, he told Wiegand, had been reporting that the Libyans were building a base from which to launch terrorist attacks. He also had noticed the steady increase of Libyans attached to the People's Bureau: In November 1985, there were seventy-seven. Thirty-four of them possessed diplomatic identity cards issued by the Ministry of Foreign Affairs, and seven carried green cards denoting nondiplomatic personnel, which nevertheless provided them carte blanche for crossing national borders, including the boundary between East and West Berlin.

Wiegand told Stuchly they would need to take action to prevent a tragedy, even though he knew that digging into Libyan affairs would spell trouble from Mielke if they were caught. The Stasi chief was not a man to fool with. Feared by his men, Mielke was utterly ruthless in matters that involved the protection of the communist state. The largest directorate within the MfS, for example, was charged with internal discipline matters. Mielke had given it extraordinary powers to watch over all state security personnel. The slightest hint of suspicion—or sometimes just a personality clash with a superior—could lead to oppressive surveillance of the hapless Stasi man and his family, hostile interrogation, and even imprisonment.

Stuchly reminded Wiegand that Mielke had provided weapons and training for Yasser Arafat's Palestine Liberation Organization and other Arab extremists. "And remember, six years ago he gave orders not to launch operations against terrorists—especially Libyans—so long as they were not committing any crimes on East German soil." The two intelligence officers argued heatedly for some hours, Wiegand trying to convince Stuchly that Mielke must be informed of the danger. "I certainly have a conscience, and I cannot allow those Arabs to blow up people in West Berlin."

Stuchly was a man who became easily excited when under pressure. "Rainer, you're going too far! You know what Mielke will do to us if he gets wind even of this discussion?" Wiegand was not swayed: "I know all that, but I can tell you that I have been bothered quite a while by this attitude on terrorism. My God, can't you see that the DDR will become involved and it will badly damage our international relations, which took years to build. More than that, we are not murderers!" Stuchly was no match for Wiegand, who had won high marks in debating dialectical materialism during his MfS political classes. Stuchly finally relented and agreed to go along.

A FIRST REPORT TO MIELKE

The two Stasi officers worked through the night composing a memorandum and an analysis, knowing all the while that they were literally putting their necks on the line. After nearly a dozen drafts, Wiegand typed the final version of the explosive document himself. It read:

> The officers in charge of Action Group Foreigners (Wiegand) and Section 15 (Stuchly), investigating independently of each other, have obtained evidence that:
>
> - The LPB is misusing its diplomatic mission and status and is almost entirely devoted to pursuing intelligence work. The bulk of the LPB

diplomats and administrative employees belong to three different residencies[3] of various Libyan secret services.
- The LPB is misusing the territory of the DDR for planning, organizing, and executing terrorist attacks in the West, specifically bombings and murders of opponents of the Libyan regime in West Berlin.
- Weapons, ammunition, and explosives are stored inside the LPB apartments of diplomats and in secretly and illegally rented apartments of GDR citizens. These items are being imported into the DDR by circumventing customs controls and are transshipped to West Berlin in diplomatic vehicles.
- Secret service employees within the LPB engage in espionage on the territory of the DDR against other foreign embassies, especially those of other Arab states, and are recruiting and controlling agents who increasingly include citizens of the GDR who have even been targeted against the MfS.
- Foreigners employed by the LPB have been identified by the MfS and by Western intelligence services as terrorists and murderers.

Wiegand signed the document and delivered it personally to his immediate superior, Lieutenant General Günther Kratsch, head of the Second Main Directorate. The Second Directorate was one of only eight directorates—out of a total of fifty-eight—that reported directly to Mielke. These eight also included the "Minister's Action Group 5," a supersecret SWAT-type outfit composed of rangers, sharpshooters, and subversion specialists.

Kratsch, after much hemming and hawing, which Colonel Wiegand countered with cogent arguments, agreed to deliver the paper to Mielke. Wiegand was more nervous than he had been at any previous time during his career. Kratsch was highly agitated when he returned. Mielke had accepted the paper "under advisement." Wiegand was surprised because he had expected the minister to explode. Wiegand wondered if the usually fierce Mielke had just swallowed one of his favorite "morning candies"—Reaktivan, an amphetamine, or Valium—before he met with General Kratsch. (It was an open secret among ranking Stasi officers that Mielke had been taking uppers and downers for some time.)

Wiegand began receiving calls from Mielke's office requesting more details and clarification of some points. He was being taken seriously. The colonel was relieved when no one asked whether he had recruited an informant from among the LPB staff in violation of the minister's orders.

The event that would brand the East German regime as an accessory to the La Belle bombing occurred in mid-December. Mielke had requested a meeting at the imposing government headquarters on Marx-

Engels Square in the heart of Berlin. Present were Honecker and Egon Krenz—next to Honecker, the most powerful man in East Germany. Krenz was a member of the Politburo and a secretary of the Central Committee, responsible for security, justice, and youth affairs. The third man at this secret parley was Herman Axen, Politburo member and Central Committee secretary for international relations. When Mielke announced the subject of the meeting, Honecker called in a fourth man. He was Günther Kleiber, the Politburo member responsible for Middle East matters.

Mielke gave each a copy of Colonel Wiegand's report and analysis. He also handed out a separate analysis of Wiegand's findings, produced by the Central Task Group/Information and Evaluation (ZAIG). When they finished reading, Mielke, as usual, collected the reports and stuffed them back into his briefcase. He was an ace in conspiratorial thinking; his interlocutors were babes in the woods, in comparison. Mielke never took the chance of leaving highly sensitive material in the hands of political functionaries. Special couriers delivered the most sensitive top secret material even to his underlings. They would have to read it in the presence of the courier, sign it to show that they had done so, and then the material went back directly to Mielke. He kept only the signed copy in his personal safe, which stood behind his desk and was secured every night with his special seal. All other copies landed in his shredder.

Before leaving the party leaders, Mielke telephoned General Kratsch and ordered him to be at the chief's office when he returned. Kratsch in turn summoned Wiegand, who was told to stand by in Mielke's reception room in case he was needed. As the colonel waited nervously, Mielke passed through. He nodded silently toward Wiegand to acknowledge his presence. The pallor of Mielke's face was more pronounced than usual. In his customary white shirt, dark tie, and dark suit, he looked more like an undertaker than a secret police chief. Wiegand strained to hear what was being said inside Mielke's office. He wanted a hint of the Stasi chief's mood. The heavy door of solid oak was virtually soundproof. Once, however, Wiegand faintly heard the high-pitched sound of the legendary oversized shredder that stood to the right of Mielke's desk. The shredder could chew up an inch-thick file in less than a minute.

When Kratsch emerged from his session, he grasped Wiegand by the forearm and wordlessly propelled him out of the reception room. Back in Kratsch's office, the general said Mielke talked about his meeting with Honecker, Krenz, Axen, and Kleiber, and that Honecker instructed him to continue surveillance but do nothing else. Wiegand was ordered not to use IMs and not to interfere in any way with the Libyans.

Kratsch was a *Linientreuer,* a man who unhesitatingly toed the party line. He described how Mielke had launched into a diatribe about the Libyan "friends" who were doing so much to help build the DDR's economy, and the importance of their trade relations. Mielke reminded the general that the Libyans had also assisted greatly in intelligence matters and were important allies in the "anti-imperialist struggle." Mielke, as Kratsch related to Wiegand, was agitated when he exclaimed that "little" Libya had no other way to defend itself against the "big" Americans with their planes and ships. "Finally, Mielke told me," said Wiegand, "that America is the archenemy and that we should concern ourselves with catching American spies and not bother our Libyan friends."

Wiegand was not surprised. He knew the East German regime had never wavered in its pursuit of Stalinism and that the ideological blinders worn by the leadership were impenetrable. As far as Wiegand was concerned, however, the dangers posed by the Libyan secret service outweighed any ideological considerations. The colonel had swallowed much during his career as a Stasi officer; but this was the day when he finally realized that his government had crossed the threshold of what could be tolerated in support of the "anti-imperialist struggle."

Notwithstanding orders to the contrary, Wiegand continued using his agents to learn more about the Libyan terrorists' plans. By early March 1986, the electronic surveillance division of the Stasi was intercepting directives sent by the CIA and the FBI to their European representatives. It became clear to MfS counterintelligence that instructions from the U.S. administration called for greater aggressiveness in locating and exposing terrorist bases. One message singled out West Berlin for increased counterterrorist intelligence activities. U.S. intelligence apparently had recognized that foreign missions in the eastern part of the city had become such bases.

By that time, Wiegand had recruited a half dozen Arabs as agents, and he intensified surveillance of U.S. installations in West Berlin. Most of his IMs were journalists from various Arab countries. He instructed some to activate their connections to the U.S. embassy in East Berlin. Others were to visit the West Berlin press club more often and get close to journalists the Stasi suspected of U.S. intelligence connections. He told them to express their dissatisfaction with the DDR regime and pass on tidbits of information he provided, information that would be of interest to the American espionage services.

THE CIA HIRES WIEGAND'S AGENTS

Within a short time, Wiegand's six agents had been recruited by U.S. intelligence. His double agents were in place—curiously, all under the same roof. Wiegand and his collaborator, Stuchly, studied their files on U.S. intelligence facilities in West Berlin and concluded that a new CIA section had been established. They assigned the new CIA operation the code name *Dom*—German for "cathedral."

Wiegand's most successful double agent was a Syrian posted to East Berlin by the Syrian Arab News Agency (SANA) who worked closely with the Allgemeiner Deutscher Nachrichtendienst (ADN), the official East German government news agency. The Syrian's information convinced Wiegand that Dom was not employing the Arab nationals for espionage against the DDR. Instead, he concluded, the CIA was using them to infiltrate suspected terrorist groups based in East Berlin and at the same time establishing them as future agents of influence. Wiegand marveled at the CIA's ability in spotting and recruiting the right people. The Americans always seemed to pick those who could not only be of immediate help but whose family ties and official connections in their home countries would stand them in good stead in the future.

With his double agents in place and without any fear that the new CIA efforts would involve general espionage, Wiegand was able to concentrate on the Libyan People's Bureau. He focused his attention on a new arrival who spent a great deal of time with a Libyan official already suspected of being a terrorist. The newcomer was Musbah Abulgasem Eter, who had been granted a multiple entry diplomatic visa by the foreign ministry. A computer check revealed that he was a member of a secret service unit led by Abdussalam Zadmah, who was responsible for actions outside Libya against opponents of the Qaddafi regime.

On March 19, 1986, Wiegand was informed by Stuchly that informer Ali Chaana, code-named Alba, had reported that more explosives had arrived. Alba unveiled plans to blow up a school bus transporting children of U.S. diplomats from East Berlin to the American sector. The bus crossed through the Berlin Wall at Checkpoint Charlie every weekday at 7 A.M. The attack was to take place before the end of the month at the intersection of Kochstrasse and Wilhelmstrasse, just around the corner from the American checkpoint. Two men were to hurl bundles of explosives at the bus. Alba, a Palestinian member of the Libyan terrorist group, also reported that plans were being made to detonate between 100 and 150 kilograms (220 and 330 pounds) of explosives concealed in an automobile at the high-rise building that housed the Springer Publishing Company. The Springer newspapers—*Die Welt, BZ, Bild Zeitung,* and *Morgenpost*—were detested by the East German regime for their anticommunist stance and by Arab extremists for their pro-Israel editorial policy. Wiegand was appalled by the size of the bomb. Although he did not know the composition of the explosives, he knew the bomb would cause incredible damage, and if set off during working hours, enormous casualties.

Wiegand once more persuaded Colonel Stuchly that they pool their resources for around-the-clock surveillance of Ali Keshlaf, Yasser Chraidi, and Elamin A. Elamin—all members of the LPB with diplomatic status. Chraidi was the most dangerous of the trio. A member at least since 1975 of the Popular Front for the Liberation of Palestine, General Command (PFLP-GC), he had conducted previous terrorist operations in West Germany and Berlin against Israeli establishments and citizens. He was suspected of several murders. In an assessment, Colonel Wiegand described Chraidi as a "person of poor mental ability, not well educated, talkative, prone to brag, loudmouthed, a liar with criminal tendencies, a womanizer who drinks alcohol to excess and uses narcotics."

Stasi surveillance teams at first observed Keshlaf reconnoitering the U.S. Army's McNair Barracks in the Lichterfelde district, the army hospital at Unter den Eichen boulevard, the U.S. military headquarters and diplomatic mission on Clay Allee boulevard, a drive-in restaurant catering mostly to Americans, and a military gas station. His clandestine meetings with other Arabs in West Berlin had increased in frequency. Keshlaf and his associates then shifted their attention to discotheques frequented by American soldiers. Ali Mansur, a Lebanese who had arrived in East Berlin only days earlier, was particularly active. He was spending all of his time watching the discotheques La Belle, Stardust, and Nashville, located in the American sector.

From March 20 on, Wiegand received information almost daily on planned attacks. Qaddafi obviously had become emboldened by European public opinion polls showing no significant popular support for military action against him. A radio message originating in Tripoli and intercepted by the East Germans was believed to signal official approval for an attack on March 26.

The information went to General Kratsch, who brought it to Stasi chief Mielke. Concurrently, Wiegand was getting requests for information from Politburo members—to him, a sure sign that the top leadership was being kept up to date.

On March 23, Wiegand was ordered by Mielke to write another report, this time for Honecker. The colonel recapitulated previous data and topped it off with a statement that all available information indicated that a bombing would take place March 26. He said immediate action was necessary to prevent the attack. Wiegand recommended that a deputy foreign minister confront the head of the Libyan People's Bureau, Abdusalam Alregee, and that the DDR ambassador in Tripoli deliver a formal protest to the Qaddafi government.

Yasser Chraidi, Libyan terrorist and planner of the 1986 bombing of the La Belle discotheque in Berlin. Courtesy Ullstein Photo.

Wiegand, together with Kratsch, was summoned to face an enraged Mielke, who told the colonel that permission to take action had been denied at the "highest level." Wiegand perceived a threat when Mielke reminded the counterespionage expert of his "sense of political responsibility." The secret police chief pointed to the "dire consequences such political action would have on relations if taken without operational evidence."

As usual, General Kratsch, the sycophant, acquiesced. Later, Wiegand briefed Stuchly on the confrontation, and both were indignant over not being taken seriously. In another memorandum the following day, March 24, Wiegand tried to persuade Honecker and company to change their minds, only to be rejected again.

After midnight March 24, Stuchly was still in Wiegand's office, discussing what they were sure was the imminent Libyan attack. "I am fed up with extremism, terrorism, and with all those comrades of ours who shut their eyes," Wiegand told his associate. "That can turn against us tomorrow . . . when you happen to sit in a plane or your family is out for a walk on Alexander Platz. . . . We can be blown up just like anybody else."

On the morning of March 25, Chraidi and Musbah El Albani, who was officially listed as a diplomatic courier, drove a Volkswagen Golf bearing East German diplomatic license plates through Checkpoint Charlie into West Berlin. As usual, communist border guards merely examined their diplomatic passes and waved them on without inspecting the car. At the American checkpoint, West Berlin police also allowed them through without any examination. (It was Allied policy not to recognize the wall as a legitimate frontier, and anyone could pass into the Western sectors without hindrance.) The two Arabs were transporting a suitcase that—Wiegand had been informed—contained two submachine guns with spare clips, three pistols equipped with silencers, and seven hand grenades.

The lethal baggage was stashed in the apartment of Imad Salim Mahmoud, a thirty-five-year-old Palestinian enrolled as a student in West Berlin's Technical University. He lived in the lower-class district of Kreuzberg, which over the years had become heavily populated with Turkish families—a place where a swarthy newcomer would not be noticed. This latest information reached Wiegand just before noon. The colonel summoned Stuchly to his office and turned up the radio, as he did habitually when there was something to discuss that he did not want others to hear. Then he raged once more against Stasi officers who took the position that "so long as we cooperate with the terrorists, they won't do anything against us."

"Now we must take matters into our own hands. . . . We must bite the bullet," Wiegand told Stuchly, who agreed fully. One slip would have meant their immediate arrest for treason. In the event that something went wrong, they agreed that they would keep their mouths shut and deny ever having discussed or even thought about such actions.

That same evening, March 25, the two colonels stationed themselves in a side street near the apartment occupied by the Libyan secret service station chief, Ali Keshlaf. When he left the building, they approached Keshlaf and pushed him into a doorway. Wiegand held out his MfS credentials. "We are from state security." Stuchly roughly grabbed the Libyan by the arm. Keshlaf angrily hissed that he could not be arrested. "We have no intention of doing that," Wiegand told the Libyan. "We just want to tell you one thing. We know what you are planning in West Berlin . . . with those discotheques. . . . We know all of it. We have passed our information on to the West Berlin police. If you go ahead with it, the DDR will show you and your friends no mercy. You are seriously endangering the relations between the DDR and Libya, and you will bear full responsibility. Consider this a warning between comrades and colleagues."[4] Stuchly released the Arab, and the two officers returned to Stasi headquarters.

Wiegand and Stuchly nervously sat out the next day and night listening to the emergency frequency of the West Berlin police, taking turns at catnaps in Wiegand's office. Nothing happened. The following morning, Stasi agents shadowed Yasser Chraidi's wife, who went by the name of Souad Mansur and who was in possession of a diplomat's pass identifying her as an LPB administrative employee. She boarded the elevated train for West Berlin and headed straight for the apartment of Imad Salim Mahmoud, where the weapons had been stored two days earlier. The woman emerged from the apartment building after only a brief stay, carrying the weapons suitcase, and returned to East Berlin. Two days later, her husband, whom Wiegand's researchers had earlier identified as an unscrupulous Libyan secret service killer and explosives expert, was observed delivering the suitcase to the People's Bureau office.

At Stasi headquarters, General Kratsch summoned Wiegand and Stuchly to his office and launched into a tirade because the predicted attack had not taken place. Wiegand countered that several of his informants had told him that the action—spraying the Stardust discotheque with submachine gun fire and lobbing hand grenades onto the dance floor—was called off at the last minute because the Libyans had noticed an increased West Berlin police presence. Furthermore, he said, the Libyans had decided that the place was too far from a border checkpoint for a quick escape. The counterespionage chief accused the two colonels of making lame excuses for falsely interpreting the reports from their double agents. Kratsch also charged Wiegand with "hyping": "You did this to make yourself appear important."[5] Kratsch ranted about Wiegand leading him and Mielke down a primrose path and how the colonel had embarrassed the party leadership. It was obvious to Wiegand that the general had been severely reprimanded by an irate Mielke, who probably got the same treatment from Honecker.

Wiegand and Stuchly said nothing about the preventive measures they had taken. They returned to Wiegand's office, weary and uncertain of their future. Nevertheless, Wiegand uncorked a bottle of Crimean champagne, and the two men toasted their success in keeping their hands clean. They were convinced that they had prevented a bloodbath and a serious international incident that would have further blackened their country's already bad image.

Wiegand was also sure that the new CIA unit in West Berlin was collecting information about the Libyan activities that at least equaled that acquired by his agents. To make certain, he used the six CIA informants, who were his agents as well, to relay information he had provided—data pointing to a possible attack. The CIA's resources in West Berlin were much better than his own, and Wiegand was hoping that the Americans might be able to better pinpoint a target and a date for the attack. At the very least, he felt, the Americans would be taking stringent security measures on the basis of what they already knew, which must have included the Libyan surveillance of the discotheques. Wiegand was sure that the Americans also had intercepted the message exchange between Tripoli and East Berlin. The U.S. National Security Agency had a listening post atop the Teufelsberg hill in West Berlin where all radio communications originating in or destined for East Germany and beyond were intercepted.

Stasi agents continued their tight surveillance, but they were unable to gather reliable information on any planned terrorist attacks. Meanwhile, radio and telephone traffic between Tripoli and East Berlin had picked up markedly. All Libyan telephones in the latter city were tapped. Video cameras concealed behind the walls of apartments occupied by the major suspects continuously recorded their moves. Wiegand studied transcripts of telephone recordings and noted that the Libyans had become more careful, obviously operating under the assumption that their activities were being monitored by the MfS. The Libyans were looking for leaks and seemed to have concluded that the appearance of police just prior to the planned attack on the Stardust disco was no coincidence but the result of cooperation between "the Germans." This was exactly the impression that Wiegand and Stuchly wanted to convey. The colonel again perused the latest surveillance reports. Although Musbah, the Libyan courier, was observed near Stardust, La Belle, and Nashville discotheques each day between April 1 and 4 during daylight hours, Wiegand still had no concrete evidence that an attack was imminent. Al-Albani returned from West Berlin on April 4, crossing at 11:45 P.M. at Friedrichstrasse intercity railway station checkpoint.

LA BELLE IS BOMBED

On April 5 between 12:30 and 2:00 A.M., Chraidi was at his apartment on Hans Loch Strasse, about a mile and a half from Stasi headquarters. He was listening to West Berlin news broadcasts and received a number of telephone calls from unidentified Arabs in West Berlin. At 1:15 A.M. a caller told him: "It hasn't been possible yet." The Libyan killer then left the apartment and drove to the Berolina Hotel on Karl-Marx-Allee in downtown East Berlin, where he was joined by Musbah. In a second-floor room expertly bugged by the Stasi, they listened to a special newscast at 5 A.M., aired by RIAS (Radio in the American Sector), reporting an explosion at the La Belle discotheque.

Wiegand became enraged when he heard the news: "The swine bluffed us! They took the weapons and explosives through the front door and brought them back out through the rear." The colonel was furious at his own negligence. He told Stuchly, "We were too anxious to believe that we had done a good deed, and overlooked the deviousness of the Arab mentality." The transport of the weapons back to East Berlin had been a ruse, and the explosives, taken earlier to West Berlin, had not been detected by Wiegand's watchers.

At the Berolina Hotel, Chraidi telephoned Keshlaf, the Libyan secret service station chief. Then he contacted Elamin A. Elamin, who had been accredited as a diplomat only a month earlier and whom the Stasi believed was sent to East Berlin specifically to organize the bombing. Both had already heard about the bombing, and they profusely congratulated one another.

Returning to Chraidi's apartment, Al-Albani and Chraidi drafted a note claiming responsibility for the bombing: "We the Arab forces on German soil and in Europe take responsibility for the bombing of the American discotheque, an answer to the American aggression in the Gulf of Sidra. Under the leadership of the Great Leader!" The two terrorists then drove to the Palast Hotel to phone a West Berlin newspaper, but they were unable to get a connection and thus the message was never sent. All telephone calls out of East Germany were under constant control of the Stasi. The Stasi listener, knowing the West would be monitoring as well, and wishing to protect the East German government, was probably acting on personal initiative in refusing to put the call through.

A SWIFT U.S. REACTION

The U.S. government's verbal reaction to the massacre was immediate: President Ronald Reagan called Qaddafi a "flaky barbarian." The State Department charged that the East German government could have prevented the bombing. The U.S. Ambassador to West Germany, Richard Burt, said radio intercepts by U.S. intelligence proved that the attackers had come from East Berlin.

Damage control became a matter of the highest priority for the East German government. On April 9, Wiegand received an unsigned top secret document from General Kratsch.[6] The colonel surmised that the paper had originated with Honecker, the chief of state and party boss. It said:

> Based on the unusually sharp political reaction of the USA toward the DDR and the USSR shortly before and after the attack in West Berlin, as well as the initial public announcements by the USA ambassador in Bonn, Richard Burt, it can be concluded that this incident will be used to strengthen the lies about terrorism. It must be expected that "evidence" will be produced.
>
> Attempts by the USA to enlist their West European allies in a united front against Libya having failed, it appears now that the intention is to

> use the "West Berlin example" for a new effort. The activities of the imperialist media (film requests from ARD/ZDF [West German TV networks] and requests for interviews from Reuter [the British news agency] point to the preparation of a major campaign to discredit the DDR and its socialist allies.

The document concluded that "further escalation must be expected" and therefore, that "possible action [on the part of the DDR] toward the Libyan side must be considered." In addition, DDR reaction, "especially toward the USA, must demonstrate that the relations between the DDR and third countries are its own sovereign affair."

Honecker was correct in saying that the European countries had refused to join an economic embargo or any other action against Libya, as had been urged by various U.S. missions, including one headed by Deputy Secretary of State John C. Whitehead.[7] They were undoubtedly influenced in that decision by their own economic ties with Libya. Italy was Libya's largest trading partner, with trade amounting to US$4.353 billion annually, followed by West Germany with US$2.881 billion. In total, the European Common Market imported Libyan oil and gas valued at US$6.4 billion a year and exported US$3.8 billion worth of varied goods. There were 40,000 Europeans living in Libya at the time.

Wiegand realized that his country's leadership feared a severe American reaction to their coddling of terrorists. The colonel read on and was astounded that he was being ordered to "take necessary action against militant forces within the Libyan People's Bureau only after such action will no longer convey the impression that it is a reaction to the demands of the USA."

Wiegand noted with satisfaction that Mielke had finally agreed that it was "urgently necessary to stop the misuse of diplomatic immunity by representatives of Arab embassies." Nevertheless, the schizophrenia of the East German communist leadership came to fore once more in this paragraph of the document:

> Considering the fact that effective interstate relations commenced only at the beginning of 1986 but have already resulted in considerable economic advantages for the DDR, necessary political steps in connection with the LPB must be in the form of friendly and frank talks. Any impression that the DDR is giving the slightest consideration to American interests must be avoided. All necessary political steps toward the Libyans must be explained as DDR measures designed to guarantee the safety of the People's Bureau and to prevent anti-Libyan activities by the imperialists.

Honecker's anger over the political fallout resulting from the policy that had made the bombing possible was perceptible. Yet, Wiegand noted, ambiguities remained in that policy. Wiegand interpreted the instructions as saying, "Go ahead and wash the bear, but don't get his fur wet." General Kratsch telephoned him to ask whether he understood the situation, and before hanging up, he admonished Wiegand to follow instructions to the letter: "For heaven's sake, don't do anything that would make the Libyans think we are allying ourselves with the Americans," he told Wiegand. "Remember, the main enemy is the American imperialists. They are attacking; Libya is not attacking the USA." Wiegand repeatedly heard Mielke say the same thing many times. Now Kratsch was using the Stasi chief's words verbatim.

The East German government had realized that it was being adversely affected by its alliance with extremist politics and terrorism, and the leadership was distressed. Facing the leadership, however, was the sacrosanct basic political and ideological position of solidarity in the "battle against imperialism and support of national liberation movements." This position did not provide the impetus to pursue consequent and clear actions to disassociate the government from dangerous entanglements.

It was in character, therefore, that Honecker would issue a statement on April 10 in which he condemned terrorism, and in a blatant attempt to shift blame, urged that West Berlin police and customs exercise proper border controls. He knew, of course, that the Western allies had never recognized his wall as a legal border, and adhering to the right of free and unhindered access, would never check anyone who was crossing from the East.

WIEGAND'S INVESTIGATION INTENSIFIES

Colonel Wiegand's investigation began to take an even a more aggressive direction. No longer bound by the need to conceal his activities from his superiors, the colonel was bent on finding the routes over which the Libyan terrorists had brought the weapons and explosives into East Germany. This had puzzled him for some time, because all diplomatic baggage was x-rayed by the MfS and customs at all entry points. That left only clandestine routes. His agents fanned out at Schönefeld Airport, which serviced the East German capital. The break he was hoping for came on March 11. An informant reported that a woman named Irena Schiffel, who was a ground stewardess of the East German government airline Interflug, was involved with Libyans in smuggling operations. Schiffel's job was to meet Libyan planes on arrival and to pick up the usual travel documents. Often, though, she would also pick up a suitcase. She would stow the suitcase in her locker, in the employees' lounge, before proceeding to the dispatcher's office with the documents. After finishing her shift, she would retrieve the case and leave the airport without being checked.

Once again Wiegand was jolted when he checked Schiffel's background. Her entire immediate family, as well as some in-laws, were full-time members of the Ministry for State Security. Her father held a high rank. Wiegand knew he could not move against the woman without getting clearance from Stasi chief Mielke. Mielke authorized only "temporary detention." Wiegand and Stuchly picked Schiffel up that evening and took her for interrogation to a safe house. She was unusually calm. Other than acknowledging her name, she said nothing during the first fifteen minutes of questioning.

"You are in trouble, and the best thing for you is to come clean fast," Wiegand told the attractive, statuesque blonde. But Schiffel remained silent. Stuchly then told the woman that she was not giving them any choice but to arrest her father. Irena Schiffel reached into her purse and retrieved a slip of paper, which she handed to Wiegand. Written on it was a telephone number that she asked Wiegand to call. He wasted no time, first checking out the number, and then making the call. Surprise! On the other end was "Kolya," the East Germans' nickname for all of their male colleagues at the KGB. The colonel identified himself, and ignoring the usual telephone security procedures, he told the Soviet colleague that he had detained a woman named Irena Schiffel who requested that he call. Wiegand held the receiver away from his ear. Smiling, he said to Stuchly, "It's Kolya, and he is mad." Wiegand then told the KGB man to come to the safe house.

When the KGB officer arrived, he told the two colonels that Irena Schiffel was one of his top agents. Turning to the woman, he ordered her to answer Wiegand's questions. Incredibly, the Soviets had known all along that the Libyans were bringing arms and explosives into East Germany. Schiffel had been recruited by the KGB in Libya, where she once had been stationed for the airline. In turn, and with KGB encouragement, she was recruited by Libyan intelligence, by none other than the terrorist Yasser Chraidi, who had been paying her large sums in hard currency.

Wiegand was aware that the Soviets often played fast and loose with their "fraternal friends." But he considered it a new milestone in perfidy that the KGB never informed the MfS about the Libyans' arms- and explosives-smuggling activities. Wiegand recalled the official Soviet statement twelve days after the La Belle bombing: Foreign ministry spokesman Vladimir Lomeiko had said it was a "cynical lie" when the U.S. government said the Soviet Union could have prevented the attack. The colonel could not believe that General Chumilov, the KGB chief for East Germany, had not reported the Libyan smuggling to Moscow Center.

There was yet another surprise in store for Wiegand: The day after his talk with Schiffel, he received a paper labeled only "translation from the Russian—top secret," which was the usual way the KGB would transmit information to the Stasi. It said a Libyan named "Omar Dargam Saleh, who is the son of Qaddafi's sister Sikkino, is planning an action against the club of the American forces in West Berlin." The report said further that delivery of weapons from Cairo to "the capital of the DDR is said to be handled by a certain Al-Hadji Ismail Sabrin, who has a car rental business near the Ambassador Hotel in Cairo." In addition, the KGB pointed out that Omar Dargam Saleh had formed an export-import business in East Berlin and that his partner was a Palestinian named Darrar. Since the paper was not dated, Wiegand had no way of knowing whether the KGB had suddenly become solicitous or whether it had been sent earlier and had gotten held up somewhere in the MfS bureaucracy. Wiegand had not previously heard of the two Arabs mentioned in the document, but he accepted the report as additional proof that the Soviets had been fully aware of Libyan terrorist activities in Berlin.

Three days after Wiegand uncovered this evidence of Soviet complicity, U.S. Air Force and Navy jets launched their attacks against Libyan Army installations and air bases, barely missing Qaddafi himself. This sent the East German leaders into another convulsion. The 11th Party Congress was to open in two days, and Honecker was loath to see the American retaliation overshadow his show. First, the government news agency (ADD) published a government denial that Libyan officials stationed in East Berlin had orchestrated the La Belle bombing. Honecker opened the congress with an attack on the United States for its "barbaric bombardment of peaceful Libyan cities." In the audience was Mikhail Gorbachev, who applauded vigorously. Had the Soviet leader been kept in the dark by the KGB?

The American furor over the Libyan bombing had by no means subsided. Alan R. Thompson, counselor to Francis J. Meehan, the U.S. ambassador to East Germany, delivered a verbal U.S. protest to the DDR Ministry for Foreign Affairs. Thompson insisted that the East German government take action against the Libyan terrorists operating out of East Berlin under the guise of diplomats. The East Germans rejected the protest, and in a public statement, said the Americans "could not present any proof" of their accusations. Ambassador Meehan had already been to the Foreign Ministry on March 27 to report that the United States had indications of hostile acts being planned against it by the LPB in East Berlin. Foreign Ministry officials were lying when they told the U.S. ambassador that they had no knowledge of such activities.

The Stasi representative present at all meetings with foreign diplomats, Colonel Ernst Herbt, left for Stasi headquarters immediately after the American envoy's presentation. He met with Wiegand and Stuchly, to whom he said, "the Americans know that somebody is protecting the Libyans." Wiegand knew Herbt as a sober and calm professional who previously had served as operations chief of the MfS residency in Moscow. Now he was two years away from his pension and had been given a cushy job as a "member of the Foreign Office." Why, Wiegand asked, was he so excited? "I'll tell you why," said Herbt: "The American slammed his fist on the deputy minister's desk. He was wild. We thought we were back in the occupation days. Thompson threatened to resort to the *Geldknüppel* (bludgeon made of money), to cut off all trade relations and get the other Western countries to do the same. He also implied that we should forget about Honecker's planned visit to the United States." Honecker had been pushing for a meeting with President Reagan, a meeting that would have been the culmination of the DDR's quest for international recognition and respectability. Then, more quietly, he told Wiegand, "If you know something, you better come clean with me, because we have to know how to deal with this. I tell you, the Americans have evidence that we had a hand in this thing." Wiegand replied that there was nothing he could say at the moment but that he would report Herbt's misgivings to General Kratsch, which he did at once. Kratsch merely smiled at Wiegand. "Forget Herbt, we will take care of Herbt." Wiegand understood: Herbt would be told to keep his mouth shut.

BLAME THE AMERICANS

As the party congress got underway, Wiegand was summoned to a meeting with General Kratsch and Lt. Colonel Siegfried Neubert, chief of the Stasi's Coordination and Planning Group. Kratsch was smiling broadly as he handed Wiegand a sheaf of papers. It was a telephone surveillance transcript covering a conversation between two West Berlin police detectives who were discussing the investigation of the La Belle bombing. One of the detectives apparently was a member of a special group formed to probe the bombing. He was being questioned by his colleague on the progress of the investigation. The man replied that he was frustrated by the Americans, who also had sent a special team. He complained of "stonewalling" and wondered out loud if perhaps "the Americans did it themselves." His colleague asked on what he based his suspicion. The detective replied that an

FBI agent had mentioned that one of the Americans killed at La Belle had kept a savings account into which a large deposit had been made that could not be explained. The detective thought it was around $50,000. FBI agents attached to the U.S. embassy in Bonn as "legal attachés" had in fact been in Berlin to offer assistance to German investigators. However, their offer was rejected, and subsequent investigations failed to produce any information on the alleged bank account.[8]

Wiegand quickly understood what Kratsch had in mind: Protecting the Libyans was more important to the East German regime than bringing murderers to justice. Addressing Wiegand, Lt. Colonel Neubert, the planning chief, said he had been charged by Stasi Minister Mielke to "find a way out of our exposed position."

"We cannot remain with our backs to the wall. You've read the transcript. There is already speculation that the Americans did it themselves to create a pretense for hitting Libya." Kratsch then ordered Wiegand to "come up with something" that could be used in a disinformation campaign. Like it or not, he had to comply. Back at his own office, Wiegand summoned his staff and asked whether anyone had any details on suspicions that the Americans had planted the bomb themselves. One of his analysts spoke up, saying he had been reading the debates in American newspapers over how to respond to terrorism in the weeks after the Rome and Vienna shootings. He thought there might be something useful in the articles.

Wiegand's staff produced an analysis that included the text of a U.S. State Department report on terrorism issued on January 9, 1986, which the Stasi had obtained from their man in Washington. It could have served to arouse public opinion against Qaddafi, but Wiegand found nothing that could be used in a disinformation campaign. The colonel then turned to the terse analysis, which actually was little more than a synopsis of certain passages from official pronouncements and speeches by government officials as reported in *The New York Times*, such as:

> (January 12) But the White House warned that with the expected departure of Americans (from Libya),[9] the United States was prepared to take drastic action in response to any future attacks for which Colonel Qaddafi could be blamed. Mr. Reagan, in an interview with European journalists, described the departure of the Americans as a move 'to untie our hands.'
>
> (Secretary of State Shultz in a television interview) Asked if the President was suggesting that the next incident probably would provoke a strong military response, Mr. Shultz today pointedly refused comment.

The analyst found another speech by Shultz, delivered on January 15, in which he had said the United States could not wait "for absolute clarity" before using "military force to strike at terrorists or countries that support them." An aide to Shultz explained that the Secretary was trying to make sure that if any other terrorist action was linked to Libya, there would be no hesitancy about striking back, now that virtually all possible economic sanctions had been imposed by the United States.

The analyst also cited a January 23 *New York Times* report that quoted CIA Director William Casey as saying, "We cannot and will not abstain from forcible action to prevent, preempt, or respond to terrorist acts." Summarizing, the analyst wrote that these statements as well as the failure of the United States to enlist its allies' solidarity in enforcing sanctions against Libya could be reasonably interpreted to mean that the world public, and especially the Western allies, was not supportive of U.S. military action against Libya. To obtain their support, the United States needed an incident that could be interpreted in such a way as to discredit Libya.

General Kratsch beamed with pleasure when he read the analysis. "We'll show that the Americans pulled it off themselves. I don't want someone to cobble something together. It has to be done with skill and care, and so I will take care of it." The matter was taken out of Wiegand's hands, and the fairy tale was concocted by the MfS disinformation department. Its dissemination was handled by the controllers of Stasi agents in West Berlin and aided by a number of left-wing German journalists who delighted in publishing anything detrimental to the *Amis*. Articles soon began to appear in various newspapers and magazines, hinting at CIA involvement in the La Belle bombing. The most enthusiastic supporter of the Stasi fairy tale was the left-wing West Berlin newspaper *Tageszeitung*. Foreign newspapers and news agencies, including some American ones, ran stories quoting the German media. The East German Communist Party newspaper *Neues Deutschland* reprinted a commentary by Yuri Lvov of the Soviet news agency TASS, relying on the "evidence" manufactured by the Stasi.

Toward the end of April, Wiegand gave Mielke an interim report on the La Belle bombing. He wrote that the MfS investigations and analyses had concluded beyond any doubt that the "attack originated at the highest level in Libya and was carried out by the secret service residency of the LPB based in the capital of the DDR." The logistical support was furnished entirely by the Libyan People's Bureau. Wiegand concluded his report:

> According to unassailable evidence obtained by the MfS, the following diplomats and administrative employees of the Libyan People's Bureau were directly responsible for the planning, preparation, security, and execution of the attack:

A. Musbah Albugasem Eter, age 33, Libyan citizen. Cover name "Dervish." As member of the headquarters of the Libyan secret service detailed specifically for this purpose to the LPB, bears the chief responsibility.
B. Elamin A. Elamin, age 48, Libyan citizen. Cover name "Nuri III." Member of the headquarters of the Libyan secret service and assigned to the LPB solely for this purpose.
C. Ali Ibrahim Keshlaf, age 38, Libyan citizen. Cover names "Nuri II" and "Khalif." Member of the LPB and resident of the Libyan Foreign Intelligence Service responsible for security of the operation.
D. El-Munir A.M.A. Madani, age 36, Libyan citizen. Resident of the Libyan Military Intelligence Service. He had knowledge of the operation and furnished some support, although IM reported that he had privately stated his opposition.
E. Yasser Chraidi, alias Yuseff Salam, alias Abdul Salam Bachir Mokh, age 27, Libyan citizen. Cover name "Nuri." Member of the secret service residency at the LPB.
F. Musbah El Albani, age 31, Libyan citizen. Member of the secret service.

Other participants, not members of the LPB:

A. Imad Salim Mahmoud, age 31, Libyan citizen. Student at Technical University, West Berlin.
B. Mohamed-Suleiman Benali, age 30, Moroccan citizen, residing in West Berlin on welfare.
C. Ali Mansur, age 32, Lebanese citizen, living in West Berlin on welfare.
D. Hamadi Abu Jabber, age 26, Moroccan citizen, living in West Berlin, unemployed.
E. Saleh Habda, 31, Syrian citizen, living in West Berlin, no known employment.
F. Faour Daher, age unknown, Palestinian, citizenship unknown. Owner of West Berlin discotheque Down Town.
G. Souad Mansur, wife of Chraidi.

One of the suspects on Wiegand's list, Faour Daher, the owner of the discotheque Down Town, was brought to East Berlin after the bombing, in a diplomatic car belonging to the LPB, and was hidden in a diplomat's apartment. He was later flown to Tripoli. One of Wiegand's agents reported that Daher was paid "at least $10,000" for his part in the bombing and that Libyan intelligence agents had hailed him as the "hero of La Belle."

Despite Wiegand's detailed report and continued U.S. diplomatic pressure on the East German government, no action was taken against the Libyans except for the "friendly, comradely discussion" Honecker had ordered immediately after the bombing. Rather than acting as a deterrent, Colonel Wiegand felt that the "friendly" talks encouraged the Libyans to continue their murderous activities in West Berlin and elsewhere in Germany.

Kratsch, Wiegand, and Stuchly met on January 29, 1987 for a comprehensive discussion of the entire Libyan terrorist situation and future Stasi action. At the end of the session, Kratsch finally made an important concession when he agreed to start an operational dossier code-named Lux, with the MfS registry number XV 1076/87.[10] The dossier contained a chronological account of Libyan terrorist activities as well as Wiegand's reports and analyses sent earlier to Stasi chief Mielke and notes that Kratsch had received from Mielke. Some of these notes bore handwritten notations by Honecker. Omitted, of course, was any record of the actions taken by Wiegand and Stuchly that violated the orders of the MfS minister and the state and party leadership.

Kratsch, Wiegand, and Stuchly agreed that they would function as codirectors of a task force dealing exclusively with the Libyan People's Bureau. Access to task force operational information was highly restricted, but this troika was able to draw on the resources of all Stasi departments. The establishment of the dossier and the task force provided a "legal" basis for operations against the Libyans. Until then, most of Wiegand's and Stuchly's activities had been "illegal" in the eyes of the Stasi chief. Nonetheless, Wiegand and Stuchly continued to resort to subterfuge because they knew certain actions would never be approved by the East German leadership.

INTIMIDATION OF U.S. DIPLOMATS

A bizarre scenario was developing within the government bureaucracy. While Wiegand's officers were consumed by efforts to contain the Libyans' activities, the Ministry for Foreign Affairs was feeding the Libyans information. When the Libyan "diplomats" and their terrorist minions were told about the heavy U.S. pressure, their behavior became more brazen and dangerous. They launched a massive campaign of intimidation against U.S. embassy personnel in East Berlin. Using cars with diplomatic plates, the Libyans menacingly pursued U.S. vehicles. They also stationed themselves outside the residences of U.S. officials and the embassy itself, acting as if they were about to resort to violence. Cynthia Miller, public affairs officer at the U.S. embassy at the time, said the "Libyans were pretty bad."[11] Libyan "diplomats" would follow U.S. officials and their families at every step. They telephoned Americans and threatened them with death and further bombings.

Wiegand's surveillance teams observed these activities, and Stasi telephone taps picked up the death threats as well as conversations between worried U.S. security officers. Several American diplomatic families were moved into more secure residences and hunkered down. The tensions became intense when a high-ranking U.S. diplomat complained to the East German Foreign Ministry, demanding that its government improve the physical security of the embassy by building a "wall" around it. This request became the subject of ironic remarks and *Galgenhumor* (gallows humor) among Stasi officers. However, it created enough of a stir in the government that Stasi chief Mielke ordered twenty-four-hour protection of the embassy by the highly trained special forces under his direct control. Sharpshooters were placed on rooftops across from the embassy, and heavily armed Stasi agents tailed every car belonging to the LPB, around the clock. On at least two occasions, Stasi vehicles deliberately rammed Libyan vehicles from behind, while officers brandished their Skorpion submachine guns at the terrorists. The Stasi countermeasures were effective, and Libyan harassment finally stopped.

ANOTHER MURDER

Alerted by a double agent to the increased activities of U.S. intelligence, the Libyans involved in the La Belle bombings began an intensive surveillance of Arabs living in West Berlin who had no connections with terrorist groups. These Arabs were suspected of working for U.S. authorities not only by the Libyans but by the MfS as well.

Among the suspects was Mohamed Ashur, a former Libyan diplomat and member of the LPB in Bonn. He had become disenchanted with the Qaddafi regime, refused to return to Libya, and moved to West Berlin. Ashur previously had maintained "unofficial contacts" with the MfS's Twenty-Second Directorate, led by Colonel Harry Dahl, which was responsible for counterterrorism. Although Ashur had a girlfriend in East Berlin, he had not been in the communist part of the city for some months prior to the La Belle bombing. A few days after the attack, Ashur was crossing into East Berlin almost daily. Wiegand's agents had been watching him and noted that Ashur was seeking to establish contacts with a number of Arabs, including members of the LPB.

Mohamed Ashur was found dead with a bullet wound to the head on the morning of May 2, 1986. The body was found in Treptow Park, close to the giant Soviet war memorial and the river Spree, which runs through East Berlin. It was subsequently determined that Ashur had been shot the day before.

The murder sounded an alarm at Stasi headquarters. Because of Ashur's previous association with the counterterrorism directorate, officials felt that he might have been liquidated because of this connection and as a warning to the MfS to stay away from the Libyans. The initial investigation was immediately taken out of the hands of the criminal investigation department of the Volkspolizei. A homicide investigation team of the Stasi's so-called "Special Commission" assumed command. This commission, known as the Department Seven, was part of the Ninth Main Directorate, the investigations arm under Major General R. Fister, who reported directly to Mielke. The commission was established to investigate crimes and incidents such as major accidents, fires, and the like, when "an attack on the security of the state" was suspected. The homicide team, led by Colonel Ewald Pycka, was staffed by outstanding criminologists and forensic experts recruited from the ranks of the People's Police and equipped with state-of-the-art technology far beyond the DDR police norm.

The homicide officers, with whom Wiegand collaborated, concluded that the murder had been committed by Musbah Abulgasem Eter, one of the La Belle participants, and Yousef El Saleh, a member of the Libyan secret service. The Stasi was able to establish that El Saleh had entered East Germany a few days earlier, specifically to carry out the execution of Ashur.

As the criminologists wound up their probe, an Arab double agent reported to Wiegand that the murder was ordered by secret service central in Tripoli. It was punishment for becoming "an agent of the CIA" and to demonstrate the "powerlessness of the U.S.A. vis-à-vis the power of Libya."

The final report of the Ashur murder investigation (dubbed "Operation Lux") said the operation had been supervised by the Libyan secret service station chief Keshlaf of the LPB. He had lured Ashur to East Berlin with an invitation to a meeting with diplomats of the LPB. The car in which Ashur had been murdered was recovered, and his blood was found on the back seat. Fingerprints of Eter and El Saleh also were identified. The murder weapon was a 7.65 caliber Beretta automatic pistol. Ballistic tests were performed on the projectile recovered from Ashur's head as well as on the spent cartridge found at the scene. The results proved that the murder weapon was identical to the gun that had been officially imported by the LPB for Keshlaf. It had been easy to identify the pistol. All weapons officially brought into East Germany were test fired, and bullets and cartridge cases were kept on file by the Stasi. After the murder, one of Wiegand's officers entered Keshlaf's apartment illegally, performing a so-called "black bag" job, and examined the weapon. It had been fired recently.

Officers of the homicide team and counterintelligence now took the initiative in accordance with the East German penal code, arresting Eter and charging him with murder. Before the Libyan could be taken to the Hohenschönhausen prison, however, Wiegand and his collaborators received a direct order from Mielke to release the man. Eter retained his diplomatic status and made several trips to Tripoli in 1986. In January 1987, he traveled again to Tripoli and was held there by Libyan authorities while he was being investigated for possible unprofessional conduct. Inspectors from the three Libyan secret services flew to Berlin, and after they uncovered the operational activities of the MfS against the LPB, Eter was exonerated. He nonetheless remained in Libya.

Despite the overwhelming evidence against Eter, the East German leaders stuck to their "principles" and blocked his arrest and trial for the Ashur murder. Ashur's murder, like the bombing of La Belle, was a necessary evil, as far as Honecker, Krenz, Axen, and Mielke were concerned. Shielding "the interests of the state" and maintaining "good fraternal relations" with the enemies of the arch foe, the United States, were paramount. El Saleh, who came to East Berlin as the executioner, was able to return to Tripoli just nineteen days after committing murder.

The Libyan terrorists lay low the remainder of 1986. Wiegand and Colonel Stuchly kept them under constant surveillance, now making sure that they knew they were being watched. The Stasi pressed them hard, even threatening some with death unless they desisted.

A NEW THREAT

Wiegand was alerted on April 9 by border watchers at Schönefeld Airport that Musbah Eter had reentered the country on a diplomatic visa. He was accompanied by another Libyan man, Sadegh Abousrewil. The two men were met by "diplomats" of the LPB, and each was taken to a different apartment. Abousrewil was ensconced in the home of a twenty-six-year-old German woman, Silvia Pfennighaus. The files of the MfS had already listed the place as an illegal residence of the LPB.

Wiegand sensed more trouble in the offing and told Stuchly of Eter's arrival. Wiegand showed Stuchly the photographs taken secretly by the MfS at the airport. Stuchly looked at the pictures, slapped his forehead, and groaned, "Oh Lord, that swine Musbah Eter is back." Stuchly pointed to the photograph of Abousrewil and said he had never seen him before, but since he was with Eter, he "must be a heavy hitter." Wiegand agreed, and the two decided to move against Abousrewil. They would not use any of their own officers, but would conduct around-the-clock surveillance themselves. The two colonels also decided that they would surreptitiously enter the apartment as quickly as possible and search the new arrival's possessions.

The day after his arrival, the new Libyan member of the East Berlin terrorist scene left the apartment in an LPB car driven by Eter. Wiegand, who stood watch, had neglected to take the usual additional precautions, such as posting lookouts. He picked the locks on the Pfenninghaus apartment. A cheap imitation leather valise was in plain view and unlocked on a kitchen table. It was crammed with documents, all in Arabic. Wiegand also found two sketches, one of which he recognized as a location at West Berlin's Tempelhof Airport that was being used almost exclusively by the U.S. military. The other showed the locations of the Pan American Airways and British Airways ticket offices at the Europa Centrum, a high-rise office building in West Berlin. Wiegand knew that he had found the plans for new terrorist attacks, and he quickly photographed them.

Back at Stasi headquarters, Wiegand told his translators that he was in a hurry and to make just a rough translation of the documents. The translations completed, the colonel saw that his guesses were correct. Simultaneous bombings of the Pan American and British Airways ticket offices were scheduled for November 25, the day before the American Thanksgiving holiday.

The last telephone check-in from Stuchly had placed Abousrewil at the bar in the Palast Hotel on Liebknechtstrasse—in the center of the city, some four miles from Stasi headquarters. He appeared to be waiting for someone. Wiegand stuffed copies of the documents and sketches into a briefcase and headed for the hotel. When he walked into the lobby, he spotted Stuchly watching the entrance to the bar, and joined him. Wiegand pulled the documents from his briefcase and told his colleague: "I have it all. Thanks to typical Arab *Schlamperei* [sloppiness], I had no trouble finding this stuff. Abousrewil is not only a member of the secret service but he is also planning new bombings."

Stuchly looked at the sketches and simply said, "Let's go." Wiegand headed into the bar while Stuchly stationed himself at the entrance and ostentatiously assumed a "cop look," making sure that the Makarov pistol he carried in a shoulder holster could be seen by the Arab. Wiegand approached Abousrewil's table. Behaving as rudely as he knew how, he waved the documents before the Arab's face. The Libyan secret service man, startled and staring wide-eyed at the papers, began to rise from his chair. Wiegand pushed him down.

"Meine Unterlagen! [my documents]" Abousrewil exclaimed in bad German, glancing uneasily at the doorway where Stuchly stood, arms crossed, pistol in plain sight, staring menacingly at the Arab. Wiegand told the man that he knew the papers were his, but not to worry, as they were only copies and the originals were still in his suitcase. The colonel then showed his credentials. "I am a ranking member of the Ministry for State Security and I am going to give you a message as a courtesy between colleagues, so to speak. We know everything you plan to do. We were bystanders once and kept our mouths shut. But not this time." Wiegand then pulled a bluff. "This morning we notified the West Berlin police about everything and gave them your photographs." He showed the Libyan a number of photos, starting with the ones taken secretly on his arrival and continuing through a series of others taken later, to make clear that he had been under constant surveillance. Wiegand told Abousrewil that he would "never get back to Libya" if he carried out his plans, and advised him to get out of East Germany quickly and never to return. "And while you're here, don't make any false moves. . . . We are very edgy." Before the Libyan terrorist could reply, Wiegand turned and left the bar.

While in Berlin, neither Arab crossed through the wall to the West. In fact, they rarely left their respective apartments. On May 20, Wiegand and Colonel Stuchly followed Abousrewil and Musbah Abulgassem to Schönefeld, where they boarded a plane for Tripoli. When the Libyan Airlines jet lifted off, Wiegand began to chuckle. Stuchly asked what the colonel found amusing. "Simple: I made another set of copies of Abousrewil's papers and sent them off to the Tripoli center with a note extending greetings from the MfS."

Two months later, on July 1, Abdukarim El Sadek, a member of Colonel Qaddafi's personal staff charged with supervising Libyan intelligence, arrived in East Berlin. Wiegand's agents inside the Libyan diplomatic mission reported that El Sadek inspected the intelligence residencies in the LPB and investigated charges of gross misconduct against Keshlaf, Chraidi, Eter, and Abousrewil. The inspector returned to Tripoli July 31. A report written by El Sadek and obtained by the Stasi through agents in Tripoli said that the LPB was "totally controlled and hamstrung by the MfS." Therefore secret operations in the DDR "have been totally compromised."

The *Operationsspiele* (operational games) played by Wiegand and Stuchly appeared to have had the desired effect on the Libyan intelligence chief, Younis Belqassim, as well. The games, as Wiegand called them, included supplying double agents with evidence of infiltration of the LPB by agents of Western intelligence services and the MfS. Wiegand had also assembled a number of videotapes and voice recordings that he had delivered to Belqassim as proof that his men had been violating the tenets of morality decreed by the Koran. Almost all had engaged in sexual orgies, had been caught drunk in public, had used narcotics, or had committed crimes such as smuggling and currency speculation.

From his agents Wiegand learned that El Sadek had recommended to the Libyan leadership that the use of the LPB as a cover for intelligence and terrorist activities be discontinued. This was accomplished in 1988. East German counterespionage officers surmised that the Libyans then began to use only illegals—i.e., deep-cover agents without diplomatic protection.

The final report of Operation Lux leaves little doubt that Wiegand's "games" prevented the bombing of the Pan American Airways and British Airways ticket counters. In addition, they most likely had deterred other terrorist attacks, including the murders of three Qaddafi opponents and the storming of a synagogue in West Berlin for the purpose of taking hostages. Planned attacks against the American school bus, the drive-in restaurant, the gasoline station, and the Springer newspaper building also were not carried out.

In summer 1990, five of the Libyan terrorists were still in East Germany, including Musbah Eter, who had returned as a correspondent for the Libyan JANA news agency. Arrest warrants issued in West Berlin were ignored. By then, the Ministry for State Security had been dissolved. Michael Diestel, the interior minister of the last East German government, who was responsible for law enforcement, allegedly refused to turn over the files on the La Belle bombing and on other terrorist actions to West Berlin prosecutors. When the files finally were given to West Berlin police, the terrorists had escaped. Also, all memoranda bearing Erich Honecker's signature or initials had been removed from the dossier.

Ali Mansur, who had scouted West Berlin locales for possible attacks, was detained briefly by West Berlin police in mid-August 1990 but was released for lack of evidence. Unsettled by Mansur's arrest, Eter quickly returned to Tripoli in summer 1990.

In January 1991, West Berlin police got lucky. Faour Daher, the owner of the Down Town disco had returned to West Berlin from his sanctuary in Libya. Daher was arrested on an unspecified sex charge, but there was no direct evidence tying him to the attack on the La Belle discotheque.

THE LA BELLE BOMBING SOLVED

The Berlin prosecutor was determined to solve the bombing. In 1994 he got his first break.[12] Investigators working with the West Germans had located Yasser Chraidi in Lebanon, where he was serving an eighteen-month prison sentence for a petty crime. A request for extradition was honored in May 1995, and Chraidi was brought back to Berlin. Eter also was arrested after he returned to Berlin. Chraidi and Eter steadfastly denied having had any part in the bombing. An investigative judge ordered that Chraidi be held in pretrial custody but ruled insufficient evidence against Eter, who was released and immediately left Berlin. Although probers had the Stasi case files on the bombing, which were turned over in 1990, as well as those Colonel Wiegand had brought with him when he defected in 1989, they were still combing the Stasi archive. In summer 1996 they found a torn file. After the file was painstakingly reconstructed, the prosecutor was able to get an arrest warrant and to wrap up the case.

In October 1996, Berlin detectives arrested Ali Chaana and his wife, Verena. On the same day, Greek police arrested Andrea Häusler, Verena Chaana's sister, at a resort south of Thessaloníki where she was vacationing with her boyfriend. She was extradited in January 1997. Murder indictments subsequently were filed against Chraidi, Ali Chaana, and his wife Verena. Häusler and Eter were charged as accessories, but Eter had disappeared. Police tracked him down in Rome, where he was arrested by an Italian antiterrorist squad on August 26, 1997 and quickly extradited to Berlin. The overwhelming evidence against these four substantially confirmed the information that Colonel Wiegand had supplied ten years earlier, although Wiegand did not know the roles played by the two women and Ali Chaana, the Stasi informer code-named Alba.

Ali Chaana had met Verena Hampel in 1971, in East Berlin, where she worked as a secretary. He was then living in West Berlin. The following year the couple applied for a marriage permit and an exit visa, intending to move to Lebanon. At this point the Stasi became involved. Permission to marry was denied them, and pressure was applied on Verena Hampel to sever her relations with Chaana. However, Verena became pregnant in January 1981. Eight months later the Stasi issued orders that Chaana be refused entry to East Berlin. Chaana then had a covert meeting with a Stasi officer during which he agreed to become an unofficial collaborator. Verena also agreed to become a Stasi informer and was given the cover name Petra Müller. As a result, permission to marry was granted and Verena was allowed to leave for West Berlin, which she did in early 1982. Both Ali Chaana and his wife pursued various minor espionage assignments, such as investigating addresses given them by their Stasi handlers and providing names for possible recruitment.

In 1984, Ali Chaana opened a restaurant. It failed after three months, and the couple was deeply in debt. Marital problems followed, but the Chaanas continued living in one apartment. Verena had not held a regular job since 1985. She had stopped spying and was living on welfare payments and her earnings as a prostitute. By that time the Stasi had paid her a total of DM14,000 (about US$4,500). Ali Chaana meanwhile worked diligently as informer Alba, maintaining contact with Libyans in general and with Yasser Chraidi in particular. When Keshlaf and Chraidi were ordered by Libyan intelligence to scout locations suitable for attack, Chraidi enlisted Ali Chaana's help. They came up with six possible locales, winnowed to three at a meeting at the People's Bureau in East Berlin on March 30. Finally, Keshlaf and Elamin, the two Libyan intelligence operatives assigned to East Berlin, decided on La Belle.

On April 3, Masud Abuagela, an explosives expert flown in from Libya, prepared the bomb while Chraidi was in West Berlin persuading Ali Chaana to have his wife take the bomb to the discotheque. Verena agreed, and Chraidi gave her DM6,000 (about US$2,500) to do the job. Her husband received DM9,000 (about US$3,750).

On the evening of April 4, Verena asked her sister Andrea, who lived in the same apartment and knew about the plot, to accompany her. They arrived at La Belle before midnight, Verena carrying a large cloth bag holding the bomb. They sat in a corner close to the bar. Andrea shielded Verena as she set the timer following Chaana's instructions. Verena order a small bottle of champagne. Later, Enzo Dinunno, the owner of the disco, instructed bartender Steve Richards to serve the two women a concoction called "Kiwi Wonder." A patron, Ralf Seefeld, talked to the two women, then danced with Andrea. After 1:00 A.M. the place began to fill up with GIs because the U.S. Army clubs had closed. At 1:35, the two women left La Belle, hailed a taxi, and returned to their apartment. It is unlikely that they heard the bomb go off five minutes later. Witnesses described the sound as a muffled bang.

Verena Chaana and her sister Andrea were later positively identified as the women who had sat at the spot where investigators determined the explosion had occurred. Musbah Eter confessed to his part as an accessory but denied killing the suspected CIA agent Ashur in May 1985. There was no word from the prosecution as to whether the women admitted playing a role. However, based on the details contained in the indictment, one can intelligently speculate that the women confessed. The trial of the five perpetrators was scheduled for spring 1997 but had to be postponed because of the death of a key witness. Because German justice proceeds at a snail's pace, an official told the author, the trial could last as long as four years.

10

PLAYGROUND FOR INTERNATIONAL TERRORISTS

THE EAST GERMAN COMMUNIST leadership's support of international terrorism began in the mid-1960s, when the Soviet Union's worldwide subversive activities were taxing its capabilities. The buildup of the country's military arsenal, especially of nuclear weapons, was taking a financial toll on Moscow.

In June 1960, the Kremlin's emissaries visited their East European allies and demanded that they participate in Third World "political activities." Motivated primarily by the desire to save money, the Soviets first assigned the Middle East and Africa to East Germany.[1] Later they added Latin America. Walter Ulbricht, the SED party leader and government chief who once worked as a Soviet secret police agent, tackled the task with fervor. Ulbricht and his Politburo saw this as a perfect chance to establish important economic ties and achieve diplomatic recognition for the GDR, at least by Third World countries. East Germany had been virtually isolated by Bonn's Hallstein Doctrine, which called for severing diplomatic relations with any nation that recognized East Germany. This situation changed in late 1960, when West German Chancellor Willy Brandt proclaimed a new policy of rapprochement with Eastern Europe—a policy that became known as *Ostpolitik*.

Contacts in the developing countries were initially clandestine, chiefly effected by Mielke's Ministry for State Security. MfS officers trained underground communist cadres and others with antipathy toward the West, especially the United States and Israel. These contacts increased to the point where the SED Politburo decided that a special institution should be established to carry out further clandestine work.[2]

Herman Axen, chief of the Politburo's International Department, became the spear carrier for this effort. He found an eager partner in Stasi chief Erich Mielke, whose own MfS school at Potsdam-Eiche was tailor-made for the task. Mielke ordered the establishment of a Department for International Relations. It was not housed within the college campus but was ensconced at a top secret location near Potsdam, just outside East Berlin. The new department opened in late 1969, and for several years, its "students" were primarily members of Yasser Arafat's Palestine Liberation Organization (PLO). Hundreds were trained in intelligence and counterintelligence operations.[3] There was no need to train them in the use of weapons, explosives, or individual combat. At the department's secret inaugural ceremony, Mielke remarked: "These people already know how to fight. They can probably teach us a thing or two about explosives."[4]

By April 1971, Mielke's devotion to his job as secret police chief had reached workaholic proportions: Besides dealing with internal security and foreign espionage and maintaining relations with international terrorists, he was keeping watch on major developments within the party. He had learned that Moscow was becoming increasingly disturbed by the obstreperous behavior of Walter Ulbricht, his enthusiasm for helping "national liberation movements" notwithstanding. When Ulbricht was shunted aside, the Soviets decided that Erich Honecker should replace him.

Honecker had been Central Committee secretary for security affairs and thus was Mielke's comrade in arms. Mielke had come to terms with Honecker without stepping on Ulbricht's toes. Thus, when the Soviets gave the signal, it was only natural that the Stasi chief would support Honecker against Ulbricht. Honecker awarded Mielke a seat in the highest policymaking body of the party, the Politburo. From then on, Mielke had an absolutely free hand in running the Stasi, so long as it did not meddle in party affairs. Especially in questions concerning East Germany's relations with terrorists, Honecker was a pliable leader who never failed to authorize a request or follow a suggestion from Mielke.

STASI SOLIDARITY WITH TERRORISTS

In spring 1974, when Mielke returned from one of his many consultations in Moscow, he immediately ordered a major conference of senior

MfS department heads. It was held in a building that sat imposingly on a mound in the center of the huge MfS compound, in the Lichtenberg district of East Berlin. Stasi officers had nicknamed the place *Feldherrnhügel,* the field marshal's mound, because Mielke made his pronouncements there in the manner of a supreme commander. He opened the meeting with his usual call for vigilance against enemies of the state. Then he explained that "our friends," as he always called the Soviets, had once again urged greater international MfS engagement, particularly in the Middle East.

Only a handful of those assembled knew that the MfS had already been training Arab terrorists in clandestine camps around Berlin. But those who were in on the secret, like Colonel Rainer Wiegand of counterintelligence, realized at once that the subject was assistance to terrorism, although Mielke never used the word. The gist of the Stasi chief's talk was that the question of whether capitalism or socialism would achieve world supremacy would be decided in the Third World.

Mielke described the Arab world as especially critical to the outcome of this epic struggle, and said that "whoever controls the intelligence organizations of those countries will contribute decisively in the battle against imperialism." The ideological position put forth by Mielke explains why he had no qualms about the massive international efforts of the MfS, or more particularly, its collaboration with Middle Eastern security and intelligence services, including groups engaged in terrorism.

Mielke's first move to reinforce Soviet efforts was made two months after the meeting on the *Feldherrnhügel* and involved the People's Republic of Yemen, Moscow's closest ideological ally in the Arab world. The capital city of Aden with its excellent harbor was of major strategic importance as a base for Soviet naval operations in the Indian Ocean. The KGB had maintained a large contingent there for years, but its agents did not have an easy time of it. They found it difficult to infiltrate the Yemeni Marxist party and to work with government security and intelligence people because of constant intrigues. This was another reason why the MfS was asked by Moscow to provide help.

Department Three of Lieutenant General Markus Wolf's foreign intelligence directorate, the HVA, was assigned the Yemen project. This department was responsible for maintaining legal residencies in countries that had recognized the DDR diplomatically, and with supporting "liberation" movements. Colonel Siegfried Fiedler began his operations in Aden with 60 officers, and achieved such remarkable initial successes that the contingent was rapidly increased to 100.

As had the KGB before it, the Stasi found the Yemeni Ministry for State Security badly organized and extremely vulnerable to infiltration by opposition intelligence services. Fiedler's initial assignment was to restructure the organization along the lines of his own ministry and to place one of his officers in every department, as an "instructor." In this way the East Germans achieved a measure of control and gained access to all operational matters, including the training and support of terrorists: South Yemen was a primary training ground for various international terrorist organizations, which received logistical support from the Yemeni intelligence service. From its vantage point, the MfS was able to compile vast dossiers on the terrorist groups and their clandestine operations. The Stasi's activities in South Yemen were among its first major collaborative efforts with international terrorism outside East Germany.[5]

Wolf's foreign espionage operations benefited from his support of the various Middle Eastern and African intelligence services. As a quid pro quo, the Department Three received vital information on Western intelligence services. West Germans who had violated local laws or had otherwise become entangled were turned over to the Stasi for recruitment as spies. The East Germans were given full operational support in eavesdropping on western embassies, businessmen, and tourists in Africa and the Middle East. "We are able to operate as if we were at home," Colonel Fiedler once told Wiegand. Numerous top espionage operations of the MfS had their genesis in Middle Eastern countries. The HVA was also able to mount special operations when East German espionage agents were to be inserted into West Germany. These operations could only be carried out with the help of Yemen's security services, which in turn were rewarded by the HVA with blank passports and other documents, some forged. Wiegand also learned from colleagues that the MfS was willing to accept offers from terrorist organizations to liquidate Stasi defectors.

It cannot be emphasized enough that support of international terrorism did not primarily involve the Twenty-Second Main Directorate, the international antiterrorism section of the Stasi, but rather Department Three of the HVA. Long before internal counterintelligence faced the problem of terrorism, the HVA had established excellent contacts with foreign terrorist organizations, especially those with roots in the Arab world.[6] "It has to be pointed out that Wolf did not have the courage of his convictions that he is trying to convey in his memoirs," said former Colonel Wiegand. "Wolf was the best-informed insider of the MfS. As a member of the Kollegium [general staff], the party leadership, and as deputy minister, Wolf was not, as he claims, only responsible for foreign espionage. Instead, he was fully informed on all matters in which the MfS was involved. Wolf had the full confidence of Mielke in the 1980s and could have influenced him but didn't."

In East Germany, the training of "national liberation fighters" was continuing at a steady pace. Wiegand, responsible for the surveillance and control of foreigners residing in the DDR, had suspected for some time that the regime's collaboration with terrorist groups was broadening. He had no evidence, however, other than observing the increasing number of officials from radical Arab countries meeting with high-ranking party and government officials.

On March 16, 1979, Wiegand met with his agent Toni, a leader of a Kurdish organization who lived in West Berlin. The meeting turned out to be far from routine. The Kurd, in exile because of his opposition to the Iraqi regime, confided that Abu Daoud would be arriving at East Berlin's Schönefeld airport within a few days for meetings with terrorists operating in West Berlin and West Germany.

At that moment Wiegand remembered how shocked and sickened he had been by the photographs of the massacre at the Munich Olympic Games in 1972, in which eleven Israeli athletes and a West German police officer were killed. Five terrorists were shot to death by police. Abu Daoud, a leader of the Black September group, collaborating with Yasser Arafat's Palestine Liberation Organization, was identified by a surviving terrorist as the mastermind of the Munich carnage. Two years earlier Daoud had fled Jordan after being exposed as the leader of a Palestinian attempt to wrest power away from King Hussein. Daoud, alias Wali Saad and Radsi Jusif bin Hanna, was born in 1937 in Shilou near Jerusalem, where at one time he studied law and worked as a teacher. His given name was Mahmoud Odeh. In 1973 he was sentenced to death in Jordan for plotting to kill King Hussein. However, after Black September attacked Saudi embassies in Khartoum and Paris and threatened further terrorism against Jordan and other Arab countries, Hussein granted Daoud a full pardon.

DAOUD IN EAST GERMANY

Had Toni not been such a dependable informant, Wiegand would have dismissed the information as rubbish. The colonel had difficulty believing that Daoud would have the courage to travel to the DDR, especially to East Berlin. Wiegand puzzled over why he would feel so secure. Considering the borders with West Berlin, the Mossad (the Israeli intelligence service) and other security agencies could have easily located and liquidated him.

Details provided by Toni, including a message received from contacts in the Middle East, convinced Wiegand that Daoud would, indeed, travel to the DDR. The informant warned that Daoud probably would meet with terrorist groups to establish new command structures for West Berlin and West Germany, and at the same time, would plan new attacks.

Wiegand's aversion to terrorism spurred him into action. It was already late at night when he returned to his office at Stasi headquarters. He telephoned a number of his officers and ordered them to join him. During the night and the next morning, they sifted through dozens of files. Finally, the colonel wrote a report to Colonel General Bruno Beater, Mielke's first deputy, rather than to Mielke himself. Wiegand had judged that Beater was the real "hands-on" leader while Mielke was the political boss. The colonel, who described Beater as perhaps the only "human being" among the Stasi hierarchy, felt the Daoud problem would get a better hearing from this veteran communist who had fought in the Soviet Army during World War II.

Wiegand's top secret report, dated March 17, 1979, detailed the meeting with the informant and precise background information on Daoud. It also recommended that Daoud be arrested on arrival, or if arrest was not feasible for political reasons or because of fear of terrorist attacks against the DDR, that entry to the DDR be denied. As Wiegand was about to hand the report to one of his officers for delivery to the deputy minister, he was called by Colonel Harry Dahl, chief of the Twenty-Second Directorate. Dahl wanted to know what Wiegand planned to do about Abu Daoud.

Wiegand became leery. "What do you know about it?" he asked Dahl. Dahl replied that he had heard of Wiegand's inquiries during the night and that he knew Wiegand had been in contact with Lieutenant Colonel Helmut Voigt of the Twenty-Second Directorate. "Well, in that case we can work together," Wiegand proposed. "Daoud is planning to arrive at Schönefeld day after tomorrow. I think we should arrest him." Dahl, a usually jovial colleague, answered in a curt and cutting tone, "You're not going to arrest anybody! You keep your paws off! Abu Daoud is not coming to the DDR illegally but by invitation, and I have been personally charged by the minister to provide Daoud with around-the-clock protection."

Wiegand thought this was a joke. Before he could say anything, though, Dahl ordered him to drop the case, and added that if he did not want a broken leg, he had better not get involved. Because Dahl's demeanor was so unusual, Wiegand realized that he had overstepped his bounds. Despite it all, he dispatched his report to General Beater, who replied immediately. He was told that the Twenty-Second Directorate was in charge in this matter and was ordered to "stop all actions."

At this stage, however, it was too late for Wiegand to attempt to comply with the order: His agent Toni had already been activated and instructed to gather more information. In turn, Toni had mobilized his own network. Furthermore, how could he tell the Kurd that the government of East Germany had invited the Palestinian killer in and was treating him as an honored guest?

Though Wiegand could not arrest Abu Daoud, he could at least observe him and record his activities for possible future use. On March 19, 1979, he went to the airport and watched the notorious terrorist emerge from the first class section of an Interflug jet that had flown in from Damascus. To Wiegand's surprise, Daoud was welcomed by a full-fledged government delegation. The colonel was even more astonished when he spotted his old friend Wolfgang Krause acting as the delegation's major domo. Krause had once been a section chief in the international relations department of the SED's Central Committee. Wiegand had not seen him in some time, and he knew only that Krause traveled periodically to Lebanon and Syria on diplomatic assignments. Officials at the airport told Wiegand that Krause was now deputy director of the International Solidarity Committee of the DDR and that he had been appointed Abu Daoud's "honor escort." Daoud was driven off in a government limousine followed by another car that Wiegand recognized as belonging to the counterterrorism directorate. The colonel followed at a safe distance. Abu Daoud's first stop was at the imposing building of the Communist Party's Central Committee, in downtown East Berlin. The terrorist was a guest of honor at the Central Committee! Wiegand decided that nothing would surprise him any longer. His faith in the leadership of East Germany was steadily declining.

Wiegand knew that a reception was held for Daoud at the Central Committee but he did not know who was present, and he was cautious enough not to ask those who might have known. He would not have been shocked, however, if party boss Erich Honecker and Stasi chief Mielke had been there. From the Central Committee, Abu Daoud was taken to the offices of the Solidarity Committee for another reception. Finally he was checked into a posh suite at the Metropol, at that time East Germany's most luxurious hotel, on Friedrichstrasse, just a few blocks from the wall and Checkpoint Charlie. Wiegand noted that Daoud was guarded by officers of the counterterrorism department and not by the MfS bodyguards usually assigned to top government officials and VIP visitors.

During the week Abu Daoud spent in East Berlin, he was also given a reception at the mission of the Palestinian Liberation Organization and met with officials at the Syrian and South Yemeni embassies. After his departure, Colonel Dahl paid Wiegand a visit. "Well, did it finally dawn on you whom you wanted to arrest? He is a friend of our country, a high-ranking political functionary." Before he could continue, Wiegand's temper took over. "My God, Abu Daoud is a terrorist!" Dahl, now again in the role of the friendly, jovial associate, reached into the briefcase he had brought along and handed Wiegand a folder. "Who has proved that he is a terrorist? If the West Germans[7] had concrete evidence against him, he would have been listed in international wanted bulletins. Have you ever seen an international warrant on Daoud? Check it out after I leave, and then take a look at the file I gave you. Amuse yourself!"

Dahl was hardly out of the door when Wiegand reached for the thick book of international wanted notices. Dahl was correct. Daoud was not listed. When he opened Dahl's file, the first thing he saw was a large photograph with a label indicating that it was taken in April 1974 at the state funeral of French President Georges Pompidou. Daoud was shown among the mourners. Next Wiegand read about how Daoud was arrested in France in 1977 but almost immediately released with apologies. It turned out that Daoud, using the alias Radsi Jusif bin Hanna, was in France as a government guest on a political mission for the Palestine National Council, of which he was a member. He had been received by Foreign Minister Louis de Guiringaud shortly before the arrest. For the remainder of his stay in France, Abu Daoud was assigned two French police officers as bodyguards. Wiegand was not surprised that some Western countries were also handling Abu Daoud with kid gloves. He doubted, however, that their actions were as steeped in ideology as were those of the East German regime. Instead, Wiegand surmised, they were probably prompted by fear that any action taken against Daoud would lead to an increase in terrorism in their countries.

After Daoud's departure, Colonel Wiegand attended a meeting with the Hungarian and Polish counterintelligence services that provided him an opportunity to exchange views on terrorism. Whenever he mentioned Abu Daoud, the reaction was always, "He is not a terrorist!" Throughout the communist bloc Daoud traveled under the mantle of Palestinian political activism, and just as in the DDR, he was assigned secret police bodyguards. He would be met at plane-side and driven off without being subjected to the usual controls. He stayed only at luxury hotels. When East Berlin's Palast Hotel was completed, it became Daoud's home away from home. Wiegand noticed that he always occupied a suite at the end of a floor where security personnel could be posted rather unobtrusively. Later Wiegand told me: "That was also the time when I learned the meaning of 'normal' Arab behavior—hypocritically swearing off alcohol and abhorring immorality but in reality enjoying the high life. Women tumbled through their beds in droves. Money was thrown around. It was disgusting."

What also irked Wiegand was that he and his fellow officers helped pay for the terrorists' lifestyle. "We were forced to contribute an amount equal to Communist Party dues to the 'International Solidarity Fund' every other month." For the colonel this amounted to between DM120 and DM150 (about US$60 to $75, at the official rate then prevailing).

Krause of the International Solidarity Committee was a key figure in the East German government's coddling of Arab terrorists over many years. His committee had always been responsible for maintaining connections that might jeopardize other sensitive Communist Party relations, especially those with the Kurds. Publicly, the committee portrayed itself as a charitable institution merely contributing blankets, medicines, and money and occasionally providing job training. Krause met with Abu Daoud even after the wall came down; and after a new government was formed, the two met again to conduct negotiations, on December 12, 1989, at the PLO's embassy in East Berlin.

MIELKE AND THE PLO

Mielke's desire to strengthen the Stasi's relations with Arab terrorists was highlighted when he received the head of PLO intelligence, Abu Iyab (the nom de guerre of Salah Khalaf), on August 22, 1979.[8] Also present was Major General Gerhard Neiber, who had just returned from Ethiopia where he had led the Stasi group aiding the secret police of dictator Mengistu Haile Mariam. The third Stasi representative was Colonel Harry Dahl, head of the Twenty-Second Directorate. To properly impress the PLO visitor, Mielke held the meeting in his suite on the second floor of the ministerial building in the Stasi compound. Before settling down to business, Mielke showed Iyab through the lavishly appointed suite, each room of which was paneled in different kinds of wood—mahogany, oak, and birch. The Stasi minister was especially proud of his trophy room, where he displayed hundreds of gifts from "friendly" secret services and his collection of dozens of busts of Karl Marx and Lenin.

The Stasi chief opened the conference by asking Iyab to relay his thanks to Yasser Arafat for refraining from "carrying out any action against the American President during the Soviet-American summit meeting in Vienna." Mielke said he was pleased that Arafat "did everything to assure that this important international event proceeded without a hitch." Mielke emphasized that the DDR government was totally sympathetic to the aspirations of the PLO under Arafat: "We are paying great attention to the Palestine resistance and the other revolutionary forces fighting against the policies of the United States and against the provocations of the Israeli aggressor. Together with the Soviet Union and other socialist countries, we will do everything to support this just battle," he told Iyab.

With protocol formalities out of the way, Mielke got down to serious business. He pledged that his ministry would supply two sniper rifles of Western manufacture, with ammunition, as the PLO had requested, as well as any quantity of hand grenades desired. Special explosive devices for blowing up ships would also be made available. Iyab expressed his gratitude when Mielke said: "We will also furnish operational technical support by way of supplying explosives and training of cadres, and if the MfS does not have the materials on hand, we will obtain them. I hope that this will serve to strengthen the work of the PLO in this area." With such top-level encouragement, it was only a matter of time until terrorists would use East Berlin as a base to plan and carry out attacks against American and German targets.

THE JACKAL IN EAST GERMANY

Within days of Mielke's meeting with the PLO security chief, Wiegand was tipped off by an IM that a man who had entered the DDR using South Yemeni diplomatic passport No. 001278 was in fact Carlos the international terrorist. The last time he had known the Venezuelan-born killer's whereabouts was four years earlier. At that time, the Hungarian state security service (AVH) told the Stasi that he had entered Hungary and that its agents had made "contact" with him.[9] The Hungarians reported that Carlos, whose real name was Ilich Ramirez Sanchez, was under control—in other words he was being watched. Wiegand recalled speculation that Carlos was operating from a Hungarian base when he led an attack on the OPEC conference in Vienna, just before Christmas in 1975. Two Arab staff members and an Austrian state police officer were killed. Carlos and his gang had captured eleven oil ministers and demanded to be flown to Libya, and later, to Algeria. After releasing several ministers from countries of lesser importance, the terrorists threatened to murder the ministers from Saudi Arabia and Iran. Both were eventually ransomed by Austria, Iran, and Saudi Arabia, for a sum believed to have been in the tens of millions of dollars—perhaps as much as $50 million. The money was said to have been deposited in a bank in Aden. After the ministers were released, the gang fled to an unidentified Arab country, presumably Libya.

Was Carlos setting up a base in East Berlin? The fact that his movements were facilitated by South Yemen, with whom the Stasi was closely cooperating, could mean that someone in Berlin had granted him safe haven. Colonel Wiegand assigned a team of officers to obtain

This wanted poster prepared by German police shows Ilich Ramirez Sanchez, commonly known as Carlos, "the Jackal," one of the deadliest terrorists active in the 1970s and 1980s. Carlos was given safe haven in East Germany and other communist countries and allowed to carry out his bloody assignments in behalf of various Arab extremist groups. In 1997, Carlos was arrested and tried in France. He was found guilty on three counts of murder of unarmed French intelligence agents in the 1970s. On December 24, 1997, Carlos was sentenced to life imprisonment. Courtesy German Federal Police.

photographs of the "visitor." Comparing the surveillance photos with pictures that over the years had circulated through the world press convinced him that the South Yemeni "diplomat" was in fact Carlos. Wiegand contacted an officer of the Twentieth Directorate, which was responsible for the security of party and state organs. This officer confirmed that the man was Carlos. Wiegand was told that the Twentieth Directorate had received word on the terrorist's stay in the DDR directly from Mielke, who had ordered that nothing be done about Carlos "except to observe." Wiegand said his contacts at the directorate found themselves in a peculiar situation.

> They started watching and were perplexed when they saw that Carlos was being escorted by officers from the counterterrorism directorate, including Lieutenant Colonel Voigt, who had also been associated with Abu Daoud. So on the one hand, they needed to observe in order to determine with whom he met; and on the other hand, he needed to be protected so that he himself would not become the victim of an attack.

Constant surveillance revealed that Carlos spent much of his time at the South Yemeni embassy and the Metropol Hotel, where he was staying. The all-night bar at Haus Berlin, the hotel in the former Stalin Allee, was also a favorite hangout of Carlos and his entourage. The bar on the top floor was attractively decorated, and a fountain surrounded by fake palm trees gave the place a tropical motif. Stasi agents also noted that in addition to being supported by South Yemen, Carlos had a car and chauffeur provided by the Syrian embassy.

When Carlos was on another visit to East Berlin, in summer 1983, the French cultural center Maison de France on West Berlin's fashionable Kurfürstendamm, the city's main boulevard, was bombed. One person was killed and twenty-four others were injured. Carlos was widely believed to have been behind the attack; but not until seven years later was it proved that he was responsible and that the Stasi counterterrorism directorate had played an active role in the crime.[10] The crime was part of a secret operation the Stasi had set up with Carlos (Operation Separat).

In winter 1982, a German terrorist identified as Johannes Weinreich traveled to East Berlin on a Syrian diplomatic passport.[11] A routine x-ray examination of his baggage revealed 24 kilograms (52.8 pounds) of explosives. Responding to the customs alert, Lieutenant Colonel Voigt, who had previously escorted Carlos during his East Berlin visits, took possession of the explosives. Weinreich, whose cover name was Steve, was questioned for a few days and then released. Voigt had learned that Weinreich was Carlos's right-hand man, and therefore Weinreich was allowed to remain in East Berlin and was given a room in the Metropol Hotel.

A few months later, Voigt and several Stasi officers visited the hotel and searched Weinreich's luggage. They found a sketch of the Maison de France, indicating where the explosive was to be placed. The terrorist explained that the bombing was intended to force the release of Magdalena Koop, a member of Carlos's gang who was then imprisoned in France. Incredibly, Voigt returned the drawing. Worse yet, he handed over the bomb as well, on condition that it would not be transported to West Berlin in a diplomatic vehicle, to make sure the East German regime could not be implicated.[12] Weinreich gave the bomb to another associate of Carlos's, a Palestinian named El Sibai. It was El Sibai who planted and set off the explosives.[13]

Not long after learning that Carlos was a special protégé of the Hungarian communist government, Wiegand attended a conference of top-level counterintelligence officials from Hungary, Poland, and Czechoslovakia. At that meeting, the East German colonel inquired about Carlos. He found that all East European countries had been visited by Carlos at one time or another, although Hungary remained his main base.[14] All of the countries had refrained from taking any action against him, on the "recommendation" of the Soviet KGB. The MfS, too, held back. Wiegand did not know then that the KGB was involved: His orders always came from Mielke, presumably in connivance with the Politburo.

Wiegand was still curious about the Soviet angle, especially when he was informed by Twentieth Directorate that Carlos was again in East Berlin, planning terrorist attacks. He contacted KGB Colonel Boris Smirnov, head of counterespionage (Department Two) at the Karlshorst headquarters, and asked for advice on how to proceed in the Carlos matter. Again Wiegand found that the Soviets "kept themselves veiled like the oracle of Delphi." Smirnov's answer was nebulous: He said only that the MfS should follow the example of others. So long as Carlos could not be clearly implicated by Western authorities, Wiegand was told, he should "let him be and just watch him." Besides, the KGB colonel added, Carlos was causing more damage to the West than any action against him would be worth. When Wiegand suggested that he should at least detain Carlos for interrogation, the KGB officer said: "I wouldn't do that. . . . You'd be pouring a bucket of water over your head." Wiegand realized then that the Soviets, too, were guided by the axiom, If you take action against an activist, your own neck might be on the block.

INTERNECINE BATTLES

Not only was East Berlin a base for terrorists waging their war against the West; for nearly two decades it was also a major arena for internecine battles among myriad Arab intelligence services. Hundreds of politically active students from various Arab countries were studying in the DDR as well as at institutions of higher learning in West Berlin. In addition, hundreds of dissidents had formed a number of organizations opposed to the various regimes—notably, those of Iraq, Iran, Libya, Syria, and South Yemen.

Colonel Wiegand observed that the activities of the secret services mirrored the Arab problem: "Sometimes they fought one another, and at other times the former foes embraced and swore an oath to brotherhood. Sometimes they even collaborated in a limited way; but on the whole, they remained distrustful of each other." The colonel's counterspy team, for example, once discovered through an Arab informer that the Libyans had recruited a third secretary of the Iraqi embassy, who worked successfully for them over long period. The Iraqis, in turn, were able to place three Kurds inside the Libyans' network in East Germany. The Stasi would take advantage of the situation and focus on diplomats who were actually intelligence officers. Wiegand's men would summon them to the foreign ministry, where the chief of consular service, Jochen Vogel, would introduce them as MfS members. The "diplomats" would be told that one of their citizens had committed some criminal offense, usually smuggling or currency speculation. However, there would be no arrest or expulsion if they could reach a "gentlemen's agreement." The Stasi officers would then provide confidential information about political opponents or other embassies. After playing this game for a month or two, the seeds sown by the Stasi would sprout, and this one-way street of suspicion became a two-way operation. "Then they came to us and dropped each other into the frying pan—the Libyans snitched on the Iraqis, the Iraqis on the Libyans, the Syrians on the Iraqis, and so forth," Wiegand recalled.

KURDS UNDER ATTACK

In time, these mutual denunciations yielded significant information. For example, toward the end of July 1980 the Syrians provided a lead that the first secretary of the Iraqi embassy, Khalid J. Jaber, and his chauffeur, Hay Ali Mahmoud, were preparing a bomb attack on a Congress of Kurdish Students in West Berlin. Mahmoud was actually the "resident," or station chief, of the Iraqi intelligence service in East Berlin. The Syrians had received their information from a Kurdish exile living in West Berlin whom the Iraqis had recruited to set off the explosives. Wiegand used another Kurd who was vehemently opposed to Saddam Hussein to tip off West Berlin authorities.

On August 1, 1980, at about 8:30 A.M., detectives of the West Berlin police special action command watched Jaber and Mahmoud drive through the U.S. Army's Checkpoint Charlie, the diplomatic crossing point through the Berlin Wall. They were in a gray Mercedes limousine bearing East German foreign office diplomatic license plates CD-21-09. The West Berlin officers followed the Iraqis to the district of Wedding, where the Mercedes stopped. Jaber and Mahmoud got out of the car, and the chauffeur retrieved an attaché case from the trunk.

Both men walked a short distance to a street corner, where another man was waiting for the attaché case. The third man was the Kurd who had tipped off the Syrians. After he walked away, the two Iraqis returned to their car.

When Jaber and Mahmoud were about to drive away, an unmarked police car stopped alongside the Mercedes and another stopped in front of it. Mahmoud reversed, sideswiped a parked car, and careened across the center strip dividing the road, but was blocked by another police car. Jaber jumped from the car and tried to flee. He was wrestled to the ground by detectives. Still at the wheel and trying to escape, Mahmoud rammed the police car. At that moment, a detective yanked the car door open and dragged the Iraqi secret service station chief out of the seat. A brief struggle ensued during which a loaded Walther PPK 9mm pistol with a silencer attached fell out of Mahmoud's jacket pocket.[15]

The attaché case was taken to a bomb squad laboratory for x-ray examination. It was equipped with a coded numerical lock set on 0. Had another number been set, the bomb would have exploded in 44 minutes. Specialists dismantled the bomb and found that it held 575 grams (1.2 pounds) of pentaerythritoltetranitrate (PETN). Experts describe PETN as one of the most powerful explosives used as a base charge in sea mines, torpedoes, and antiaircraft shells.

Meanwhile, the Kurd, identified as Hussain Said, told West Berlin police that he had met the Iraqis on July 28 in West Berlin. Jaber, the first secretary, gave him 500 marks (about US$200) and conveyed "greetings from President Saddam Hussein." He was to take an attaché case with "some noisemakers" to the meeting room at a youth hostel, where the Kurdish students were assembled, "just to scare them a little."

An arrest warrant was issued for Jaber and Mahmoud. They were charged with thirty-five counts of attempted murder (the number of students in the conference room at the time the bomb was to have been detonated). But there would never be a trial: The Iraqi government warned that the lives of two West German engineers held as hostages in Iraq were in jeopardy. German Foreign Minister Hans-Dietrich Genscher, a liberal Free Democratic Party member, was already serving in a coalition government ruled by the Social Democratic Party under Chancellor Helmut Schmidt. Genscher insisted that the Iraqi terrorists be deported. West Berlin, however, was still subject to Allied occupation laws, which stipulated severe penalties for illegal possession of explosives and firearms. Since the Iraqis were arrested in the French sector, French authorities could have assumed jurisdiction, but they did nothing. At the same time, the West German government had no authority over then Socialist Governing Mayor Dietrich Stobbe, who initially stood firm and insisted that the Iraqis be tried.

Stobbe eventually succumbed to heavy political pressure and agreed to the extradition, saying that the Bonn government had requested it on "urgent foreign policy and security policy grounds." In addition, the mayor said, "improving cooperation in international counterterrorism activities also played a role." In return for gaining the freedom of its diplomats, the Iraqi government said in the future it would "not assist in any terrorist attacks or other criminal activities in Berlin." It also pledged closer cooperation in antiterrorist activities and the denial of safe haven to German terrorists on Iraqi territory. Lastly, the Iraqi government assured the West Germans that the diplomats would not return to their posts in East Berlin.

On September 17, 1980, Jaber and Mahmoud were flown to Frankfurt and placed on a direct flight to Baghdad. West Berlin authorities were astounded when the names of the two terrorists reappeared on the East German diplomatic accreditation roster issued November 1, 1980. Mahmoud, the secret service station chief, also was given a job with the ADN, the official news agency of the East German government. Once again the communist leadership had taken potential mass murderers under its wing.

The bombing of the Kurdish students probably would have occurred had it not been for the vicious rivalry among East Berlin's Arab "diplomats." So far as Colonel Wiegand was concerned, all the solemn avowals of Arab unity were nothing more than hackneyed propaganda. "They fought each other like pit bulls and delivered one another to the knife." Citing an example, Wiegand said: "When the situation about the poison gas factory in Rabta (Libya) made news in 1986, you wouldn't believe the information we obtained from the Iraqi embassy. I believe that the Iraqis wanted the information to be known so that the Americans would take action against Libya and destroy Qaddafi, who had made no secret of his ambition to be the leader maximus of the Arabs. Therefore, I believe that Saddam was already at that time pursuing a clear strategy to become the supreme Arab leader. Something else, no other secret service operated on our territory so brutally and with so much contempt for human life as that of Iraq." Wiegand would not forget seeing Iraqi dissidents, especially Kurds, whose bodies displayed evidence of extreme torture. "I had never experienced that with the Libyans. . . . It was gruesome."

IRAQI MAYHEM

Iraqi "diplomats" created a stir in summer 1981 when they seized an Iraqi dissident in broad daylight at the busy Alexanderplatz in the heart of East Berlin.[16] They dragged him by the hair and feet to a car bearing diplomatic plates assigned to the Iraqi embassy. But before they could stow the hapless victim in the trunk of the automobile, several passersby intervened and foiled the abduction. The police report had not even reached the Stasi when the Iraqi ambassador appeared at the foreign ministry to protest "a provocation of imperialist forces" against his people on Alexanderplatz.

Beginning in 1981, Colonel Wiegand's counterintelligence team carried out a series of operations under the code name Orient. It was an effort to protect dissident Iraqi students, especially those who were members of the Iraqi Communist Party, from attacks by agents of Saddam Hussein's secret service. Wiegand told me: "Some barely escaped the murder squads by jumping out of dormitory windows several floors above ground. We kept others hidden for weeks in MfS safe houses to save them from the Iraqi murderers."

The Iraqi government delivered a note protesting the MfS action to the East German ambassador in Baghdad and presented photographs of MfS surveillance teams. The Iraqis also accused the Stasi of planning the execution of members of the Baath Party who were living in the DDR. Although Honecker, the party leader and head of government, and Stasi chief Mielke were kept up-to-date on the terror attacks and attempted murders by the Iraqi secret service in East Germany, the Iraqi government's complaint was heeded. Wiegand and his associates were reprimanded and ordered to keep their hands off.

Iraqi citizens living in the DDR, especially students, were under the constant surveillance of Iraqi intelligence. The Stasi noticed time and again that students would fail to return from semester breaks without notifying their schools. They just disappeared. Wiegand figured that the Iraqi government killed anyone who had fallen out of favor. "They seemed to be operating according to the idea that it is better to kill an innocent person than to allow one dissident to run around loose."

The ruthlessness of the Iraqis also caught the attention of the Stasi's Twentieth Directorate headed by Major General Paul Kienberg. Among this directorate's tasks was the control of churches and the suppression of underground political movements. Rainer Eppelmann, a Lutheran pastor who had formed a group opposing the communist regime, was a particular thorn in the side of the directorate. Rather than arrest Eppelmann and risk a further escalation in antigovernment activities, the Stasi church controllers resorted to a dastardly scheme. In 1988 they sent a postcard to the Iraqi embassy in East Berlin denouncing Eppelmann as an enemy of Islam. It said the pastor hated and had cursed the Islamic religion.

One evening after church service, Eppelmann was visited by the Iraqi embassy's first secretary Chalabi, who said he had heard about the pastor's political activities and just wanted to meet him. In the course of the meeting, Chalabi questioned Eppelmann on religion and on his feelings about Islam. At the end of their chat, Chalabi showed the postcard to Eppelmann. "I see that somebody doesn't like you and wants to get rid of you," the Arab diplomat said. "When we received this card, we had our doubts, and I needed to talk to you before sending it to Baghdad, because if we had done that, you would have been put on a liquidation list." Eppelmann had come close to being killed, and he knew then that the postcard had been sent by the Twentieth Directorate.[17]

ABU NIDAL RETURNS

Hotel Neptune in the Baltic port city of Warnemünde was the site of a clandestine meeting late in April 1988, between Colonel Wiegand and an agent code-named Carsten Berg. The colonel was accompanied by one of his section chiefs, Major Klaus Schilling. Two years had elapsed since the bombing of the La Belle discotheque in West Berlin, and Wiegand was more aggressive than ever in using informants to locate potential terrorists. Even though the SED leadership and Mielke still enforced the hands-off-terrorists order, they had at least approved of surveillance, undoubtedly in order to make certain that no bombs went off on DDR territory.

Carsten Berg was a Lebanese studying at a college near Cottbus, a grimy industrial town southeast of Berlin, close to the Polish border. The three men were enjoying their dinner after the informant had been debriefed on his latest assignment, and the conversation turned to small talk. Suddenly the informant said he and a friend were in Berlin on a recent Saturday and met an Arab who tried to recruit them for the Abu Nidal organization. Wiegand continued to eat and paid no attention. "I think this guy is beginning to see white elephants," the colonel said sotto voce to Major Schilling, who nodded in agreement. Wiegand knew that Abu Nidal had been in East Germany briefly in 1985. But the colonel and other competent counterespionage officers had been convinced for years that his organization was not operating in East Germany. Nevertheless, the Stasi had remained watchful, because Abu Nidal, otherwise known as Sabri Khalil al-Banna, was the ringleader of the most ferocious of all terrorist groups.

When Wiegand showed no interest, Berg repeated what he had said, and finally the colonel replied laconically that he would listen. The agent then told them that he had gone to the Berolina Hotel, an Arab hangout on East Berlin's Karl-Marx-Allee, with a fellow Lebanese student, Al Chimmy. There they met an Arab whom Berg knew by sight.

The man was a scientist teaching at Leipzig's Karl Marx University, but the informant didn't know his name. As Wiegand listened, he realized that there had indeed been an attempt to recruit his agent. Carsten Berg took several copies of the Abu Nidal publication *The Fighter* from his briefcase and handed them to the colonel. He also had an Abu Nidal training pamphlet on how to spot agents of the Mossad, the Israeli intelligence service, and their operational methods.

Wiegand studied the papers and recognized that they were identical to the Nidal publications obtained abroad by HVA, the foreign intelligence arm of the MfS. Abu Nidal material had never surfaced in the DDR. Wiegand decided to take the matter seriously. He instructed his IM to meet again with this mysterious acquaintance but to turn down recruitment. (Wiegand had been using Berg to spy on the Libyan intelligence service and felt a double-track operation could collide at some point.) However, he told the agent to talk his friend Al Chimmy into joining the Abu Nidal group. Wiegand figured that Al Chimmy would pick up additional information, which would reach him via Berg.

Wiegand and Major Schilling returned to Berlin late that night. The following morning, Wiegand telephoned Lieutenant Colonel Wolfgang Stuchly, the counterespionage officer with whom he had worked on the La Belle case. "Listen, Wolfgang, I had a *Treff* yesterday and heard an unbelievable story about somebody recruiting for Abu Nidal, and I even obtained some Abu Nidal publications." Stuchly became excited and wanted to know where Wiegand's clandestine meeting had taken place. Wiegand, conscious of the first rule of espionage—that an agent's identity must be totally protected—replied that it was none of his business. He demanded to know why Stuchly was so excited. "Because I heard the same thing yesterday, and now I believe we are sharing an agent right here in Berlin." Wiegand urged his associate to calm down and to come to his office, where they would discuss the matter. They compared notes on the meetings, which had taken place at different times and places but which had yielded nearly identical information—not an ironclad verification by any means, but at least an indication that there might be something to the story. Stuchly's agent also could not identify the man who had approached him—the superficial description could have fit a hundred Arabs. They decided to send a surveillance team to cover the next meeting between Berg and the mysterious Abu Nidal recruiter.

A week later Wiegand showed Stuchly photographs taken of Berg and his Abu Nidal contact. "It can't be true, it can't be true!" shouted the impulsive Stuchly, pointing to the photograph the Stasi watchdogs had taken secretly. Berg's contact was none other than Hassan, one of Stuchly's own agents.

Stuchly explained that he had been Hassan's control officer for seven years. The man was an assistant professor of natural sciences at Karl Marx University. He had been granted permanent residence as a political refugee and was one of Stuchly's most important sources on Iraqi and Libyan secret service agents and their diplomatic connections at the embassies of those countries. Wiegand asked whether the man was reliable. Instead of replying, Stuchly ran to his office and returned with the Hassan file, which Wiegand read with astonishment. He had never known of an informant who denounced Arab diplomats so fanatically and so vehemently. Hassan had reported on major smuggling operations, currency speculations and manipulation, illegal gold dealings, and counterfeit money operations by diplomats attached to the Iraqi and Syrian embassies in East Berlin. Wiegand had been aware of extensive criminal activities involving diplomats. Because of the strict rules on protection of sources, however, he did not know that the bulk of the information had come from a single man. In fact, Wiegand's staff had become preoccupied with investigating such activities between 1978 and 1980. Although they had made many arrests in connection with organized international criminal activities, they had less time for their primary counterespionage task—keeping their eyes on foreign intelligence services and terrorist activities. For that reason Colonel Wiegand had urged the establishment of a new section to deal exclusively with smuggling by diplomats and international criminal activities involving foreigners residing in the DDR. Stuchly had relinquished control of Hassan to that section when it became fully operational because he had been so successful in ferreting out criminals. In his final evaluation of his agent, Stuchly wrote that he was "so totally devoted to the Koran that he goes crazy when these Arabs come here and whore around, engage in sex orgies, wallow in alcohol, and use narcotics."

Wiegand read the notation and sensed that he had solved another puzzle. He was sure now that Hassan really was in league with Abu Nidal: Wiegand had read a lot of background on Nidal, who seemed to be as zealous as Hassan when it came to the teachings of the Koran. Both abhorred the loose life some Arabs were enjoying. As a result, Wiegand theorized, Abu Nidal and like-minded Arabs would not shy away from using the Stasi when they themselves were unable to settle problems of behavioral self-discipline among Arabs. Wiegand was chagrined that the MfS had been "working all the while for the Abu Nidal organization when we threw out Arab diplomats or jailed nondiplomats." Hassan had triggered probes into forty or fifty such cases.

Hassan had been so important that Stuchly personally controlled him for a long time and went to the clandestine meetings himself. "Mein Gott, I told him so often that I am interested in terrorism and information on possible espionage. But he never had anything . . . always had this stuff on smuggling, money speculation . . . these things that violated the Koran."

Stuchly found it difficult to believe that he had been so thoroughly fooled, and he remained skeptical. For that reason Wiegand was elated when the first positive report arrived from agent Berg and his friend Al Chimmy. The two had met again with Hassan on a Saturday at East Berlin's Berolina Hotel. Apparently, Hassan could only come to East Berlin on weekends, when he did not have to teach. Berg told him that he could not join, and Hassan accepted the decision, saying they needed only fighters, not cowards. Before dismissing him, he warned Berg that he would be liquidated if he talked to anyone about this contact. His friend Al Chimmy remained behind and later told Berg that he had signed up, describing how he had to copy by hand an unusually long commitment agreement in Arabic. That fact alone was accepted by Wiegand as evidence of the conspiratorial structure and resources of the operation. Hassan obviously felt perfectly secure in carrying such incriminating documents on his person. More importantly, he could send them out of the country without fear of interception. According to Berg, the agreement said his friend pledged to participate in the armed struggle—they didn't use the word *terrorism*—and that he was willing to travel to Lebanon for training during his next semester break.

With this new information in hand, Stuchly joined Wiegand in writing a report for the head of the Main Directorate for Counterespionage, General Günther Kratsch. Besides giving a factual account of the situation, they also recommended that Hassan be detained for intensive interrogation. The ambitious and self-centered Kratsch now found himself in an awkward and embarrassing position. He could not go to Stasi chief Mielke and boast that his directorate had uncovered a dangerous agent whom another directorate had trusted. Hassan had not been with the new section long enough for that—he had been an IM for counterespionage over a much longer period, and he had been recruited by Kratsch's own directorate. Therefore, Wiegand also had to work hard to convince Kratsch that the Abu Nidal group was in fact operating in East Germany. Wiegand's officers were ordered to painstakingly recheck all leads and information before Kratsch agreed to face Mielke. When the Stasi chief read the detention recommendation, he turned purple, threw up his arms, and launched into a tirade. "What, Abu Nidal . . . terrible! He has never done any harm in the DDR, so stay away."

Wiegand was perplexed when he read Mielke's order: "We will take no notice of this fact." Considering what had transpired in the aftermath of the La Belle bombing, Wiegand thought this an extraordinary decision. He recalled how Mielke had his men scrambling to undo the damage caused to the image of the regime because of its protection of the Libyan terrorists. Kratsch told Wiegand that Mielke had a good reason for ordering that he not use IMs against Hassan. Should one turn out to be a double agent—in other words, working for the terrorists as well—then Hassan could "get wind of it and he would know that the MfS knows everything but is doing nothing about it." If this were to happen, Kratsch went on quoting Mielke, "we would become accessories if the Nidal people did something."

Clearly, Mielke was thoroughly conscious of the trouble the La Belle killings had caused. Why would Mielke react differently now than he had in a previous matter concerning Abu Nidal, which came to light just a month after the La Belle bombing? At that time, on May 9, 1986, Mielke had received a memorandum stating that an Abu Nidal group was planning a "terrorist action" at the international book fair under way in Düsseldorf, West Germany.[18] The information came from the MfS foreign intelligence directorate, which in turn said it had gotten it from the Americans, who had pointed out "that a number of Western personalities are attending the fair, including the former U.S. secretary of state H[enry] Kissinger." The memorandum continued:

> Action is warranted, since the Americans, when they gave us this information, intimated that according to their knowledge Abu Nidal surfaced in the past year in several countries of the Warsaw Pact. It is not known if the American details are total inventions or if they are based on facts. Nevertheless, we find it appropriate to inform the leadership of several Arabic countries as well as Y. Arafat. We should point out that any new terrorist acts, no matter what their motivation, would only play into the hands of the Reagan Administration and would allow Washington to pursue more actively its policy of using force against sovereign states and national liberation movements under the slogan of its battle against terrorism.

The memorandum added that besides informing the leadership of the DDR, it would be in "our mutual interest if the 'friends' would exert pressure on the various Palestinian groups with which they have contacts to prevent the realization of any kind of terror acts in Europe." The MfS always used the word *friends* when referring to the Soviet Union. Therefore, the memorandum suggested that the Soviets be asked to give the Stasi a hand.

Stasi chief Mielke had reacted immediately. He discussed the matter with his KGB counterpart, who apparently agreed that Abu Nidal had to be stopped. Mielke then issued an order to General Wolf, the head of the foreign intelligence directorate, and to General Neiber, who supervised the antiterrorist directorate, to carry out the suggestions. There were no incidents at the Düsseldorf book fair.

Wiegand concluded that as far as Hassan was concerned, Mielke had decided that allowing him to run loose in the DDR was preferable to incurring the wrath of Abu Nidal's organization. Mielke did approve continued surveillance of the assistant professor. What had really set off Mielke was something that neither Wiegand nor Kratsch knew: Mielke was angry because he had been deceived by the terrorist. When Abu Nidal visited in 1985, he had pledged to stay out of East Germany in exchange for substantial weapons deliveries to Libya. Alexander Schalck-Golodkovsky, a Stasi colonel operating under deep cover as a state secretary of the Ministry for Foreign Trade, sold Qaddafi more than 4,000 Skorpion submachine guns and a million rounds of ammunition. He made the deal through a commercial firm secretly owned by East Germany's Communist Party. The shipment went via Poland to hide its origin, and Qaddafi paid the equivalent of more than US$470,500 in hard currency.[19] Abu Nidal acted as middleman and was paid a substantial commission by the East Germans.

In summer 1988, Stasi surveillance officers presented Wiegand with another surprise. Hassan was observed and photographed at several meetings with Yasser Chraidi, the Libyan killer—one of the chief planners of the La Belle bombing. In addition, the surveillance agents documented that Hassan had close contacts with diplomats of the Libyan People's Bureau who had been identified as members of Qaddafi's intelligence service. Wiegand now realized that the Libyans were pursuing a dual-track strategy: They controlled the East German segments of the Abu Nidal group but kept them on a short leash and had not yet used them for any terrorist actions. However, the weapons used in the December 1986 attacks at the airports in Rome and Vienna most likely had been part of the East German shipment that went to Libya a year earlier.[20]

Confronted with the Chraidi connection, Mielke authorized the arrest of the Libyan killer. On June 20, 1988, Wiegand and a few of his junior officers picked up Chraidi and detained him at a safe house on the outskirts of East Berlin. Chraidi was interrogated for six days, and MfS officers wrung a detailed confession from him. He admitted that he had hired Ghassan Ayaub, a Palestinian living in West Berlin, to carry out the 1984 murder of Mustafa Elashek in Bonn, West Germany, and described his role in the La Belle bombing and in other terrorist actions. In addition, he supplied information on terrorist activities that had been planned and controlled by the intelligence services and organizations of various Arab countries. Again the communist government refused to prosecute Chraidi and decided to expel him.

A STASI COLONEL DEFECTS

The political decisions by Honecker and Mielke not to take rigorous measures against terrorists had become a severe psychological burden for Colonel Wiegand. There were times when he felt close to a breakdown. A former star player on the national handball team, Wiegand saw his weight shoot up from 155 pounds to close to 200: Considering his modest height and his small frame, he was overweight. His job was consuming him and had led to the breakup of his marriage. There was no one in whom he could confide when he decided to defect to the West. Toward that end, he had been covertly copying top secret documents that proved the communist leadership's complicity in terrorism. At the same time, he used a double agent in 1988 to send signals to the West German Bundesnachrichtendienst that he was preparing to defect. He had already packed several hundred of the purloined documents in a suitcase when he saw his first opportunity—a chance to turn his back on the country he had served for more than three decades and on the ideology on which he had been weaned.

On January 23, 1989, Wiegand met with fifteen of his officers stationed at the various Stasi district headquarters. It was the annual conference of Wiegand's counterespionage task force dealing with foreign citizens in the DDR. The colonel's lecture included a merciless analysis of East Germany's political and economic problems and their causes. In fact, Wiegand predicted the very events that occurred later that year.

Wiegand left for Belgrade the day after the conference to attend a meeting with Yugoslav intelligence officials. Wiegand had contrived this meeting in order to rendezvous with West German intelligence officers and discuss final arrangements for his defection. The date was set for June 28, when another conference was scheduled to be held in Belgrade. From Yugoslavia he would be taken clandestinely to Austria.

When Wiegand returned to Berlin, he immediately sensed that something was wrong. It became obvious that someone present at the meeting with his subordinates had denounced him for his frank lecture. "I could feel the distrust toward me, changed attitudes of colleagues, and hard-liners conspiring against me. At General Kratsch's meeting with division heads, the favorite theme had become the 'battle against deviants and traitors.'" Wiegand's seeming paranoia proved to be valid intuition when he was told by a close friend that he was under surveillance and his telephone and apartment had been bugged. The last piece of evidence that he was in deep trouble fell into place on February 11. It was a Saturday morning, and Wiegand was still asleep after returning home late from a party with KGB colleagues, when the telephone rang at 8:15. It was Kratsch's adjutant, who ordered Wiegand to deliver his diplomatic passport to the general's office immediately. For years Wiegand had enjoyed the privilege of retaining the passport in his personal safe rather than having to deposit it at the Stasi document center. Except for Kratsch's deputy, Major General Wolfgang Lohse, Wiegand was the only officer of the counterespionage directorate allowed to travel to a Western country.

Wiegand spent the next four months acting the part of true believer. He lectured his staff on the political situation without deviating from the party line. At home he played to the microphones and acted the true, convinced, and dependable Stasi officer and communist. "Even those whom I had indoctrinated to my line of thinking began to have doubts about me, and I lost their respect. But at least the hard-liners and my guardians did not have a chance to gather new evidence against me."

In the meantime, Wiegand continued to gather and copy secret Stasi documents, which he hid at various places. By now he had made so many copies that he needed a second suitcase. "I was scared, I was terribly afraid. I could hardly sleep anymore. When I closed my eyes, I could see the images of Captain Werner Teske of the HVA, Navy Captain Winfried Zakrovski of military intelligence, and Major Gert Trebbeljahr of the MfS. All three tried to make contact with the West and were caught. Each died with a bullet in the back of the head."

The tension was taking its toll on Wiegand's health. For the first time he experienced heart problems. He stopped his compulsive eating, and within three months he had lost more than forty pounds. "Then I decided to follow the example of Werner Stiller of the HVA, who collected documents for three years before defecting in 1979. I admired his sangfroid and adopted a devil-may-care attitude. That gave me some inner peace."

The afternoon before his departure on June 28, 1989, Wiegand went to the office of his boss, General Kratsch, to pick up his passport. The trip to Yugoslavia had already been approved by the Stasi's political directorate. Thus, Wiegand was totally unprepared for the reception that awaited him. "The trip is canceled," Kratsch said. "You will never see your diplomatic passport again. I don't trust you anymore." Wiegand protested, and Kratsch confronted him with a report from a political officer on his January 23 lecture. "If I could, I would throw you out, or even better, lock you up." As Wiegand listened to the general, he began to fear that colleagues from the investigations directorate were already searching his apartment and would find his secret hoard. "I deeply regret your attitude. I am loyal and was only interested in protecting the party and the DDR." Say anything, Wiegand told himself, and just get out of the general's office quickly.

He was relieved when Kratsch remarked that no further action would be taken and that he would remain head of his department. Kratsch obviously had decided that Wiegand was too well known in the MfS, where he had performed brilliantly over many years as a counterespionage expert. Mielke had personally pinned the highest decorations on him, and a dismissal, particularly at a time of extreme tension between the regime and the East German people, might have caused turmoil within the Stasi.

When he left the general's office, Wiegand went immediately to his apartment and retrieved the dangerous suitcases. Before leaving the apartment, the colonel stood at his fifth-floor window for a few minutes, observing the neighborhood. When he was satisfied that he was not under surveillance, Wiegand grabbed the suitcases and went to his car. He drove to a nursery on the edge of East Berlin. He bought a large gooseberry bush. He already had a dozen of these growing in the garden at his weekend bungalow, and one more would arouse no suspicion if the place were searched. The bungalow was fifteen miles north of Berlin, in Wandlitz, where the top government leadership lived in a compound of luxurious villas. In fact, Wiegand's place stood less than one and a half miles from Erich Honecker's villa and was surrounded by shrubbery and pine trees. There was practically no chance that anyone might spot Wiegand burying the suitcases, which he had wrapped in a sheet of plastic. The sandy soil made digging easy, and after stuffing the cases end up into a two-foot hole, he planted the gooseberry bush over them. Now he had to bide his time and keep a low profile.

Wiegand's colleague Stuchly also had become more outspoken in his opposition to party policies. Stuchly had not been as prominent in MfS affairs as Wiegand, which made it easier for Kratsch to discipline him. He was relieved of his duties as chief of the Fifteenth Division and transferred to an obscure desk job. The official reasons given for his demotion were flimsy. But Stuchly was lucky that he was not jailed.[21]

The Berlin Wall crumbled on November 9, 1989, and within days the East German border with the West was wide open. The DDR was to exist another year, the Stasi only a few more months. Colonel Wiegand was ready to leave at once, but then he faced an unexpected complication. When he went to his office for the last time, he was approached by his executive assistant, Lieutenant Helga Schröder.[22] "I know what you are going to do. You are going to take off," the woman officer said quietly. "Don't worry, I am not going to denounce you. You know that my marriage is over, too, and I am as fed up here as you are. I just want you to take me and my two children along."

Wiegand agreed without hesitation. Still, he had to be cautious. The Stasi was not yet dead, and some of the more radical officers could still hunt him down. Wiegand decided to wait until December 31, when everyone would be celebrating New Year's Eve. The last hour before the new year was the most tense of Wiegand's life. The roads were icy as he drove to his bungalow to retrieve the suitcases. The ground was frozen solid. Wiegand labored more than an hour with pickax and shovel before he could remove the suitcases. When he drove back to Berlin to pick up the Schröders, his car skidded on the icy road and clipped a traffic sign; however, no one saw the mishap, and he was able to drive away under cover of darkness. Frau Schröder and the children were ready when he reached their previously arranged rendezvous point on the outskirts of the city. Six hours later, they were safe at the headquarters of the Bundesnachrichtendienst in the Bavarian town of Pullach, at the foot of the Alps near Munich.

Colonel Wiegand was the first high-ranking Stasi defector who decided to make a clean break with communism. The evidence that he brought with him allowed authorities a first glimpse at a morally corrupt regime that had condoned murder and mayhem in the name of "social justice." Even after German reunification, there was no assurance that all terrorist groups had left eastern Germany. In his debriefing by West German intelligence officials, Wiegand warned that the Iraqis in particular had established a well-functioning intelligence and terrorist apparatus in Germany that could be activated at any time. There were fifteen or sixteen Iraqi secret agents living in the DDR at the time Germany was reunified, and all had German names. Wiegand revealed that East German citizens had been recruited by the Iraqis as well and had been active for years: "That means they could well have established secret caches of weapons, explosives, and money."

Following his extensive debriefings by German intelligence and counterespionage authorities, Wiegand settled down in Munich and formed a management consulting firm. He also brought Portuguese construction workers to Germany for building projects in Berlin and in the former East Germany.

DEATH OF A STAR WITNESS

Wiegand was informed in spring 1996 that he would be called as the prosecution's chief witness in the trial against the perpetrators of the La Belle bombing. However, it was not to be: On June 17, 1996, Wiegand and his wife died under mysterious circumstances while traveling on business in Portugal. There are three different version of their deaths. One was that while driving at night, Wiegand rammed his car into the rear of a truck at high speed. Another had it that his car was rolled over and crushed by a heavy construction rig. A third version said the Wiegands were in a head-on collision with a truck.

No one who knew Wiegand and his wife identified the bodies before they were cremated. Their ashes were shipped to Germany, but none of Wiegand's personal belongings ever turned up. A business associate said Portuguese police officials told him they had launched a secret investigation. Subsequently, police said they could almost rule out murder. However, German intelligence officials, a member of the federal prosecutor's office, and a former Stasi associate who defected shortly after Wiegand told me privately that they believe Wiegand and his wife were murdered by Libyan assassins. A spokeswoman for Berlin's judicial authorities described Wiegand's death as "a heavy blow" for the prosecution handling the trial of the alleged bombers of La Belle discotheque. Nevertheless, the trial was proceeding with the prosecution privately expressing confidence of victory because of the abundance of evidence found in Stasi files. In addition, Wiegand's erstwhile comrade in arms, former Colonel Stuchly, was listed in the indictment as a prominent witness. Prosecutors believed the trial would take about four years because of the tediously slow pace of German court proceedings generally.

The only other trial in Germany of a terrorist—that of Johannes Weinreich, who was charged in the 1983 bombing of the Maison de France in West Berlin—was still in progress in summer 1998.

11

SAFE HAVEN FOR THE RED ARMY FACTION

MURDER, KIDNAPPING, EXTORTION, bank robbery, and arson were felonies under the East German criminal code. However, if these offenses were committed under the banner of the "anti-imperialist struggle," the communist government would look the other way. Moreover, it had assigned the Stasi to make sure that terrorists were properly trained for murder and mayhem. There was no limit to the East German regime's involvement with terrorism, so long as it could be ideologically justified.

A series of arrests that began on June 6, 1990 would expose yet again the moral bankruptcy of the East German government led by Erich Honecker and its secret police directed by Erich Mielke. Detectives of the People's Police, working under the new, noncommunist German government, captured ten former members of the Red Army Faction (RAF), a Marxist-Leninist terrorist group. Most of this group's members came from upper-middle-class West German families. Since the 1970s, the RAF had been kidnapping and killing German industrialists, bankers, and policemen. They had murdered U.S. soldiers, robbed banks, and bombed U.S. military bases. The RAF was the most vicious terrorist organization then operating in Germany. International warrants for the arrest of its members had been issued a decade earlier by the West German attorney general.

Susanne Albrecht was the first RAF member arrested after authorities were tipped off by a former member of the East German Ministry for State Security's counterterrorism directorate (the Twenty-Second Directorate). Albrecht, thirty-nine years old at the time, was wanted for participating in the murders of two prominent German businessmen, the West German attorney general, and six bodyguards. The daughter of a Hamburg attorney, Albrecht was a close family friend of Jürgen Ponto, the chairman of the Dresdner Bank. In July 1977, she had visited Ponto at his home near Frankfurt. Ponto suspected nothing when he opened the door to his villa and saw that the caller was Albrecht. He also had no reason to be wary of her companions—who opened fire and killed him as he stood in the doorway. The other murders in which Albrecht was declared an accessory were those of Attorney General Siegfried Buback, in April 1977, and of Hanns Martin Schleyer, president of the West German Association of Industries. Schleyer was kidnapped, held for six months, and then killed. Albrecht was also charged with participating in the bomb attack on General Alexander Haig in June 1979. Haig, later U.S. Secretary of State, was commander of the North Atlantic Treaty Organization in Brussels at the time. He was not injured, but his armored Mercedes limousine was damaged beyond repair.

By the end of June 1990, nine more RAF suspects had been taken into custody. Three were released because the statute of limitations had expired. Transferred to West German prisons were Werner Lotze, age 38, who was suspected of complicity in the murders of a police officer, an industrialist, and a diplomat; Henning Beer, 31, wanted for taking part in a bomb attack at a U.S. Air Force base; Sigrid Sternebeck, 41, Silke Maier-Witt, 40, and Monika Helbing, 36, all suspected of having participated in the Ponto and Schleyer murders; and Inge Viet, 46, charged with complicity in the 1974 murder of West Berlin superior court president Günter von Drenkmann and in the kidnapping of a top conservative politician in 1975. Lotze turned state's evidence, and in January 1991, received a reduced sentence of nine years in prison.

The RAF prisoners were interrogated by federal criminal investigators and prosecutors. Investigators finally had proof of a monstrous alliance between the RAF terrorists and the communist state. West German officials had begun to suspect in the late 1980s that such an alliance existed, a number of Stasi defectors having divulged information to that effect during their interrogations by intelligence and counterespionage officers; however, the East Germans had unwaveringly denied all allegations. Now, although some of the suspected RAF terrorists refused to talk, the new Kronzeugen law under which an accused could be offered leniency for turning state's evidence was proving effective among others: Faced with prison terms up to life, most followed Lotze's example and talked.

When the arrests were first made, in summer 1990, authorities believed that the Stasi, acting on orders of the SED leadership, had done nothing more than provide new identities and asylum to RAF members who wanted to quit the terrorist business. The "retired" terrorists initially insisted that the East German regime had merely given them the opportunity to live in their native country rather than in external exile somewhere in the Middle East. Besides, they said, the active RAF members thought East Germany more secure for those who had bailed out and who were already emotionally unstable. Had the latter been cut loose in a distant land, they might have been tempted to surrender to West German diplomatic representatives.

For more than a decade, the RAF "retirees" were under the care of none other than Colonel Harry Dahl, the chief of the MfS counterterrorism directorate. Over many years, Dahl and his officers had sheltered and wined and dined the most notorious of international terrorists, among them Carlos and Abu Daoud, mastermind of the massacre at the Olympic Games in Munich.

Dahl, of course, was not a solo player. He was carrying out the orders of Colonel General Gerhard Neiber, deputy MfS minister, responsible for seven major directorates, including the one responsible for preventing escapes from East Germany. Neiber, in turn, was acting on behalf of Stasi chief Erich Mielke and the government leadership. Neiber also granted safe haven to a neo-Nazi terrorist, Odfried Hepp, in 1983. Hepp fled to East Berlin after setting off bombs beneath automobiles belonging to U.S. soldiers (none of whom was hurt) and committing a number of bank robberies that netted him a total of DM600,000 (about US$261,000). The Stasi officers who initially questioned the neo-Nazi wanted to send him back to the West. General Neiber ruled against it. Hepp told Stasi interrogators about his contacts with right-wing extremists. The information he provided helped them to compile a genealogy of the West German neo-Nazi scene. In July 1983, Hepp was allowed to fly to Syria. He was later nabbed in Paris, extradited to West Germany, and sentenced to fifteen years in prison.

ANARCHISTS AND THE STASI

The RAF-Stasi relationship began in March 1978, after intensive West German police operations resulted in a number of arrests, prompting the remaining terrorists to flee West Germany. While a number of RAF members escaped to Paris, Inge Viet decided to head for East Germany. For a criminal, it was an easier border to cross. West German authorities did not check anyone crossing to the East, maintaining the myth of freedom of movement in all of Germany. And a myth it was, for on the communist side the controls were the most stringent in the

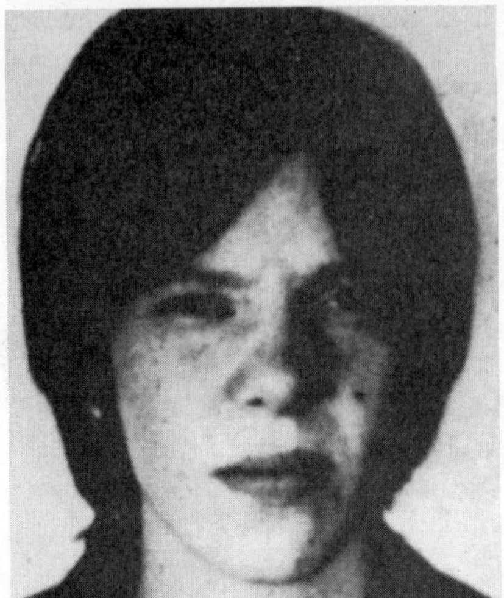

Susanne Albrecht

Werner Bernhard Lotze

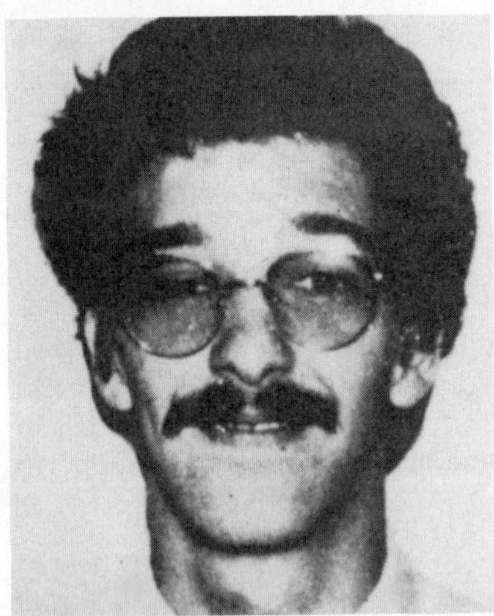

Henning Beer

Sigrid Sternebeck

Photos 11.1–11.7 show members of the extreme left-wing terrorist group Red Army Faction (RAF) who were trained in East Germany by the Stasi or were given sanctuary by the communist government. The photos are reproduced here from wanted posters distributed by German police.

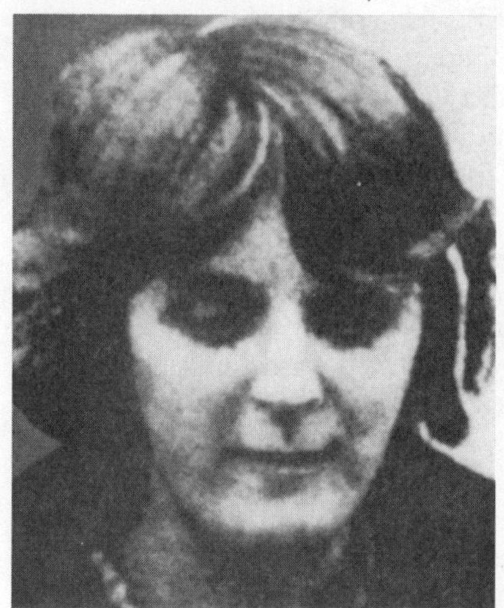

Silke Maier-Witt

Monika Helbing

Inge Viet

world. Viet arrived at the East German end of the checkpoint at Lauenburg, some twenty-five miles southeast of Hamburg, armed with a pistol. There she asked to speak with a Stasi representative and was detained until Colonel Dahl arrived from Berlin. Dahl questioned the woman and obtained permission from General Neiber to admit her to the DDR. Viet spent several days as a guest of the Stasi at a villa outside Berlin. Then she flew to South Yemen, where many RAF terrorists were trained in camps maintained by the South Yemeni secret service and the Palestine Liberation Organization, the plane ticket being provided by the Stasi. Viet maintained her contact with Colonel Dahl and later was instrumental in the resettlement of the "retirees," whom she joined in 1983.

On April 18, 1991, Attorney General Alexander von Stahl was ready to act. Based on the statements of Stasi defectors and jailed terrorists as well as on Stasi files found in East Berlin, von Stahl issued six arrest warrants. The charges: Aiding and abetting in attempted murder and illegally detonating explosives. Five days later, on April 23, detectives of the Bundeskriminalamt (BKA), the German equivalent to the FBI, converged on the eastern part of Berlin, the former capital of the DDR, to execute five of the warrants. Along with Neiber and Dahl, they arrested Günter Jäckel, former colonel and deputy chief of the counterterrorism directorate; Gerhard Plomann, former lieutenant colonel and chief of staff to Neiber; and former Major Gerd Zaumseil of the counterterrorism directorate, who was charged with looking after the RAF "retirees." A sixth warrant was served on former Stasi chief Erich Mielke at Berlin's Plötzensee prison, where he had been confined since winter 1990 on two counts of murder. A seventh target, former Lieutenant Colonel Helmut Voigt, had trained and chaperoned terrorists for more than a decade. He managed to escape to Greece, where he was captured in 1994. Extradited and tried for complicity, Voigt went to prison for four years. Proceedings against Mielke and the other five Stasi officers on these charges were dropped when it was determined that the statute of limitations of five years had expired.

Particularly damning was the ex–Stasi officers' involvement in *Ausbildungsprojekte Stern I und Stern II,* training camps code-named Star I and Star II, where RAF cadres were instructed in the use of explosives, antitank rockets, and various other weapons. At the camps, MfS experts on explosives demonstrated a bomb-triggering device consisting of a battery-fed photoelectric beam, which could be employed against moving objects. Interruption of the beam would detonate the bomb.

On November 30, 1989, a shaped-charge grenade containing 150 pounds of high explosives tore into an armored Mercedes limousine carrying Alfred Herrhausen. The fifty-nine-year-old head of Deutsche Bank, one of West Germany's most brilliant business executives and a top adviser to Chancellor Helmut Kohl, was killed. A photoelectric beam of the kind that RAF killers were taught to assemble by Stasi experts had triggered the grenade. It had been strapped to a bicycle placed at the roadside near Herrhausen's home in Bad Homburg, near Frankfurt, along the only route that Herrhausen could have used in driving to his Frankfurt office. The charge itself had been built and positioned in such a way that it was propelled like an antitank missile into the right rear door, causing the blast to be directed inward, blowing out all four armored doors of the limousine.

A letter to police from "Commando Wolfgang Beer" claimed responsibility. The letter bore the imprint of a five-pointed red star, on which a submachine gun and the acronym *RAF* were superimposed. This was

An armored Mercedes limousine after it was struck by an explosive projectile fired by a member of the West German extreme left-wing Red Army Faction. The projectile, similar to an antitank weapon in its deadly effectiveness, killed Alfred Herrhausen, one of Europe's most influential bankers. Courtesy AP/Wide World.

the logo that the RAF used in its communications about acts of terrorism. Wolfgang Beer, an RAF terrorist, was later killed in an auto crash, in 1980. Wolfgang's brother, Henning, surfaced later in East Germany and made extensive admissions regarding Henning's RAF involvement.

In less than a year, the RAF struck again. This time the target was Hans Neusel, the sixty-three-year-old state secretary of the West German Interior Ministry, responsible for internal security affairs. On July 27, 1990, a high-explosive projectile slammed into the right side of his armored BMW limousine as it was turning onto an autobahn exit ramp near Bonn. Neusel had given his driver the day off and was driving himself, which saved his life. He suffered only minor injuries. The bomb trigger was identical to the one used in the Herrhausen murder—a photoelectric beam. Again the RAF claimed responsibility.

The terrorists were also trained by Stasi experts on such weapons as the 9mm Heckler & Koch submachine gun of West German manufacture; the G-3 automatic rifle, a standard weapon of the West German Army; an American .357 magnum Smith & Wesson revolver; and the Soviet AK-47 Kalashnikov automatic rifle. The weapons training phase in March 1981 was followed by practice with the Soviet RPG-7,

Deutsche Bank Chief Alfred Herrhausen, assassinated November 30, 1989, when a member of the extreme left-wing Red Army Faction fired an explosive projectile into his armored Mercedes limousine. Courtesy AP/Wide World.

an antitank rocket weapon that was a longtime favorite of communist insurgents around the world. Under intensive interrogation by BKA detectives, former Stasi Major Hans-Dieter Gaudig described how mannequins fashioned of cloth and stuffed with sawdust and a German shepherd dog were placed in a Mercedes limousine. The instructors were bent on creating as realistic a situation as possible. The mannequins and the dog were torn to pieces by the three RPG-7 rounds. The "students" then were shown how to construct explosive and incendiary devices and position them where Stasi experts deemed the vehicle most vulnerable. Finally, RAF terrorists learned how to make an explosive from chemicals readily available in any drug store. This explosive was packed in fire extinguishers, which were placed beneath front and rear automobile fenders and detonated. According to Inge Viet, these exercises took place in March 1981.

Five months later, on August 31, 1981, a bomb was set off in front of the main administration building of the U.S. Air Force European headquarters in the southwest German town of Ramstein. The blast occurred at 7 A.M., when base personnel were arriving for work. It injured twenty people, including Brigadier General Joseph D. Moore, assistant deputy chief of staff for operations, and the air staff operations officer, Lieutenant Colonel Douglas R. Young. Experts of the Federal Criminal Investigation Agency found that the bomb had been "very professionally rigged" inside a Volkswagen. A second bomb was also in the car but failed to explode. Two days after the explosion, the West German news agency Deutsche Presse Agentur in Hamburg received a letter from the Red Army Faction, saying the bombing was carried out by the "Sigurd Debus Commando Unit." Debus was an RAF terrorist who had died in April 1981 in a Hamburg prison, as the result of a hunger strike.

ATTACK ON A U.S. ARMY COMMANDER

General Frederick J. Kroesen, commander of U.S. Forces in Europe, and his wife Rowene were traveling in an armored Mercedes sedan on route 37 in the scenic Neckar river valley the morning of September 15, 1981. Police had told the general a fortnight earlier that they believed he was on a terrorist hit list. The Germans had insisted that he accept an armored sedan—the car in which the couple was now traveling to the general's headquarters in Heidelberg. RAF terrorists Christian Klar, Helmut Pohl, and Ingrid Jacobsmeier were positioned on a hillside just below the ruins of Heidelberg castle. From that carefully selected spot in a lush, mixed forest of oak, beech, birch, and pine, they had a clear view of the road and a manually operated pedestrian traffic light about two hundred yards away. The area, normally busy with joggers and strollers, was nearly deserted that morning. Thus, no one noticed the fourth member of the hit team, Adelheid Schulz, who was the lookout and the traffic light operator. When the general's yellow Mercedes approached, she pushed the button that switched the light to red, and walked away.

The German police driver took his foot off the brake pedal and the car inched forward. It had moved three feet from the stop line when, at 7:17 A.M., Klar fired an RPG-7 projectile at the general's car. The rocket penetrated the trunk and exploded; but instead of plowing into the passenger compartment, the armored piercing core veered off to the right and exited through the fender. Part of the trunk's Scandia armor lid was pushed against the rear window. The armor-plated rear seat absorbed metal fragments and shielded the general and his wife from the blast. The shooter's calculations had been thrown off by the car having moved forward and beyond the point where it was supposed to have stopped. With Klar still pointing the launcher, Pohl pushed another rocket into the rear of the firing tube. Klar fired again and missed. The rocket exploded in the street behind the car. Mrs.

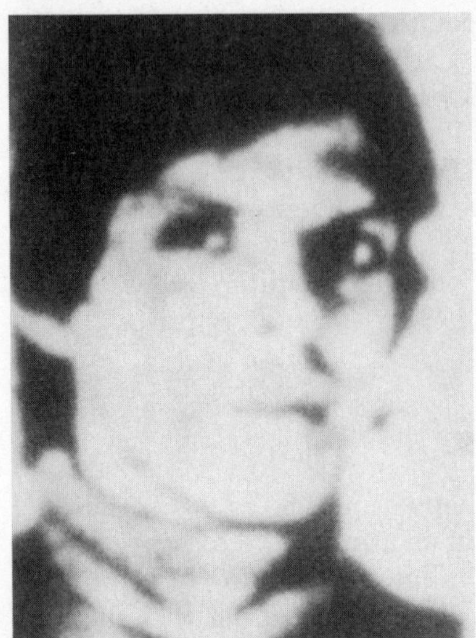

Christian Klar, member of the extreme left-wing terrorist Red Army Faction (RAF), pictured on a German police wanted poster.

RAF member Adelheid Schulz, pictured on a police wanted poster.

Kroesen regained her wits quickly. "Let's get out of here," she said. "Does the car still run?" The dazed driver pushed down the accelerator and sped off, undoubtedly saving their lives. The terrorists had just loaded a third round and were ready to fire.[1]

Klar and Schulz, twenty-eight and twenty-six years old respectively at the time of the attack, were captured in 1982. Pohl, at thirty-seven the oldest of the killer team, was arrested in 1984, and twenty-seven-year-old Jacobsmeier, in 1986. They were sentenced to prison for life. Klar has never talked about his RAF involvement. However, some four years later his former comrades, eager to bargain for lesser prison terms, said that Klar had spent three days practicing with the Soviet-made bazooka under Stasi supervision. The training was conducted at the top secret Stasi base known as Objekt 74, at Briesen, a bucolic location about forty miles southeast of East Berlin. According to a top secret Stasi document[2] originating with thc Twenty-Second Directorate and dated May 25, 1987, Objekt 74 is the same base where members of the PLO and other Middle Eastern and Latin American terrorists were trained by Stasi specialists and members of the F. E. Dzerzhinski Guard Regiment.

The statements made by the former RAF terrorists and the Stasi trainers were identical in every detail except one: the dates when the training took place. The former terrorists insisted that the training took place early in 1981. Obviously aware of their own culpability, the Stasi officers insisted that it was a year later, from mid-February to mid-March 1982—i.e., several months after the attacks at Ramstein Air Base and on General Kroesen. To prove it, they produced the visitors' registration book from Objekt 74. Experts of the Federal Criminal Police Agency declared the entries forgeries. "And stupid forgeries at that," one official commented. For example, some Stasi officers were listed with ranks to which they had been promoted after 1982.[3] Inge Viet remained adamant that the training took place in 1981, because in 1982 she was in South Yemen.

A FINAL ASSASSINATION

As the Stasi-RAF connection began to unravel, a new terrorist outrage reemphasized the impotence of the West German security establishment.[4] At 11:30 P.M. on March 31, 1991, Detlev Rohwedder, a prominent German businessman, entered the second-floor study at his home in Düsseldorf. The room was lit only by one 25-Watt bulb in a desk lamp. The second bulb had burned out some time earlier. After checking his airline ticket for the flight schedule to Berlin the next day, he returned it to a briefcase that stood on a desk near the window. As Rohwedder turned to head back to the adjoining master bedroom, his back was toward the window and his six-foot-three-inch frame could only be seen from the outside as a shadow. At that moment an assassin fired two shots. The first smashed into Rohwedder's back, tearing into his trachea and aorta. The second bullet missed; but Rohwedder was already dead as he hit the floor. His wife, Hergard, heard the noise and thought it was the burned-out light bulb exploding as her husband replaced it. Hergard, who had always been a little afraid of "electrical things," got out of bed to see if she could help her husband. As she entered the study, the murderer again saw a shadow and fired a third time, hitting her left arm.[5]

Rohwedder was chairman of the Treuhandanstalt, a government trusteeship established to handle the privatization of former state property in eastern Germany, including 8,000 industrial plants. Until buyers could be found, the trust was to administer the industries' operations. However, the decrepit condition of many operations after forty years of communist mismanagement led Rohwedder to close hundreds of plants. The resulting unemployment became manna for communists who were irate over their spectacular fall from power and desper-

Detlev Rohwedder, head of the trust agency in charge of restructuring East German industry, was shot and killed by a Red Army Faction assassin in April 1991. Courtesy AP/Wide World.

ate to regain their popularity: Now they could point to yet another example of the "heartlessness" of capitalism. Rohwedder became their favorite whipping boy. The party's official newspaper *Neues Deutschland* called the Treuhandanstalt the "bony hand of the grim reaper." As a consequence, Rohwedder, who had already been placed on a police list of threatened executives, became a logical RAF target.

The weapon used to murder him was a G-3 rifle, the standard automatic weapon of the West Germany Army. It was the same weapon from which more than 100 shots had been fired at the U.S. Embassy at Bonn-Mehlem on February 13, 1991.[6] Although some rounds penetrated windows, there were no casualties. The RAF claimed responsibility for that shooting, as it had for the Rohwedder killing.

Detectives reported that Rohwedder's killer must be an "extraordinarily well-trained shooter," having hit a shadowy target from a distance of about 70 yards, standing behind a hedge. The G-3 rifle was one of the weapons on which Stasi officers had trained RAF terrorists. However, investigators were unable to come up with any clues to the killer's identity. Detectives also theorized that the RAF had been tipped off by a Stasi agent employed by the security firm that had installed the bullet-proof glass in the ground-floor windows of Rohwedder's home. Security experts evidently had assumed that the special glass was unnecessary on the second floor.

Police experts on the RAF eventually determined that Rohwedder's killer belonged to the "third generation" of RAF terrorists. The first was the Bader-Meinhof Gang (named after its leaders, Ulrike Meinhof and Andreas Bader), which was active in the 1970s. Meinhof and Bader were arrested and sentenced to life imprisonment. Bader starved himself to death and Meinhof hanged herself in a prison cell. RAF killers active in the 1980s and those who had "retired" to the DDR belonged to the second generation.

The first two generations of RAF terrorists delighted in thumbing their noses at police. They deliberately left clues to their identities at crime scenes, taunting law enforcers to catch them. Christian Klar went so far as to plant his fingerprints on the Soviet-made rocket launcher that he abandoned after firing at General Kroesen's Mercedes limousine. But no usable clues had been uncovered since the 1985 fatal shooting of Ernst Zimmermann, chairman of Motor & Turbinen Union, a major defense contractor.

The shrill denunciations by left-wingers and civil libertarians of *Rasterfahndung,* a system of identifying enemy spies that was devised by the BKA, seriously undermined the work of investigators. *Rasterfahndung* involved the establishment of fact-based profiles indicating potential terrorists, and the use of investigative methods similar to those employed by U.S. Customs and Drug Enforcement Administration agents to ferret out drug couriers. For example, the Bader-Meinhof Gang and the second-generation RAF killers were known to rent apartments and houses as hideouts, asking for three-month leases and paying in advance. They also had a penchant for fast and expensive cars such as Porsches, Mercedeses, and BMWs, typically paid for with the loot from bank robberies. The police would receive tips about individuals fitting the profile and would establish covert surveillance of those individuals, until they were satisfied either that they had gathered enough evidence to obtain an arrest warrant or that there were no grounds for further investigation. The public pressure brought to bear on federal criminal investigators because of *Rasterfahndung* became so intense that Horst Herold was forced to resign as president of the Bundeskriminalamt in 1981. His offense was "overzealousness" in collecting and computerizing data on possible terrorists, which left-wing and liberal critics charged had grossly violated individuals' civil liberties. Yet not a single case of police harassment of an innocent citizen was ever established, whereas many terrorists were caught by *Rasterfahndung.*

GENERAL WOLF'S FINGERPRINTS

Given the obvious skill with which the third-generation RAF killers were eluding authorities, it appeared that they had received expert advice in covert operations and security methods practiced by espionage agents. It seemed likely, therefore, that Stasi experts were their tutors in this area as well. There was no solid evidence that such training had taken place in East Germany. However, exactly that kind of schooling was conducted in Africa, the Middle East, and Latin America for two decades by Department Three of the HVA, the Main Administration for Foreign Intelligence, led by Colonel General Markus Wolf. Department Three was particularly active in South Yemen, where many RAF members had lived from time to time. Colonel Rainer Wiegand, the MfS counterintelligence officer who secretly tried to curb terrorists, said that when he visited the HVA station in Aden, officers had talked about their contacts with German terrorists. Wolf's officers also were used to ward off any suspicion by West German authorities that RAF fugitives were living in East Germany. At one point, Stasi officers brought Susanne Albrecht to Aden and paraded her around the city, making sure she was seen near the embassies of West Germany and other Western powers. The Stasi knew that the West Germans were always scouting the city, on the lookout for familiar faces.

Wolf had vehemently denied any knowledge of Stasi involvement with RAF terrorists. However, Wiegand dismissed Wolf's denial, saying that there was "absolutely no chance that Wolf was not fully informed, and furthermore, just about the entire Politburo knew about it." In a paper prepared for (West) German security authorities after his defection, Wiegand wrote:

> Honecker and Mielke were not solely responsible (for supporting terrorists). Also involved with them was the Central Committee secretary responsible for state security affairs, Egon Krenz, and all first secretaries of the districts,[7] because of their authority over the district MfS chiefs. These facts weigh against the "I knew nothing" attitude of Krenz. Herr Krenz knew of all Honecker decisions, including the support of the RAF by the DDR. The MfS was obliged to carry out the policy decisions that were formulated at the highest level by party leaders such as Honecker, Krenz, Axen, and Kleiber. Kleiber is implicated because of his special role as the Middle East emissary in negotiations with chiefs of governments and parties in the Arab area.[8]

Wiegand pointed out that the RAF terrorists were not just random "illegal border crossers." Instead, their asylum and training were the results of deliberate political considerations by the East German state and party leaders, and of those leaders' connections to the PLO as well as to the governments of South Yemen, Libya, Ethiopia, Syria, and Iraq. Wiegand proved right.

Major General Werner Irmler submitted a report to Stasi chief Mielke on August 5, 1979, in which he comprehensively detailed the activities of terrorists residing in the DDR. Mielke had only eight copies made, one of which he sent to Markus Wolf. The document[9] was so sensitive that it was labeled "top secret, only for personal information, return is requested." Mielke had personally written out the distribution list, and Wolf's name was in third place.

The report named RAF terrorists Inge Viet, Ingrid Siepman, and Regine Nicolai as having been "housed in a Stasi safe house from June 28 to July 12, 1978." Then they were flown to Baghdad "under operational control," meaning that Stasi officers accompanied the trio to the Iraqi capital, where the terrorists had told the Stasi they had their "operational base." The Stasi felt obliged to accord the terrorists special protection because earlier, Bulgarian authorities had arrested other members of the group, who had been allowed to escape through East Germany after they had broken convicted murderer Till Meyer out of a West Berlin prison. The Bulgarians had turned these individuals over to West German police for trial. Nonetheless, all of the RAF terrorists, including those harbored by the East German communist regime, were eventually tried, convicted, and sentenced to prison terms ranging from seven years to life.

On April 20, 1998, an anonymous eight-page statement was received by the Bonn office of the British news agency Reuters. It was laden with the left-wing anarchistic rhetoric typical of RAF documents and contained not a word of apology for the murders and other high crimes the group had committed. It ended with the words: "Today we are ending this project. The urban guerrilla group in the form of the RAF is now history." Emblazoned on the statement was the RAF's emblem—a red, five-point star superimposed over a sketch of a submachine gun. This emblem had always been stamped on notes sent to the news media after a murder or a bombing. An expert of the Federal Criminal Police Agency (BKA) attested to its authenticity, and German newspapers quoted Horst Herold, former BKA president, as saying: "With this statement the Red Army Faction has erected its own tombstone."

12

SHATTERED SHIELD, BROKEN SWORD

MIKHAIL GORBACHEV'S TENTATIVE relaxation of central controls over Soviet society, with the new policies of glasnost and perestroika introduced in 1986, was felt throughout the Eastern bloc. East Germans began to ask why similar policies of liberalization were not being adopted by their own regime. Small groups of dissident intellectuals and Lutheran churchmen, which had sprung up two or three years earlier, were rapidly growing. At the same time, Mielke's suppressive operations were shrinking: Although the Stasi was still arresting and jailing hundreds of individuals, it was exercising greater caution in moving against highly visible dissidents, because the opposition had learned how to use the Western media. Prior to any planned public protest, West Berlin newspapers and television would be informed. Any arrests would immediately make headlines in the West. East Germany's communist leadership had become more sensitive to criticism, especially in view of internal Stasi reports indicating that arrests merely strengthened the resolve of the opposition.[1] Instead of jailing dissident leaders, Stasi officers would merely detain them for a day or two to keep them off the streets during holidays, when public protests might be expected. From time to time the regime would expel a particularly vocal dissident to West Berlin.

Increasingly concerned over the growing popular opposition, Stasi Minister Mielke early in 1989 ordered the creation of a special elite unit for crushing disturbances.[2] Its personnel were carefully selected members of the counterespionage and counterterrorist directorate. They were equipped with special batons similar to electric cattle prods but much more powerful. In a secret speech to top-ranking Stasi officers on June 29, Mielke warned that "hostile opposing forces and groups have already achieved a measure of power and are using all methods to achieve a change in the balance of power."[3] Former Stasi Colonel Rainer Wiegand told me he was horrified when Mielke compared the situation with that in China two months earlier. Chinese students in Beijing had begun massive protests in April, and in May, during a student demonstration in Tiananmen square, security troops had opened fire on them, killing hundreds. "Mielke said our situation was comparable and we had to be ready to counter it with all 'means and methods,'" Wiegand recalled. "Mielke said the Chinese leadership had succeeded in smothering the protests before the situation got out of hand."

In early summer 1989, Hungary, which was undergoing its own transition to greater individual liberty, made the first dent in the Iron Curtain. The barbed wire fences along its borders were dismantled, and the number of border guards was dramatically reduced. Hundreds of East Germans vacationing in Hungary decided then and there not to return home and instead headed for Austria, although the official opening of the border would not be announced until the end of August. By early September, thousands had traveled through Czechoslovakia to Hungary, whence they stampeded to the West. About 15,000 fled westward in a single week. Prodded by Mielke in a Politburo meeting, the regime persuaded the Czech government to close its borders to East Germans. Thousands of men, women, and children were thus trapped in Prague, and some 2,500 sought asylum in the West German embassy there, transforming its spacious garden into a refugee camp. West German officials negotiated with the Czech government to bring the refugees out, and on September 29 Erich Honecker announced that he would honor a request from the "Czechoslovakian comrades" to let the refugees leave for West Germany aboard a special train. In an interview with his government's news agency (AND), Honecker called the refugees "antisocial elements who trample upon moral values" and added that "one should not waste a tear on them." When the train arrived in the East German city of Dresden on the night of September 4, thousands of citizens converged on the main railroad station: They, too, wanted to defect. Mielke's elite units, alongside riot squads from the People's Police, went into action, clubbing hundreds into submission. These would-be defectors were thrown onto army trucks and hauled away to detention centers.

From then on, the political climate deteriorated rapidly. Protest marches erupted throughout the country. The burghers of Leipzig were particularly resolute, despite beatings from Stasi goons and police. Beginning in September, two to three thousand demonstrators, many carrying lighted candles, marched through downtown Leipzig to gather for prayers in front of Nikolai church every Monday evening. Except for the occasional shouted demand for democratic reforms and free travel, the crowds were peaceful. Their ranks swelled by thousands every Monday. In East Berlin, Mielke informed his commanders of plans calling for the Stasi goon squads to attack the demonstrators, split them into three groups, and arrest their leaders.[4] He added that paratroop units were assembled outside the city in case reinforcements were needed. Police commanders had orders to fire, though these orders were issued verbally rather than in writing. As former Stasi Colonel Wiegand later commented to me, "All it would have taken to start a civil war was a single shot."

GORBACHEV'S WARNING

Despite the unrest, the regime celebrated its fortieth with a huge, pompous ceremony in Berlin on October 7, while tens of thousands of jeering citizens stood outside the ornate building of the State Council. The People's Police cordons were utterly ineffectual. As Stasi minister Erich Mielke drove up and was greeted by General Günther Kratsch, the counterintelligence chief, Mielke screamed at police: "Club those pigs into submission!"[5] The police ignored Mielke's ranting.

Soviet President Mikhail Gorbachev was also in attendance as a guest of honor, although his East German allies had rejected his policies of glasnost and perestroika and had banned the sale of Soviet publications, labeling them subversive. He watched as thousands of demonstrators waved, many shouting "Gorby, help us!" Just prior to his trip to Berlin, the Soviet president had received a top secret analysis that Colonel Rainer Wiegand had prepared for the KGB on his own initiative and at great personal risk. "If Mielke had found out, I would have been finished," the officer later told me, drawing a finger across his throat. In this report he had described the situation in the DDR as verging on chaos and had warned the Soviets against being taken in by "Potemkin villages." Perhaps with this briefing in mind, Gorbachev pointedly remarked in an impromptu speech before East German party functionaries, "Life will punish those who arrive too late."

Erich Honecker, secretary-general of the party and head of state, ignored this warning, and was stripped of his posts eleven days later. Egon Krenz, a Politburo member charged with the supervision of the state security apparatus and a longtime Mielke ally, became the new party leader and head of state. Nothing essential was altered by this changing of the guard, although Krenz tried to ingratiate himself with the people, claiming that he had prevented the outbreak of civil war on October 9 by countermanding Honecker's orders to fire on the estimated 200,000 anticommunist demonstrators in Leipzig. This time the demonstrators had carried signs demanding free elections—an act that was punishable just a decade earlier by at least ten years' hard labor. Large banners reading "no violence!" were stretched across the entrance to the imposing Stasi district headquarters in downtown Leipzig.

Regardless of Krenz's claims, the man the people credited with preventing a bloodbath was Kurt Masur, the musical director of the renowned Leipzig Gewandhaus orchestra. Masur is an imposing man not only because of his status in the international cultural world but also in physical stature. A bear of a man standing well over six feet, he towered over most of the protesters and politicians whom he passionately debated. Western news media were reporting these debates, forcing the party hierarchy to heed the pleas of the world-famous conductor.

THE BEGINNING OF THE END

On November 9, the Politburo surrendered to public pressure and decided to issue a statement that unhindered travel to the West would be allowed. Günter Schabowski, Politburo member and Berlin district party secretary, read the decision before television cameras at a news conference that evening. While still on live camera, he was asked when the new rule would take effect. "Immediately," he answered, looking flustered. Captain Bruno Nevyhosteny of the Stasi passport control unit at the Berlin Wall crossing point Bornholmer Strasse, north of the city center, was at home that night but had not been watching television.[6] He received a telephone call from headquarters saying that there was an alert and ordering him to return to his post. As he drove through the streets, he saw thousands of people streaming toward the control point. Nevyhosteny got there just before the crowd arrived demanding to be let through. Major Harald Jäger, deputy chief of the unit, was beside himself. There were only sixty men at the post. The people were pounding on the steel gate, ready to destroy the entire facility, and Jäger's superiors had nothing more to tell him than that he should try to placate them. Shortly after 11:00 P.M. he took matters into his own hands and ordered the gates opened. Captain Nevyhosteny complied, and the crowd roared in jubilation. The Berlin Wall was breached forever—but dangerous tensions remained.

Emboldened by the disarray within the Communist Party and the government, the people directed their verbal attacks against the Stasi as well. In a top secret report of October 30, 1989 to the party leadership, Mielke said groups of dissidents had repeatedly attempted to provoke MfS officers at their various offices into taking "uncontrolled measures." They shouted "burn the house down," "Stasi pigs, get out," "beat them to death," or "the knives have been honed and the ropes are ready." Throughout those turbulent weeks, the Soviets kept their own troops of 380,000 in the barracks. President Gorbachev had decided not to interfere with armed force, even though it meant the loss of the Soviet Union's most important ally and trading partner.[7] For the first time in his career, Mielke was on his own, his Soviet friends having left him to dangle in the winds of political change.

The people's hatred of the Stasi, which had been simmering for more than four decades, erupted in public outrage. Throughout the late fall and early winter, Stasi offices in the provinces were stormed by irate East Germans. In the city of Halle, Stasi officers set up machine guns at the windows of their building to mow down intruders, but capitulated before *Bürgerkommittee*s, citizens' committees that were formed to prevent violence and oversee an orderly transition. During ugly confrontations throughout East Germany, Stasi officers barricaded themselves in their offices behind steel doors, their shredders and furnaces working overtime to destroy incriminating documents. In Dresden, the local Stasi boss was kicked in the buttocks by irate burghers as he left his office. He and his colleagues in the cities of Suhl and Neubrandenburg, committed suicide. Miraculously, the only incidents of violence against Stasi officials involved beatings. The public rage could easily have led to lynching, as was the case during the 1956 Hungarian revolution, when a number of members of the Hungarian secret police were stoned to death, hanged, and shot.

Mielke, the powerful secret policeman and intriguer, now eighty-two years old, was nearing the end of his bloodstained career. On November 13 he was called before the Chamber of People's Deputies, the communist parliament, to deliver an analysis of the security situation. As he summarized the events and claimed that his MfS was still solidly in control, deputies began to boo and whistle in derision. Mielke was totally unprepared for such behavior. Never before had anyone dared raise a voice against him. He stuttered and squirmed, and finally, raised his arms like an evangelist. "I love every one of you . . . but I really do love all of you," he shouted, his face grief-stricken and pale. Even his staunchest supporters burst into derisive laughter. Mielke was finished.

On December 6, when Germans observe St. Nicklaus Day by presenting their children small pre-Christmas gifts, Egon Krenz threw in the towel and resigned. It was like a St. Nicklaus Day gift to the people. The day before, the Attorney General of the DDR had instituted proceedings against General of the Army Erich Mielke. Mielke was

Young Berliners raid a Stasi safe after tens of thousands stormed the secret police headquarters in East Berlin on January 15, 1990, signaling the end of the regime. Courtesy AP/Wide World.

suspected of having damaged the national economy by ordering and condoning a number of building projects for the private use of party functionaries. He was arrested and placed in solitary confinement. On January 7 the investigation was broadened to include high treason and conspiracy with Honecker to order nationwide surveillance of telecommunications and mail. In addition, Mielke was accused of violating the constitution by ordering the violent smashing of peaceful demonstrations. Meanwhile, Honecker was in the hospital, undergoing cancer surgery.

With Mielke in jail, the People's Chamber, once a rubber-stamp parliament, ordered that the Ministry for State Security be reconstituted as the Amt für Nationale Sicherheit (AfNS), the Office for National Security. All of Mielke's deputies and the seventeen chiefs of the larger MfS directorates were fired. Still hoping to salvage the DDR, the hard-liners appointed another Stasi veteran, Lieutenant General Rudi Mittig, to head the new office. Hans Modrow, district party leader in Dresden, was chosen to lead the party and the government.

However, public demands for the total disbandment of the Stasi had increased to the point where they could no longer be ignored, and the government was forced to dissolve the Office for National Security just eight days after it was formed. The people demanded that the Stasi's headquarters be opened to public scrutiny. The government balked, and tens of thousands of Berliners, mostly young men and women, assembled at the huge, fortress-like complex housing the Stasi on the bitterly cold evening of January 15.[8] Rocks and bricks pounded the steel gate. Appeals for order and reason by members of the Citizens' Committees were drowned out by the roar of the crowd, which was screaming "we are the people!" and ignoring signs pleading "no violence." The small detachment of police inside gave up and opened the gates shortly after five o'clock. The crowd surged through and headed for the various buildings, smashing doors and windows and systematically sacking the offices of their former tormentors. Files and furniture were thrown out of windows. Portraits of Honecker and Brezhnev, the former Soviet leader, were trampled.

The protesters did not know that among them were agents of the Bundesnachrichtendienst, the West German intelligence service. They made a beeline for Building No. 2, which housed the counterespionage directorate. With schematic drawings provided by Colonel Rainer Wiegand, who had defected a fortnight earlier, the agents searched offices of particular interest for the most sensitive material. Their job done, they disappeared quietly into the night.[9] By now a group of protesters had discovered the supply room for the colonels' and generals' cafeteria. Their rage assumed even greater dimensions when they opened cartons of canned delicacies that most East Germans had never tasted. Several women burst into tears. "That can't even be bought in the *Delikatladen*!" one exclaimed, referring to the special stores where Western goods could be purchased only with a Western currency. The wine cellar was stocked with French wines and domestic champagne and cognac. Before continuing to sack the offices, the protesters had a meal of shrimp, smoked eel, and turkey, washed down with plenty of wine and brandy. Dessert was peaches and pineapple. They used the Stasi's silver, Meissen china, and crystal wine glasses and cognac snifters. When they were through, one sarcastic diner crossed "shrimp and smoked eel" off a menu he had found and wrote "bread and water."[10]

Shortly before seven o'clock, the new party leader and premier, Hans Modrow, drove into the courtyard of Stasi headquarters. Demonstrators pounded on his car, shouting "red pig!" He left his car and mounted a lectern that the demonstrators had set up in the center of the yard. His appeal to halt the destruction was met with derisive boos and whistles. Modrow gave up when people began shouting, "Down with the SED!" Pastor Rainer Eppelmann, a major dissident figure and

Stasi target, also showed up. "Violence is only water on the mills of the old Stalinists," he shouted to the crowd, and asked them to disperse. At eight o'clock they began their exit, many staggering from the Stasi's wine and liquor. Outside, demonstrators gleefully passed out souvenirs of their conquest of Stasi headquarters. Producing the most laughter were commemorative badges that were to be issued less than a month later, on February 8, to mark the fortieth anniversary of the founding of the secret police organization.

Mielke remained in prison under investigative detention. New charges were brought against him in 1991, for the 1931 murders of two police officers. In addition he was indicted for manslaughter in connection with the shooting of defectors and for misuse of office, breach of trust, and incitement to pervert justice. He was tried first on the murder charges, and after a twenty-month trial, in October 1993, was found guilty and sentenced to six years. After 1,904 days behind bars, he was released. It was then 1995, and Mielke's prosecution on the other charges had been suspended on the grounds of his advanced age. However, his bank account, which held more than 300,000 marks (about US$187,500), was confiscated. Before his arrest in 1989, the most feared man in East Germany had lived in a luxurious home with access to an indoor pool. In addition, he owned a palatial hunting villa, complete with movie theater, trophy room, 60 servants, and a 15,000-acre hunting preserve. After he was released from prison Mielke was obliged to move into a two-room, 600-square-foot flat. Like all Stasi pensioners, he would thenceforth have to live on 802 marks (about US$512) a month.

There is no question that Mielke was surrounded by crooks: Jürgen Wetzenstein, one of Mielke's lawyers during the murder trial and once a feared communist judge, fled the country the day before prosecutors issued a warrant for his arrest on charges of embezzlement. He allegedly had absconded with DM14 million (about US$8.75 million) from the bank account of a company formerly owned by the Stasi. In 1997 he was living in Cuba. In a similar case, Rolf-Peter Devaux, the major general believed to have sold lists of Stasi spies to the CIA, disappeared with what authorities believed was more than DM1 million in cash, also obtained from an old Stasi firm. Manfred Kittlaus, head of the Berlin police group probing these and other government crimes, said in 1997 that investigations were continuing into the embezzlement of Stasi hard currency funds believed to be in the millions. The primary targets were former Stasi officers who had established suspiciously lucrative businesses.[11]

A number of entrepreneurial former secret policemen set themselves up as private detectives. Others, according to chief investigator

Kittlaus, entered the business world with forged curricula vitae and even new identities. Of all the former high-ranking Stasi officers, foreign espionage chief Markus Wolf seemed to have fared best, having left his job in 1986, claiming political differences with Mielke. Former Colonel Karl Grossmann, who worked under Wolf, later told me that these claims were a smoke screen: "Mielke got rid of him because of his outrageous womanizing." Nevertheless, Wolf was given a spacious apartment in the posh Nikolai Viertel, an upper-class residential area that had been rebuilt as a showcase of communism. The apartment was furnished at no expense to Wolf by the Stasi-controlled Commercial Coordination group, at a cost of 545,752 West marks (about US$363,834). If Wolf really quit the service over differences with Mielke, why did he still have an office and a secretary at Stasi headquarters, and an official car? Wilhelm Schlomann, a lawyer and author of books on Stasi espionage, told me that Wolf never quit. The 1989 salary list of Stasi officers shows a Jens Neffe in second place behind Mielke, earning only 6,138 marks less than the Stasi boss. Rudi Mittig, a three-star general and Mielke's deputy, was paid 1,674 marks less than Neffe. According to Neffe's age and the code number for his assignment, he would have been a twenty-two-year-old general in the passport and customs unit of the Stasi's Potsdam district office. Obviously, *Neffe* is a pseudonym for a highly placed Stasi man. Whoever was responsible for his listing in the salary folder committed a grievous error in not making him older and listing a more plausible assignment. Speculation continues that Neffe is Wolf, in which case Wolf's departure was as phony as the legends he created for his spies.

Although Wolf was convicted of kidnapping in 1997, he was given only a two-year suspended sentence and a fine of DM50,000. In the meantime, his autobiography—a book full of distortions, in which he named only those of his former spies who were either convicted or dead—has become a best-seller in Germany. So was Hitler's *Mein Kampf*.

NOTES

INTRODUCTION

1. Meaning "Red Banner," the German Communist Party (KPD) newspaper in Berlin for which Mielke worked in 1921.

2. On August 9, 1931, two Berlin police officers were shot and killed during a communist demonstration. In a subsequent trial, Mielke and a compatriot were named by witnesses as the killers. The incident will be examined in detail later in this book.

3. In early 1991, a high-ranking German counterespionage official told the author that only about 100 out of more than 100,000 Stasi officers have been willing to reveal details of their activities.

CHAPTER ONE

1. Figures compiled by custodians of the archives of the East German Ministry for State Security.

2. By comparison, U.S. security agencies—the FBI, the CIA, and the NSA—have a combined staff of roughly 100,000 for a population of 250 million. Proportionally, the U.S. security services would need a staff of some 1.8 million if they wanted to emulate the Stasi's personnel structure.

3. Interview in October 1991 with Joachim Gauck, federal commissioner in charge of the Stasi archives in Berlin.

4. From my interview with Wiegand in September 1990, in Munich.

5. From my interview with Wiesenthal in October 1991, in Vienna.

6. There were other Nazi security services, such as the Sicherheitsdienst and the Abwehr, but none was directly involved in political surveillance of the population.

7. Interview in October 1991 with Joachim Gauck, federal commissioner in charge of the archives of the MfS, in Berlin.

8. Ibid.

9. *Die Welt,* March 3, 1995.

10. These figures were reported by the federal government to parliament on January 27, 1997.

11. Ibid.

12. From an interview published in the news magazine *Der Spiegel,* December 1994.

13. From my interview with Professor Scholz, in September 1991, in Bonn.

14. From my interview with Sauer in October 1991, in Braunschweig.

15. Ibid.

16. From my interview in 1991 with Günther Buch, a leading historian of the Federal Institute for All-German Affairs in Berlin, who investigated and registered political offenses for more than forty years.

17. Ludwig Rehlinger, *Freikauf: Die Geschäfte der DDR mit politisch Verfolgten, 1963–1989* (Berlin: Ullstein, 1991).

18. Interview with Günther Buch, historian and archivist at the Federal Institute for All-German Affairs in Berlin.

19. Rüdiger Knechtel and Jürgen Fiedler, *Stalins DDR: Berichte von politisch Verfolgten* (Leipzig: Forum, 1991).

20. Ibid.

21. Ibid.

22. *Statut der Sozialistischen Einheitspartei Deutschlands* (Berlin: Dietz, 1972), p. 25.

23. From my interview with Prof. Scholz in 1991, in Bonn.

24. From my interview with Joachim Gauck in 1991, in Berlin.

25. Ibid.

26. Ibid.

27. From my interview with Gauweiler in October 1991, in Munich.

28. Ibid.

29. Ibid.

30. Interview with William L. Stearman, former U.S. State Department official and member of the National Security Council staff, in Washington, D.C., in 1992. Stearman said that in the 1952 election campaign, Dulles had pledged, "We will roll back the Iron Curtain." Stearman, a Soviet affairs expert, also reported: "Every Hungarian official and those who participated in the uprising told me later that they were encouraged by Dulles's remarks, which had been broadcast to Hungary, and that they fully expected U.S. intervention."

31. I was reporting from Berlin at the time for the Associated Press, and obtained this information from high-ranking U.S. and British officers on the condition of their anonymity.

32. Stearman has asserted that many other courses of action might have been taken to respond to these events. For example, the city of Budapest was in the hands of the freedom fighters on October 28 and 29, and Allied observers and a U.S. peacekeeping force could have been flown into the city. "It certainly would have restricted Soviet action. But nothing was done, and on November 1, the Red Army pushed into the city and steamrolled the resistance." When Czechoslovakia was invaded, Stearman charged, President Lyndon B. Johnson was "more concerned about maintaining good relations with Brezhnev to further détente, which had gotten under way during his Glassboro Summit with Kosygin. Also, he badly wanted to start arms control negotiations."

33. From my interview with the prosecutor, Sauer, in October 1991, in Braunschweig.

34. Interview with Gauweiler in October 1991.

35. Interview with Wiesenthal in 1991, in Vienna.

36. The documents are in my possession.

37. I located this file in East Berlin and later presented it to the former U.S. president on his eighty-third birthday.

38. Interview with Karl Grossmann, former HVA colonel and intimate associate of Markus Wolf during the formation of the Stasi's foreign espionage directorate.

39. Interview with Rainer Wiegand, former colonel in the Stasi counterintelligence directorate.

40. A copy of this document is in my possession.

41. Interview with Bert Rombach, formerly a ranking member of the Bundesverfassungsschutz, the Office for the Protection of the Constitution, which was charged with surveillance of espionage activities and radicalism. In 1991 Rombach became a leading official in the internal security department of the German Federal Ministry of the Interior.

42. From my interview with Knechtel by telephone in 1991.

43. Hans Kroll, *Lebenserinnerungen eines Botschafters* (Berlin: Kiepenheuer & Witsch, 1967).

CHAPTER TWO

1. Margarete Buber-Neumann, *Von Potsdam nach Moskau* (Berlin: Deutsche Verlags-Anstalt, 1957).

2. Bernd Kaufmann, Eckard Reisener, Dieter Schwips, and Henri Walther, *Der Nachrichtendienst der KPD, 1919–1937* (Berlin: Dietz, 1993).

3. The events leading up to the murder were reconstructed from detailed police interrogations of participants arrested in 1932 and 1933 and were extensively reported by the Berlin press.

4. The photograph showing both men sharing the platform is on file at Ullstein photo archives, Berlin.

5. The events of the day were meticulously reported by the newspaper *Berliner Morgenpost* on August 10, 1931.

6. This information comes from Willig's testimony during the trial on July 8, 1934. Willig had recovered after fourteen weeks in the hospital and was promoted to police lieutenant.

7. In a 1997 interview, Dora—the only surviving member of the Anlauf family—said her oldest sister had been engaged and that she quickly married so that the underage Dora could live with her and avoid becoming a ward of the state. Dora later married and lived quietly in East Berlin. She was never harassed by the Stasi, probably because she was careful never to discuss her past with anyone but her husband and her daughter. Her only run-in with the regime occurred when she refused to join the East German communist party (SED) and was demoted from her job as an office manager to a menial position. Her husband died in 1984.

8. *Berliner Morgenpost,* August 10, 1931.

9. From my interviews with former officers of the Ministry for State Security. Another version of the story that emerged during the 1934 trial was that Mielke and Ziemer were provided with false passports, money, and railroad

tickets by Mrs. Kippenberger and left Berlin directly for Moscow by train. This seems unlikely, since the shooting prompted police to seal off all railroad stations and to inspect travelers' documents meticulously.

10. From my conversation with former Lieutenant General Günther Kratsch, former head of the East German Ministry for State Security's counterespionage directorate. Kratsch was allowed by the KGB to see Mielke's Comintern dossier in order to prepare a testimonial for presentation to Mielke on his eightieth birthday. When Mielke learned of Kratsch's mission, he angrily terminated it and forbade the preparation of the testimonial, without any further explanation. "Perhaps he didn't want too much of his background to become public knowledge," Kratsch hypothesized.

11. Mielke's addition of "Prussia" was a source of amusement to former General Kratsch, who told me, "Apparently he was proud of his Prussian heritage, and he certainly acted like a Prussian martinet in his later life."

12. A copy of the document is in my possession.

13. A copy of the document is in my possession.

14. Defenders of Mielke would later claim that confessions had been obtained under torture by the Nazi Gestapo. However, all suspects were in the custody of the regular Berlin city criminal investigation bureau, most of whose detectives were SPD members. Some of the suspects had been nabbed by Nazi SA men and probably beaten before they were turned over to police. In the 1993 trial of Mielke, the court gave the defense the benefit of the doubt and threw out a number of suspect confessions.

15. When I interviewed Margot Kippenberger in 1997, she told me that she had lived for several years with Ivan Chernavin, whom she was not allowed to marry because she was German. The couple had five children, who were allowed to move with her to East Germany. Her common-law husband was kept behind in Russia until she appealed to Khrushchev during the latter's visit to East Berlin in 1960. Two weeks later Chernavin was allowed to leave the Soviet Union. However, he had become an alcoholic, and Margot could no longer live with him. He returned to Soviet Russia, where he died in 1984. Margot and her children were thoroughly fed up with communism. Three of her children had been arrested for antistate activities. Only her connections with old party functionaries saved them from long jail terms. In 1981, the family applied for permission to leave for the West. It was granted, and they now live in Berlin.

16. From my conversation with Walter Janka in 1991. Janka fled from a French internment camp and made his way to Mexico. In 1947, he returned to Germany and became head of the Communist Party's publishing company. Over the years, he became disenchanted at the course that his party was taking in the Stalinization of East Germany. He was arrested in 1956 and interrogated by his old nemesis Mielke. At one point during the questioning, Mielke grabbed Janka by his jacket collar, made a fist, and raised his arm as if to punch him. "Let go of my jacket," Janka said he told the irate Mielke. "You know that threats do not impress me." Mielke: "You underestimate your position and our patience. Don't play the strong man. Here we have brought other people to their knees." Janka was sentenced to five years at hard labor on

charges ranging from spying for the West German Social Democratic Party to having been an organizer of a counterrevolution.

17. A copy of the letter was found in Mielke's prosecution file and is in my possession.

18. Hugh Thomas, *The Spanish Civil War,* revised and enlarged edition (New York: Harper & Row, 1977).

19. F. P. Martin, *Know Your Enemy* (London: Independent Information Center, 1982).

20. This information comes from my 1991 conversations with former MfS Colonel Rainer Wiegand, who told of Mielke bursting into the wartime songs during office parties. At these parties he always preferred the company of Karl Kleinjung, a German communist who served in Soviet partisan units and repeatedly parachuted into Germany. Kleinjung served for years as a Stasi lieutenant general.

21. A copy of the questionnaire is in my possession.

22. From my conversation with Kaufmann in February 1997, in Berlin.

23. Gerhard Finn, *Die politischen Häftlinge der Sowjetzone, 1945–1959* (Pfaffenhofen: Ilmgauverlag, 1960).

24. The Soviets handed the court records to Mielke. Instead of destroying the incriminating papers, he locked them in his private safe, where they were found when his home was searched in 1990. They were used against him in his trial for murder.

25. Documents concerning the Kühnast case are in my possession.

26. According to the newspaper *Bild,* the Mielkes secretly adopted an orphan girl named Ingrid, who was born in 1950. Along with Frank, she was said to have attended the Wilhelm Pieck School, an institution restricted to offspring of high-ranking party functionaries, and eventually served as a captain in the Stasi. The same newspaper reported that she was married to a Stasi first lieutenant, Norbert Knappe, who had refused to talk to *Bild*'s reporters.

27. Finn, *Die politischen Häftlinge.*

28. I have a copy of the directive, 350.09 (CIC/S–3/PG), issued by Headquarters, Counter Intelligence Corps, United States Forces, European Theater, then located at Frankfurt-am-Main.

29. William L. Stearman, *The Soviet Union and the Occupation of Austria* (Bonn: Siegler & Co., 1961).

30. Carola Stern, *Ulbricht: Eine politische Biographie* (Cologne: Kiepenheuer & Witsch, 1964).

31. Unless otherwise indicated, all figures regarding the revolt were released in April 1993 by the Institute for All-German Affairs in Berlin.

32. From my conversations with Rainer Wiegand, former MfS counterespionage colonel, in 1991.

33. Peter Przybylski [former spokesman for the DDR attorney general], *Tatort Politbüro: Die Akte Honecker* (Berlin: Rowohlt, 1991).

34. From my conversations in 1975 with Gitta Bauer, journalist for the Springer Foreign News Service, formerly the wife of Leo Bauer, a veteran communist who was arrested in 1950 and sent to a Soviet labor camp. Mrs. Bauer

was also imprisoned eight years by the MfS, first at Bautzen and later at the Waldheim women's prison. After her release she became an ardent anticommunist. She said she had gotten the information on Mielke's game of intrigue from Leo Bauer after he was released from prison and settled in West Germany, where he became an intimate of Willy Brandt.

35. Nadja Stulz-Herrnstadt, *Das Herrnstadt-Dokument* (Hamburg: Rowohlt, 1990).

36. Zaisser died in obscurity in 1958. Unlike other purge victims, he was never rehabilitated.

37. *Der Spiegel* magazine reported in 1971 that a West German agent working for General Gehlen had infiltrated the school. Soon after his reports reached the general's headquarters near Munich, a series of shipping accidents occurred that "bore Wollweber's signature." The *Empress of Canada* burned in Liverpool harbor on January 25, 1953; and that same month there were fires aboard the *Queen Elizabeth* and the *Queen Mary.* Sabotage was also discovered aboard the British aircraft carriers *Warrior, Triumph,* and *Indomitable,* as well as aboard several cruisers, destroyers, and submarines.

38. Markus Johannes Wolf, former MfS colonel general and espionage chief, in a series of articles in *Stern* magazine, nos. 47, 48, and 49 (1990).

39. Wollweber and Schirdewan were expelled from the Central Committee and the party in February 1958. Wollweber died in 1967.

40. From a 1959 report by an informant of the Ministry for All-German Affairs. A copy of the report is in my possession.

41. Ibid.

42. A copy is in my possession.

43. From my conversation in 1997 with Heinz Busch, former colonel in charge of military analysis in the foreign espionage directorate and a graduate of the Frunze Military Academy in Moscow.

44. Informants of the (West German) Ministry for All-German Affairs.

45. From my conversation with former HVA colonel Busch.

46. Ibid.

47. All refugee figures are based on reports of the Ministry for All-German Affairs, issued in 1966.

48. From a presentation by Vladislav M. Zubok, a leading Russian historian on the Cold War, at the "Conference on Cold War Military Records and History," March 1994, in Washington, D.C.

49. Ibid.

50. Zubok, citing documents found in Soviet archives.

51. Ibid.

52. Ibid.

53. Interview with Rainer Wiegand, former colonel in the Stasi's counterespionage department.

54. The preceding statistics are from the Ministry for All-German Affairs.

55. Central Party Archives in Berlin, cited in Przybylski, *Tatort Politbüro, Pt. 2* (Berlin: Rowohlt, 1992).

56. From the notes of Rainer Wiegand, former colonel in the Stasi's counterespionage directorate. (These notes are in my possession.)

57. Interview with former Stasi colonel Rainer Wiegand.

58. Ibid.

59. Ibid.

CHAPTER THREE

1. From my interview in 1991 with former Colonel Rainer Wiegand, of the MfS counterintelligence directorate.

2. A copy of the agreement is in my possession.

3. The KGB retained its offices until 1994, when all Soviet troops were removed from Germany. All powers accorded the KGB by the DDR regime were withdrawn after reunification, and the KGB's officers became subject to German law for infractions occurring outside military establishments.

4. This document is in my possession.

5. The descriptions in this book of MfS activities in Poland and elsewhere in Eastern Europe are based on my interviews with former Stasi Colonel Rainer Wiegand in 1991 and 1992, in Munich.

6. Interviews with former Stasi colonels Rainer Wiegand of the counterintelligence directorate and Heinz Busch, who headed the analysis department (the Seventh Department) of the espionage directorate.

7. In summer 1991, I learned from a high-level intelligence source in Europe who wished to remain anonymous that Männchen had been offering to sell his knowledge to the highest Western bidder. At the same time, during a German television interview, he hypocritically denounced Stasi defectors as traitors.

8. The entire episode was recounted by former Colonel Rainer Wiegand in a written report and an hour-long tape recording, of which he gave me copies during our meeting in July 1992, in Munich.

9. The exchange rate at the time was about US$1.60 to the ruble.

10. Vinogradov spent about ten years in Germany. His last assignment was completed in Hamburg, West Germany, under the guise of a representative of the Soviet shipping line. He was so successful that the newly assigned chief of the KGB for Germany, based in East Berlin, Major General Gennady F. Titov, saw him as a professional rival and had him transferred back to Moscow.

11. After recording the Brauner case in 1992, Wiegand said pensively: "Today I often see photos of Larissa Brauner in the boulevard press. Meanwhile she has become a member of high society in Europe. Accompanying her husband, she travels through the whole world. She is a wealthy woman. I doubt she is still working for the KGB."

12. Felfe had been a Nazi SS intelligence officer. He was recruited by Skorik in 1951 and joined the fledgling West German Federal Intelligence Service, the Bundesnachrichtendienst (BND). When he was finally arrested in 1961, he was head of the BND's counterintelligence department. Sentenced to fourteen years' imprisonment, he was exchanged in 1969 for Western spies caught in East Germany. Felfe's espionage activities were among the most damaging to

West Germany. Felfe later obtained a doctorate in criminology and became a professor at East Berlin's Humboldt University.

13. Lieutenant Colonel Vladimir Vurfamalenko, the ambitious and unscrupulous son of a high-ranking party functionary with ties to KGB chief Viktor Chebrikov, was after Skorik's job. But Skorik was the KGB's sacred cow, a virtual monument of the successful KGB officer who was fawned over by his boss, Colonel General Markelov, who addressed him as "my esteemed, my dear Misha." Vurfamalenko surreptitiously acquired the records of Skorik's department over a three-year period, probably acting at the behest of Colonel Gennady F. Titov, who was after the top job in East Germany which came with a promotion to major general and which Skorik also coveted. Vurfamalenko cobbled together an analysis purportedly showing that the entire Second Department (counterintelligence) had been resting on its laurels for years. During a visit to Moscow, MfS Colonel Rainer Wiegand was invited to the apartment of the intriguer, who showed the East German the records. "See here, they paid 2,000 rubles for a single piece of information, but they had not had a single success in three years," Vurfamalenko reportedly told Wiegand. "Instead they spent the money on boozing, expensive dinners, and whoring with agents, and nothing comes of it." Skorik wound up as head of counterintelligence in Afghanistan, and Titov got the job in East Berlin.

14. Wandlitz is an idyllic village on a lake near East Berlin. The top members of the regime lived there in a highly secure compound.

15. Interview with former Colonel Rainer Wiegand in 1992. The KGB's cheating was reconfirmed by Werner Bierbaum, former chief of the political analysis division of the espionage directorate, during my interview with him in 1997.

16. This account of the Ivankovic incident is based entirely on my interviews in 1993 with the victim and with former Stasi Colonel Rainer Wiegand.

17. A copy of the handwritten statement is in my possession.

18. This case is discussed in another chapter.

19. Titov was KGB resident in Norway, where he controlled a number of agents. He was expelled in 1977 and became an assistant to General Vladimir A. Kryuchkov, chief of foreign espionage, who later became head of the KGB. In 1985 Titov was assigned to East Germany as deputy to Colonel General Oleg Shumilov, whom he succeeded in 1987.

20. Oleg Gordievsky, former colonel and chief of the London KGB station, who defected in 1985, said in his book *KGB: The Inside Story* (New York: HarperCollins, 1990): "Titov was deeply unpopular among his KGB colleagues (though not his superiors), and save for a small group of protégés, feared by his subordinates."

21. Interview with Grossmann.

CHAPTER FOUR

1. The details of this case recounted here come from my interviews with Erdmann in 1993, in Berlin; from Stasi files; and from court records.

2. From my interview with Erdmann on September 24, 1991, in Berlin.

3. Ibid.

4. A tape recording of the trial was found by Erdmann after reunification and was made available to me.

5. Interview with Günther Buch, historian and archivist of the Federal Institute for All-German Affairs.

6. Gerhard Finn, *Die politischen Häftlinge der Sowjet Zone, 1945–1959* (Pfaffenhofen: Ilmgauverlag, 1960).

7. From my interview with Erdmann.

8. Ibid.

9. Rüdiger Knechtel and Jürgen Fiedler, *Stalins DDR* (Leipzig: Forum, 1991).

10. From my interview with Knechtel in 1993.

11. Kneifel's story, retold here, is based on my 1993 interviews with Kneifel and his wife in Nürnberg as well as on Stasi records.

12. Ibid.

13. Interview with Knechtel in 1993.

14. Interview with Kneifel.

15. Ibid.

16. Interview with Mrs. Kneifel.

17. The order was found in Kneifel's Stasi file, which was made available to me.

18. Statement by Frank Hiekel, who was installed as deputy director of the Bautzen prison in 1991.

19. Interview with the Berlin newspaper *Bild.* Lustik retired on a pension of DM2,300 (about US$1,500) and lives in a villa built by prisoners.

20. By 1995 all had retired, and pretrial investigations were under way into those against whom former prisoners had filed charges of torture.

21. Conversation in 1990 with Gitta Bauer (since deceased), who also was arrested and spent six years in various prisons, among them Bautzen. After her release she became a foreign correspondent for the Berlin-based Springer newspapers, reporting for many years from New York. Similar stories have been reported by other communist functionaries who had fallen into disfavor, especially stories of Mielke's threats to hack off heads.

22. Wolfgang Leonard, member of the Communist Party's division of agitation and propaganda, who returned from Soviet exile, reported in a February 1990 speech: "Max Fechner, chairman of the SPD Central Committee in Berlin, received from the Soviets a new automobile and 300,000 marks for a book he was writing. The son of Erich W. Gniffke, another SPD functionary, was released from a Soviet prison camp and flown to Berlin aboard a special Red Army plane. Otto Grotewohl, a leading member of the SPD Central Committee, was promised a leading position in the new party by Marshal Georgy K. Zhukov, the Soviet commander."

23. All figures were reported by the SPD's Friedrich Ebert Foundation in 1994.

24. Interview with Hildebrandt in Berlin in 1961, shortly after the Berlin Wall was built.

25. Conversation with General Howley in 1969. He died on July 30, 1993, at the age of ninety.

26. Report in West Berlin's daily newspaper *Morgen-Echo,* October 18, 1948.

27. Conversation in 1992 with former Stasi Colonel Rainer Wiegand, who said that during Stasi cadre meetings Knye would rail against officers who dared asked questions he thought were nonsensical. "Knye branded them deviationists in a manner so brutal that they shook in their boots for days, wondering when they would be arrested."

28. Interview with Rainer Hildebrandt in 1991.

29. Ibid.

30. Ibid.

31. Ibid.

32. Johannes Hedrich, a high-ranking officer of the East German State Security Service who defected in June 1953, told U.S. intelligence interrogators that it was indeed an attempted kidnapping. One car was to ram Hildebrandt as he was riding his bicycle, causing him to fall. Then they were to speed away. A second vehicle was to pick up Hildebrandt, ostensibly to take him to a hospital. In actuality, it would cross the sector border and deliver him to waiting Soviet MVD officers.

33. Conversation in 1995 with Günther Buch, former official of the Institute for All-German Affairs in West Berlin.

34. Ibid.

35. Kai-Uwe Merz, *Kalter Krieg als antikommunistischer Widerstand* (Munich: R. Oldenburg, 1987).

36. Conversation in 1995 with Peter Sichel, former CIA station chief in Berlin.

37. Less than a year after Heckscher was reassigned to Laos, four members of the KgU who had served as Stasi informants returned to East Berlin. The communist press reported their "defection," saying they "voluntarily turned themselves in to state security organs" because they no longer wanted to be associated with a terrorist group. It was a well-orchestrated propaganda campaign.

38. Interview with Bailey in 1994 in Munich.

39. Conversation with Peter Sichel in 1995, in New York.

40. *Kurier* (Berlin), March 20, 1958.

41. *Bild Zeitung,* April 1958.

42. Melnikov's role as mastermind of the UFJ was revealed to me by an unimpeachable U.S. intelligence source on condition of anonymity. Although an obviously brilliant intelligence officer, Melnikov simply applied a variation of the so-called Trust formed in the 1920s by GPU Chief Feliks Edmundovich Dzerzhinski as an ostensibly anti-Bolshevik organization. The Trust was used to infiltrate the numerous White Russian émigré groups in Western Europe that Lenin saw as a danger to his young Bolshevik state. With Trust operations stretching over several years, the GPU succeeded in neutralizing émigrés' attempts to destabilize Bolshevik Russia and reestablish a non-Bolshevik government.

43. I served as an interpreter at a U.S. Army Signal Corps radiotelephone relay station a few miles outside Belzig in 1946. The station handled communications between the U.S. Army's European headquarters and the Berlin garri-

son. It was established in the Soviet zone by special agreement between General Eisenhower and Marshal Zhukov. Station personnel were under around-the-clock surveillance by the Soviets, who delighted in petty harassment. One evening the station commander was summoned by the Soviets to 25 Brandenburgerstrasse in Belzig. When he asked directions to that address from a local woman, she exclaimed: "My God, don't go there! That is the GPU's place." The Germans at the time still called the secret police by its old name. When the station chief and I presented ourselves at the given address, we were met by a short, heavy-set Russian carrying a shotgun and wearing a civilian coat over military breeches that were tucked into jackboots. Another Russian addressed him as "Tovarishch General." The general appeared friendly and explained that he wanted us to drive him in our three-quarter-ton weapons carrier across nearby fields so he could shoot jackrabbits he hoped would be caught in the beams of the headlights. Our excursion lasted a few hours, netted a dozen rabbits, and concluded with the general passing around a bottle of vodka. During the drinking bout I asked what the general's name was, and one of the Russians replied, "Melnikov." When my Signal Corps group was detained a few weeks later for accidentally having taken a road not listed on our Soviet passes, we were brought to MGB headquarters and ran into Melnikov as he was leaving the building. I tried to speak to him, but he looked at me stone-faced and continued on his way without uttering a word. We were released a few hours later, after a lecture about map reading. Later I saw Melnikov on yet another occasion in uniform, beating a young Red Army private whom he had spotted holding hands with a farm girl.

44. No relation to Stasi victim Horst Erdmann, whose story is told earlier in this chapter.

45. The Latvian guerrillas were supported by the British intelligence service using former German Navy S-boats with German crews to land supplies and infiltrators on the Baltic coast. The Soviet deception operation is described by Gordievsky in *KGB: The Inside Story* (New York: HarperCollins, 1990).

46. Anonymous U.S. intelligence source.

47. Interview with Günther Buch in 1995.

48. Interview with Günther Buch in 1995; *Der Spiegel,* April 1952.

49. Anonymous U.S. intelligence source who had access to the files.

50. A copy of the pledge is in my possession.

51. The details of the kidnapping, of its planning, and of the subsequent interrogation are recorded in a three-inch-thick Stasi file, a copy of which is in my possession. The file contains a copy of Linse's application for a position with the UFJ, including a detailed questionnaire that UFJ Chief and Soviet agent Erdmann had him complete. A highly reliable U.S. intelligence source told me on condition of anonymity that Walther Rosenthal, Erdmann's deputy and also a Soviet agent, set up Linse for the kidnapping.

52. Copies of the transcripts are in my possession.

53. The interrogation protocols are in my possession.

54. Copies of the Soviet trial records are in my possession.

55. A copy of the thesis written by Colonel Thomas Rieger is in my possession.

56. Conversation in 1993 with former MfS Colonel Rainer Wiegand.
57. The order, classified as secret, is in my possession.
58. A copy of the document is in my possession.
59. Interview in 1992 with former Stasi Colonel Rainer Wiegand.
60. Statement made in August 1990 by the last DDR deputy attorney general, Lothar Reuter.
61. This information is from the Postal Ministry in Bonn.
62. After World War II, Felfe was recruited by the KGB and joined the West German Federal Intelligence Service. After more than a decade as a successful mole, he was uncovered in 1963 and was sentenced to fourteen years in prison. He was exchanged six years later for Western agents held by the East Germans.
63. A copy of the report is in my possession.
64. A copy is in my possession.
65. I have such a tape in my collection.
66. A copy of the Stasi pay roster is in my possession.
67. Interview with the driver of a Stasi general on condition of anonymity.
68. Interviews with Günther Buch of the Federal Institute for All-German Affairs and with former Stasi Colonel Rainer Wiegand.

CHAPTER FIVE

1. Cited in 1992 by the Office for the Protection of the Constitution, responsible for counterespionage.
2. Comments from our conversation in April 1997.
3. Ibid.
4. Information given me by the office of the prosecutor general.
5. A copy of the report is in my possession.
6. Bernd Kaufmann, Eckard Reisener, Dieter Schwips, and Henri Walther, *Der Nachrichtendienst der KPD, 1919–1937* (Berlin: Dietz, 1993).
7. Interview with Günther Buch, Institute for All-German Affairs.
8. Information obtained from a West German counterintelligence official on condition of anonymity.
9. Interview on condition of anonymity with a high-ranking West German government official who was an observer at hearings of a special parliamentary commission probing the Guillaume affair in summer and fall 1974. The commission was chaired by the eminent professor of law Theodor Eschenburg, University of Tübingen, and became known as the Eschenburg Commission.
10. Ibid.
11. Ibid.
12. Ibid.
13. Interview with Ambassador Rush in 1974.
14. Statement by West German government spokesman Rüdiger von Wechmar, June 26, 1974.

15. Interview in 1962 with Inspector Johannes Neumann of the Federal Criminal Police (Bundeskriminalamt), the West German equivalent of the U.S. FBI.

16. Interview on condition of anonymity with two former members of the West German counterespionage agency, the Bundesamt für Verfassungsschutz (Office for the Protection of the Constitution).

17. Conversation in 1997 with Fritz Michel, former department head with the equivalent rank of colonel in the Office for the Protection of the Constitution.

18. Interview, on condition of anonymity, with an official observer at the Eschenburg Commission.

19. Testimony at the 1993 treason trial of Markus Wolf, former head of the Stasi's foreign espionage directorate.

20. *Der Spiegel,* October 1974.

21. When the Office for the Protection of the Constitution was formed in the late 1940s, the West German parliament decreed that the agency would be restricted to observing subversive activities by both the left and the extreme right and to counterespionage. Lawmakers decided against giving the agency powers of arrest because they did not want to create an institution identical in structure and powers to the Nazi Gestapo.

22. Conversation with the late Johannes Neumann, federal criminal police inspector.

23. *Bunte Illustrierte,* September 1981.

24. *Quick* magazine, August 1988.

25. I obtained these details about the Kuron affair in confidential conversations with former counterintelligence officials as well from trial testimony in 1992.

26. West Germany had never recognized East Germany in a diplomatic sense. In an agreement to "normalize" relations, however, the two states established representatives who carried out ambassadorial functions.

27. Interview in 1997 with Klaus Wagner, presiding judge at the provincial high court in Düsseldorf.

28. Interview with Hellenbroich in 1993.

29. Testimony at the 1992 trial of Kuron.

30. Interview with Gerlinde Garau published in *Quick* magazine, 1992.

31. From my interview in 1993 with Karl Grossmann, former colonel and deputy head of counterintelligence in the Stasi's foreign espionage directorate (the Main Administration for Foreign Intelligence).

32. Ibid.

33. A copy of this dissertation is in my possession.

34. Interview with presiding judge Klaus Wagner.

35. Interview in 1993 with Karl Grossmann.

36. Neither was ever indicted. In 1995 the West German Supreme Court ruled that officers of the Stasi's foreign espionage directorate could not be tried if they worked only from East German territory.

37. Presiding judge Klaus Wagner of the provincial high court in Düsseldorf.

38. *Bild am Sonntag,* February 1997.

39. Ibid.

40. Details of the Krase case were provided by a retired high-ranking West German intelligence officer on condition of anonymity. In addition, I gleaned relevant facts from the indictment of former Lieutenant General Günther Kratsch, who led the Stasi's counterespionage directorate (the Second Directorate).

41. Ibid.

42. This incident and others that took place during the conference were described to me on condition of anonymity by an intelligence officer who participated in the meeting and who was close to Count Hardenberg.

43. Related to me on condition of anonymity by a former intelligence official.

44. Ibid.

45. Details of the Gieren case are listed in the indictment of Lieutenant General Günther Kratsch et al. for treason. The case against Kratsch and officers under his command was dismissed by the West German supreme court because they operated solely on DDR territory.

46. Gieren indictment.

47. German newspapers identified the defector as Karl Grossmann, who had been deputy chief of the counterintelligence division before his retirement in 1987. In an interview with me in 1992, Grossmann denied this but confirmed Gast's role as a spy.

48. The following details of the Gast case come from court testimony and from my conversations with intelligence officers on condition of anonymity.

49. Interview in 1997 with Judge Wagner.

50. Conversation in 1991 on condition of anonymity with a high official of the BND.

51. Conversation with Buch in July 1998.

52. Conversation in 1995 with Ferdi Breidbach, former Christian Democratic member of the federal parliament.

53. Testimony before the high provincial court in Düsseldorf, 1993.

54. Ibid.

55. Lubig indictment.

56. Ibid.

57. Ibid.

58. Ibid.

59. Ibid.

60. Interview with Busch in 1993.

61. *Bildzeitung,* July 1991.

62. Trial testimony in 1961.

63. The journalist, who is now dead, confided this story to me in the 1960s. I have withheld his name in deference to his family.

64. *Focus* (news magazine), no. 19, May 1993.

65. Interview in 1996 with Günther Buch, former chief archivist and historian with the Ministry for All-German Affairs.

66. Peter-Ferdinand Koch, *Die feindlichen Brüder* (Munich: Scherz, 1994).
67. *Süddeutsche Zeitung,* April 1991.
68. Trial testimony.
69. Trial testimony in June 1992.
70. Interview with former Ambassador Günter Diehl, and information provided by the prosecutor general's office.
71. Conversation with retired Ambassador Günter Diehl.
72. Information provided by the federal prosecutor general's office.
73. Trial testimony.
74. Statement by the federal prosecutor general.
75. Trial testimony.
76. Statement by the federal prosecutor general.
77. Trial testimony.
78. Interview in 1996 on condition of anonymity with a former high-ranking West German counterespionage official.
79. Ibid.
80. 1993 indictment of Stasi Lt. Gen. Kratsch, whose counterintelligence directorate controlled Gebauer.
81. *Berliner Morgenpost,* February 1996.
82. Interview with Schröder in summer 1992, after he was indicted for espionage. Schröder, who worked for me when I was in charge of the Bonn bureau of the Associated Press, denied that he had been a spy.

CHAPTER SIX

1. Unless otherwise indicated, this account of the safe caper has been constructed from documents provided me by U.S. Army counterintelligence agents and by individuals identified in later notes.
2. From my interview in 1991, in Port Charlotte, Florida, with retired Colonel Franz H. Ross, who investigated the Hesse case for the chief of U.S. Army Military Intelligence. Much of the story as retold below comes from this interview.
3. Ibid.
4. Interview with Leyden in 1991, in Washington, D.C.
5. Interview with Colonel Ross.
6. As reported in the newspaper *Main-Post,* June 30, 1956.
7. Interview with Colonel Ross.
8. Ibid.
9. Reported in detail, with photographs, in the newspaper *Main-Post,* July 11, 1956.
10. Ibid.
11. A copy of the letter is in my possession.
12. Copies of this and preceding memoranda are in my possession.
13. From my interview in 1992, in Juan-les-Pins, France, with Willms, who was my superior when I was assigned to the 513th MI Group as a reserve officer.
14. I was present at this meeting in 1960.

15. From my interview with Wiegand (Munich, 1992) about his attendance at the Stasi counterespionage school.

16. Ibid.

17. My interview with retired Colonel William G. Leyden in Washington, D.C., in 1992.

18. The details of the story retold here are from my interview in 1997 with Christa Trapp, who now is a U.S. citizen and has a different name.

19. By agreement between the Western Allies and the Soviets, this was the only transit route by which Westerners could reach the city.

20. A cable classified as secret was sent on July 22, 1955, to Secretary of State John Foster Dulles by the Berlin mission, which said: "We have concluded that giving publicity to Erdmann and Trapp cases might serve to give them both protection from further harassment or possible recrimination by SSD [the State Security Service, a forerunner of the Ministry for State Security] agents, on theory that SSD less likely bother these individuals in future if SSD's past action were well known to the public. At the same time publicity would serve to alert other local employees to penetration efforts of East Germany and thus better enable to ward off SSD approaches, in particular by avoiding trips to East Berlin or by surface through Soviet Zone." Twenty-eight days later, the mission called a news conference to announce the incidents.

21. The plan was found in the Stasi archive in 1990. A copy is in my possession.

22. Interview with Christa Trapp.

23. From the kidnapping plan.

24. Interview with Christa Trapp.

25. Trial transcript.

26. I interviewed Koch in summer 1991 at the former colonel's country cottage, northeast of Berlin. Although reluctant to talk at first, Koch confirmed details of the Hall case when I told him no harm could come to his ex-agents, since Hall was already in prison and had fully confessed.

27. While researching the matter in Berlin in summer 1990, I was given copies of documents that Hall had sold to the East Germans, which were found at Stasi headquarters. Because the documents originated with the National Security Agency and were highly classified, I complied with federal law and turned them over to U.S. intelligence authorities.

28. Interview with former Stasi counterintelligence Colonel Rainer Wiegand in Munich in 1991.

29. From a statement by Hall, videotaped in December 1988, and from a copy of the transcript of Yildirim's trial, both in my possession.

30. Ibid.

31. Ibid.

32. Ibid.

33. Ibid.

34. Ibid.

35. From my interview in 1991 with Karl Grossmann, former Stasi colonel and deputy chief of foreign counterintelligence.

36. I have changed the name to protect his identity.

37. Interview with former Stasi Colonel Grossmann.

38. Interview in 1991, on condition of anonymity, with a ranking official of West Berlin's criminal investigation department.

39. Ibid.

40. Colonel Herrington is the author of *Silence Was a Weapon* and *Peace With Honor?* (San Francisco: Presidio Press, 1982 and 1983, respectively).

41. I have a copy.

42. From my interview with Walter in 1997, in Savannah, Georgia.

43. Ibid.

44. Ibid.

45. From my conversation with Boeden in 1997, in Bonn.

46. From my interviews with Grossmann in 1990 and early 1991, in Berlin.

47. In his book, *Man Without a Face* (New York: Times Books, 1997), ex–spy chief Markus Wolf claimed that Carney had contacted his department from Texas, saying he wanted to desert. Wolf claimed that Carney left the United States on a false Cuban passport and was flown to East Berlin via Havana and Moscow. I know this is untrue, as is Wolf's statement that Carney disappeared from a hiding place in southern East Germany in early 1990 and was believed to have been kidnapped by CIA agents.

48. I brought copies out of Berlin and relinquished them to U.S. authorities, in compliance with federal espionage laws.

49. My interview with former Stasi Colonel Karl Grossmann.

50. A copy of the letter is in my possession.

51. Interview in 1992, in Munich, with former Colonel Heinz Busch, military analyst and head of the task force.

52. Interview with General Lynn by telephone in 1992.

53. Interview with Koch in 1992, in Stolzenhagen, Germany.

54. Interview with Wiegand in 1991, in Munich.

55. Interview in 1991 with former Stasi Colonel Karl Grossmann.

56. Ibid.

57. Ibid.

58. Ibid.

59. I was allowed access to these files by the German government commission in control of the Stasi archive in May 1996. Because of government regulations, files involving Germany's allies could not be copied.

60. Interview on condition of anonymity with German intelligence sources.

61. From a conversation in 1997 with the official, who requested anonymity.

62. Interview with Busch in 1992.

63. Ibid.

64. Ibid.

65. This has never been confirmed officially. However, I was told in 1997 by a highly reliable German intelligence source that authorities have been searching for Devaux for several years. Some believed he was provided a new identity and is living in the United States. However, in May 1997, authorities were reportedly concentrating their search on Belgium, where a man resembling Devaux had made a bank deposit of more than DM1 billion (about

US$625 million) that was believed to have originated with a covert, Stasi-owned company.

66. From the trial record.

67. Interview in *Die Zeit* magazine, March 1997.

68. Interview in 1997 with former Colonel Heinz Busch, who said Rogalla was the only agent with the first name Jürgen who occupied a high position and who was known to criticize the regime with impunity.

69. Trial testimony.

70. Indictment of June 20, 1994.

71. Interview with Judge Wagner by telephone in 1997.

72. Ibid.

73. From my interview in 1996 with Presiding Judge Ina Obst-Öllers of the provincial high court in Düsseldorf.

74. Ibid.

75. Trial testimony.

76. A copy of the report is in my possession.

77. Evan C. Reeves, *President Kennedy: Profile of Power* (New York: Simon and Schuster, 1993).

78. Ibid.

79. From my 1997 interview, on condition of anonymity, with a former high-ranking counterespionage official.

80. Copies of Scholz's Stasi dossier are in my possession.

81. Copies of reports contained in Naor's Stasi dossier are in my possession.

82. A professor at the University of Maine who wished to remain anonymous recalled during a conversation with me in 1998 that Naor had twice been awarded Fulbright scholarships for study in Eastern Europe, but the informant could not recall the dates.

83. A copy of the briefing paper is in my possession.

84. Interview in 1992, in Munich, with former Colonel Heinz Busch.

85. The entire account, except when otherwise noted, originated with former Colonel Rainer Wiegand. The woman's clear name is known to me, but under U.S. federal law it would be a felony to publish it.

86. Günter Bohnsack and Herbert Brehmer, *Auftrag Irreführung: Wie die Stasi Politik im Westen machte* (Hamburg: Carlsen, 1992).

87. Ibid.

88. The file was found by a young dissident who took part in the storming of Stasi headquarters on January 15, 1990. He had forgotten about it until I contacted him in fall 1991, in search of Stasi documents. After I purchased a number of Stasi files from him, I asked whether he had anything else concerning America. He suddenly remembered the Reagan file, which he had hidden behind a bookcase. At first I suspected a forgery, but the details the file contained could only have been assembled by an experienced intelligence officer from espionage reports. I presented the original of the file to President Reagan on his eighty-first birthday, February 6, 1992.

89. I traveled in Europe as a government consultant in May 1987, and spoke with a broad spectrum of government and political party officials as well as the media, eliciting their views on the proposed treaty to withdraw intermedi-

ate range missiles from Europe. My analysis was shared with President Reagan and with the U.S. secretary of state. Thus, I was familiar with sensitive discussions on the subject within the administration.

90. Copies are in my possession.

91. Interview with Bierbaum in 1997, in Berlin.

92. From my interviews with numerous former Stasi officers, including Heinz Busch, HVA chief military analyst, and Karl Grossmann, onetime deputy head of external counterintelligence.

93. Report by former Colonel Rainer Wiegand after his defection to the West German Federal Intelligence Service. A copy is in my possession.

94. Ibid.

CHAPTER SEVEN

1. Interview in 1992, in Munich, with former Colonel Rainer Wiegand, who served two decades under Kratsch.

2. Ibid.

3. I have several such warrants signed by Mielke.

4. The death list is in my possession.

5. Interview with former Colonel Wiegand.

6. Ibid.

7. Ibid.

8. A tape recording of the trial, as well as about a thousand pages of the Stasi investigation, including the protocol of the execution, are in my possession.

9. General Reinhard Gehlen was the Wehrmacht's intelligence chief for the eastern front. In 1945 he surrendered to the U.S. Army and offered to place his organization at the disposal of the United States until such time as West Germany regained her sovereignty. In 1956, the organization became the Bundesnachrichtendienst, the Federal Intelligence Service. Gehlen retired in 1968.

10. Interview in 1996 in Berlin and correspondence with Müller.

11. From a letter written by Frau Müller to me in 1996.

12. From my interview in 1996 with Juretzko and from documents concerning his case.

13. I have a copy of this letter.

14. Indictment in 1993 for espionage of former Colonels Rolf Wagenbreth and Rolf Rabe, chief and deputy, respectively, of the Stasi foreign espionage directorate's disinformation and active measures department. The charges were eventually dropped, after the German Supreme Court ruled that former Stasi espionage officers could not be tried because they had acted under laws of a sovereign government and had not actually spied on West German territory.

15. Ibid.

16. Interview with former Stasi counterespionage officer Colonel Rainer Wiegand.

17. This account of the Liebing affair is based on Stasi documents provided me by Reinhard Borgman of Radio Free Berlin.

18. Interview with Günther Buch, former chief archivist and historian for the West German Ministry for All-German Affairs.

19. From a letter I received from Günther Jahn in 1996.

20. Ministry for State Security arrest report of September 14, 1967.

21. These details are from my interview with Wiedenhoeft in 1997.

22. The United States established diplomatic relations with the German Democratic Republic in fall 1974.

23. From my interview in 1997 with Maxwell Rabb, who served as U.S. ambassador to Italy during Ronald Reagan's presidency.

24. President Johnson wrote Rabb in June 1969: "Your own efforts in East Germany and your successes in obtaining the release of the young Americans imprisoned there were outstanding examples of what most gratifies me about our country and the unselfish good people it produces. Please know that I am grateful, as all your countrymen should be."

25. Interview in 1993, in Munich, with former Colonel Rainer Wiegand of the Stasi's counterespionage directorate.

26. Ibid.

27. Ibid.

28. From a 1988 report to the counterespionage directorate by the Ninth Main Directorate (charged with investigations). The report also listed names of identified CIA and British Secret Intelligence Service officers. I am prevented by U.S. federal law from revealing the names, but a copy of the report is in my possession.

29. Interview with former Colonel Rainer Wiegand.

30. Ibid.

31. Ibid.

32. Interview in 1991, in Berlin, with former General Kratsch.

33. Ibid.

34. The entire sensor story is based on an extensive report former Colonel Rainer Wiegand provided Western intelligence after his defection in 1989. Wiegand gave me a tape recording of this report.

CHAPTER EIGHT

1. From my interview with former Stasi Colonel Rainer Wiegand in 1992, in Munich.

2. Ibid.

3. Ibid.

4. A copy of the report is in my possession.

5. A copy of the protocol is in my possession.

6. Internal Stasi document, a copy of which is in my possession.

7. Thirty-page meeting protocol, a copy of which is in my possession.

8. A copy of the report is in my possession.

9. Stasi follow-up report of February 18, 1981, in my possession.

10. General Damm's proposal to Mielke, a copy of which is in my possession.

11. I have copies of these documents.

12. A copy of the cable is in my possession.

13. Top secret Stasi report, a copy of which is in my possession.

14. A copy of the memorandum is in my possession.

15. Excerpt from Honecker's account 628 with the German Trade Bank in East Berlin. The account was opened in 1974 on Honecker's orders, which decreed that it must have a continuous balance of 100 million convertible West marks and be at his sole disposition. A copy of the balance sheet is in my possession.

16. I have a copy of this cable, which was found in the Stasi archive.

17. From my 1992 interview with former Stasi Colonel Rainer Wiegand, in Munich.

18. Ibid.

19. A copy of the order is in my possession.

20. A copy of the letter is in my possession.

21. Nathaniel Davis, *The Last Years of Salvador Allende* (Ithaca: Cornell University Press, 1985).

22. Ibid.

23. Guided by a former Stasi man who wished to remain anonymous and who had been close to General Günther Kratsch, I visited the site after the Stasi's demise in 1990.

24. Interview with Wiegand in 1992.

25. The Associated Press, August 14, 1986.

26. Letters to party secretary-general Erich Honecker from the financial administration of party-owned firms. Copies of these letters are in my possession.

27. Honecker fled to Moscow in winter 1990, after the Soviets had given him asylum in a military hospital near Berlin. When the Soviet Union collapsed, the new Russian leader, Boris Yeltsin, ordered that Honecker be turned over to the German judiciary, which wanted to try him on manslaughter charges in the shooting of people trying to escape from East Germany. Pressured relentlessly by the German government, the Chilean government ordered his expulsion from the embassy in July 1992, and Honecker returned to Berlin. In January 1993, a Berlin court ruled that he was unfit to stand trial. He flew to Chile on January 14 to rejoin his wife and daughter. He died a year later of liver cancer.

28. Interview with former Stasi Colonel Rainer Wiegand in 1992.

29. Ibid.

30. Interview with William L. Stearman, former U.S. National Security Council expert on Soviet and liberation movement affairs, in 1997, in Washington.

31. A copy of the decision is in my possession.

32. Morgan Norval, *Inside the ANC* (Washington, D.C.: Selous Foundation Press, 1990).

33. Interview with former Stasi Colonel Rainer Wiegand.

34. I have the report.

35. Ibid.

36. Interview with William L. Stearman, former member of the U.S. National Security Council and expert on Soviet and national liberation movement affairs, and adjunct professor for international affairs (1973–1993) at Georgetown University, Washington, D.C.

37. In this connection, Stearman commented: "Foreign correspondents' obvious unconcern about the SACP is, I believe, due partly to ignorance, but mostly to a reluctance to discredit the popular new regime. Furthermore, SACP members keep silent about their affiliation and are *acting* more like capitalists than communists, which communists normally do and have done in similar circumstances; proceed very cautiously, slowly, and with guile in imposing 'socialism'—in this case, to avoid, inter alia, discouraging foreign investments and encouraging white flight and to buy time needed for incrementally consolidating control of the levers of power and influence."

38. Interview in 1992, in Berlin, with Günther Buch, former chief archivist and historian of the Ministry for All-German Affairs.

39. Documents provided me by Kästner.

40. Interview in 1992, in Munich, with former Stasi Colonel Rainer Wiegand.

41. *The Economist,* July 1994.

42. A copy of the document is in my possession.

43. A copy of the order is in my possession.

44. Interview in 1992, in Munich, with former Stasi Colonel Rainer Wiegand.

45. Ibid.

46. Oleg Gordievsky, *KGB: The Inside Story* (New York: HarperCollins, 1990).

47. Copies of the contracts are in my possession.

48. A copy of the memo authorizing the payment is in my possession.

49. Interview with Wiegand in 1992, in Munich.

CHAPTER NINE

1. Statement in 1990 by Vaclav Havel, Czechoslovakia's noncommunist president.

2. The details of Stasi involvement in the La Belle bombing are based on my extensive recorded interviews in 1991 and 1992 with former Colonel Rainer Wiegand and on written reports that he provided.

3. Intelligence jargon for branches.

4. Interview with Wiegand in 1991, in Munich.

5. Ibid.

6. The document is in my possession.

7. From my conversation with Mr. Whitehead in 1991.

8. Statement made to me on February 1, 1991 by Thomas F. Jones, FBI inspector in charge of the public affairs office.

9. President Reagan ordered that American businesses withdraw their U.S. employees from Libya.

10. I have in my possession the final Operation Lux report, which was written on December 28, 1989.

11. Conversation with Cynthia Miller.

12. All details of the case recounted here are based on the legal record.

CHAPTER TEN

1. Interview with former Colonel Rainer Wiegand in 1991, in Munich.
2. Ibid.
3. Ibid.
4. Former Stasi Colonel Rainer Wiegand, who at the time of these events was a counterintelligence officer with the National People's Army.
5. Ibid.
6. Ibid.
7. A wanted notice was issued by West German authorities in 1952 for Daoud, who was suspected of having masterminded the Munich attack.
8. Meeting recorded in an MfS protocol dated August 23, 1979, a copy of which is in my possession.
9. Having made "contact" was an understatement at best. In June 1990, the new noncommunist Interior Minister, Balasc Horvath, made public a letter signed "Carlos." This letter was addressed to Janos Kadar, the Communist Party chief and head of the Hungarian government, and expressed appreciation for Hungary's hospitality. Horvath also turned over thirteen AVH files to the prosecutor general. These files showed that "Carlos" carried a diplomatic passport issued by the government of South Yemen and that he was asked to leave Hungary in 1981. Nevertheless, he returned several times thereafter. His last stay in Hungary was in fall 1985, and when he departed, according to the interior minister, he left behind sixty rocket launchers and forty pounds of explosives.
10. Statement to officials of the Federal Criminal Investigation Agency by former Colonel Günter Jäckel of the Stasi's antiterrorist directorate.
11. From a statement issued to the press by the Berlin prosecutor's office in 1991.
12. Voigt's admission in a June 1991 German television interview after he eluded arrest.
13. Arrest warrant issued by the West Berlin prosecutor against El Sibai and stating the involvement of Carlos, Weinreich, and Voigt, whose names also were on the wanted list.
14. A high-ranking West European police official told me in March 1991, on condition of anonymity, that Carlos had been in Warsaw several months earlier and that Western security authorities knew it but had taken no action against him. The official also said that Carlos was in Bulgaria for several days in 1986. He was accompanied on this trip by several women and was armed. Bulgarian officials met him at the airport. This information also was relayed to police in Western Europe and presumably to intelligence organizations as well.
15. The episode was recounted to me by a Berlin police official on condition of anonymity.
16. Interview in 1991 with former Colonel Rainer Wiegand.
17. Conversation with Rainer Eppelmann, who became minister of defense after the ouster of the communist government in 1990. He served until reunification, and then entered the parliament in Bonn.

18. A copy of the memorandum is in my possession.

19. Documents of the MfS's Twenty-Second Directorate (for counterterrorism).

20. Interview with investigating magistrate Rosario Priore in Rome in 1992.

21. After the Stasi was dissolved in 1990, according to Rainer Wiegand, Stuchly was running a sausage stand near the Alexander Platz, in downtown East Berlin.

22. I have changed the name to protect the former officer's identity.

CHAPTER ELEVEN

1. Conversation with General Kroesen in 1993.

2. I have a copy of the document.

3. From my conversation with a German police official in 1992 on condition of anonymity.

4. Police reports.

5. Interview with Caecily Rohwedder, the Rohwedders' daughter, who was twenty-three years old at the time and completing studies for a master degree in international relations at New York's Columbia University.

6. Conversation in 1991 with Gerhard Heuer, deputy undersecretary of the Department of Interior and in charge of internal security. He was the deputy to State Secretary Hans Neusel, whom RAF terrorists tried to kill with a bomb.

7. The DDR was apportioned into fifteen administrative districts called *Bezirke,* each headed by a first secretary of the SED who wielded extraordinary power and was responsible only to the Council of Ministers and the party leadership in Berlin. A district secretary was the immediate superior of the district Stasi chief.

8. A copy of the report is in my possession.

9. I have a copy of this report (No. 285/79), which was found in Mielke's personal safe.

CHAPTER TWELVE

1. Interview with former Stasi Colonel Rainer Wiegand in 1992, in Munich. As head of a special task force in the counterespionage directorate, Wiegand was privy to the most secret Stasi directives and analyses on internal security.

2. Ibid.

3. Ibid.

4. Ibid.

5. Interview in 1991 on condition of anonymity with the driver of a high-ranking East German official, who witnessed the scene.

6. *Der Spiegel* (news magazine) no. 45, 1996.

7. Valentin Falin, secretary for international affairs, Central Committee of the Communist Party of the USSR, in a letter to *Der Spiegel* magazine dated May 1991.

8. I was in West Berlin at the time and interviewed participants later that night and the following day.

9. Interview in 1992 with former Colonel Wiegand.

10. *BZ* (West Berlin newspaper), January 16, 1990.

11. Interview in 1997 with Manfred Kittlaus, chief of the Berlin criminal police group investigating government crimes.

INDEX